THE BEST PLAYS OF 1976–1977

THE
BURNS MANTLE
YEARBOOK

THE
BEST PLAYS
OF 1976-1977

EDITED BY OTIS L. GUERNSEY JR.

*Illustrated with photographs and
with drawings by* HIRSCHFELD

DODD, MEAD & COMPANY
NEW YORK • TORONTO

Copyright © 1977 by Dodd, Mead & Company, Inc.

ISBN: 0-396-07501-0

Library of Congress Catalog Card Number: 20-21432

Printed in the United States of America

EDITOR'S NOTE

IN THIS NEW YORK THEATER season of 1976-77 it has been clear to everyone that the showcase called Broadway is blazing as gloriously as ever; but it has all but abandoned its function as an incubator of new material, for reasons of economics and decentralization as obvious as the fact itself. Our whole country is now one vast incubator in a coast-to-coast network of regional, university and little theaters (including New York's off off Broadway) breeding new talent and new scripts for the stages of the world.

The *Best Plays* yearbook was the first to give national recognition to this important new trend of theater production in Ella A. Malin's first comprehensive listing in the 1967-68 volume. We still follow this development wherever it leads, with Ms. Malin's complete city-by-city and play-by-play record of professional regional productions (with expanded coverage by Rick Talcove in Los Angeles and David Richards in Washington, D.C.). We are also pioneering with Camille Croce's comprehensive listing of hundreds of off-off-Broadway productions.

In addition, in *The Best Plays of 1976-77,* we are featuring a detailed individual example of an outstanding new play produced outside New York, selected by the 125-member, countrywide American Theater Critics Association and presented in these pages in the form of a synopsis with examples from the text exactly like the ten New York Best Plays. Further information about the purposes and method of this ATCA selection, together with short descriptions of other outstanding cross-country scripts nominated in the ATCA process, appears with the synopsis at the beginning of "The Season Around the United States" section of this volume.

To say that we have retained the mixture as before in these pages is a prideful, not a routine, statement. Jonathan Dodd of Dodd, Mead & Company, publishers of the *Best Plays* series from Burns Mantle's first volume in the season of 1919-20, has supervised this one with his customary care and devotion, and the book has benefited from a similar effort by the editor's faithful and persevering wife. Our sincerest thanks are extended to them and to our painstaking group of compilers including Rue Canvin (necrology, books and records listings and other coverage), Stanley Green (cast replacements and touring companies), Jeff Sweet (a Best Play synopsis) and Thomas W. Mallow of American Theater Productions, Inc. (split-week tours); and informants/advisers including Henry Hewes, Clara Rotter of the New York *Times,* Hobe Morrison of *Variety,* Ralph Newman of the Drama Book Shop, the Off-Off-Broadway Alliance and the many, many other patient and forbearing staff members of theater production offices who supply the facts in the complete listing of shows produced on and off Broadway.

Equal thanks are extended to the embellishers of this volume: to Al Hirschfeld for his brilliant, prototypical interpretations of the season's major events and personalities; to David Mitchell, Theoni V. Aldredge and Santo Loquasto for the illustrations of their scenery and costume designs; to Martha Swope for her photographs of *Annie* and other productions, and to the other photographers in New York and elsewhere whose work enhances these pages, including the Joseph Abeles Studio, Sy Friedman, Merwin Goldsmith, Gerry Goodstein, Roger Greenawalt, Steven Keull, John Wulp and Michael Szczesiul.

Finally and annually, all of us who love the theater including the publishers, editors, contributors and readers of the *Best Plays* series must express our special thanks to the authors of the new scripts and scores which are the true glory of each New York theater season. We are most grateful to those Best Plays authors whose work is synopsized in this volume, and also to the other playwrights, composers and lyricists who brought this New York theater season of 1976-77 to life, whether for brief moments in short-lived productions or long moments in the bests and near-bests. May their dedication be fulfilled, if it is not already, and may we hear from them soon again.

OTIS L. GUERNSEY Jr.

June 1, 1977

CONTENTS

Drawings by HIRSCHFELD

SUMMARIES
OF THE
SEASONS

THE SEASON IN NEW YORK

By Otis L. Guernsey Jr.

"WE ARE LIVING in a vulgar, brutal time and audiences go to the theater and movies to relieve their anxieties. Today, it's a theater of shock," Dore Schary remarked at a theater forum, going to the heart of the matter of the 1976-77 theater season in New York. Mr. Schary was not speaking of *all* audiences, any more than a New York *Times* Sunday article was speaking of all playwrights when it mentioned a group of newcomers who "are not afraid of offending, even alienating, an audience." But certainly the cutting edge of the theater year was sharpened with shock and alienation, whatever crowd-pleasers may have come along behind.

The year's most powerful script was a clinically detailed study of a painful, bloody miscarriage — David Rudkin's *Ashes* — a parable of our disturbed times and an almost unbearable theatergoing experience for all but the case-hardened and anxiety-ridden (but exactly how the latter might derive some relief from this experience is beyond my understanding). A one-acter by a promising new playwright — Albert Innaurato's *The Transfiguration of Benno Blimpie* — raised the audience's gorge with images of an emotional defective fattening himself for an ultimate goal of self-cannibalism and suicide by meat cleaver. Next to these 1976-77 shock and alienation pace-setters, the contemplation of death looming over three terminal patients and their families in Michael Cristofer's Pulitzer Prize-winning Broadway play *The Shadow Box* was a laff-riot.

An artistic current as strong as this one inevitably generates its own back-eddies and counter-currents; the reaction of warm-hearted optimism in *Annie*, self-indulgent farce in *Sly Fox*, nostalgia in a series of revivals like *Fiddler on the Roof* and *The King and I*. But it was shock that was making the history this year from the bleeding aristocrats in *Comedians* to the foul language of the Critics Award-winning *American Buffalo*, along with the icy alienation of another Critics Award-winner *Otherwise Engaged*, making the apparently masochistic audience's heart beat faster and drawing its attention away from such offerings as Dore Schary's literate but disappointingly short-lived biography of the founder of Zionism, *Herzl*, or Preston Jones's *A Texas Trilogy*, the latter popular in every other corner of the United States (c.f. David Richards's account of its Washington reception in "The Season Around the United States" section of this volume) but quickly outcast in New York.

There was 18 per cent more action along Broadway in 1976-77 than in the previous season and the money was fabulous on a scale of Ali Baba's cave — but, the best news of all was the encouraging increase in the number of new

3

The 1976-77 Season on Broadway

PLAYS (17)

CALIFORNIA SUITE
Checking Out
A Texas Trilogy:
  Lu Ann Hampton
    Laverty Oberlander
THE LAST MEETING OF
  THE KNIGHTS OF THE
  WHITE MAGNOLIA
THE OLDEST LIVING
  GRADUATE
Wheelbarrow Closers
Best Friend
Herzl
SLY FOX
Something Old,
  Something New
The Trip Back Down
AMERICAN BUFFALO
Unexpected Guests
THE SHADOW BOX
Ladies at the Alamo
Gemini (transfer)
Vieux Carré

MUSICALS (6)

Godspell (transfer)
The Robber Bridegroom
  (return engagement)
Music Is
*Your Arms Too Short
  to Box With God*
I Love My Wife
ANNIE

REVUES (2)

Let My People Come
  (transfer)
*Side by Side by
  Sondheim*

FOREIGN PLAYS IN ENGLISH (8)

Days in the Trees
Poor Murderer
Siamsa
Don't Step on My
  Olive Branch
No Man's Land
COMEDIANS
**Dirty Linen &
  New-Found-Land**
OTHERWISE ENGAGED

FOREIGN-LANGUAGE PLAYS (4)

Nat'l Theater of Greece:
  Oedipus at Colonus
  Knights
Ipi-Tombi
La Guerre de Troie
  N'Aura Pas Lieu

REVIVALS (17)

Circle in Square 1976:
  Pal Joey
  Guys and Dolls
  Going Up
  Oh! Calcutta!
  Porgy and Bess
Circle in Square 1977:
  Night of the Iguana
  Romeo and Juliet
  The Innocents
  The Eccentricities of
    a Nightingale
Fiddler on the Roof
Vivian Beaumont:
  The Cherry Orchard
  Agamemnon
  Caesar and Cleopatra
Anna Christie
*The Basic Training
  of Pavlo Hummel*
The King and I (transfer)
Happy End (transfer)

SPECIALTIES (11)

An Evening With
  Diana Ross
Shirley MacLaine
For Colored Girls, etc.
  (transfer)
Debbie
I Have a Dream
A Party With Betty Comden
  and Adolph Green
Piaf . . . a Remembrance
Mark Twain Tonight!
  (return engagement)
*Lily Tomlin in Appearing
  Nitely*
Mummenschanz
*Toller Cranston's
  The Ice Show*

HOLDOVERS WHICH BECAME HITS IN 1976-77

The Belle of Amherst
Chicago
Me and Bessie

Categorized above are all the plays listed in the "Plays Produced on Broadway" section of this volume.
Plays listed in CAPITAL LETTERS have been designated Best Plays of 1976-77.
Plays listed in *italics* were still running June 1, 1977.
Plays listed in **bold face type** were classified as established or likely hits in *Variety*'s annual estimate published June 8, 1977.

American playscripts in Broadway production. We count 65 new shows this season, the same number as last, but 17 of them were new American plays compared with only ten last year (see the one-page summary accompanying this report). Unhappily, there was a big slump in musical production to only six this year from 13 last — but three of the six seem to be hits at this writing and some of the slack was taken up by outstanding musical revivals. The best measure of Broadway activity is its playing-week total (if ten shows play ten weeks, that's 100 playing weeks) which rose to 1,347 in 1976-77 from 1,136 last year, continuing its climb from the historic low of 852 in 1973-74.

"Legit Posts Its Greatest Season" was the way *Variety* put it in a banner page one headline over a story announcing that its estimate for the total Broadway gross during the 52 weeks of the 1976-77 season was a whopping $93,406,082, 31.85 per cent higher than last year's all-time record $70.8 million, towering above the previous historical high of $58.9 million in the season of 1967-68. Broadway shows on the road also enjoyed huge prosperity, grossing what *Variety* called a "sensational" $82,627,309, bringing the 1976-77 combined total for Broadway shows to $176,033,391, 42.62 per cent over last year's all-time record — right out of the ball park.

Within this incredible context *Porgy and Bess* set a new record for a week's Broadway gross, taking in $239,233 at the Uris Theater the week of Oct. 4. As the season gathered momentum in November its collection of Broadway attractions began registering $2 million weeks and finally set a new all-time record for a week's total Broadway gross of $2,671,286 for the week ending Jan. 2. The road business that week brought the total take of Broadway shows to $4,560,202 for that single seven-day period.

Taking these long figures apart to see what really glues them together, we remember that the price of a top ticket broke through the $15 barrier last season and reached upward through $17.50 to touch the inevitable $20 at *Fiddler on the Roof* — but this accounts for only a drop in the season's enormous bucket. There were a few high-grossing newcomers like *For Colored Girls, Sly Fox* and the late-opening musicals *Annie, I Love My Wife* and *Side by Side by Sondheim*, but they don't account for the season-long boom in ticket sales. Taking a closer look at one Broadway week — not a record grosser, but a mere $1.8 million-er from the latter part of the season when Broadway had already passed the $70 million mark but before the three musicals had opened — we can see how the money was distributed, according to *Variety* estimate:

Holdovers more than one year old (9)		$ 776,534
Holdovers one year old (2)		183,986
		$ 960,520
Revivals (4)		290,352
		$1,250,872
New American plays/musicals (6)	$331,275	
New foreign plays (2)	106,404	
Specialties (3)	155,850	
	$593,529	593,529
		$1,844,401

It would seem from the above that an increase in the theatergoing audience or attendance (estimated by *Variety* to be 8,815,095, 22.57 per cent more than last season), not in the number or quality of new shows, produced that $93 million record gross. Certainly 1976-77 was no circus parade of gala new offerings trooping through town — not, at least, until the musicals followed each other on in April, trunk to tail. Broadway was more like an investment portfolio of gilt-edged capital assets — the long-run holdovers and attractive revivals — generating something like two-thirds of the theater's box office by attracting new audiences to a gilt-edged backlog of entertainments like *Grease* and *Fiddler on the Roof.* These new audiences may be observed any evening, rain or shine, freeze or swelter, lined up for last-minute cut-rate admissions at the TKTS booth at Duffy Square (TKTS sold more than three quarters of a million such tickets this season for Broadway and off-Broadway shows). As the 1976-77 record shows, these new audiences like what they see and are coming back at full prices and bringing their friends.

Audiences are plentiful, but not yet adventurous; the hit syndrome still troubles the outwardly thriving commercial theater. The number of 1976-77 shows estimated by *Variety* to be hits or likely-to-become hits was an enormous eighteen — count 'em, 18 — but any individual show was apt to starve in the midst of this plenty unless it could establish itself with some fancy-capturing advantage, like shock voltage. Quality alone was no guarantee of success — c.f. the short run of Jones's Texas plays or the $100,000 estimated loss of the Critics Award-winning *American Buffalo.* The exotic enticement of foreign origin didn't always help, either — the distinguished British play *Comedians* dropped its original investment of $300,000 plus $50,000 more during its Broadway run, according to *Variety* estimate.

The most spectacular losses took place out of town, however, where David Merrick's musical *The Baker's Wife* folded in Washington for an estimated $1 million and Alexander H. Cohen's updated *Hellzapoppin,* with Jerry Lewis, collapsed in Boston for an estimated $500,000 more than its original cost of $750,000. A tight little show like *Music Is* (not George Abbott's best work but, remarkably, his 119th) carried a price tag of $650,000 for its brief Broadway appearance. Samples of artistically creditable but financially expensive ventures at the straight-play level were *The Trip Back Down* ($200,000), *Poor Murderer* ($250,000) and the somewhat more ambitiously-mounted *Herzl* ($350,000). Broadway's shortest-lived attraction was Henry Denker's *Something Old, Something New* which played one performance on Jan. 1 and then called it a year.

On the good-news side of the box office, *Sly Fox* recouped its $300,000 cost by the end of the season according to *Variety* estimate, and the three April musicals were headed in the same direction. *For Colored Girls,* etc. was transferred to Broadway in mid-September and was still playing to SRO, 102 per cent of capacity, at the end of May. *Same Time, Next Year* was in its third year with a $2.2 million-plus profit on its initial $230,000 investment already in its backers' pockets. Among the older shows, *Fiddler* had returned 1,308 per cent (and came back for another dip), *Hello, Dolly!* 1,298 per cent, *Gypsy* 182 per cent, while *Pippin* had returned $1,659,207 on its $500,000 investment and road grosses of

LILY TOMLIN IN "APPEARING NITELY"

Raisin had mounted up to more than $5 million — etc., etc., in sufficient volume to keep the hopes and dreams of backers alive, and a respectable number of new shows coming.

On the subject of success, 1976-77 was a glory year on Broadway for individuals like Ntozake Shangé as author and one of the six performers in *For Colored Girls,* the one-of-a-kind, avant-garde lyric choreopoem which climbed all the way up the ladder from OOB to decorate the tip of the Broadway season . . . Fred Gwynne as a crusty old Texas autocrat in two plays of *A Texas Trilogy* . . . Ralph Richardson and John Gielgud proving that great performers *can* fascinate an audience merely by reading the telephone book, in the telephone-book stasis of Harold Pinter's *No Man's Land* . . . Jonathan Pryce as a clown in deadly earnest, a searing portrayal in *Comedians* . . . George C. Scott as the *Sly Fox,* together with his crony Hector Elizondo and his dupes Bob Dishy and Jack Gilford . . . Zero Mostel and Yul Brynner dusting off past masterpieces in *Fiddler on the Roof* and *The King and I* . . . Tom Courtenay, translucent under Harold Pinter's close directorial scrutiny in *Otherwise Engaged* . . . Betty Comden and Adolph Green in a repeat performance of their famous *Party* . . . Robert Duvall and Kenneth McMillan in Santo Loquasto's junkshop to end all junkshops, in *American Buffalo* . . . The members of the ensembles of *The Shadow Box* and *Ladies at the Alamo* . . . Liv Ullmann, Irene Worth, Al Pacino, Robert Guillaume, Clamma Dale, Ernestine Jackson, Paul Rudd and others who put their stamp on revival productions . . . Sandy and all the people in and around *Annie* . . . Meryl Streep glowing (and singing) with Christopher Lloyd in *Happy End* . . . Gene Saks with a stand-up directing double (*California Suite* and *I Love My Wife*) and Alan Schneider with a ground-rule triple (*A Texas Trilogy*).

Off Broadway there were Brian Murray and Roberta Maxwell under Lynne Meadow's relentless *Ashes* direction . . . Mike Kellin in the monologue *Duck Variations* and Michael Lipton and Martin Balsam in the duologue *Cold Storage* . . . The *Club* ensemble under Tommy Tune's direction, as well as those of *A Tribute to Lili Lamont* (including William Hindman and Leueen MacGrath), *G. R. Point,* David Storey's *The Farm* under Marshall W. Mason's direction, *Gemini,* and the Schiller *Waiting for Godot* . . . James Coco and Rosemary De Angelis as two among many *Monsters* . . . Douglas Turner Ward in command of the barracks in *The Brownsville Raid.*

Joseph Papp continued in 1976-77 to show other harried producers how it's done, adding the transfer hit *For Colored Girls* to his durably smash-hit-popular *A Chorus Line;* following his standout revival of *Threepenny Opera* at Lincoln Center with standout revivals of *The Cherry Orchard* and *Agamemnon;* repeating the Best Play distinction of last year's *Streamers* with this year's *Ashes* — plus Public Theater productions of *Marco Polo Sings a Solo* and *Hagar's Children* as well as the Central Park season. Stealing some of his thunder in off-Broadway country was Marshall W. Mason's Circle Repertory Company which came up with an outstanding 1976-77 schedule including *The Farm, A Tribute to Lili Lamont* and *Gemini.* The Brooklyn Academy of Music organized a whole new performing company under Frank Dunlop's leadership and attracted to its stage such performers as Margaret Hamilton, Blythe Danner, Rosemary Harris, Rene Auberjonois, Denholm Elliott, Ellen Burstyn, Tovah Feldshuh, Austin Pendleton and Barnard Hughes — not at the head of nine casts, but bunched together in only two.

Among the wheeler-dealer impresarios, David Merrick was bogged down in his finally failed attempt to repeat the success of *Fanny* with a musical version of Marcel Pagnol's *The Baker's Wife.* Alexander H. Cohen remained in the limelight with the Best Play *Comedians,* the star vehicle *Anna Christie,* and the Tony Awards show on TV. Roger L. Stevens and Robert Whitehead were occupied with quality productions of prestigious playscripts: *A Texas Trilogy,* Harold Pinter's *No Man's Land,* Arthur Miller's *The Archbishop's Ceiling* (at Kennedy Center) and the revivals of *Fiddler* and *Caesar and Cleopatra* (through

YUL BRYNNER IN THE REVIVAL OF "THE KING AND I"

Kennedy Center). The Shubert Organization was helping to fill its own theaters by co-producing *Fiddler*, *Sly Fox*, *Your Arms Too Short to Box With God* and the *Godspell* transfer.

Mike Nichols produced *Annie*, directed *Comedians* but neglected to star in something to complete the circle. Harold Pinter wrote one (see above) and directed two: *Otherwise Engaged* and *The Innocents*. The career pinnacle of the late Kermit Bloomgarden was his original production of *Death of a Salesman*, but his last was a peak too, the Czechoslovakian Pavel Kohout's striking *Poor Murderer*. Arthur Cantor had a busy year with the revival of *The Innocents*, plus the popular Betty Comden-Adolph Green specialty, plus the effort to show-case Carol Channing in a British comedy, *The Bed Before Yesterday*, which closed out of town — plus Emlyn Williams as Dylan Thomas and the annual sponsorship of the Baird Marionettes off Broadway.

If you judge a book not by its cover but by its best chapter, then the theater season in New York should be viewed through the rose-colored glasses of its Best Plays, be they theater of shock, theater of alienation, theater of nostalgia, theater of the obscure and whatever else it was — and indeed it *was* — in 1976-77. Our list of the year's ten Best Plays is a stylistic kaleidoscope, with David Rudkin's powerful antithesis of entertainment, *Ashes,* alongside Neil Simon's multiply entertaining *California Suite* and Larry Gelbart's well-made farce *Sly Fox.* The classic differences between "comedy" and "serious" drama have all but disappeared in the whirlpools and cross-currents of modern playwriting: Trevor Griffiths' *Comedians* is a shocker full of laughs, while Michael Cristofer's *The Shadow Box* is a reassuring play about death. Alienation by illiteracy is a major thrust of David Mamet's *American Buffalo,* as is alienation by literacy in Simon Gray's *Otherwise Engaged. Annie* by Thomas Meehan, Charles Strouse and Martin Charnin is in a class by itself in more ways than the most obvious one of being the only musical on the list. And also there are two of Preston Jones's appealing and revealing reconstructions of Southwest Americana, *The Oldest Living Graduate* and *The Last Meeting of the Knights of the White Magnolia.*

Only one of the above — *Sly Fox* — was an original Broadway production. Three — *Comedians, Otherwise Engaged* and *Ashes* — originated on the London stage. The other six were first produced in regional theater — demonstrating its great importance as an incubator of American theater in the 1970s — as follows: *California Suite* (Los Angeles), *The Oldest Living Graduate* and *The Last Meeting of the Knights of the White Magnolia* (Dallas), *American Buffalo* (Chicago), *The Shadow Box* (Los Angeles and New Haven) and *Annie* (East Haddam, Conn.). In recognition of the growing innovative strength of cross-country theater, we have included in this volume (in "The Theater Around the United States" section) a special Best-Play-like synopsis of an outstanding new play produced outside New York during the 1976-77 season, selected by the American Theater Critics Association: *And the Soul Shall Dance* by Wakako Yamauchi, produced in Los Angeles by East West Players.

This year's list consists of one off-Broadway and nine Broadway productions (last year the split was even, five and five). Their authorship includes, most encouragingly, the professional New York theater debuts of four American dramatists — Preston Jones, David Mamet, Michael Cristofer and Thomas Meehan — as well as two British authors new to New York — Trevor Griffiths and David Rudkin. The return of Neil Simon, Larry Gelbart, Simon Gray, Charles Strouse and Martin Charnin to Broadway was equally an event. Only the tyranny of numbers prevents us from including many others new and experienced who came so close that there is scarcely even a shade of difference between their work and the bests, including the authors of *Gemini* and *The Transfiguration of Benno Blimpie, I Love My Wife, The Brownsville Raid, G. R. Point, Cold Storage, A Tribute to Lili Lamont, Poor Murderer, Ladies at the Alamo* and *The Trip Back Down.*

The ultimate insignia of New York professional theater achievement (we in-

MIKE NICHOLS, DIRECTOR AND PRODUCER

sist) is selection as a Best Play in these volumes, a designation which is 16 years older than the Critics Award and only three years younger than the Pulitzer Prize. Our Best Play selection is made with the script itself as the first consideration, for the reason (as we've stated in previous volumes) that the script is the spirit of the theater's physical body. The script is not only the quintessence of the present, it is most of what endures into the future. So the Best Plays are the best scripts, with as little weight as humanly possible given to comparative production values. The choice is made without any regard whatever to a play's type — musical, comedy or drama — or origin on or off Broadway, or popularity at the box office or lack of same.

If a script of above-average quality influences the very character of a season, or if by some function of consensus it wins the Critics, Pulitzer or Tony Awards, we take into account its future historical as well as present esthetic importance to the season as a whole. This is the only special consideration we give, and we don't always tilt in its direction, as the record shows.

On the other hand, we don't take scripts of other eras into consideration for Best Play citation in this one, whatever their technical status as American or New York "premieres" which don't happen to have had a previous production of record. And we draw a line between adaptations and revivals, the former eligible for Best Play selection but the latter not, under close scrutiny on a case-by-case basis.

The ten Best Plays of 1976-77, named in the paragraphs above, are listed here for visual convenience in the order in which they opened in New York (a plus sign + with the performance number signifies that the play was still running on June 1, 1977).

California Suite
(Broadway; 406+ perfs.)

The Last Meeting of the Knights of the White Magnolia
(Broadway; 22 perfs.)

The Oldest Living Graduate
(Broadway; 20 perfs.)

Comedians
(Broadway; 145 perfs.)

Sly Fox
(Broadway; 194 + perfs.)

Ashes
(Off Broadway; 145+ perfs.)

Otherwise Engaged
(Broadway; 135+ perfs.)

American Buffalo
(Broadway; 109+ perfs.)

The Shadow Box
(Broadway; 69+ perfs.)

Annie
(Broadway; 46+ perfs.)

Broadway

It was a playwrights' season on Broadway in 1976-77. Neil Simon enhanced the whole year with a new script, Tennessee Williams and Paul Zindel came in from the cold for brief visits and Arthur Miller got as far as Washington. They found themselves in the thick of new talent cropping up all over the place, flowering in purple and orange hues of shock and alienation, or in some cases softer colors.

Most promising of the Broadway debuts was one of the latter kind: Preston Jones's with his three Texas plays compassionately chronicling the agonies of slowly-dying pride and prejudice in a small Southwest Texas town. His *The Last Meeting of the Knights of the White Magnolia* uncovered the last vestiges of racism, become almost as pitiful as contemptible, in the events of a tacky lodge meeting. His *The Oldest Living Graduate* saw new money clashing with old values. His *Lu Ann Hampton Laverty Oberlander* watched a cheerleading beauty queen become a lonely barfly, amid fading social standards. This last and

ZERO MOSTEL IN THE REVIVAL
OF "FIDDLER ON THE ROOF"

least of Jones's three plays was stretching a one-act point into three acts, a weakness which even a strong performance by Diane Ladd in the title role couldn't redeem. But the first two were well-made plays about victims of cultural transition clinging to remnants of the past, but drowning nevertheless — well-made with a structure and mobility of events as well as of emotional bias. In these two Best Plays Fred Gwynne found a rich character in an aged, half-senile — but absolutely undefeated — old Texas patriarch and World War I veteran whose proudest boast is that the great Black Jack Pershing once spoke to him and told him to shut up. Patrick Hines's redneck booze-seller, Red Grover, also made an indelible impression. Preston Jones is an actor and a writer-in-residence at the Dallas Theater Center, where the plays of *A Texas Trilogy* were first produced. But that's not all — Jones is a play-maker, too. His works seem native-born to the stage where they are sure to prosper mightily, their weak New York reception to the contrary notwithstanding.

Another actor-playwright made his New York debut this season: Michael Cristofer whose *The Shadow Box* won the Pulitzer Prize and the Tony best-play award at the same time he was making his New York acting debut in *The*

Cherry Orchard at Lincoln Center. In contrast to Jones, Cristofer is a scene-writer. His play is remarkable more for texture and tone than momentum, as it shares its attention among three terminally ill patients and the relatives and friends keeping them company in separate versions of the same situation, interlocked in the play without touching each other (no one in one group ever says so much as "hello" to anybody in another). One of the patients is a family man (Simon Oakland) insisting that his wife set aside her fear so that they can enjoy these last days together. Another is an intellectual bisexual (Laurence Luckinbill) who hopes that his still-fond ex-wife (Patricia Elliott) and his male lover (Mandy Patinkin) won't sour this last of the wine by picking a quarrel with each other. The third is an old woman (Geraldine Fitzgerald) clinging painfully to life while an unappreciated daughter (Rose Gregorio) helps her pretend her favorite, long-dead daughter is still alive. Cristofer handled his subject — not death itself, but life before death — with emotional maturity, with a touch of gallows humor but no trace of morbidity. Like Preston Jones, he has a regional theater writing-acting affiliation — the special Tony Award-winning Mark Taper Forum in Los Angeles whose artistic director, Gordon Davidson, staged this difficult piece in all its versions from the Taper to Broadway and won this year's play-directing Tony.

Jones is a play-maker; Cristofer a scene-writer; and a third 1976-77 newcomer, David Mamet, is a dialogue-writer whose ear for contemporary speech distinguishes his work. His professional New York debut had a sort of preview last season with off-off-Broadway productions at St. Clements of *American Buffalo* and *Sexual Perversity in Chicago* which won him an Obie Award as the best new playwright. Both plays made the debut official in commercial productions this season. *Sexual Perversity,* a juggling act of comic sexual cliches, was a season-long success off Broadway on a bill with Mamet's short *Duck Variations,* an exercise in making mountains of character out of molehills of conversation between two old men sitting on a park bench. Mamet's more substantial work, *American Buffalo,* came all the way up to Broadway, winning the Critics Award for best American play and a Best Play citation as an outstanding — if certainly not flawless — new theater work. In it, two over-the-hill petty crooks and their young stooge plan to steal a coin collection — planning and planning, reacting to each other but never taking action, until it becomes obvious that like the arrival of Godot, this crime will never take place.

In the opening scenes of *American Buffalo* Mamet surely intended to shock and alienate his audience with some of the foulest language ever heard on a stage. The language cools off a bit finally (or seems to). The dialogue is like a violin finely tuned to the vibrations of a junk-shop owner (Kenneth McMillan) and his small-time hoodlum friend (Robert Duvall), the words in perfect pitch at each delicate touch of the excellent acting and the direction by Ulu Grosbard, who coped brilliantly with this difficult play. Santo Loquasto's junk-shop setting, surely the year's most imaginative design, was a sight to make sore eyes much sorer, and indeed "entertainment" is a word not easily applicable to *American Buffalo.* Virtuosity, yes — Mamet has mastered a verbal instrument of high quality, and we can expect that his next number will carry a more rewarding tune.

BING CROSBY

Highly promising and performing new playwriting growth wasn't limited to the Best Plays list either on or off Broadway. Like David Mamet, Albert Innaurato came heavily upon the professional theater scene this season with two startlingly effective plays: the one-acter *The Transfiguration of Benno Blimpie* off Broadway and *Gemini* both off and on. The interrelation of emotional and physical distortion is the preoccupation of both works. The former, one of the season's premier shockers, is a study of a misfit child unloved even by his mother (Rosemary De Angelis in a mesmerizing performance) who stuffs and smears food into his mouth in compensation, fattening himself for ritual slaughter like a suicidal pig. Poor Benno was played to disgusting and pitiable perfection by James Coco under Robert Drivas's remorseless direction.

The latter, *Gemini,* which began off Broadway at Circle Repertory Company and moved uptown in late spring, played out a double-twin motif in a Philadelphia backyard setting: a brother and sister both feel a sexual attraction for a college chum who in turn feels some sexual attraction for both of them. The play's air is full of Italian family warmth (notably provided by Danny Aiello and Anne DeSalvo), somewhat counterbalanced by the presence of another Benno Blimpie, an awkwardly fat youth (Jonathan Hadary) driven to weird excesses. Innaurato's concepts were often so far out of human scale in both plays that they tended to acquire the shortcomings as well as the advantages of a cartoon.

Another newcomer, John Bishop, made the journey from the boondocks of OOB to the bright lights of Broadway with his first professionally-produced script, *The Trip Back Down,* about a racing car driver whose career has reached its peak — or never peaked very conspicuously — and is now on the downslide. As played by John Cullum, the driver was appealingly devoid of self-delusions on a visit to family and friends in his old home town, trying to renew his energy for another go-round of the tracks. His victory over his own doubts takes place very slowly and somewhat monotonously at first, but it picks up momentum for a touching scene in which the driver invites his daughter to come along with him on the auto-racing circuit but advises her "I never win" with a shy sort of pride. Like Jones, Cristofer, Mamet and Innaurato, Bishop is a name to be remembered among the extraordinary new playwriting talent that surfaced in the professional theater this season.

The happiest 1976-77 results among the previously-established dramatists were achieved by Larry Gelbart in his adaptation of Ben Jonson's durably comic *Volpone* into Broadway's richly comic *Sly Fox.* Gelbart re-entered the territory fenced off by Jonson and made it over into a gag-filled playground for the kind of one-dimensional but unforgettable characters to be found in his TV series *M.A.S.H.;* characters a director like Arthur Penn could juggle hilariously and actors could bounce off all three walls of the auditorium. The latter included, memorably, George C. Scott as the fox tricking the greedy with promises of riches in his will, Hector Elizondo as his henchman (the Mosca character in *Volpone*), Jack Gilford as a scabrous old money-lender and Bob Dishy as an insanely jealous but even more avaricious husband.

Another Best Play by an experienced hand was *California Suite* by Neil Simon, a matched set of four hotel-room episodes. Simon is what Jean Kerr has called the master of the garde play, and he makes doing his thing seem so easy that new Simon hits are not only taken for granted, they're an obligatory part of any Broadway season in the 1970s. In his latest, in the manner of *Plaza Suite,* four different sets of people follow each other into the same hotel accommodations and lift up a corner of their lives to reveal themselves. The ensemble under Gene Saks's sure direction consisted of Barbara Barrie, Tammy Grimes, George Grizzard and Jack Weston moving in and out of the four playlets as (1) an acerbically articulate and divorced New York couple (Grimes and Grizzard), (2) a Philadelphia family man caught by his wife *in delictu* so *flagrante* as to be forgivable (Weston and Barrie), (3) a conveniently married British movie star and antique dealer in town for the Academy Awards (Grizzard and Grimes again) and (4) two Chicago couples at each other's throats at the end of a shared vacation (all four). After *God's Favorite* in 1974-75, Neil Simon took a well-documented powder to California, so that he neglected to supply Broadway with its annual Simon treat last season. As the season of 1976-77 began (his new play opened in June) it was certainly good to have him back.

Tennessee Williams also returned to town this season with a new script, *Vieux*

Carré, his first professional New York production since his unhappy attempt at absurdism in *Out Cry* four years ago. The style was as fondly remembered in his best work: moody, poetic, with sexual obsessions and deprivations of the inhabitants of a run-down New Orleans boarding house viewed through a gauze of memory. It was indeed a shadowy play, episodic and incoherent, informed by the author's insights but not his craft. Paul Zindel had better luck with *Ladies at the Alamo,* a clash of tigresses in a take-over attempt behind the scenes of a major Texas regional theater operation (is Alamo an intentionally alliterative suggestion of Alley?). Frank Perry directed it like an animal trainer cracking his whip over an ensemble of five intensely striving actresses led by Estelle Parsons. It was effective, and it might have made a stronger impression outside this season's theater-of-shock context.

This year of 17 new American plays was like a new beginning for Broadway, but it repeatedly contemplated endings in scripts like Allen Swift's *Checking Out,* with an aged Yiddish actor stage-managing his own death; and Louis La Russo II's *Wheelbarrow Closers,* with Danny Aiello as a vigorous wheeler-dealer kicking against the pricks of his own inevitable retirement. Also on the playbill were Michael Sawyer's study of a malevolent woman in *Best Friend* and Jordan Crittenden's of a problematical marriage in *Unexpected Guests.*

British authors were well represented but didn't dominate the season or its best lists as has sometimes happened in the past. The best of their Broadway offerings was *Comedians* by Trevor Griffiths, in his American playwriting debut with an abrasive play about aspiring comics sweating through a tryout engagement at a third-rate social club and then analyzing their performances after the show. Mike Nichols directed its changes of key back and forth between standup gags and painful introspection with perfect timing. The performances had to be very good, and they were — none better than Jonathan Pryce's conscientious clown determined to pursue the truth at all costs, exacerbating class hatreds in his routine as a bully harassing a pair of papier-mache dummies in evening dress.

The other British Best Play on Broadway this season was Simon Gray's Critics Award-winning *Otherwise Engaged,* like his previous Best Play *Butley* a meticulous study of disintegration. It isn't the personality of the protagonist that is coming apart here (as in *Butley*), but his connections with other members of the human race. He is at the center of a gathering storm of relationships with friends and family, at the calm center where he insists on remaining. He maintains a cool, rational detachment when others expect heated involvement, and therefore he is increasingly incapable or unwilling to share in others' lives or permit others a share in his. Tom Courtenay played the central role in a performance precision-engineered under Harold Pinter's direction.

Pinter's other major contribution to the 1976-77 Broadway season was his play *No Man's Land,* providing a vehicle for two of the most accomplished heavyweights in the business: John Gielgud and Ralph Richardson. The tilt of Richardson's chin and the slant of Gielgud's eyebrow sufficed to send shock waves to the farthest reaches of the balcony, as they performed a strange encounter of two writers chatting over drinks and cigars, while menacing servants enter and exit on unexplained errands. The performances had to suffice, because the play itself was an enigma, an audience do-it-yourself project with either a few pieces or a few lines of instruction missing, or both. Finally from Britain there was Tom Stoppard's *Dirty Linen,* an evanescent gag farce about a Parliamentary committee investigating sex scandals. It was so vaporous that in fact it vanished altogether at one point to make room for a long monologue inset (delivered earnestly by Jacob Brooke), *New-Found-Land,* describing a journey across North America in cartoon images of tourist attractions.

On the darker side, the Czechoslovakian play *Poor Murderer,* by Pavel Kohout, appeared in English translation in an absolutely first-rate production with Laurence Luckinbill (in one of his two important performances this season), Maria Schell, Kevin McCarthy, Ruth Ford, Larry Gates and others under Herbert Berghof's direction. This play concentrated intensely on the interrogation of an actor, a prisoner in an insane asylum, who is prepared to believe he has actually killed the actor playing Polonius while playing Hamlet in the bedroom scene. This script is said to have political overtones, and its New York production took place at a time when Kohout and some of his fellow-writers were suffering a wave of oppression in their native land. In a program note in *Playbill* Kohout explained that his own country refused him permission to come to the United States to see his play. Kohout added, "They tell me I can emigrate. Were I to do so, I could spend my whole life going from one opening night to the next and see or even influence the production of all my writing. But I cannot, for the sake of the characters I've created on paper, abandon the people of real flesh and blood, my children, my friends and the audience which remains my audience even though their grandchildren might be the first ones to see my play."

A translation from the French of *Days in the Trees* by Marguerite Duras was the leadoff production of Circle in the Square's season, with Mildred Dunnock playing a mother with a special affection for her ne'er-do-well son — "one son in reserve for when the bad times come" — affirming their kinship even as they clash over the details of their lives. The 1976-77 program of foreign works in English also included visits from the National Folk Theater of Ireland (*Siamsa*) in an evening of emerald-green folklore and an Israeli musical revue of satiric and patriotic comment, *Don't Step on My Olive Branch.*

Broadway's visiting foreign-language productions ranged from the imposing National Theater of Greece repertory of Sophocles's *Oedipus at Colonus* and Aristophanes's *Knights* (the first professional New York production of record of this comedy in any language), through Tréteau de Paris's *La Guerre de Troie N'Aura Pas Lieu* (known in English as *Tiger at the Gates*), to the somewhat controversial South African musical *Ipi-Tombi,* a colorful and rhythmic expression of the black South African spirit in various village, tribal and even big-city rituals and celebrations.

On our own musical stages, it was as though invention had evaporated and the production of new shows had come to a standstill, until April 17 when presto! the West Forties came alive with the sound of music. *I Love My Wife* appeared on that date, followed the next night by *Side by Side by Sondheim* and three nights later by *Annie* — and about a week later the Chelsea production of the Brecht-Weill *Happy End* moved over to Manhattan to add a fourth part to this late-season harmony of shows. Granted that *Happy End* is a revival and the revue assemblage of Stephen Sondheim numbers is a new collection but not new work; still, the freshness of their approach and presentation contributed importantly to this late-season musical bonanza.

Annie immediately drew the longest lines at the box office, together with a faint echo of scorn drifting downwind, for its manner and substance even more simplistic, possibly, than the *Little Orphan Annie* comic strip from which the show was derived. We're convinced that *Annie* was the musical of the year, with a consistent soft-sell style of music, performance, design and humor that for once wasn't so over-seasoned with gags that it lost the taste of wit (remember, Mike Nichols produced this show for Broadway). When Dorothy Loudon as the keeper of an orphanage comes in to rouse her little girls as roughly as possible with a police whistle, blows it, and nearly takes the top of her own head off because of a hangover she's forgotten she has, you know that *Annie* is going to be all right: it isn't going to be sentimental about either victims or villains, it is never going to reach for the sugar when the salt is handy. When poor little Annie (Andrea McArdle, a cheerful and forthright young personality) arrives as a Christmas charity guest at the grand mansion of Daddy Warbucks (Reid Shelton), is asked ingratiatingly, "Now, Annie, what do you want to do first?" and replies, "The floors. I'll scrub them, then I'll get to the windows," you wonder where you'd find a more satisfying line than that these days, however far upwind.

Dorothy Loudon was wonderful as the orphans' harsh mistress, a function which until *Annie* has remained an unappealing stereotype, even in cartoons; Sandy was wonderful; Robert Fitch danced up a breeze as a small-time con man; David Mitchell's New York skyline sets and Theoni V. Aldredge's costumes were as stylish as the staging and choreography by Martin Charnin and Peter Gennaro. Charles Strouse's music was eminently hummable as well as singable (notably in "Tomorrow" and "Easy Street"). For those who insist on profound social comment in the framework of the musical stage, well, *Annie* is a statement of values in total revolt from the present conventional theater of shock and alienation. *Annie* dares to be different. It insists that a child has a right to its innocence as it stares with wide eyes upon such ugliness as a Depression; that blank pupils may perceive subtle purposes that hard glares are sure to miss. It further insists that once in a while even the New York audiences of the 1970s deserve the unashamed relief of shiny entertainment, a proposition with which the editor of this volume joyfully agrees.

I Love My Wife was vastly entertaining, too, in a more conventional 1970s package. It explored the obligatory 1970s subject — sexual adventure — and the show was for it, sort of, in a book about two Trenton, N.J. couples determined to celebrate Christmas Eve with a wife-swapping orgy. The title was a tipoff to the outcome; in the meantime, the one joke was worked and reworked, wrung out, rinsed off and wrung out again under Gene Saks's resourceful Tony-winning direction. The performance of Lenny Baker as the most eager and least skillful of the quartet stood out in good company. The jazzy Michael Stewart-Cy Coleman score was the year's best. It was played by four musicians right on the stage, taking little direct part in the action but serving as a sort of Greek-chorus commentary as they came on in different costumes playing different instruments and harmonies reflecting the events and mood of the show at the moment. Their Act II opening number "Hey There, Good Times" was a show-stopper.

A rousing Gospel musical *Your Arms* (sic) *Too Short to Box With God*, conceived by Vinnette Carroll from the Book of Matthew and developed in her Urban Arts Corps via a Washington tryout with music and lyrics by Alex Bradford and Micki Grant, was for many, many weeks the only new musical game in town. The season's other early-opening new show, George Abbott's effort to make another modern musical out of Shakespeare's *Twelfth Night* in *Music Is*, was a very brief candle.

Broadway's musical program was augmented with revivals, with the transfer of the marathon-running *Godspell* (another inspiration from the Book of Matthew) from off Broadway, and with the return engagement of last year's *The Robber Bridegroom* with Barry Bostwick making another of his strong impressions and winning the Tony Award in the title role. The sex-centered off-Broadway cabaret revue *Let My People Come* also transferred for a moment in the Broadway limelight, where it had more of a negative impact on the League of New York Theaters and Producers, who regarded it as "antithetical," than a positive impact on theater audiences. A late-coming but major element of the musical season's enjoyment was the revue *Side by Side by Sondheim* brought over from London with its indefatigable and inimitable British cast singing up a storm of memorable Sondheim lyrics and tunes by himself and other composers with whom he has collaborated.

Specialties, like revivals, were numerically and artistically important this season. Ntozake Shangé's touching "choreopoem" *For Colored Girls Who Have Considered Suicide/When the Rainbow Is Enuf* was a major adornment after it transferred uptown from the Public Theater in September. It was categorized as a "play" on the Tony nominations list, but that is a courtesy title — it is an original theatrical entity of dance, poetry and performance which created its own category and made a big space for itself on Broadway.

A Party With Betty Comden and Adolph Green brightened up the place for weeks with a new version of the performers' popular two-person show. Martin Luther King Jr. was warmly remembered in his own words and Billy Dee Williams's performance in *I Have a Dream,* as was Edith Piaf in song and Juliette Koka's performance in *Piaf . . . a Remembrance,* and as was Mark Twain in a return engagement of Hal Holbrook's celebrated one-man impersonation *Mark Twain Tonight!* The Swiss *Mummenschanz* pantomine-and-mask show paid Broadway a visit, and the Palace became a winter wonderland in May, housing a Canadian skater's spectacle, *Toller Cranston's The Ice Show.*

The comedienne Lily Tomlin captivated Broadway audiences with a repertory of characterizations ranging from wide-eyed schoolgirl to drug-addicted babe, in a solo show called *Lily Tomlin in "Appearing Nitely."* Many other solo bookings were spotlighted on 1976-77 Broadway scene, some of them billed as "revues" and some as "concerts" in Broadway theaters, attracting fans to join and mingle with the crowds of theatergoers at curtain time. For the record, Diana Ross, Debbie Reynolds and Shirley MacLaine appeared in one-woman "shows." Somewhat differently presented but equally popular in "concert" were Bing Crosby, Barry Manilow, Nana Mouskouri, Al Green and many other pop stars and combos — as well as two entire musicals, *She Loves Me* and *Knickerbocker Holiday,* performed in concert versions at Town Hall by such stars as Madeline Kahn, Rita Moreno, George Rose and Richard Kiley. There was even a new Robert Wilson theatrical what-is-it, *Einstein on the Beach,* presented for a couple of special, unclassifiable performances at the Metropolitan Opera House.

Here's where we list the *Best Plays* choices for the top individual achievements of the season. In the acting categories, clear distinctions among "starring," "featured" or "supporting" players can't be made on the basis of official billing, in which an actor may appear as a "star" following the title (not true star billing) or as an "also starring" star, or any of the other career-building typographical gimmicks. Here in these volumes we divide acting into "primary" and "secondary" roles, a primary role being one which carries a major responsibility for the show; a role which might some day cause a star to inspire a revival in order to appear in that character. All others, be they vivid as Mercutio, are classed as secondary (and of course there are a few plays that don't have any primary roles at all, like *The Shadow Box*).

Our problem isn't definition but an embarrassment of riches as we proceed to name the single best in each category. Here, then, are the Best Plays bests of 1976-77:

PLAYS

BEST PLAY: *The Last Meeting of the Knights of the White Magnolia* by Preston Jones

BEST FOREIGN PLAY: *Comedians* by Trevor Griffiths

BEST REVIVAL: *The Cherry Orchard* by Anton Chekhov in the New York Shakespeare Festival production of a new English version by Jean-Claude van Itallie directed by Andrei Serban

BEST ACTOR IN A PRIMARY ROLE: George C. Scott as Foxwell J. Sly in *Sly Fox*

BEST ACTRESS IN A PRIMARY ROLE: Roberta Maxwell as Anne in *Ashes*

BEST ACTOR IN A SECONDARY ROLE: Jonathan Pryce as Gethin Price in *Comedians*

BEST ACTRESS IN A SECONDARY ROLE: Rosemary De Angelis as Mother in *The Transfiguration of Benno Blimpie*

BEST DIRECTOR: Gordon Davidson for *The Shadow Box;* special citation to Gene Saks for *California Suite* and *I Love My Wife*

BEST SCENERY: Santo Loquasto for *American Buffalo* and *The Cherry Orchard*

BEST COSTUMES: Santo Loquasto for *The Cherry Orchard* and *Agamemnon*

MUSICALS

BEST MUSICAL: *Annie*

BEST BOOK: Thomas Meehan for *Annie*

BEST SCORE: Cy Coleman and Michael Stewart for *I Love My Wife*

BEST REVIVAL: *Porgy and Bess* by George Gershwin, Ira Gershwin and DuBose Heyward in the Houston Grand Opera production directed by Jack O'Brien

BEST ACTOR IN A PRIMARY ROLE: Lenny Baker as Alvin in *I Love My Wife*

BEST ACTRESS IN A PRIMARY ROLE: Meryl Streep as Lt. Lillian Holiday ("Hallelujah Lil") in *Happy End*

BEST ACTOR IN A SECONDARY ROLE: Robert Fitch as Rooster Hannigan in *Annie*

BEST ACTRESS IN A SECONDARY ROLE: Dorothy Loudon as Miss Hannigan in *Annie*

BEST DIRECTOR: Martin Charnin for *Annie*

BEST CHOREOGRAPHER: Peter Gennaro for *Annie*

BEST SCENERY: David Mitchell for *Annie*

BEST COSTUMES: Theoni V. Aldredge for *Annie*

Off Broadway

Exactly what is "off Broadway"? By our lights, an off-Broadway show is one with an Equity cast giving a regular schedule of 8 performances a week in an off-Broadway theater, after inviting public comment by critics on opening night(s). And according to Paul Libin, president of the League of Off-Broadway Theaters, an off-Broadway theater is a house seating 499 or fewer and situated in Manhattan *outside* the area bounded by Fifth and Ninth Avenues between 34th and 56th Streets, and by Fifth Avenue and the Hudson River between 56th and 72d Streets.

Obviously, there are exceptions to each of these rules. There is nothing exactly exact about off Broadway. In each *Best Plays* volume we stretch these definitions somewhat in the direction of inclusion — never of exclusion. For example, the word "Manhattan" means what we want it to mean, *Alice in Wonderland*-wise, when we include Brooklyn's Chelsea Theater Center and Academy of Music programs. Casts are sometimes only part-Equity and schedules sometimes take in only 7 and in rare cases 6 performances a week (but we don't list 5-a-weekers, which are distinctly off off Broadway, more familiarly known in these pages as OOB). In one recent case we included a long-run show — *Let My People Come* — which deliberately refrained from subjecting itself to review by the critics.

The point is that off Broadway isn't an exact location, it's a state of the art (generally advanced), a structure of production costs (generally reduced, but now climbing and threatening the existence even of some of the institutional producers), a level of expertise and effort as well as a physical function measurable in locale, credentials and rhythm. In any single season, OOB groups rise to it, touch it, break through or fall back; OB groups sink back into workshop or exalt their material above the best of Broadway. Off Broadway isn't the expense-sheltered haven for experiment, the opportunity to fail that it once was and OOB now often is, but it is still unfrozen, ever-changing, with both surprise and disappointment still possible.

Off Broadway in 1976-77 the program was loaded with revivals as usual, what with the Roundabout, CSC, LOOM and other organizations concentrating heavily in this area of production. The numbers yielded ground grudgingly in the vital category of new American shows, plays and musicals: 22 and 9 in 1976-77 (see the one-page summary accompanying this report), only one down from last year's total of 26 and 6, but well off the pace of 30 and 12 the year before. A rise in the number of foreign plays in English from three last year to nine this year additionally shores up the total. Institutional production dominated independent more than ever, especially in the huge output of revivals and in the new-play category.

Only one off-Broadway script, *Ashes,* made the Best Plays list this season, as compared with last season's record-breaking five — not because of diminishing quality but because of the marked numerical and qualitative increase in the Broadway competition. Off-Broadway plays like *G.R. Point, The Brownsville Raid, The Transfiguration of Benno Blimpie, 'A Tribute to Lili Lamont, Gemini,* and *Cold Storage* might well have made the list in other seasons.

Ashes was the New York playwriting debut of its British author, David Rudkin, as it progressed from OOB production at the Manhattan Theater Club to its commercial booking under the sponsorship of Joseph Papp and his New York Shakespeare Festival Public Theater. *Ashes* was the peak of the off-Broadway season and the spearpoint of the theater of shock (not quite as disgusting as *Monsters,* but more penetrating), in a parable of the Northern Irish political tragedy reflected in the personal agonies, both mental and physical, of a childless husband and wife trying to preserve their heritage at all costs, no matter the clinical indignities, no matter the blood and pain of their heroic but miscarrying efforts. It is hard to imagine how the acting of Brian Murray and Roberta Maxwell as the couple and the brutally direct staging by Lynne Meadow could have been bettered. It was effective to the point where it risked shattering the audience's suspension of disbelief with theater of *unendurable* shock, that dangerous esthetic territory where even the ancient Greeks feared to tread.

Also on Papp's schedule at the Public was another tell-it-like-it-is closeup, this one of a shelter for emotionally disturbed teen-agers, *Hagar's Children,* written in changing keys of violence and compassion by Ernest Joselovitz, a onetime staff member of just such a haven. Papp's downtown schedule was additionally filled out with *On the Lock-In,* a musical about prison life by David Langston Smyrl; *Marco Polo Sings a Solo,* a melange of absurdist comment and characterization in John Guare's individualistic comic style; and revivals of the Strindberg one-acters *The Stronger,* and *Creditors,* plus workshop activity some of which is listed in the "Plays Produced off off Broadway" section of this volume.

If Papp came up with the best off-Broadway play this season, Marshall W.

The 1976-77 Season off Broadway

PLAYS (22)

Negro Ensemble 1976:
Livin' Fat
Beware the Jubjub Bird
Sexual Perversity in Chicago & Duck Variations
Circle Repertory 1976:
Mrs. Murray's Farm
American Place:
Jack Gelber's New Play: Rehearsal
Comanche Cafe & Domino Courts
Isadora Duncan Sleeps With the Russian Navy
Cold Storage
Does Anybody Here Do the Peabody?
Circle Repertory 1977:
A Tribute to Lili Lamont
My Life
Gemini
Phoenix Theater:
Ladyhouse Blues
Marco Polo
G.R. Point
Lincoln
The Brownsville Raid

Public Theater:
Marco Polo Sings a Solo
Hagar's Children
Monsters
Jockeys
I Was Sitting on My Patio This Guy Appeared I Thought I Was Hallucinating

FOREIGN PLAYS IN ENGLISH (11)

The Farm
Bingo
The Prince of Homberg
Canadian Gothic & American Modern
A Sorrow Beyond Dreams
The Crazy Locomotive
ASHES
The Perfect Mollusc
Curtains
The Sunday Promenade
Scribes

MUSICALS (9)

Becoming
The Club
Joseph and the Amazing Technicolor Dreamcoat
The Cockeyed Tiger
Castaways
Movie Buff
On the Lock-In
Der Ring Gott Farblonjet
New York City Street Show

REVUES (5)

Lovesong
2 by 5
Nightclub Cantata
Jules Feiffer's Hold Me!
Starting Here, Starting Now

SPECIALTIES (3)

Dylan Thomas Growing Up
Davy Jones' Locker
In My Father's Time

REVIVALS (34)

Roundabout 1976:
The World of Sholom Aleichem
Actors' Alliance:
The Tavern
Lullaby
Hay Fever
Delacorte:
Henry V
Measure for Measure
Light Opera Manhattan:
H.M.S. Pinafore
The Mikado
The Pirates of Penzance
Ruddigore
Princess Ida
The Merry Widow
Naughty Marietta
The Vagabond King
The Yeomen of the Guard
Utopia, Limited

Roundabout 1977:
The Philanderer
The Rehearsal
John Gabriel Borkman
Endgame
Dear Liar
Classic Stage Company:
Heartbreak House
The Homecoming
Tartuffe
The Balcony
The Plough and the Stars
All the Way Home
Happy End
BAM Theater:
The New York Idea
Three Sisters
The Great Macdaddy
Creditors
& The Stronger
Peg o' My Heart
Exiles

FOREIGN-LANGUAGE PLAYS (3)

Kraljevo
Rodogune
Waiting for Godot

Categorized above are all the plays listed in the "Plays Produced off Broadway" section of this volume.
Play listed in CAPITAL LETTERS has been designated a Best Play of 1976-77.
Plays listed in *italics* were still running June 1, 1977.

Mason's Circle Repertory Company came up with the most interesting group of shows. Like New York Shakespeare, Circle mined gold out of peripheral production in bringing Albert Innaurato's *Gemini* (described in the previous chapter of this report) from the PAF Playhouse in Huntington, L.I., into the off-Broadway and finally the Broadway limelight. Also at the Circle, Arthur Whitney's *A Tribute to Lili Lamont* (his second professionally-produced script) reminded us in an encounter of a once-was movie star (Leueen MacGrath) with the remnants of her last surviving fan club that fan-ism is a two-way street — fans need identification with their idol to bolster their self-esteem every bit as much as the star needs their adoration to feed her ego.

Mason also imported for Circle production a brooding David Storey play about a craggy Yorkshire farmer and his self-possessed daughters, *The Farm;* and he brought in Corinne Jacker's *My Life,* an exploration of motives in one man's memories of his past. Mason also filled out his 1976-77 schedule with a revival, *Exiles,* James Joyce's only play. Season after season, production after production, Circle Repertory has consistently rivalled the best in town, and this year was no exception.

T. Edward Hambleton's Phoenix Theater did its usual number of rising from the flames with a refreshed identity and came on with an international show-casing program of six new scripts. Kevin O'Morrison's *Ladyhouse Blues* was a backward glance at an America that once was in 1919 but is no more, with a cast of five women waiting for their men to come home from World War I and take up a life that is immediately going to suffer radical change. This sensitive play had been selected by American Playwrights Theater for production by its member university, regional and community theaters across the United States. Equally effective in more somber colors at the Phoenix was a backward glance at a corner of America's participation in the Vietnam War, David Berry's *G.R. Point,* about members of a Graves Registration unit adapting each in his own way to the presence of death confronted in battle and storehoused in green plastic body bags. John Heard (a recruit) and Lori Tan Chinn (a Vietnamese maid-of-all-work) led a fine ensemble under the direction of Tony Giordano. From other lands the Phoenix offered a translation from the German of Peter Handke's *A Sorrow Beyond Dreams,* a dramatic monologue with Len Cariou as a writer expressing the many ways of his grief and bewilderment over his mother's suicide; a program of one-acters, *Canadian Gothic* and *American Modern,* by Canada's Joanna M. Glass; and *Scribes* by Barrie Keeffe, about the tribulations of a small-town British newspaper. A *Marco Polo* for children completed the Phoenix's season.

American Place was a new-play haven as usual under Wynn Handman's supervision. Its season began well with a script self-described in the title — *Jack Gelber's New Play: Rehearsal.* This one turned inward to examine the personalities and processes of the theater itself in a rehearsal-within-a-play depicting actors, director, author, producer at work. The group went on to a program of William Hauptman one-acters, *Comanche Cafe* and *Domino Courts;* played host to the Tréteau de Paris's production of Corneille's *Rodogune* for a week's visit; offered Jeff Wanshel's fanciful and semi-biographical *Isadora Duncan Sleeps With the Russian Navy;* and ended the season on a high note in a key of contemplative drama, Ronald Ribman's *Cold Storage,* with Martin Balsam and Michael Lipton as a pair of wheel chair-bound patients on a hospital rooftop contemplating death in some of its past and ever-present forms. The popular success of American Place's season came out of its American Humorists series in the Subplot Cafe, where Caymichael Patten staged a revue collection of Jules Feiffer cartoon characters that went out to a commercial run at the Chelsea Westside Cabaret Theater under the title *Jules Feiffer's Hold Me!*

Chelsea itself was attracted to English translations of foreign material this season, including the American professional premiere of Von Kleist's *The Prince of Homberg,* a 165-year-old German political conundrum about a prince in moral conflict with the state he serves heroically; and Witkiewicz's *The Crazy Locomotive,* a between-World-Wars Polish play about the imminent demise of civilization. Chelsea's 1976-77 popular success was a new adaptation by Michael Feingold of the Bertolt Brecht-Kurt Weill musical *Happy End* (classified by the Tony Nominations Committee as a "new" musical but viewed here as an extraordinarily skillful and imaginative revival) which leapt from Brooklyn to Broadway. An interesting anomaly on the 1976-77 Chelsea program was Saul Levitt's multimedia *Lincoln,* a one-performer (Fritz Weaver) show with multiple sound and visual effects built up around the character of the great Civil War president. Chelsea made it a regular policy this season to bring its programs across the river to Theater Four for midtown Manhattan bookings, following their Brooklyn engagements.

Season after season Negro Ensemble Company comes up with an outstanding new work. This year's was *The Brownsville Raid* by Charles Fuller, a historical drama of a 1906 incident in which a black Army regiment stationed in Texas was falsely and racistically accused of participating in a violent public disturbance, for which the whole regiment was unjustly punished with a dishonorable discharge, with the collusion of authorities including President Theodore Roosevelt. Directed by Israel Hicks and performed by Douglas Turner Ward at the head of an NEC ensemble, this was an eloquent re-examination of history in the form of first-rate theater. For the second offering of its season, the group revived its own previously-produced symbolical drama, *The Great Macdaddy.*

Two emergent ex-OOB groups came up with new work on their 1976-77 schedules. T. Schreiber Theater presented Enid Rudd's *Does Anybody Here Do the Peabody?,* a nostalgic 1930s movie-style romance of a poor, sweet widow and an attractive scoundrel, as well as the American premiere of the British play *Curtains* by Tom Mallin about a couple's disintegrating relationship. Christopher Martin's Classic Stage Company (CSC) slipped the New York professional premiere of Edward Bond's *Bingo,* the pessimistic portrait of a disillusioned Shakespeare nearing the end of the line, into its schedule of revivals.

Individual production of off-Broadway shows was a rarity in 1976-77, and sometimes of great value. For example, David Mamet's professional New York theater debut took place off Broadway in June at the Cherry Lane with the Lawrence Goossen-Jeffrey Wachtel production of two short Mamet works, *Sexual Perversity in Chicago* and *Duck Variations,* described in the previous chapter of this report. And in this season of alienation, no program was more forbidding (or horribly fascinating, to put a positive face on it) than Adela

Holzer's off-Broadway production *Monsters*. This consisted of the two one-acters *Side Show* by William Dews, with Drivas (who directed the whole program) and Richard De Fabees as Siamese twins who have just slaughtered the hated parents who first abhorred and then exploited them; and the more substantial *The Transfiguration of Benno Blimpie* by Albert Innaurato, described with his other work in the previous chapter of this report. Also among independent productions there appeared another of Robert Wilson's perplexing divertissements, laboriously and comma-lessly entitled *I Was Sitting on My Patio This Guy Appeared I Thought I Was Hallucinating*, produced off Broadway by Richard Barr for some reason in the season's final week.

In off-Broadway musical production, it was a cheerful and fruitful year. Circle in the Square (Downtown) brought Eve Merriam's *The Club* in from the Lenox, Mass. Arts Center. The show satirized male attitudes and vanities with a cast of women playing turn-of-the-century clubmen in consummate style under Tommy Tune's direction, carrying the joke even so far as to bill themselves in the program by sexless initials in place of first names (example: G. Hodes instead of Gloria Hodes), with a score of selected songs of the period. Still another off-Broadway musical hit imported from Lenox's Music-Theater Performing Group (overseen by Lyn Austin and Mary D. Silverman) was Elizabeth Swados's *Nightclub Cantata* at the Top of the Gate, a rich cabaret assortment of musical commentary varied in subject but consistent in skill and imagination (this was a fruitful year for Miss Swados, who also wrote the exceptionally effective background music for *The Cherry Orchard* and *Agamemnon* at Lincoln Center). The year's off-Broadway program of revues also took in two notable collections of show tunes: *2 by 5*, a John Kander-Fred Ebb medley, and *Starting Here, Starting Now,* an OOB-originated collage by Richard Maltby Jr. and David Shire.

The *Jesus Christ Superstar* authors, Tim Rice and Andrew Lloyd Webber, turned to the Old Testament for their *Joseph and the Amazing Technicolor Dreamcoat*, produced with considerable success by London's Old Vic under the direction of Frank Dunlop, who came across the Atlantic to stage this musical at Brooklyn Academy of Music and remained to help set up the new BAM Theater Company. The 1976-77 off-Broadway musical program also included *Movie Buff*, one of this season's several reminiscences of 1930s movies; a Charles Ludlam-Ridiculous Theatrical Company burlesque of Wagnerian opera *Der Ring Gott Farblonjet;* and Peter Copani's street musical *New York City Street Show.*

A special event of the off-Broadway year was the limited engagement at BAM of the German-language *Waiting for Godot*, directed by Samuel Beckett himself in the Schiller Theater production. Other visitors from abroad were the Gavella Theater of Zagreb, Yugoslavia in a Croation play *Kraljevo* (The Kermess); the Abbey Theater troupe in O'Casey's *The Plough and the Stars;* and Emlyn Williams and Eamon Kelly in their one-man shows, *Dylan Thomas Growing Up* and *In My Father's Time,* respectively. Our home-grown, perennial and cherished specialty, the Bil Baird Marionettes, presented the Mary Rodgers-Waldo Salt-Arthur Birnkrant musical *Davy Jones' Locker* throughout the season.

As a whole, 1976-77 was a busy and productive year off Broadway in every category of shows, but mostly grouped together in one category of production: organizational. Off Broadway helped introduce outstanding new playwrights and provided a showcase for small-scale, innovative musicals. Its costs may have been creeping in the direction of Broadway, but the perceptions of its most impressive work were not. It was doing its own thing, offering an alternative New York theater at a professional level for both artists and audiences.

Revivals on and off Broadway

The New York revival scene has broadened in this decade like a wide-angle lens, until in 1975-76 revivals outnumbered the total of new American plays and musicals on Broadway and nearly reached it off. In 1976-77 their presence on Broadway attenuated somewhat, with "only" 17 as opposed to 28 the previous year, but they predominated off Broadway with a grand total of 34. In both areas they were a Presence with a capital P, making a world festival of our stages.

The Broadway revival season was distinguished by the number and high quality of life-sized copies of musicals which, far from laying on any veneer of newness, strove mightily to recapture the exact thrust and glamor of the original. The Gershwins' *Porgy and Bess* came to town in a Houston Grand Opera production that was larger than life-size, in that it presented the work in its seldom-seen original version, uncut, with operatic recitatives in place of conventional dialogue. Gifted singers (including Clamma Dale and Larry Marshall, nominated for Tonys) alternated in the leads. The show itself won the Tony for "most innovative revival" and was indeed one of the most rewarding events of the musical season, which also took in a snappy *Guys and Dolls* with an all-black cast headed by Robert Guillaume as Nathan Detroit; Zero Mostel and Yul Brynner recreating their towering original roles for *Fiddler on the Roof* and *The King and I*, as well as regroupings of *Pal Joey* (at Circle in the Square) and even *Oh! Calcutta!* In a class by itself as usual was Light Opera of Manhattan (LOOM) which put on a repertory of ten operetta revivals under William Mount-Burke's direction including well-loved works by Lehar, Friml, Herbert and a cluster of Gilbert & Sullivan from *H.M.S. Pinafore* to the seldom-produced collector's item *Utopia, Limited*.

Topping the list of revivals which strived for a kind of newness was Chelsea's *Happy End*, a Bertolt Brecht-Kurt Weill musical shaped so imaginatively that it almost seemed like a new work. *Almost,* we repeat, because we consider *Happy End* a revival even though it was nominated for a Tony in the new-musical category after it moved from Brooklyn to Broadway. It is "new" by virtue of the fact that it has never been professionally produced in New York, though its material, written in 1929, has been excerpted in at least two Broadway shows. We agree that a *Sly Fox* becomes a new play in *total* adaptation of setting, characters, dialogue, style, etc., retaining only the original concept, the Holinshed of the matter; but we don't accept a technicality by which ancient Greek plays which have never received a professional New York production would qualify as "new" — and we did not consider the revamped *Candide* of a few seasons back a "new" musical.

If not a new work, this *Happy End* was certainly a creative one, particularly in Michael Feingold's free adaptation of the book and lyrics. A scholarly note in the Chelsea program informs us that the book was credited to Elisabeth Hauptmann, Brecht's secretary, who had supposedly based it on a play by a nonexistent "Dorothy Lane." Feingold's book was more than a translation; Weill's and Brecht's "The Bilbao Song" would stop any show; and Meryl Streep (a competent singer as well as a consummate actress) and Christopher Lloyd played a Salvation Army lass and a gangster of the 1920s as though they'd never met before, not even in *Guys and Dolls.*

Another musical work revised in the direction of newness for modern audiences was *Going Up*, a 1917 musical with a Louis Hirsch-Otto Harbach score and several ice cream flavors in its adventure of a daring young man showing off to a maiden fair by going aloft solo in an airplane, though he's never flown one before. These days, even revivals have cross-country origins: *Going Up*, like the equally innocent *Annie*, was first launched at the Goodspeed Opera House in East Haddam, Conn.; and *Happy End* tried out in Yale Repertory Theater before coming to New York.

In the straight-play category, Joseph Papp turned Andrei Serban loose on *The Cherry Orchard* (in a new English adaptation by Jean-Claude van Itallie which, it was reported, the Tony Eligibility Committee had considered classifying a "new" play) and Aeschylus's mighty *Agamemnon* at the Vivian Beaumont. In both cases, but most lucidly in the former, Serban achieved imposing and startling effects of ritualistic theater, with Irene Worth leading the intricate ensemble measures of the Chekhov play. Papp recruited Michael Moriarty and Paul Rudd for *Henry V* and Sam Waterston and Meryl Streep for *Measure for Measure* in his outdoor summer season in Central Park and ended his indoor winter season with a program of Strindberg one-acters.

The Broadway revival as star vehicle was much in evidence. Liv Ullmann gave us an *Anna Christie* clear as glass, shining through every detail of the Eugene O'Neill character under José Quintero's direction. Al Pacino reshaped the role of the nonentity caught in the tide rip of the Vietnam War in David Rabe's *The Basic Training of Pavlo Hummel* and made it his own. Rex Harrison and Elizabeth Ashley did Shaw's *Caesar and Cleopatra* conspicuously but briefly. Claire Bloom moved gracefully through *The Innocents* (based on Henry James's *The Turn of the Screw*) under Harold Pinter's direction, and Paul Rudd and Pamela Payton-Wright concentrated on the love story in Theodore Mann's abridged version of *Romeo and Juliet.* Tennessee Williams added less to his reputation with his new play than he did with his Broadway revivals this season: *The Eccentricities of a Nightingale,* the rewrite of *Summer and Smoke* previously produced in London, off Broadway and in the present, still further rewritten version first produced at Studio Arena in Buffalo; and *The Night of the Iguana,* revived under Joseph Hardy's direction and Circle in the Square's unfailingly competent production auspices.

Shaw's *The Philanderer* and Ibsen's *John Gabriel Borkman,* with Gale Sondergaard, were highlights of the Gene Feist-Michael Fried Roundabout

Theater Center's 1976-77 schedule on its busy stages. Christopher Martin's Classic Stage Company (CSC) put on the first New York production of Jean Genet's full script of *The Balcony,* in a repertory that ranged from Pinter's *The Homecoming* to Molière's *Tartuffe.* A new group, the BAM Theater Company, was formed at the Academy of Music with the help of Frank Dunlop of London's Old Vic, attracting a number of stellar performers to do *Three Sisters* and a 1906 Langdon Mitchell comedy, *The New York Idea,* under Dunlop's intercontinentally renowned direction. Various OOB groups were making the effort to emerge at the commercial level with revival productions, including Actors' Alliance *(The Tavern, Lullaby* and *Hay Fever),* T. Schreiber Theater *(All the Way Home)* and Lion Theater Company *(Peg o' My Heart).*

The whole of the New York Theater revival festival of 1976-77 was greater than the sum of its parts. As entertaining, as revealing, as stimulating as many of the individual attractions were, there was a greater service to the theatergoer in making *all* of them available in the same place within the same short time frame. This informal but impressive festival took in not only Shakespeare, Shaw, Ibsen and Chekhov, but Coward, Beckett, O'Neill and O'Casey — and Pinter, Rabe, Anouilh and Williams — and Gershwin, Loesser, Rodgers and Harbach. From *Agamemnon* to *The Basic Training of Pavlo Hummel,* from *Tartuffe* to *Waiting for Godot* is a world of theater not too wide for the New York stage to encompass.

Offstage

The clinking of coins and the clicking of credit cards at the Broadway box offices was the most conspicuous offstage activity of the 1976-77 season, but the second most conspicuous was the downward slide of the neighborhood — slowed a bit, perhaps, but unchanged in direction. Boarded-up stores, half-lit hotel foyers uncleaned in this century and trash-filled doorways lined the approaches to Broadway. The best that can be said for the Sixth Avenue-to-Broadway blocks these days is that they provide audiences with a suitable preparation for a theater of shock and alienation.

Thanks to the persistent efforts of New York City departments, who are perfectly aware of the theater's enormous value to both the economy and lifestyle of the city, Broadway and its approaches were at least kept safe for theatergoers. The neighborhood isn't inviting, but its only negative impact during theater hours is esthetic.

Competing with the theater for public attention in the Broadway area, and having far outstripped the movies there, is the blatant marketing of sex, an intrusive presence which both theater and city oppose at every level, apparently unavailingly. In June, 1976 Gov. Hugh Carey of New York State signed an anti-loitering bill designed to keep prostitutes off certain streets. Broadway's sidewalks nevertheless teem with their annoying shills with their massage-parlor handouts and their cries of "Check it out!" which has replaced the newsboy's "Whatdya read?" as Broadway's background noise (it's hard to find a place to buy a newspaper there these days). The unceasing efforts of the League of New York Theaters and Producers to inhibit and shut off the porno traffic boomeranged when Lester Osterman, a League member, booked off Broadway's self-styled "sexual musical" *Let My People Come* into the Morosco. A special meeting of the League's Board of Governors declared this action "antithetical" to their policies. The show's producer, Phil Oesterman (no relation to the theater operator) immediately branded the League's action as censorship. The show went into the Morosco for a short and uneventful run and the controversy died down; but the League remains on record in its Aug. 31 resolution that "a cause for dismissal from membership in the League shall be deemed to exist when . . . . . a League member shall be found to have produced and/or presented and/or booked a play which shall be antithetical to the programs of the League seeking to upgrade the physical appearance of ths theatrical district; to eliminate sex-related businesses, such as massage parlors, peep shows, prostitution hotels, street prostitution, topless bars and pornographic motion picture theaters from the theater district; and to generally improve the urban environment in the midtown area."

Later in the season, a revival production of the erotic revue *Oh! Calcutta!* slid quietly into the smallish Edison Theater on West 47th Street, alternating performances with *Me and Bessie* and then staying on alone after *Bessie* closed, without raising any objections, a sort of if-you-can't-lick-'em-join-'em response to the theater's present environmental predicament.

Speaking of the Morosco, hard times in real estate and good times in the theater have caused postponement and possible abandonment of the plan to raze the Broadway end of the 45th-46th Street block to put up a hotel and office complex that would have wiped out the Morosco and Helen Hayes Theaters (we erroneously identified the latter as the Ethel Barrymore in our 1975-76 volume and hasten to correct this regrettable error). "The Hayes and Morosco are two of the better theaters in New York," Lester Osterman declared, and he means to refurbish and run them on a long-term lease. There will also be some sprucing-up around the Broadway block which takes in the old Astor Theater facade. And now for the bad news: the newly-refurbished Harkness Theater on the fringe of Lincoln Center was sold to real estate interests, gutted and will probably be razed.

Joseph Papp also announced theater-refurbishing plans for the Vivian Beaumont; and then, just as everyone was beginning to speculate where he was going to get the $6.5 million he wanted to do this, he threw in the towel entirely and gave up on the Lincoln Center operation. Papp never found his feet uptown; he tried new plays, toyed with the idea of Shakespeare repertory, grudgingly lowered his sights to take aim at the subscription audience with a series of first-rate revival productions he hoped might be crowd-pleasers. Still, Papp's dedication to excellence emerged through all the problems; and whatever happens to the Beaumont now, it will be a long time before it matches Papp's finest hour there last season with the new adaptation of *Threepenny Opera* in the big theater and *Streamers* in the little Newhouse Theater in the basement.

The theater season's loudest street quarrel took place over the arrival in New York of the South African musical *Ipi-Tombi* for a booking at the Harkness Theater, following its long and successful London engagement. Well-organized protesters gathered under the marquee trying to make a political issue of the show, passing out literature which argued, "*Ipi-Tombi* is not simply an African musical symbolical of 'happiness.' If anything other than another cultural ripoff, *Ipi-Tombi* represents just the opposite: a sad and dangerous burlesque of the very real day-to-day victimization of our brothers and sisters in Azania (South Africa)."

Pickets castigated the show as a subliminally racist indoctrination of audiences with "a bogus air of happiness" and an exploitation of the performers for this purpose. The producers maintained that it was a non-political entertainment and a tribute to its participants' cultural achievements. The cast cried out that, far from being exploited, they were being very well paid indeed and wanted to keep on doing their thing in New York. None of the protesters we questioned had actually seen the show, which indeed ignored any white presence in South Africa (except for the starkly inhuman atmosphere of a city scene) and indeed showed great respect for the tribal arts of music and dance. In any case, the show wasn't a strong enough attraction, and it soon closed without any help from the pickets. The lyrics made one reverberating comment in the line, "I smile, but is this my face?" — but nothing could have impressed protesters who objected to begin with that the musical didn't spell its title, meaning "Where are the girls?", in a fashion more respectful of its language of origin: "Iphi-Ntombi."

In September, a group of producers instituted a court challenge to United Scenic Artists, Local 829 over its status — union or illegal combination in restraint of trade — in much the same way that the Dramatists Guild and the Society of Stage Directors and Choreographers have been challenged previously. In another part of the forest, the producers and stagehands settled on a new three-year contract with built-in raises of 10 per cent the first year and 8 per cent for each of the next two years (by which time, no doubt, the $20 ticket will be an ubiquitous Broadway reality). Robert Whitehead ushered Kevin Sanders, a TV drama critic, out of the theater at the premiere of *The Oldest Living Graduate* because Sanders had arrived 25 minutes late and, the producer claimed, had arrived late for the curtains of the two previous plays in the Preston Jones trilogy.

Alexander H. Cohen had a short-lived difference of opinion with the Tony administration over contractual arrangements for the TV awards show. Apparently it was soon settled to his satisfaction and that of his wife and co-producer Hildy Parks, because they were in charge as usual when the Tony Awards went on the air in June. The annual controversy over Tony classifications was re-heated when *Variety* reported in March that the pre-nomination Eligibility Committee (Jerry Gross, Susan Harley and Stuart Little) was considering declaring the likes of *Porgy and Bess, Threepenny Opera, Side by Side by Sondheim* and *The Cherry Orchard* eligible for the new-play and new-musical categories, because of new conceptions or translations. The committee did no such thing but set up a new Tony category for "most innovative production of a revival" to honor excellence in that field. The final list of Tony nominees, selected by still another and larger committee, included in the new-play category *Streamers,* a year-old off-Broadway swan whose ugly duckling-like presence in this nest of nominees needs explaining: 1) at some point during the 1976-77 season this drama was declared a "Broadway" show though it never moved from the little Newhouse Theater in the basement of the Beaumont and 2) it opened after last season's early Tony cutoff date in March. The cutoff date was moved ahead this year to early May, close to the actual end of the season June 1, which should prevent the intrusion of stragglers like *Streamers* into future lists. The new date was especially fortuitous this season, because if the cutoff had come in March as it did last year there would have been slim pickings for best musical, as none of the three 1976-77 nominees opened in New York until mid-April.

If these ways of concensus for Tony Award-giving seem strange, they are at least not unique — c.f. the very strange ways of this year's consensus in the voting for the New York Drama Critics Circle's Awards, detailed in the awards section of this volume.

Major changes of personnel taking place in theater circles this season included a changing of the guard in the powerful position of daily drama critic of the New York *Times*. The paper announced that Clive Barnes's occupancy of this post would come to an end with the 1976-77 season, and that he would concentrate on his duties as dance critic while Richard Eder, a 44-year-old former foreign correspondent and present member of the *Times* amusement staff, would take over in drama (while Walter Kerr remains as Sunday drama critic). In an informal valedictory as a footnote to his final review, that of *Scribes*, Clive Barnes wrote, "Nearly ten years ago at the beginning of the 1967-68 season, the first play I reviewed for this paper was *Stephen D*, starring Stephen Joyce. Now, completely by chance, in this, my last drama review for the paper, Mr. Joyce turns up again. All I can say is that I trust that Mr. Joyce has had as good a time with the theater in the last decade as I have. It has really been fun."

Still another of the longtime Critics Circle regulars, Henry Hewes, resigned as drama critic of the *Saturday Review*. In another major theater personnel change, Kitty Carlisle (Mrs. Moss) Hart was named by Gov. Carey to succeed Joan Davidson in the important and prestigious post of chairman of the New York State Council on the Arts.

One last backward glance at the 1976-77 theater season in New York: shock and alienation were its dominant tones, yes, but it was as diverse as perverse. The 180-degree opposition of lifestyles portrayed in *Annie* and *I Love My Wife*, its two best musicals, is a point-counterpoint symbol of this season, together with the foul language of *American Buffalo* opposite the meticulously weighed-up phrases of *Otherwise Engaged*, the bloody tissues of *Ashes* opposite the tennis rackets of *California Suite*. The award-giving at season's end reflected the diverse more than the perverse nature of the season, with the Pulitzer Prize and Tony Award going to *The Shadow Box* and the Critics Awards to *Otherwise Engaged* and *American Buffalo*. The Circle's significant first ballot of *first* choices for best play was so diversified that there was a four-way tie for second place.

Our Best Plays selection for the best-of-bests this season is none of the above. Our conviction that Preston Jones's *The Last Meeting of the Knights of the White Magnolia* was the best American and Trevor Griffiths' *Comedians* the best foreign play of the year remains unshaken by any fluke of consensus. We insist on our difference, and in the season of 1976-77 that makes us typical.

○
○
○

THE SEASON
AROUND THE UNITED STATES

with

A DIRECTORY OF PROFESSIONAL
REGIONAL THEATER

and

AN OUTSTANDING NEW PLAY
CITED BY
AMERICAN THEATER CRITICS
ASSOCIATION

○
○
○

*Including casts and credits of new plays, selected
Canadian programs, children's programs, dinner theater
and extended coverage of the Los Angeles and
Washington seasons*

AS WE REPORTED in the 1974–75 Best Plays volume, 23 American theater
critics met at the O'Neill Foundation in Waterford, Conn. in August of that
season and formed the American Theater Critics Association, complementing
the trend of nationwide theater production with the first nationwide critics'
organization. Two years later, the Association membership numbers more than
125 working critics in all media in cities from New York to Los Angeles, Chicago to Houston.

THE SEASON AROUND THE UNITED STATES

One of the group's stated purposes was "To increase public awareness of the theater as an important national resource." To this end, we offer as an introduction to our coverage of "The Season Around the United States" a synopsis of an outstanding new play produced outside New York in the 1976–77 season, cited by the Critics Association and presented here in exactly the same manner as one of the ten Best Plays of the New York season.

The critics selected *And the Soul Shall Dance* by Wakako Yamauchi for presentation in this volume in the following manner: member critics everywhere were asked to call the Critics Association's attention to outstanding new work in their specific areas. Scripts of these plays nominated were read by a committee whose chairman was Dan Sullivan, drama critic of the Los Angeles *Times*. Like this volume's New York Best Plays choices, the Critics Association's choice was made on the basis of script. There were no eligibility requirements (such as Equity cast or resident-theater status) except that it be the first full professional production of a new work outside New York City within this volume's time frame of June 1, 1976 to May 31, 1977.

A list of all the 1976–77 plays cited by members of the American Theater Critics Association as outstanding presentations in their areas follows the synopsis, with brief descriptions of these cited plays written by the critics who saw and nominated them. The synopsis itself was prepared by the *Best Plays* editor.

*Cited by American Theater Critics
as an Outstanding New Play
of 1976–77*

AND THE SOUL SHALL DANCE

A Play in Two Acts

BY WAKAKO YAMAUCHI

Cast and credits appear on page 70

*WAKAKO YAMAUCHI was born into an Imperial Valley farming family in
Westmorland, Calif. in 1924. She attended high school in Brawley and Ocean-
side, Calif. and spent so much of her spare time reading that finally, in her middle 30s, she decided to try writing herself. Short stories were her chosen medium,
and when she wasn't immediately successful she took up painting (abstractions
in acrylics and inks). She has made her mark in both arts.*

And the Soul Shall Dance *appeared as a short story in Frank Chin's*
Aiiieeeee, An Anthology of Asian American Writers. *Mako, who will be
remembered by New York audiences for his recent portrayal of the Narrator in*
Pacific Overtures, *is the artistic director of a Los Angeles Theater group called
East West Players, and he persuaded Ms. Yamauchi to try writing it as a play.
She did, with the help of a 1976–77 Rockefeller Playwright-in-Residence Grant.
It was produced by East West Players (Norman Cohen administrator), with
Mako and Alberto Isaac co-directing, for 14 weeks beginning Feb. 23, 1977.*

And the Soul Shall Dance *is Ms. Yamauchi's first work for the stage. She is
now writing her second, which also has a farm background. She is divorced, with
one child, lives in Gardena, Calif. and serves as drama critic for the local paper,
the* Valley News.

Time: The early 1930s

Place: On and between two small farms in Southern California's Imperial Valley

ACT I

Scene 1: Murata's kitchen

SYNOPSIS: The interior is sparsely furnished with kitchen table, chairs, a bed, a phonograph, towels hanging on pegs, etc. Hana Murata, *"35, Issei wife, in a drab house dress"* is scolding her 11-year-old daughter Masako for her carelessness with the coals heating the water in the outside bath-house. She has set it afire and all her father's efforts can't prevent it from burning to the ground.

Murata — Hana's husband and Masako's father — enters, exhausted, having given up the struggle to put out the fire. He is 40, dressed in old clothes, inclined to be forgiving about the accident. "I didn't do it on purpose," says Masako. She withdraws to the bed area and takes up a book.

Hana is worrying about how they'll manage to bathe, when a neighbor, Oka, *"45, short and stout, dressed in faded work clothes,"* comes in and offers to help Murata move the metal tub, which hasn't burned; but the ashes are still too hot and Murata still so exhausted from his effort that he can hardly move his own body.

Hana serves sake and chiles to the men while Oka explains that he's on his way to the prosperous Nagatas' to see if they'll buy his horse.

MURATA: . . . . . What the hell; if you need a few bucks, I can loan you . . .

OKA: A few hundred. I need a few hundred dollars.

MURATA: Oh, a few hundred. But what the hell you going to do without a horse? Out here a man's horse is as important as his wife.

OKA (*seriously*): I don't think Nagata will buy my wife.

> *The men laugh, but Hana doesn't find it quite so funny. Murata glances at her. She fills the cups again. Oka makes a half-hearted gesture to stop her. Masako watches the pantomime carefully. Oka swallows his drink in one gulp.*

I better get moving.

MURATA: What's the big hurry?

OKA: Like to get the horse business done.

MURATA: Ehhh, relax. Do it tomorrow. He's not going to die, is he?

OKA (*laughing*): Hey, he's a good horse. I want to get it settled today. If Nagata-san won't buy, I got to find someone else. You think maybe Kawaguchi . . .

MURATA: Not Kawaguchi. Maybe Yamamoto . . .

HANA: What is all the money for, Oka-san? Does Emiko-san need an operation?

OKA: Nothing like that.

HANA: It sounds very mysterious . . .

OKA: No mystery . . . . .

Hana fills the cups and goes back to Masako.

HANA (*muttering*): I see we won't be getting any work done today. (*To Masako.*) Are you reading again? Maybe we'd still have a bath if you . . .

MASAKO: I didn't do it on purpose.

MURATA (*loudly*): I sure hope you know what you're doing, Oka. What'd you do without a horse?

OKA: I was hoping you'd lend me yours now and then . . . I'll pay for some of the feed . . .

MURATA (*emphatically waving his hand*): Sure! Sure!

OKA: The fact is, I need that money. I got a daughter in Japan and I just got to send for her this year.

The Muratas had supposed that Oka and his wife Emiko were childless. Indeed they are — but Oka had been married before to Emiko's sister and has a 15-year-old daughter, Kiyoko, living in Japan with her grandparents. Oka had been apprenticed to his wife's family, who "always looked down their noses at me" and made Oka's work hard and humiliating. Oka and his wife Shizue decided that Oka should come to America, save up enough money to come back and take Shizue and the baby away to another province, on their own, away from her family.

Oka worked hard in America and sent every penny to Shizue — but suddenly Shizue died. Almost before he knew it, the grandparents arranged to have Oka remarried to their other daughter, Shizue's sister Emiko.

OKA: Before the body was cold! No respect! By proxy! The old man wrote me they were arranging a marriage by proxy for me and Emiko. They said she'd grown to be a beautiful woman and would serve me well . . .

HANA: Emiko-san is a beautiful woman . . .

OKA: And they sent her to me. Took care of everything! Immigration, fare, everything . . .

HANA: But she's your sister-in-law . . . Kiyoko-san's aunt . . . It's good to keep the family together.

OKA: That's what I thought. But hear this: Emiko was the favored one. Shizue was not so pretty, not so smart. They were grooming Emiko for a rich man — his name was Yamato — lived in a grand house in the village. They sent her to schools; you know, the culture thing: the dance, the tea ceremony, you know, all that. They didn't even like me, and suddenly they married her to me . . .

MURATA: Yeah, you don't need all that formal training to make it over here. Just a strong back.

HANA: And a strong will . . .

Furthermore, the grandparents have been mistreating Kiyoko, telling her that her father has forgotten about her. Kiyoko knows better, through her father's letters — but Oka feels that he must send for her at once. Hana agrees and offers

Masako's help to get Kiyoko started in America. Oka invites all the Muratas to come to his house this evening for their baths. They accept, and Oka exits.

After Oka has gone, Hana confesses that she's uneasy about going over there. In the three or four years she's been a neighbor, Emiko has continued stand-offish, never making Hana feel welcome, never even offering a cup of tea, for all her supposed graces. The Muratas discuss bringing some sort of present to the Okas.

HANA (*looking around*): We'll have to take something . . . There's nothing to take . . . Papa, maybe you can dig up some carrots . . .
MURATA: God, Mama, be sensible. They got carrots. Everybody's got carrots.
HANA: Something . . . Maybe I should make something . . .
MURATA: Hell, they're not expecting anything.
HANA: It's not good manners to go empty-handed.
MURATA: We'll take the *sake.*
    Masako sees the record player.
MASAKO: I know, Mama, we can take the Victrola! We can play records for Mrs. Oka. Then nobody has to talk.
    Murata laughs. Hana looks at Masako. Fade out.

Scene 2: Oka's yard and beyond

That evening the Muratas arrive in front of the Okas' house, with its weather-beaten wall, screen door and wide bench standing outside. It is almost sunset. Through the window Emiko can be seen walking up and down. She is an *"Issei woman, 30 . . . . . she wears a drab cotton dress but her grace and femininity come through. Her hair is bunned back in the style of Issei women of the era."*

Oka is sitting outside on the bench fanning himself, and he jumps up to wel-come the Muratas. Emiko comes to the door. As Hana is politely begging par-don for this intrusion, it becomes clear that Oka hasn't told Emiko about invit-ing the Muratas over. Oka tries to be hospitable, noticing the bottle of sake the Muratas have brought and asking Emiko to bring out some cups. Emiko ig-nores this request and sits in a chair next to the bench outside. Instead of insist-ing, Oka simply goes to get the cups himself.

Hana and Masako sort Victrola records and offer a choice to Emiko. She refuses to respond and instead rolls and lights a cigarette. Hana selects a record and puts it on the player. Emiko listens, smoking; apparently the nostalgic appeal of the record reaches her, because there seem to be tears in her eyes as she rises abruptly, goes back into the house and *"stands forlornly and slowly drifts into a dance."*

Oka seems unaware of his wife's distracted behavior. Hana sends Masako off to take her bath. Hana stops the record and substitutes a more lively one. The three are tapping their feet to the music, when *"From the side of the house Emiko appears. Her hair is down, she wears an old straw hat. She dances in front of the Muratas. They are startled. After the first shock, they watch with frozen smiles. They try to join Emiko's mood but something is missing. Oka is grieved. He finally stands as though he's had enough. Emiko, now close to the door, ducks into the house . . . . . Oka settles down and grunts."*

Masako returns from the bath, having performed her ablutions quickly because the water was too hot to suit her. Hana and Murata go off to take their baths.

OKA: So . . . you don't like hot baths, eh?

MASAKO: Not too hot.

OKA (*laughing*): I thought you liked it real hot. Hot enough to burn the house down. That's a little joke.

> *Masako busies herself with the records to conceal her annoyance.*

I hear you're real good in school. Always top of the class.

MASAKO: It's a small class. Only two of us.

OKA: When Kiyoko comes, you'll help her in school, yeah? You'll take care of her . . . a favor for me, eh?

MASAKO: Okay.

OKA: You'll be her friend, eh?

MASAKO: Okay.

OKA: That's good. That's good. You'll like her. She's a nice girl too . . . (*Stands, yawns, stretches.*) I'll go for a little walk now.

> *He touches his crotch to indicate his purpose and leaves. Masako turns her attention to the records and selects one, "The Soul Shall Dance" and begins to sway to the music. The song draws Emiko from the house. She looks out the window, sees Masako is alone and begins to slip into a dance.*

EMIKO: Do you like that song, Masa-chan?

> *Masako is startled and draws back . . . . . She doesn't know what to do. She nods.*

That's one of my favorite songs. I remember in Japan I used to sing it so often . . . my favorite song . . . (*Sings along with the record*):

> Akai kuchi biru
> Kappu ni yosete
> Aoi sake nomya
> Kokoro ga odoru . . .

Do you know what that means, Masa-chan?

MASAKO: I think so . . . The soul will dance?

EMIKO: Yes, yes, that's right . . . The soul shall dance. "Red lips against a glass/Drink the green . . . "

MASAKO: Wine?

EMIKO (*nodding*): Drink the green wine . . .

MASAKO: Green? I thought wine is purple . . .

EMIKO (*nodding*): Wine is purple . . . but this is a green liqueur . . .

> *Emiko holds up one of the china cups as though it were crystal, and looks at it as though the light were shining through it and she sees the green liquid.*

It's good . . . it warms your heart.

MASAKO: And the soul dances . . .

EMIKO: Yes . . .

MASAKO: What does it taste like? The green . . .

EMIKO: Oh, it's like . . . it's like . . .

> *The second verse starts: "Kurai/yoru no yume/Setsunasa yo/Aoi sake nomya/Yume mo odoru . . . "*

MASAKO: In the dark night . . .

EMIKO: Dreams are unbearable . . . insufferable . . . (*She turns sad.*)

MASAKO: Drink the . . .

EMIKO (*nodding*): Drink the green wine . . .

MASAKO: And the dreams will dance . . . . .

Emiko confides to Masako that she dreams of the day when she can return by herself to her real home — Japan. As the music stops, the women see Oka approaching. Emiko slips away.

Oka is curious to find out what the women were talking about. Masako tells him they were talking about the song, and the nature of the soul (Emiko has no soul, Oka implies scornfully).

Oka mentions his daughter Kiyoko's name. Emiko, overhearing inside the house, sings so loudly that Oka and Masako find themselves shouting in order to continue their conversation. Enraged, Oka goes into the house and silences Emiko forcefully and violently. Masako is a little bit afraid of Oka when he comes back outside and lights the lantern in the gathering dusk.

The Muratas return, having enjoyed their hot bath. Emiko comes out of the house, now with *"a large purple welt on her face,"* which the Muratas embarrassedly pretend not to notice. They begin the formalities of leave-taking — but Emiko, now become as conspicuously talkative as she had been conspicuously silent, delays them, speaking of the music, of her parents' belief that singing was an improperly frivolous occupation for young ladies, of her classic training in the city, ended abruptly when she was sent to America.

Oka tells the Muratas that Nagata is interested in his horse and will probably buy it, so he'll soon be sending for Kiyoko. Emiko tries to continue talking about her former life — "I had more freedom in the city . . . I lived with an aunt and she let me . . . She wasn't so strict" — but the others pay no attention to her. The Muratas finally manage to make their departure.

On the way home, Hana explains to Masako that Emiko is not *kitchigai* — crazy — she merely had a little too much to drink this evening. Emiko cannot bend to the new, strong winds of American life, and so she is in danger of cracking. Hana confesses that she'd like to go back to Japan some day — "Everyone does" — but Masako is quick to remark that *she* doesn't.

Hana sees that Emiko is very lonely, without friends and living on memories. Perhaps Kiyoko will be company for her. The Muratas would like to befriend Emiko, but Hana finds it very difficult: "She either closes up, you can't pry a word from her or else she goes on and on . . . all that . . . that . . . about the *koto* and tea and the flower . . . I mean what am I supposed to say. She's so unpredictable. And the drinking . . . "

Masako informs her parents that Emiko's bruise was inflicted by Oka — she saw the episode through the window. The Muratas decide that from now on until a new bath-house is built it will be better to bathe in a bucket at home than to accept the Okas' hospitality.

Scene 3: Oka's yard

That same evening after the Muratas have left, Emiko pours herself another drink while Oka voices his disgust at her behavior. Oka grabs her shoulders to command her attention, but she pulls away from him and forbids him to touch her.

Their quarrel flares, as Oka accuses her of being "a second hand woman" whose affairs with men in Tokyo were notorious. Oka knew all about Emiko's behavior from Shizue's letters.

EMIKO: I'm not ashamed of it . . .

OKA: You're not ashamed! What the hell. Your father thought he was pulling a fast one on me . . . thought I didn't know nothing . . . thought I was some kind of dumb ass . . . I didn't say nothing because Shizue's dead . . . Shizue's dead. I was willing to give you a chance . . .

EMIKO (*laughing*): A chance?

OKA: Yeah. A chance! Laugh! Give a *joro* another chance . . . Sure, I'm stupid . . . dumb . . .

EMIKO: I'm not a whore . . . I'm true . . . he knows I'm true . . .

OKA: True! Ha!

EMIKO: You think I'm untrue just because I let . . . let you . . . There's only one man for me . . .

OKA: Let me (*Obscene gesture.*) you? I can do what I want with you. Your father palmed you off on me — like a dog or cat — an animal . . . couldn't do nothing with you . . . Even that rich dumb Yamato wouldn't have you . . . Your father . . . greedy father . . . so proud . . . making big plans for you . . . for himself . . . Ha! The whole village laughing at him . . .

Emiko hangs her head.

Shizue told me. And she was working like a dog . . . trying to keep your goddamn father happy . . . doing my work and yours.

EMIKO: My work?

OKA: Yeah, your work too! She killed herself working! She killed herself . . . (*He has tender memories of his dull, uncomplaining wife.*) Up in the morning getting the fires started, working the bellows, cleaning the furnace, cooking, and late at night working with the sewing . . . tending the baby . . . (*He mutters.*) The goddamn family killed her . . . And you . . . you out there in Tokyo with the fancy clothes, doing the (*He sneers.*) dance, the tea, the flower, the *koto,* the . . . (*Obscene gesture.*)

Emiko swears she is true to her one lover, and Oka mocks her for supposing that her lover will wait for her to come back to Japan. He challenges Emiko to go back to Japan right now — he doesn't need her. He pushes her off the bench, hurting her. Emiko begs him for the horse money for her passage home, but that is to be spent on his daughter's passage to America.

Emiko tells Oka she was away when Shizue died, she loved her and would have helped her if she could have.

EMIKO: . . . . . I loved her. I didn't want her to die . . . I . . .

OKA (*softening*): I know that. I'm not blaming you for that . . . and it's not my fault what happened to you either . . .

> *Emiko is silent and Oka mistakes that for a change in attitude. He is encouraged.*

You understand that, eh? I didn't ask for you. It's not my fault you're here . . . in this desert . . . with . . . with me . . .

> *Emiko weeps. Oka reaches out.*

I know I'm too old for you . . . It's hard for me too . . . but this is the way it is. I just ask you to be kinder . . . understand it wasn't my fault. Try to make it easier for me . . . for yourself too . . .

> *Oka touches her and she shrinks from his hand.*

EMIKO: Ach!

Oka asks why they must live this way, alienated, always fighting, and waits for an answer. When it doesn't come he realizes the situation is hopeless. Worn out from the quarrel, he goes into the house.

> *Emiko watches him leave and pours herself another drink. The storm has passed, the alcohol takes over. She turns to the door Oka disappeared into.*

EMIKO: Because I must keep the dream alive . . . the dream is all I live for. I am only in exile now . . . Because if I give in, all I've lived before . . . loved and hurt for . . . will mean nothing . . . will be for nothing . . . nothing . . . Because if I let you make me believe this is all there is to my life, the dream would die . . . I would die . . . wither and die . . .

> *She pours another drink and feels warm and good. Fade out. Curtain.*

ACT II

Scene 1: Murata's kitchen and yard

In mid-September, Hana and Masako are discussing the imminent arrival of Oka's daughter Kiyoko, speculating about how tall she'll be, whether she'll wear kimonos, when she'll be arriving (Oka has gone to San Pedro to fetch her, but Emiko stayed at home). Masako is looking forward to having a friend with whom she can share her interest in books and stories, though perhaps Kiyoko won't be able to read when she first arrives. Masako is reading a tale of the prairie pioneers which reminds her of her own family's life here in California.

The arrival is signaled by the sound of Oka's car. Kiyoko enters behind her obviously proud father. "*She is short, chunky, broad-chested and very selfconscious. Her hair is straight and banded in two shucks. She wears a conservative cotton dress, white socks, two-inch heels."* She bows deeply to the Muratas. Her appearance is strange to Masako, who is put off by it and has to be reminded of her manners by her mother.

Oka tells them of how his daughter — "just a big country girl" — is enjoying the new experiences of America. Each time attention is cast on her, Kiyoko covers her mouth and giggles.

Murata enters, wipes the soil off his hand to greet the newcomer. Shyly, Kiyoko remains silent while the men discuss the trip: the fan belt broke on the way home.

OKA: Lucky I was near a gasoline station. We were in the mountains. Waited in a restaurant while it was getting fixed.

HANA: Oh, that was good.

OKA: Guess they don't see Japanese much. Stare? Terrible! Took them a long time to wait on us. Dumb waitress practically threw the food at us. Kiyoko felt bad.

HANA: Ah! That's too bad . . . too bad. That's why I always pack a lunch when we take trips.

MURATA: They'll spoil the day for you . . . those barbarians!

OKA: Terrible food too. Kiyoko couldn't swallow the dry bread and bologna.

HANA: That's the food they eat . . .

They go into the house, where Hana serves wine. Questioned about her "mother," Emiko, Kiyoko tells the Muratas that she barely remembers her as a very pretty woman who was away in Tokyo most of the time.

Masako goes outside. The lights on the scene inside the house dim as Emiko walks into the yard and looks through the window. Masako invites Emiko to come inside, but the two women both sense that they don't belong in that family group.

Masako confides to Emiko that she doesn't have a boy friend and doesn't want one. Emiko assures her that love will come some day: "It's good, Masa-chan. And this feeling you'll remember the rest of your life . . . will come back to you . . . haunt you . . . keep you alive . . . five, ten years . . . no matter what happens . . . keep you alive."

Emiko leaves when Hana comes out to fetch Masako. Masako doesn't want to go back inside. She doesn't like Kiyoko, she feels that at 15 Kiyoko is already an old lady more suitable as her mother's friend. Hana reminds Masako of her promise to Oka to take Kiyoko under her wing.

Masako can't stand Kiyoko's habit of giggling. Hana tells her daughter, "That's the way girls do in Japan." Seeing she can't get Masako to come in, Hana goes into the house and brings Kiyoko out, then leaves the two girls alone.

> *Kiyoko and Masako stand awkwardly, Kiyoko glancing shyly at Masako.*

MASAKO: Do you like it here?

KIYOKO (*nodding*): Eh.

> *There's an uncomfortable pause.*

MASAKO: School will be starting next week . . .
KIYOKO (*nodding*): Ah.
MASAKO: Do you want to walk to school with me?
KIYOKO (*nodding*): Ah.
    Masako rolls her eyes and tries again.
MASAKO: I leave at 7:30 . . .
KIYOKO: Ah.
    There's a long pause. Masako finally gives up and moves offstage.
MASAKO: I have to do something . . .
    Kiyoko watches her leave and uncertainly moves back into the house. Hana looks up at Kiyoko coming in alone, sighs and quietly pulls out a chair for her. Fade out.

Scene 2: Murata's kitchen

The family is seated around the kitchen table, Hana sewing, Masako studying, Murata reading the paper, while lightning flashes outside. At Hana's request, Masako reports on Kiyoko's progress at school: she's skipped a grade in mathematics but is something of a joke among the other pupils, has made no new friends and just follows Masako around. Hana advises Masako she ought to help Kiyoko learn to talk properly as the others do, and to fit in.

Looking at another flash of lightning, Murata hopes the storm won't be followed by a freeze. As it begins to rain, there's a knock on the door. A trembling Kiyoko enters, bare-legged and wearing a kimono, looking for help. Oka and Emiko are "fighting like animals," and Kiyoko fears they may kill each other unless someone intervenes. Hana reassures her that every family has its quarrels, some very unpleasant, but that they are a normal part of life and no outsider can interfere.

Oka and Emiko often drink home brew which "makes them crazy," Kiyoko complains, weeping as she reports how they fight drunkenly, rolling about on the floor. Meanwhile, she has more than enough troubles of her own keeping up in school where "It's hard . . . hard . . . I'm too old for the class and the children." She envies Masako, Kiyoko tells Hana, nothing is going right in her own life. She doesn't even have a mother.

HANA: Emiko-san is almost a real mother to you . . . She's blood kin.
KIYOKO: She hates me. She never speaks to me. She's so cold. I want to love her but she won't let me. She hates me.
HANA: I don't think that's true, Kiyoko-san.
KIYOKO: I know it's true.
HANA: No, I don't think you have anything to do with it. It's this place. She hates it . . . This place is so lonely and alien . . .
KIYOKO: Then why didn't she go back? Why did they stay here?
HANA: You don't know. It's not so simple . . . Sometimes I think . . .
KIYOKO: Then why don't they make the best of it here? Like you?
HANA: That isn't easy either. Believe me.
    She goes to the stove to stir the soup.
Sometimes . . . sometimes the longing for homeland fills me with despair. Will I

never return again? Will I never see my mother, my father, my sisters again? But what can one do? There are responsibilities here . . . children. (*She draws a sharp breath.*) And another day passes . . . another month . . . another year. Eventually everything passes.

Kiyoko hasn't had any supper, but she's used to not eating, the Okas don't cook when they are drinking. Hana advises Kiyoko to take care of herself and make what she can of her own life. She doesn't have to go home tonight, however, she can sleep here.

There is another rap on the door — it's Oka, come to fetch Kiyoko. Oka tries to pretend Kiyoko merely came over for a visit but Hana tells him bluntly that the family quarreling frightened his daughter. Hana speaks her mind: "You sent for Kiyoko-san and now she's here. You said yourself she had a bad time in Japan, and now she's having a worse time. It isn't easy for her in a strange new country; the least you can do is try to keep her from worrying . . . especially about yourselves. I think it's terrible what you're doing to her."

Oka is ashamed and promises that it won't happen again. He tells Kiyoko he is sorry he upset her and leads her away, covered in Murata's borrowed robe, as Hana goes to the bed and, protectively, pulls the covers over Masako.

Scene 3: Murata's yard

The next morning, Masako waits for Kiyoko to walk with her to school. Kiyoko comes in red-eyed and without a lunch box, carrying Murata's robe borrowed the previous night. She is a pitiful figure arousing Masako's instinct to help.

Masako drills Kiyoko in some of the difficult English words and shows her how Americans laugh — openly, not giggling behind their hands. They begin to communicate, and Kiyoko begins to understand that sometimes Masako is laughing with, not at, her mispronunciations. They exchange tongue-twisters, Kiyoko showing off her proficiency in Japanese, Masako hers in English. As they move off toward school, they've started to become friends who are going to share their single lunch.

Hana and Murata return from surveying the storm damage. It wasn't as bad as expected.

HANA (*quietly*): Papa, where will it end? Will we always be like this . . . always at the mercy of the weather . . . prices . . . mercy of the gods?
MURATA (*patting Hana's back*): Things will change. Wait and see . . . We'll be back in Japan by . . . in two years . . . guarantee . . . Maybe sooner . . .
HANA (*dubiously*): Two years . . .
MURATA (*noticing the robe on the bench*) Ah, look, Mama. Kiyoko-san brought back my robe.
HANA (*sighing*): Kiyoko-san . . . poor Kiyoko-san . . . and Emiko . . .
MURATA: Ah, Mama. We're lucky . . . we're lucky, Mama . . .
    Hana smiles sadly at Murata. Fade out.

Scene 4: Oka's yard

Oka is dressed to go out and Kiyoko joins him, now resplendent in a bright-colored new dress and a permanent wave and carrying a movie fan magazine. They are bound for the movies, though it's such a nice day Oka feels they shouldn't waste it indoors. But Kiyoko loves the movies as she loves her curly hair, both forbidden to Masako by her mother. Oka, in contrast, gives Kiyoko everything her heart desires and can hardly wait to do more for her if they have a good harvest this year. Furthermore, he promises that soon they'll move to some place where there will be more young men around. His lease on the farm will expire next year: "In America Japanese cannot own land. We lease and move every three years."

Kiyoko wants to take her magazine with her to the movies — the last time she left the house she returned to find all the others torn in half. Before they can leave, Emiko comes out of the house, disheveled, shaking an empty tin can. Oka sends Kiyoko on ahead and turns to confront his wife.

EMIKO (*shaking the can*): Where is it? What did you do with it?
OKA (*feigning surprise*): With what?
EMIKO: You know what. You stole it. You stole my money.
OKA: *Your* money?
EMIKO: I've been saving that money . . .
OKA: Yeah? Well, where'd you get it, eh? You stole it from me! Dollar by dollar . . . You stole it from me! Out of my pocket . . .
EMIKO: I saved it . . .
OKA: From my pocket!
EMIKO: It's mine. I saved for a long time . . . Some of it I brought from Japan . . .
OKA: *Bakayuna!* What'd you bring from Japan? Nothing but some useless kimonos!
Oka starts to leave but Emiko hangs on to him.
EMIKO: Give back my money! Thief!
OKA (*swings around and balls his fist but doesn't strike*): Goddamn! Get off me!
EMIKO (*now pleading*): Please give it back . . . please, please . . .
She begins to stroke him. Oka pulls her hands away and pushes her from him . . . . .
EMIKO: It's mine . . . give it back . . .
OKA: The hell! You think you can live off me and steal my money too? How stupid you think I am?
EMIKO (*tearfully*): But I've paid . . . I've paid . . .
OKA: With what?
EMIKO: You know I've paid.
OKA (*scoffing*): You call that paying?
EMIKO: What did you do with it?
OKA: I don't have it.
EMIKO: It's gone?

OKA: Yeah! It's gone. I spent it. The hell! Every last cent.

EMIKO: The new clothes . . . the curls . . . restaurants . . . pictures . . . shoes . . . My money . . . my going home money . . .

Oka tells Emiko she can swim to Japan for all he cares, and walks away. Emiko's shoulders shake, but her grief is soundless as she stands alone with the empty can. *"She wipes the dust gently from the can as though comforting a friend. Her movements become sensuous, her hands move on to her own body, around her throat, over her breasts, to her hips, caressing, soothing, reminding her of her lover's hands. Fade out."*

Scene 5: Murata's Yard

In late afternoon of the same day, Hana sweeps the yard while Masako hangs a glass wind chime, a present from Kiyoko, on the wall of the house. Its sound reminds Hana of Japan and maybe some day will remind Masako of her life here with her parents on the farm.

Emiko comes in rather unsteadily, carrying a bundle wrapped up in a scarf which she places on the bench. Hana comments on how pretty Kiyoko looked in her new dress and permanent wave when she came by on her way to the movies.

Hana sends Masako inside to make tea, while Emiko, her hand still on her package, strokes it and seems to be letting her thoughts stray elsewhere as she makes small talk with Hana. Finally the two women sit silent, the package in Emiko's lap, listening to the sound of the wind chime.

Masako comes back with the tea and serves it. Emiko opens her package and reveals its contents: two beautiful kimonos she brought with her from Japan. Masako fingers the gold threads and admires the robes, as Emiko suggests they would be appropriate for Masako to wear on special occasions — if only Hana could give Emiko a little money in exchange for them.

The kimonos are worth hundreds, Hana replies. Murata couldn't possibly afford them. Emiko answers that she will take any sum Murata can afford. Masako wants them, but Hana is firm: the kimonos are a luxury which they cannot permit themselves. *"Hana folds the gowns and puts them away. Masako is disappointed. Emiko is decimated."*

Emiko pulls herself together as best she can, while Hana tries to reassure her that someone with daughters will buy them — maybe some well-to-do Terminal Island fisherman.

HANA: . . . . . Have your husband take them there . . . I know you'll get your money . . . He'll find a buyer. I know he will.

EMIKO: Yes . . .
Emiko finishes folding and ties the scarf. She sits quietly.

HANA: Please have your tea. I'm sorry . . . I really would like to take them for Masako but it just isn't possible. You understand, don't you?
Emiko nods.
Please don't feel so . . . so bad . . . It's not really a matter of life or death, is it? Emiko-san?

Emiko nods again. Hana sips her tea.
MASAKO: Mama? If you could ask Papa . . .
HANA: Oh, the tea is cold. Masako, could you heat the kettle?
EMIKO: No more. I must be going . . .
She picks up her package and rises slowly.

Hana offers to send Masako to accompany her home, but Emiko refuses. She leaves with Hana calling out after her, "I'm sorry . . . . . "

Hana is stroking her daughter's straight hair lovingly as Murata comes in from the fields. It looks like rain, and Murata, suddenly remembering that he's forgotten to shut off the irrigation water, sends Masako off to do it. The couple have noticed that their daughter seems to be growing up, becoming more responsible. They enter their house, where *"Hana glances at him and quietly sets about preparations for supper. Murata removes his shirt and sits at the table with a paper. Lights fade slowly."*

Scene 6: Desert

In the desert, Masako hears the sound of Emiko's voice singing "The Soul Shall Dance." Masako conceals herself. Emiko appears dressed in one of her beautiful kimonos and carrying a branch of sage, singing in Japanese.

> *Emiko breaks into a dance, laughs mysteriously, turns round and round, acting out a fantasy. Masako stirs uncomfortably. Emiko senses a presence. She stops, drops her branch and walks offstage, singing as she leaves: "Aoi sake nomya/Yume mo odoru . . . "*
> *Masako watches as Emiko leaves. She rises slowly and picks up the branch Emiko has left. She looks at the branch, moves forward a step and looks off to the point where Emiko disappeared. Light slowly fades until only the image of Masako's face remains in the mind. Fade out. Curtain.*

Other Plays Cited
By American Theater Critics Association Members

As to the Meaning of Words by Mark Eichman (Stamford, Conn.: Hartman Theater Company) — After the prologue in a Boston hospital admissions unit, the play shifts into a courtroom. Dr. Winston Gerrard, a black physician who performed an abortion at the patient's request, is on trial for manslaughter. The parade of witnesses, which includes fellow-physicians and a nurse, skillfully counterposes the arguments of abortion advocates with those of the Right to Life movement. Dr. Gerrard, with his passionate regard for his patient's rights, becomes a pawn caught between a shrewd, ambitious prosecutor, Ned "Scooter" Ryan, and a deft, legal-eagle defense counsel, Alexander Thomas.

Thomas allows his humane considerations for Dr. Gerrard's feelings to override his legal savvy, and finally Dr. Gerrard is convicted.

Come Back to the Five and Dime, Jimmy Dean, Jimmy Dean by Ed Graczyk (Atlanta: Alliance Theater) — In a small-town dime store in West Texas, the disciples of James Dean gather for their 20th reunion. Now a gaggle of middle-aged women, the disciples were teen-agers when Dean filmed *Giant* two decades ago in nearby Marfa. One of them, an extra in the film, has a child whom she says was conceived by Dean on the *Giant* set; the child is the Jimmy Dean of the title, now off in town somewhere and apparently not quite right in the head. The ladies' reminiscences mingle with flashbacks to their youth; then the arrival of a stunning and momentarily unrecognized woman sets off a series of confrontations that upset their self-deceptions and expose their well-hidden disappointments. A funny, touching comedy-drama with a fine ear and a sympathetic sense of character.

Counting the Ways and **Listening** by Edward Albee (Hartford, Conn. Stage Company) — The former is a sentimental, playful comedy of marriage after 20 years, unlike anything its author has written previously. It is based on an exploration of the Robert Browning-Elizabeth Barrett relationship, with a married couple counting the ways in which they love one another, trying to understand the nature of married love after 20 years. The latter demonstrates ways in which people hear one another but fail to listen for the real meaning of what is being said.

The Dog Ran Away by Brother Jonathan, O.S.F. (Milwaukee Repertory Theater Company) — On a lonely Long Island Estate that once served as active novitiate for their Franciscan order, three monks — one senile and petulant, one young and newly amorous, one indifferent to all save his roaming hound — struggle with each other and their faith in God. A most honest and surprising portrait of religious life and human commitment, with humor and pain conveyed in taut, naturalistic language and deeply personal characterizations.

Family Business by Dick Goldberg (Stockbridge, Mass. Festival) — Four sons sort out their lives in the wake of their father's death. Home truths are exchanged — not pleasant ones — but the family will, in some sense, endure.

The Gin Game by D.L. Coburn (Louisville, Ky.: Actors' Theater) — On the sun porch of a nursing home, two senior citizens sit down to play gin rummy. Fonsia, a seemingly prim woman, has never played before; Weller, an irascible man, considers himself an expert. But Fonsia wins every hand, and Weller grows increasingly violent. Commanding attention on its own terms, the game also serves as a device enabling the characters to face their self-deceptions, to reveal themselves as the products not of chance but of their own smallnesses and cruelties; in the end, they become almost symbiotically yoked by hate. Initially comic, the play grows progressively darker as it accumulates dramatic tension.

A History of the American Film by Christopher Durang (Hartford, Conn. Stage Company. Los Angeles: Center Theater Group, Mark Taper Forum. Washington, D.C.: Arena Stage) — An elaborate spoof of mainstream movies from the flickers to the latest disaster epics. Durang's chief aim is amusing his audience and getting them to play Spot That Reference. But some serious notions are available on the dangers of confusing life and life in the movies.

Ice by Michael Cristofer (Los Angeles: Center Theater Group, Mark Taper Forum) — Caught in the long night of an Alaskan winter, two young men and a young woman find themselves at shifting points of an uneasy and finally fatal triangle. A post-1960s play which examines several facile notions of the period, particularly about the innocence of the dropout.

A Life in the Theater by David Mamet (Chicago: Goodman Theater, Stage 2) — A comedy in which scenes of an older actor and a younger actor talking backstage are interspersed with parody-scenes of the play they're in. Underneath the talk of the mystique of theater are such personal matters as the young man's ambition and the older man's sadness.

A DIRECTORY OF PROFESSIONAL REGIONAL THEATER

Compiled by Ella A. Malin

Professional 1976-77 programs and repertory productions by leading resident companies around the United States, plus selected Canadian programs and major Shakespeare festivals including that of Stratford, Ontario (Canada), are grouped in alphabetical order of their locations and listed in date order from May, 1975 to June, 1976. This list does not include Broadway, off-Broadway or touring New York shows (unless the local company took some special part), summer theaters, single productions by commercial producers or college or other non-professional productions. The directory was compiled by Ella A. Malin for *The Best Plays of 1976-77* from information provided by the resident producing organizations at Miss Malin's request. First productions of new plays — American or world premieres — in regional theaters are listed with full cast and credits, as available. Figures in parentheses following title give number of performances and date given is opening date, included whenever a record of these facts was obtainable from the producing managements.

Augmented reports on other than regional theater production in Los Angeles by Rick Talcove and Washington, D.C. by David Richards are included under those cities' headings in this listing. A section on U.S. dinner theater by Francine L. Trevens appears at the end of this Directory.

Summary

This Directory lists 517 productions of 387 plays (including one-acters, workshop and plays-in-progress productions) presented by 55 groups in 85 theaters in 49 cities (41 in the United States, eight in Canada) during the 1976-77 season. Of these, 212 were American plays in 150 full productions and 67 workshop productions. 59 were world premieres, 15 were American premieres and 57 were workshop premieres. In addition, 17 groups presented 39 children's theater productions of 36 plays, plus improvisational story theater and participation programs at their theaters and on tour. Other groups presented their regular repertory at special matinees for junior and senior high school students. There was an increase in the number of guest productions presented (not included in this summary) and more community involvement in the form of outreach projects: theater classes, special productions for senior citizens, hospitals, penal institutions and with the physically handicapped.

Frequency of production of individual scripts was as follows:

   1 play received 7 productions (*Vanities*)
   6 plays received 5 productions (*A Christmas Carol, Equus, Hamlet, King Lear, A Midsummer Night's Dream, Sizwe Banzi Is Dead*)
  10 plays received 4 productions (*A History of the American Film, Cat on a Hot Tin Roof, The Glass Menagerie, Man and Superman, Private Lives, When You Comin Back, Red Ryder?, Relatively Speaking, Sleuth, The Tempest, Who's Afraid of Virginia Woolf?*)
  18 plays received 3 productions (*Artichoke, The Devil's Disciple, Death of a Salesman, The Importance of Being Earnest, Jacques Brel Is Alive and Well and Living in Paris, Knock Knock, Ladyhouse Blues, The Matchmaker, Much Ado About Nothing, Misalliance, Of Mice and Men, The Sunshine Boys, The Show-Off, A Streetcar Named Desire, The Sea Gull, Twelfth Night, Travesties, Tartuffe*)
  44 plays received 2 productions
308 plays received 1 production

Listed below are the playwrights who received the greatest number of productions. The first figure is the number of productions; the second figure (in parentheses) is the number of plays produced, including one-acters.

Shakespeare	46 (22)	Mamet	6	(6)
Shaw	20 (10)	Stoppard	6	(5)
Williams	16 (7)	Albee	6	(4)
Coward	10 (4)	Kaufman	6	(4)
Brecht	8 (7)	Chekhov	6	(3)
O'Neill	9 (6)	Durang	6	(3)
Ayckbourn	9 (5)	Peter Shaffer	6	(2)
Molière	8 (6)	Ibsen	5	(5)
Fugard	7 (3)	Pinter	5	(4)

Hellman	5	(3)	Bond	2	(2)
Arthur Miller	5	(2)	Connelly	2	(2)
Joanna Glass	4	(3)	Cristofer	2	(2)
Shepard	4	(3)	Guare	2	(2)
Wilson	4	(3)	Inge	2	(2)
Moss Hart	4	(2)	Linney	2	(2)
Beckett	3	(5)	Orton	2	(2)
Preston Jones	3	(2)	Tremblay	2	(2)
Simon	3	(2)	Wedekind	2	(2)
Auletta	2	(2)	Zigun	2	(2)

ABINGDON, VA.

Barter Theater: Main Stage

(Founder, Robert Porterfield; artistic director-manager, Rex Partington)

THE THREEPENNY OPERA (25). By Bertolt Brecht and Kurt Weill. June 2, 1976. Director, John Going; musical director, Byron Grant. With Mark Dempsey, James Tolkan, Dorothy Marie, Michelle Reilley, Joseph Costa, Gloria Zaglool, Mary Shelley.

DEMOCRACY (25). By Romulus Linney. June 23, 1976. Director, John Olon-Scrymgeour. With Cleo Holladay, Robert Blackburn, Esther Dudley, George Clark Hosmer.

THE MATCHMAKER (31). By Thornton Wilder. July 14, 1976; April 5, 1977. Director, Rex Partington. With Virginia Mattis, Rex Partington, Gwendolyn Brown, George Clark Hosmer.

THE GLASS MENAGERIE (8). By Tennessee Williams. August 3, 1976, Director, Owen Phillips. With Dan Deitch, John Christopher Jones, Virginia Mattis, Sharon Morrison.

YOU CAN'T TAKE IT WITH YOU (8). By George S. Kaufman and Moss Hart. August 10, 1976. Director, Charles Maryan. With Harry Ellerbe, Cleo Holladay, Peggity Price, Paul Meacham, Holly Cameron, Gale McNeeley.

RELATIVELY SPEAKING (31). By Alan Ayckbourn. August 18, 1976; May 25, 1977. Director, Owen Phillips. With Gwyllum Evans, Cleo Holladay, George Clark Hosmer, Peggity Price.

SWEET MISTRESS (23). Book by Ira Wallach; lyrics by Susan Dias; music by David Spangler; inspired by Carlo Goldoni's *Mistress of the Inn.*

September 8, 1976 (world premiere). Director, Charles Maryan; scenery, Bennet Averyt; lighting, Don Coleman; costumes, Sigrid Insull; musical director, John Lesko; choreographer, William Van Keyser.

Marquis of Forlipopoli	George F. Maguire
Count of Albafiorita	Donald Drake
Mirandolina	Lynn Ann Leveridge
Fabrizio	Robert Sevra
Domenico Pallavicini	Mike Dantuono
Ortensia	Rita Gardner
Dejanira	Ilsebet Tebesli
Nicolo Paganini	Gwyllum Evans

Time: The 1830's. Place: A traveller's wayside inn, Italy. One intermission.

Musical Numbers — Act I: Overture, "Here in the Inn," "You're the First," "Sweet Mistress," "The Cavalier's Lament," "Just Another Guest," "Think of It," "I'd Love to Hate Her," "Since We Met." Act II: Entr'Acte, "Here in the Inn" (Reprise), "Mazzini and Mankind," "Everything You Are," "None of My Dreams," "I'll Go On," "We Give Her Up," "Sweet Mistress" and "You're the First" (Reprise).

BEYOND THE FRINGE (22). By Allan Bennett, Peter Cook, Jonathan Miller and Dudley Moore. September 29, 1976. Director, Dorothy Marie. With Gwyllum Evans, George Clark Hosmer, John Christopher Jones, Robert Rutland.

THE TAMING OF THE SHREW (18). By William Shakespeare. May 3, 1977. Director, Owen Phillips. With Beth McDonald, John Spencer, George Clark Hosmer, Jane Ridley.

Designers: scenery, Bennett Averyt, Parmelee Welles, Carr Garnett; lighting, Don Coleman, Tony Partington, Grant Clifford Logan; costumes, Sigrid Insull, Elizabeth Covey, Carr Garnett.

Barter Theater: Barter Playhouse

Showcase Intern Ensemble: Stanley J. Flood, Carol Haynes, Sara Hofman, Wayne Eliot Knight, Ellen Painter, Peggity Price, Michelle Reilley, Robert Rutland, Tyson Stephenson, Alicia Quintano.

THE GREAT SWITCHEROO (14). By Eric Conger; adapted from Molière's *Sganarelle*. July 1, 1976. Director, Eric Conger; scenery, Bruce Rayvid; costumes, Martha Christian. With the entire ensemble.

ASTERIAN CANTICLES (12). By Daffi Nathanson. August 26, 1976. (world premiere). Director, Gloria Maddox; scenery, Bruce Rayvid; costumes, Martha Christian.

Ambsace; Amaxa	Dan Beebe
Ampersand; Amba	Carol A. Chittum
Mage	Eric Conger
Maynard	Stanley J. Flood
Emerald	Carol Haynes
Black Astor	Sarah Hofman
Shellac Ohms	Wayne Eliot Knight
Maze	Ellen Painter
Kid; Angel	Alicia Quintano
Dr. Walrus; Electrics	Tyson Stephenson

Selections from TRANSFORMATIONS (9). Adapted from Anne Sexton's poem-stories, reworked and transformed by her from the Grimms' fairy tales. July 16, 1976 (world premiere). Director, Dorothy Marie. With Holly Cameron, Dorothy Marie, Ellen Painter, Peggity Price, Alicia Quintano.

Children's Theater Apprentice Ensemble: Dan Beebe, Bonnie Blake, Janet Brown, Mary Ann Brownlow, Carol A. Chittum, Martha Groseclose, R. Scott Lank, Denise Pitts, Hilda Stark, Timothy Thomas, Sandra Ward, Arthur Whitehead.

THE JACK TALES (23). By Linde Hayen Herman. June 30, 1976 (world premiere). Director, Owen Phillips; scenery, Hilda Stark; lighting, Stephen Arnold, Martha Mainous; original music, R. Scott Lank; performed by R. Scott Lank, Timothy Thomas, Martha Groseclose; narrator for all the tales, Martha Groseclose.

The Fox, The Possum, And The Rabbit

Fox	Hilda Stark
Possum	Carol A. Chittum
Rabbit	Denise Pitts
Scarecrow	Arthur Whitehead

Graveyard; Fence: Dan Beebe, Bonnie Blake, Mary Ann Brownlow, Janet Brown, R. Scott Lank, Sandra Ward

Water Ho

Duck	Mary Ann Brownlow
Dog	Sandra Ward
Pig	Bonnie Blake
Woodpecker	Janet Brown

Quare Jack

Jack	Timothy Thomas
Bill	Dan Beebe
Tom	R. Scott Lank

Peter Francisco

Young Peter; Sam	Dan Beebe
Judge	Janet Brown
Older Peter	R. Scott Lank
Flossie the Mule	Carol A. Chittum
Mike; British Officer	Arthur Whitehead
Innkeeper	Bonnie Blake
Gen. Washington	Hilda Stark
Aide	Timothy Thomas

Sailors; British Troops; Revolutionary Soldiers: Mary Ann Brownlow, Janet Brown, Carol A. Chittum, Denise Pitts, Hilda Stark, Arthur Whitehead

A MIDSUMMER NIGHT'S DREAM (13). Adapted and directed by Peggity Price. August 7, 1976. Designed and performed by Apprentice Ensemble.

Note: Barter interns and apprentices were selected by countrywide auditions to participate in the two-year training/performance program. They performed with the regular company at the Barter Playhouse and on tours in Virginia and neighboring states.

ASHLAND, ORE.

Oregon Shakespearean Festival: Elizabethan Stagehouse (outdoors)

(Founder, Angus L. Bowmer; producing director, Jerry Turner; general manager, William W. Patton)

MUCH ADO ABOUT NOTHING (34). By William Shakespeare. June 18, 1976. Director, James Edmondson. With Cal Winn, Marilyn Jones, Jean Smart, Allen Nause, Judd Parkin, Larry R. Ballard, Ron Woods, David Williams, Rex Rabold, Will Huddleston.

HENRY VI, Part 2 (24). By William Shakespeare. June 19, 1976. Director, Jerry Turner. With John Warren Tyson, Gordon Townsend, Brian Lynner, Brian Thompson, Bruce Williams, Jean Smart, Kathleen Worley.

KING LEAR (35). By William Shakespeare. June 20, 1976. Director, Pat Patton. With Denis Patton, Christine Healy, Roberta Levitow, Sands Hall, James Edmondson, Ron Woods, Allen Nause, Rex Rabold.

Oregon Shakespearean Festival: Angus Bowmer Theater (indoors)

THE LITTLE FOXES (37). By Lillian Hellman. June 19, 1976. Director, James Moll. With Christine Healy, William Ferriter, Denis Arndt, Mary Turner, Dan Kremer, Sands Hall, Jerry Jones, Delores Y. Mitchell, Keith Grant.

THE DEVIL'S DISCIPLE (25). By George Bernard Shaw. June 20, 1976. Director, Michael Leibert. With Barry Mulholland, Joseph De Salvio, Christine Healy, Denis Arndt, Kathleen Worley, Ruth Cox, Shirley Patton.

THE COMEDY OF ERRORS (42). By William Shakespeare. June 21, 1976. Director, Will Huddleston. With Brian Mulholland, Barry Mulholland, Allen Nause, Joseph De Salvio, Virginia Bingham, Roberta Levitow, Ruth Cox, David Williams, Cal Winn, Brian Thompson.

Oregon Shakespearean Festival Stage II: Angus Bowmer Theater

THE RIVALS (20). By Richard Brinsley Sheridan. February 11, 1977. Director, William Glover. With Michael Santo, Mimi Carr, William Moreing, Allen Nause, Joseph De Salvio, Catherine Butterfield, Kenned MacIver, Ronald Edmundson Woods.

MEASURE FOR MEASURE (19). By William Shakespeare. February 12, 1977. Director, Jerry Turner. With James Edmondson, Christine Healy, Judd Parkin, Dan Kremer, Jahnna Beecham, Shirley Patton.

ANGEL STREET (19). By Patrick Hamilton. February 13, 1977. Director, Pat Patton. With Catherine Butterfield, Gordon Townsend, Kenned MacIver, Mary Turner, Ronald Edmundson Woods.

Oregon Shakespearean Festival Stage II: Black Swan Theater

A TASTE OF HONEY (39). By Shelagh Delaney. February 12, 1977. Director, James Edmondson. With Cameron Dokey, Margaret Rubin, Patrick DeSantis, Keith Grant, Rex Rabold.

Designers: Scenery, Richard L. Hay; lighting, Dirk Epperson, Robert Peterson, Thomas White; costumes, Jeannie Davidson.

BALTIMORE

Center Stage

(Managing director, Peter W. Culman; artistic coordinator, Stan Wojewodski Jr.)

SHE STOOPS TO CONQUER (36). By Oliver Goldsmith; as conceived by Boris Tumarin. October 26, 1976. Director, Stan Wojewodski Jr.; scenery, Eldon Elder; lighting, Ian Calderon; costumes, Dona Granata. With Paul C. Thomas, Tana Hicken, Christine Baranski, Jim Broaddus, Dan Szelag.

WHEN YOU COMIN BACK, RED RYDER? (36) By Mark Medoff. November 26, 1976. Director, Stan Wojewodski Jr.; scenery and lighting, Charles Cosler; costumes, Walker Hicklin. With Thomas G. Waites, Tana Hicken, Dan Diggles, Pat Karpen, Michael Medeiros, John Straub, Paul C. Thomas, Donna Welby.

MISALLIANCE (36). By George Bernard Shaw. December 31, 1976. Director, Arne Zaslove; scenery, Peter Harvey; lighting, Ian Calderon; costumes, Bob Wojewodski. With Linda Alper, Davis Hall, Nannette Rickert, Joseph Warren, Paul C. Thomas.

TOYS IN THE ATTIC (36). By Lillian Hellman. February 4, 1977. Director, Stan Wojewodski Jr.; scenery, Peter Harvey; lighting, Ian Calderon; costumes, Elizabeth P. Palmer. With Anne Lynn, Lois Markle, Beeson Carroll, Deborah Offner.

THE FIRST BREEZE OF SUMMER (36). By Leslie Lee. March 11, 1977. Director, Woodie King Jr.; scenery and lighting, Charles Cosler; costumes, Elizabeth P. Palmer. With Claudia McNeil, Bill Cobbs, Juanita Bethea, Elizabeth Van Dyke, Norman Mizell Wilkerson III.

KNOCK KNOCK (36). By Jules Feiffer. April 15, 1977. Director, John Henry Davis; scenery, Charles Cosler; lighting, Arden Fingerhut; costumes, Elizabeth P. Palmer. With Robert Pastene, Herman O. Arbeit, Edmond Genest, Bess Armstrong.

Center Stage: Guest Production

A SORROW BEYOND DREAMS (16). By Peter Handke; translated by Ralph Manheim; adapted and directed by Daniel Freudenberger. May 17, 1977. The Phoenix Theater production with Len Cariou.

Note: The Young People's Theater of Center Stage toured elementary and high schools during 1976–77 with two productions. *Way Back When* by Ray Aranha, tales and ditties set in Puritan New England of 1680, was directed by Jeffrey O. Rodman; and *Workers,* based on Studs Terkel's *Working.* The YPT Company: Preston Boyd, Vendia Evans, Kurt Everhart, Chris Forth, Tana Hicken, Walker Hicklin, Chequita Jackson, Timothy Jenkins, Michael Jeter, Larry Riley.

BERKELEY, CALIF.

Berkeley Repertory Theater

(Producing director, Michael Leibert; associate director, Douglas Johnson)

ROPE (39). By Patrick Hamilton. June 11, 1976. Director, Michael Leibert. With Tuie Kinsolving, Rick Casorla, Douglas Johnson, Linda Lee Johnson, John Oldham.

THE IMPORTANCE OF BEING EARNEST (39). By Oscar Wilde. July 23, 1976. Director, Michael Addison. With Joe Spano, Douglas Johnson, Karen Ingenthron, Linda Lee Johnson, Anne Swift.

CANDIDA (39). By George Bernard Shaw. September 17, 1976. Director, Michael Leibert. With Joy Carlin, Joe Spano, Roderic Prindle.

BUS STOP (39). By William Inge. October 29, 1976. Director, Douglas Johnson. With Linda Lee Johnson, Rick Casorla, Al McVay Jr., Anne Swift.

TWELFTH NIGHT (46). By William Shakespeare. December 10, 1976. Director, Michael Addison. With Anne Swift, Karen Ingenthron, Al McVay Jr., Rick

Casorla, Michael Leibert, Paul Laramore, Alice Rorvik.

THE PHILANTHROPIST (39). By Christopher Hampton. January 28, 1977. Director, Douglas Johnson. With Joe Spano, Rick Johnson, Linda Lee Johnson, Alice Rorvik.

MANN IST MANN (39). By Bertolt Brecht; adapted and directed by Michael Leibert from a translation by Roderic Prindle (with thanks to Eric Bentley and Gerhard Neihaus). March 11, 1977. Original music, John Aschenbrenner; additional music, Kurt Weill; puppets created by Peggy Van Patten; makeup, Paul Laramore. With Dale Elliott, Peggy Van Patten, Al McVay Jr., Karen Ingenthron, Paul Laramore.

THE COUNTRY WIFE (39). By William Wycherley. April 22, 1977. Director, Michael Addison. With Alice Rorvik, Linda Lee Johnson, Rick Casorla, Robert Haswell.

Designers: scenery, Jeffrey Whitman, Lesley Skannal, Andrew DeShong, Gene Chesley; lighting, Matthew Cohen; costumes, Diana Smith, Lesley Skannal.

BUFFALO

Studio Arena Theater

(Executive producer, Neal Du Brock)

THE ECCENTRICITIES OF A NIGHTINGALE (39). By Tennessee Williams. October 8, 1976. Director, Edwin Sherin; scenery, William Ritman; lighting, Marc B. Weiss; costumes, Theoni V. Aldredge. With Betsy Palmer, David Selby, Shepperd Strudwick, Nan Martin.

DEATH OF A SALESMAN (40). By Arthur Miller. November 12, 1976. Director, Warren Enters; scenery, James Tilton; lighting, David Zierk; costumes, Clifford Capone. With Pat Hingle, Joan Lorring, Marcus Smythe, Richard Greene, Ralph Farnworth, Pat McNamara, Suzanne Gilbert.

VANITIES (39). By Jack Heifner. December 17, 1976. Director, Larry Carpenter; scenery, Jack Arnone; lighting, Patrika Brown; costumes, David James. With Ann McCurry, Nancy New, Cecilia Riddett.

SIZWE BANZI IS DEAD (39). By Athol Fugard, John Kani, Winston Ntshona. January 21, 1977. Director, Woodie King Jr.; scenery and costumes,

Karl Eigsti; lighting, Peter Gill. With D'Urville Martin, Joe Seneca.

ELIZABETH THE QUEEN (39). By Maxwell Anderson. April 1, 1977. Director, Tony Tanner; scenery, Scott Johnson; lighting, Marc B. Weiss; costumes, Clifford Capone. With Kim Hunter, George Chakiris, Marshall Borden, Kermit Brown, Eric Conger, Harriet Hall, Edward Holmes.

A VERY PRIVATE LIFE (40). By Neal Du Brock. May 13, 1977 (world premiere). Director, Terry Schreiber; scenery and lighting, Ben Edwards; costumes, Jane Greenwood; musical number staged by Tommy Tune; musical arranger, William R. Cox.

Myra Matthews .... Celeste Holm
Gary Alan .... Thomas Callaway
Carole Benton (Kay) .... Betty Buckley
Houseboy (Teddy) .... Franklyn Seales
    Time: Two years of the recent past. Place: A living room in a large Bel Air house on Stone Canyon Road — "Hollywood" — and in bits of places about the world. One intermission.

Studio Arena Theater: Guest Production

CHARLES DICKENS (26). Selected, adapted and performed by Emlyn Williams in scenes from the famous novels and stories. February 22, 1977.

BURLINGTON, VT

Champlain Shakespeare Festival: Royall Tyler Theater, University of Vermont

(Producer-director, Edward J. Feidner)

THE COMEDY OF ERRORS (18). By William Shakespeare. July 8, 1976. Director, Edward J. Feidner; scenery and lighting, W. M. Schenk; costumes, Polly Smith. With Greg Patnaude, Dan Baumgarten, Steven Pimsler, Kent Cassella, Lorraine Barrett, Michele Benedict.

KING LEAR (17). By William Shakespeare. July 15, 1976. Director, Gerard E. Moses; scenery, Lisa M. Devlin; lighting, E. Keith Gaylord; costumes, Polly Smith. With Edward J. Feidner, Sara O'Neil, Michele Benedict, Lorraine Barrett, Dennis Lipscomb, Jock MacDonald, Charles Kerr, Alan Altshuld.

KING RICHARD II (9). By William Shakespeare. August 4, 1976. Director, Edward J. Feidner; scenery and lighting, Lisa M. Devlin; costumes, W. K. Fauser. With Dennis Lipscomb, Charles Kerr, Bruce Teifer, John Bruce Patton, Alan Altshuld, Kent Cassella, Susan Dunlop, Michele Benedict.

CHARLOTTESVILLE, VA.

Heritage Repertory Company: Culbreth Theater — University of Virginia

(Artistic Director, George Black; producing director, David W. Weiss; general manager, Steve Reed)

THAT MAN JEFFERSON (22). By David Cupp and William Martin. May 6, 1976 (world premiere). Director, William Martin.
Cast: Mr. Jefferson — Richard Bowden. With Richard Babcock, David Cupp, Celia Howard, Lisa Sloan. Ensemble: Lloyd Bowers, Mary Charbonnet, Peter Hagan, Art Hanket, Deborah Hogg, Caroline Huggins, Mark Maslyk, Susan McVeigh, Randall Short.
Time: New Year's, 1772, through July 4, 1826. The play was presented in three acts.

SHE WOULD BE A SOLDIER (22). Book by Anthony Stimac; music by Don Pippin; lyrics by Steve Brown; based on the play by Mordecai M. Noah. June 3, 1976. Director, William Martin. With Jerry Bradley, Susan Loughran, Richard Babcock, Celia Howard, Richard Bowden.

THE LITTLE FOXES (20). By Lillian Hellman. June 10, 1976. Director, George Black. With Celia Howard, Susan Loughran, Richard Babcock, Richard Bowden, Vivian Stephens, Lisa Sloan.

THE PHILADELPHIA STORY (20). By Philip Barry. June 17, 1976. Director, Richard Bowden. With Lisa Sloan, Susan Loughran, Richard Babcock, Jerry Bradley.

BEGGAR ON HORSEBACK (17). By George S. Kaufman and Marc Connelly. June 25, 1976. Director, George Black. With Reginald Robinson, Mary Charbonnet, Arthur Hanket, Richard Babcock, Celia Howard, Peter Hagan, Lisa Sloan.

Designers: scenery, William Molyneux; lighting, Gersh; costumes, Lois Garren. Production stage manager, Bronson Platt.

CHICAGO

Academy Festival Theater: Drake Theater, Lake Forest

(Producer, William Gardner; associate producer, Sharon Griggins)

A STREETCAR NAMED DESIRE (23). By Tennessee Williams. June 8, 1976. Director, Jack Gelber. With Geraldine Page, Rip Torn, Jack Hollander, Flora Elkins, Beatrice Winde.

HUGHIE (24). By Eugene O'Neill. July 13, 1976. Director, José Quintero. With Jason Robards, Jack Dodson.

DIRTY JOKES (23). By Arthur Giron. August 3, 1976 (world premiere). Director, Lee Sankowich; scenery, Eric Head; lighting, Lowell B. Achziger; costumes, Laura Crow.

Scoutmaster Hennessey .... Michael Moriarty
Scoutmaster Pyle .... Guy Boyd
Constanza Demarais .... Allison Giglio
Honorary Scoutmaster Bates .. Maurice Copeland
Gene Dilbeck .... Matthew Cowles
Randy Hennessey .... Michael Kearney
    Time: The present. Place: A Boy Scout encampment in the northern woods. One intermission.

MISALLIANCE (31). By George Bernard Shaw. August 31, 1976. Director, Austin Pendleton. With Irene Worth, Lynn Redgrave, Donald Moffat, William Atherton, Robert Moberly, Emery Battis.

Designers: scenery, John Wulp, Eric Head; lighting, Lowell B. Achziger; costumes, Laura Crow.

Goodman Theater Center: Goodman Theater Company — Main Stage

(Artistic director, William Woodman; managing director, John Economos)

DESIGN FOR LIVING (43). By Noel Coward. October 1, 1976. Director, William Woodman. With Carrie Nye, Brian Murray, David Dukes.

LONG DAY'S JOURNEY INTO NIGHT (43). By Eugene O'Neill. November 12, 1976. Director, George Keathley. With Edward Binns, Frances Hyland, Drew Snyder, John V. Shea, Sonja Lanzener.

THE SHOW-OFF (43). By George Kelly. December 31, 1976. Director, Gene Lesser. With Woody Eney, Jane Hoffman, Carol Williard, Carolyn Kirsch, Edgar Meyer, W. H. Macy.

RICHARD III (43). By William Shakespeare. February 11, 1977. Director, William Woodman. With Norman Snow, Barry Boys, Nicholas Surovy, Michael Hawkins, Benjamin Hendrickson, Jack Roberts, Pauline Brailsford.

STREAMERS (43). By David Rabe. March 25, 1977. Director, Gregory Mosher. With W. H. Macy, Donald Corren, Robert Christian, Richard Cox, Meshach Taylor, Michael O'Dwyer, J. J. Johnston.

DON JUAN (43). By Molière; translated by Christopher Hampton. May 6, 1977 (American premiere). Directors Michael Montel with William Woodman; scenery, Joseph Nieminski; lighting, Gilbert V. Hemsley Jr.; costumes, Virgil C. Johnson; fights staged by Michael Tezla.

Sganarelle	Robert Guillaume
Guzman; Ragotin	Glenn Kovacevich
Don Juan	Nicholas Surovy
Elvira	Brenda Curtis
Charlotte	Judith Ivey
Bandit; Pierrot	Andrew Rohrer
Ghost; Mathurine	Fay Hauser
La Ramee; Bandit	Bruce Rodgers-Wright
Beggar; Dimanche	Joseph Bell
Don Carols	Gus Kaikkonen
Don Alonso	Michael Tezla
Commander	Steve Merle
La Violette; Bandit	Steven Williams
Don Luis	William Mowry

Act I, Scene 1: Don Juan's home. Scene 2: A seacoast. Scene 3: A forest. Act II, Scene 1: Don Juan's home. Scene 2: A graveyard. One intermission.

Designers: Scenery, James Nieminski, Marjorie Kellogg; lighting, Pat Collins, F. Mitchell Dana, John Jensen, Gilbert V. Hemsley Jr.; costumes, James Edmund Brady, Virgil C. Johnson, Marsha Kowal.

Goodman Theater Center: Stage Two — Ruth Page Auditorium

SIZWE BANZI IS DEAD (14+). By Athol Fugard, John Kani, Winston Ntshona. November 3, 1976 (reopened May 11, 1977). Director, Gregory Mosher. With Meshach Taylor, Lionel Smith.

THE SPORT OF MY MAD MOTHER (21). By Ann Jellicoe. December 1, 1976. Director, Dennis Zacek. With Judith Ivey, Arlene Schulfer, Keith Szarabajka, Donald Corren.

A LIFE IN THE THEATER (21). By David Mamet. February 3, 1977 (world premiere). Director, Gregory Mosher; scenery, Michael Merritt; lighting, Robert Christen; costumes, Marsha Kowal.

Robert	Mike Nussbaum
John	Joe Mantegna

Place: Various spots around a theater. No intermission. (See synopsis in the introduction to this section.)

KASPAR (18). By Peter Handke; translation by Michael Roloff. March 3, 1977. Director, Gary Houston. With J. Pat Miller, Mark Hutter, Christopher Raynolds, Randall Smith, Robert Strom, Harold Yee.

GEORGE JEAN NATHAN IN REVUE (21). Conceived and directed by Sidney Eden; based upon the writings of George Jean Nathan. April 21, 1977 (world premiere). Scenery, Michael Merrit; lighting, Robert Christen; costumes, Marsha Kowal.

George Jean Nathan — Tony Mockus; 1st Player (Clarence Darrow, H. L. Mencken, James J. Corbett, J. J. Shubert, George Bernard Shaw) — Ray Rayner; 2d Player (Sinclair Lewis, Eugene O'Neill, Ty Cobb, Sean O'Casey) — Tony Lincoln; 3d Player (Eleanora Duse, Ethel Barrymore) — Geraldine Kay.

One intermission.

New Playwrights Project: Staged Readings (Works-in-Progress premieres)

TIME'S UP (2). By Lance Lee. November 12, 1976. Director, William Woodman.

Him	Jack Wallace
Her	Cordis Fejer

Time: Now. Place: Seven scenes in the Chicago Northside Crisis Center at one-week intervals, except Scene 6, which is the day after Scene 5.

CITY JUNKET (2). By Kenward Elmslie. November 19, 1976. Director, Mac McGinnes.

Z	Nesbitt Blaisdell
Street Urchin	Bobby Di Cicco
Desk Clerk; Transistor; Waiter Guide;	
Ben; Swishy Man	J. Pat Miller
Georgette; Steel Genius	Ina Jaffe
Bebe	Arlene Schulfer
Bobbi	Cordis Fejer

A family's trip to the Paris Exhibition of 1889.

Designers, Stage Two: Scenery, Beverly Sobieski, Dean Taucher, Michael Merritt, Mahar Ahmad; lighting, Robert Christen; costumes, Michelle R. Demichelis, Marsha Kowal.

Note: The new playwrights project was suspended after the second play because of Equity contract changes for the Goodman Theater. The Goodman School of Drama's Children's Theater and Studio Theater, under professional direction, are no longer part of the Goodman Theater Company. Both had active seasons, however. The Children's Theater presented the following: *Just So Stories* by Rudyard Kipling, dramatized by Aurand Harris, directed by Joseph Slowik. Summer, 1976. *Aladdin and the Wonderful Lamp* (28) by James Norris; music and lyrics by Errol Pearlman, directed by Bella Itkin. October 16, 1976. *The Adventures of Pinocchio* (33), conceived and directed by Terry Zehr; based on the story by Carlo Collodi. December 4, 1976. *The Unwicked Witch* (27) by Madge Miller, directed by Stewart Hawk. January 29, 1977. *Androcles and the Lion* (29), a musical version by Aurand Harris in comedia dell'arte style; director/choreographer, Estelle Spector. March 19, 1977. Between October 28, 1976 and May 15, 1977, the Studio Theater presented: *The Hostage* by Brendan Behan; adapted and directed by Joseph Slowik. *Summer of the 17th Doll* by Ray Lawler; director, Bella Itkin. *The Mad Dog Blues* by Sam Shepard; director, Edwin C. Schmidtke. *Hamlet* by William Shakespeare; director, Charles McGaw. *The Real Inspector Hound* and *Albert's Bridge* by Tom Stoppard; director, Dale McFadden. *Spring's Awakening* by Frank Wedekind; director, Joseph Slowik.

St. Nicholas Theater Company: Mainstage

(Artistic director, Steven Schachter; managing director, Peter Schneider; co-founder and playwright-in-residence, David Mamet)

THE COLLECTED WORKS OF BILLY THE KID (43). By Michael Ondaatje. September 15, 1976. Director, Mike Nussbaum; scenery, David Emmons; lighting, Robert Christen; costumes, Julie A. Nagel; music, Elliot Delman. With W. H. Macy, Donald Corren, Tom Mula, Cynthia Baker Johnson, Warren Leming, Ann Ryerson, Gregg Flood.

MERT AND PHIL (37). By Anne Burr. November 10, 1976. Director, Steven Schachter; scenery, Dean Taucher; lighting, Robert Shook; costumes, Kaye Nottbusch. With Guy Barile, Madonna Niles, Patricia Malekov.

JOPLIN (30). By Kathleen Lombardo; music by Scott Joplin and Robert Lombardo; adapted for the stage by the author and William H. Macy. January 27, 1977. Director, Steven Schachter; scenery, Joseph C. Nieminski; lighting, Robert Shook; costumes, Julie A. Nagel; musical director/arranger, Robert Lombardo; choreographer, Siri Sat Nam Singh. With Hank Berrings, Timothy Oman, Angelina Reaux, Jackie Taylor, Steven Williams.

DOMINO COURTS by William Hauptman and A SLIGHT ACCIDENT by James Saunders (32). March 22, 1977. Director, Gerald Gutierrez; scenery, David Emmons; lighting, Rita Pietraszek; costumes, Julie A. Nagel. With M. Patrick Hughes, Linda Kimbrough, Audrie J. Neenan, William J. Norris.

THE WATER ENGINE: AN AMERICAN FABLE (31+). By David Mamet. May 11, 1977 (world premiere). Director, Steven Schachter; scenery; David Emmons; lighting, Kathleen Daly; costumes, Jessica Hahn; music, Alaric Jans; sound, John Carey.

Leon; Cop #1 .... Steve Anders
Lawrence Oberman .... Guy Barile
Secretary; Mrs. Varec .... Belinda Bremner
Chainletter; Dave Murray; Lecturer   Dan Conway
Charles Lang .... W. H. Macy
Postal; Cop #2; Rewrite .... John Mahoney
Martin Keegan; Deitz .... Michael O'Dwyer
Rita .... Gail Silver
Mr. Wallace; Guard .... Norm Tobin
Bernie .... Joseph Weisberg
Time: 1934. Place: Chicago. One intermission.

St. Nicholas Theater Company: Children's Theater

(Fall through spring, 1976-1977; two performances each weekend)

THE ADVENTURES OF CAPTAIN MARBLES AND HIS ACTING SQUAD: EPISODE III, CLIFF NOTES. By William H. Macy and David Kovacs; based on characters conceived by John Stasey. Director, Commander Hector Fluff; scenery, John Morris; lighting, Howard Roth; costumes, Julie A. Nagel; music composed and performed by Alaric Jans.
Cliff Notes .... Gregg Flood

First Bass .... Annie Hat
Rokko .... Alaric Jans
Witch .... Joan Lazzerini
Astronaut .... Herb Lichtenstein
Captain Marbles .... James D. Murphy
Treetrunk Eel .... Tom Mula
Frances .... Natalija Nogulich
Ballerina .... Gretchen Trapp

St. Nicholas Theater: Show Case

THE MARRIAGE OF BETTE AND BOO (12). By Christopher Durang. October 12, 1976. Director, Anne Claus; scenery, Pam Peniston; lighting, Rita

Pietraszek; costumes, Gay Crusius; choreographer, Gerald James; music, Alaric Jans.
Bette Marshall .... Claudia Bohard

Margaret Marshall .... Lesley Abrams
James Marshall .... Alan Baranowski
Paula Marshall .... Juanita Marie Walsh
Miriam Marshall .... Coleen Maloney
Boo Dunlop .... Michael J. Fijolek
Ferd Dunlop .... Dale Woolley
Mud Dunlop .... Elaine Andrews
Father Delaney; Doctor .... Peter Ryan
Matthew .... Russell Fear

MATTRESS (12). By William H. Macy. June 8,
1977. Director, Daniella Violet-Green; scenery, James
Boley; lighting, Dave Garretson; costumes, Rosalyn
Kriener.

Linda ....,.......... Natalija Nogulich
Michael .... Michael Sassone
Susan .... Patricia Stewart
George .... Jim Scholle

Note: St. Nicholas Theater's Show Case project was designed to give new playwrights, directors, actors, designers and technicians the opportunity to develop their skills through practical production experience. Personnel working with the playwrights were outstanding students selected from St. Nicholas Theater's Professional Classes.

CINCINNATI

Playhouse in the Park: Robert S. Marx Theater

(Producing director, Michael Murray; general manager, Robert W. Tolan)

CAT ON A HOT TIN ROOF (32). By Tennessee Williams. October 26, 1976. Director, Michael Murray. With Ellen Barber, Ronnie B. Baker, Richard Dix, Elizabeth Moore.

OLIVER! (32). Book, music and lyrics by Lionel Bart; based on *Oliver Twist* by Charles Dickens. December 7, 1976. Director, John Going; musical director, Fred Goldrich; dance sequences, Jack Louiso. With Tim Waldrip/Tim Rail, John Wylie, David Parkes, Joy Garrett, George Massey.

A MONTH IN THE COUNTRY (32). By Ivan Turgenev; adapted by Michael Murray. January 11, 1977. Director, Michael Murray. With Brenda Curtis, Mitchell Edmonds, Paul Collins, Chris Sullivan, Susan Wills.

WHEN YOU COMIN' BACK, RED RYDER? (32). By Mark Medoff. February 15, 1977. Director, Robert Brewer. With Kent Broadhurst, Mia Dillon, Sharon Goldman, Duncan Hoxworth, Patrick McCullough, Raynor Scheine, Karen Shallo, Luke Sickle.

HEARTBREAK HOUSE (32). By George Bernard Shaw. March 29, 1977. Director, Michael Murray. With John Wylie, Stephen Arlen, Nancy Cushman, Richard Dix, Douglas Fisher, Jo Henderson, Kathleen O'Meara Noone, Keith Perry, Ron Steelman, Claudia Zahn.

THE HOSTAGE (32). By Brendan Behan. May 10, 1977. Director, Geoff Garland. With Joyce Krempel, Moultrie Patten, Ron Steelman, Jane Lowry, Linda Dunlevy.

Playhouse in the Park: Shelterhouse Theater — Guest Production

WHAT'S A NICE COUNTRY LIKE US DOING IN A STATE LIKE THIS? (8) Created and per-

formed by the Footlighters Inc. April 26, 1977. Director, Elinor Dial; choreographer, David Holdgriewe.

Designers: scenery, Paul Shortt, John Lee Beatty, Karl Eigsti; lighting, Neil Peter Jampolis, Jane Reisman; costumes, Annie Peacock Warner, Elizabeth Covey, Dennis Parichy.

Note: The Cincinnati Playhouse presented 5 performances each of *Cat on a Hot Tin Roof, Oliver!, Heartbreak House* and *The Hostage* to high school students in the tri-state area — Ohio, Indiana and Kentucky.

CLEVELAND

The Cleveland Play House: Euclid-77th Street Theater

(Managing director, Richard Oberlin)

THE SUNSHINE BOYS (23). By Neil Simon. October 6, 1976. Director, Larry Tarrant; scenery and lighting, Richard Gould; costumes, Harriet Cone. With Richard Halverson, Norm Berman, James Richards, George Simms, Evie McElroy.

ARE YOU NOW OR HAVE YOU EVER BEEN? (29). By Eric Bentley. November 5, 1976. Director,

Larry Tarrant; scenery and lighting, Tim Zupancic; costumes, Harriet Cone. With members of the Company.

THE YELLOW JACKET (40). By George C. Hazelton and J. H. Benrimo. December 17, 1976. Director, William Rhys; scenery and lighting, Richard Gould; costumes, Estelle Painter. With Richard

Halberson, Jonathan Farwell, Tedd Rawlins, Cynthia Brown, Wayne S. Turney, Jo Farwell, John Buck Jr

LADYHOUSE BLUES (32). By Kevin O'Morrison. February 4, 1977. Director, Larry Tarrant; scenery, lighting, costumes, Richard Gould. With Christina Moore, Sharon Bicknell, Mary Gallagher, Jo Farwell, Evie McElroy.

TABLE MANNERS (39). By Alan Ayckbourn. March 18, 1977. Director, Paul Lee; scenery and lighting, Richard Gould; costumes, Harriet Cone. With John Buck Jr., Kenneth Albers, June Gibbons, Sharon Bicknell, Jonathan Farwell, J. J. Lewis.

The Cleveland Play House: Drury Theater

THE CAT AND THE FIDDLE (32). By Jerome Kern and Otto Harbach. October 15, 1976. Conceived and directed by Jack Lee; staged by Eddie Gasper; scenery, James Tilton; lighting, Joseph P. Tilford; costumes, Richard Gould. With John Leslie Wolfe, Charlotte Fairchild, Lizbeth MacKay, Wayne S. Turney, Jonathan Farwell, David O. Frazier.

A MOON FOR THE MISBEGOTTEN (33). By Eugene O'Neill. November 26, 1976. Director, Dorothy Silver; scenery and costumes, Maura Smolover; lighting, Joseph P. Tilford. With Evie McElroy, Kenneth Albers, Andrew Lichtenberg, Paul Lee, Larry Tarrant.

MAN AND SUPERMAN (38). By George Bernard Shaw. January 7, 1977. Director, Paul Lee; scenery and lighting, Joseph P. Tilford; costumes, David Smith. With Clayton Corzatte, Lizbeth Mackay, Robert Snook, Wesley Grant, Allen Leatherman, John Danielich, J. J. Lewis.

MACBETH (44). By William Shakespeare. February 25, 1977. Director, John Dillon; scenery, Stuart Wurtzel; lighting, Arden Fingerhut; costumes, Estelle Painter. With Charles Keating, William Rhys, Wesley Grant, Yolande Bavan, Richard Halverson, Lizbeth Mackay.

The Cleveland Play House: Brooks Theater: Guest Productions

CHARLES DICKENS (7). Compiled, adapted and performed by Emlyn Williams. September 28, 1976.

THE TWAIN SHALL MEET (4). Compiled, adapted and performed by Susan Ludlow and Clayton Corzatte. December 29, 1976.

Note: The Cleveland Play House also co-sponsored a guest appearance of *A Party With Betty Comden and Adolph Green* (2) at the Masonic Auditorium, April 17. The Play House Youtheater, under the directorship of Jo Farwell, presented three productions: *The Puppet Play*, adapted and directed by Eugene Hare (4), October 30, 1976 and *Golliwhoppers!*, a collage of American folk tales by Flora Atkins (4), December 28, 1976 were given at the Brooks Theater. *My Client Curly* (2), by Norman Corwin, April 2, 1977 was seen at the Drury Theater. Play House Company members directed, designed and choreographed the productions.

Between July 1 and August 21, 1976, The Chautauqua Summer Theater of the Cleveland Play House presented the following plays from the 1975-76 season: *The World of Carl Sandburg* by Norman Corwin, *Relatively Speaking* by Alan Ayckbourn, *The Dark at the Top of the Stairs* by William Inge, *Scapino!* by Frank Dunlop and Jim Dale, *Get-Rich-Quick Wallingford* by George M. Cohan, *Caesar and Cleopatra* by George Bernard Shaw, *Of Mice and Men* by John Steinbeck and, previewing the 1976-1977 season, *The Sunshine Boys* by Neil Simon.

COSTA MESA, CALIF.

South Coast Repertory Theater

(Artistic directors, David Emmes and Martin Benson)

THE RULING CLASS (44). By Peter Barnes. September 17, 1976. Director, David Emmes; scenery and lighting, Susan Tuohy; costumes, Sondra Huber. With Charles Lanyer, Don Tuche, John Ellington, Leslie Jones, Richard A. Ryan, Hal Landon Jr., Anni Long.

SATURDAY, SUNDAY, MONDAY (46). By Eduardo de Filippo; adapted by Keith Waterhouse and Willis Hall. November 5, 1976. Director, Martin Benson; scenery, Susan Tuohy; lighting, Thomas Ruzika; costumes, Sondra Huber. With Barbara Van Holt, Hal Landon Jr., William Brady, Ann Sienna-Schwartz.

OLD TIMES (44). By Harold Pinter. January 7, 1977. Director, David Emmes; scenery, Michael Devine; lighting, Thomas Ruzika. With Cherie Patch, Charles Lanyer, Irene Roseen.

THE TWO GENTLEMEN OF VERONA (44). By William Shakespeare. March 11, 1977. Director, Daniel Sullivan; scenery, Michael Devine; lighting, Thomas Ruzika; costumes, Charles Tomlinson. With Richard Doyle, Ronald Boussom, John Ellington, Elizabeth O'Toole, Martha McFarland, Don Tuche, John-David Keller.

EQUUS (46). By Peter Shaffer. April 29, 1977. Director, Martin Benson; scenery, Michael Devine; lighting, Brian Gale; costumes, James Reeves. With Charles Lanyer, Ronald Boussom, Mimi Smith, Don Tuche, Sheila Crofut, Steve Gray, Anni Long.

JACQUES BREL IS ALIVE AND WELL AND

Expedition Show

THE DARING DARDOLASES: OR LOVE FINDS COSMO C. COSMO (4). By Steve DeNaut and Ronald Boussom. March 19, 1977. Director, Ronald Boussom; lighting, Reginald Roos; costume coor-

LIVING IN PARIS (44+). By Eric Blau and Mort Shuman, based on Jacques Brel's lyrics and commentary; music by Jacques Brel. June 17, 1977. Director, John-David Keller; musical direction, John Ellington; choreographer, Diane dePriest. With Teri Ralston, Martha McFarland, Richard Doyle, James E. dePriest.

dinater/choreographer, Anni Long; sound engineer, Paul Gracey; graphics designer, Joe LaJeuness. With John Ellington, Anni Long, Howard Shangraw, Reginald Rook.

Note: South Coast Repertory Theater had an extensive touring program from October 1976 through June 1977 to schools in Los Angeles and Orange Counties, and one, *Vanities* by Jack Heifner, played prisons, colleges and community centers throughout the state. The productions were: *What This Country Needs Is a Good 5¢ Bubble Gum* (182), book, music and lyrics by Robin Frederick; *Orange Trees* (188), book and lyrics by Doris Baizley, music by Glen Barkley; *All Singing, All Dancing, No Talking* developed and directed by John-David Keller, who also directed the other productions; and *The Actor's Mime Theater* (42), developed by Ronald Roussum and Reginald Rook; directed by Reginald Rook. Performers and designers were from the regular company.

DALLAS

Dallas Theater Center: Kalita Humphreys Theater

(Managing director, Paul Baker)

SHERLOCK HOLMES AND THE CURSE OF THE SIGN OF FOUR (42). By Dennis Rosa; based on the novel by Sir Arthur Conan Doyle. June 1, 1976. Director, Ken Latimer; scenery, John Henson; lighting, Linda Blase; costumes, Cheryl Denson. With Randy Moore, John Figlmiller, Ryland Merkey, Norma Moore, Randolph Tallman, Preston Jones/Matt Tracy, Steve Lovett.

SAM (33). By Sally Netzel. July 13, 1976 (world premiere). Director, Bryant J. Reynolds; scenery, Steve Wallace; lighting, Randy Moore; costumes, Pamela Jensen.

Brown	John Figlmiller
Livy Clemens	Jacque Thomas
Sam Clemens	Ryland Merkey
Burglar	Jan Ensign
Mrs. Stowe	Mary Sue Jones
Jame Clemens	Cheryl Denson
Jean Clemens	Laura Thompson
Clara Clemens	Gretchen Brady
Susy Clemens	Laura Worthen
Frau Kruger	Celeste Varricchio
Paper Boy	Steve Lovett
Mr. Burrows	John Henson
Mrs. Orielle	Rebecca Logan
Mrs. Gashly	M. G. Johnston
Robert Chabbal	John Logan

Act I, Scene 1: The Clemens home, July 2, 1885, early evening. Scene 2: July 3, early morning. Act II, Scene 1: Later that afternoon and evening. Scene 2: July 4, evening.

ONCE IN A LIFETIME (33). By George S. Kaufman and Moss Hart. October 5, 1976. Director, Ryland Merkey; scenery, John Henson; lighting, Robin Crews; costumes, Cheryl Denson. With Ken

Latimer, Mona Pursley, Randolph Tallman, Judith Davis, John Figlmiller, Sallie Laurie, Synthia Rogers, Barnett Shaw, Matt Tracy, Lynn Trammell.

SCAPINO! (41). By Frank Dunlop and Jim Dale; adapted from Molière's *Les Fourberies de Scapin*. November 16, 1976. Director, Robyn Flatt with John R. Stevens; scenery, Yoichi Aoki; lighting, Sally Netzel; costumes, Denise Drennen. With Steven Mackenroth, Paul Buboltz, Robert A. Smith, Carolyn Pines, John R. Stevens, Cliff Samuelson, Randy Moore, Martha Robinson Goodman, Earl J. Fisher.

THREE SISTERS (33). By Anton Chekhov; translated by Robert W. Corrigan. January 11, 1977. Director, Ken Latimer; scenery, Kathleen Latimer; lighting, Randy Moore; costumes, Pamela Jensen. With Norma Moore, Mona Pursley, Mary Rohde, John Figlmiller, Robyn Flatt, Ryland Merkey, Randolph Tallman, Matt Tracy.

SOMETHING'S AFOOT (33). Book, music and lyrics by James McDonald, David Vos and Robert Gerlach; additional music by Ed Linderman. January 22, 1977. Director, John Henson; scenery, Peter Wolf; lighting, Randy Moore; costumes, Paul Buboltz; musical direction, Pam Nagle; choreographer, Sally Kushner. With Paul Buboltz, Cheryl Denson, Russell Henderson, Rebecca Logan, Jonathan Smoots, Matt Tracy, Celeste Varricchio, Alex Winslow, Allyn Winslow, Steven John Yuhasz.

SANTA FE SUNSHINE (33). By Preston Jones. April 19, 1977 (world premiere). Director, John Logan; scenery, Yoichi Aoki; lighting, Wayne Lambert; costumes, Michael Krueger.

Gino Bruno	Ken Latimer

Hendry Anaya .... Louis Landa/
                         David Romero/Rob Stone
Lyman Cotswald .... Michael Scudday
Henrietta Chipping .... Sally Netzel
Perfecto Candilaria .... Robert A. Smith
Claude Nordley .... Randy Moore
Liz Watkins .... Ruth Cantrell

Thurman Vogel .... Paul Buboltz
Mrs. P. J. Davenport .... Judith Davis
    Time: The spring of 1957. Place: Gino Bruno's
house in Santa Fe, New Mexico. Prologue: Evening.
Act I, Scene 1: Morning. Scene 2: About 9 o'clock
that night. Act II: about 8 o'clock the next night.

Dallas Theater Center: Down Center Stage

(Producer, John Figlmiller)

LADYHOUSE BLUES (12). By Kevin O'Morrison.
October 28, 1976. Director, John Logan; scenery, Lin-
da Blase; lighting, Allen Hibbard; costumes, Randy
Bonifay. With Libby Blackwell, Gail Henderson,
Rebecca Logan, Cheryl Denson, Deborah Allen.

KENNEDY'S CHILDREN (19). By Robert Patrick.
December 9, 1976. Director, Judith Davis; scenery,
Mary Sue Jones; lighting, Allen Hibbard; costumes,
Celeste Varricchio. With Michael Scudday, Sally
Netzel, Mark Momberger, Andrew C. Gaupp, Karon
Cogdill, Chantal Westerman.

GET HAPPY (13). By John Henson, John Logan,
Randolph Tallman, Steven Mackenroth; a musical
revue of the 1930s. February 3, 1977 (world premiere).
Director, Bryant J. Reynolds; scenery, Allen Hibbard;
lighting, Suzanne Chiles; costumes, Rodger Wilson;
projections, Linda Blase; musical direction, Randolph
Tallman, Steven Mackenroth, Mark Momberger;
choreographer, Dallas L. McCurley. With Joslyn
Anderson, Fitzhugh G. Houston, John Logan, Judy
Bridges, Jim Marvin, Shelley McClure, James Myers,
Shannon Wilson. Band: Mark Momberger, Steven
Mackenroth, Earl J. Fisher.
    Musical Numbers — Act I: "Tomorrow's Gonna
Be Another Fine Day," "Apples," "You Wanna
Juana?," "We Don't Need No Dames," "I've Got
You Beat," "Alphabet Soup," "Dust Bowl Blues,"
"Last Bean Blues," "Everybody Who's Anybody," "I
Love You Wally Simpson," "One of These Days," "I
Guess I Gotta," "Old Man Depression." Act II: "Get
Happy (No. 1)," "We Always Solve the Crime," "The
Touch of Your Hand," "Lover Lover," "Sugar and
Spice," "Mighty Orphan Mandy," "Rocket Love,"
"Scat Cat," "Banana," "Tom Dix," "It's Time to
Say Goodbye," "Get Happy (No. 2)."

WAR ZONE (12). By Paul R. Bassett. March 10,
1977 (world premiere). Director, Randy Bonifay,
scenery, M. G. Johnston; lighting, Robin Crews;

costumes, Rayanne Miller.
Warrent Officer Hickock .... Fritz Lennon
Warrent Officer Patterson .... Tim Green
E-6 Bernie .... Mark Brenton Henager
1st Lt. Delano .... Robert Putman
1st Lt. Lancaster .... Wayne Lambert
2nd Lt. Simmons .... James Myers
Nhu .... Susan Sleeper
1st Lt. Crandall .... Michael Scudday
Capt. Ralston .... Cliff Samuelson
Capt. Cruzik .... Allen Hibbard
Titi .... Riho Mitachi
Maj. Moody .... Bill Wheat
1st. Lt. Hale .... Rod Downey
    Time: January-March, 1971. Place: The officer's
club of the 68th General Maintenance Compound near
Qui Nhon, South Vietnam. Act I, Scene 1: 1730
hours. Scene 2: A week later, 1730 hours. Act II,
Scene 1: A month later, 1900 hours. Scene 2: A month
later, 1900 hours.

HERMIT'S HOMAGE (12). By Lewis Cleckler.
April 28, 1977 (world premiere). Director, Matt
Tracy; scenery, Denise Drennen; lighting, Leko
Fresnel; costumes, Libby Blackwell.
Cotton .... Fritz Lennon
Preacher Nix .... Glenn Allen Smith
Check .... Randy Bonifay
J. W. .... Roger Richards
Arnold .... Ron Larson
Mayor White .... Tim Green
Cecil .... Mark Brenton Henager
Butterfly Light .... Bill Wheat
    CB Radio Voices: Robert Putman (Prairie Dog),
Neil A. Jarrell (Mr. Creator), Andrew C. Gaupp
(Eightball), Wayne Lambert (Fence Post), Roy Hud-
son (Buzz Bomb), Gail Henderson (Town Rattler),
Sandy Moore (Sugarfoot), Janelle Haley (Funny Bun-
ny).
    Time: July 2-5, 1976. Place: Check's Barber Shop,
Bernecker, Texas.

Dallas Theater Center: Magic Turtle Children's Theater

(Producer, Ken Latimer)

MARCO POLO (7). By Jonathan Levy. October 16,
1976. Director, Pamela Jensen; scenery, M. Randall
Russell; lighting, Wayne Lambert; costumes, Carolyn
Pines. With Jim Marvin, Steven Yuhasz, Susan
Sleeper, Fitzhugh G. Houston.

CINDERELLA, script by the performers; director,
John R. Stevens; and HANSEL AND GRETEL,

developed by the DTC Mime Troupe; directors,
Robyn Flatt, John R. Stevens; music by Humperdink
(7). December 4, 1976. Scenery, Shannon Wilson;
lighting, Michael Krueger; costumes, Kristi Wheeler;
Magic Turtle, Allyn Winslow. With Riho Mitachi,
Karon Cogdill, Shirley McClure, Joslyn Anderson,
Sandy Moore, Robert Putman.

THE TALE OF THE MOUSE (7). By Anita Gustafson. February 5, 1977. Directors, Synthia Rogers, Robert A. Smith; scenery, Roy Hudson; lighting, Robin Crews; costumes, Rayanne Miller; Magic Turtle, Jim Marvin. With Michelle Clay, James Eddy, Andrew C. Gaupp, Janelle Haley, Mark Brenton Henager, Jaye Z. Restivo.

SLEEPING BEAUTY (8). By Brian Way. April 2, 1977. Director, Jane Farris; scenery, John Nichols, Susan Sleeper; lighting, Neil A. Jarrell; costumes, Sandra Howell; Magic Turtle, Earl Fisher. With Sandy Moore, Andrew C. Gaupp, Janis Meyer, Hanna Revitte.

Note: Dallas Theater Center toured two productions during the 1976-1977 season: *Get Happy* (4) and *Hamlet ESP* (20), a new concept of Shakespeare's *Hamlet* conceived and directed by Paul Baker in association with Randolph Tallman, through Texas, Tennessee, Louisiana, Arkansas, Kansas, Nebraska, North and South Dakota. DTC continued its affiliation with Trinity University in San Antonio, providing staff for the theater arts program from the professional company. Journeymen and apprentices, who work from three to four years in a comprehensive professional career program, augment the resident professional company.

HARTFORD, CONN.

Hartford Stage Company

(Artistic director, Paul Weidner; managing director, William Stewart; resident director, Irene Lewis)

THE GLASS MENAGERIE (44). By Tennessee Williams. September 17, 1976. Director, Irene Lewis; scenery and costumes, Santo Loquasto; lighting, Ian Calderon. With Lois Holmes, Terry O'Quinn, Cynthia Crumlish, Chip Lucia.

THE BLOOD KNOT (44). By Athol Fugard. October 29, 1976. Director, Paul Weidner; scenery, Hugh Landwehr; lighting, David Chapman; costumes, Claire Ferraris. With William Jay, Nick Smith.

THE WALTZ OF THE TOREADORS (44). By Jean Anouilh. December 17, 1976. Director, Paul Weidner; scenery, John Conklin; lighting, Peter Hunt; costumes, Caley Summers. With John Newton, Margaret Phillips, Carol Mayo Jenkins, Stephen Stout, Richard Mathews, Cynthia Crumlish, David O. Petersen.

COUNTING THE WAYS and LISTENING (44). By Edward Albee. January 28, 1977 (world premieres). Director, Edward Albee; scenery, David Jenkins; lighting, John McLain; costumes, Robert Mackintosh.
Counting the Ways (A Vaudeville)
She .... Angela Lansbury
He .... William Prince
Listening (A Chamber Play)
Woman .... Angela Lansbury
Man .... William Prince
Girl .... Maureen Anderman

One intermission. (See synopsis in the introduction to this section.)

A HISTORY OF THE AMERICAN FILM (44). By Christopher Durang. March 11, 1977 (world premiere). Director, Paul Weidner; scenery, Hugh Landwehr; lighting, John McLain; costumes, Claire Ferraris; music, Jack Gaughan; musical director/accompanist, Richard DeRosa.
Loretta .... Cynthia Herman
Jimmy .... Jerry Zaks
Bette .... Alice White
Hank .... Stephen Stout
Eve .... Mary McTigue
Edward Mortimer .... Ted Graeber
Allison Mortimer .... Anne Shropshire
Clara Mortimer .... Veronica Castang
Michael .... Dan Diggles
Piano Man .... Mel Johnson Jr.
Mickey .... Jeff Brooks
Ma Joad .... Ruth Maynard
God .... David O. Petersen
One intermission. (See synopsis in the introduction to this section.)

CANDIDA (44). By George Bernard Shaw. April 29, 1977. Director, John Going; scenery, Hugh Landwehr; lighting, Steve Woodring; costumes, Claire Ferraris. With Barbara Caruso, Jack Ryland, Thomas Hulce, Beth Dixon, Walter Flanagan, Dan Diggles.

Note: The 1976-1977 Southern New England Tour once again presented *Workman! Whoever You Are,* based on Studs Terkel's *Working,* devised by the company and Oriole O'Neill; director, Irene Lewis; designer, Hugh Landwehr; with Samuel Barton, Elaine Bromka, Jeffrey Horowitz, Neil Napolitan.

HOUSTON

Alley Theater: Large Stage

(Producer-Director, Nina Vance. Designers: scenery, Matthew Grant, John Kenny, Michael Olich; lighting, Jonathan Duff, Larry Reed; costumes, Michael Olich, Julie Jackson)

THE STY OF THE BLIND PIG (45). By Phillip Hayes Dean. October 21, 1976. Director, Beth Sanford. With Frances Foster, Louise Jenkins, Gilbert Lewis, Carl Gordon.

YOU NEVER CAN TELL (45). By George Bernard Shaw. December 9, 1976. Director, Ted Fellows; assistant director, Beth Sanford. With Jane MacIver, Pamela Brook, Christine Rose, Rutherford Cravens, Michael Ball, Bob Thompson, Kenneth Dight, David Wurst.

THE CORN IS GREEN (37). By Emlyn Williams. January 27, 1977. Director, Leslie Yeo; assistant director, David Wurst. With Kate Reid, Christopher Gaze, Bob Thompson, Cristine Rose, Maggie Askey, Concetta Tomei, Philip Davidson, Carl Davis.

THE RUNNER STUMBLES (37). By Milan Stitt. March 10, 1977. Director, Beth Sanford. With Anthony Manionis, Cristine Rose, Bettye Fitzpatrick, Philip Davidson, Lillian Evans, Randy Cheramie, Bob Thompson, Concetta Tomei.

HOW THE OTHER HALF LOVES (52). By Alan Ayckbourn. April 21, 1977. Director, Pat Brown. With Roberts Symonds, Lillian Evans, David Wurst, Cristine Rose, Trent Jenkins, Judy Mueller.

Alley Theater: Arena Stage

THE COLLECTION by Harold Pinter and THE DOCK BRIEF by John Mortimer (13). November 3, 1976. Director, Nina Vance. With Michael Ball, Kenneth Dight, Margo McElroy, Brian Tree, Kenneth Wickes.

LOOT (13). By Joe Orton. February 2, 1977. Director, Beth Sanford. With Bernard Frawley, Trent Jenkins, David K. Johnson, Sarah Hardy, Kenneth Dight.

ENDGAME (13). By Samuel Beckett. March 30, 1977. Director, Robert Symonds. With Sheldon Epps, Bernard Frawley, Victoria Zussin.

Note: The Merry-Go-Round, Alley Theater's training wing for young people, presented *The Yellow Brick Road,* adapted by Iris Siff from *The Wizard of Oz* in January and in May, 1977. Director, Bob Feingold; music, George Morgenstern; with Dr. William Glick and company.

INDIANAPOLIS

Indiana Repertory Theater: Main Stage

(Artistic director, Edward Stern; producing director, Benjamin Mordecai)

THE LAST MEETING OF THE KNIGHTS OF THE WHITE MAGNOLIA (22). By Preston Jones. October 15, 1976. Director, John Going; scenery, Raymond C. Recht; lighting, Ralph John Merkle; costumes, Carol H. Beule. With Hank Frazier, Dale Helward, Robert Blackburn, Leo Burmester, William Trotman, Robert Scogin.

WHEN YOU COMIN' BACK, RED RYDER? (21). By Mark Medoff. November 12, 1976. Director, Edward Stern; scenery, Van Phillips; lighting, Ralph John Merkle; costumes, Carol H. Beule. With Leo Burmester, Lisa Goodman, Dale Helward, Michael Hendricks, Bernard Kates, Sharon Madden, Robert Scogin, Sara Woods.

THE THREEPENNY OPERA (26). Book and lyrics by Bertolt Brecht; music by Kurt Weill; English adaptation by Marc Blitzstein. December 10, 1976. Director, Arne Zaslove; scenery, John Doepp; lighting, Michael Orris Watson; costumes, Susan Tsu; musical

director, Charles Greenwell. With Jeffery V. Thompson, Igors Gavon, Bella Jarrett, Diane Tarleton, Kurt Beattie, Demetra Pittman.

THE TEMPEST (22). By William Shakespeare. January 21, 1977. Director, Leland Moss; scenery, Christopher Hacker; lighting, Michael Orris Watson; costumes, Susan Denison; music, Michael Levenson. With Randall Duk Kim, Margaret Whitton, Linda Atkinson, Jeffery V. Thompson, Michael Hendricks.

PRIVATE LIVES (22). By Noel Coward. February 18, 1977. Director, Edward Stern; scenery, Eric Head; lighting, Timothy K. Joyce; costumes, Carol H. Beule. With Sara Woods, Nicholas Hormann, Priscilla Lindsay, John Abajian, Katherine Carlson.

SLEUTH (22). By Anthony Shaffer. March 18, 1977. Director, Edward Stern; scenery, Ursula Belden; lighting, Ralph John Merkle; costumes, Carol H. Beule. With Bernard Kates, Thomas Stechschulte.

Indiana Repertory Theater: 2nd Stage

WHO'S AFRAID OF VIRGINIA WOOLF? (23). By Edward Albee. December 15, 1976. Director, Charles Kerr; scenery, Thomas Taylor Targownik; lighting, Charles Gotwald. With Tanya Berezin, Bernard Kates, Gun-Marie Nilsson, Robert Elliott.

THE BRIXTON RECOVERY (18). By Jack Gilhooley. January 19, 1977 (world premiere). Director, Edward Stern; scenery, Thomas Taylor Targownik; lighting, Susan Dandridge, Bridget Beier; costumes, Carol H. Beule.

Mickey .... Leo Burmester
Shirley .... Elizabeth Van Dyke

Time: The mid-1970s. Place: Shirley's flat in the Brixton section of London. One intermission.

MISS JULIE (18). By August Strindberg. March 23, 1977. Director, William Guild; scenery, Thomas Taylor Targownik; lighting, Joel Grynheim; costumes,

Florence L. Rutherford. With Janice Fuller, Leo Burmester, Linda Selman.

Note: Indiana Repertory Theater gave special morning performances for junior and senior high school students of *The Threepenny Opera, The Tempest, Private Lives, Sleuth, Who's Afraid of Virginia Woolf?* and *Miss Julie.* For younger children, IRT toured the State with *Lift Ev'ry Voice,* a look at black culture in America, conceived and acted by Jeffery V. Thompson; music composed and performed by A. Paul Johnson; director, John S. Patterson; scenery, Thomas Taylor Targownik; costumes, Carol H. Beule. On returning to Indianapolis, there were performances at Indiana Central University and the Children's Museum. The second production for the elementary schools was *Musical Mirage Express '77,* dramatizations of fairy tales, nursery rhymes and children's stories, with music by A. Paul Johnson, played by Theresa Metzger; director, Gerardine Clark; scenery, Thomas Taylor Targownik; costumes, Florence L. Rutherford; with Gerald Burgess, Michael Hendricks, Demetra Pittman, Elizabeth Machlan, Alvin Lee Sanders. The seven-week tour concluded with 7 performances at the Children's Museum in Indianapolis.

KANSAS CITY, MO.

Missouri Repertory Theater: University of Missouri at Kansas City

(Director, Patricia McIlrath)

THE DRUNKARD, OR THE FALLEN SAVED (15). By Francis J. Cullinan: adapted from the W. H. Smith text. June 24, 1976. Director, Francis J. Cullinan; scenery, James L. Joy; lighting, Joseph Appelt; costumes, Vincent Scassellati. With Barrie Mason, Ellen Crawford, Richard C. Brown, Paul Hough, Carolgene Burd.

DON JUAN OF FLATBUSH (15). By Stanley Taikeff. July 1, 1976 (world premiere). Director, Thomas Gruenewald; scenery, James L. Joy; lighting, Joseph Appelt; costumes, Barbara E. Medlicott; sound, David D. Richardson.

Shmul	David Dannenbaum
Mr. Cohen	Lou Malandra
Gertz	John Maddison
Judy	Lynn Cohen
Mrs. Cohen	Etta Marie Carlisle
Lottie Korn	Liza Cole
Winek	Richard K. Allison
Lydia Fox	Alice White
Max Gruber	Walter W. Atamaniuk
Drifter	Earnest L. Hudson

Place: Shmul's Knish Store in the Flatbush section of Brooklyn. One intermission.

THE GREAT WHITE HOPE (14). By Howard Sackler. July 8, 1976. Director, John O'Shaughnessy; scenery, G. Philippe de Rozier; lighting, Joseph Appelt; costumes, Vincent Scassellati. With Earnest L. Hudson, Walter W. Atamaniuk, Marty Greene, Ellen Crawford, Gloria P. Terrell.

THE HEIRESS (15). By Ruth and Augustus Goetz; based on the Henry James novel *Washington Square.* July 15, 1976. Director, John Reich; scenery, John Ezell; lighting, Curt Ostermann; costumes, Baker S.

Smith. With Alice White, Ken Graham, Richard K. Allison, Lynn Cohen.

WHO'S AFRAID OF VIRGINIA WOOLF? (14). By Edward Albee. July 29, 1976. Director, Jim Assad; scenery, Judie A. Juracek; lighting, Curt Ostermann; costumes, Barbara E. Medlicott. With Lynn Cohen, Walter W. Atamaniuk, Nina Furst, Michael LaGue.

ONCE IN A LIFETIME (14). By George S. Kaufman and Moss Hart. August 5, 1976. Director, Thomas Gruenewald; scenery, Frederic James; lighting, Curt Ostermann; costumes, Barbara E. Medlicott. With Lou Malandra, Susan Borneman, Dalton Cathey, Liza Cole, Jackie Riggs, Ronald M. Johnson, Richard C. Brown, Steven Benson.

THE GLASS MENAGERIE (14). By Tennessee Williams. February 3, 1977. Director, James Assad; scenery, Max A. Beatty; lighting, Joseph Appelt; costumes, Vincent Scassellati. With Edith Owen, Robert Elliott, Marla Frumkin, James Daniels.

THE ORPHANS (14). By James Prideaux. February 4, 1977 (world premiere). Director, Gavin Cameron-Webb; scenery, Frederic James; lighting, Joseph Appelt; costumes, Vincent Scassellati; sound, Douglas Faerber.

Lily Spangler	Frances Peter
Catherine Spangler	Robin Humphrey
Lawrence Ervin	Walter Atamaniuk
Herman Goldfarb;	
Ronald Osborne	William Turner
Florette Lamour	Marilyn Lynch
Mr. Franklin	James Daniels

Time: A day in March, 1937. Place: Room 743 of the Chalfont Hotel on West 23rd St. in New York City. One intermission.

Note: Missouri Vanguard Theater, the touring unit of Missouri Repertory Theater, presents major productions and children's programs to outlying towns and communities throughout the state. *The Glass Menagerie* and the world premiere production of *The Orphans,* on completing their resident runs at the MRT Playhouse, toured 18 Missouri communities during March and April, 1977.

LAKEWOOD, OHIO

The Great Lakes Shakespeare Festival: Lakewood Civic Auditorium

(Artistic director, Vincent Dowling)

THE TEMPEST (13). By William Shakespeare. June 25, 1976. Director, Vincent Dowling. With Henry Strozier, Leslie Geraci, Robert Elliott, Debbie Stover, Robert Black.

DEAR LIAR (13). By Jerome Kilty; adapted from the correspondence of George Bernard Shaw and Mrs. Patrick Campbell. July 1, 1976. Director, Vincent Dowling. With Sally Mertz, V.G. Dowling.

AH, WILDERNESS! (17). By Eugene O'Neill. July 8, 1976. Director, John Dillon. With Henry Strozier, Edith Owen, John Q. Bruce Jr., Tom Blair, Bernard Kates, Leslie Geraci, Sally Mertz.

THE DEVIL'S DISCIPLE (14). By George Bernard Shaw. August 5, 1976. Director, Vincent Dowling. With Robert Elliott, Jonathan Farwell, Sally Mertz, Bernard Kates, Edith Owen, Debbie Stover, Robert Scogin.

ROMEO AND JULIET (14). By William Shakespeare. August 12, 1976. Director, William Glover. With Bonnie Sacks, Robert Black, Edith Owen, Richard Miller, Bernard Kates.

Designers: scenery, John Ezell, David Cunningham; lighting, Mark Krieger, William Plachy; costumes, Susan Tsu, Susan Murar.

LOS ANGELES

Center Theater Group: Ahmanson Theater

(Managing director, Robert Fryer)

THE GUARDSMAN (50). By Ferenc Molnar; English version by Grace I. Colbrun and Hans Bartsch; acting version by Philip Moeller. December 17, 1976. Director, Robin Phillips; designer, Daphne Dare; lighting, F. Mitchell Dana. With Maggie Smith, Brian Bedford, Victor Buono, Mary Savidge.

LONG DAY'S JOURNEY INTO NIGHT (69). By Eugene O'Neill. February 18, 1977. Director, Peter Wood; designer, Carl Toms; lighting, H. R. Poindex-ter. With Charlton Heston, Deborah Kerr, Andrew Prine, Robert Burke, Nora Heflin.

MERTON OF THE MOVIES (51). By George S. Kaufman and Marc Connelly; based on the novel by Harry Leon Wilson. April 22, 1977. Director, Burt Shevelove; scenery, John Conklin; lighting, Tharon Musser; costumes, Noel Taylor. With Richard Thomas, Annette O'Toole, Byron Webster, Brian Avery, Peggy Rea.

Center Theater Group: Mark Taper Forum — Mainstage

(Artistic director, Gordon Davidson; associate director, Edward Parone; director of Forum/Laboratory, Robert Greenwald; director of Improvisational Theater Project, John Dennis)

THE ROBBER BRIDEGROOM (54). Book and lyrics by Alfred Uhry; composed and arranged by Robert Waldman; based on the novella by Eudora Welty. July 15, 1976. Director, Gerald Freedman; scenery, Douglas W. Schmidt; lighting, David F. Segal; costumes, Jeanne Button; choreographer, Donald Saddler. With Barry Bostwick, Stephen Vinovich, Rhonda Coullet, Barbara Lang, Lawrence John Moss, Ernie Sabella.

ICE (30). By Michael Cristofer. September 16, 1976 (world premiere). Director, Jeff Bleckner; designer, John DeSantis.
Murph . . . . Cliff DeYoung
Ray . . . . Ron Rifkin
Sunshine . . . . Britt Swanson
   One intermission. (See synopsis in the introduction to this section.)

VANITIES (54). By Jack Heifner. November 4, 1976.

Director, Garland Wright; scenery, John Arnone; lighting, F. Mitchell Dana; costumes, David James. With Lucie Arnaz, Stockard Channing, Sandy Duncan.

In repertory:
TRAVESTIES (40) by Tom Stoppard, January 27, 1977 and THE IMPORTANCE OF BEING EARNEST (22) by Oscar Wilde, January 29, 1977. Director, Edward Parone; scenery, Ralph Funicello; lighting, Tharon Musser; costumes, Peter J. Hall. With Coral Browne, Jane Connell, David Dukes, Neil Flanagan, Herbert Foster, Anita Gillette, Nicholas Hammond, Jean Marsh, Richard Sanders.

In repertory:
A HISTORY OF THE AMERICAN FILM (38). By Christopher Durang. Director, Peter Mark Schifter. With Udana Power, Robert Walden, June Gable, Alice Playten, Richard Lenze, Teri Ralston.

ANGEL CITY (20). By Sam Shepard. April 15, 1977. Director, Robert Calhoun. With Ron Silver, Paul Sand, Loren Pickford, Edward Winter, Larry Hankin, Aileen Fitzpatrick.

Designers: scenery, John Conklin; lighting, F. Mitchell Dana; costumes, Joe I. Tompkins.

In repertory:
LEANDER STILLWELL (18). By David Rush. June 7, 1977 (world premiere). Director, John Dennis; scenery and costumes, Charles Berliner; lighting, F. Mitchell Dana.

Eliza Stillwell	Dorothy Chace
Author	Nathan Cook
Louisa	Brenda J. Davis
Jack Medford	Doug Franklin
Ellen Steward	Noreen Hennessy

Billy Banfield	E. Lamont Johnson
Perry Hatcher	Hal Landon Jr.
Jeremiah Oliver Stillwell	Allan Lurie
Press Allender	Michael McNeilly
Leander Stillwell	Tony Papenfuss
Joey Carlton	Randy Pelish
Enoch Wallace	Rick Vartorella
Jane Mary	Alfre Woodard.

One intermission.

BUGS/GUNS (13). By Doris Baizley. June 9, 1977. Director, John Dennis; scenery, Charles Berliner; lighting, F. Mitchell Dana; music composed and arranged, Harry Aguado; lyrics, Doris Baizley and Harry Aguado. With Nathan Cook, Brenda J. Davis, Noreen Hennessy, Hal Landon, Jr., Michael McNeilly, Tony Papenfuss, Rick Vartorella, Alfre Woodard.

Center Theater Group: Mark Taper Forum — Forum/Laboratory

(All programs workshop premieres)

CONJURING AN EVENT (3). By Richard Nelson. July 17, 1976. Director, John Dennis; designers, Charles Berliner, Julie Weiss, Brian Gale; music by Steven Wells; performed by the Urban Bourbon Band. With Brenda J. Davis, Philip Baker Hall, Milt Kogan, Michael McNeilly, Barry Moore, Tony Papenfuss.

HEY, RUBE! (3). By Janet McReynolds. October 11, 1976. Director, Robert Calhoun; designers, Erik Brenmark, Julie Weiss, Pamela Cooper. With Frances Bay, Vincent Cobb, Al Dunlap, Elizabeth Farley, Aileen Fitzpatrick, Elizabeth Franz, Lorry Goldman, Nora Heflin, Betty Jinnette, Karyn Kronenbourg, Lauren Levian, James Luisi, V. Phipps-Wilson, Mallory Sandler, Diana Scarwid.

DADDY'S DUET (3). By Clifford Turknett. November 2, 1976. Director, Gordon Hunt; designer, Dawn Chiang. With Neil Flanagan, Barbara Iley, Robert LuPone, Paul Zegler.

A HOUSE FOR ROSIE (3). By Leonora Thuna. December 16, 1976. Director, Jeremy Blahnik; designers, Bill Leavitt, Barbara Ling, Louise Hayter. With Phillip R. Allen, Dimitra Arliss, Bert Conway, Frank Geraci, Robert Machray, Richard Marion, Ruth Manning.

SAFE HOUSE (3). By Nicholas Kazan. January 7, 1977. Director, Vickie Rue; designers, Barbara Ling, Susanna Miers, Everett Frost, Mike Hodell, Bill Yaharus. With Catlin Adams, Jonathan Banks, Terri Carson, Michael Cavanaugh, Jane Elliot, Art LaFleur, L. Gray, Alex Henteloff.

THE MIDDLE AGES (3). By A. R. Gurney Jr. January 22, 1977. Director, Gordon Hunt; designers, Robert Breen, Carol Brolaski, Bruce Lane, Ralph Swickard. With Cliff DeYoung, Keene Curtis, Toni Lamond, Kitty Winn.

LEANDER STILLWELL (3). By David Rush. March 18, 1977. Director, designers and cast same as in main stage listing.

GETHSEMANE SPRINGS (3). By Harvey Perr. April 25, 1977. Director, John Sullivan; designers, P. Reid Hart, Julie Weiss, Pamela Cooper, Richard Allen, Marco Alpert. With Eileen Brennan, Tyne Daly, David Darlow, Devin Goldenberg, Arlene Golonka, Melanie Mayron, Ron Rifkin, Carol Rossen, Robert Rovin, Harvey Solin, Joyce Van Patten.

NEVADA (3). By David Kranes. May 28, 1977. Director, Jack Bender; designers, Russell Pyle, Armand Coutu. With Kay Cole, Hugh Gillin, Susan Heldfond, Ed Lowe, Adrienne Marden, Frank McCarthy, John Medici, Dennis Redfield, John Ritter, Tom Sauber.

FORCE OF HABIT (3). By Thomas Bernhard; translated by Michael Feingold. June 13, 1977. Director, Don Winton; designers, Dawn Chiang, Bill Barbe, Roger Gorden, Richard Allen; musical director, Lisa Marsnik. With Sara Ballantine, Jack Collins, Jeff Katz, George McDaniel.

Note: Forum/Laboratory also assisted in productions by the Terminal Island Correctional Institution Drama Workshop by providing directors, designers (and, in one case, a writer) for *Convictions, No Place To Be Somebody* and *Jump Street*. Also under the auspices of Mark Taper Forum/Lab, the East West Players gave a staged reading of *The Fisher King*. The Improvisational Theater Project for young theatergoers presented a fall season (September 30 through December 31, 1976) and a spring season (April 11 through July 16, 1977). Director, John Dennis; writer, Doris Baisley; designer Charles Berliner; music by Harry Aguado; lyrics by Doris Baizley and Harry Aguado. One of the projects developed into BUGS/GUNS (see mainstage production listing).

The Season Elsewhere in Los Angeles

By Rick Talcove

Theater Critic of the Van Nuys, Calif. *Valley News*

The 1976-77 theater season in Los Angeles turned out to be a most surprising one. We had the usual amount of vanity productions that expired quickly, and under-rehearsed workshop presentations, but the better offerings were definitely reaching higher, gaining more attention, running far longer than in the rigid days of limited runs.

There was a surprising amount of new material trying out on the small theater scene, and making a go of it. Most successful were Bill Solly and Donald Ward (of *Boy Meets Boy* fame) whose *Great American Backstage Musical* arrived at the Matrix in December — and was still going strong in June at the Odyssey in West Los Angeles. Solly and Ward had the enviable task of rehearsing a replacement cast while the original company readied itself for a San Francisco opening at season's end.

On the new non-musical front, Frank Salisbury (cited in these pages in the previous volume for his *Seagulls of '33*) came forth with *The Ice Cream Sunday,* a sophisticated comedy in the Feydeau tradition that should enjoy wider exposure beyond its Actors Alley premiere. Gardner McKay expanded his television script *Me* into a compelling evening by the new California Theater Ensemble. Steve Brown's *Merger* at the Beverly Hills Playhouse was a lively look at corporate politics, while Gregory Rosakis's *Persons Unclaimed* gave its author-star, and actress Doris Dowling, memorable moments in its vital study of Greenwich Village derelicts.

For local authors, Oliver Hailey organized U.S. Playwrights and offered to provide a forum to *any* playwright who took the initiative of organizing a cast for a staged reading of his play. The first public venture of the organization, William Whitehead's *And If That Mockingbird Don't Sing,* was a most promising start, greatly aided by Marcia Rodd's performance in the leading role.

The Los Angeles Actors Theater had a busy season, though only two of its productions attracted more than casual interest. LAAT's production of *Waiting for Godot* had the theater's reservation book solidly filled for weeks in advance. Though the production was eventually taped for public television, this writer thought only Donald Moffat's performance lived up to the venture's extravagant reviews. On the other hand, it was hard to find anything good to say about Miguel Piñero's *Midnight Moon at the Greasy Spoon,* a world premiere partially funded by the New York Shakespeare Festival. The author of the gripping *Short Eyes* seemed to meander forever in his new work, a study of customers in an all-night restaurant.

April 1 brought the arrival of *The American Nightmare,* the so-called "West Coast premiere of the award-winning Skaneateles New Vic Festival Theater Company" — complete with missing actress Stephanie Spelvin. The brainchild of C. Robert Holloway, the show was a hilarious send-up of staged readings in the tradition of *Don Juan in Hell.*

Three potent revivals added greatly to the season. Paddy Chayefsky's *The Tenth Man* put the Solari Theater Ensemble on the map. The playhouse, converted from the Beverly Canon film theater, opened with a mediocre presentation of one-acts. The Chayefsky revival, however, was extremely popular with an expert cast that included Richard Dreyfuss. Leon Charles projected a tormented yet humorous portrayal of *Oscar Wilde,* the old Stokes play that included — for this production — actual transcript from Wilde's celebrated trial. Finally, George Coulouris offered a well-defined *King Lear* at the Shakespeare Society.

The following is a selection of the most noteworthy Los Angeles productions of the year. The list does not include numerous touring shows nor the Center Theater Group productions at the Ahmanson and Mark Taper Forum (see the regional theater listing above). A plus sign (+) with the performance number indicates the show was still running on June 1, 1977.

THE ICE CREAM SUNDAY (51). By Frank Salisbury. December 3, 1976 (world premiere). Director, Logan Ramsey; lighting, Gary Raileanu; costumes, Saralena Martin. At Actors Alley.

Travis	T.J. Jordan
Miranda	Michele Bernath
Cordelia Massenet	Margaretta Ramsey
Edward Mayes	Stanley Brock
Augusta Massenet	Betsy Bartlett
Theron Mayes	George Cederberg
April Carter	Elizabeth Martyn
Elzora Hatch	Molly McClure
Blandine Hatch	Carrie Dieterich

No intermission.

THE GREAT AMERICAN BACKSTAGE MUSICAL (60+). Book by Bill Solly and Donald Ward; music and lyrics by Bill Solly. December 5, 1976 (world premiere). Director, Robert Talmage; scenery; Terrell Rodefer; lighting, Keith Gonzales; costumes, Christine Lewis and Quintell Apacanis. At the Matrix Theater.

Kelly Moran	Gaye Kruger
Banjo	Jerry Clark
Sylvia	Marsha Kramer
Harry	Joe Barrett
Johnny Brash	Tim Bowman
Constance Duquette	Tamara Long

No intermission.

KING LEAR (25). By William Shakespeare. December 18, 1976. Director, Stephen Roberts; costumes, Karen Jean Sanders; lighting, George Gizienski. With George Coulouris, Oren Curtis, Victoria Carver, Sarah Boulton, Phylis Ward Fox. At the Shakespeare Society.

THE TWO-CHARACTER PLAY (24). By Tennessee Williams. February 22, 1977. Director, John Hancock; scenery and costumes, Robert LaVigne; music, Fred Karlin; lighting, Alan Blacher. With Dorothy Tristan, Scott Wilson. Produced by Ken Kitch at the Callboard Theater.

AND THE SOUL SHALL DANCE (46). By Wakako Yamauchi. February 23, 1977 (world premiere). Directors, Mako and Alberto Isaac; scenery and lighting, Rae Creevey; costumes, Betty Muramoto; choreography, Mme. Kansuma Fujima; music, Hiroshima; lyrics, Wakako Yamauchi; arrangements, Dan Kuramoto, June Kuramoto, Peter Hata; vocals, Masako Hiraoka, Mako. At the East West Players, Mako artistic director, Norman Cohen administrator, Rae Creevey executive producer.

With the East West Players Ensemble (two actors alternating in each role): Shizuko Hoshi, Susan Inouye, Jim Ishida, Mimosa Iwamatsu, Denice Kumagai, Pat Li, Haunani Minn, J. Maseras Pepito, Yuki Shimoda, Sab Shimono, Diane Takei, Keone Young.

One intermission. (Cited by the American Theater Critics Association as an outstanding new play of the 1976-77 season; see synopsis in the introduction to this section.)

THE TENTH MAN (66+). By Paddy Chayefsky. March 9, 1977. Director, Paul Aaron; scenery, James Freiburger; costumes, Florence Wall; lighting, James D. Sale. With Richard Dreyfuss, Howard George, Martin Garner, Louis Guss, Joseph Mell, Sandra Shotwell, Sam Nudell. At the Solari Theater Ensemble.

ME (21). By Gardner McKay. March 11, 1977 (world stage premiere). Director, Jonathan Estrin; scenery, David Sackeroff; lighting, Russell Pyle. At the California Theater Ensemble.

Lisa Jerome	Elise Caitlin
Greg Jerome	Peter Zapp
Louise Jerome	Margaretta Ramsey
Lloyd Jerome	Harvey Vernon
Thomas Jerome	Mathew Anden

One intermission.

MERGER (28). By Steve Brown. March 18, 1977 (world premiere). Director, James Cady; scenery, William Hultstrom; lighting, Bill Quent. Produced by Elliot Apstein at the Beverly Hills Playhouse.

Keith Lawrence	Kenneth Harper
Carl Hugel	Frank Birney

Katherine McCullen .... Melinda Cordell
Lincoln Reed .... David Young
Franklin Escher .... Robert E. Oram
Ward Harris .... Donald Hotton
Marion Horowitz .... Doris Dowling
Diane Escher .... Deborah Loomis
Richard Dratz .... Logan Ramsey
Elwyn Sanborn .... Michael Byron
  Two intermissions.

AND IF THAT MOCKINGBIRD DON'T SING.
(12). By William Whitehead, March 24, 1977 (world
premiere). Director, Michael Flanagan; scenery, Nor-
ton Fairfax; costumes, Sharon Himes; lighting, Gary
Shore. Produced by U.S. Playwrights, Oliver Hailey
producer, at the Circle Theater.
K.C. Wofford .... Marcia Rodd
Darlene .... Roberta Jean Williams
Cecil Ruddleman .... Lion-el Mark Smith
Earl Wofford .... John Bennett Perry
  One intermission.

THE AMERICAN NIGHTMARE (24+). By
Thomas Benton Sterns; adapted for the stage by C.
Robert Holloway and Richard N. Levine. April 1,
1977 (world premiere). Director, C. Robert Holloway.
At the Chamber Theater.
Tyrone Craig .... Anthony Geary
Alonzo Martindale .... George D. Wallace
Daphne Houselow .... Sandra Caron
Vida Fontanne .... Jane A. Johnston

Frederic Atherton .... Donald Phelps
Alfred Adams .... Joe Warfield
Hugh Hayes .... John Milford
"Mimsie" Hayes .... Buzz Halliday
Baron Novarco .... Bryan Da Silva
Eva Braun .... Stephanie Spelvin
  No intermission.

SAME TIME, NEXT YEAR (32). By Bernard Slade.
April 12, 1977. Director, Warren Crane; scenery,
William Ritman; costumes, Bob Mackie; lighting,
Tharon Musser. With Carol Burnett, Dick Van Dyke.
Produced by Martin Gottlieb at the Huntington Hart-
ford Theater.

PERSONS UNCLAIMED (41). By Gregory
Rozakis. April 17, 1977 (world premiere). Director,
Frank Cavestani; scenery, Michael Riva; lighting,
Barbara O'Keefe. At the Venture Theater.
Bambi .... Gregory Rozakis
Gardenia .... Tara Tyson
Marguerite .... Doris Dowling
Ms. Murph .... Anne Ramsey
  One intermission.

OSCAR WILDE. (16+) By Leslie and Sewell Stokes.
May 13, 1977. Director, Mike Road; scenery and
lighting, George Gizienski; costumes, Noel Taylor.
With Leon Charles, Terence Scammell, Russ Marin,
Myron Natwick. At the Cast Theater.

LOS GATOS, CALIF.

The California Actors' Theater: Old Town Theater

(Artistic director, James Dunn; executive director, Sheldon Kleinman)

HAMLET (27). By William Shakespeare; adapted
and directed by James Dunn. October 1, 1976. With
Byron Jennings, Kurtwood Smith, Karen Hensel,
Dakin Matthews, John Vickery, Susan Leigh
Brashear, Terry Wills.

BLITHE SPIRIT (27). By Noel Coward. October 29,
1976. Director, Terry Wills. With Bonnie Gallup,
Dakin Matthews, Karen Hensel, Karen Kreider,
Carolyn Reed.

THE GOOD WOMAN OF SETZUAN (27). By Ber-
tolt Brecht; English adaptation by Ralph Manheim.
November 26, 1976. Director, James Dunn. With
Bonnie Gallup, Anita Birchenall, Terry Wills, Byron
Jennings, Karen Hensel.

THE ODD COUPLE (27). By Neil Simon. December
31, 1976. Director, G. W. Bailey. With Dakin
Matthews, Terry Wills, Carolyn Reed, Bonnie Gallup,
Tom Ramirez.

THE RAINMAKER (27). By N. Richard Nash.
January 28, 1977. Director, James Dunn. With
Carolyn Reed, Kurtwood Smith, David Daniel
Haney, G. W. Bailey, Martin Ferrero, Richard
Bradshaw, Tom Ramirez.

THE INNOCENTS (27). By William Archibald;
based on Henry James' *The Turn of the Screw*.
February 25, 1977. Director, Anne McNaughton.
With Bonnie Gallup, Kelly Durkin, Craig Waletzko,
Richard Bradshaw, Tracy Hannah, Anita Birchenall.

RASHOMON (27). By Fay and Michael Kanin.
March 25, 1977. Director, Kurtwood Smith. With
Scott Paulin, Gina Franz, Matthew J. Locricchio,
Tom Ramirez, Terry Wills.

BIERCE TAKES ON THE RAILROAD! (27). By
Philip A. Bosakowski. April 20, 1977 (world
premiere). Director, James Dunn; scenery, Ronald
Krempetz; lighting, Robert Klemm; costumes, Bar-
bara Affonso.
William Randolph Hearst .... John Vickery
Hartford T. Kent .... Tary Ismond
Ambrose Bierce .... Kurtwood Smith
Molly Bierce .... Sarita Johnson
Day Bierce .... Martin Ferrero
Senator Roger Merton .... Scott Paulin
Emily Wilton .... Anita Birchenall
Pancho Villa .... Tom Ramirez
  Chorus: Shannon Bryant, Bonnie Gallup, Michael

Martin, Scott Paulin, Carolyn Reed, David Silverman, Terry Wills.

Time: The turn of the century. Place: The United States of America. One intermission.

Designers: scenery, Ronald Krempetz; lighting, Robert Klemm, Ray Garrett; costumes, Barbara Affonso, Sara Gadbois.

Note: California Actors' Theater initiated a play reading program, Operation CATalyst, January to April, 1977, which they expect to expand in the future. Plays given were *Nights and Days in the Gardens* by Yale Udoff, *Manchild* by Nikos Kazantzakis, *The Counterfeit Rose* by George Hitchcock, *The Feeding* by Pat Pfeiffer, *Of Angels and Eskimos* by Oscar Mandel, *Lazy Mary* by Janet McGinniss.

LOUISVILLE, KY.

Actors' Theater of Louisville: Pamela Brown Auditorium

(Producing director, Jon Jory; resident designers: Paul Owen, Vincent Faust, Kurt Wilhelm)

THE BEST MAN (28). By Gore Vidal. October 7, 1976. Director, Jon Jory. With William Cain, Marji Dodrill, Victor Jory, John Newton, Adale O'Brien, John H. Fields, Ruth Maynard.

MUCH ADO ABOUT NOTHING (29). By William Shakespeare. November 4, 1976. Director, Jon Jory. With Jim Baker, Adale O'Brien, Nan Wray, Daniel Hugh-Kelly, Michael Kevin, William McNulty, Ray Fry.

A CHRISTMAS CAROL (33). By Charles Dickens. December 2, 1976. Director, Robert Brewer; scenery, Richard Kent Wilcox. With Ray Fry, Bob Burrus, Michael Kevin, William McNulty, Jeff Murphy.

THE RESISTIBLE RISE OF ARTURO UI (27). By Bertolt Brecht; English version by George Tabori. January 6, 1977. Director, Jon Jory; lighting, Ronald Wallace. With Andrew Davis, Dawn Didawick,

Joseph Costa, Vaughn McBride, William Metzo, Patrick Tovatt.

THE MATCHMAKER (27). By Thornton Wilder. February 3, 1977. Director, Jon Jory. With Adale O'Brien, Dawn Didawick, Lee Anne Fahey, John H. Fields, William McNulty, Daniel Zippi.

THE DIARY OF ANNE FRANK (33). By Frances Goodrich and Albert Hackett; based on the book, *Anne Frank: Diary of a Young Girl*. March 3, 1977. Director, Israel Hicks; lighting, James E. Stephens. With Marcell Rosenblatt, Deborah Trissel, Harry Groener, Adale O'Brien, Bob Burrus.

TABLE MANNERS (27). By Alan Ayckbourn. April 7, 1977. Director, Jon Jory; scenery, Richard Gould. With Adale O'Brien, Peggy Cowles, James Secrest, Ray Fry, William McNulty, Vinnie Holman.

Actors' Theater of Louisville: Victor Jory Theater

SEXUAL PERVERSITY IN CHICAGO by David Mamet, directed by Charles Kerr, and REUNION (world premiere) by David Mamet, directed by Ray Fry (8) October 12, 1976. *Sexual Perversity* with Joseph Costa, Andrew Davis, Dawn Didawick, Marcell Rosenblatt. *Reunion* with Bob Burrus as "Bernie" and Nan Wray as "Girl."

MEDAL OF HONOR RAG (5). By Tom Cole. October 13, 1976. Director, Elizabeth Ives. With Damien Leake, Joseph Costa, Andrew Davis.

VANITIES (12). By Jack Heifner. October 16, 1976. Director, Charles Kerr. With Lee Anne Fahey, Marcell Rosenblatt, Dawn Didawick.

WHO'S AFRAID OF VIRGINIA WOOLF? (18). By Edward Albee. January 5, 1977. Director, Daniel Sullivan. With Adale O'Brien, Ray Fry, Lee Anne Fahey, Harry Groener.

INDULGENCES IN THE LOUISVILLE HAREM (9). By John Orlock. March 2, 1977 (world premiere). Director, Patrick Henry; scenery and lighting, Paul Owen; costumes, Kurt Wilhelm.

Viola . . . . Kathleen Doyle
Florence . . . . Vinnie Holman
Winfield . . . . Ken Jenkins
Amos . . . . Michael Kevin
Time and place: Louisville, 1902. One intermission.

THE GIN GAME (8). By D. L. Coburn. March 5, 1977 (world premiere). Director, Steven Robman; scenery and lighting, Paul Owen; costumes, Kurt Wilhelm.

Fonsia Dorsey . . . . Georgia Heaslip
Weller Martin . . . . Will Hussung
Place: The sunporch of the Bentley Nursing and Convalescent Home. One intermission. (See synopsis in the introduction to this section.)

Actors' Theater of Louisville: Victor Jory Theater — Guest Production

TEA WITH DICK AND JERRY (24). Devised and directed by Erik Brogger. October 4, 1976. With Bill

Schoppert, Michael Laskin, Vaughn McBride. Edinburgh Festival Production.

MADISON, N.J.

New Jersey Shakespeare Festival: Drew University

(Artistic director, Paul Barry)

THE TEMPEST (20). By William Shakespeare. June 29, 1976. Director, Paul Barry. With J. C. Hoyt, Eric Booth, Earl Hindman, Susanne Marley, Clayton Berry.

HENRY V (20). By William Shakespeare. July 6, 1976. Director, Paul Barry. With Eric Booth, William Preston, Ronald Steelman, Edwin J. McDonough, J. C. Hoyt.

THE BEST MAN (19). By Gore Vidal. July 23, 1976. Director, Paul Barry. With Kenneth Gray, J. C. Hoyt, Ronald Steelman, Patricia Kilgarriff, Katherine McGrath, Naomi Riseman, Robert Machray.

THE DEVIL'S DISCIPLE (19). By George Bernard Shaw. August 11, 1976. Director, Paul Barry. With Clayton Berry, Michael McCarty, Katherine McGrath, Patricia Kilgarriff, J. C. Hoyt, Robert Machray.

PRIVATE LIVES (20). By Noel Coward. August 29, 1976. Director, Davey Marlin-Jones. With Katherine McGrath, Edwin J. McDonough, Clayton Berry, Susanne Marley.

STOP THE WORLD — I WANT TO GET OFF (21). Book, music and lyrics by Leslie Bricusse and Anthony Newley. October 5, 1976. Director, Paul Barry. With Paul Barry, Ann McCurry.

THE PLAYBOY OF THE WESTERN WORLD (21). By John Millington Synge. October 26, 1976. Director, Paul Barry. With Timothy Meyers, Molly Scoville, Lynn Cohen, Earl Theroux, Ronald Steelman, Michael Zeke Zacarro.

OF MICE AND MEN (21). By John Steinbeck. November 16, 1976. Director, Paul Barry. With Michael Capanna, Paul Barry, Earl Theroux, Timothy Meyers, David Connell, Molly Scoville.

Designers: Scenery, David M. Glenn; lighting, Gary C. Porto; costumes, Jean Steinlein.

Note: New Jersey Shakespeare Festival presented 12 "Monday Night Specials" consisting of dance, music, mime and poetry, July 5-September 20, 1976. In addition, *Dinny and the Witches* by William Gibson, directed by Ronald Steelman and performed by the 1976 Festival Intern Workshop, was presented for 3 performances, August 18-20, 1976.

MILWAUKEE

Milwaukee Repertory Theater Company: Todd Wehr Theater

(Artistic director, Nagle Jackson; managing director, Sara O'Connor)

DEATH OF A SALESMAN (44). By Arthur Miller. September 17, 1976. Director, Nagle Jackson. With William McKereghan, Ruth Schudson, James Secrest, John Mansfield, Montgomery Davis, Durward McDonald.

THE TRIAL OF THE MOKE (44). By Daniel Stein. October 29, 1976 (world premiere). Director, Robert Lanchester; scenery and lighting, Christopher M. Idoine; costumes, Ellen M. Kozak.
Gentlemen (in order of rank):
Col. Pennypacker;	
West Pt. Capt.	Bennett Sargent
Col. William Shafter	Durward McDonald
Capt. Clous;	
Southern Gentleman	Montgomery Davis
Capt. Merritt Barber	James Secrest
Lt. Henry Ossian Flipper	Franklyn Seales
Lt. Carl Wilhelmi	John Mansfield
Lt. Charles Nordstrom	Tom Blair
Sgt. Ross	Daniel Mooney
Private	Allan Cobb
Pvt. Bentz	James Pickering
Cadet Captain; Gentleman	Kevin Schwartz
Cadet James Smith	Bob Gossett
Cadet Clark	T. A. Taylor
Cadet Johnson Whittaker	Bill Henry Douglass
Cadet Sentry	Michael Plunkett
William Chamberlain	Kelvin Davis
Joseph Sender	William McKereghan
Ladies:	
Molly Reilly	Shellie Chancellor
Miss Cooper	Cheryl Kennis
Miss Jackson	Alverna Jones
Ladies	Karla Koskinen, Patricia Schmidt
Lucy Smith	Emma Angeline Butler

Time: 1881. Place: Fort Davis, Tex., and the memory, mind and imagination of Lt. Henry O. Flipper, 10th Regiment, U. S. Cavalry. Two intermissions.

PRIVATE LIVES (44). By Noel Coward. December 10, 1976. Director, William Glover. With Peggy Cowles, Steven Ryan, Daniel Mooney, Mary Lowry.

VOLPONE (44). By Ben Jonson. January 28, 1977. Director, Nagle Jackson. With Jim Baker, Sirin Devrim Trainer, Bruce Somerville, G. Wood, Durward McDonald, James Crow, Shellie Chancellor.

VANITIES (44). By Jack Heifner. March 11, 1977.

Director, Kent Paul. With Shellie Chancellor, Elaine Hausman, Eda Zahl.

THE DOG RAN AWAY (44). By Brother Jonathan,

O.S.F. April 22, 1977. Director, Nagle Jackson. With Tom Blair, Peter MacLean, William McKereghan. (See synopsis in the introduction to this section.)

Designers: Scenery and lighting, Christopher M. Idoine, R. H. Graham; costumes, Ellen M. Kozak, Linda Fisher, Elizabeth Covey.

Milwaukee Repertory Theater Company: Pabst Theater

A CHRISTMAS CAROL (24). By Charles Dickens; adapted and directed by Nagle Jackson. December 8, 1976. Designer, Christopher M. Idoine; costumes,

Elizabeth Covey. With G. Wood, James Pickering, Rose Pickering, Tommy Vicini, Montgomery Davis, Franklyn Seales.

Milwaukee Repertory Theater Company: Court Street Theater

THE BIRTHDAY PARTY (17). By Harold Pinter. March 17, 1977. Director, Sanford Robbins; scenery, Pete Davis; lighting, R. H. Graham; costumes, Rosemary Ingham. With James Pickering, Rose Pickering, William McKereghan, Jim Baker, Daniel Mooney, Penelope Reed.

DOMINO COURTS (17). By William Hauptman. April 7, 1977. Director, Walter L. Schoen; scenery, Valerie Kuehn; lighting, Seth Price; costumes, Ellen M. Kozak. With James Pickering, Penelope Reed,

John Mansfield, Rose Pickering. And: IN MEMORY OF (17). By Kevin Schwartz. April 7, 1977 (world premiere). Director, Daniel Mooney; scenery, Sam Garth; lighting, Seth Price; costumes, Joanne Karaska.

Bob .... Jim Baker
Arthur .... Bennett Sargent
Judy .... Penelope Reed
Young Man .... Michael Plunkett
Time: the present. Place: A hospital room.

MINNEAPOLIS

The Cricket Theater

(Producing director, William Semans; artistic director, Lou Salerni)

ARTICHOKE (28). By Joanna M. Glass. October 16, 1976. Director, Lou Salerni; designer, Dick Leerhoff. With David Willis, Bob Breuler, Zoaunne LeRoy, Frank Scott, Allen Hamilton, Susan Fuller, William Emmons.

SUBJECT TO FITS (26). By Robert Montgomery. November 20, 1976. Director, John Soliday; designer, Dick Leerhoff; musical director, Rob Struzinski. With Andrew Miner, Sedgwick Howard, Michael Laskin, Kathleen Perkins, Mari Rovang.

THE MOUND BUILDERS (21). By Lanford Wilson. December 31, 1976. Director, Rustin Greene; scenery and lighting, Dick Leerhoff; costumes, Laraine Lee. With Louis Plante, Zoaunne LeRoy, Tena May Murray, Rosemary Hartup, David Ode, Mary Ann Lippay, Joe Horvath.

AND WHERE SHE STOPS NOBODY KNOWS (21). By Oliver Hailey. February 5, 1977. Director, Lou Salerni; scenery, Jack Barkla; lighting, Dick Leerhoff; costumes, Christopher Beesley. With Camille Gifford, Don Amendolia.

THE LAST MEETING OF THE KNIGHTS OF THE WHITE MAGNOLIA (22). By Preston Jones. March 12, 1977. Director, Lou Salerni; scenery and lighting, Dick Leerhoff; costumes, Christopher Beesley. With William Preston, William Schoppert, William Halliday, David Willis, Clive Rosengren, James Murray, Michael Laskin, Sedgwick Howard, Bob Breuler.

A TRIBUTE TO LILI LAMONT (21). By Arthur Whitney. April 16, 1977. Director, Lou Salerni; filmed sequence conceived and directed by Rustin Greene; scenery, Jerry Williams; costumes, Christopher Beesley; original music, Norman Berman. With Merle McDill, Nancy Bagshaw, John Lewin, Philip Blackwell, Don Amendolia, Clive Rosengren, Jane McDonough.

WHO'S AFRAID OF VIRGINIA WOOLF? (25). By Edward Albee. May 21, 1977. Director, Lou Salerni; scenery, Thom Roberts; costumes, Christopher Beesley. With Zoaunne LeRoy, Allen Hamilton, Joe Horvath, Helena Power.

The Guthrie Theater Company: Guthrie Theater

(Artistic director, Michael Langham; managing director, Donald Schoenbaum)

THE MATCHMAKER (62). By Thornton Wilder. June 14, 1976. Director, Michael Langham. With Barbara Bryne, Tony Mockus, Helen Carey, Peter Michael Goetz, Barnaby Tucker.

DOCTOR FAUSTUS (24). June 16, 1976. By Christopher Marlowe. Director, Ken Ruta. With Mark Lamos, Michael Gross, Jeff Chandler, Fran Bennett.

CAT ON A HOT TIN ROOF (36). By Tennessee Williams. June 30, 1976. Director, Stephen Kanee. With Victoria Thompson, Christopher Pennock, Tony Mockus, Barbara Bryne.

ROSENCRANTZ AND GUILDENSTERN ARE DEAD (34). By Tom Stoppard. August 18, 1976. Director, Stephen Kanee. With Jeff Chandler, Mark Lamos, Christopher Pennock, Karen Landry, Russell Gold, Susan Dafoe, Wiley Parker.

AN ENEMY OF THE PEOPLE (32). By Henrik Ibsen. September 1, 1976. Director, Adrian Hall.

With Ken Ruta, Barbara Bryne, Tony Mockus, Helen Carey, Peter Michael Goetz.

THE WINTER'S TALE (36). By William Shakespeare. October 27, 1976. Director, Michael Langham. With Ken Ruta, Peter Michael Goetz, Helen Carey, Karen Landry, Jeff Chandler.

A CHRISTMAS CAROL (28). By Charles Dickens. December 8, 1976. Director, Stephen Kanee. With Jeff Chandler, Mark Lamos, Dwyer Reilly.

THE NATIONAL HEALTH (29). By Peter Nichols. January 19, 1977. Directors, Peter Nichols and Michael Langham. With Lance Davis, Richard Ramos, Cheryl Tafathale Jones, Fran Bennett, Lela Bonynge, Oliver Cliff, Susan Dafoe.

Designers: Scenery, Desmond Heeley, Ralph Funicello, John Conklin, Jack Barkla, Sam Kirkpatrick; lighting, Duane Schuler; costumes, Desmond Heeley, Robert Morgan, John Conklin, Jack Edwards, Sam Kirkpatrick.

Guthrie Theater: Special Productions

GUTHRIE VARIETY SHOW, January 23, 1977. An evening of song, dance and comedy, directed, designed and performed by members of the Guthrie Theater Company.

THE BELLE OF AMHERST (4). By William Luce; compiled by Timothy Helgeson from the poems, letters and family recollections of Emily Dickinson. March 3-5, 1977. With Julie Harris.

A PARTY FOR TWO, created and performed by Dominique Serrand and Barbra Berlovitz. March 28, 1977. Animateur, Emily Mann; lighting, Robert Bye;

special costume effects and masks, Beth A. Sanders. In two parts: Jeux de Masques (Mask Game) and PAF (A Tiny Explosion).

A SORROW BEYOND DREAMS (4). By Peter Handke; translated by Ralph Manheim; adapted from the novel and directed by Daniel Freudenberger. April 7-9, 1977. Performed by Len Cariou.

BULLY (8). By Jerome Alden; based on Teddy Roosevelt's books and writings. April 25-30, 1977. With James Whitmore.

The Guthrie Theater Company: Guthrie Two

DEAR LIAR (14). By Jerome Kilty; adapted from the letters of George Bernard Shaw and Mrs. Patrick Campbell. December 14, 1976. Director, Mark Lamos. With Patricia Conolly, Ken Ruta.

ANNULLA ALLEN — THE AUTO-BIOGRAPHY OF A SURVIVOR (16). Adapted by Emily Mann from conversations and taped interviews of Mrs. Allen. March 16, 1977 (world premiere).

Directed by Emily Mann; scenery and costumes, Barry Robison. With Barbara Bryne.

Annulla Allen's memories and philosophy of life: flight from Galicia (Russia) during the revolution, to Berlin, to Austria and marriage; her husband's arrest by the Nazis and incarceration in Dachau from which she managed to free him; England through the war years and the present.

Note: A Party For Two toured the upper Midwest — Minnesota, Michigan, Iowa, Wisconsin, the Dakotas — from January to April, 1977. Among its other community outreach programs, the Guthrie Theater has developed an extensive series of theater classes in acting, design and production for children and adults, which are given by members of the professional acting, design and technical staff.

NEW HAVEN

Long Wharf Theater

(Artistic director, Arvin Brown; executive director, M. Edgar Rosenblum)

ALPHABETICAL ORDER (37). By Michael Frayn. October 8, 1976 (American premiere). Director, Steven Robman; scenery, Marjorie Kellogg; lighting, Ronald Wallace; costumes, Carrie F. Robbins.
Geoffrey . . . . Roderick Cook

Leslie . . . . Jeanne Ruskin
Arnold . . . . Josef Sommer
John . . . . John Horton
Lucy . . . . Valerie French
Nora . . . . Mary Fogarty

Wally .... Richard Mathews
Place: The library of a small English newspaper.
One intermission.

THE AUTUMN GARDEN (37). By Lillian
Hellman. November 12, 1976. Director, Arvin Brown;
scenery, David Jenkins; lighting, Judy Rasmuson;
costumes, Bill Walker. With Joyce Ebert, Carolyn
Coates, Victor Garber, Carmen Mathews, James No-
ble, Josef Sommer, Alice Drummond, Susan Sharkey,
John McMartin, Charlotte Moore, Mary Fogarty,
Robert Bernard Turner.

HOME (37). By David Storey. December 17, 1976.
Director, Michael Lindsay-Hogg; scenery, Steven
Rubin; lighting, Jamie Gallagher; costumes, Mary
Strieff. With Emery Battis, J. Frank Lucas, Bette
Henritze, Mary Fogarty, Everett McGill.

THE SHADOW BOX (37). By Michael Cristofer.
January 21, 1977. Director, Gordon Davidson;
scenery, Ming Cho Lee; lighting, Ronald Wallace;
costumes, Bill Walker. With Josef Sommer, Clifton
James, Vincent Stewart, Joyce Ebert, Laurence
Luckinbill, Patricia Elliott, Mandy Patinkin, Rose
Gregorio, Geraldine Fitzgerald.

ST. JOAN (37). By George Bernard Shaw. February
25, 1977. Director, Martin Fried; scenery, Marjorie

Kellogg; lighting, Ronald Wallace; costumes, Bill
Walker. With Kitty Winn, Kristoffer Tabori, Everett
McGill, Emery Battis, William Swetland, Josef
Sommer, Timothy Jerome, Ben Kapen.

ABSENT FRIENDS (37). By Alan Ayckbourn. April
1, 1977 (American premiere). Director, Eric Thomp-
son; scenery, Edward Burbridge; lighting, Ronald
Wallace; costumes, Michele Suzanne Reisch.
Diana .... Anne Jackson
Evelyn .... Dale Hodges
Marge .... Christina Pickles
Paul .... Joseph Maher
John .... Jacob Brooke
Colin .... Eli Wallach
Act I: 3 p.m. Saturday. Act II: 4:15 Saturday. One
intermission.

THE ROSE TATTOO (37). By Tennessee Williams.
May 6, 1977. Director, Steven Robman; scenery, John
Conklin; lighting, Judy Rasmuson; costumes, Bill
Walker. With Rita Moreno, Toni Kalem, Steven
Keats, Estelle Omens, Glenn Close, Linda Hunt.

THE GIN GAME (33). By D. L. Coburn. June 8,
1977. Director, Mike Nichols; scenery, David
Mitchell; lighting, Ronald Wallace; costumes, Bill
Walker. With Jessica Tandy, Hume Cronyn.

Long Wharf Theater: Monday Night Special Events

AN EVENING OF ONE ACTOR PLAYS (6).
November 22, 1976. FAITH HEALER by Brian
Friel, director, Jamie Brown, with John Leighton; and
DR. KHEAL by Maria Irene Fornes, with Linda
Hunt.

A CHRISTMAS PROGRAM (2). December 27,
1976. With Eileen Atkins, Victor Garber, Don Scardino, John Tillinger, Joan Sommer.

THE NEXT MOVE REVUE (6). April 4, 1977.
Boston's Next Move Theater Company in an evening
of improvisation. Company: Martin R. Anderson,
Cynthia Caldwell, Brad Jones, Andy Gaus, Geraldine
Librandi, Karen McDonald, Gil Schwarts, Steven
Warnick, Lanie Zera.

Long Wharf Theater: Monday Night New Play Readings

(Series director, John Tillinger. Workshop premieres, one performance each)

WHAT PEACHES, WHAT PENUMBRAS? by
Daniel Sklar. January 31, 1977. With Roy Cooper,
Michael Goodwin, Bette Henritze, Dorothy Lyman,
Howard Rollins, Susan Sharkey, Terrence Sherman,
Lewis J. Stadlen.

EMINENT DOMAIN by Percy Granger. February
7, 1977. With Frank Converse, John Gallogly,
Timothy Jerome, Terrence Sherman, Lois Smith,
William Swetland.

CORNBURY by William M. Hoffman and Anthony
Holland, with Rise Collins, Lindsay Crouse, Richard
Dunn, Anthony Holland, Timothy Jerome, Nick
Kepros, Sharon Laughlin, Joseph Maher, Roberta
Maxwell, Robert Murch, Sarah Peterson; and TIDE
IN THE AFFAIRS OF WOMEN by Phillip Martin,
with Shirley Bryan, Lindsay Crouse, Dale Hodges,
Neil Hunt, Barbara Lester, Geraldine Sherman.
February 14, 1977.

EARTHWORMS by Albert Innaurato. March 7,
1977. With Lance Davis, Rosemary De Angelis, Peter
Evans, Michael Goodwin, Barnard Hughes, Ben
Masters, Keith McDermott, Sarah Peterson, Susan
Sharkey, Terrence Sherman.

DWARFMAN by Michael Weller. March 14, 1977.
With Emery Battis, Louis Beachner, Sully Boyar, Bob
Dishy, Bara-Cristin Hansen, Patrick Hines, Timothy
Jerome, Dorothy Lyman, Caroline McWilliams,
Deborah Offner, Terrence Sherman, Josef Sommer,
Ray Zifo.

LUNCH GIRLS by Leigh Curran. March 21, 1977.
With Carol Androsky, Octavio Ciano, Leigh Curran,
Edward Herrmann, Marybeth Hurt, Dorothy Lyman,
Roberta Maxwell, Ellen Sandler, Terrence Sherman,
Meryl Streep.

Yale Repertory Theater

(Director, Robert Brustein; associate director, Alvin Epstein)

In repertory:
JULIUS CAESAR (25). By William Shakespeare. October 1, 1976. Director, Alvin Epstein; scenery, Tony Straiges; lighting, William B. Warfel; costumes, Jeanne Button. With Jeremy Geidt, Robert Drivas, Thomas Hill, Ron Leibman, Eugene Troobnick, Norma Brustein, Carmen de Lavallade.
SUICIDE IN B FLAT (23). By Sam Shepard. October 15, 1976 (world premiere). Director, Walt Jones; scenery, Michael Yeargan; lighting, Paul Gallo; costumes, Jess Goldstein; original music, Lawrence Wolf.

Pianist	Lawrence Wolf
Pablo	Clifford David
Louis	Joe Grifasi
Petrone	William Hickey
Laureen	Alma Cuervo
Niles	Paul Schierhorn
Paullette	Joyce Fideor

No intermission.

IVANOV (31). By Anton Chekhov; translation by Jeremy Brooks and Kitty Hunter Blair. November 19, 1976. Director, Ron Daniels; scenery, Michael Yeargan; lighting, William B. Warfel; costumes, Jeanne Button. With Alvin Epstein, Elzbieta Chesevska, Robert Brustein, Eugene Troobnick, Norma Brustein, Margaret Whitton.

In repertory:
THE VIETNAMIZATION OF NEW JERSEY: AN AMERICAN TRAGEDY (24). By Christopher Durang. January 14, 1977 (world premiere). Director, Walt Jones; scenery, Christopher Phelps Clarens; lighting, James H. Gage; costumes, Kathleen M. Armstrong.

Ozzie Ann	Kate McGregor-Stewart
Harry; Larry	Charles Levin
Et	Stephen Rowe
Hazel	Ben Halley Jr.
David	Richard Bey
Liat	Anne Louise Hoffmann
Father McGillicutty	Jeremy Geidt

Place: Piscataway, N. J. Act I: 1968–75. Act II: 1976. One intermission.
THE DURANGO FLASH (17). By William Hauptman. January 28, 1977 (world premiere). Director, Kenneth Frankel; scenery and projections, Michael Yeargan; lighting, Thomas Skelton; costumes, Jeanne Button.

Leon LaPresto	Guy Boyd
Bartender; 3d Cowboy	Richard Grusin
Monte Murray	William Carden
C.C. LaPresto	Lynn Oliver
Bonnie Good	Carmen de Lavallade
1st Cowboy; Photographer	Tony Sherer
2d Cowboy; Photographer	William McGlinn

Ben Stoner	Thomas Hill
Howard Oates	Eugene Troobnick
Cisco Boyd	Alvin Epstein
Paula Boyd	Joyce Fideor
Script Girl; Press Agent	Rebecca Nelson
Joe Bob Foley	Paul Schierhorn
Cicero	Ben Halley Jr.
Dennis Blair	Stephen Rowe
Little Joe	Damon Ortega/Donovan Withers

Film Crew: Anthony Antonelli, Richard Castagna, Misia Celichowski, David Churbuck, David Ford, Luis Gonzales, Lynn Goodwin, Karen Siderman, John Wolf.

Act I: Hollywood, 1939. Act II: Hollywood, 1943; Abilene, 1948. One intermission.

PUNTILLA (29). By Bertolt Brecht; translated by Gerhard Nellhaus; music by William Bolcom; lyrics adapted by Michael Feingold. March 4, 1977. Director, Ron Daniels; scenery, David Lloyd Gropman; lighting, Thomas Skelton; musical direction, Paul Schierhorn. With Thomas Hill, Ron Faber, Shaine Marinson, Richard Bey, Eugene Troobnick, Jeremy Geidt, John Doolittle, Nancy Mayans, Alma Cuervo.

WHITE MARRIAGE (28). By Tadeusz Rozewicz; translated by Adam Czerniawski. April 15, 1977 (American premiere). Director, Andrzej Wajda; scenery and costumes, Krystyna Zachwatowicz; lighting, William B. Warfel, Lewis Folden; music consultant, Paul Schierhorn; movement consultant, Carmen de Lavallade.

Bianca	Carol Williard
Pauline	Blanche Baker
Father	Eugene Troobnick
Mother	Elzbieta Chezevska
Cook	Alma Cuervo
Grandfather	Alvin Epstein
Benjamin	Steven Rowe
Milkmaid	Polina Klimovitskaya
Aunt	Norma Brustein
Mr. Felix; Huntsman	William Roberts

Guests: David M. Grant, Timothy Hagan, Douglas Simes, Roy B. Steinberg, Shaine Marinson, Patrizia Norcia, Julia Przybos.

Time: About 1900. Place: A country estate. Tableau 1: The girls' bedroom. Tableau 2: Glass and china. Tableau 3: Oh come ... Tableau 4: The confessional. Tableau 5: Blood in the girls' bedroom. Tableau 6: Wedding and mourning. Tableau 7: In a black forest — past and present. Tableau 8: Sweets. Tableau 9: Description. Tableau 10: The rehearsal. Tableau 11: The bride's trousseau. Tableau 12: Kiss her! Kiss her! Tableau 13: I am. One intermission.

Yale Repertory Theater: Special Production

THE BANQUET YEARS (8). Conceived by Carmen de Lavallade, Robert Gainer, Joe Grifasi and Jonathan Marks; texts by Alfred Jarry, Pierre Louys, Max Jacob, Erik Satie, Jonathan Marks; music by

Erik Satie, Claude Debussy, Francis Poulenc. December 30, 1976. Director, Robert Gainer; choreographers, Carmen de Lavallade, Joe Grifasi. With members of Yale Repertory Company. A celebration of turn-of-the-century Paris in words, music, dance and song.

Note: Yale Repertory Theater and School of Drama sponsor Yale Cabaret, Experimental Theater, studio projects (including playwrights workshops and Sunday series of new play readings) with students, faculty and members of the professional company; as well as a Student Repertory subscription series, all of which were open to the public. In the Experimental Theater, the Playwrights' Projects (1976-1977) presented *Lion Dancers* by James Yoshimura, *Evenings In* by Robert N. Sandburg, *Dottie's Home* by Lewis Black, *His Master's Voice* by Richard Zigun (*Equal Rights* by Zigun was one of the Studio projects, as well). The Sunday Series of staged readings of new plays (October 17, 31, December 5, 1976, February 6, 13, April 24, May 1, 1977) included *They Are Dying Out* by Peter Handke, *Mississippi Mud* by Robert Auletta, *The Woods* by David Mamet, *Euripides at Bay* by Aristophanes in a translation by William Arrowsmith, *Reunion* by David Mamet. The Drama School's main stage productions were *The Revenger's Tragedy* by Cyril Tourneur, directed by Thomas Hill; *Earth Spirit* by Frank Wedekind, directed by Lee Breuer. Workshop productions were *Terra Nova* by Ted Tally, directed by Travis Preston; *The Sea Gull* by Anton Chekhov, directed by Louis Criss. The Student Repertory gave *The Government Inspector* by Nikolai Gogol, directed by Denise Gordon, *Henry IV* by William Shakespeare, directed by Allen Mokler. In addition to *Equal Rights,* studio projects included Henrik Ibsen's *Hedda Gabler,* directed by Richard Gilman, and *Little Eyolf,* student-directed. Finally, Cabaret productions between October and May 1977 included one-man and one-woman shows, improvised comedy, a musical puppet show, a variety of other nightclub-type acts and vaudevilles, as well as the following plays: *In the Russian Manner* (tales from Chekhov), directed by Alan Mokler; *Fits and Starts* by Grace McKeaney, directed by Bruce Siddons; *The Little Mahagonny* (Brecht-Weill) directed by Tom Gardner; *Adaptation* by Elaine May, directed by Walt Jones; *Foreplay, Door Play* by Robert Auletta, directed by John Weil; *All Men Are Whores* by David Mamet: *Doc: The Trial of the Salt Seller* by Ed Gold: *Frontal Nudity* by Peter Blanc: *Taking Care of Business* by Robert Sandberg and *Noam Chomski Monologue* by James Kuslan.

PHILADELPHIA

The Philadelphia Drama Guild: Walnut Street Theater

(Artistic director, Douglas Seale; managing director, James B. Freydberg).

HEARTBREAK HOUSE (23). By George Bernard Shaw. November 3, 1976. Director, Douglas Seale. With Valerie Von Volz, Tony Van Bridge, Louise Troy, Moya Fenwick, Gillie Fenwick, James Valentine, Ronald Bishop, Jeffrey Jones, Edward Atienza, Betty Leighton.

ENTER A FREE MAN (23). By Tom Stoppard. December 1, 1976. Director, Douglas Campbell. With Edward Atienza, Domini Blythe, Sam Kressen, Betty Leighton, Louise Troy, Eric Uhler, James Valentine, Rudolph Wilrich.

FIVE FINGER EXERCISE (23). By Peter Shaffer. January 5, 1977. Director, Douglas Seale. With Carolyn Coates, John Glover, Lee Toombs, Jack Gwillim, Linda Hunt.

BLITHE SPIRIT (23). By Noel Coward. February 2, 1977. Director, Douglas Seale. With Louise Troy, Ann Crumb, Carolyn Coates, Peter Page, Betty Leighton.

HAMLET (23). By William Shakespeare. March 9, 1977. Director, Douglas Seale. With John Glover, Sherry Steiner, David Leary, Louise Troy, William Le Massena, Powers Boothe, Donald Symington.

Designers: Scenery, John Kasarda; lighting, Spencer Mosse; costumes, Dona Granata.

PRINCETON, N.J.

McCarter Theater Company: McCarter Theater

(Producing director, Michael Kahn)

A STREETCAR NAMED DESIRE (15). By Tennessee Williams. October 7, 1976. Director, Michael Kahn; scenery, Michael Yeargan, Larry King; lighting, John McLain; costumes, Jane Greenwood. With Shirley Knight, Kenneth Welsh, Glenn Close, George Dzundza.

MAJOR BARBARA (15). By George Bernard Shaw. November 4, 1976. Director, Kenneth Frankel; scenery, Marjorie Kellogg; lighting, Pat Collins; costumes, Carrie F. Robbins. With Maria Tucci, William Swetland, Robert Stattel, Louis Beachner,

Patricia Falkenhain, Christopher Gaze, George Hosmer.

THE NIGHT OF THE TRIBADES (15). By Per Olov Enquist; translated by Ross Skideler. December 2, 1976 (American premiere). Director, Michael Kahn; scenery, Michael H. Yeargan and Larry King; lighting, John McLain; costumes, Jane Greenwood.

August Strindberg . . . . Donald Madden
Siri . . . . Patricia Elliott
Marie Caroline David . . . . Kathryn Walker
Viggo Schiwe . . . . Ted Graeber
Photographer . . . . Lawrence Holofcener

Time: 1889. Place: On stage at Copenhagen's Dagmar Theater, during a rehearsal of Strindberg's *The Stronger*.

THE PHYSICISTS (15). By Friedrich Duerrenmatt. February 3, 1977. Director, Gene Lesser; scenery, Tony Straiges; lighting, John McLain; costumes,

Jeanne Button. With Anthony Holland, Nicholas Kepros, James Noble, Vivian Nathan, Alice Beardsley, George Touliatos.

ANGEL CITY (14). By Sam Shepard. March 3, 1977 (world premiere). Director, Michael Kahn; scenery, David Jenkins; lighting, John McLain; costumes, Laura Crow; composer, Fred Hess.

Miss Scoons . . . . Christine Baranski
Tympani . . . . Stephen Long
Rabbit Brown . . . . Anthony McKay
Wheeler . . . . Lewis J. Stadlen
Saxaphonist . . . . Fred Hess

One intermission.

DESIGN FOR LIVING (14). By Noel Coward. March 31, 1977. Director, Stephen Porter; scenery and costumes, Zack Brown; lighting, John McLain. With Meg Wynne Owen, Michael Allinson, Patrick Horgan.

McCarter Theater Company: McCarter Theater — Guest Production

I WAS SITTING ON MY PATIO THIS GUY APPEARED I THOUGHT I WAS HALLUCINATING (1). By Robert Wilson. May 5, 1977. With

Robert Wilson, Lucinda Childs. Sound, film and music by Robert Lloyd.

PROVIDENCE, R.I.

Trinity Square Repertory Company: Lederer Theater — Upstairs

(Producer-director, Adrian Hall)

OF MICE AND MEN (52). By John Steinbeck. November 23, 1976. Director, Adrian Hall. With William Damkoehler, Norman Smith, David C. Jones, Tom Griffin, Peter Gerety, Mina Manente.

THE BOYS FROM SYRACUSE (50). Book by George Abbott; music and lyrics by Richard Rodgers and Lorenz Hart; based on William Shakespeare's *The Comedy of Errors*. January 4, 1977. Direc-

tor/choreographer, Don Price. With Robert Black, William Damkoehler, Peter Gerety, Timothy Donahue, Nancy Nichols, Melanie Jones, Barbara Orson.

KING LEAR (43). By William Shakespeare. March 1, 1977. Director, Adrian Hall. With Richard Kneeland, Mina Manente, Melanie Jones, Bonnie Sacks, Ed Hall, Peter Gerety, David C. Jones, Daniel Von Barggen.

Trinity Square Repertory Company: Lederer Theater — Downstairs

SEVEN KEYS TO BALDPATE (26). By George M. Cohan; adapted from the novel by Earl Derr Biggers. September 14, 1976. Director, Adrian Hall. With Richard Kneeland, Barbara Orson, Richard Kavanaugh, Richard Jenkins, Margo Skinner.

A FLEA IN HER EAR (45). By Georges Feydeau. September 24, 1976. Director, George Martin. With Richard Jenkins, Margo Skinner, Richard Kavanaugh, David Kennett, Melanie Jones.

KNOCK KNOCK (41). By Jules Feiffer. November 30, 1976. Director, Robert Mandel. With George

Martin, Howard London, Richard Kavanaugh, Margo Skinner.

RICH AND FAMOUS (43). By John Guare. February 1, 1977. Director, George Martin; music director, Vern Graham; choreographer, Sharon Jenkins. With Richard Jenkins, Cynthia Strickland, Barbara Meek, Timothy Crowe.

BAD HABITS (32). By Terrence McNally. April 12, 1977. Director, Robert Mandel. With George Martin, Tom Griffin, David C. Jones, Bradford Gottlin, Barbara Orson, Margo Skinner.

Designers: scenery, Eugene Lee, Robert D. Soule; lighting, John Custer, Mark Rippe; costumes, Betsey Potter, James Berton Harris, Franne Lee.

Note: Trinity Square's production of *Knock Knock* was presented at the Charles Playhouse in Boston for six weeks. *Rich And Famous* was moved to the Wilbur Theater in Boston for four weeks. *Of Mice And Men* and *King Lear* were presented for 50 performances as part of Trinity Square's *Project Discovery*, a theater experience program offered to high school students.

RICHMOND, VA.

The Repertory Company of the Virginia Museum Theater

(Artistic director, Keith Fowler; general manager, Loraine Slade)

THE COUNTRY WIFE (23). By William Wycherley. October 1, 1976. Director, Keith Fowler; scenery, Terry A. Bennett; lighting, Michael O. Watson; costumes, Frederick M. Brown. With Wyman Pendleton, Jeremiah Sullivan, Janet Bell, Ken Letner, Sarah Brooke, William Pitts.

THE MOUSETRAP (27). By Agatha Christie. October 29, 1976. Director, James Kirkland; scenery and lighting, Richard Carleton Hankins; costumes, Frederick N. Brown. With Kathleen Klein, Maury Erickson, Brad O'Hare, Beth Dixon, Philip LeStrange.

OH COWARD! (25). Words and music by Noel Coward; devised and directed by Roderick Cook. November 26, 1976. Scenery, Richard Bryant; lighting, James D. Bloch; costumes, Paige Southard. With Dalton Cathey, Kimberly Gaisford, W.M. Hunt.

THE CARETAKER (24). By Harold Pinter. January 7, 1977. Director, James Kirkland; Scenery and lighting, Richard Carleton Hankins; costumes, Frederick N. Brown. With Michael Martin, Keith Fowler, Dillon Evans.

HAMLET (28). By William Shakespeare. February 4, 1977. Directors, James Kirkland, Keith Fowler; scenery and costumes, Terry A. Bennett; lighting, Michael O. Watson. With Keith Fowler, Margaret Gwenver, Pamela Lewis, Brooks Rogers, Edward Stevlingson, Michael Martin.

CHILDE BYRON (25). By Romulus Linney. March 4, 1977 (world premiere). Director, Keith Fowler; scenery, Sandr La Ferla; lighting, Michael O. Watson; costumes, Paige Southard; muscial director, William Stancil; fights choreographer, Joseph Martinez.

Byron .... Jeremiah Sullivan
Ada .... Marjorie Lerstrom
Girl .... Pamela Lewis
Boy .... David Addis
Young Woman .... Janet Bell
Young Man .... James Kirkland
Woman .... Rachael Lindhart
Man .... William Stancil
Time: November 27, 1852. Place: The bedroom of Augusta Ada, Countess of Lovelace, Somerset, England.

ROCHESTER, MICHIGAN

Oakland University Professional Theater Program: Meadow Brook Theater

(Artistic director, Terence Kilburn; managing director, David Robert Kanter; resident costume coordinator, Mary Lynn Bonnell)

MAN AND SUPERMAN (29). By George Bernard Shaw. October 7, 1976. Director, Terence Kilburn; scenery, Peter Hicks, lighting, Nancy Thompson. With William Hurt, Elizabeth Horowitz, Donald C. Moore, Cheryl Giannini, Richard Hilger, Fred Thompson.

THE NIGHT OF THE IGUANA (29). By Tennessee Williams. November 4, 1976. Director, Charles Nolte; scenery, Lance Brockman; lighting, Jean A. Montgomery. With David Canary, Marie Wallace, Elizabeth Orion, Richard Hilger, Melanie Resnick.

THE SCHOOL FOR WIVES (29). By Molière; English verse translation by Richard Wilbur. December 2, 1976. Director, Terence Kilburn; scenery, Peter Hicks; lighting, Fred Fonner. With Cheryl Giannini, Elizabeth Horowitz, Dan C. Bar, Donald Ewer, William Halliday, Carl Schurr, Richard Hilger, James Winfield.

WHEN YOU COMIN' BACK, RED RYDER? (29). By Mark Medoff. December 30, 1976. Director, Charles Nolte; scenery, C. Lance Brockman; lighting, Nancy Thompson. With Lynne Bradford, J. L.

Dahlmann, John Petlock, William Le Massena, Thomas C. Spackman, Elizabeth Dallas, Elizabeth Horowitz, Richard Hilger.

SLEUTH (29). By Anthony Shaffer. January 27, 1977. Director, Vincent Dowling; scenery and lighting, Larry A. Reed. With Clive Rosengren, Fred Thompson.

THE MERCHANT OF VENICE (29). By William Shakespeare. February 24, 1977. Director, Terence Kilburn; scenery, Peter Hicks; lighting, Larry A. Reed. With Booth Colman, Fran Brill, John Petlock, Dan C. Bar, Cheryl Giannini, Richard Hilger, Patricia Reilly.

THE SHOW-OFF (29). By George Kelly. March 24, 1977. Director, John Ulmer; scenery, Robert Joseph Mooney; lighting, Fred Fonner. With Richard Jamieson, Polly Rowles, Patricia Harless, Harry Ellerbe, Fred Thompson.

DAMES AT SEA (29). Book and lyrics by George Haimsohn and Robin Miller; music by Jim Wise. April 21, 1977. Director, Don Price; scenery, Peter

Hicks; lighting, Larry A. Reed; musical direction, Jim Hohmeyer. With Dennis Bailey, Thom Bray, Brenda Broome, Kevin Daly, Corinne Kason, Marcia Lynn Watkins.

Note: At the end of the run at the Meadow Brook Theater, *The Show-Off* toured 16 cities in Michigan, April 22 to May 13, 1977.

ST. LOUIS

Loretto-Hilton Repertory Theater

(Managing director, David Frank; consulting director, Davey Marlin-Jones)

BILLY BUDD (29). By Louis O. Coxe and Robert Chapman; based on Herman Melville's novel. October 15, 1976. Director, David Frank. With Robert Spencer, Louis Edmonds, Nicholas Surovy, Robert Darnell, Joneal Joplin, Benjamin Henrickson, James Anthony.

THE ECCENTRICITIES OF A NIGHTINGALE (29). By Tennessee Williams. November 19, 1976. Director, Davey Marlin-Jones. With Margaret Winn, Stephen Keep, Joan Matthiessen, Joneal Joplin, Patricia Kilgarriff, Henry Strozier.

THE BEAUX' STRATAGEM (29). By George Farquhar. December 31, 1976. Director, Harold Scott. With Robert Spencer, Wil Love, Alan Clarey, Robert Darnell, Joneal Joplin, Henry Strozier, Brendan Burke, Ellen Crawford, Ann McDonough, Cara Duff-MacCormick, Margaret Winn.

THE HOUSE OF BLUE LEAVES (20). By John Guare. February 4, 1977. Director, Carl Schurr. With Henry Strozier, Robert Spencer, Margaret Winn, Cara Duff-MacCormick, Robert Darnell, Susanne Marley.

THE FRONT PAGE (29). By Ben Hecht and Charles MacArthur. March 11, 1977. Director, Davey Marlin-Jones. With Robert Spencer, Robert Darnell, Margaret Winn, Susanne Marley, Brenden Burke, Wil Love, Henry Strozier, Ellen Crawford.

Designers: scenery, Atlin Pace, John Kavelin, Karen R. Connolly; lighting, Peter E. Sargent, Glenn Dunn; costumes, Bill Walker, John Carver Sullivan, Catherine Reich.

Note: *The Pied Piper,* conceived, written and directed by Loretto-Hilton's Young People's Touring Company, toured Missouri and was performed at the theater. The YPT Company consisted of Addie Walsh, Josie Lawrence, Eric Singerman, Stephen Benson and Mickey Talbott. The Webster College Conservatory of Theater Arts, from which the Loretto-Hilton Repertory Theater developed as a professional theater, shares the performing arts center, resident designers and actors who are part of the teaching faculty. Outstanding Conservatory students work on staff, backstage and in productions.

SAN FRANCISCO

American Conservatory Theater: Geary Theater

(General director, William Ball)

OTHELLO (28). By William Shakespeare. October 16, 1976. Director, Allen Fletcher. With John Hancock, Daniel Davis, Deborah May, Elizabeth Huddle, Stephen St. Paul.

MAN AND SUPERMAN (28). By George Bernard Shaw. October 19, 1976. Director, Jack O'Brien; associate director, Dolores Ferraro. With Peter Donat, Barbara Dirickson, Francine Tacker, James R. Winker, Charles Hallahan, Michael Keys-Hall, William Paterson, Ray Reinhardt, Marrian Walters.

EQUUS (14). By Peter Shaffer. October 28, 1977. Director, William Ball; associate director, Eugene Barcone. With Raye Birk/Peter Donat/Earl Boen/Michael Keys-Hall.

A CHRISTMAS CAROL (23). By Charles Dickens; adapted by Dennis Powers and Laird Williamson. December 7, 1976. Director, Laird Williamson; associate director, James Haire; music, Lee Hoiby, choreographer, Angene Feves. With William Paterson, Earl Boen, John Hancock, Al White, Raye Birk, James R. Winker, Todd Harley, Charles Hallahan.

KNOCK KNOCK (26). By Jules Feiffer. January 18, 1977. Director, Tom Moore. With Elizabeth Huddle, Sydney Walker, Ray Reinhardt, Tony Teague.

THE BOURGEOIS GENTLEMAN (24). By Molière; translated by Charles Hallahan and Dennis Powers. February 8, 1977. Director, William Ball; associate director, Eugene Barcone. With Charles Hallahan, Barbara Dirickson, Daniel Davis, James R. Winker, Raye Birk, Deborah May, Stephen St. Paul.

VALENTIN AND VALENTINA (22). By Mihail Roschin; translated by Irene Arn Vacchina and Edward Hastings. March 8, 1977 (American premiere). Director, Edward Hastings; scenery, Robert Blackman; lighting, F. Mitchell Dana; costumes, Cathy Edwards; sound, Bartholomeo Rago.

Valentin ....J. Steven White
Valentina ....Janice Garcia
Valentina's Mother ....Anne Lawder
Valentina's Grandmother .... Joy Carlin
Valentina's Sister .... Francine Tacker
Valentin's Mother .... Elizabeth Huddle
Valentin's Sister .... April Hyatt
Valentin's Classmates:
Bouhov ....Harry Hamlin
Karandashov .... Sabin Epstein
Ochkarik .... Delores Y. Mitchell
Dina ....Amy Ingersoll
Pavlik ....Gregory Itzin
Beloglazik .... Lawrence Hecht
Katiusha .... Susan E. Pellegrino
Rita .... Candace Barrett
Volodia .... Tony Teague
Gousev .... Michael Keys-Hall

Passerby .... William Paterson
Time: The present. Place: Moscow. The story of a modern Romeo and Juliet in contemporary Soviet society. Two intermissions.

TRAVESTIES (27). By Tom Stoppard. March 29, 1976. Director, Nagle Jackson; associate director, Eugene Barcone; music, Larry Delinger; choreographer, Tony Teague. With Raye Birk, James R. Winker, Sydney Walker, Earl Boen, Joseph Bird, Deborah May, Barbara Dirickson, Franchelle Stewart Dorn.

PEER GYNT (11). By Henrik Ibsen. April 26, 1977. Director/translator, Allen Fletcher; associate director, David Hammond; music, Larry Delinger; choreographer, John Pasqueletti. With Daniel Davis, Joy Carlin, Francine Tacker, J. Steven White, Joseph Bird, Franchelle Stewart Dorn, Sydney Walker/John Hancock.

Designers: Scenery, Robert Blackman, Richard Seger, Robert Dahlstrom, Ralph Funicello; lighting, F. Mitchell Dana, Richard Devin, Dirk Epperson; costumes, Robert Fletcher, Robert Morgan.

American Conservatory Theater: Marines' Memorial Theater

VANITIES (43+). By Jack Heifner. November 16, 1976. Director, Garland Wright; assistant director, Larry Carpenter; scenery, John Arnone; lighting, Patrika Brown; costumes, David James. With Valerie Strong/Rebecca Taylor, Sarah Harris, Patricia Richardson.

MISS MARGARIDA'S WAY (20). Written and directed by Roberto Athayde. April 4, 1977

(American premiere). Scenery and lighting, Richard Seger; costumes, Walter Watson; slide photography, Judith Ogas; assistant to the director, Timothy Bishop. With Michael Learned.

A sadistic schoolteacher berates and terrorizes her 8th grade class into submission with horrible lessons in history, mathematics, biology and religion, demonstrating her fanatic view of the world as a contest between the powerful and their victims.

Note: ACT presented several special events: at the Geary, March 27, 1977, An Evening With Tom Stoppard, directed by Nagle Jackson, with Tom Stoppard (scenes from his plays performed by ACT acting company and the playwright reading from his own work and answering questions from the audience); at the Marines, Recitations and Cogitations, conceived and performed by Peter Donat (poetry and play reading from Chaucer to Dylan Thomas), and On The Harmfulness Of Tobacco by Anton Chekhov. ACT's Young Conservatory presented a varied touring program in 1976–1977 Season. This included Antigone, Hansel and Gretel, Step on a Crack, Androcles and the Lion and The Medieval Mystery Plays, adapted by Raye Birk and staged by Conservatory director Candace Barrett for young audiences. From June 7–19, 1977, ACT presented its fifth consecutive Hawaiian season at Leeward Community College Theater, outside Honolulu. Productions from the regular season were Man and Superman by George Bernard Shaw and Molière's The Bourgeois Gentleman in the Hallahan-Powers translation. In addition to its advanced, three-year conservatory training program, ACT has added an evening extension theater program for the community and a Black Actors Workshop.

SARASOTA, FLA.

Asolo State Theater: Ringling Museum's Court Playhouse — Mainstage

(Artistic director, Robert Strane; managing director, Howard J. Millman; executive director/founder, Richard G. Fallon)

THE MUSIC MAN (23). By Meredith Willson. June 4, 1976. Director/choreographer, Jim Haskins; music director, John Franceschina. With Kelly Fitzpatrick, Martha J. Brown, Ken Costigan, Miles Larsen, Barbara Lewis.

LOOK HOMEWARD, ANGEL (20). By Ketti Frings; based on the novel by Thomas Wolfe. July 2, 1976. Director, Richard G. Fallon. With Dennis

Michael, Bette Oliver, Ken Costigan, Steven Va Benschoten, Pamela Lewis, Isa Thomas, Bradfor Wallace, Martha J. Brown.

WIN WITH WHEELER (16). By Lee Kalcheim. July 30, 1976 (world premiere). Director, Bradford Wallace; scenery, Bennet Averyt; lighting, Martin Petlock, Dan Gwin; costumes, Catherine King.
Sam Duffy .... David S. Howar

P.J. Whitlesee .... Steven Ryan
Mason Sternwell .... Kelly Fitzpatrick
Kathy Myer .... Donna Pelc
Reese Mandell .... Stephen Van Benschoten
Sarah Pryor .... Isa Thomas
Bellboy .... Peter Ivanov
Cleaning Woman .... Nora Chester
Harvey .... Clark Niederjohn
Florence Wheeler .... Barbara Reid
Cong. Jack Davis .... Bradford Wallace
Time: The present. Place: A medium-sized
American city. Act I: A room in a second-class hotel.
Act II, Scene 1: Same, a moment later. Scene 2:
Same, three days later, late at night.

THE RULING CLASS (23). By Peter Barnes. February 17, 1977. Director, Robert Strane. With Frederick Sperberg, Bradford Wallace, David S. Howard, Isa Thomas, Trent Jones, Susan Borneman, Steven Ryan, William Leach.

MUMMER'S END (20). By Jack Gilhooley. February 25, 1977. Director, Peter Maloney. With William Leach, David S. Howard, Bette Oliver, Isa Thomas, Kelly Fitzpatrick, Molly DePree.

CAT ON A HOT TIN ROOF (24). By Tennessee Williams. March 4, 1977. Director, Amnon Kabatchnik. With Deanna Dunagan, Steven Ryan, Walter Rhodes, Bette Oliver, Milt Tarver, Mary Ed Porter.

THE WALTZ OF THE TOREADORS (25). By Jean Anouilh; translated by Lucienne Hill. April 1, 1977. Director, Bradford Wallace. With David S. Howard, Bette Oliver, Mary Ed Porter, Frederick Sperberg, Susan Borneman, Deborah Unger.

DESIRE UNDER THE ELMS (24). By Eugene O'Neill. April 8, 1977. Director, Howard J. Millman. With William Leach, Deanna Dunagan, Trent Jones, Kelly Fitzpatrick, Milt Tarver.

MY LOVE TO YOUR WIFE (33). Book by Brian J. McFadden; music and lyrics by John Franceschina; based on William Wycherley's The Country Wife. May 6, 1977 (world premiere). Conceived and directed by Neal Kenyon; scenery, John Scheffler; lighting, Martin Petlock; costumes, Catherine King; musical/choral director and arranger, John Franceschina; special staging, Jim Hoskins.
Town Crier .... Joseph Reed

Dr. Quack .... William Leach
Mr. Arnold (Judy) .... Howard A. Branch Jr.
Mr. Carter (Punch) .... John C. Wall
John Wilmot .... Arthur Hanket
George Villiers .... Peter Ivanov
Lady Buckingham .... Lou Ann Csaszar
Charles Sedley .... Steven J. Rankin
Samuel Pepys .... Fred Davis
Nell Gwynn .... Molly DePree
Moll Makepiece .... Deborah Unger
Ebenezer Clasp .... Robert Walker
Aphra Behn .... Maryann Barulich
Frank Harcourt .... Frederick Sperberg
Dick Dorilant .... Kelly Fitzpatrick
Sir Jasper Fidget .... David S. Howard
Lady Fidget .... Isa Thomas
Dainty Fidget .... Mary Ed Porter
Mrs. Squeamish .... Bette Oliver
Jack Pinchwife .... Bradford Wallace
Margery Pinchwife .... Susan Borneman
Will B. Thayer .... Bill Herman
Harry Horner .... Steven Ryan
Bob Sparkish .... Milt Tarver
Alithea Pinchwife .... Deanna Dunagan
Lucy Daley .... Beth Lincks
Parson Goodly .... Kim Ivan Motter
Time: 1677. Place: London. Act I, Scene 1: The exterior of a theater. Scene 2: Lobby of the theater. Scene 3: Interior of the theater, Horner's box. Scene 4: Men's theater lounge. Scene 5: Pinchwife's theater box. Scene 6: Exterior of the theater. Scene 7: The Cup and Kettle Tea House. Scene 8: An adjacent mall. Scene 9: Margery's room. Scene 10: Bartholomew Fair. Act II, Scene 1: A wedding chapel. Scene 2: Pinchwife's house. Scene 3: Horner's lodgings. Scene 4: Pinchwife's house. Scene 5: Horner's lodgings.
Musical Numbers: Act I — Overture, "Poor, Poor Harry Horner," "The Passepartout of the Town," "Fugue for Fops" "All the Pretty People," "My Wife," "My Wife" (Reprise), "The Signs of Love," "What's the Use of Honor Any More," "Perfect Employment," "I Want to Go to Town!" "Bartholomew Fair," "Who Loves You More?" "If You Weren't a Boy," "Something to Remember Me By!" Act II: Entracte, "Hymen, Hymen," "Someone Loves Me," "Never Take a Wife to the City," "China," "What to Do With Her," "Brand New Feelings," "The Letter," "When Does the Loving Start?" "Brimmer," "I Wish You Joy, Madam," "My Love to Your Wife."

Designers: Scenery, John Scheffler, Bennet Averyt, David Chapman, Robert C. Barnes; lighting, Martin Petlock, Dan Gwin; costumes, Catherine King, Flozanne John.

Asolo State Theater: Downtown Theater — Stage Two

KNOCK KNOCK (6). By Jules Feiffer. November 24, 1976. Director, Howard J. Millman. With Bradford Wallace, Patricia Oetkin, David S. Howard, Alan Brooks.

THE SEA HORSE (20). By Edward J. Moore. December 28, 1976. Director, Isa Thomas. With Nora Chester, Gene Lindsey.

OH COWARD! (20). Devised by Roderick Cook; words and music by Noel Coward. January 20, 1977. Director, Jim Hoskins; musical direction, Marifran Casey. With Stephen Joseph, Marilyn Wassell, John York.

TWO FOR THE SEESAW (22). By William Gibson.

February 26, 1977. Director, Philip LeStrange. With Robin Bartlett, Scott Porter.

SERENADING LOUIE (25). By Lanford Wilson.

March 24, 1977. Director, Stephen Rothman. With Lynda Myles, Lou Bedford, Stephanie Lewis, Donegan Smith.

Designers: Scenery, John Scheffler, Ray Perry, Jeffrey W. Dean; lighting, Martin Petlock, Dan Gwin, David Loftin, Jim Rynning; costumes, Catherine King, Sally A. Kos.

Asolo State Theater Company: Theater for Young People

1776 . . . AND ALL THAT JAZZ! (16). Conceived and directed by Neal Kenyon. August 5, 1976 (world premiere). Scenery, Sam Bagarella; lighting, Bob Hippenmier; costumes, Martha Spaulding. Original sketches by Neal Kenyon, Bill Herman, Paul Murray and John C. Wall; music and lyrics by Fred Davis, John Franceschina, Gary Geld and Peter Udell, Neal Kenyon, John Lennon and Paul McCartney, Cole Porter, Steven J. Rankin, William Roy, Jule Styne, Betty Comden and Adolph Green; additional material from Vachel Lindsay, Henry Wadsworth Longfellow, Washington Irving. With Fred Davis, Molly DePree, Bill Herman, Peter Ivanov, Beth Lincks, Paul Murray, Steven J. Rankin, Deborah Unger, John C. Wall.

Note: Asolo Touring Theater presented four productions in Florida public and high schools, September 1976-May, 1977: *Step on a Crack* by Susan Zeder, directed by Paul Prece (also played 4 performances at the Kennedy Center in Washington, D. C.); *Hey There — Hello!* by Gennadi Mamlin, a Soviet play translated by Miriam Morton; *The Doctor In Spite of Himself* by Molière; and *Queen Bird and the Golden Fish*, improvised by the Company (Barry Carter, Chris Ceraso, Kathy Danzer, Sally Dunn, Abbe Hurwitz, Tom Shreier, Bill Schwartz). Asolo State Theater's Conservatory of Acting continues to provide a two-year MFA program for actors and theater technicians.

SEATTLE

A Contemporary Theater

(Artistic director, Gregory A. Falls; general manager, Andrew M. Witt)

SIZWE BANZI IS DEAD (25). By Athol Fugard, John Kani and Winston Ntshona. June 17, 1976. Director, Gregory A. Falls. With Mel Johnson Jr., Joe Fields.

THE TIME OF YOUR LIFE (25). By William Saroyan. July 15, 1976. Director, Gregory A. Falls. With Kurt Beattie, Tom Hill, Dean Gardner, Patricia Estrin, Robert MacDougall, A. C. Weary, Christopher Duncan.

SCAPINO! (24). By Frank Dunlop and Jim Dale; adapted from Molière's *Les Fourberies de Scapin*. August 12, 1976. Director, Gregory A. Falls. With Jim Jansen, Kurt Beattie, A. C. Weary, Maury Cooper, Robert E. Oram, Jo Leffingwell, Patricia Estrin.

DESIRE UNDER THE ELMS (23). By Eugene O'Neill. September 9, 1976. Director, Robert Loper. With Tanny McDonald, Robert Cornthwaite, Richard Marion, John Aylward, Robert McDougall.

RELATIVELY SPEAKING (23). By Alan Ayckbourn. October 7, 1976. Director, Paul Lee. With Donald Ewer, Margaret Hilton, Katherine Ferrand, Mark Geiger.

BOCCACCIO (35). Book and lyrics by Kenneth Cavander; music by Richard Peaslee; based on *The Decameron* by Giovanni Boccaccio. November 4, 1976. Director, Gregory A. Falls; music director, Stan Keen. With Megan Dean, Beth McDonald, Robert MacDougall, Marnie Mosiman, Frederick Sperberg, Kelly Walters, A. C. Weary.

A CHRISTMAS CAROL (24). By Charles Dickens; new version by Gregory A. Falls; music by Robert MacDougall. December 16, 1976. Director, Gregory A. Falls. With John Gilbert, Jim Royce, Mark Sather, Karen Eastman, John Hosking, Robert MacDougall, Barbara Bercu.

FIRE! (6). By John Roc. February 25, 1977. Director, Eileen MacRae Murphy. With members of the Company.

Designers: Scenery, William Forrester, Jerry Williams, Shelley Henze Scherman; lighting, Richard Devin, Phil Schermer, Al Nelson; costumes, Sally Richardson.

Note: During 1976-1977, A Contemporary Theater sent two productions for children on a five-state tour to Oregon, Montana, Wyoming, Idaho, Nevada. They were *Absurd Musical Revue* and *The Whistlestop Revue*.

OUTSTANDING PERFORMANCES

Above, Brian Murray and Roberta Maxwell as Colin and Anne in David Rudkin's *Ashes*

Left, Ralph Richardson and John Gielgud as Hirst and Spooner in Harold Pinter's new play *No Man's Land*

Left, Kenneth McMillan and Robert Duvall as Donny Dubrow and "Teach" Cole in a scene from David Mamet's *American Buffalo*

George C. Scott as Foxwell J. Sly in *Sly Fox*

Irene Worth as Mme. Ranevskaya in *The Cherry Orchard* (FAR RIGHT)

Estelle Parsons as Dee Cooper in *Ladies at the Alamo* (FAR LEFT)

Jonathan Pryce as Gethin Price in *Comedians*

Martin Balsam as Joseph Parmigian in *Cold Storage*

Fred Gwynne as Col. J. C. Kinkaid in *A Texas Trilogy* (FAR RIGHT)

Rosemary De Angelis as Mother (FAR LEFT) and James Coco as Benno in *The Transfiguration of Benno Blimpie*

nny Baker as Alvin in
Love My Wife

eryl Streep as Lt. Lil-
n Holiday in *Happy*
d (FAR RIGHT)

Dorothy Loudon as Miss
Hannigan in *Annie* (FAR
LEFT)

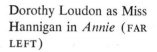

Tom Courtenay as Simon
Hench in *Otherwise En-*
gaged

k Weston as Marvin
chaels in *California*
te

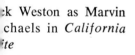

n Cullum as Bobby
rvath in *The Trip*
ck Down (FAR RIGHT)

Liv Ullmann as Anna
Christie in *Anna Christie*
(FAR LEFT)

Al Pacino as Pavlo Hum-
mel in *The Basic Train-*
ing of Pavlo Hummel

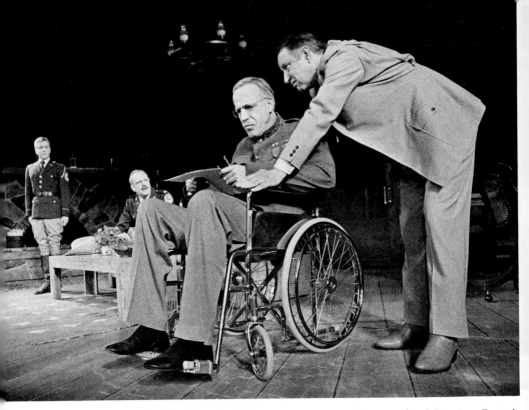

A TEXAS TRILOGY—On this page are scenes from each of Preston Jones's three plays. *Above, left to right,* Paul O'Keefe, William Le Massena, Fred Gwynne and Lee Richardson in *The Oldest Living Graduate. Below left,* Henderson Forsythe (*seated*) and Patrick Hines in *The Last Meeting of the Knights of the White Magnolia. Below right,* Diane Ladd in the title role of *Lu Ann Hampton Laverty Oberlander*

TWO BRITISH BEST PLAYS—*Above,* Larry Lamb (*on floor*), David Margulies, Jarlath Conroy, Jonathan Pryce and John Lithgow in *Comedians* by Trevor Griffiths. *Below,* Tom Courtenay and Nicolas Coster in *Otherwise Engaged* by Simon Gray

CALIFORNIA SUITE

Pictured on this page are the four episodes of Neil Simon's comedy

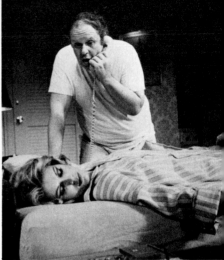

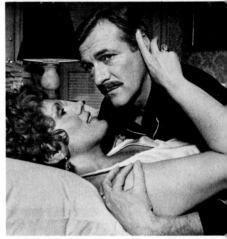

Right, at top of page, Jack Weston and Leslie Easterbrook in *Visitor From Philadelphia*

Above and right center, Tammy Grimes and George Grizzard in *Visitor From New York* and *Visitors From London. Right,* Barbara Barrie, Jack Weston, Tammy Grimes and George Grizzard in *Visitors From Chicago*

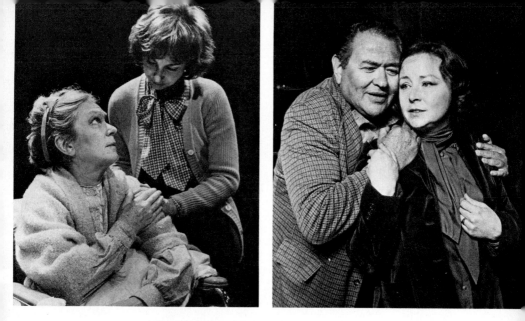

THE SHADOW BOX

Pictured on this page are the three sets of characters in Michael Cristofer's
Pulitzer Prize-winner

At top of page, left,
Geraldine Fitzgerald
and Rose Gregorio;
above, right, Simon
Oakland and Joyce
Ebert; *at right,* Laurence
Luckinbill, Patricia El-
liott, Mandy Pantinkin

SLY FOX—Howland Chamberlin, George C. Scott and (*in front row*) Gretchen Wyler, John Heffernan, Hector Elizondo (in shirtsleeves), Jack Gilford, Bob Dishy and Trish Van Devere in courtroom scene of Larry Gelbart's adaptation of *Volpone*

DIRTY LINEN—*Below,* Merwin Goldsmith, Cecelia Hart and Leila Blake in Tom Stoppard's comedy; *right,* Jacob Brooke in the play's *No-Man's-Land* scene

MUSICALS

Right, the orgy of *I Love My Wife:* Ilene Graff, Lenny Baker, James Naughton (*at top*), Joanna Gleason

Below, left to right, the gang of *Happy End:* Benjamin Rayson, Tony Azito, Christopher Lloyd, Grayson Hall, Donna Emmanuel, Robert Weil, Raymond J. Barry, John A. Coe

DESIGN FOR *ANNIE*

On opposite page at top are Theoni V. Aldredge's *Annie* costume designs for Daddy Warbucks's secretary's black party dress and the orphans' night clothes. *Below,* photos of David Mitchell's model for an *Annie* scene in which the New York skyline changes and simulates the movement of Daddy Warbucks's Dusenberg and a 1930s taxi (*top*). The limousine "progresses" to the Warbucks mansion (*center row*) while the taxi (*bottom row*) "moves" past the Empire State and Chrysler Building into the Broadway night. A photosynopsis of *Annie* appears elsewhere in this volume

SIDE BY SIDE BY SONDHEIM—Ned Sherrin, Julie N. McKenzie, David Kernan and Millicent Martin in revue imported from London

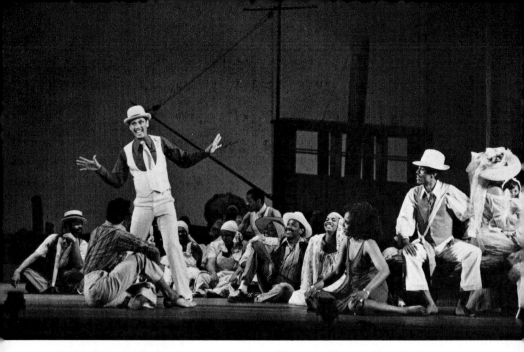

OUTSTANDING REVIVALS

Above, Houston Grand Opera's *Porgy and Bess,* with Larry Marshall as Sportin' Life (*standing*) and Clamma Dale as Bess (*seated on floor*)

Below in foreground, Priscilla Smith, Irene Worth and George Voscovec in the Joseph Papp-Andrei Serban *The Cherry Orchard* at Lincoln Center (see examples of Santo Loquasto's costume designs *at right, on opposite page*)

Santo Loquasto's distinguished 1976-77 designs included the Maharam Award-winning scenery for *American Buffalo* (*above*) and the costumes for *The Cherry Orchard* (*below*)

OFF BROADWAY

Left (clockwise from top), Marlene Dell, Memrie Innerarity, Gloria Hodes, Joanne Beretta, Julie J. Hafner, Carole Monferdini, Terri White in Eve Merriam's musical *The Club*

Below, Paul Dooley and Cynthia Harris in the American Place production of *Jules Feiffer's Hold Me!*

Below, Shelly Plimpton (*lower left*), Paul Kandel, Mark Zagaeski, Rocky Greenberg, Karen Evans, JoAnn Peled, David Schechter in Elizabeth Swados's *Nightclub Cantata*

AT THE PUBLIC THEATER—
Left, Rip Torn in *Creditors; above,*
Sigourney Weaver and Ann Jackson
as they appeared in John Guare's
Marco Polo Sings a Solo

AT BAM THEATER
COMPANY — *Right,*
Rosemary Harris, Tovah
Feldshuh and Ellen Bur-
styn in *Three Sisters*

AT THE ROUND-
ABOUT—*Left,* Jan Far-
rand, Gale Sondergaard
and Robert Pastene in
John Gabriel Borkman

CROSS-COUNTRY THEATER

LOS ANGELES—*Below,* Shizuko Hoshi, Keone Young, Jim Ishida and Pat Li in Wakako Yamauchi's *And the Soul Shall Dance* at East West Players, selected by American Theater Critics Association as an outstanding new 1976-77 play

HARTFORD — *Above,* William Prince, Angela Lansbury and Maureen Anderman in Edward Albee's *Listening* at Hartford Stage Company

LOS ANGELES — *Above,* Britt Swanson and Cliff DeYoung in Michael Cristofer's *Ice* at the Mark Taper Forum

CHICAGO—*Left,* Joe Mantegna and Mike Nussbaum in David Mamet's *A Life in the Theater* at Goodman Theater Center

Seattle Repertory Theater: Seattle Center Playhouse — Main Stage

(Artistic director, Duncan Ross; producing director, Peter Donnelley; resident costume designer, Lewis D. Rampino)

MUSIC IS (30). By George Abbott; adapted from William Shakespeare's *Twelfth Night;* music by Richard Adler; lyrics by Will Holt. October 13, 1976 (world premiere). Director, George Abbott; musical numbers and dances staged by Patricia Birch; scenery, Eldon Elder; lighting, H. R. Poindexter; costumes, Lewis D. Rampino; orchestrations, Hershy Kay; musical direction, Don Smith; dance and vocal arrangements, William Cox.

William Shakespeare; Clown .... Daniel Ben-Zali
Valentine .... William McClary
Duke Orsino .... David Holliday
Curio; 1st Officer .... David Brummel
Viola .... Catherine Cox
Captain .... Seymour Penzner
Maria .... Laura Waterbury
Sir Toby Belch .... David Sabin
Malvolio .... Christopher Hewett
Olivia .... Sherry Mathis
Antonio .... Marc Jordan
Sebastian .... Joel Higgins
Sir Andrew Aguecheek .... Joe Ponazecki
2d Officer .... Doug Carfrae

Members of the Court: Helena Andreyko, Doug Carfrae, Jim Corti, Ann Crowley, Dennis Daniels, Dana Kyle, Wayne Mattson, Jason McAuliffe, Carolann Page, Susan Elizabeth Scott, Denny Shearer, Melanie Vaughan, Mimi Wallace.

Musical Numbers: "When First I Saw My Lady's Face," "Masquerade," "The Time Is Ripe for Loving," "Should I Speak of Loving You," "Big Bottom Betty," "Paeans of Paradise," "Needing No One," "Time Gone By," "Sing Hi," "I Am It," "Tennis Song," "No Matter Where," "the Duel," "Please Be Human," "What You Will."

ANNA CHRISTIE (23). By Eugene O'Neill. November 17, 1976. Director, Duncan Ross; scenery, Robert Blackman; lighting, Richard Devin. With Kaiulani Lee, Jonathan Frakes, Wallace Rooney, Molly Dodd.

THE MOUSETRAP (24). By Agatha Christie. December 15, 1976. Director, Reginald Denham; scenery, Jerry Williams; lighting, Cynthia J. Hawkins. With Dennis Robertson, Eda Zahl, Jeffrey Jones, Richard Brestoff, John Capodice, Katherine Ferrand, Gardner Hayes, Joan Norton.

CAT ON A HOT TIN ROOF (24). By Tennessee Williams. January 12, 1977. Director, Garland Wright; scenery, Robert Blackman; lighting, Cynthia J. Hawkins. With Katherine Ferrand, David Darlow, Walter Flanagan, Marjorie Nelson.

THE SHOW-OFF (24). By George Kelly. February 9, 1977. Director, John Going; scenery, Robert Dahlstrom; lighting, Cynthia J. Hawkins. With Robert Moberly, Sydney G. Smith, Josephine Nichols, Darcy Pullium, Anne Gee Byrd, Warren Buck.

EQUUS (34). By Peter Shaffer. March 16, 1977. Director, Duncan Ross; scenery, Michael L. Mayer; lighting, Richard Devin. With James Ray, Mark Buchan.

Seattle Repertory Theater: Second Stage

BINGO (13). By Edward Bond. February 22, 1977. Director, Robert Loper; scenery, John Shaffner; lighting, Cynthia J. Hawkins; costumes, Nanrose Buchman. With John Aylward, Marjorie Nelson, Cynthia Crumlish.

ONCE UPON A TIME (13). By Aleksei Arbuzov; translated by Ariadne Nicolaeff. March 15, 1977 (American premiere). Director, Gwen Arner; scenery, John Shaffner; lighting, Scott Hawthorn; costumes, Lewis D. Rampino.
Fedya .... Philip Minor
Kuzma .... Robin Haynes
Khristofor Blokhin .... John Gilbert
Viktosha .... Lisa Goodman
Levushka .... Charles Michael Wright
Fatty .... Ralph Steadman

Time: Today. Place: Moscow. Part I, Scene 1: Fedya's studio, evening. Scene 2: Late that same evening. Scene 3: A week later. Part II, Scene 1: The following day. Scene 2: Ten days later. Scene 3: A day later. One intermission.

SUZANNA ANDLER (13). By Marguerite Duras; translated by Barbara Bray. April 5, 1977 (American premiere). Director, Duncan Ross; scenery, Michael L. Mayer; lighting, Cynthia J. Hawkins; costumes, Lewis D. Rampino.
Suzanna Andler .... Eve Roberts
Michel Cayre .... Joe Horvath
Monique Combes .... Judith Anna Roberts
Riviere .... Gardner Hayes.

The action takes place in the course of one day. Act I, Scene 1: Les Colonnades, a summer house by the sea near St. Tropez on the French Riviera, late morning in winter. Scene 2: A few days later. Act II: The beach below the house, later that afternoon. Act III: Les Colonnades, about 6 p.m. that day.

BOESMAN AND LENA (13). By Athol Fugard. April 26, 1977. Director, Glenda Dickerson; scenery, John Shaffner; lighting, Cynthia J. Hawkins; costumes, Nanrose Buchman. With William Jay, Zaida Coles, Paul Makgoba.

VANITIES (13). By Jack Heifner. May 17, 1977. Director, Larry Carpenter; scenery, Michael L. Mayer, Bill Bartelt; lighting, Cynthia J. Hawkins; costumes, Nanrose Buchman. With Jane Bray, Dawn Didawick, Nancy New.

Note: *The Show-Off* played 12 special matinees for high school students and, following its regular run, toured 12 cities in Washington, Oregon, Montana, Idaho and Utah for 7 weeks, March 11-April 23, 1977. SRT's second traveling troupe, The Mob (Mobile Outreach Bunch) staged 42 performances of *The Rhythm Show*, a revue using mime, dance, poetry and storytelling to illustrate the affect of rhythm in everyday life, at junior high schools in the same area. From May 2-14, 1977, The Mob toured 10 Alaskan communities. The original script by Megan Dean was directed by Julian Schembri; with Steve Tomkins, Marnie Mosiman, Maureen Hawkins, Donald Matt, Gail Hebert.

STAMFORD, CONN.

Hartman Theater Company

(Producing directors, Del and Margot Tenney; managing director, Daniel B. Miller)

THE REASON WE EAT (34). By Israel Horovitz. November 3, 1976 (world premiere). Director, Mel Shapiro; scenery, Akira Yoshimura; lighting, John McLain; costumes, Gerda Proctor.

Edna Wrath .... Estelle Parsons
Edmund Scorn .... Ron Faber
Ted Something .... Robert Balaban
Edith Tempt .... Diane Davila
Place: A clinic. Act I, Scene 1: Night, the first day. Scene 2: Night, three days later. Act II, Scene 1: Night, two weeks later. Scene 2: Day, two days later.

ARSENIC AND OLD LACE (33). By Joseph Kesselring. December 15, 1976. Director, Jerry Blunt; scenery, J.D. Ferrara; lighting, David McWilliams; costumes, Gerda Proctor. With Carol Teitel, Lenka Peterson, Austin Pendleton, Tina Cartmell, Gary F. Martin, Theodore Sorel.

TARTUFFE (26). By Molière; English verse translation by Richard Wilbur. January 19, 1977. Director, Del Tenney; scenery and costumes, Zack Brown; lighting, Roger Meeker; music, Barbara Damashek; choreographer, Ara Fitzgerald. With Austin Pendleton, George Morfogen, Margot Tenney, Lenka Peterson, Eric R. Christiansen, Theodore Sorel.

DEATH OF A SALESMAN (26). By Arthur Miller. February 23, 1977. Director, Del Tenney; scenery, Robert Verberkmoes; lighting, John McLain; costumes, Gerda Proctor. With Mike Kellin, Lenka

Peterson, Ralph Byers, Theodore Sorel, Earle Hyman, Alfred Hinckley.

AS TO THE MEANING OF WORDS (26). By Mark Eichman, March 30, 1977 (world premiere). Director, John Dillon; scenery, Akira Yoshimura; lighting, Roger Meeker; costumes, Gerda Proctor.

Admitting Clerk .... Rina Rose Rosselli
Dr. Winston Gerrard .... Earle Hyman
Alexander Thomas .... Paul Collins
Ned Ryan .... George Dzundza
Judge Horace J. Wheeting ...... Alfred Hinckley
Dr. Madelyn Foster .... Deloris Gaskins
Dr. Ramon Norriega .... Theodore Sorel
Dr. Clarence Parrish .... Dominic Chianese
Dr. Jonathan Wallace .... Ralph Byers
Gloria Sanders .... Margot Tenney
Time: Winter of 1975. Place: A courtroom in Boston, Mass. One intermission. (See synopsis in the introduction to this section.)

HE WHO GETS SLAPPED (25). By Larry Arrick; free adaptation from Leonid Andreyev's play. April 27, 1977. Director, Larry Arrick; scenery, Akira Yoshimura; costumes, David Murin; lighting, Roger Meeker; lyrics and music written and directed by Barbara Damashek; acrobatics coordinator, Bill Patton. With Richard Kavanaugh, Ed Waterstreet Jr., A. Linda Bove, Deborah Offner, Carmen de Lavallade, James Brick, Joel Kramer, Dominic Chianese, Theodore Sorel, Gregory Salata, Earle Hyman.

Note: The Hartman Theater Company presented its Conservatory students in performances of *Under Milk Wood* by Dylan Thomas, directed by David F. Eliet; *Old Paint* by Miklos Horvath, directed by Robert Eichler; *East/West* by Andrei Amalrik, directed by Jonas Jurasas; *The Sea Horse* by Edward Moore, directed by Timothy Warren, June 23-August 28, 1976. Between February 17 and May 2, 1977, the Conservatory presented *Olympian Games* by Kenneth Cavander, directed by Larry Arrick; *Exit the King* by Eugene Ionesco, translated by Donald Watson, directed by Wendy Chapin; *A Midsummer Night's Dream* by William Shakespeare.

STRATFORD, CONN.

American Shakespeare Theater

(President, Konrad Matthaei; artistic director, Michael Kahn. Designers: scenery, David Jenkins; lighting, John McLain; costumes, Jane Greenwood)

THE CRUCIBLE (21). By Arthur Miller. June 8, 1976. Director, Michael Kahn. With Don Murray,

Maria Tucci, Tovah Feldshuh, Anna Levine, Anne Ives, George Hearn, Sarallen.

THE WINTER'S TALE (19). By William Shakespeare. June 9, 1976. Director, Michael Kahn; music, Lee Hoiby. With Philip Kerr, George Hearn, Wyman Pendleton, Josef Sommer, Maria Tucci, Bette Henritze.

AS YOU LIKE IT (42). By William Shakespeare. July 20, 1976. Director, Michael Kahn; music, Lee Hoiby. With Eileen Atkins, Tovah Feldshuh, Kenneth Welsh, Josef Sommer, Theodore Sorel, Philip Kerr, April Shawhan.

SYRACUSE

Syracuse Stage

(Producing director, Arthur Storch; managing director, James C. Clark)

A QUALITY OF MERCY (24). By Roma Greth. October 16, 1976 (world premiere). Director, Arthur Storch; scenery, John Doepp; lighting, Judy Rasmuson; costumes, Lowell Detweiler.

Lily Fisher .... Sheila Coonan
Shirley Meneely .... Janet Ward
Mary May Meneely .... Kathleen Tolan
Martha Meneely .... Prudence Wright Holmes
Henry Fisher .... William Carden
Verney Meneely .... Brad Sullivan
    Time: 1972. Place: A small town. Act I: Late May. Act II: Later that evening.

WHAT THE BUTLER SAW (24). By Joe Orton. November 13, 1976. Director, Marshall Oglesby; scenery, Virginia Dancy, Elmon Webb; lighting, James E. Stephens; costumes, Patricia McGourty. With Robert Moberly, Elaine Bromka, Madeleine le Roux, John Guerrasio, Nicholas Hormann, Douglas Fisher.

TWELFTH NIGHT (24). By William Shakespeare. December 18, 1976. Director, Bill Ludel; scenery, Sandro La Ferla; lighting, Lee Watson; costumes,

Nanzi Adzima. With Deborah Mayo, Stephanie Braxton, Joseph Regalbuto, Alan Rosenberg, Haskell Gordon, Bobo Lewis, Alan Kass, Tony Aylward.

THE SEA GULL (24). By Anton Chekhov. January 15, 1977. Director, Arthur Storch; scenery, John Doepp; lighting, Judy Rasmuson; costumes, Lowell Detweiler. With Rita Gam, Pirie MacDonald, Trish Hawkins, Mark Winkworth, Tony Aylward, Suzanne Toren, Rudy Bond.

SLEUTH (24). By Anthony Shaffer. February 12, 1977. Director, Robert Mandel; scenery, Marjorie Kellogg; lighting, Edward Effron; costumes, Jennifer Von Mayrhauser. With Sam Gray, Nicholas Woodeson.

A STREETCAR NAMED DESIRE (24). By Tennessee Williams. March 12, 1977. Director, John Going; scenery, Stuart Wurtzel; lighting, Arden Fingerhut; costumes, James Berton Harris. With Virginia Kiser, David Canary, Dorothy Fielding, Conrad McLaren.

Note: Syracuse Stage presented *Twelfth Night* at the Regent Theater for 7 special student performances and toured *Sleuth* around Central New York, following the regular run.

TUCSON

Arizona Civic Theater

(Producing director, Sandy Rosenthal; managing director, David Hawkanson).

IN FASHION (18). Book, Jon Jory; lyrics, Lonnie Burstein; music, Jerry Blatt; adapted from Barnett Shaw's translation of Georges Feydeau's *A Gown For His Mistress*. November 4, 1976. Director and choreographer, David Pursley; scenery, Reagan Cook; lighting, Dan Willoughby; costumes, Sandra Mourey; musical direction, Daniel Gordon. With Nancy Davis Booth, Anna Gianiotis, Lowell Harris, Francesca Jarvis, David Keeley, Virginia Lee, Joe Orton, David Pursley.

SIZWE BANZI IS DEAD (11). By Athol Fugard, John Kani and Winston Ntshona. December 2, 1976. Director, Dean Irby; scenery, John Walker, Cynthia Beeman; lighting, Dan Willoughby; costumes, Sandra Mourey. With Robert Delegall, Zakes Mokae.

AH, WILDERNESS! (17). By Eugene O'Neill. January 13, 1977. Director, David Pursley; scenery, Reagan Book; lighting, Dan Willoughby. With James Lawless, Ruth Warshawsky, Wayne Bryan, Joe Orton, Carol Calkins.

HAMLET (17). By William Shakespeare. February 10, 1977. Director, Robert Ellenstein; scenery and lighting, Peter Wexler; costumes, Sandra Mourey. With James Occhino, Molly McKasson, John McMurtry, Roxana Stuart, Philip Bourneuf, John Herzog.

VANITIES (11). By Jack Heifner. March 10, 1977. Director, Ryland Merkey; scenery, Reagan Cook; lighting, Dan Willoughby; costumes, Sandra Mourey.

With Penny Metropulos, Barbara Sammeth, Rebecca Taylor.

JACQUES BREL IS ALIVE AND WELL AND LIVING IN PARIS (18). By Eric Blau and Mort Shuman, based on Jacques Brel's lyrics and commentary; music by Jacques Brel. March 31, 1977. Director, Sandy Rosenthal; scenery, Reagan Cook; lighting, Dan Willoughby; costumes, Sandra Mourey; music director, Daniel Gordon. With Bill Copeland, Gary Krawford, Denise LeBrun, Penny Metropulos.

WALTHAM, MASS.

Brandeis University: Spingold Theater

(Chairman, Theater Arts Department, Charles Werner Moore; general manager, John-Edward Hill)

MISALLIANCE (9). By George Bernard Shaw. October 20, 1976. Director, Charles Werner Moore; scenery, Daniel Veaner; lighting, Harry Feiner; costumes, Francis Blau. With Jennifer A. McLogan, Michael Kluger, Carl Whidden, Thomas Peacocke.

A MIDSUMMER NIGHT'S DREAM (10). By William Shakespeare. December 8, 1976. Director, James H. Clay; scenery, Christine Kaseta; lighting, Steven C. Berkowitz; costumes, Amy Koplow With Sandra Guberman, Lawrence Reese, Patricia Riggin, Carl Whidden, David A. Lewis, Diane Dowling, Michael Guido.

THE PLOUGH AND THE STARS (9). By Sean O'Casey. March 2, 1977. Director, Ted Kazanoff; scenery, Harry Feiner; lighting, Frances Blau; costumes, Melinda Leeson. With Michael Kluger, Jennifer A. McLogan, David A. Lewis, Annette Miller, Jeannie Lindheim.

BONJOUR, LA, BONJOUR (9). By Michel Tremblay; translated by John van Burek and Bill Glassco. April 27, 1977 (American Premiere). Director, Daniel Veaner; scenery, Jim Moran; lighting, Daniel Veaner; costumes, Amanda J. Klein.
Gabriel .... Charles Werner Moore
Serge .... Lawrence Reese
Albertine .... Edith Agnew
Charlotte .... Harriet Rogers
Lucienne .... Sandra Guberman
Monique .... Pamela Pascoe
Denise ....Diane Simmons
Nicole .... Diane Dowling
  Time: The present. Place: Montreal. No intermission.

Brandeis University: Laurie Theater

BAAL (5). By Bertolt Brecht; adapted and directed by Ken Baltin. October 13, 1976. Scenery, Amanda Klein; lighting, Melinda Leeson; costumes, James Moran. With David A. Lewis, Scott Richards, Mary Clifford, Ed Houser, Michael Angelo Castellana, Bob Kolsby.

FELDSHUH & BRACKETT (5). By Linda Segal. December 1, 1976 (world premiere). Director, Annie Thompson; scenery, Steve Saklad; lighting, Dennis J. Cohen; costumes, Gail Brassard.
Harold Brackett .... Ted Kazanoff
Nancy Ludensky ....Sarah Pearson
Mike Gardener .... Mark R. Kramer
Dan Serkin .... Randall Forsythe
Claude Wygrelevitchka .... Ken Baltin
Elise Hoben .... Jeannie Lindheim
Muriel Hoctor ....Edith Agnew
J. Mardman-Smith .... Scott Richards
Benjamin Pitager .... Marshall Hambro
George Rolnick .... Jim Luse
  Place: The office of Feldshuh & Brackett, a New York law firm. Act I: A hot morning in August. Act II: A week and a half later, one o'clock in the afternoon.

THE MISANTHROPE (5). By Molière; English version by Tony Harrison. February 23, 1977. Adapter/director, Cheryl G. McFadden; scenery, Michael L. Lincoln; lighting, Robert Little; costumes, Kati Slaton. With Michael Guido, Ken Baltin, Kerry Ruff, Deborah Quayle, Annie Thompson, Lawrence Reese.

THE HOT L BALTIMORE (5). By Lanford Wilson. March 23, 1977. Director, James Luse; scenery, Paul W. Gorfine; lighting, Rob Weiss; costumes, Julie DeChaine. With Daniel J. Fins, Julia Figueras, Lin Parker, Scott Richards, Bill Borenstein, Linda Moskowitz.

ALL'S WELL THAT ENDS (5). By Robert Kolsby. April 20, 1977 (world premiere). Director, Ken Baltin; scenery, Karen Gerson; lighting, Chris Kaseta; costumes, Charlene Tuch.
Michael Furey .... Randall Forsythe
Linda Bernstein ....Sarah Pearson
Ralph Messersmith ....Kerry Ruff
Lou Chummer ....Marshall Hambro
Marla Mooney .... Deborah Quayle
Fern Gerber ....Robi Schwartz
  Place: A beach house in Margate, N. J., a suburb of Atlantic City. Act I: Late May. Act II: Two weeks later.

Brandeis University: Merrick Theater—Playwrights Festival

In Repertory April 13–15, 1977, 5 performances each, world premieres. Designers: scenery, Dennis J. Coval; lighting, Mark C. Anderson; costumes, Ellen K. Brower, Steve Saklad.

SHOWMAN by Daniel Lyon. Director, Christopher Wheatley.
Man ....Michael Kluger
Woman ....Amy Lerner
P.T. Barnum .... Scott Richards

TAKEN AT THE FLOOD by Plave Dunbar. Director, Linda Segal.
Henry ....David A. Lewis
Alice .... Mary Clifford
Maurice ....Bill Borenstein
Place: The rooftop of an apartment building in a major metropolitan city.

TEMPORARY TECHNICAL DIFFICULTIES, written and directed by Frederick Zollo.

Arthur .... Michael Guido
Agnes .... Jennifer McLogan
A Television Set ....Vaughn West
Scene 1: Late Friday evening. Scene 2: One week later. Scene 3: One week later. No intermission.

NOT A THURSDAY AFTERNOON by Ellen Joan Pollock. Director, Annie Thompson.
Tilly ....Lin Parker
Maralyn .... Patricia Riggin
Judith ....Hillary Davis
Lisa .... Christal Miller
Nina .... Paula Singer
Time and Place: A Friday afternoon in suburban New Jersey.

WASHINGTON, D.C.

Arena Stage: Kreeger Theater

(Producing director, Zelda Fichandler; executive director, Thomas C. Fichandler)

PLAY, THAT TIME and FOOTFALLS (18). By Samuel Beckett. December 3, 1976. Director, Alan Schneider; scenery and costumes, Zack Brown; lighting, William Mintzer. Play, with Sloane Shelton, Dianne Wiest, Donald Davis: That Time (American premiere), Face and Voice — Donald Davis; Footfalls (American premiere), May — Dianne Wiest, Mother's Voice — Sloane Shelton.

STREAMERS (46). By David Rabe. January 7, 1977. Director, David Chambers; scenery, Tony Straiges; lighting, William Mintzer; costumes, Jennifer Von Mayrhauser. With David Garrison, Joel Colodner, Damien Leake, Terry O'Quinn, Brent Jennings, Howard Witt, Robert Prosky.

CATSPLAY (46). By Istvan Orkeny; adapted by Clara Gyorgyey. March 11, 1977 (American premiere). Director, Edward Payson Call; scenery, Karl Eigsti; lighting Hugh Lester; costumes, Linda Fisher; incidental music, Robert Dennis.
Mrs. Orban ....Helen Burns

Arena Stage: Arena Theater

SAINT JOAN (39). By George Bernard Shaw. October 15, 1976. Director, Martin Fried; scenery, Karl Eigsti; lighting, Hugh Lester; costumes, Marjorie Slaiman. With Laurie Kennedy, Michael Mertz; Kristoffer Tabori, Stanley Anderson, John P. Ryan, Robert Pastene, James Tolkan, Gary Bayer.

SATURDAY, SUNDAY, MONDAY (39). By Eduardo de Filippo; English adaptation by Keith Waterhouse and Willis Hall. November 26, 1976. Director, Norman Gevanthor; scenery, Karl Eigsti; lighting, William Mintzer; costumes, Marjorie

Giza ....Katherine Squire
Paula ....Eunice Anderson
Waiter .... Joseph Bieber
Mousie .... Paula Trueman
Ilona ....Phyllis Somerville
Yoshka .... Michael Mertz
Victor .... I. M. Hobson
Adelaida .... Joan Croydon
The Correspondents: Mrs. Bela Orban, 127 Csatarka St., Budapest, Hungary and her sister Giza, Leutberg Manor, Garmisch-Partenkirchen, Bavaria, Federal Republic of Germany. Time: Mid-1960s. One intermission.

A HISTORY OF THE AMERICAN FILM (46). By Christopher Durang. May 13, 1977. Director/choreographer, David Chambers; scenery, Tony Straiges; lighting, William Mintzer; music, Mel Marvin. With April Shawhan, Gary Bayer, Swoosie Kurtz, Joan Pape.

Slaiman. With Dolores Sutton, James Tolkan, Robert Prosky, Grace Keagy.

THE AUTUMN GARDEN (12). By Lillian Hellman January 27, 1977. Director, Martin Fried; scenery, Grady Larkins; lighting, Hugh Lester; costumes. Marjorie Slaiman. With Leora Dana, Stanley Anderson, Leslie Cass, Ann Williams, Terrence Currier, Richard Bauer, Meg Myles, Laurie Kennedy, Halo Wines.

THE LOWER DEPTHS (38). By Maxim Gorky.

April 1, 1977. Director, Liviu Ciulei; designer, Santo Loquasto; costumes, Marjorie Slaiman. With Stanley Anderson, Richard Bauer, Leslie Cass, Terrence Currier, Eric Weitz, Halo Wines.

Arena Stage: Old Vat Room Cabaret Theater

FOREVER YOURS MARIE-LOU (17). By Michel Tremblay; translated by John Van Burek and Bill Glassco. January 13, 1977 (American premiere). Director, David Chambers; scenery, Sally Cunningham; lighting, Hugh Lester; costumes, Marjorie Slaiman.

Marie-Louise .... Leslie Cass
Leopold .... Howard Witt
Carmen .... Laura Esterman
Manon .... Marilyn McIntyre
A working class family's disintegration told through stylized flashbacks. No intermission.

In the Process (Plays-in-Progress Premieres):
SINGERS (8). By Steven Stosny. January 16, 1977. Director, Douglas C. Wager.

Singer .... Jay O. Sanders
Jack .... James Tolkan
Andy .... Gary Bayer
Manager .... Mark Hammer
Sharon .... Lisa Sloan
Man .... Christopher McHale
Kelly .... Tania Myren
Time: A three-month span. Act I: The present. Act II: Two weeks later.

PORCH by Jeffrey Sweet and EXHIBITION by Janet Neipris, directed by Thomas Gruenewald; SCOOPING by Richard Nelson, directed by Douglas C. Wager (8). February 4, 1977.

Porch
Mr. Herbert .... Mark Hammer
Amy .... Elaine Kerr
Sam .... Gary Bayer
Early evening, a front porch of a house in the suburbs.

Exhibition
Katy Valentine .... Elaine Kerr
Alex Ainbinder .... Gary Bayer
Bennie Gibson .... Mark Hammer
The present, late afternoon on the day before Christmas, a museum.

Scooping
Buba, a reporter .... Jay O. Sanders.

LIVING AT HOME (8). By Anthony Giardina. February 25, 1977. Director, Thomas Gruenewald.

Eddie Bogle .... Max Gulack
John Bogle .... David Garrison
David Bogle .... John B. Jellison
Alice Langree .... Lisa Sloan
Mary Langree .... Linda Patchell
Miggsy Bogle .... Tania Myren
Chip Holtzman .... Steven Sullivan
Mary Laughton .... Dulcie Arnold
Act I, Scene 1: The kitchen of the Bogle house in Watertown, Mass. 9 a.m. Scene 2: That evening. Scene 3: Sunday. Act II, Scene 1: Sunday. Scene 2: Monday evening.

Note: *Living Stage*, a professional improvisation theater directed by Robert Alexander, was originally a touring workshop for children and youth. It has become the outreach company of Arena Stage. In addition to working with educationally disadvantaged and physically handicapped children, Living Stage has gone into the community to work improvisationally with penal institutions, senior citizen and parent-teacher groups to establish that "creativity is a full-time way of life." Using the techniques of improvisation, music, mime, movement and ritual, the company created a script, *Faces of Fascism,* based on Ken Wooden's book *Weeping in the Playtime of Others — America's Incarcerated Children,* which was publicly performed at the Old Vat Room (3 performances), March 25–27, 1977. Professional performers in the company were Rebecca Rice, Jennifer Nelson, Larry Samuels, Gregory R. Jones and musical director, Joan Berliner.

Folger Theater Group

(Producer, Louis W. Scheeder)

THE FOOL (35). By Edward Bond. October 17, 1976 (American premiere). Director, Louis W. Scheeder; scenery, Raymond C. Recht; lighting, Arden Fingerhut; costumes, Bob Wojewodski.

John Clare .... Paul Collins
Miles; Arny .... David Garrison
Lawrence; Man in
  Straitjacket .... Steven Nowicki
Darkie .... Terry Hinz
Patty .... Linda Atkinson
Mary .... Anne Stone
Lord Milton .... Frederic Warriner
Parson .... Albert Corbin
Wadlow; Michael .... Louis Schaefer
Hilary; Referee .... Richard Madden

Bob .... John Gilliss
Peter .... Kenneth Kelleher
Betty .... Pat Gebhard
Hamo; Jackson; Attendant ..... Barry MacMillan
Hicks; Tommy .... James Dean
Governor .... Donald Parker
Mrs. Emmerson .... June Hansen
Porter .... Joseph Pinckney
Charles Lamb .... David Cromwell
Mary Lamb .... Joanne Hrkach
Lord Radstock; Napoleon .... Earle Edgerton
Dr. Skrimshire .... Robert Hagen
Lord Milton's Guests: Kenneth Kelleher, Pat Gebhard, Donald Parker, David Cromwell, Joanne Hrkach, Robert Hagen. Gentlemen: David Crom-

well, Robert Hagen, Donald Parker; Porter's Backers: Steven Nowicki, Kenneth Kelleher. Jackson's Backers: David Garrison, Louis Schaefer.

Time: 19th century. Place: East Anglia, England. The brutal and tragic life of rural poet John Clare in an England that is gearing up for the Industrial Revolution. One intermission.

MUCH ADO ABOUT NOTHING (58). By William Shakespeare. December 3, 1976. Director, Jonathan Alper; scenery, Raymond C. Recht; lighting, Hugh Lester; costumes, Jennifer Von Mayrhauser; choreography, Virginia Freeman; music, William Penn. With Mary Carney, Etain O'Malley, Steven Gilborn, Steven Nowicki, Clement Fowler, Albert Corbin.

MUMMER'S END (36). By Jack Gilhooley. February 4, 1977 (world premiere). Director, Louis W. Scheeder; scenery, David Chapman; lighting, Elizabeth Toth; costumes, Bob Wojewodski.

Cookie O'Rourke	Jean Barker
Peaches Catania	Marie Wallace
Shooter O'Rourke	Frederic Warriner
Gaspari Catania	John LaGioia
Trixie Catania	Mary Carney
Spike O'Rourke	Joseph Sullivan
Denise Walker	Anne Stone

Franjo Catania .... John Gilliss
Time: An afternoon between Christmas and New Year's day, 1975; New Year's night, 1976. Place: The den in a row house in a blue-collar Philadelphia neighborhood. Three generations of the O'Rourke clan find a way to continue participating in Philadelphia's traditional Mummer's Parade, after 92-year old Shooter inadvertently disrupts the festivities with a gun and gets the family banned. One intermission.

BLACK ELK SPEAKS (36). By Christopher Sergel. March 25, 1977. Director, Jonathan Alper; scenery, John Kasarda; lighting, Arden Fingerhut; costumes, Karen M. Hummel; movement, Virginia Freeman; native dances, Jane Lind. With Clayton Corbin, Henry "Kaimu" Bal, Jane Lind, Carlo Grasso, Carlos Carrasco, Michael Medeiros.

A MIDSUMMER NIGHT'S DREAM (21+). By William Shakespeare. May 13, 1977. Director, Harold Scott; scenery, Franco Colavecchia; lighting, Elizabeth Toth; costumes, Bob Wojewodski; music and songs, William Penn; choreography, Virginia Freeman. With Anthony Call, Elizabeth Perry, Steven Nowicki, Terry Hinz, Andrew Davis, Count Stovall, Marcell Rosenblatt, Deborah Mayo.

The Season Elsewhere in Washington

By David Richards

Drama Critic of the Washington *Star*

This just may have been the season that Washington decided it had a mind of its own. Zelda Fichandler, the uncommonly alert producing director of Arena Stage, has been saying as much for 27 years and programming her theaters accordingly. But this city has always paid a certain deference to New York and acknowledged its primacy in matters theatrical.

Of course, Washington remains a lucrative stop for shows on their way to or from Broadway, and the extraordinary success of the Kennedy Center has New York producers more eager than ever to book their wares into the Eisenhower, the Opera House or, failing that, the National. Tryouts are attended zealously here and their fates are followed with more than passing interest.

This season, however, there seemed to be a subtle shift in values. Washington was beginning to take pride in its own creative climate. At the same time, it was coming to the belated conclusion that New York may have different, but not necessarily better, tastes.

Was it a sign that producer Stuart Ostrow moved his Musical Theater Lab from New York to the Kennedy Center, which now co-sponsors its investigations into new musical forms? Or that the Center is currently setting up a library of the performing arts in conjunction with the Library of Congress? Roger L. Stevens, the Center's chairman, certainly believes so. He likes to talk about how the Center is going into its second phase of development. (The first phase was simply to get the building up and demonstrate that it could work.) The goal, openly advertised, is to turn the place into a beehive of creative endeavor and it will no doubt be considerably helped along when the Center completes its fourth theater, an experimental house on the top floor. (The Japanese government pledged the necessary funds as a Bicentennial gift to the U.S.A. and architectural studies are underway.)

Ironically, in a city that has a black majority population, black theater groups have been hard pressed to make a go of it. The D.C. Black Repertory Company, founded four years ago by Robert Hooks, finally went under, a victim of its own ambitions and lackadaisical attendance. Likewise, the American Theater, which under Paul Allen's direction had a black emphasis, couldn't make ends meet and folded after a year, leaving only a faltering non-Equity company, the Paul Robeson International Center for the Performing Arts and Humanistic Studies, to carry on under a decidely wordy banner.

But elsewhere the pot was starting to boil. The New Playwrights' Theater of Washington, another non-Equity group, took over an abandoned brick gymnasium on a quaint tree-lined street near Dupont Circle and rallied a significant amount of local enthusiasm to its cause. Its exclusive orientation is original works, and Joseph Papp thought enough of its production of *Hagar's Children* to take it pretty much intact to New York. The NPTW also produced a couple of fruitcake revues, *Sirocco* and *Bride of Sirocco,* the latter transferred to the West End Theater (the former Washington Theater Club, now functioning as an intimate booking house) for an extended run.

The American Society of Theater Artists, a downtown storefront theater that has existed mainly on dreams, caught fire at least twice this season with startlingly good non-Equity productions of *The Indian Wants the Bronx* and *In the Jungle of Cities,* while the Folger Theater Group, now a member of LORT, attracted national attention with its American premiere of Edward Bond's *The Fool.*

Despite the nucleus of a resident company, the Folger's productions of Shakespeare (*Much Ado About Nothing, A Midsummer Night's Dream*) are highly erratic, but the theater does have an intoxicating willingness to venture off the beaten track, as it did with *Black Elk Speaks,* Christopher Sergel's account of the winning of the West as seen by the losers, the Indians, and also with Jack Gilhooley's *Mummer's End,* which examined one Philadelphia family's devotion to the annual Mummer's Parade.

Meanwhile, Ford's Theater sent a gospel musical, *Your Arms Too Short to Box With God,* to New York, saw it take and then settled down with another long-running revue, *The All Night Strut* — this one made from the music and dance crazes of the 1930s and 40s.

The strongest voice, however, continued to come from Arena Stage, which now counts three theaters in its complex — the Arena, the Kreeger and the Old Vat Room in the basement, home of works "In the Process." International in the scope of its fare, Arena mounted plays from England (Shaw's *Saint Joan*), Italy (Eduardo de Filippo's *Saturday, Sunday, Monday*), Russia (Gorky's *The Lower Depths*), Canada (Michel Tremblay's *Forever Yours Marie Lou*),

Hungary (Istvan Orkeny's *Catsplay*), and France (Samuel Beckett one-acters), without overlooking such home-grown works as Lillian Hellman's *The Autumn Garden*, David Rabe's *Streamers* or Christopher Durang's *A History of the American Film*. With Orkeny, Rabe and Beckett, the theater attained the sublime, and with Durang, the sublimely ridiculous. But Arena's audiences are the real miracle, patiently and carefully nurtured over the years to accept such fare as vital to their lives. Mrs. Fichandler has done as much as anyone to raise the town's theatrical consciousness.

The sharpest blow for independence, though, may have been inadvertently struck by a Texan, Preston Jones, and his three-play chronicle of Texas life, *A Texas Trilogy*, in which Washington took a near-proprietary interest. It ran 17 capacity weeks in the Eisenhower, engaging a whole spectrum of theatergoers from cabbies to society dowagers, and could easily have run 17 more. The cool disdain that greeted *A Texas Trilogy* in New York was perceived here as an affront — not only to Jones, but to Washington itself. Only this time, no one was willing to grant New York the final say.

Ford's Theater

FORGE OF FREEDOM (8). Musical by John Allen; music by Shelly Markham; lyrics by Annette Leisten. July 12, 1976. Director, Jay Harnick; scenery, Jim Hamilton; lighting, Jo Carbo; costumes, Dianne Finn Chapman; choreography, Rick Atwell. With Scot Stewart, Grace Keagy, William March, Christy Lawrence, Jack Bittner.

VANITIES (31). By Jack Heifner. October 19, 1976. Director, Garland Wright; scenery, John Arnone; lighting, Patrika Brown; costumes, David James. With Valorie Armstrong, Sarah Harris, Patricia Richardson.

THE ALL NIGHT STRUT (197+). Musical revue conceived by Fran Charnas. December 16, 1976 (world premiere). Director, Fran Charnas; scenery, Richard Ferrer; lighting, Barry Arnold; costumes, Carol Oditz; choreography and musical staging, Arthur Faria; orchestrations, Luther Henderson. With Jonelle Allen, Barbara Heuman, Michael Davis, Irving Lee.

One intermission.

Musical Numbers: Act I — "One O'Clock Jump," "Jukebox Saturday Night," "Moonlight Serenade," "A Tisket, a Tasket," "If I Didn't Know," "Java Jive," "Stormy Weather," "Beat Me Daddy, Eight to the Bar," "The Lindy," "Blue Champagne," "Let's Fly Away," "I Get Ideas," "Begin the Beguine," "Cuanto La Gusto," "Broadway Rhythm," "Brother, Can You Spare a Dime." Act II — "Military Tap," "G. I. Jive," "Shoo Shoo Baby," "A Nightingale Sang in Berkeley Square," "Don't Sit Under the Apple Tree," "Rosie the Riveter," "You're a Lucky Fellow, Mr. Smith," "Comin' In on a Wing and a Prayer," "Praise the Lord and Pass the Ammunition," "I'll Be Seeing You," "New Orleans Rag," "Ain't Misbehavin'," "Hard Hearted Hannah," "Wish That I Could Shimmy Like My Sister Kate," "Why Do You Do Me Like You Do Do Do," "Just Imagine," "Dream," "You Do Something to Me," "The Continental."

John F. Kennedy Center: Eisenhower Theater

THE MAGNIFICENT YANKEE (37). By Emmet Lavery. July 1, 1976. Director, Peter Hunt; scenery and lighting, James Riley; costumes, Noel Taylor. With James Whitmore, Audra Lindley, Emery Battis, Jack Murdock, Louis Beachner. An American Bicentennial Theater production, produced for Kennedy Center by Zev Bufman and presented in conjunction with the Xerox Corporation.

TRAVESTIES (45). By Tom Stoppard. January 6, 1977. Director, Peter Wood; scenery and costumes, Carl Toms; lighting, Robert Ornbo. With John Wood, Charles Kimbrough, Lynne Lipton, James Booth, Katherine McGrath, Jack Bittner. Produced for Ken-

nedy Center by Roger L. Stevens and Edmonstone F. Thompson.

THE AMERICAN COLLEGE THEATER FESTIVAL. Ninth annual two-week festival of representative college productions, selected from across the country. April 4-17, 1977. Produced by the Kennedy Center in conjunction with the Alliance for Arts Education, the American Theater Association and Amoco Oil Company.

MEG (4). By Paula Vogel. April 4, 1977. Director, Phil Karnell; scenery, Josh Dachs; lighting, Phil Miller; costumes, Candace Warner. Produced by Cornell University. Winner of the ACTF playwrighting competition.

Meg .... Cindy Recker
Sir Thomas More .... Peter Winn
Alice More .... Harriet Winkleman
William Roper .... Robert Schenkkan
Thomas Cromwell .... Bruce Probst
Time: 16th century. Place: England. The martyrdom of Sir Thomas More, as viewed by his daughter Meg. Two intermissions.

The festival also included: HISTORIAS PARA SER CONTADAS (STORIES TO BE TOLD) (4) by Osvaldo Dragun, Texas A & I University; LEAR (3) by Edward Bond, University of Alabama; HAY FEVER (3) by Noel Coward, Webster College; UPSTREAM TOWARD LETHE (3) by George Moran, University of California, Los Angeles; WHO'S HAPPY NOW? (3) by Oliver Hailey, Midwestern State University; WAITING FOR GODOT

(3) by Samuel Beckett, Virginia Polytechnic Institute and State University; ROUND TRIP TICKET (2) by Bruce Jones, Mankato State University.

THE ARCHBISHOP'S CEILING (42). By Arthur Miller. April 30, 1977 (world premiere). Director, Arvin Brown; scenery, David Jenkins; lighting, Ron Wallace; costumes, Bill Walker. Produced by Robert Whitehead, Roger L. Stevens and Konrad Matthaei.

Adrian .... Tony Musante
Sigmund .... John Cullum
Maya .... Bibi Andersson
Martin .... Josef Sommer
Marcus .... Douglass Watson
Irena .... Bara-Christen Hansen
Time: The present. Place: A capital in Europe. A dissident writer discusses his fate with his small circle of friends in an apartment that may be bugged by the state. One intermission.

Note: The Eisenhower season also included a touring production of *The Belle of Amherst* and pre-Broadway productions of *A Texas Trilogy, No Man's Land, Music Is, Annie* and *Dirty Linen*. The latter was first presented by the Kennedy Center at the West End Theater for 56 performances, then was transferred to the Eisenhower for an additional 32 performances, before going to New York.

Note: The John F. Kennedy Opera House season included pre-Broadway productions of *Fiddler on the Roof, The Baker's Wife, Caesar and Cleopatra,* and touring productions of *Mark Twain Tonight,* the D'Oyly Carte, *Shenandoah* and the Shirley MacLaine show.

John F. Kennedy Center: Musical Theater Lab

HOT GROG (12). Musical by Jim Wann; music and lyrics by Jim Wann and Bland Simpson. March 15, 1977. Director, Edward Berkeley; lighting, Joan Arhelger; costumes, Hilary Rosenfeld; choreography and musical staging, Patricia Birch.

Dr. Heathcliff Hayti .... William Bryan
"Blackbeard" Teach .... Frederick Coffin
Stede Bonnet .... Homer Foil
Wife #5 .... Rebecca Gilchrist
William Rhett .... Roger Howell
Anne Bonney .... Cassandra Morgan
Wife #13 .... Kathi Moss
Gov. Charles Eden .... William Newman
"Calico Jack" Rackham .... Terry O'Quinn
Mary .... Melinda Tanner
Wife # .... Mimi Wallace
Musical Numbers: Act I — "Make Way," "Seizure to Roam," "Got a Notion," "Come on Down to the Sea," "Hot Grog," "The Pirate's Life," "The Difference Is Me," "Only a Woman." Act II — "Sea Breeze," "Hack 'Em," "Break Me Out," "Skye Boat Song," "Marooned," "High Summer," "The Head Song," "Bastards Have the Best Luck," "Drinking Fool," "Bound Away."

NEVERLAND (8). Musical by Jim Steinman. April 26, 1977. Director, Barry Keating; scenery, Daniel Leigh; lighting, Martin Tudor; costumes, Bosha Johnson; choreography, Edmond Kresley; musical direction, Paul Jacobs.

Historian .... Barry Keating
Baal .... Richard Dunne
Tink .... Larry Dilg
Max .... Baxter Harris
Emily .... Johanna Albrecht
Wendy .... Ellen Foley
Lost Boys: Mark Kapitan, Tim Millett, Toby Parker. Obsidianites: Rodney Reiner, Robert Rhys, Brian DeStazio, Don Swanson.
Time: The long and distant future. Place: The coast of Southern California; the metropolis of Obsidian.
Musical Numbers: Act I — "The Formation of the Pack," "City Night," "Midnight Serenade," "Bat Out of Hell," "Heaven Can Wait," "The Hunt," "The Assassins' Song," "Gods." Act II — "Dance in My Pants," "The Malediction," "Kingdom Come," "The Annihilation."

Olney Theater

MARY, MARY (21). By Jean Kerr. June 1, 1976. Director, Leo Brady; scenery and lighting, James D. Waring; costumes, Kaye A. Byars. With Roger Newman, Caroline McWilliams, Henry Sutton, Robert Milli, Kathleen O'Meara Noone.

THE IMPORTANCE OF BEING EARNEST (21). By Oscar Wilde. June 22, 1976. Director, James D.

Waring; scenery and lighting, James D. Waring; costumes, Kaye A. Byars; musical score, Emerson Meyers. With Steven Sutherland, Max Wright, Katherine McGrath, Cecilia Hart, Anita Dangler, Dorothy Blackburn, Henry Sutton.

SPIDER'S WEB (21). By Agatha Christie. July 13, 1976. Director, Leo Brady; scenery and lighting,

James D. Waring; costumes, Kaye A. Byars. With Kathleen O'Meara Noone, Richard Bauer, Cecilia Hart, Peter Vogt, J. Robert Dietz, Anita Dangler.

ALL THE NICE PEOPLE (21). By Hugh Leonard. August 3, 1976 (American premiere). Director, James D. Waring; scenery and lighting, James D. Waring; costumes, Kaye A. Byars.

Fran Corish	Judith McGilligan
Old Heegan	J. Robert Dietz
Christine Lambert	Halo Wines
Charlie Lambert	Richard Bauer
Mrs. Corish	Columba Hoban
Lily Heegan	Pauline Flanagan
Bertie Totterdel	Max Wright
Humphries	George Vogel
Mick Humphries	Timothy Crowe

Shakespeare Summer Festival

THE TEMPEST (30). By William Shakespeare. July 6, 1976. Director, Tony Tanner; scenery, C. H. Vaughan III; lighting, Victor En Yu Tan; music, Jim Smith. With Tony Tanner, Richad Vernon, Richard

Wolf Trap Farm Park

SHENANDOAH (5). Musical by James Lee Barrett, Peter Udell and Philip Rose; music by Gary Geld; lyrics by Peter Udell. June 14, 1976. Director, Philip Rose; scenery, Kert Lundell; lighting, Tom Skelton; costumes, Pearl Somner, Winn Morton; choreog-

Colm	John Synk

Party Guests: Nannette Rickert, Melissa Vogel, Monica Yates.

Time: The present. Place: Charlie Lambert's home, a few miles south of Dublin; a pub; a railway bridge. After eight lonesome years as a London barmaid, Fran Corish returns home to Ireland to visit all the nice people she left behind and discovers that they have failings like everybody else. One intermission.

UNCLE VANYA (21). By Anton Chekhov. August 24, 1976. Director, John Going; scenery, Rolf T. Beyer; lighting, James D. Waring; costumes, Kaye A. Byars. With John Wylie, Lynn Milgrim, Richard Bauer, Brenda Curtis, Richard Greene, Louise Campbell, J. Robert Dietz.

Niles, Sarah Rice, Tobias Haller, Jon Polito, Norman Allen, Richard Lupino. Produced by Ellie Chamberlain in cooperation with the National Park Service.

raphy, Theodore Agress. With John Cullum, Leslie Denniston, Penelope Milford, Joel Higgins, Roger Berdahl, Richard Flanders, Tony Holmes, Paul Corey.

WATERFORD, CONN.

Eugene O'Neill Theater Center: National Playwrights Conference

(President, George C. White; artistic director, Lloyd Richards; assistant to artistic director, Nancy Quinn; designers, Fred Voelpel, Spencer Mosse, Arden Fingerhut. All programs new works in progress)

Barn Theater (Indoors)

DADDY'S DUET (2). By Clifford Turknett. July 21, 1976. Director, Dennis Scott; dramaturg, Michael Feingold.

Nelson	Edward Herrmann
Charles	Andy Backer
Stanley	Richard Backus
A Nurse	Dianne Wiest

No intermission.

LADYHOUSE BLUES (2). By Kevin O'Morrison (2). July 24, 1976. Director, Tony Giordano; dramaturg, Marilyn Stasio.

Eylie	Christine Estabrook
Helen	Cara Duff-MacCormick
Dot	Cynthia Herman
Liz	Jo Henderson
Terry	Gale Garnett

Time: August 1919. Place: South St. Louis. One intermission.

SECRETS OF THE RICH (2). By Arthur Kopit. July 29, 1976. Director, Lynne Meadow; dramaturg, Marilyn Stasio.

Dodge Burden	Edward Herrmann
Benedict	Keith Gordon
Miranda	Jill Andre
Dyer	Robert Blumenfeld
Grace	Carol Ostrow
Voice on Telephone	Frank Hamilton
Mazie Douzens	Cara Duff-MacCormick

Workmen: Dick Bruno, Jim Metzler, Joel Wald. One intermission.

WINDS OF CHANGE (2). By Barbara Field. August 2, 1976. Director, Tony Giordano; dramaturg, Marilyn Stasio.

Theo Van Maas	Richard Backus
Marya Broeken	Gale Garnett
Madame Van Maas	Jo Henderson
Prof. Van Maas	Roger DeKoven
Gelb	Frank Hamilton
Ans Van Maas	Dianne Wiest

Time: 1915. Place: The Van Maas home, Louvain, Belgium. One intermission.

SUCKERS (2). By Werner Liepolt. August 6, 1976.

Director, Peter Mark Schifter; dramaturg, Michael Feingold; songs, Stephen Fechtor; additional music arranged and performed, Steven Gordon Crist.

Clown .... Jeffrey DeMunn
Barnum .... Edward Herrmann
Man #2 .... Richard Backus
Boy .... Keith Gordon
Man #1 .... Bryan Clark
Mr. Nemesis .... Roger DeKoven
Man #3 .... Jerry Zaks
Female .... Gale Garnett
Charity .... Dianne Wiest
    One intermission.

THE SUGAR BOWL (2). By Stanley Taikeff.

Amphitheater (Outdoors)

PIRATES (2). By Amlin Gray. July 27, 1976. Director, John Dillon; dramaturg, Michael Feingold.
Jack Rackham .... Paul Collins
Basil .... Bob Christian
George .... Richard Backus
Gusset .... Roger Robinson
Mulga .... Lou Ferguson
Roussin .... Robert Blumenfeld
Targove .... Andy Backer
Jakes .... Francisco Prado
Flecken .... Brent Jennings
Mary .... Dianne Wiest
    Sailors: David Berry, Chris Durang, Mike Chin.
    Place: A pirate ship. No intermission.

THE DEFENSE (2). By Edgar White. July 30, 1976. Director, Dennis Scott; dramaturg, Edith Oliver.
Dread .... Lou Ferguson
Woman of Silence .... Ramona Perry
Barabbas .... Francisco Prado
Girl Gambler; Miss Ming .... Lori Tan Chinn
Root; Apollo; Mugger .... Brent Jennings
Viola; Guemada .... Mila Conway
Ella; Tenant; Mugged Woman .... Delores Gaskins
Kate .... Deatra Lambert
Nenen .... Rosanna Carter
Deacon .... Robert Christian
Cousin Sutton .... Roger Robinson
Jestina Sutton; Dwen .... Marie Thomas
Sharon; Prostitute .... Arlene Quiyou
Terika .... Ceal Coleman
Mr. Calavary .... Andy Backer
    Place: The Lower East Side of New York and in the mind of Dread. One intermission.

G.R. POINT (2). By David Berry. August 7, 1976. Director, Tony Giordano; dramaturg, Edith Oliver.

Instant Theater (Outdoors)

BENIFIT (Sic) OF A DOUBT (2). By Edward J. Clinton. July 22, 1976. Director, Lynne Meadow; dramaturg, Edith Oliver.
Sadie .... Dee Victor
Laurie Cassidy .... Toni Kalem
John Cassidy .... Bryan Clark
Kay .... Jill Andre
Eileen Cassidy .... Carolyn Coates

August 13, 1976. Director, Tony Giordano; lighting, Malcolm Ewen; dramaturg, Michael Feingold.
Jack Diamond .... Andy Backer
Moe .... Roger DeKoven
Susie .... Toni Kalem
Zeke .... Joe Cortese
Ritchie .... Robert Blumenfeld
Stanley .... Edward Herrmann
Chuck .... Jeffrey DeMunn
Fatso .... Clarence Felder
Lucky .... John Heard
    Time: 1970. Place: The Sugar Bowl, a candy store in Brooklyn, New York. Act I: An afternoon in summer. Act II: Same, the action is continuous. Act III: Evening of the same day. Two intermissions.

Deacon .... Roger Robinson
Tito .... Francisco Prado
Straw .... Donald Warfield
Mama San .... Lori Tan Chinn
Micah .... John Heard
Shoulders .... Robert Christian
Zan .... Gary Bayer
K.P .... Brent Jennings
Lt. Johnston .... Joseph Cortese.
    Time: 1969. Place: Tay Loi, Vietnam. One intermission.

A HISTORY OF THE AMERICAN FILM (2). By Christopher Durang. August 12, 1976. Director, Peter Mark Schifter; dramaturg, Marilyn Stasio; music, John J. Gaughan Jr.; lyrics, Christopher Durang; additional music arranged and performed, Steven Gordon Crist.
The Stars:
    Loretta .... Cynthia Herman
    Jimmy .... Jerry Zaks
    Bette .... Gale Garnett
    Hank .... Richard Backus
The Contract Players:
    Mickey; etc. .... Gary Bayer
    Piano Man; etc .... Robert Christian
    Victor Henreid; etc .... Bryan Clark
    Clara; etc .... Cara Duff-MacCormick
    Allison Mortimer; etc .... Jo Henderson
    Ma Joad; etc .... Dee Victor
    Michael O'Reilly; etc .... Donald Warfield
    Eve .... Dianne Wiest
    Salad Girls .... Barbara Keiler, Rima Miller
    God .... Frank Robbins.
    One intermission

Dandelion .... Roger Robinson
Father Pat .... Bob Christian
    Two intermissions.

AS TO THE MEANING OF WORDS (2). By Mark Eichman. August 4, 1976. Director, John Dillon; dramaturg, Edith Oliver.
Dr. Winston Gerrad .... Roger Robinson

Alexander Thomas . . . . Paul Collins
Ned Ryan . . . . Clarence Felder
Judge Horace J. Wheeting . . . . John Wylie
Dr. Madelyn Foster . . . . Jo Henderson
Dr. Ramon Norriega . . . . Francisco Prado
Dr. Clarence Parrish . . . . Robert Blumenfeld

Dr. Jonathan Wallace . . . . Joseph Cortese
Gloria Sanders . . . . Cara Duff-MacCormick
Radio Announcer . . . . Frank Hamilton
Grand Jury Voice . . . . Jill Andre
Man's Voice . . . . Andy Backer
One intermission.

WEST SPRINGFIELD, MASS.

Stage West: Main Stage

(Managing director, Stephen E. Hays; artistic director, Rae Allen)

SLEUTH (28). By Anthony Shaffer. November 13, 1976. Director, Grover Dale; scenery, Jerry Rojo; lighting, Jamie Gallagher; costumes, Sigrid Insull. With Peter Walker, Chris Romilly.

YOU CAN'T TAKE IT WITH YOU (30). By George S. Kaufman and Moss Hart. December 18, 1976. Director, Rae Allen; scenery, Laurence King; lighting, Ronald Wallace; costumes, Sigrid Insull. With Elizabeth Parrish, Nancy Sellin, Brad Sullivan, Wyman Pendleton, Chris Waering, Chris Romilly.

In repertory (January 20, 1977, 25 performances):
THE TOOTH OF CRIME by Sam Shepard. Director, Davey Marlin-Jones; scenery, Robert Alpers; lighting, Jamie Gallagher; costumes, Carr Garnett. With Clyde Burton, Sharon Ernster, Renos Mandis, Ray Aranha, Chris Romilly.
WHEN WE DEAD AWAKEN by Henrik Ibsen. Director, Rae Allen; scenery, Jerry Rojo; lighting,

Ronald Wallace; costumes, Sigrid Insull. With Ronald Bishop, Nancy Sellin, Gwyllum Evans, Dorrie Kavanaugh, Brad Sullivan.

THE HOT L BALTIMORE (32) By Lanford Wilson. February 26, 1977. Director, Rae Allen; scenery, Fredda Slavin; lighting, Barley Harris; costumes, Carr Garnett. With Clyde Burton, Kathleen Tolan, Elizabeth Parrish, Dorothy Marie, Carol Morley, Wyman Pendleton, Timothy Near, Jeremy Lawrence.

JACQUES BREL IS ALIVE AND WELL AND LIVING IN PARIS (34). By Eric Blau and Mort Shuman, based on Jacques Brel's lyrics and commentary; music by Jacques Brel. April 2, 1977. Director, Rae Allen; associate director, Steven Woolf; scenery, Jerry Rojo; lighting, Barley Harris; costumes, Susan Tucker; musical direction, Avram Schackman. With Rae Allen, Jim Canavan, Nina Menge, William Michael, Avram Schackman.

Stage West: Stage Two

(Staged readings — 2 performance each)

SONGS AT TWILIGHT by Maureen Howard. December 19, 1976. Director, Michael Montel. With Anthony Howland, Carey Gold, Josef Sommer, Tudi Wiggins, Judith Barcroft.

LOVESONG by Robert Lehan, directed by Dan Eaton and UNTITLED by Dan Eaton, directed by Robert Lehan. February 6, 1977. With Gwyllum Evans, Elizabeth Parrish, Wyman Pendleton, Dorothy Marie, Steven Worth, Deborah Davison.

AKOSU'A OF THE FIRST AND FINAL DAY

written and directed by Ray Aranha. March 13, 1977. With Rosanna Carter, Sam Williams, Michelle Shea, Basil Wallace, Lou Ferguson, Arthur French, Bari K. Willerford, Bill Henry Douglass, John Harris, Chuck Wise.

QUAIL SOUTHWEST by Larry Ketron. April 23, 1977. Director, Andy Wolk. With Munson Hicks, Drew Snyder, Dick Latessa, Tara Loewen, Zina Jasper, Amy Nathan, Ellen Barber, Margot Stevenson.

Note: The Tooth of Crime was presented at the Loeb Drama Center, January 26-29, 1977, for 5 performances, then returned to Stage West. The Children's Touring Theater Company of Stage West performed Take A Fable, written and directed by Marjorie Sigley, October 4-November 20, 1976, and Golliwhoppers by Flora Atkins, directed by Timothy Near, April 25-May 20, 1977, at schools in Massachusetts and Connecticut.

CANADA

CALGARY, ALBERTA

Theater Calgary

(Artistic director, Harold G. Baldridge)

THE SUNSHINE BOYS (21). By Neil Simon. October 1, 1976. Director, Harold G. Baldridge; designer, Richard Roberts. With Milt Kamen, Eugene Elman, David Rosenbaum, Mel Tonken, Stephen Hair.

THE GLASS MENAGERIE (21). By Tennessee Williams. October 29, 1976. Director/designer, Richard Roberts. With Helen Hughes, Lynne Griffin, Robert Armstrong, Terry Waterhouse.

TIME AND TIME AGAIN (21). By Alan Ayckbourn. November 26, 1976. Director, Harold G. Baldridge; designer, Walter Foster; lighting, Richard Roberts. With Stephen Hair, David Yorston, Debra Stott, Helene White, Darryl Beschell.

HEDDA GABLER (21). By Henrik Ibsen. January 21, 1977. Director, Bernard Hiatt; designer, Pat Flood; lighting Ted Roberts. With Patricia Collins, Helen Hughes, Eleanor Beecroft, Brian Gromoff, Richard Farrell.

FESTIVAL! (21). Conceived and written by Tink Robinson; original music by Allan Rae and Tink Robinson. February 25, 1977 (world premiere). Director/choreographer, Tink Robinson; musical su-

pervisor, Allan Rae; designer, Harold G. Baldridge; lighting, Ted Roberts; costume coordinator, Robin Benjamin; vocal arranger/director, Judy Armstrong; musical arrangers, Allan Rae, Eric Friedenberg; additional lyrics, Wally Grieve; sound, Tim Dubber.

Granny	Judy Armstrong
Stella Reingold	Lorraine Butler
Penelope Farquirst	Jennifer Higgin
Mr. O'Flanigan	David Dunbar
Henri LaTogue	Sam Moses
Underarm Tom	Tink Robinson

Musical revue from 1890s to 1977, commissioned for Calgary's Festival of the Arts, 1977. Act I: 1890 to 1910; Act II: 1912 to 1977.

EQUUS (20). By Peter Shaffer. March 25, 1977. Director, Harold G. Baldridge; designer, Richard Roberts; original background sound score, Allan Rae. With Fred Euringer, Brian Paul, Patricia Benedict, Felixe Fitzgerald, Des Smiley and the Arête Mime Troupe.

A THOUSAND CLOWNS (21). By Herb Gardner. April 25, 1977. Director, John Plank; designer, Donald J. Halton; lighting, Gordon King. With Patrick Christopher, Stephen Hair, Elan Ross Gibson, Jack Northmore, Mina Mina.

Note: Theater Calgary Caravan is a professional touring company for children, performing in schools in Calgary and Southern Central Alberta. From October 1976 through January 1977, the Arête Mime Troupe gave 65 performances in junior high schools. From April 1976 through June 1977, Sarah's Play by Rex Deverell and scenes from The Miracle Worker, with special permission from William Gibson, were given 65 performances at elementary schools; directed by Shirley Tooke and performed by Shirley Harris, Sharon Stone, Jeane Stuart and Nigel Beamish. During December 1976, Please Don't Sneeze was performed by Pamela Prodan, Jayne Edmonds, Duval Lang, Don Rae, Jim Grouix.

HALIFAX, NOVA SCOTIA

Neptune Theater Company

(Artistic director, John Wood)

KING LEAR (21). By William Shakespeare. January 10, 1977. Director, John Wood; scenery, John Ferguson; lighting, Michael J. Whitfield; costumes, Peter Blais. With Eric Donkin, Janet Doherty, Patricia Gage, Denise Fergusson, Max Helpmann, Rodger Barton, Richard Blackburn, Don Goodspeed.

EQUUS (21). By Peter Shaffer. February 7, 1977. Director, John Wood; designer, John Ferguson; lighting, Michael J. Whitfield; horse-head designer, Linda Whitney. With David Renton, Richard Greenblatt, Max Helpmann, Joan Gregson, Denise Fergusson, Melody Ryane, Rodger Barton, Stephen Russell, Nicola Lipman.

WILLIAM SCHWENCK AND ARTHUR WHO? (25). Conceived and directed by Alan Laing and John Wood; words and music by W. S. Gilbert and Arthur Sullivan. March 14, 1977 (world premiere). Script and additional lyrics, John Wood; arrangements and additional music, Alan Laing; designer, Robert Doyle; lighting, R. A. Elliott.

Director/Gilbert	David Renton
Rehearsal pianist/Sullivan	Richard Greenblatt

Company: Lee J. Campbell, Janet Doherty, Denise Fergusson, Charles Fletcher, Craig Gardner, Rita Howell, Alan Laing, Frank MacKay, Jill Orenstein, Joan Orenstein, Sharron Timmins

One intermission

BACK TO BEULAH (25). By W.O. Mitchell. March 15, 1977. Director, John Wood; designer, Susan Benson; lighting, R. A. Elliott. With Joan Orenstein, Rita Howell, Denise Fergusson, Lee J. Campbell, Janet Doherty, Craig Gardner, Frank MacKay.

SCAPIN (21). By Molière. March 19, 1977. Adapted and directed by John Wood; designer, Sue LePage; lighting, R. A. Elliott; music composed and performed by John Bird. With Richard Greenblatt, David Renton, Janet Doherty, Joan Orenstein.

MA'S TRAVELLING CIRCUS AND VAUDE-VILLE SHOW (14). Devised by John Wood and Alan Laing. April 2, 1977 (world premiere). Director, John Wood; designed and performed by members of the company.

Note: *Ma's Travelling Circus and Vaudeville Show* toured the province from April 25 through May 25, 1977.

MONTREAL, QUEBEC

Centaur Theater Company: Centaur 2: Main Stage

(Artistic director, Maurice Podbrey)

THE PLAYBOY OF THE WESTERN WORLD (33). By John Millington Synge. October 7, 1976. Director, Maurice Good; scenery and costumes, Barbra Matis; lighting, Harry Frehner. With Graham McPherson, Diana Barrington, Richard Farrell, Maggie Griffin, Roland Hewgill.

ANATOL (33). By Arthur Schnitzler; English version by Frank Marcus. November 18, 1976. Director, Jean Gascon; scenery, Wendell Dennis, lighting, Vladimir Svetlovsky; costumes, Francois Barbeau. With Albert Millaire, Roland Hewgill, Martha Henry, David Francis.

ARTICHOKE (33). By Joanna M. Glass. January 6, 1977. Director, Elsa Bolam; scenery and costumes, Barbra Matis; lighting, Vladimir Svetlovsky. With Jennifer Phipps, Dan MacDonald, Margaret Bard, Tim Whelan, James B. Douglas, Griffith Brewer, Doug Peterson.

SIZWE BANZI IS DEAD (33). By Athol Fugard, John Kani and Winston Ntshona. February 17, 1977. Director, Maurice Podbrey; designer, Wendell Dennis; lighting, Harry Frehner. With Alton Kumalo, Errol Slue.

COMEDIANS (33). By Trevor Griffiths. March 31, 1977. Director, Pam Brighton; scenery and costumes, Michael Eagan; lighting, Harry Frehner. With Jeff Braunstein, Walter Massey, Tom Butler, David Francis, Peter MacNeill, Louis Negin, Brian MacGabhann, Griffith Brewer, Ivan Smith, Doug Peterson.

Centaur Theater Company: Centaur Theater 1: Small Stage

NOTHING TO LOSE (12). By David Fennario. November 11, 1976 (world premiere). Director, Guy Sprung; designer, Barbra Matis; lighting, Harry Frehner.

Claude	Denys Nadon
Chabougamou	Jean Archambault
Foreman	Tony Angelo
Gros Gas	Raymond Belisle
Fred	Walter Bolton
Murray	Lubomyr Myktiuk
Jerry	Don Scanlan
Jackie	Peter MacNeill
Frank	Simon Malbogat.

No intermission.

LES CANADIENS (12). By Rick Salutin; assisted by Ken Dryden. February 10, 1977 (world premiere). Director, Guy Sprung; designer, Astrid Janson; lighting, Steven Hawkins. With The Hockey Team: Raymond Belisle, Pierre Lenoir, Steven Hawkins, Ray Landry, Luce Guilbeault, Eric Peterson, Sebastien Dhavernas, Michael Rudder.

Act I: The past. Act II: The day of a game, this season. One intermission.

THERESE'S CREED and QUILLER (12). By Michael Cook. March 24, 1977 (world premieres). Director, John Juliani; designer, Wendell Dennis; lighting, Harry Frehner.

Therese's Creed

Therese	Donna Butt

Quiller

Quiller	Roland Hewgill
Mrs. I	Donna Butt
Neighbor	Janet Feindel

Children (alternating): Morgan Poteet, Aaron Poteet, Richie Hall

Two one-act plays about Newfoundland.

OTTAWA, ONT.

National Arts Center Theater Company: English

(Director/artistic director, Jean Roberts)

THE FANTASTICKS (21). Book and lyrics by Tom Jones; music by Harvey Schmidt; suggested by Edmond Rostand's *Les Romantiques*. November 29, 1976. Director, Marigold Charlesworth; designer, Art Penson; lighting, Andis Celma; musical director, Peter Yakimovich. With Diane Stapley, Donald Hunkin, Douglas Chamberlain, Grant Roll.

SAINTE MARIE AMONG THE HURONS (22). By James W. Nichol. January 10, 1977. Director, Heinar Piller; scenery and costumes, Art Penson; lighting, David Wallett. With Colin Fox, Jan Muszynski, Wayne Burnett.

MAN AND SUPERMAN (21). By George Bernard Shaw. January 31, 1977. Director, Peter Dews; scenery and costumes, Brian H. Jackson; lighting, Nick Cernovitch. With Bernard Lloyd, Tedde Moore, Tony Van Bridge, Amelia Hall.

PRIVATE LIVES (20). By Noel Coward. February 28, 1977. Director, Eric Thompson; scenery, Michael Eagan; lighting, Nick Cernovitch; costumes, Brian H. Jackson. With Elizabeth Shepherd, Neil Vipond.

DON JUAN IN HELL (18). By George Bernard Shaw. March 21, 1977. Director, Peter Dews; and costumes, Brian H. Jackson; lighting, Nick Cernovitch. With Edward Atienza, Bernard Lloyd, Tony Van Bridge, Tedde Moore.

WHEN WE ARE MARRIED (20). By J. B. Priestley. April 18, 1977. Director, Peter Dews; scenery and costumes, Brian H. Jackson; lighting, Nick Cernovitch. With Edward Atienza, Amelia Hall, Gillie Genwick, Betty Leighton, Louise Nicol, Sandy Webster.

National Arts Center Theater Company: French

(Artistic director, Jean Herbiet)

WOYZECK (24). By Georg Buechner. October 4, 1976. Directors, Jean Herbiet and Felix Mirbt; scenery, Michael Eagan; costumes, Janet Logan.

TARTUFFE (28). By Molière. February 14, 1977.

Director, Olivier Reichenbach; scenery, Guy Neveu; costumes, Francois Barbeau. With Jean-Marie Lemieux, Jean-Pierre Ronfard, Lenie Scoffie, Christiane Raymond.

Note: During the 1976-77 Season, theater groups from all over Canada, both English and French, presented productions of plays, one-man shows, West End tours, European French companies, marionette shows, too numerous to mention here. The Center is exactly that, a bilingual production company and host to other Canadian and European theater companies.

STRATFORD, ONT.

Stratford Festival: Festival Stage

(Artistic Director, Robin Phillips; director Festival Stage, William Hutt; founder, Tom Patterson; lighting, Gil Wechsler)

THE WAY OF THE WORLD (20). By William Congreve. June 7, 1976. Director, Robin Phillips; designer, Daphne Dare; music, Louis Applebaum; choreographer, Earl Kraul. With Domini Blythe, Jeremy Brett, Alan Scarfe, Maggie Smith, Jessica Tandy, Tony Van Bridge.

THE MERCHANT OF VENICE (53). By William Shakespeare. June 8, 1976. Director, Bill Glassco; designer, Susan Benson; music, Morris Surdin. With Hume Cronyn, Jackie Burroughs, Lewis Gordon, Denise Fergusson, Domini Blythe, Max Helpmann, Bernard Hopkins.

ANTONY AND CLEOPATRA (26). By William Shakespeare. June 9, 1976. Director, Robin Phillips; designer, Daphne Dare; music, Louis Applebaum.

With Maggie Smith, Keith Baxter, Alan Scarfe, Lewis Gordon, William Needles, Patricia Idlette.

MEASURE FOR MEASURE (15). By William Shakespeare. June 30, 1976. Director, Robin Phillips; designer, Daphne Dare; music, Louis Applebaum. With Martha Henry, William Hutt, Richard Monette, Douglas Rain, Tony Van Bridge.

A MIDSUMMER NIGHT'S DREAM (25). By William Shakespeare. August 18, 1976. Director, Robin Phillips; designer, Susan Benson; lighting, Michael J. Whitfield; music, Alan Laing. With Jessica Tandy, Robin Nunn, Richard Partington, Denise Fergusson, Mia Anderson, Nick Mancuso, William Needles, Jeremy Brett, Hume Cronyn.

Stratford Festival: Avon Theater

HAMLET (49). By William Shakespeare. June 7, 1976. Directors, Robin Phillips, William Hutt; designers, Daphne Dare, John Pennoyer. With Nicholas Pennell/Richard Monette, Marti Maraden,

Pat Galloway/Patricia Bentley-Fisher, Michael Liscinsky, Eric Donkin, Richard Partington.

THE TEMPEST (29). By William Shakespeare. June

8, 1976. Directors, Robin Phillips, William Hutt; designers, Daphne Dare, John Ferguson. With William Hutt, Marti Maraden, Nicholas Pennell, Richard Monette, Jack Wetherall.

THE IMPORTANCE OF BEING EARNEST (27). By Oscar Wilde. June 10, 1976. Director, Robin Phillips; scenery, Daphne Dare; costumes, Molly Harris Campbell. With Nicholas Pennell, Barry MacGregor, Pat Galloway, Marti Maraden, William Hutt, Amelia Hall.

EVE (11). By Larry Fineberg; based on *The Book of Eve* by Constance Beresford-Howe. July 14, 1976 (world premiere). Director, Vivian Matalon; designer, John Ferguson; lighting, Gil Wechsler.

Eva .... Jessica Tandy
Burt .... James Edmond
Neil .... Les Carlson
Pat .... Richard Partington
Johnny ....: Louis Zorich
Kim .... Melody Ryane
One intermission.

THREE SISTERS (14). By Anton Chekhov. September 1, 1976. Director, John Hirsh; designer, Daphne Dare. With Keith Baxter, Pat Galloway, Martha Henry, William Hutt, Marti Maraden, Alan Scarfe, Maggie Smith.

All Avon Theater productions: lighting, Gil Wechsler.

TORONTO, ONT.

Tarragon Theater

(Artistic director, Bill Glassco; general manager, Robert Lowe)

ARTICHOKE (37). By Joanna M. Glass. October 9, 1976. Director, Bill Glassco; designer, John Ferguson; lighting, John Stammers. With Patricia Hamilton, Marie Romain Aloma, Les Carlson, Charles Palmer, Antony Parr, Larry Reynolds, Hagan Beggs.

LULU (35). By Frank Wedekind; adapted and directed by Bill Peters. December 31, 1976. Designer, Astrid Janson; lighting, Bjarne Christensen. With Zoe Alexander, David Bolt, David Clement, George Merner, Gary Schwartz, Sarah Albertson.

JOHANNES AND THE TALMUD (37). By Basya Hunter. February 19, 1977 (world premiere). Director, Bill Glassco; scenery, Eoin Sprott; lighting, John Stammers; costumes, Pat Flood; music, Morris Surdin.
Father Simon .... George Merner
Pfeffercorn .... David Stein
Shmuel .... James Kirchner
Beryl .... Ron Barry
Rabbi Margolit .... Kurt Freund
Johannes Reuchlin .... David Hemblen
Erasmus .... Maurice Good
Von Ritten .... Ken Le Maire
Elling .... John Gilbert
Hoogstraten .... David Calderisi

Cardinal Gramini .... Claude Bede
Kollin .... Ralph Small
Jews, Priests, Clerks, etc.: Howard Rypp, Joseph Vayda, Matt Walsh.
Time: The early years of the 16th Century. Place: Germany. Act I — Scene 1: The Rabbi's dwelling adjoining the synagogue. Scene 2: Reuchlin's study. Act II — Scene 3: Hoogstraten's palace. Scene 4: Another room in the Inquisitorial Palace. Act III — Scene 5: The Inquisitorial Court. Scene 6: A prison in the Inquisitorial Palace.

ONE NIGHT STAND (28). By Carol Bolt. April 9, 1977 (world premiere). Director, Eric Steiner; designer, Shawn Kerwin; lighting, Bjarne Christensen.
Rafe .... Brent Carver
Daisy .... Chapelle Jaffe
Sharon .... Carole Strypchuk
Act I: 11:30 p.m. Act II: 4 a.m.

THE SEAGULL (31). By Anton Chekhov; new translation by David French. June 4, 1977. Director, Bill Glassco; designer, Maurice Strike; lighting, Bill Williams. With Claude Bede. Clare Coulter, Nicky Gaudagni, Thomas Hauff, Don L. McManus, Eric Peterson, Patricia Phillips, Gordon Pinsent, Anna Reiser, Sandy Webster.

Tarragon Theater: Guest Production

THE FINAL PERFORMANCE OF VASLAV NIJINSKY (10). By Jeremy Long. November 27, 1976. Director, Suzie Payne; lighting and sound, Tom

Braidwood, Steve Miller; costumes, Palarbo. With members of Vancouver's Tamahnous Theater Workshop.

Tarragon Theater: Writers-in-Residence Staged Readings

(Dramaturge, Bena Shuster. May-June, 1977, 2 performances each)

EARTHLY DELIGHTS by Christine Foster; director Sean Mulcahy. ON THE LEE SHORE by

Christopher Heide; director, Lewis Baumander. COMFORT By Doris Cowan; director, Brian

Meeson. CHARMED CIRCLE by Shelagh Hewitt; director, Hutchison Shandro. EXACT CHANGE by Bruce Dowbiggin; director, John Van Burek.

NORTH END STORY by Brad Leiman; director, Rene Aloma. With members of the professional company.

VANCOUVER B. C.

Playhouse Theater Center of British Columbia: Queen Elizabeth Theater—Mainstage

(Artistic director, Christopher Newton)

TARTUFFE (24). By Molière; English verse translation, Richard Wilbur. November 8, 1976. Director, Derek Goldby. With Heath Lamberts, John Gardiner, Terence Kelly, Margaret Robertson, Alex Diakun, Joy Coghill.

THE COUNT OF MONTE CRISTO (24). By Ken Hill; songs by Ian Armit and Ken Hill; adapted from the novel by Alexandre Dumas. December 13, 1976. Director, Christopher Newton; musical director/arranger, Roger Perkins. With Jim Mezon, John Innes, Terence Kelly, Al Kozlik, Glen MacDonald, Margaret Robertson, Robert Seale, Donna White.

KING LEAR (24). By William Shakespeare. January 31, 1977. Director, Philip Hedley. With Powys

Thomas, Donna White, Heather Brechin, Margaret Robertson, Heath Lamberts, Tom McBeath, Jim Mezon.

TRAVESTIES (24). By Tom Stoppard. March 7, 1977. Director, Philip Hedley. With Heath Lamberts, Christopher Newton, Andrew Gillies, Terence Kelly, Heather Brechin, Shirley Broderick, John Innes, Margaret Robertson.

CAMINO REAL (24). By Tennessee Williams. April 11, 1977. Director, Christopher Newton. With Terence Kelly, Rodney Christensen, Joy Coghill, Al Kozlik, Christopher Newton, Jo Jo Rideout, Margaret Robertson, John Innes.

Designers: Scenery and costumes, Cameron Porteous; lighting, Jeffrey Dallas, Paul Reynolds.

Playhouse Theater Center of British Columbia: David Y. H. Lui Theater — New Series

DIRTY LINEN and NEW-FOUND-LAND (16). By Tom Stoppard. October 18, 1976. Director, Susan Ferley. With Shirley Broderick, David Glyn-Jones, John Innes, Colin Miller, Christopher Newton, Briain Petchey, Angela Slater, Powys Thomas, Robert Clothier, Andrew Gillies.

THE BLUES (16). Written and directed by Hrant Alianak. January 10, 1977. With Susan Wright, Alex Diakun, Booth Savage, Angela Slater.

THE SOUND OF DISTANT THUNDER (16). By Christopher Newton. March 21, 1977 (world premiere). Director, Kathryn Shaw; designer, Judith Lee; lighting, Jeffrey Dallas; musical direction, Roger Perkins; musical staging, James Hibbard.

Cast: Aunt Enid, Clare, Glove Model, Jessie, Voice 10, Woman 3 — Sherry Bie; Carmen Miranda, Girl on Trolley, Usell Triplet, Soldier's Gal, Glove Model, Voice 4 — Charlene Brandolini; Ray, V-Bond Drive Leader, German Singer, Air Commodore, Patriot, Soldier, Salvage Drive Leader, Voice 7 — Donald Cant; Reporter, Churchill, Zoot Suiter, Admiral,

Bert, Conductor, Newsman, Voice 1 — Alex Diakun; German Consul, General, Aide to MacKenzie King, Arp Warden, Roosevelt, Chairman, King George V, Voice 5 — Al Kozlik; MacKenzie King, Kenny, Alan Chipping, M.C.2, Soldier 1; Voice 9 — Glenn MacDonald; Mabel, British Woman, Glove Model, Child 2, Voice 8 — Jo Jo Rideout; Fred, Happy Gang Leader, Sgt. Major, Joe, Mayor, Voice 3 — Robert Seale; Umbrella Girl; Usell Triplet; Darlene; Queen Elizabeth; Woman 4; Voice 6 — Linda Third; Mabel's Mother, Fashion Show Narrator, Usell Triplet, Japanese Girl, News Reader, Mothers 1, 2 and 3 — Donna White.

Time: The Present. One intermission.

72 UNDER THE O (16). By Allan Stratton. May 2, 1977 (world premiere). Director, Paul Reynolds; designer Judith Lee; lighting, Jeffrey Dallas.

Weldon Plum . . . . Norman Browning
Linda McCloud . . . . Nicola Cavendish
David Pearce . . . . Andrew Gillies
Margaret Bip . . . . Beth Kaplan
George Bip . . . . William Webster

Designers: Scenery and costumes, Judith Lee; lighting, Jeffrey Dallas

Note: Playhouse Theater Center gave 16 performances of *72 Under the O,* May 17-June 11, 1977, throughout British Columbia. Theater-in-Education presented *Interaction* (30) for adults, January-March 1977 and *The Return of the Story Teller* (20) in schools, April-May 1977. Both programs were led by professional actor/teachers.

WINNIPEG, MANITOBA

Manitoba Theater Center: Mainstage

(Artistic director, Arif Hasnain)

TWELFTH NIGHT (29). By William Shakespeare. October 15, 1976. Director, Edward Gilbert; scenery and costumes, Mark Negin; lighting, Nicholas Cernovitch. With Anton Rodgers, Marrie Mumford, Deborah Kipp, Richard Blackburn, Ron O'Krancy, James Blendick, John-Peter Linton, Irene Hogan.

ALL OVER (27). By Edward Albee. November 19, 1976. Director, Arif Hasnain; scenery and costumes, Peter Wingate; lighting, Bill Williams. With Anne Shropshire, Myra Carter, Budd Knapp, Walter Massey, Anne Murray.

RELATIVELY SPEAKING (27). By Alan Ayckbourn. January 7, 1977. Director, Richard Digby Day; scenery and costumes, Peter Wingate; lighting, Robert C. Reinholdt. With Marti Maraden, Peter Dvorsky, Robin Bailey, Irene Hogan.

DAMES AT SEA (27). Book and lyrics by George Haimsohn and Robin Miller; music by Jim Wise. February 11, 1977. Director/choreographer, Voigt Kempson; scenery and costumes, Robert Doyle; lighting, Bill Williams; music director/conductor, Victor Davies. With Trudy Bayne, Edda Gburek, Cynthia Parva, Michael Ricardo, Patrick Young, Don Bradford.

THE CRUCIBLE (27). By Arthur Miller. March 18, 1977. Director, Arif Hasnain; scenery and costumes, Joseph Cselenyi; lighting, Neil McLeod. With James Blendick, Deborah Kipp, Philip Kerr, Alexe Duncan, Cynthia Parva, Sean Sullivan, Robin Bailey.

SHE STOOPS TO CONQUER (27). By Oliver Goldsmith, April 22, 1977. Director, Richard Cottrell; scenery and costumes, Peter Wingate; lighting, Donald Acaster. With R. H. Thomson, Fiona Reid, James Blendick, Ian Deakin, Robin Bailey, Margaret Barton, Zoe Alexander.

Manitoba Theater Center: Warehouse Theater

BERLIN TO BROADWAY WITH KURT WEILL (20). Text and format by Gene Lerner; music by Kurt Weill; arrangements by Newton Wayland; lyrics by Maxwell Anderson, Marc Blitzstein, Bertolt Brecht, Jacques Deval, Michael Feingold, Ira Gershwin, Paul Green, Langston Hughes, Alan Jay Lerner, Ogden Nash, George Tabori, Arnold Weinstein. September 30, 1976. Director Alex Dmitriev; scenery and costumes, Grant Guy; lighting, Bill Williams; music director, Victor Davies. With Ross Douglas, Joan Karasevich, Dorothy Poste, Don Samuels.

CANADIAN GOTHIC and AMERICAN MODERN (15). By Joanna M. Glass. November 25, 1976. Director, Eric Steiner; scenery and costumes, Grant Guy; lighting, Brynn Finer. With Irene Mayeska, Neil Vipond, Janet Barkhouse, Tim Sikeya.

WAITING FOR GODOT (15). By Samuel Beckett. February 24, 1977. Director, Alex Dmitriev; scenery and costumes, Doug McLean; lighting, Bill Williams. With Peter Rogan, Dennis Robinson, George Buza, Clive Endersby, Michael Davis.

ALPHA BETA (15). By E.A. Whitehead. March 31, 1977. Director, Alex Dmitriev; scenery and costumes, Doug McLean; lighting, Bill Williams. With Peter Rogan, Elisabeth LeRoy.

Manitoba Theater Center: Theater for Young Audiences

BEAUTY AND THE BEAST (10). By William Glennon. December 24, 1976. Director, Alex Dmitriev; scenery and costumes, Grant Guy; lighting, Bill Williams. With Janet Laine Green, Tom Butler, Frank Adamson, Alexe Duncan, Gloria Bien, Robert More. (Mainstage matinees)

FABLES HERE AND THEN (40). By David Feldshuh. January 17, 1977. Director, David Calderisi; scenery and costumes, Grant Guy; lighting, Bill Williams; music, Jay Brazeau. With David Bentley, Jay Brazeau, David Gillies, Gina Laight, Lynda Langford, Sharon Noble, Robin Nunn. (Warehouse theater matinees).

Note: After its run at the Warehouse Theater, *Fables Here and Then* toured Northern and Southern Manitoba for two weeks, February 11-23, 1977.

DINNER THEATER

Coming of Age

By Francine L. Trevens

Playwright and co-founder of Readers and Playwrights Theater, Springfield, Mass.

"Dinner theaters have a bright future if unions and management can come to closer terms," predicted Jay Devlin, a frequent headliner in the countrywide dinner theater network. He was expressing a matter on many a manager's mind these days, as theaters fluctuate from Equity to non-Equity, attempting to survive the strange economics of our era. This year, most dinner theaters report heavy to sellout business on weekends. What's more, there are nine more Equity theaters than a year ago, and new theaters continue bravely to open their doors.

The bright news in the field is that more dinner theaters are successfully staging new plays, that these plays often go on to other dinner theaters, stock or publication. Many big names who once turned up their noses at dinner theater, now have whiffed the sweet scent of dollar signs and have appeared on the various proscenium, arena, and thrust stages of this phenomena. Producers find that stars or well-known shows generally draw better than new plays. Nevertheless, many theaters which have been in business over five years find they are running out of light, bright fare the dinner-theater audiences eat up, and are hungry for new plays. Revues have filled many a bill, as have new scripts. Musicals remain the most popular productions for the steak and stage set, not surprising when one acknowledges that the majority of dinner-theater audiences have never gone to other types of live theater.

Northgate in Glen Cove, N.Y. is one of the few theaters that has a separate seating area of 522 in addition to the 540 seats at dinner. It's a large, lavish operation which needs tremendous crowds to keep functioning. Broadway successes hold the stage here.

Florida's Golden Apple Dinner Theater with its total of 292 seats is far cozier and far less cautious in its stage fare. It can even afford to do children's theater as well as premiere plays.

Large theaters can also be successful with new plays. Dallas's Country Dinner Playhouse with its 440 seats premiered Richard Egan in *Hanky Panky* a comedy. Newest dinner theater this year is Peoria's Left Bank Dinner Playhouse, which casts in New York where it keeps its executive offices, much as Windmill Dinner Theaters did seven years ago. Left Bank, under the astute guidance of Jack Batman, opened its 200-seat house in September, 1976 and was delighted when *Dial "M" For Murder* was a big hit in the spring. Batman figured it was because businessmen prefer mysteries to the light comedies most dinner theaters serve as standard fare. Others who tried mysteries in their theaters agree.

Fred Steinharter of the Colonial Tavern Dinner Theater in Oxford, Conn. proudly notes that his professional theater of only 180 seats had one of its two premiere productions published by Samuel French. Pheasant Run Playhouse in St. Charles, Ill. scored a hit this year with Richard Hatch in *P.S. Your Cat is*

Dead, a recent play with a brief Broadway history. Its homosexual questions are a bit different in subject matter than most dinner theaters attempt, although *Norman, Is That You?* has enjoyed tremendous success. The hit of Beverly Dinner Playhouse in Jefferson, La., was *Cat on a Hot Tin Roof* starring Michael Cole.

So this year mysteries, dramas, unusual subjects and premieres all fared well in dinner theaters which surely indicates this kid sister in the theater world has come of age. Major 1976-77 premiere productions were the following:

GOLD DIGGERS OF 1963 (3½ weeks) by Lee Goldsmith; music by Lawrence Hurwit; lyrics by Lee Goldsmith. May 18, 1976. Directed by Robert E. Turoff; scenery Lee Furmak; lighting, Tony Falconer; costumes, Paige Southard; musical direction, Janet Aycock; choreography, Ginger Prince. With Ralston Hill, Kenneth Prescott, Forrest Rankin, Ginger Prince, B. G. Fitzgerald, John Roberson. Golden Apple Dinner Theater, Sarasota, Fla. (Dallas Country Playhouse Aug. 3, 1976 with Hans Conried.)

NEVER GET SMART WITH AN ANGEL (5 weeks) by George Tibbles. May 24, 1976. Directed by Richard Vath; scenery and lighting, Lynn Massingill. With Don Ameche, Mel Miller, Mary Hennessy, Travis Dean, Sarah B., Irwin Charone. Country Dinner Playhouse, Austin, Tex.

THREE ON A RUNWAY (5 weeks) by Donna de Mateo. June 22, 1976. Directed by Carl Stohn Jr; scenery, Jeffrey Harris. With Jerry Stiller, Marlene Paulette, Andrea Braun, Edi Howard. Pheasant Run Playhouse, St. Charles, Ill.

HOT LINE TO HEAVEN (6 weeks) by Larry Maraviglia. Sept. 21, 1976. Directed by Storer Boone; scenery, David Raphael; lighting, S. Stamai. With Pat

O'Brien, Eloise O'Brien, Doug Roberts, Arnold Coty, John Creamer, Francine Segal. Beverly Dinner Playhouse, Jefferson, La.

UP A TREE (6 weeks) by Robert Nichols. Oct. 19, 1976. Directed by Buff Shurr; scenery and lighting, Francisco Vela; costumes, Jo McDaniel. With Ron Scott, Olive Seale, Patsy Magruder, Kirk McClanahan, Michael Donn, E.D. (Bud) Manley, Melonie Magruder. Country Dinner Playhouse, Dallas, Tex.

HANKY PANKY (4½ weeks) by Larry Maraviglia. January 4, 1977. Directed by Richard Vath; scenery and lighting, Francisco Vela. With Richard Egan, Kathleen Singleton, Michael White, Chris Wilson. Country Dinner Playhouse, Dallas, Tex.

RED, HOT AND COLE! (2 weeks+) by Randy Strawderman, Muriel McAuley, James Bianchi; music and lyrics by Cole Porter. May 14, 1977. Directed and choreographed by Randy Strawderman; scenery, Tim Priddy; lighting, David Kilgore; costumes, Lydia Longaker; musical direction, Dougee Zend. With James Bianchi, Nancy Kilgore, Burt Edwards, Tye Heckman. Barksdale Theater, Hanover, Va.

THE TEN
BEST PLAYS

Here are the synopses of 1976–77's ten Best Plays. By permission of the publishing companies which own the exclusive rights to publish these scripts in full in the United States, our continuities include many substantial quotations from crucial/pivotal scenes in order to provide a permanent reference to the style and quality of each play as well as its theme, structure and story line.

Scenes and lines of dialogue, stage directions and descriptions quoted in the synopses appear *exactly* as in the stage version or published scripts unless (in a very few instances, for technical reasons) an abridgement is indicated by five dots (. . . . .). The appearance of three dots (. . .) is the script's own punctuation to denote the timing of a spoken line.

SLY FOX

A Play in Two Acts

BY LARRY GELBART

BASED ON *VOLPONE* BY BEN JONSON

Cast and credits appear on pages 297-298

LARRY GELBART was born in Chicago Feb. 25, 1928 and did his first radio writing at 16 just before his two years' service in the Army in 1945–46. He contributed to Duffy's Tavern, Jack Paar, Jack Carson *and* Bob Hope *on radio 1945–51 and to* Hope, Red Buttons, Sid Caesar *and* Art Carney *on TV 1949–1960. His adaptation of the movies* M*A*S*H *into a TV series is a long-run (about 100 episodes so far) smash hit which he co-produced and has frequently directed. On the large screen his work has included* The Notorious Landlady *(1960),* The Wrong Box *(1966),* Not With My Wife You Don't *(1966),* Little Me *(1968) and* The Ecstasy Business *(1968).*

On Broadway, Gelbart provided the book for The Conquering Hero, *a musical version of the Preston Sturges movie* Hail the Conquering Hero, *which lasted only 8 performances beginning Jan. 16, 1961. His next stage venture was the book (in collaboration with Burt Shevelove), based on works of Plautus, of the extremely successful* A Funny Thing Happened on the Way to the Forum, *which ran for 964 performances beginning May 2, 1962 and won its authors a Tony Award. His second classic-based script,* Sly Fox, *is his first straight play on Broadway. Still another Gelbart play,* Jump, *has been produced in England.*

The collection of Gelbart TV accolades includes Emmy, Sylvania, Peabody, Humanitas and Writers Guild of America Awards. Gelbart is married with three children, makes his home in Ghent, N.Y. and maintains an office in London.

Time: One day in the late 1800s
Place: San Francisco

ACT I

Scene 1: Sly's bedroom

SYNOPSIS: A large canopied bed with curtains is the principal feature of the well-appointed bedroom of Foxwell J. Sly. A short flight of steps leads to an entrance at right. The windows, up center, are shuttered now, and other doors lead into the room up and down left.

Simon Able, Foxwell J. Sly's right-hand man, enters and opens the shutters. He instructs three servants who enter the room after him, "Sweeten the air. His bed is awash in sweat. Mister Sly spent another night in agony. I doubt he slept an hour. The poor bugger gets no rest at all. If he's to die in his sleep, God'll have to be on his toes."

Able cautions the servants to pretend to be all the more cheerful as Sly's condition deteriorates. There is a groan offstage, and Able goes to help his master come into the room, dressed in his nightgown and grimacing in pain. Sly is barely able to thank his servants for their attentions and totter to the bed. But once the servants have left the room and Able assures his master that they have gone, Sly is miraculously "cured" of his ailments.

SLY (*standing up on the bed*): No one's better! No one's more fit! (*Getting out of bed.*) I've got enough health to start another man! Catch me sick with a new day dawning; the bay shimmering like diamonds, the hills as green as cash and the sun the color of gold. Ah, bright, glimmering, warming gold — the centerpiece of the sky! Gold, hiding and teasing under the ground. To find it, to fondle it, the best reason for living. To lie next to it in the earth, the only advantage of dying. (*Crosses up to the window.*) Able. (*As Able crosses to join him.*) Look at those pathetic fools. (*They look down at the scene below.*) Dumber'n their donkeys. They'll do anything for gold. Panhandler, miner, thief — they'll beg, burrow or steal it. Each one burning with a fine, high fever. Night brings no sleep and they dream all through the day, dream of gold, only gold; God with an "l", gold. But I have no need to dream. Mine's come true. I already own what those simps below slobber and kill for. (*Crosses to the chest at the foot of the bed, sits in a chair next to it.*) And my back has yet to bend; I've used only the muscle of my mind. For all that I have, I have gained by wit — using my own and what others lack of it.

> Unlocks the chest, throws it open. Gazing fondly at the gleaming contents of the chest.

This is where gold belongs. Not in the sky above or the earth below, but here with me for the sight of it, the feel of it; here, where it serves the delightful double purpose of enriching me while depriving someone else.

A pensive Able sits on the bed.
Able, what's wrong? I detect a sudden, unseemly lack of greed.
  ABLE: What I feel is pity, sir.
  SLY: Pity? No man pities me.
  ABLE: Pity for the gold — jailed up in there.
  SLY: And you? What would you do with it?
  ABLE: If I had the power, I'd give it wings.
  SLY: Fool! You don't free gold. You coddle it. You nurse it, you love it. Fondle a coin long enough and it begins to feel like skin. Polish your gold and it gets even golder. Able, are you saying that were I to leave you all this in my will — a document I have no need of since they're only for people who are going to die — are you saying you'd get rid of it all?
  ABLE: Every bit! Fast as I could! For the best of all possible uses! For women!

Able runs some of the coins through his fingers. Sly admonishes him that gold is meant to rest quietly while attracting the greedy. "Have you ever seen one coin escape that chest?" Sly challenges Able, who must admit he hasn't, though his master lives lavishly well. Sly needs only to let it be known that he is rich, childless and without an heir, and dying (a rumor spread carefully by Able), and "people fall out of the trees, crawl out of the woodwork, they squeeze through the plumbing to offer you everything."

Indeed, the day's first caller, Lawyer Craven, is already at the door. They get ready for their scene, Able setting out a tray of medications while Sly gets into bed and reassumes his role of a dying man.

Craven enters dressed in black and carrying a briefcase from which he produces a will with the heir's name left blank and a golden goblet as a token of friendship to help persuade the "dying" Sly to fill in Craven's name. Able takes the goblet to Sly and presses it into his trembling hands as Craven comes over to the bed.

  CRAVEN: Dear friend Sly. I've come to wish you health, certainly better than you've enjoyed.
  SLY: I am grateful, sir. I would've thanked you, had I lived.
  CRAVEN: Surely, you still do.
  SLY: Living is all that keeps me from dying. My body is a container of pain; its main ingredient is bile, its chief industry indigestion and my kidneys have gone into business for themselves.
  ABLE: Maybe Mr. Craven's gift'll change your luck, sir.
  SLY (*holding it close to his "failing" eyes*): It's gold, am I right? Gold?
  CRAVEN: If only I could bring you comfort instead.
  SLY: Indeed. What good are my riches now, now that my heart beats only once an hour.
  CRAVEN (*kneels on the chest at the foot of the bed*): Oh, how I pray for you.
  SLY: It cannot last much longer. May the Lord pardon my sins. I was too attached to money and now it suffocates my soul! I have swindled people!
  CRAVEN: You? Never! You are the most honorable man I know in all San Francisco.

SLY: How can I thank God enough for letting me know men like you? Craven, Craven! Good friend — best friend!

Able closes the curtains around the bed. Craven, convinced that Sly is really dying and ready to sign Craven's name to the will, dances for joy. Grudgingly, he gives Able a coin as a down payment for his good will. There is a knock at the door, and a servant enters to inform Able that the money-lender Jethro Crouch has come to call and is being helped up the stairs.

CRAVEN: Crouch! What's that bloodsucker up to? He doesn't take a step except for profit.

ABLE: He's coming to appraise the jewels, the estate. You'd better go.

CRAVEN: And leave that vulture alone with what's to be mine?

ABLE: I'll guard your interests.

    Crouch enters, an ancient, tottering man, supported by a gold-handled cane which he uses at times to thrash out at people.

CRAVEN: Well, Jethro Crouch in the flesh. Or at least what's left of it.

CROUCH: I'm still alive. The Lord's been kind to me.

CRAVEN: God is respectful of his elders.

CROUCH: Spare me, Craven. I know your mind. No better'n your credit!

CRAVEN (*getting ready to leave*): The sight of you is always reassuring, sir. You are absolute proof of life after death. I wish you luck getting across the room.

    He exits. Able goes to door, shuts it.

CROUCH: What's *he* want here?

ABLE: Just hovering, waiting to pick the pocket in Sly's shroud, making lazy circles over the bed.

CROUCH (*parts the bed curtains with his cane, peeks in and cackles*): I love to look at dying men. I've seen so many, but you never see the same one twice. In my eighty years I've buried four brothers, my sisters, father, mother, friends, enemies, a wife I was deeply devoted to, three mistresses and I'm still alive. I been pallbearer to men I seen christened. I watched 'em go from pink babies to blue stiffs.

Apparently Sly's act is good enough to fool even this connoisseur of deathbeds. Crouch prods the supine Sly with his cane, then orders Able to have Sly's will ready so that the moment after Sly dies Crouch can receive twenty thousand dollars in repayment for ten he has lent the dying man. Able flourishes the golden goblet and warns Crouch of Lawyer Craven's pressing for new clauses in the will. Able suggests that Crouch advance his own cause by presenting Sly with the valuable ring he's wearing. Crouch refuses. But when Able opens the chest to put in the goblet, *"Crouch sees the open chest, gold plates and coins shimmering. Almost doubled in half with greed, he beckons to Able as he removes his ring."*

Crouch leaves after pressing the ring and a coin on Able — just in time, because Sly could hardly hold in his laughter another moment. Sly congratu-

ates Able on his performance but takes his coins along with the ring and gob-
et.

SLY: I'll put these against your account.

ABLE (*a wry smile*): Oh, thank you, sir. At this rate, we'll be even in two hundred years.

SLY (*at his desk, writing in his ledger*): Now, now. It wasn't I who misspent
your youth, my boy. I'm not the gambler who changed cash into chips and chips
into chits and handed out enough IOUs to paper the Taj Mahal.

ABLE (*fondly*): Well, whatever I lost at the tables, I'm ahead in memories.
And remember he does.) Champagne for breakfast. Beautiful nights, some last-
ng weeks at a time. Finding surprise cash in forgotten pockets. Green felt
covered with bets; lovelies at my elbow, slender hands at my back. And then, as
hey will, the cards froze, went cold — so cold every King, Queen and Jack went
outh, leaving me for company only threes and fours and all the other vagrants
n the deck.

SLY: You put your trust in luck. I'm not a great believer in either. You'll learn
rom me. Better than in that debtor's prison I took you from. And when you've
aid back all the money I laid out for you . . .

ABLE: Plus interest.

SLY: Only the nominal usury.

ABLE: Of course.

SLY: From then on, you'll play people, not poker. . . .

Able pours wine for Sly into the goblet left by Craven. Sly declares his affec-
ion for Able as "the son I never had" and at the same time voices his utter con-
empt for his hypocritical, greedy victims. The doorbell rings, signaling the
arrival of a third eager victim, the joyless Abner Truckle. Sly leaps back into
bed and reassumes his pose of a dying man.

ABLE (*cheerfully*): Good morning, Mr. Truckle.

TRUCKLE (*the same*): Good morning. Is he dead?

ABLE: He's napping.

TRUCKLE: Again? All he does is nap. What would he miss if he was dead?

ABLE: You can afford patience, sir. You know he means to leave you every-
hing. That's all I work for.

TRUCKLE: How close is he?

ABLE: He prays to God to let him die.

TRUCKLE: I've brought a little something to add power to his prayer.
     Producing a small bottle.
Just one drop in a glass of wine and he'll never sleep more deeply.
     He pours some into Sly's wine glass on the desk.

ABLE: That smells of foul play.

TRUCKLE: It smells of nothing, that's what's so good about it. You can tell
him it's for his rest, you won't be lying.

ABLE: He'll never take it. He has no faith in medicines. I keep trying to get
him a good doctor . . .

HECTOR ELIZONDO, JACK GILFORD, GRETCHEN WYLER, JOHN HEFF

ISHY, TRISH VAN DEVERE AND GEORGE C. SCOTT IN "SLY FOX"

TRUCKLE: For God's sake, no doctors! If a man's going to die, let him die. This long, drawn-out torture; the pain, the agony — how much can I take?
ABLE: I know it's been hell for you, sir.
TRUCKLE: I have a friend! (*Crosses to window, points offstage.*) He works across the road at the ship chandler's. He can put a harpoon through a whale from two hundred feet. Tomorrow morning, get Sly to the window for a breath of air, and bam! (*Smacks his forehead.*) Right through his blow-hole!

Able warns Truckle that he'd better not kill Sly because the will still lacks Sly's signature. And now Lawyer Craven is interfering, dispensing free legal advice. Upset, Truckle reaches for the wine glass absent-mindedly and almost drinks his own poison by mistake. Able stops him and pours the mixture into the street.

Truckle has brought some gold dust with him just in case he needs to reinforce his best-friend status with Sly. Truckle presses the gold into Sly's failing grasp, naming Sly his partner and being rewarded with gasping words of gratitude from the "dying" man.

   Truckle pulls Able aside.
TRUCKLE: Able, he's got to sign the will! He can't last the day! Fetch a notary!
   Pushes Able toward the door.
ABLE: I can't leave him!
TRUCKLE: Go! He's toyed with me long enough! What's mine's been his; now, what's everyone's'll be mine!
ABLE (*thinking fast*): And may you and your most generous wife use it well, sir.
TRUCKLE (*troubled*): Generous? Most generous? My wife?
ABLE (*innocently*): Mrs. Truckle, sir, the apple of many an eye.
TRUCKLE (*reddening*): I'll not have her name on your tongue!
ABLE: But Mrs. Truckle's the toast of the Coast. Market Street's never fuller than when she sashays down to church. They say the only sight nicer'n seeing her approach is watching her going away.
   Truckle, too incensed to speak, tries to strike Able, who dodges.
I'm only repeating what I heard, sir.
TRUCKLE: What you heard is nothing I want to hear! (*A troubled beat.*) When she goes to church, you say?
ABLE (*nods*): Every morning.
TRUCKLE (*snaps*): Who asked you?
ABLE: *You* did.
TRUCKLE: Well, just shut up when you answer!
ABLE: Yes, sir.
TRUCKLE (*crazed, as he storms out door*): I'll teach her to go to church in front of everyone! (*Exits.*)

Sly congratulates Able on his performance. He also suggests that if Mrs. Truckle is such a tasty dish she should be "set before the king." Miss Fancy, the whore who caters to Sly without charge, knocks at the door. Sly makes his escape before she comes in — he means to go out in disguise to get a glimpse of Mrs. Truckle.

Miss Fancy wants very much to see Sly, but Able puts her off on various pretexts. Like the others, Miss Fancy produces a paper she hopes Sly will sign — only this one is a marriage license. She is pregnant and wants a father for her child. Able suggests that Sly is too far gone for such a masquerade and sends her off to try her luck with Jethro Crouch who is also single, very old and very moneyed.

Sly comes back, wearing the disguise of a Chinese servant, which he throws off at once. Sly has seen Mrs. Truckle and is obviously smitten by her, reminding himself of "How cunningly her features rest on that slender, tantalizing neck which thrusts upward from that pillowy bosom. And all of those delicacies above are supported by a pair of hips below so tempting, yet reserved, that they run to hide behind her, thereby creating a bottom that is one, or should I say two, of a kind."

Able reminds his boss of the impossibility of satisfying his desires. Truckle is extremely jealous and Mrs. Truckle impregnable. But Sly insists and offers Able $500 off his debt to think of a way to procure her. Furthermore, Sly wants Abner Truckle to hand her over in person: "My boy, you could drill into Abner Truckle for a year and never strike decent. If you can convince him that he's out of my will unless I have his wife, he'll serve me and the good lady our breakfast in bed."

As for their other victims, Craven has obviously given them his all, but there is more to be had from Jethro Crouch, Sly believes.

ABLE: I can't imagine him parting with another buck.

SLY (*an inspiration*): Then have him give away someone else's! His son's!

ABLE: Cheat his own son? He'll never do it!

SLY: He will! He's as low as Truckle. You're going to learn the underbelly of human nature today, boy. Don't ever think too little of people. There's always a little less to be thought. On your way now. You've got your morning's work cut out.

ABLE: Right. All I have to do is get one man to betray his son and the other to pimp for his wife.

SLY: If it makes it any easier for you . . .

ABLE: Yes?

SLY: You don't have to serve lunch until one.

Blackout.

Scene 2: The Truckle living room

Mrs. Truckle is working at her embroidery frame in a room decorated conspicuously with religious objects. There is a window at right and and archway up left, in which Truckle makes his manic appearance, accusing his wife of sewing out a message to someone. He notices that the window is open and suggests that she's been hanging out of it, showing passers-by her body. He shuts and wedges it closed, without interrupting his tirade: "My God, two eyes are too few to watch over one wife! A man's got to be rich! They steal poor men's brides. If I had money, *real* money; if Sly would only breathe his last foul breath! I'll have the windows walled up, buy me a house with a garden on the *inside* where you can breathe your head off with no lechers peeking up your nostrils!"

There is a knock on the door. Truckle sends his wife to her room before admitting Able who has come with bad news: Sly has had "a sudden attack of health" and is much improved. Now he wants a women, but Able fears that making love might kill him. Get him two women, Truckle advises, "and we can bury him in an hour with a smile on his face!"

Able warns Truckle that Lawyer Craven has offered to deliver his 16-year old virgin daughter to Sly, a gift so precious that Truckle can no longer hope to remain the principal object of Sly's affection and beneficiary of his will. Truckle gets the message, but his tongue and throat will not form the words he stutteringly tries to speak: "Mrs. Truckle, my wi . . . , my wi . . . my wife."

Truckle manages to persuade himself that it's his duty to help his friend: "Surely, I can do as well by my friend as any common opportunist. Go! Tell Sly that out of reverence for our friendship, I'll bring Mrs. Truckle to him."

Able congratulates Truckle on this stroke of policy and departs. When Mrs. Truckle enters, Truckle is all soothing words and consideration. Finally Truckle informs her that they are going calling.

MRS. TRUCKLE: Where? On who?

TRUCKLE: My friend, Foxwell Sly. To show you how true I know you to be, I'll leave you at his side to nurse him, to minister to him with these little fingers on your saintly hands.

MRS. TRUCKLE: He means this much to you?

TRUCKLE: His life is very valuable to me. I can't even *guess* how much. Perhaps your piety and your virtue will restore him.

MRS. TRUCKLE: This is a great honor you pay me, husband.

TRUCKLE: I'll get mine. Let's go.

MRS. TRUCKLE: First, I must pray.

TRUCKLE (*impatiently*): *Now?*

MRS. TRUCKLE: I must pray to the Madonna.

TRUCKLE: Not now!

MRS. TRUCKLE: I must thank her for sending me on this mission.

TRUCKLE: You can pray on the way! Come, come!

MRS. TRUCKLE (*starting for archway*): I'll need my Bible.

TRUCKLE: He's got a Bible. I looked at it; it's just like yours. "In the beginning God created . . . " Right?
Blackout.

Scene 3: Crouch's office

Crouch, jeweler's loop hung around his neck, is closing the safe in an office that is a dusty disarray of ledgers, papers, etc. His Chinese servant announces the arrival of Miss Fancy. The servant then ushers her in and exits.

MISS FANCY: It's swell of you to give me your valuable time, Mister Crouch.

CROUCH: Time's not as valuable as money. There's many's got more years than dollars.

MISS FANCY: How wise you are.

CROUCH: I knew that before you came. State your business.

MISS FANCY: Mind if I sit, sir?

CROUCH: Sit, sit, sit.

> *He nods at the divan. In sitting, Miss Fancy notices something behind it, screams loudly and jumps to her feet.*

MISS FANCY: Is that a dead cat?

CROUCH: You know what it costs to feed 'em? Sit, sit!

Miss Fancy tells Crouch a tale: she is rich and pretty but tired of the world's ways. She's thinking of entering a nunnery and wants to turn her jewels into money to give to the nuns. She holds out a ring for Crouch to appraise. He takes a square of green felt, comes over to the divan, sits beside Miss Fancy, examines the ring on the spread-out felt and finds it of the highest quality. "It's only one of the little ones daddy left me," Miss Fancy murmurs, meanwhile stroking Crouch's leg. He can feel it, but he gets no ideas from it.

CROUCH (*returns the ring*): What else you want to sell?

MISS FANCY: How 'bout this?

> *She opens her dress a bit, baring a good deal of bosom and coming even closer to him.*

CROUCH (*squinting at chain through his glass*): Gold . . . heavy gold . . .

MISS FANCY: The medallion's the real prize. (*Addressing the medallion.*) Let's go, little bird. (*Purrs to Crouch.*) Doesn't want to leave its warm nest.

> *Pulls the medallion slowly, tantalizingly, out of her bodice.*

CROUCH: Mmmm.

MISS FANCY (*edging closer*): Take a *good* look.

> *Crouch lays his square of green felt on her bare chest, using it as a work surface, then looks at the medallion through his glass.*

CROUCH: You've got some nice things.

MISS FANCY: Thank you. And what about the jewelry?

CROUCH: Worth five thousand easily. I'd give you three for it right now.

Even though she insists that Crouch replace the medallion between her breasts, he remains all businesslike. Her increased efforts to seduce him merely put him to sleep. Miss Fancy gives up. The servant enters to announce Able, who pays his respects to Miss Fancy as she departs.

Able warns Crouch that Truckle and Craven are pressing upon Sly gifts more valuable than Crouch's ring. Crouch insists he has no more wealth to bestow on Sly, and Able suggests that it would be the ultimate gesture of friendship for Crouch to make Sly his sole heir. He would thus disinherit his son, but only briefly. Sly cannot last the night, Able attests, and Crouch's son would be twice as rich by morning.

Crouch's greed is such that he is almost running as he goes off to have a new will notarized. Able is congratulating himself on the success of his mission when Crouch's son (a captain, *"big, brusque exaggeratedly military"*) enters, sees Able and calls him "scum" and "lackey." Able defends himself as "one of those picked out by God himself to see the world doesn't get boring," but the Captain is not amused or impressed.

CAPTAIN (*dumping Able on divan*): *Worm!* is your vanity so pumped up by favor seekers, you've forgotten how to show respect for second generation wealth?

ABLE (*snaps*): Too bad you'll never see a penny of it!

CAPTAIN: And what is that meant to convey?

ABLE: I'm afraid you'd be miserable if you knew. Which is probably the best reason for telling you. (*Pause.*) As everyone knows, your old man's very rich.

CAPTAIN: For a fact.

ABLE: He doesn't spend a wrong buck.

CAPTAIN: Right.

ABLE: Any doubts were dispelled when he buried your mother in a fruit box.

CAPTAIN: So?

ABLE: Naturally, you reckon you'll get it all when he dies, but I know better.

CAPTAIN: What?!

ABLE: At this moment, he's preparing to cut you out of his will, to make someone else his only heir.

CAPTAIN: You're lying!

ABLE: Ordinarily, that'd be true. But not today.

The Captain, dumfounded, demands proof. He chases Able up the stairs and out. *Blackout.*

Scene 4: Sly's bedroom

The room is empty until Able comes in, followed by the Captain. Able hides him behind one of the doors so that he can hear all that follows. Sly enters and hears from Able that both Crouch and Truckle are on their way, one with his will and the other with his wife.

Truckle arrives first and pretends to be glad to see Sly sitting up. Truckle suggests, however, that Sly make pretense of being in bed sick so that his wife will have no suspicion of Sly's real intentions. Sly obliges only too happily. Truckle brings in his wife who, seeing the "desperately sick" man, immediately suggests praying to the Madonna to make him well and frighten away all bad thoughts.

Meanwhile, Able is troubled because Truckle came first and not Crouch — Able doesn't want the hiding Captain to overhear Sly's lovemaking. Able goes off to try to rearrange matters. He soon comes back, obviously having received a swift kick from the Captain, still in his place of concealment.

Able departs with Truckle, leaving Mrs. Truckle alone in the bedroom with Sly. Sly bids her come closer; finally she is close enough so Sly can take her hand.

MRS. TRUCKLE: Grandmother Violet in Boston, when she was aged and plagued by gout, always used to lay little dogs on her legs and it never failed to help her. Let me bring you another blanket.

SLY (*not realeasing her hand*): Do you *really* want me to get better, my dear?

MRS. TRUCKLE: Oh, surely, sir. I'll say five Hail Marys for you and three Our Fathers.

SLY: Forget about Marys, Fathers and covering me with puppies. I know a magic cure. It was taught me by a hundred-year-old Indian who died on his wedding night.

MRS. TRUCKLE: Truly?

SLY: Put your hand here — under the quilt — now, move it lightly and think only the kindest of thoughts.

MRS. TRUCKLE (*complying, tentatively*): I never heard of this.

SLY (*moving her hand with his*): It's written out on buffalo skin. We can read it later. (*Enjoys the proceedings a moment, then:*) Ah, yes, very good.

MRS. TRUCKLE: I'm doing it right?

SLY: Lightly, lightly. Are you thinking kind thoughts?

MRS. TRUCKLE (*nods*): Thoughts of virtue, sir.

SLY: Suit yourself.

MRS. TRUCKLE (*surprised*): Am I mistaken, sir?

SLY: Not yet.

MRS. TRUCKLE: You seem to be getting stronger.

SLY: Yes.

MRS. TRUCKLE: . . . and stronger.

SLY: Mmm . . . (*He sits up.*)

MRS. TRUCKLE (*startled*): Sir! You have risen!

SLY Let me count the ways!

MRS. TRUCKLE: It's a miracle! Madonna, a miracle!

Mrs. Truckle tries to get Sly to lie back, but he keeps groping for her with ever-increasing strength. Mrs. Truckle wants to make a votive offering for the miracle, and she looks around for a candle. She goes to find one in the armoire, not realizing that Sly has gotten out of bed and is following her across the room. Unknowingly, she knocks Sly down when she opens the armoire door. Sly gathers himself together and jumps at her; still unknowingly, she moves aside so that Sly sails past her and bounces off the bed onto the floor. Now she sees him, and, thinking he's just fallen out of bed, goes to help him.

Sly tries to take further advantage of Mrs. Truckle, but at this moment the irate Captain, who has been listening at the door, bursts into the room, interrupts the proceedings and shouts for the police. Able rushes in. The Captain grabs him and pins him to the chest at the foot of the bed, as the Police Chief and two policeman enter to see what is the matter.

CAPTAIN: I want to prefer charges!

CHIEF: Which charges do you prefer?

CAPTAIN: I caught that degenerate lump in a sexual assault on this good woman!

CHIEF (*crossing to Mrs. Truckle*): Rape is a very serious charge ma'am. I'll want to know all the details. You might have to repeat them several times, *slowly*. I'll want to know about his hot, probing hands and how you fought and scratched him as your own breath became very hot and both of you were panting, panting heavily and you scratched his hot face with your sharp nails and then you rolled across the carpet, your body tumbling over his, your hot cheeks on fire —

MRS. TRUCKLE: I never did that!

CHIEF (*eagerly*): Would you like to?

MRS. TRUCKLE: I was here to offer a prayer.

ABLE: Right! It was a little religious frenzy, that's all! Just some good-natured praying!

CHIEF: Who're you?

CAPTAIN: He set the whole scene up! They both should hang!

ABLE (*pointing to Sly*): See for yourself, sir. The man can't stand, let alone swing!

          Truckle enters, overhearing.

CHIEF (*to policemen, regarding Sly*): Fetch his servants to carry him!

TRUCKLE (*as policemen exit*): Is he dead?

MRS. TRUCKLE: Oh, Abner!

          She runs into his arms.

CHIEF: Are you the husband of the rapee?

TRUCKLE: The what-ee?

CAPTAIN: Yes, he's the husband! And he *brought* her here to be ravaged! I heard it all!

CHIEF (*eager once more*): You did? You remember any of the words?

ABLE (*to Sly, explaining the Captain's presence*): He forced his way in. He forced me to hide him!

          Crouch enters, waving a document.

CROUCH: I've got it! Here's my new will!! (*Seeing the Captain.*) Sonny boy!

CAPTAIN (*grabbing the will*): Give me that, you old poop! (*Scanning the will.*) " . . . being of sound mind and body . . . " (*To Crouch.*) If you had *anything* like the first, you'd know you don't have the second!

Servants and police enter, and the former prepare Sly to be carried off to jail. Sly is upset by the thought that his chest with its precious contents must be left behind in the custody of the police. The servants blindly follow Able's orders to preserve a cheerful mien, telling Sly how wonderful he looks as they carry him out. *Blackout Curtain.*

ACT II

Scene 1: A jail cell

Behind bars, Sly and Able receive a visit from Miss Fancy who has a proposition to save Sly from hanging for rape: sign her marriage license application and she'll testify that "the only way a man sick as you could make love was to be raised and lowered on a pulley." She departs to let Sly think it over.

The prisoners' next caller is Lawyer Craven, who informs them that the Captain is pressing charges. Craven offers to defend Sly; his fee is to be named Sly's sole heir. Sly agrees (and the defense will include Able, whose fate is tied to Sly's).

Craven warns them the court has been plagued lately with an unfortunate string of honest judges. The one they'll appear before is one of the worst, "A Baptist of the first water, a man with the strength of countless convictions." Before leaving, Craven advises Sly to look as frail and sick in court as he can manage.

Sly declares that he will be a changed man if he gets out of this fix, no longer covetous, promising to give all his wealth to charity, and observing: "Good God! I wonder what poor people use for promises?" *Blackout.*

Scene 2: The courtroom

The courtroom in which Sly is to be tried is *"in fact, a saloon with the furniture rearranged. Craven enters, looking for Truckle. A handcuffed Able is brought to the defendant's table. The Captain, Miss Fancy, the Police Chief and the Bailiff enter. The Court Clerk, who will record the proceedings in a painfully slow hand, sits sharpening his quill with a pocket knife. The Bailiff straightens the Judge's papers on the table that sits on the saloon stage and serves as the Judge's bench. Spectators enter and seat themselves."*
Truckle insists to Craven that no injury was done his wife and therefore her name should not be mentioned in these proceedings. Crouch enters, and Craven suggests Crouch testify that the will disinheriting his son was merely his little joke to please a dying man, not a request of Sly's. Craven warns both Truckle and Crouch that if Sly is found guilty and hanged his entire estate could become the property of the court.

The Judge enters and sits high above the crowd on the "bench" at left. He is played by the same actor who is playing Sly. In his Judge's role he is muscular and commanding, with jet-black hair and moustache, booted and dressed in black in the frontier manner. As the Judge sits, so does everyone else except Craven.

CRAVEN: Your Honor!
JUDGE: Sit down!
CRAVEN: But I am the lawyer for the defendant.
JUDGE: That's *your* red wagon! Sit down!
　　　Bangs his gavel. Craven sits.
Now, we have before us a very trying case. All the way back to Biblical times of yore, rape has been one of the most heinous offenses known to man. And it can be pretty rough on women, too.
　　　The courtroom breaks into laughter. The Judge disapproves.
I'm warning everybody present here that, because of the delicate nature of this charge, I won't put up with anyone sniggering so much as a titter.

Consulting his papers.

Do we have all the witnesses that have been cited in this, the case of the Territory versus Foxwell J. Sly and his servant, Simon Able; the second, the accomplice of the first, who is accused by Captain Luther Crouch of the alleged molestation of Mrs. Abner Truckle?

CRAVEN (*rising*): Everyone is present, Your Honor, except for Mr. Sly, who languishes in his cell, his life hanging by a mere thread.

JUDGE: *I* decide who hangs by what around here! (*To Bailiff.*) Fetch the defendant!

Bailiff starts to exit, stops.

CRAVEN: It would be impossible for His Honor to be impartial were you to see him. His presence will move the court to tears. His quivering pale blue lips will stir your pity.

CAPTAIN (*jumping up*): Rot! He's getting paid by the lie!

JUDGE (*banging his gavel*): Sit down! I object to your interruption and my objection is sustained! Sit down!

The Captain does so. The Bailiff goes out on his errand. At the Judge's command, the Police Chief tries to tell what happened, but he has to admit. "On looking around there was no sex act to be seen anywhere. Which is pretty much the way my luck's been running lately."

Mrs. Truckle sobs into her handkerchief. The Captain takes credit for stopping Sly before any act could take place. Able was there too (the Police Chief testifies) and so was Miss Fancy.

The Captain is asked to testify and tells the court he had learned his father was going to disinherit him and hid in Sly's house to try to find out why. While he was hidden, the incident under scrutiny took place.

The Judge asks Mrs. Truckle for her view. She tells the court that she made physical contact with Sly, massaging his bare chest under his nightgown. Her testimony so inflames the Police Chief that he tries to tear her clothes off, then regains control of himself and apologizes. Mrs. Truckle continues her testimony: while she was stroking Sly, a "miracle" happened. "His strength arose!"

JUDGE (*aside, to Clerk*): The woman's a bimbo. (*To Mrs. Truckle.*) What happened then? Did he insist his body on yours? Did he force himself husbandlike upon you?

MRS. TRUCKLE: A husband is different, Your Honor. A wife expects him to force himself on her. That's a good Christian marriage.

JUDGE: But he behaved like a animal?

MRS. TRUCKLE: Only on our wedding night. He wanted to keep a light on.

JUDGE: I was talking about Sly.

MRS. TRUCKLE (*flustered*): Oh, let me go home, Your Honor! My shame is unbearable!

TRUCKLE (*rising, taking Mrs. Truckle back to her seat*): Both our shames, sir. This has been a big day for us, shamefully speaking.

JUDGE: You must be Mister Truckle.

TRUCKLE: Yes, sir! I must. I have no other choice.

JUDGE: How do you come to know Foxwell Sly?

TRUCKLE (*taking the stand*): I'm an accountant, sir. I mind other people's business. For some time now, I've looked after Sly's affairs.

JUDGE: And did it ever occur to you he might want to make out of your own wife one of them?

TRUCKLE: Never! If even then. The man is a saint. I trust him as I would have my own brother, if I hadn't had only sisters, except one was very masculine.

JUDGE: Mister Sly is very wealthy, is he not?

TRUCKLE: I'm sure I don't know.

JUDGE (*bearing down*): Didn't you say you were his accountant?

TRUCKLE: That's right, I did. And he's very wealthy.

JUDGE: Were you interested in getting your hands on his money?

TRUCKLE: Most of his money I gave him. What reason would I have?

JUDGE: To get it back!

TRUCKLE: Yes. That would be a reason.

JUDGE: To get your own back — and more.

TRUCKLE (*worried*): What is His Honor suggesting, Your Honor?

JUDGE: That the Captain's charge is true! That you delivered your own wife for another man's abusement!

TRUCKLE: False!

CAPTAIN (*jumping up*): I heard you! (*Pointing at Able.*) And that one arranged it!

ABLE: *I* did?

CRAVEN: With *Truckle?*

ABLE: A husband *that* jealous?

CRAVEN: To the point of insanity?

TRUCKLE: I am! (*Crossing to Mrs. Truckle.*) Tell the Judge! Have I ever let another man see so much as your ankles?

MRS. TRUCKLE: He bought me chastity shoes!

CRAVEN (*to the Captain*): *Now* who's the liar?!

CAPTAIN (*reaching for his sword*): Shut your cakehole or I'll cut you up for jerky!

JUDGE (*bangs gavel*): Order! Order! One more outburst, Captain, and I'll hold you in even more contempt than I do now! Sit down!

CAPTAIN (*crossing to the bench*): Your Honor, understand my anger. (*Producing a document.*) My father's will, signed by his own hand, cutting me off without a cent!

JUDGE (*studying the will*): Mm . . .

CRAVEN (*whispers hoarsely*): Mr. Crouch! You're on!

CROUCH (*rising and crossing to the bench*): Your Honor, I am Jethro Crouch.

JUDGE: The father of the Captain.

CROUCH (*salutes*): Yes, sir!

JUDGE: Pretty fishy business, this will, Crouch.

CROUCH: I can explain, Your Honor. Sly is very dear to me.

CAPTAIN (*shouts*): Dearer than a son!

CROUCH (*to the Captain*): Please! (*To the Judge.*) The navy's made him so cranky! That will was for Sly's benefit.

JUDGE: Obviously.

CROUCH: But I wasn't serious. It was meant as a joke.

JUDGE: A joke?

CROUCH: Yes, sir.

JUDGE: You find death funny?

CROUCH: Yes, sir. In the daytime.

JUDGE: Well the humor of it escapes me.

ABLE (*rising*): He did it to cheer Sly up, sir. To make the poor man think he'd outlived him.

CROUCH (*to the Judge*): What he said is what I meant.

ABLE: And I in turn, Your Honor, enjoyed the little joke of fooling the Captain. I thought I'd make him jealous, let him hear it all acted out, but it was all a joke, Your Honor, honest. (*To the Clerk.*) Put that down: "It was all a joke."

CLERK (*writing, mutters*): " . . . the woman's a bimbo . . . "

A cot is wheeled onstage. On it, covered up, is what purports to be Sly, apparently more dead than alive. The Captain draws his sword and prepares to test Sly's masquerade of illness. Police restrain him, but the courtroom is thrown into confusion by Mrs. Truckle's screams when the Police Chief bares his chest to her.

After the Judge manages to restore order, Craven calls a surprise witness — Miss Fancy, whose marriage application the desperate Sly has signed. Miss Fancy testifies that she and Sly were once intimate, but as his illness progressed he became incapable of a physical relationship: "On our last nights together I would just read to him."

Crouch and Truckle chime in with praise of Sly, and the Judge finally comes to a decision: the rape testimony has been contradicted by the very husband of the supposed victim, and "the miserable condition of the accused makes the possibility of a act of sex dependent only on a act of God." The Judge finds Sly and Able not guilty. The spectators applaud the verdict — except for the Captain, who protests that the witnesses were perjurers and the Judge himself may have been bribed in the bargain. The Judge, indignant, sentences the Captain to 60 days and the police drag him away, still making angry noises.

JUDGE (*to the Clerk*): He's sucking around for a noose! (*To Able, gesturing to Sly.*) Better get him home. If he don't make it, my funeral parlor's right next door. Court's adjourned!

> He exits. All immediately crowd around Sly and follow his cot as it is wheeled off by police.

MISS FANCY: My darlin' Sly . . .

CRAVEN: Did you hear me defend you? I saved your life.

CROUCH: I saved some of it, too!

TRUCKLE: It was *my* words saved you! I told every kind of truth!

MISS FANCY: You don't have to move. We can be married lyin' down.

MRS. TRUCKLE: With it all, how I pity the man. I will pray for him.

TRUCKLE (*moving her*): Don't pray so close, my dear.

ABLE (*watches them go; then turns to the audience*): They'll never cease to amaze me. Each had so much to gain, had the judge found us guilty, as indeed we are. Each could've retrieved through the court what Sly's pulled through their noses. Yet, each, as a witness, was as false as his smile. Any amusement they've given me is giving way to fear. Jail today, the docket. If the stakes are going to be raised this high, it's time I had more say in the game. The longer I play it this way, the longer I'm in danger. The longer I'm used as someone's pawn, the longer I could be —

CLERK (*still writing*): " . . . sucking around for a noose . . . "
    Blackout.

Scene 3: Sly's bedroom

Sly enters, dressed in a sumptuous robe and carrying a carpetbag, followed by Able. Able is happy about their escape, but Sly realizes what a close shave it was. He instructs Able about packing the bag and leaving "before that flock of vultures flies in for the payoff." In the case of Miss Fancy, Sly has some protection in the form of documentary proof that he already has a wife, in Toledo.

Sly plans to depart for Africa, where "there are diamonds in the ground. . . . and the same fools walk the earth above." First, though, he wants one last crack at his San Francisco dupes. He instructs Able to spread the news of Sly's death. The would-be heirs are to be summoned for the reading of the will, which is to make Able sole beneficiary. Able is afraid the victims will turn on him, but Sly disagrees: "They'll fly to their lawyers! Their lawyers'll fly to lawyers! By the time the dust settles, you and I will be aboard our clipper, dining at the captain's table, seeing if we can't talk him out of his wheel."

Able is afraid they are pressing their luck. Sly insists, pulls the cord for the servants and gets into bed with his carpetbag. Able closes the bed curtains, then stares reflectively at Sly's will on the desk.

Able strikes a pose of respectful grief, as the servants enter and are told that their master is dead. The servants are sent off to spread the news of Sly's death, while Able sits at the desk to inventory Sly's possessions.

First to arrive and ask about the will is Craven, soon followed by Truckle and Mrs. Truckle. Crouch is not far behind. Each is certain that Sly's estate is to be his alone.

TRUCKLE (*to Crouch*): Come to buy and bargain, have you?

CRAVEN: Nothing here's for sale.

CROUCH: Me, buy? I've got all I want! The only thing I need is more! (*Cackles.*) I came to hear the will! The will's the words — in there's the music!
    He raps the chest with his cane.

TRUCKLE: Of course! The will! Able, read us the will!

CROUCH: Yes, the will!

CRAVEN: Wait! We can't read it yet.

TRUCKLE: Why not?

CROUCH (*overlapping*): Why?

CRAVEN: We need a witness from the court, everything must be done legal-like.

CROUCH: Since when?
TRUCKLE: I waited long enough.
CROUCH: Time is money!

Able sends a servant off to fetch the Judge. Miss Fancy comes in and suspects Sly may be shamming, but Able manages to prevent her from opening the bed curtains to investigate. Crouch suggests holding a lighted match to the soles of Sly's feet. Truckle favors a stab in the heart just to make sure, but before they can take any action the Judge strides in.

Craven attests that the will is genuine. The Judge breaks the seal on the will and reads: "I name as my sole heir . . . to be the unconditional possessor of all my goods and gold, my beloved companion . . . and faithful servant — Simon Able." The others are stunned, except for Miss Fancy, who transfers her attentions to Able at once.

CROUCH (*bangs his cane*): This is treachery!
TRUCKLE (*seizing the will*): This document is a forged fake!
CRAVEN: I contest it!
JUDGE: You just said you wrote it!
CRAVEN: Well, I wrote it, but I didn't write *it*.
TRUCKLE: Something's rotten here! Sly absolutely assured me I was to inherit it all!
CROUCH: He assured me the same!
TRUCKLE (*gathering Sly's clothes, cushions, anything*): No! only *me*!
CROUCH: You lie! Sly and *I* were the only me!
CRAVEN: Wrong! I am the only only! I was his friend! His *best* friend!
CROUCH: I was a *better* best friend.
TRUCKLE: *I* was the closest! I gave him all kinds of gifts!
CROUCH: You gave him crap! I know! I sold whatever you gave him and I only sold you crap! *I* gave him gold, jewelry, a fortune . . . my *whole* fortune! Willed him everything, disinherited my own son!
TRUCKLE: Your son! *I* gave him Mrs. Truckle; gave him my own wife!
JUDGE: What? Is that true?
TRUCKLE (*not realizing the implications*): I swear it!
JUDGE: But you swore the opposite in court!
TRUCKLE (*flustered*): I probably didn't understand the question!

The angry Judge orders a policeman to go get the obviously innocent Captain out of jail. The Judge threatens to hang everybody, including Sly even though he's already dead. Furthermore, if the will turns out to be invalid the court will put Sly's estate to good use.

Able saves the situation by reporting Sly's dying words: ' "Give back all I stole from my friends,' he said. 'Beg them to forgive me so I can face them when we meet once more. I make you my heir so you can give back all the silver, the gold, the jewels I stole.' I promised I would. Only as his heir can I keep that sacred vow."

Grasping for their third of a loaf, each of the three would-be heirs does an about-face and agrees that the will is a valid document. Since there is no objection, the Judge validates it. Able begs the Judge to spare Sly's remains any indignity and let Able bury them. The Judge agrees, commenting, "You can throw the stiff in the bay for all I care," as he exits.

The Captain bursts in, now wearing a prison uniform and hell-bent to avenge himself on Sly. Able sends him off with Miss Fancy to pamper him with a warm and soothing bath to cleanse his body and calm his nerves. Able invites the others to a farewell feast in Sly's honor at 8:30 that evening, "a real send-off for the man we all agree died for the best — ours!" The others leave, now friends with Able and looking forward to the celebration.

Alone in the room with Able, Sly steps from the bed and congratulates his manservant on his fine performance. They have a carriage waiting at the back, and Sly organizes the packing of his possessions.

SLY (*handing Able Craven's goblet*): And be sure to leave room for this little beauty.

ABLE: No. No, I don't think so.

SLY: Pardon?

ABLE: The goblet's part of the estate, sir. It cannot be removed.

SLY: Very amusing. Remind me to laugh on the boat. Come now, boy, it's time to move.

ABLE: Move if you like, sir. (*A beat.*) But I'm not leaving my house.

SLY: ... *Your* house?

ABLE: And all that's in it. As you heard at the reading of the will. Along with the witnesses. *And* His Honor.

SLY: I see. You figure I did myself in.

ABLE: Who else but you could've outfoxed you?

SLY: It won't work, Able.

ABLE: What can you do? Haul me into court? If that judge you double-tweaked today finds out you're still alive, he'll sentence you to life in front of a firing squad. No, sir, I'm afraid that out of the mob of sole and only heirs, I am the sole and onliest, if I so choose.

SLY: And, of course, you do.

ABLE: I am neither Craven nor Truckle, sir, and centuries away from being Crouch.

Opening desk drawer.

The IOU's are my prize. All I want is to own the face I see in the mirror once more.

SLY (*tearing up the IOUs*): These are all you want? I certainly owe you no less. You could have gone for the whole works.

ABLE: Owning myself is more than enough.

SLY: Well done, Able! Not only am I pleased that you're your own man again; I'm particularly proud that you swindled me to do it.

ABLE: Thank you, sir.

SLY: Now let's get going! (*Nodding at door.*) Miss Fancy can't keep swabbing the Captain's deck forever. You'd better take one of my coats. It gets cold as hell out at sea.

ABLE: I won't need one. (*Beat.*) I won't be going.

Able informs his master he's lost the taste for fraud, he's tired of looking at only the seamier side of everybody. Sly hates to break up such a good team, but he sees that Able really means it. Good naturedly, Sly wishes Able luck and Able returns the compliment. Sly turns to go.

ABLE (*noticing Craven's goblet on the desk*): Sir, the goblet.
SLY (*refusing it, graciously*): Think of it as a graduation gift.
ABLE: Thank you, Mister Sly.
SLY (*correcting him*): Ah, ah. Wrong again.
          He takes a business card from his pocket and hands it to Able.
ABLE (*reads, quizzically*): "The Reverend Slywell J. Fox?"
SLY (*explaining*): A new place, a new name. (*Gesturing toward bed.*) After all, Foxwell J. Sly *is* dead. (*He heads for the door again.*)
ABLE (*reminding him*): Sir, the chest!
SLY (*at the door*): Chest? (*Grandly.*) There are chests all over the world waiting to be filled!
          He exits, closing the door behind him. A beat, then Able, intrigued,
          crosses to the chest and opens it. It is empty. Sly reenters.
SLY: There's only one way to take it with you, my boy. (*Beat.*) Send it on ahead.
          Curtain.

ASHES

A Play in Three Acts

BY DAVID RUDKIN

Cast and credits appear on pages 336-337

DAVID RUDKIN was born in England in 1936 and was educated at King Edward's School and St. Catherine's College, Oxford. His first play, Afore Night Come *was written in 1960 and won him the London* Evening Standard *award for most promising playwright when produced by Royal Shakespeare Company at New Arts, London, in 1962. There followed* Burglars *(1968, a play for children),* The Fifth Hunt *(1972),* Ashes *(1974, produced by the Open Space in London),* The Sons of Light *(a Wagnerian epic produced by Tyneside Theater Company of Newcastle in 1976) and in 1977 an adaptation of* Hecuba *put on by Royal Shakespeare. Rudkin's work for other media has included collaboration on the* Fahrenheit 451 *movie script with Francois Truffaut and on the adaptation of Genet's* Mademoiselle *with Tony Richardson. He has adapted Aeschylus and Euripedes for radio presentation, translated a number of operas and his many TV credits include* Cries From Casement as His Bones Are Brought to Dublin *(1973) and* Brenda's Pen *(1974).*

Rudkin's only previous American productions were Afore Night Come *at the Long Wharf Theater in New Haven in 1975 and* Ashes *at the Mark Taper Forum in Los Angeles in 1976 and at Manhattan Theater Club off off Broadway prior to its professional New York premiere at New York Shakespeare Festival. Rudkin is married and lives in England.*

Time: Now

Place: England

ACT I

SYNOPSIS: There is no formal setting. A movable raised platform serves symbolically as bed, sofa, etc. Traverse curtains at mid-stage divide the playing area as needed. A desk, three plain chairs, a lounger, a waste basket and some small pieces of medical equipment become part of the environment as required.

The stage is in darkness, but voices can be heard of a man and woman making love. They are Colin (*"early 30s, Northern Irish, was a writer, now a teacher"*) and Anne (*"late 20s, his wife, West Riding, was an actress, now a teacher"*). We will see later that they are *"an averagely presentable couple, neither sexually glamorous nor pathetically unprepossessing. Colin cared more how he dressed five years ago: a good pair of unflared corduroys he wore for best then, he uses at work today; plain shirt, tie, quilted anorak, hush puppies. Anne had more style, but now they live far from shops and have less money — a neutral grey smock, fashionable once, now she knocks about in."* One actor and one actress play all the other characters they encounter, which has no thematic significance but is in keeping with the play's atmosphere of frugality.

Colin and Anne are obviously enjoying their lovemaking. Once it is finished, however, she soon persuades him to shift his weight.

> *Sounds of them shifting. Long pause.*

ANNE: Perhaps we did it this time.

> *Snap up stagelight. White traverse curtain masks all but Anne's half of the bed, on which Anne lies supine, head toward us, bare legs raised in a coital posture. Doctor — fresh-faced, early 30s, slight hint of the farmer — gently, firmly palps her lower belly to feel that everything is in its proper place.*

DOCTOR (*faintest last trace of rural speech; frank, unpatronizing*): How long have you and your husband been trying for a conception, Mrs. Harding?

ANNE: Two years.

DOCTOR: Then you *do* have a problem. Forgive me: are you doing it right?

ANNE: Do we look fools?

DOCTOR: I've had couples trying to conceive through the navel.

> *Manipulates; palps.*

No sign of damage or deformity, no displacement. . . . Very nice set of organs, Mrs. Harding; compact. . . . Your husband is potent, you say; your blood groups compatible; your cycle short and regular —

ANNE (*bitter*): Clockwork.

DOCTOR: Which I like. Well. First I think we should take a PC sample —

ANNE: Post-coital.

DOCTOR (*surprised she knows*): Have you been a nurse?

ANNE: No.

DOCTOR (*pause; comes away, peels off a disposable glove into the waste basket*): Well you can probably work out for yourselves what a post-coital test involves. Round about the tenth or eleventh day of your next cycle —

The stage darkens again and an alarm clock rings. It is very early morning. Colin and Anne must rouse themselves to make love again, by the clock, to provide the laboratory with "a characteristic sample of our mixture."

When the lights come up, the doctor is inserting a medical implement between Anne's raised legs, taking a smear with the help of a white-coated aide, Jennifer, who sets the slide in the microscope. Examining it, the doctor concludes that all the spermatozoa are dead, so now it is Colin's turn to be examined.

The screen is drawn, masking Anne and revealing Colin naked, waiting to have his genitals examined. The doctor draws another part of the curtain to preserve Colin's privacy except for the vague image of a standing man seen through the translucent material. The doctor finds everything in order; there is no apparent reason why Colin's semen should be useless. He gives Colin a letter to a clinic for further study of his problem.

The doctor-shadow behind the curtain exits as Colin appears, pulling on his clothes.

> *While as yet keeping us at some distance, he puts on an act for us.*

COLIN (*imitates a woman receptionist*): "Yes, sir, can I help you?" (*Self.*) I have this letter. It is about a sperm count. (*Woman.*) "Oh, this is Family Planning. You want Fertility. Up the stairs, sir."

> *His trousers are up now. He looks at us, making us feel a little easier in his company. Now he goes into another act, a vocal send-up of a lab assistant.*

"Here y'are then, friend: a room apart. Produce your sample, bring it back to the lab when yow've done. We send yow the bill for two smacker, yowr doctor the results in twenty-one days, Venetian blind don't work, I'm sorry to say, but nobody to overlook yow. Lock on the door don't work either, I'm sorry to say, but they all know here what this room is for. (*Confidential.*) Some blokes has to get their wives to help them wi this at home, then bring the product in to us by buz. Take your time."

> *Colin is staring us out again; his expression never breaks, yet somehow he is charming us into a humorous sharing of his absurd predicament. . . .*

With great difficulty, and once interrupted by the intrusion of a young woman who has somehow found the wrong room, Colin finally supplies the sample of his semen in a small glass bottle.

The locale changes to the doctor's office, where Colin is told the results: there are live sperm in his semen, but not enough. He is to improve production by wearing boxer shorts from now on instead of tight underwear and bathing his testicles in cold water twice a day for six weeks, after which the clinic will take another sperm count.

The doctor disposes of the semen bottle in the waste basket and exits while Colin jokes to the audience on the physical difficulties of soaking this part of one's anatomy with cold water without getting cold and wet all over and flooding the bathroom.

It is obvious after his second test at the clinic that the treatment has succeeded, however, and now the focus is on Anne as she enters, reading a letter from the Doctor telling her that her husband's sperm motility is normal. What's more, Anne is now overdue for the first time in her life: "I say no, it's a freak. Or hysterical. Twenty-nine days, for me unheard of. Thirty. He's telling himself, stop thinking about it, stop hoping: watched pot and that. We've clicked or we haven't. Thirty-one days. If I can hang on till only Monday, hang out the flags, I'm qualifying for a Urine Test! Thirty-two days. Every time I'm out of the room now, I can hear his ears pricked for the sound of the door of the cupboard where I keep my pads. Thirty-third day. No gutrot. No pain in the back, no heaviness in the breasts. Just the blood."

Colin and Anne are both deeply disappointed. Colin proceeds to take the next step: he goes to see a specialist, a seminologist whom his patients dub "the Guru." Colin tells the doctor of his youthful homosexual feelings and how he adapted them successfully to a heterosexual life, despite the stunting emotional influences of the school he attended, "the usual seedbed of gentle Christian fascism. . . . My sexual world is very discordant now, but for all the vain yearning my several lusts put me in, I am glad in their diversity and would not be without one of them."

The Guru assures Colin that so long as he performs the sexual act properly, his emotional state has nothing to do with conception: "The trouble in your case most possibly lies with neither wife nor you, but in the combination of your genetic chemistries." The Guru suggests that Colin stretch the skin tighter during his cold baths and advises him: "Your diligence has been excessive: there is no need for the alarm clock, intercourse the night before is quite sufficient."

Anne joins Colin in consultation with the Guru, whose relentlessly clinical attitude soon strips the husband-wife relationship of any remaining modesty, even dignity. He poses Anne in "a posture of performing dogs" and with an oversized anatomy-class phallus demonstrates to Colin "the most efficient angle of insemination. Compared with which, the conventional Anglo-American attitude, from the spermatozoon's point of view, is all uphill." The Guru departs after handing Colin a small glass vial for a new sample which the Guru himself will test.

Colin speculates on whether his condition makes him less of a man — or more of a man because it frees him from the chore of propagation to indulge in and give pure pleasure. Anne admires Colin's ability to perform the sex act to order. Only once, while trying for the Guru's post-coital test, Colin was unable to rouse himself; but then later in the night he and Anne made it, half-asleep.

At the Guru's office, Anne is being examined. Colin's sperm is now normal, the Guru tells her, so she is probably killing them through some obscure chemical rejection process: "Your doing, but not your fault." The Guru gives her a device for reducing her acidity with bicarbonate of soda at the crucial moment, while admonishing her that it is her duty to humanity to try as hard as she can to have children: "The one inheritance man is short in is reason. Even if you and your husband look like the back end of buses, you've more than an average share of reason to bequeath. That is your duty to the world. If man is to survive, he must evolve up out of his mythic mire; and soon. So tell your husband to keep up the cold water treatment and the diet; and you combine the posture and the alkali."

The Guru exits and the curtain reveals Colin lying on the bed, prepared to make love to Anne. Then they remember that Anne must use the douche contraption, and the mood is broken. They proceed anyway, joylessly but as best they can, using the prescribed treatment and posture, as the lights go to black. In the dark can be heard a sound as of a slot machine turning over and over mechanically. Then the lights come up again.

COLIN: To think we were a year on the pill before we married.

ANNE (*to the audience*): Repeat on the thirteenth and fifteenth nights of the cycle. Two cycles. Five.

COLIN (*slowly withdrawing*): Remembering always to come away carefully, not spilling any.
   Lies away from her, speaking over pillow to the audience.
Sacrament, my arse. Four stages of a childless marriage: "Children?" (*Mild.*) "Not yet." "Children?" (*Slightly rebuking.*) "Give us time." "Children?" (*Gentle, sad.*) "No." "Children?" (*Defiant.*) "No."
   Anne relaxes into Little Mermaid pose, drawing blanket round self.

ANNE: "Try changing the wall paper," they say. Aunts, mother-in-law, sisters. "It's nothing to do with the *function*," I tell them: "That part of it's all right."
   Now there appears behind her a young married, Valerie, nursing baby and obscenely pregnant, a mixture of the affected-vulgar and intellectual pretension.

VALERIE: Try buying some different colored nighties, dear.

ANNE: I've told you, Valerie: that part's in order!

VALERIE: Get him away, a romantic holiday, a second honeymoon — or would it be the third or fourth, dear, including those you had with him before you were married?

ANNE: It's nothing —

VALERIE: George had his troubles, too. A warm climate's the thing —

COLIN (*unpresent to them, mockingly indicates his testicles*): Warm!

ANNE: It's chemistry, Valerie. Not the sex, the chemistry.

VALERIE: Perhaps he should take up football. On second thoughts, perhaps not, knowing his past. (*Disappears.*)

ANNE (*almost tearful*): It's nothing to do with that! It's chemistry!

Anne complains to herself about all the young wives so openly proud of their fecundity, making Anne feel inadequate.

Now Colin and Anne consult a gynecological surgeon who suggests that perhaps Anne isn't ovulating. He gives them a conspicuously oversized temperature chart, with orders about taking Anne's temperature regularly and keeping a record: "If, round your tenth day or so, the graph you are making suddenly dips, say five or six points of a degree, and the next day rises again by as much and a little more, you can normally assume ovulation has occurred. Whereupon, I recommend you two initiate an orgy. After six months, if you have indeed not conceived before then, make an appointment to bring me the charts, so that I can see what ovulation pattern, if any, is suggested by them."

The surgeon adds that they should mark the points on the graph where intercourse takes place. He approves of the antacid in moderation but puts little faith in the circus-dog posture. The surgeon raises the question of sperm volume.

SURGEON: I don't mean the quantity of the load, I mean its density in sperms. Your sperms can be the most motile under heaven, but if they are few, say a mere fifty million per milliliter, then all the cold water in the world will not make you fertile.

COLIN: I know the drill.

SURGEON (*bringing up from the drawer a long printed envelope that slightly bulges*): Good. The more sperms you put into circulation at any one time, the better your chances, I think you see that. The contents are self-explanatory: two forms, a sealable container. By post to the Path Lab, or drop it by: for this purpose, a time-lag will not matter; even if all the sperms die in the post, it is merely a question of our counting the corpses.

Colin takes the envelope, Anne the charts.

If that, and these, are in order, I see no reason why the two of you should not be expectant by midsummer.

COLIN: You will send the bill.

SURGEON: Yes. And the charts and the thermometer together will come to an extra eighty pence. (*Stands, quiet.*) Don't be despondent. (*Goes.*)

Anne and Colin are at home, working on their complicated chart, upon which they can as yet see no sign of encouragement. Each in turn feels a degree of guilt over the situation. Colin is on the phone to the lab, trying to get the results of his density test. But no amount of argument will turn the bureaucratic wheels to get him an answer.

Not till they return to the surgeon's office does Colin find out that the test shows him normally potent. Anne hands her charts to the surgeon who comments on their sloppiness (the thermometer broke here, the pencil there), making Anne feel like an errant schoolgirl deficient in her homework. Finally the surgeon shuffles the papers and makes sense of them: Anne's ovulation pattern is erratic, but not enough so to prevent conception which, according to the surgeon, should be taking place. There's nothing more to be done except proceed along these same lines, the surgeon tells them: "You have approached the problem with realism and courage. I am sure your pertinacity will be rewarded."

Back at home, in darkness, Anne announces triumphantly the arrival of an ovum, and Colin proceeds to try to fertilize it. In the darkness, there is the mechanical sound of the slot machine turning over and over — and then the sound of money pouring out in a jackpot. Still in darkness, via the speaker, the student nurse Jennifer tells the doctor that Anne's urine sample is positive.

Organ, orchestra, choir titanically burst out: first half-dozen bars

Mahler VIII, Veni, Veni Creator Spiritus. *Up pencil spot on desk now draped altar-like with white cloth, central on it a tall specimen jar, chalice-like, filled with straw-colored liquid. Spot tightens on jar until it glows like Holy Grail. Brutally, in mid-paean, cut music, light. Silence, darkness.*

ACT II

Without intermission and with little or no delay in the action, the scene becomes pastoral, with Anne lying on the ground in her smock in the warm sunlight and Colin, dressed in trousers and open shirt, stroking her and murmuring metaphysical poetry which he remembers poorly. His affection has sexual overtones, to which Anne is ready to respond.

After a long kiss, Anne gets up and goes off behind the screens as though searching for a spot to relieve herself. Colin *"lies langorous,"* searching his memory again for the lines of the poem, Traherne's *Salutation.*

COLIN: Who shall . . . who shall he or she be . . . ? that out of nothing comes . . . A nothing: that all a sudden — is . . . Where there was empty darkness, a sudden eye, seeing . . . Sudden in emptiness, new-minted limbs. Out of the dark silence, a forming tongue . . . Child — (*Ulsterish.*) Jamie . . . or (*Ulsterish.*) Annie . . .

> *Silence, Anne emerging, afraid to move. Something wrong. Colin turns sharply to her.*

ANNE: (*quiet, hard*): No sex. Take me home. I'm passing these.

> *Thrusts into his and our sight a white tissue in her cupped hands; in it, black clots of blood.*
> *A moment. Shock goes off in Colin like a deep mine — no other reaction shown. Blackout.*

The doctor is helping Anne in to bed, telling her she has a "pregnancy at risk" and must stay in bed until 48 hours after the bleeding stops — which it must, he reassures her, because she doesn't have "an inexhaustible supply." The doctor goes off, leaving Colin to tend a waste basket full of bloody paper tissues and commenting to the audience, "The child is lost. I don't mean I foresee that — we'll do everything mortal possible to prevent that. I mean, it is now that in the heart the loss takes place."

After a light change, the doctor returns to learn that Anne's bleeding did indeed stop — only to start again after she felt well enough to take a little mild outdoor exercise helping Colin plant potatoes and tomatoes. Anne has been up and down with the bleeding, and she asks for a drug to help stop it. But the doctor advises her: "If there's a good reason for a foetus to miscarry then miscarry we must let it. I know you have very much wanted this child, but you at least know now how you can conceive."

Anne protests that she isn't getting any younger and wants to know her chances this time. The doctor gives her about a 50-50 chance to complete the pregnancy. He departs.

Colin wheels in Anne's breakfast. Anne, who repeatedly tests her condition with the white paper tissue, finds it reddened; she is bleeding again.

Colin is trying to take care of Anne, but he hasn't done Anne's breakfast egg properly and has left several items off the tray; and the more he tries to set it right, the more he bungles until the whole tray is overturned and the bed becomes a mess of cornflakes, coffee and milk. Colin manages to clean up some of the debris with dust pan and brush and goes off while Anne reluctantly tackles what's left of her breakfast.

ANNE (*taps egg*): Egg smells funny.
> *Beheads egg with knife. Suddenly a most convulsive recoil — she hurls herself from bed, reels down — with a shock we see her night-dress stained where she bleeds. She crouches shudderingly, utterly upturned.*
>
> *Colin re-enters; sees her gone; looks into egg. Utters almost inaudible choke of abomination; covers egg with first thing to hand; stands, bottling nausea, shock.*

ANNE (*to self*): What am I trying to save? Some monster to be born, they'll take one look at —
> *Colin stumbles out with egg. Light change; Anne feels belly, wondering what horror might be forming there.*

Or a Mozart, Darwin? My will is blind. But is it itself willed, by some other will, that *sees?* That wills into being — man's share of monstrosity or his share of light? Is it either of these? Or is the world's will wild? Without mercy, senseless? At the heart of things, what if there *is* no purpose, no logic, no love at all?
> ..... *Anne slowly dons a plain long-worn dressing gown. Colin comes bringing a garden lounger, unfolds this, erects it, dressed as returned from school.*

COLIN (*no sarcasm*): Have you thought how lucky we are? .....
> *Brings bedclothes down.*

Think how lucky. We know exactly *how* to click, and that's so damn roundabout a method, the thing itself is really Love without Fear. Think of the rabbit. She ovulates every time she's entered. Homo sapiens is at least some way advanced on that. Perhaps you and I and others in our predicament are one stage even more evolved.

ANNE (*eases self carefully onto lounger*): Right now I'd rather be an ammonite.

COLIN (*tucks her in*): Extinction hurts too. We're wrong to patronize the dinosaur, by the way. One of the kids was saying. The dinosaur lasted five hundred times longer than man is likely to. It seems man's last end, though, will be the moral same.

ANNE: Out of step with his environment.

COLIN: Worse than that. It seems there were tiny termites, millions of them, eating their way up the dinosaur's legs. His nerve-system was so slow, out of touch with his condition, the pain didn't reach the brain till all his nethers were eaten away.

Anne reaches out another bloodied tissue, Colin automatically brings waste basket.
So what are *our* termites. What danger-signal is the human brain not getting?

Colin goes out without waiting for an answer, as Valerie comes in to visit Anne. Her sympathetic attentions to Anne seem patronizing, even demeaning. Valerie goes to brew Anne some coffee and manages to break a jug that was a memento of Colin's from his would-be playwriting days.

Anne is wondering how to bring up her child as an independent spirit. Valerie comes in with the coffee, complaining to Anne about her own pregnancy. The child isn't her husband's and she doesn't want it; how different from Anne's struggling situation Valerie is quick to point out.

Colin enters wearing his apron and refuses to let Valerie get away with insinuating a slight to his manhood because of it: "I don't see how it is manlier somehow to let one's clothes get wet." He escapes and doesn't return until Valerie has left with a parting shot at Anne: "God, the trouble I had carrying Jason. *He* simply *refused* to be born. George was driving me over level-crossings, foreways and backways, the little bugger simply refused to be born. Christ, when he did come, such a relief, my dear: to be able to see your toes again. . . . . When you're up and about again, my dear, you must come and have tea with me and the children, and we'll have a jolly old cow."

Colin returns, commenting on Valerie's wanton cruelty. He reaches out to pat Anne's belly, but she stops him; there is something wrong, she feels, the movement seems to have stopped.

Colin has brought Anne some potatoes to peel, and he distracts her by calling for the answer to a puzzle word: H E blank I T A blank E. Anne immediately guesses "heritage," but Colin tells her the answer is "hesitate," philosophizing, "Heritage my arse. He-si-tate. To stutter, to stammer, to stumble, to *be unsure, that.* . . . . is our determined role."

Colin has forgotten to turn on the oven and goes to do it, while *"Anne quietly moves paper, peelings a little down; rests hand on belly. Uneasy. From under pillow takes out a clean tissue. Makes cautious essay beneath blanket. Brings tissue out: no visible stain, yet something on it she does not like. She looks carefully, fearfully sniffs. Folds tissue carefully, stows into dressing gown pocket to keep for doctor."*

Anne continues peeling potatoes, then tries to adjust the lounger's headrest. It falls backward, and she has to ease herself off the lounger. As she does so, she slips, her foot overturns the bowl full of water and potatoes, and she falls into the mess as Colin returns. He tries to help her up, but she informs him that her wetness is not just from the overturned bowl: "My waters have broken."

An ambulance driver — *"gentle, heavy-sized"* — comes in with a stretcher while Colin gets together what Anne will need in the hospital. The driver comments, "This lady now sees, for the first time she fully sees: she'm in danger of death. Some 'at about our sympathy, in how familiar we are with her condition, in how serious and careful it makes *us* of her, strikes the scale from her eyes. . . . . To her, to this woman, this ambulance is the valley of the shadow, that sad little shadow through which one in five of British mothers pass. . . . . Look, a tear. Swells up out of nothing in the socket of her eye. The salt drop from the gland: fills, bulges, quivers. Makes her look so stupid. You could want to smash her face in, for looking so stupid. Weak face, stupid, helpless; slack jaw, so helpless, stupid. It tears your heart in two for pity, and your right hand itches up to strike that stupid face."

The curtain is drawn around Anne and the driver. Colin, alone, cleans up the potato mess, then sits and muses: "Now think. Think, how this happens from some good cause. If a bomb or a soldier had done it, you could be bitter. Think, how it can have some — rightness. The way of nature. Yet, was it in the way of nature, what we did? Lend her a helping hand. Nature might — take unkindly to our — 'help.' I rescued a shrew once, from the cat: yet the shrew ran straight off the shovel into a drain. The struggling in the water; the sound of the little blind thing struggling in the water. 'Helped.'

"It is true: what happens to us in the world, bears no resemblance to 'morality.' Yet, from that — inequity, might there not be a lesson to be learned? We are so near the letters, how can we see the word? (*Silence.*)

"In nature there is no annihilation. The dead are eaten. What remains rots down in corruption. In corruption itself murmur the bubbles of rebirth. Even what was burned, from ashes the fields are fertilized.

"For all that: however a cosmos might absorb calamity, extinction's final for the thing extinct."

The lights change, Colin goes off and Anne is now in a hospital being attended by a nurse. She tells us that "the cervix contracted, it almost closed," and they nearly saved the unborn child. But suddenly and definitely it aborted; Anne screams at the memory of it.

Anne's face is "a terrible white, eyes red" as Colin pulls up a chair by her bedside, a bouquet of wildflowers in his fist.

ANNE: There were two. Two babies. One came, then I was unconscious; then the other, it woke me in the night. I said, "Is it a boy?" "Nothing," she said, "it's only clots." But it was a baby. I know it was. There were two. They were twins. One must have gone wrong, you see. One must have been wrong from the start. So it died in the womb, it brought them both out, the good one with the bad. (*Motionless throughout.*) The nurse won't tell me. I only want to know it wasn't a monster. Or that it *was* a monster. I don't know what it is I want to know.
        Pause.
They're in the fridge. They take them to the end of the ward and — put them in the fridge. In the next ward you can hear the good ones crying, the ones that have been born. You have to have the different gyny wards together, that's only sense . . .

COLIN: Next ward's where we'll be. Next time.

ANNE (*motionless, seems not to hear him*): I said to the doctor, I won't go through all this again. Oh he's a patronizing bastard, the nurses queue up to kiss his arsehole — he's only a *doctor!* I won't go through this again, I told him:

bugger this for a tale. Next time I start to bleed I'll go down to my husband's school and hire the trampoline.

COLIN: Next time we'll be in there. This happens to one couple in five first time. We'll be in there next time.

ANNE (*utterly motionless; at last*): He said, "There isn't going to be a next time, Mrs. Harding. I'm sorry. We have had to take the womb away." (*Pause.*) "I'm sure your GP will recommend you for adoption."

Silence. Anne suddenly buries her head in Colin's breast.

I'm sorry, love, I'm sorry —

COLIN (*stunned*): Why "sorry" — ?

Anne says something indistinct about giving children.

No . . . No . . .

Anne says something indistinct about wanting to have his children.

No, no . . . Stop being so Arab. It's not "giving children," it's having. *Our* children, not mine. No. No.

ANNE (*constrained movement, orchestrating her pinned anguish*): I can see the smoke. From the incinerator. burning my womb — !

They remain motionless, silent.

COLIN (*at last; very quiet*): Gone then. Gone. Gone. We must do what we can with what remains. All that, is gone.

Anne utters one nigh-audible gasp of grief. Shakes bitterly, silent. (*Deathly quiet.*) Gone.

They remain so, motionless, silent, a cruel time. Then blackout.

ACT III

Without intermission, the lights slowly come up on a Social Services Officer — "*mid-30s, compassionate, quite smooth*" — and the Area Adoptions Officer — "*a woman in her early 30s, smart, conventional, clipboard on lap*" — seated in front of a map of the county districts. The woman is making a surreptitious notation from time to time. The man is speaking as though to a semi-circle of attentive couples, breaking it to them as gently as possible that adoptive children are very scarce and their chances of being picked to adopt one are very small. He understands their feelings but warns them: "Sad though your path has so far been, it may yet lead to further sadness."

The Social Services Officer is sympathetic but unyielding: the child's welfare is to be considered above everything else, even the feelings of the would-be parents whose nerves must already be raw as they re-think their roles after being excluded from the "common human heritage" of natural parenthood. He warns the couples that they must be prepared for deeper and possibly more painful probing than they have yet experienced: "You will flinch from this inquisition; at times feel laid out on our slab just once too often."

Even if they qualify, the officer tells them, there may not be an exactly suitable child available for adoption. "In such a case, we prefer to get your disappointment over and done with straight away. Our reasons, however, for not accepting you, whatever they are, we never give. Painful though it is, to be found unsuitable and wondering forever why, we find that on balance it is safer for you to be left in the dark. We marvel constantly at the courage would-be adoptive parents show. You begin to see now how much you really need."

The officers disappear as the lights change. Colin comes on in his underwear, obviously just having gone through a physical exam. As Colin dresses, he thinks of his native Ireland: "What sort of son am I, to such fine fathers? White sterile son, dead branch of the tribe. . . . No. No. All that's behind me. Progenitive fantasy, all behind me. For fatherhood I was not made. Nature was wise, she cast me from the start: dead seed, best fit to mix with excrement — ashes to ashes. (*Sarcastic.*) But I knew better. 'I knowed better.' I would be a 'mahn.' A 'father.' With cold water and bicarbonate of soda, chart calendar and clock — 'Hi, oul' bitch Nature!' I said, 'I'll worst ye yet!' If I had been content — (*Pauses.*) Content . . . (*Sees truth of it.*) Content . . . my wife would have her womb this day."

Colin has completed a long interview and forms, and he goes off as Anne comes in to be interrogated by the Area Officer, who notes how persevering Colin and Anne were in their efforts to have a child. The Area Officer wants to know what they'd do if they were turned down. Anne replies they'd be bitter, then accept, then go on to the next thing. Under questioning, Anne tells her she thinks Colin's worst fault is pigheadedness. She sketches the outline of their lives: their careers as actress and playwright were going nowhere, so they went back to teaching, and domestic matters began to become more important to them.

AREA OFFICER: How strong do you think your marriage is?
   Anne thinks.
What do you think is the greatest threat to it?
   ANNE: (*at last*): If one knew that . . .
   AREA OFFICER: Your husband's answer to this question was: (*Brief glance at notes.*) "When the earthquake happens, the buildings that survive are the ones that swayed." How do you think he means your marriage could sway? His rather unorthodox sexuality, you think because of that?
   ANNE: I don't think he meant the *marriage* could sway. I think he meant about people rolling with the punches that nature gives them.
   AREA OFFICER: You say he is pigheaded.
   ANNE (*candid*): He's learning. (*Yes: she has been the stronger all along.*) Anyway. I don't think his sexuality is unorthodox. His acknowledgment of it might be. We have to tell you these things.
   AREA OFFICER: That he can consciously feel for his own sex, do you think that threatens your marriage?
   ANNE: I feel safer.
   AREA OFFICER: Safer?
   ANNE: Safer than if he had a roving eye for other women. Anyway, I've told him: if he has to have a bit of the other sex once in a while, just be sure to come back clean. It's how he's made; he has only one life. Likewise me. If I *have* to succumb to the milkman, he says, just not in *our* bed. It's a joke but . . . a grain of truth. If that shocks you, I'm sorry.

AREA OFFICER: It doesn't *shock* me —

ANNE: We don't abuse each other's liberality — Anyway, men with open homosexual emotions are supposed to make good fathers. It's just a rotten consequence of natural logic so few of them get the chance.

The Area Officer continues probing Colin's and Anne's sex life, and Anne can't resist answering her bluntly: "He's not the great greasy bullcock of my dreams, what woman's husband is? It's probably better to find your man tolerable company for fifty years than be hooked on his cock." The Area Officer keeps her cool as the interview ends, with Anne declaring that the only thing they would have to offer a child would be a share in their lives, such as they are.

The lights go to black and when they come up the scene has shifted to the airport, where Anne is meeting Colin returning from a trip to Belfast. Colin pours out his feelings to Anne: he is still under a spell of horror at the obscenely bloody aftermath of a bomb blast in which a great many innocent persons including his own Uncle Tommy had been blown into numerous and very sickening pieces.

Colin remembers his Aunt Annie asking him why he hadn't come to live in Belfast years ago. Colin answered: "Truth to tell, Aunt Annie, I was afeared to come. Forbye, because I am so torn. 'Between what?' Between the baker's half-dozen wrongs of this all. Torn, I tried to tell her, torn wondering where best — no, not where best; where at all we go now. 'Aunt Annie' — my heart was in my mouth as I said it — 'we've known from the year one the old North of Ireland had to go some time.' "

Colin remembers how the rivalry and challenges, the sense of moral cause he felt in his childhood, grew into riots and then bombs: "Awful to say, but only these bombs have made me really think. If an undertribe can commit themselves to such atrocity, there must be some terrible misery they are trying to communicate."

His generation has now reaped the whirlwind, and Colin reflects: "Derry . . . . . has nourished a monster, and the lining's torn from her belly in its birth, Our only hope: did the seed of anything good come out? . . . . . Our only hope, see what — new people we have it in us to become."

But Aunt Annie insisted on showing Colin, "safe in England all this time," what lay in the room at the back: the horribly mutilated, quadriplegic but still living body of her son Sam's girl friend. Sam means to marry her still, and to keep on fighting the Catholic "enemy." Colin insisted to Sam that he loves Ireland as much as ever but doesn't believe in violence as a solution to her troubles. Sam said, "If we do not fight now, we shall be wiped out. All we stand for shall vanish, as though we had never been."

Trying to find a way to persuade Sam, Colin admitted to the past greatness of the Protestant identity and purpose in turning back first the Catholic kings of Europe and then Hitler. He remembers that he told Sam: "Can we rise to the occasion this third time, then? turn a third tyranny back? the tyranny of our own — (*Now it hits Colin, and the clarity of it is freeing him.*) inheritance? Our inheritance is glorious, we are a brave clan, quite hard in the head and I think very straight: we have the puritanical vices and virtues. But all that has to be behind us now. Shed. I just — I just think we have to — try to see, what new selves we can rise up out of this, and become. Oh, Sammy, if we can do that, oh then we are a brave tribe."

Sam's reply at Uncle Tommy's funeral was to push Colin away from the coffin, telling him, "You'll carry no Ulsterman's coffin to no grave. Stay here wi the weemen." Colin was able to endure the ostracism; but at the same time, he tells Anne, "I felt so severed. (*No self-pity, but an absolute new clear-seeing.*) I know it is the strongest feeling in the world, to be alone. And I did feel strong. Yet, the land, from whose earth I belong, the clan, from whose loins I come, had turned me out; to my own loins no child of tomorrow shall come: and I felt so — (*At last.*) severed. . . . . So. There's another — 'self' for the rubbish heap with all the rest. My self as 'tribal son.' Yet: if we do not change, tomorrow has no place for us."

The lights go to black and come up on Anne digging and sorting potatoes, musing about good years and bad, blight and sterility; about forcing the earth to bear more crops than it naturally should, whatever the cost to future generations. Her thoughts turn into a remembered nightmare of a barren, hopeless world in which everything was being destroyed, even in the act of love, and everyone, including Colin, was poisoned, the flesh becoming scaly, and dying.

ANNE: . . . . . I came out across the marsh. The sky was red like blood. The land was black. The cabbages had been blasted from their stalks, the stalks stood gnarled and knotted in rows, unnaturally gleaming. I was weak. I could see my body was turning scaly as his had done. I dragged myself to where I could lean against a thorntree. I lay there. A child came. No child that I would call a child. A child of ice, moving without seeming to move, crossing the black flat of the marsh beneath the red sky. He-she-it, featureless, white, its head in a dome like a child from space. I was so frightened, so weak I could not lift myself at all; I felt I was going out, like water down a drain: into extinction. (*Thinks, does not say: "But no." New tone of coming resurrection.*) I woke. A voice overlapped from the dream: the child's and mine: the same. "Take *off* your dead."

> *Quietly Colin comes in, in anorak, opened letter in hand.*

COLIN (*terse*): From the County.

> *Face, voice show nothing. Anne snatches letter, glancing at his face; then reads. Colin . . . . . reads newspaper without taking any of it in; a covert glance at Anne. She is looking up, forward, out, letter in hand on lap. Colin waits till it is time for him to speak.*

(*Not cold; but only stricken of all expression.*) That's it. Another "us" to shed: mummy and daddy.

> *Looks down at newspaper again. Eye catches something.*

(*With tiniest chuckle.*) "Day-old boy found in lavatory pan in Worcester." The world is like this.

> *Anne says nothing. Colin does not look up.*

(*A there-it-is tone.*) Laughter of children in our house, not for us. Whatever *is*.

> *Yes. Whatever is. This road must now be abandoned also. Anne sees it; inly she has known it all along. It is pitiful, but they are released. Their hopes for parenthood lie in ashes, but on some other road must lie what is for them. After a moment she turns herself, without stand-*

ing, toward Colin; with right hand she quite strongly seizes his hair, forcefully raises his face to her own. On his face suddenly the beginning of a strange light, Cut immediately. Curtain.

○○○
○○○
○○○
○○○
○○○
○○○
○○○ ANNIE

A Musical in Two Acts

BOOK BY THOMAS MEEHAN

MUSIC BY CHARLES STROUSE

LYRICS BY MARTIN CHARNIN

Cast and credits appear on pages 308-309

THOMAS MEEHAN (book) was born in New York City Aug. 14, 1929. He wanted to write as long as he can remember and kept on doing it at Hamilton College and after graduation, when he persisted in writing plays but never was able to get a production. Finally, in 1956, he got a job as a staff writer on the New Yorker, *to which he is still a contributor (a collection of his pieces entitled* Yma, Ava; Yma, Aga; Yma, Uta; Yma, Ida . . . and Others *was recently published).*

As a TV writer, Meehan received two Emmy nominations for That Was the Week That Was *sketches. His work on TV specials finally won him an Emmy for his contribution to an Anne Bancroft show created by Martin Charnin. Charnin persuaded Meehan to try again in the theater, after reading one of Meehan's unproduced playscripts (Meehan thought the* Little Orphan Annie *idea was a good deal less than sensational when it was first proposed, but it finally grabbed him). The rest is history, with Meehan, Charnin and Charles*

146

Strouse going all the way with Annie *from the Goodspeed Opera House in East Haddam, Conn. through the Washington, D.C. tryout to Broadway on April 21, 1977 and a Best Play citation, the Critics Award and the Tony Awards for best musical, best book and best score.*

Meehan lives in Rockland County, N.Y. He is married, with two children.

CHARLES STROUSE (music) was born in New York City June 7, 1928 and has composed since the age of 12. He studied at Eastman School of Music (Mus.B., 1947), in private lessons with Aaron Copland and Nadia Boulanger and as a scholarship student at Tanglewood.

All Strouse's Broadway works prior to Annie *were done in tandem with Lee Adams as lyricist. Their first show was* Bye Bye Birdie *(1964), followed by* All American *(1962),* Golden Boy *(1964),* "It's a Bird It's a Plane It's SUPERMAN" *(1966, a Best Play) and* Applause *(1970), a Best Play and the Tony Award winner for best musical). His other work for the theater has included the incidental music for the Phoenix Theater's 1975* The Member of the Wedding *and the whole script — book, music and lyrics — for the 1971 off-Broadway revue* Six. *His other compositions have included the theme song for the TV series* All in the Family, *the movie scores for* Bonnie and Clyde, The Molly Maguires, The Night They Raided Minsky's *and* There Was a Crooked Man. *He has recently completed a piano concerto and an opera to be published by G. Schirmer.*

Strouse and his lyricist Martin Charnin won the best-score Tony for Annie, *their first collaboration. The composer is married to the dancer Barbara Siman, who was featured in* My Fair Lady. *They have two sons and a daughter.*

MARTIN CHARNIN (lyrics) was born Nov. 24, 1934 in New York City and was educated at the High School of Music and Art and Cooper Union. He began his theater career as an actor and singer, creating the role of Big Deal in West Side Story *(1957), including the "Gee, Officer Krupke" number. After writing short stories and magazine pieces, Charnin wrote his first Broadway lyrics for* Hot Spot *(1963) and the same year contributed to the Los Angeles-produced* Zenda *and the off-Broadway revue* Put It in Writing, *and later to another of the same,* Wet Paint *(1965).*

Continuing in the theater, Charnin wrote the lyrics for Mata Hari *(1967), the off-Broadway musical* Ballad for a Firing Squad *(1968, which he also directed) and* Two by Two *(1970), with music by Richard Rodgers. He conceived and directed the Ogden Nash revue collection* Nash at Nine *(1973); directed an American-music cavalcade* Music! Music! *(1974) directed* The National Lampoon Show *(1975) for off-Broadway presentation; and, finally, directed and wrote the lyrics for* Annie *which, in addition to its best-show awards, won the best-score Tony for Charnin and Strouse.*

Charnin has also been active in night club production and in TV, where his nine specials have won him four Emmys and a Peabody Award. He is the possessor of a gold record for which he wrote the music and lyrics (Barbra Streisand's The Best Thing You've Ever Done); *the author of a children's book entitled* The Giraffe Who Sounded Like Ol' Blue Eyes; *and the proud parent of two children, a boy and a girl. Charnin lives in New York City.*

Our method of representing Annie *in these pages differs from that of the other Best Plays. The musical appears here in a series of photographs with synopsis and quotes from the script and lyrics, recording the overall "look" of a 1977 Broadway musical, with its visually expressive concept and characters as well as its story structure and style.*

The photographs of Annie *depict scenes as produced by Mike Nichols, Lewis Allen and Alvin Nederlander Associates, Inc. and as directed by Martin Charnin and choreographed by Peter Gennaro, as of the opening April 21, 1977 at the Alvin Theater, with scenery by David Mitchell and costumes by Theoni V Aldredge.*

Our special thanks are tendered to the producers and their press representative, David Powers, for making available these selections from Martha Swope's excellent photographs of the show.

ANNIE

ACT I

1. In December, 1933 in a New York City orphanage, a little girl named Annie (Andrea McArdle, *right*) wakes in the night. She longs for the parents who left her years ago with half of a silver locket and a note promising to come back to get her as soon as possible.

2. Annie sings to herself— "Maybe":

Maybe far away,
Or maybe real nearby
He may be pouring her coffee
She may be straight'ning his tie!

Maybe in a house
All hidden by a hill
She's sitting playing piano,
He's sitting paying a bill!

Betcha they're young
Betcha they're smart
Bet they collect things
Like ashtrays, and art!
Betcha they're good—
(Why shouldn't they be?)
Their one mistake
Was giving up me!

So, maybe now it's time
And maybe when I wake
They'll be there calling me "baby"—

Maybe.

3. Annie tries to run away, but she's caught (*left*) by the orphanage keeper, Miss Hannigan (Dorothy Loudon).

4. The whole group i
punished. They act ou
their resentment (*left*) b
pretending little Moll
(Danielle Brisebois) i
Miss Hannigan. The or
phans sing their lament
"It's the hard-knock lif
for us!...Steada treate
we get tricked! / Stead
kisses, we get kicked!...
It's the hard-knock life!

5. Next morning, Annie makes good her
escape, in a laundry hamper. She soon be-
friends another hunted waif and names
him Sandy (himself, *right*), reassuring him
in song:

> The sun'll come out
> Tomorrow
> Bet your bottom dollar
> That tomorrow
> There'll be sun!
>
> Just thinkin' about
> Tomorrow
> Clears away the cobwebs,
> And the sorrow
> 'Til there's none!
>
> When I'm stuck with a day
> That's gray
> And lonely,
> I just stick out my chin
> And grin,
> And say,
> Oh

> "The sun'll come out
> Tomorrow"
> So ya gotta hang on
> 'Til tomorrow

> Come what may!
> Tomorrow!
> Tomorrow!
> I love ya

> Tomorrow!
> You're always
> A day
> Away!

6. Annie and Sandy find shelter and a meal at a Depression-era shantytown, a "Hooverville" (*above*), where hapless but hospitable residents sing: "We'd like to thank you, Herbert Hoover/You made us what we are today." Police come to drive away the "bums." They catch Annie (Sandy escapes) and return her to the orphanage —but Miss Hannigan's troubles are far from over.

7. Rich Oliver Warbucks's secretary, Grace (Sandy Faison, seated in photo at *right*), comes to choose an orphan to be a guest in the Warbucks mansion over Christmas. She picks Annie, increasing Miss Hannigan's bitterness as she sings "Little Girls":

Some day I'll land
     in the nut house
With all the nuts
     and the squirr'ls
There I'll stay
Tucked away
'Til the prohibition of
Little girls.

8. Annie arrives at the mansion and is soon singing "I Think I'm Gonna Like It Here." Oliver Warbucks (Reid Shelton, *right*) comes in to find phone messages from President Roosevelt and Bernard Baruch. But he decides to spend the evening strolling with Annie and Grace in "NYC" (*below*):

NYC
The shadows at sundown
The roofs that scrape the sky
NYC
The rich and the rundown
The big parade goes by

What other town has the
Empire State
And a mayor five foot two
No other town in
The whole forty-eight
Can half compare with you

Oh NYC
You make 'em all postcards
You crowd, you cramp
You're still the champ
Amen
For NYC.

9. Another waif still roams a friendless city (*right*).

10. Grace visits the orphanage to tell Miss Hannigan that Warbucks has decided to adopt Annie. On her way out she passes Miss Hannigan's ex-con brother and his friend Lily (Robert Fitch and Barbara Erwin, *above*). Rooster recalls how their mother advised them to live, by hook or by crook, on "Easy Street":

Easy Street
Easy Street
Where the rich folks play
(Play all day)
Move them feet
To Easy Street
When you get there,
Stay.

11. Instead of rejoicing at the gift of a new locket, Annie dissolves in tears— she still hopes to find her real parents. Warbucks comforts her (*right*) with the self-sacrificing promise, "I'll find your parents for you." The staff gathers to assure Annie in song, "You Won't Be an Orphan for Long." Annie reflects:

Maybe now it's time
And maybe when I wake
They'll be there calling me "Baby"—
Maybe.

(*The curtain slowly falls.*)

12. One of Warbucks's first moves is to go on Bert Healy's "Oxydent Hour of Smiles" radio program and offer $50,000 to Annie's parents to get in touch with him. The orphans (*above*) listen in and imitate the Healy performers singing "You're Never Fully Dressed Without a Smile." Later, they tell Miss Hannigan of Warbucks's offer.

13. Next, Warbucks visits the White House, where FDR (Raymond Thorne, in wheelchair *below*) and his cabinet are helplessly bemoaning the Depression. Annie cues them to cheer up with a chorus of "Tomorrow." FDR orders his cabinet to join in the song. He decides what the country needs is a fresh outlook—a New Deal.

14. Back at the Warbucks mansion, a thousand fakes have pretended to be Annie's parents. Warbucks sings to Annie of his feelings—"Something Was Missing":

I've made me a fortune
(That fortune made ten)
Been headlined
And profiled
Again and again
But something was missing
(I never quite knew)
That something was missing—
But who? . . . . .

The world was my oyster—
But where was the pearl?
Who dreamed I would find it
In, one little girl.
Yes, something was missing—
But dreams can come true
That something
Is no one
But you.

Warbucks offers again to adopt Annie and hugs her when she replies, "If I can't have my real mother and father, there's no one in the world I'd rather have for a father than you!" and joins him in singing "I Don't Need Anything But You." Annie goes to get dressed for the adoption ceremony. The staff warms to the occasion, singing "Annie/Annie/Annie/Everything's humming now/Annie/Annie/Annie/Good times are coming now/Since you came our way/It's Christmas, Christmas every day."

15. As Annie comes back, hair curled and wearing her red dress, Lily and Rooster Hannigan (third and fourth from left, *above*) enter in disguise, pretending to be Annie's real parents, supporting their story with inside information about the locket and a forged document. Strangely, Annie seems downcast instead of happy. But FDR comes to the rescue with an FBI report that Annie's parents are dead. Rooster and accomplices, Lily and Miss Hannigan, are arrested for fraud.

16. Now for the celebration. Annie's orphan friends (*above,* right) will suffer no longer under Miss Hannigan but are to attend school. There are Christmas gifts all around. *"A policeman comes to the door and beckons to Warbucks, who goes to the door and briefly confers with him. A moment later, two of the liveried servants bring in a huge Christmas package and set it on the floor. Annie goes to it and opens it. In the box is Sandy"* (as *above*), and now Annie, Sandy and Warbucks are a happy, united family (*below,* right). Everyone including the President of the United States joins in singing "A New Deal for Christmas":

ALL:
  Fill every stocking with laughter
  We haven't got room
                 for any more gloom
  Let's ring every bell from its rafters
WARBUCKS:
  And chime across the land
ANNIE:
  Tomorrow's at hand
WARBUCKS (*speaks*): Those happy days
  that we were promised
ROOSEVELT:
  Are finally here
ALL:
  We're getting a New Deal for Christmas
  We're getting a New Deal
              for Christmas . . . . .
  This year.

                      (*Curtain.*)

CALIFORNIA SUITE

A Comedy in Two Acts and Four Playlets:
VISITOR FROM NEW YORK
VISITOR FROM PHILADELPHIA
VISITORS FROM LONDON
VISITORS FROM CHICAGO

BY NEIL SIMON

Cast and credits appear on pages 284-285

NEIL SIMON was born in the Bronx, N.Y. on July 4, 1927. After graduation from DeWitt Clinton High School he managed to find time for writing while serving in the Army, and writing soon became his profession without the formalities of college (except for a few courses at New York University and the University of Denver). His first theater work consisted of sketches for camp shows at Tamiment, Pa., in collaboration with his brother Danny. He became a TV writer, supplying a good deal of material for Sid Caesar and Phil Silvers in scripts for Caesar's Hour *and* Sergeant Bilko.

On Broadway, Simon contributed sketches to Catch a Star *(1955) and* New Faces of 1956. *His first Broadway play was* Come Blow Your Horn *(1961), followed by the book of the musical* Little Me *(1962). His next play, the comedy* Barefoot in the Park *(1963) was named a Best Play of its season, as was* The Odd Couple *(1965). Neither of these had closed when the musical* Sweet Charity, *for which Simon wrote the book, came along early in 1966; and none of the three had closed when Simon's* The Star-Spangled Girl *opened the following season in December, 1966 — so that Simon had the phenomenal total of four shows running simultaneously on Broadway during the season of 1966–67. When the last of the four closed the following summer, they had played a total of 3,367 performances over four theater seasons.*

Simon immediately began stacking another pile of blue-chip shows. His Plaza Suite *(1968) was named a Best Play of its year. His book of the musical* Promises, Promises *(1969) was another smash, and* Last of the Red Hot Lovers *(1969) became his fourth Best Play and third in still another group of Simon shows in grand simultaneous display on Broadway.* Plaza Suite *closed before* The Gingerbread Lady *(1970, also a Best Play) opened, so that Simon's second stack was "only" three plays and 3,084 performances high.*

There followed The Prisoner of Second Avenue *(1971, a Best Play),* The Sunshine Boys *(1972, a Best Play),* The Good Doctor *(1973, a Best Play) and* God's Favorite *(1974). There was no new Neil Simon play on Broadway the following year because he was moving himself and his family from New York to California partly for personal reasons and partly to write for the screen. Movies or no movies, by April 1976 he had* California Suite *ready for production at Center Theater Group in Los Angeles and brought it to the Eugene O'Neill Theater — which he owns — immediately afterward as his 15th Broadway show and ninth Best Play.*

In addition to the recent Murder by Death, *Simon's movie scripts have included* The Out-of-Towners *and* The Heartbreak Kid *in addition to the screen versions of his own* Barefoot in the Park, The Odd Couple, Plaza Suite, The Prisoner of Second Avenue *and* The Sunshine Boys. *Simon's second wife is the actress Marsha Mason. He has two daughters by his first marriage.*

Place: Suite 203 and 204 in the Beverly Hills Hotel

ACT I

Scene 1: Visitor From New York

SYNOPSIS: The living room of this hotel suite is at right and the bedroom at left, *"cheerful and brightly colored . . . . . It has elegant reproductions of Van Gogh and Renoir on the walls, large color TV sets in both rooms, a fireplace in the living room."*

About 1 p.m. of a sunny, warm day in late fall, Hannah Warren is standing by the window at right smoking a cigarette, with her bags packed, ready to leave. She is *"a bright, intelligent and sophisticated woman . . . . . wearing a tailored woolen suit."* The phone rings. Hannah answers it, invites the caller to come up and orders one tea and one scotch from room service.

The bedroom phone rings. While Hannah is explaining to a friend that she can't wait to get back to New York where it's snowing, her ex-husband Billy Warren comes into the living room. *"He is about 45, quite attractive. He is well tanned and trim. He wears brush denim slacks, an open sport shirt, a cashmere V-neck sweater and tan sneakers."*

Hannah finishes her phone conversation and goes into the living room. Even their first greeting takes the form of repartee between two highly articulate people who barb every comment to each other.

BILLY: Shouldn't we kiss or shake hands or something?

HANNAH: Let's save it for when you leave . . . I love your California clothes.

BILLY: They're Bloomingdale's in New York.

HANNAH: The best place for California clothes . . . You look so — I don't know — what's the word I'm looking for?

BILLY: Happy?

HANNAH: Casual . . . It's so hard to tell out here. Are you dressed up now or is that sporty?

BILLY: I didn't think a tie was necessary for a reunion.

HANNAH: Is that what this is? When I walked in, I thought we were going to play tennis.

BILLY: Well, you look fit enough for it.

HANNAH: Fit? You think I look fit? . . . What an awful shit you are. I look gorgeous.

BILLY: Yes you do, Hannah. You look lovely.

HANNAH: No, no. *You* look lovely. *I* look gorgeous.

BILLY: Well, I lost about ten pounds.

HANNAH: Listen to what I'm telling you, you're *ravishing* . . . I love the way you're wearing your hair now. Where do you go, that boy who does Barbra Streisand?

BILLY: You like it, you can have my Thursday appointment with him . . . If you're interested, I'm feeling *very* well, thank you.

HANNAH: Well, of course you are. Look at that tan. Well, it's the life out here, isn't it? You have an office outdoors somewhere?

BILLY: No, just a desk near the window . . . Hey, Hannah, if we're going to banter like this, give me a little time. It's been nine years, I'm rusty.

HANNAH: You'll pick it right up again, it's like French.

This obviously has been their regular style of communication, what there was of it over the years. Hannah has heard that out here they call him "Billy" instead of "Bill," and she comments: "It's adorable . . . A forty-five-year-old Billy . . . Standing there in his cute little sneakers and sweater," but Billy refuses to rise to her baiting. He has tried to make a new life for himself since their divorce, and this includes regular exercise, no more hard liquor, a careful watch on diet, vitamins and health foods in place of pills. Hannah's supercilious New York sarcasms are unable to shake Billy: he is impervious to them now, having taken up such stimulating pursuits as guitar-playing and mountain-climbing, and he can even get along without the services of a psychiatrist.

Hannah still lives in their old apartment and has taken a lover, a 54-year-old Washington *Post* reporter with "the second-best mind since Adlai Stevenson." Hannah annoys Billy by asking him about *his* love-life. Billy would prefer to cut the chatter and talk seriously about their daughter, Jenny, now 17, but Hannah clings to her sarcasm, commenting on the shape of the swimming pool at Billy's French farmhouse in Beverly Hills. Billy replies: "You're terrific. You haven't spent fifteen days of your life out here but you know exactly how we all live, don't you? . . . Too bad you're going back so soon . . . You're gonna miss the way we spend our holidays. Wouldn't it *thrill* you to see a pink painted Christmas tree on my lawn . . . or a three-flavored Baskin and Robbins snowman wearing alligator shoes . . . with a loudspeaker on the roof playing Sonny and Cher singing 'Silent Night.' "

Hannah keeps after Billy about his love life. Billy was married to a singer after his divorce from Hannah, was divorced again and is now seeing an actress who has an 11-year-old boy.

HANNAH: And is marriage contemplated? Am I being too nosy?

BILLY: Not for a Newsweek editor . . . Yes. Marriage is contemplated . . . It is being discussed, it is being considered. Strange as it seems, I like being married.

HANNAH: Right . . . And will there be room for all of you in the little French farmhouse or will you have to move to an Italian palazzo on Wilshire Boulevard?

BILLY: What the hell are you so bitter about? . . . You used to be bright and witty. Now you're just snide and sarcastic.

HANNAH: It comes with age. When you don't have a fastball any more, you go to change-ups and sliders.

BILLY: Oh, please. Spare me your sports metaphors. You never knew a bunt from a double. The only reason you went to the games is because you thought you looked butch. Are you through with your interrogation?

HANNAH: I'm still interested in this new girl.

BILLY: Her name is Betsy LaSorda. Her father used to be a damned good director. She can catch a trout and she can beat me in tennis. I think she's peachy. What else?

HANNAH: Well, I know you've been bouncing around a lot, Billy. Do you really care for her or do you have someone who gets you a break on marriage licenses?

BILLY: God, I can just hear the quips flying when you and the second best mind since Adlai Stevenson get together. Sitting there freezing under a blanket at the Washington Redskin game playing anagrams with the names of all the Polish players . . . I'll tell you something, Hannah: For one of the brightest women in America, you bore the hell out of me. Your mind clicks off bric-a-bracs so goddamn fast, it never has a chance to let an honest emotion or thought ever get through.

HANNAH: And you're so *filled* with honest emotions, you fall in love every time someone sings a ballad. You're worse than a hopeless romantic, you're a *hopeful* one. You're the kind of a man who would end the world's famine problem by having them all eat out . . . preferably at a good Chinese restaurant.

Billy has had enough and starts to go but remembers that they must settle the problem of their daughter Jenny, who wants to stay in California with her father for a year instead of returning to New York with her mother. Hannah takes a snobbish view of Jenny's intellectual opportunities back East as compared with California, but Billy argues that New York is not the center of the universe.

BILLY: . . . . . I went to a charity luncheon in East Hampton to raise money for the California grape pickers . . . There was this teeming mob of women who must have spent a total of twelve thousand dollars on new Gucci pants in order to raise two thousand dollars for the grape pickers . . . why the hell didn't they just mail them the pants?

HANNAH: You were terrific when you used to write like that . . . I didn't see the last picture you wrote, but they tell me it grossed very well in backward areas.

BILLY: Jesus, was I anything like you before?

HANNAH: I couldn't hold a candle to you.

BILLY: No wonder no one spoke to me here for the first two years.

Hannah insists that Billy has a right to his daughter's company only in the summers, but Billy claims that Jenny ought to be able to live as she pleases. Jenny feels stifled by her mother (Hannah admits, "She loves me but she doesn't like me. She's afraid of me"). It's Hannah's view that Jenny *should* rebel to some extent against the parent she lives with for the longest time of the year. She means to take Jenny back, and she threatens Billy that she will hire the best lawyer and even call her friend the U.S. Attorney General if Jenny isn't on the afternoon plane to New York.

Billy believes that Hannah leaves Jenny alone too much, but Hannah contends, "She has two dogs, a Dominican cook and twelve different girls who sleep over every time I'm away." Hannah admits that if left to choose, Jenny would stay with her father, but she's not going to give up her daughter just because they have normal conflicts in their relationship. Billy senses that Hannah is really afraid she may lose Jenny.

BILLY: . . . . . This is an event. It's the first time I think I've ever actually seen you nervous.

HANNAH: Wrong. I was nervous on our wedding night . . . Unfortunately, it was *after* we had sex.

BILLY: Please. No cheap shots. It's not like you . . . I mean, we may have had a very narrow chance for happiness, but sex was never a stumbling block.

HANNAH: Neither was it an architectural marvel . . . Oh, I'm not blaming *you* . . . Actually you were very skillful in bed . . . You could ravage me for hours without ever mussing the sheets . . . But the moment it was over, you would heave a deep sigh and tell me your plans for the future . . . the sex was stimulating but the plans were so freaking boring.

BILLY: Boring? And I have made love to women with the television on before, but *never* watching Eric Severeid.

HANNAH: Sometimes we need our private fantasies to help us get to the top of Magic Mountain.

BILLY: You know something, Hannah . . . I don't like you any more.

HANNAH: It's okay. I'm not always fond of me either . . . . .

Nevertheless she wants her daughter back. This is Hannah's last year to enjoy Jenny's company. After that, she'll go away to college and come back four years later "a revolutionary or a nun . . . Or even worse, like you or me."

There is a trace of an appeal in Hannah's tone as she confides to Billy that her

GEORGE GRIZZARD, TAMMY GRIMES, JACK WESTON A

BARA BARRIE IN "CALIFORNIA SUITE"

Washington *Post* friend won't be around for the long pull, having recently had open-heart surgery. Billy, with a modicum of sympathy, suggests that Hannah move to California for the winter months — that way she'll be able to see Jenny all she wants. Hannah rejects this proposal absolutely.

Billy informs Hannah that Jenny is downstairs in the car with her bags packed, waiting to accept any decision her parents make. Hannah sees this as a no-win situation: "If we say she goes back to New York, she'll think I coerced you. And if we say stay here, she'll think I didn't even put up a fight for her."

Billy perplexes Hannah even further by offering to abide by any decision she makes. Crisply, efficiently, Hannah decides to cut her losses: Jenny can stay with Billy for the next six months, after which Hannah will select a school for her. Billy tries to be generous, inviting Hannah to stay over the weekend to make up her mind, but Hannah refuses bluntly: "If I have to give her up to get her back, then let's do it."

Billy admits that Hannah's decision leaves him somewhat frightened at the prospect of taking on new responsibilities as a parent — but he's grateful to Hannah for letting go.

BILLY: I think you're doing a terrific thing, Hannah.

HANNAH: So do I.

BILLY: And if for any reason I feel things aren't working out, I'll send her back to you.

HANNAH: The hell you will. You're a father now, Billy.

BILLY: I suppose you want to see her before you leave.

HANNAH: Well, you suppose wrong. I've seen her . . . I'll call her when I get to New York.

BILLY: What should I tell her?

HANNAH: Tell her I hope she'll be very happy and that I'm selling her record collection . . .

BILLY (*starts towards the door*): You know, we couldn't have been too bad together. We produced a hell of a girl.

HANNAH: You got that a little wrong . . . I think the two of you produced a hell of a mother.

BILLY: Maybe you're right . . . Can we shake hands now? I'm about to leave.

HANNAH: Sure. Why not? What more can I lose?

They shake hands. He holds on.

Serve her plenty of broccoli and lima beans.

BILLY: She likes them?

HANNAH: *Hates* them . . . But from now on, what do I care?

BILLY: Goodbye, Hannah . . . It was good seeing you again.

HANNAH: I suddenly feel like an artist selling a painting he doesn't want to part with.

BILLY: I'll frame it and keep it in a good light.

HANNAH: Do that . . . And take care of Jenny, too.

Billy looks at her and kisses her on the cheek. He wants to say something else, then changes his mind, opens the door quickly and leaves.

She stands there a moment, then crosses to the window and looks down . . . Then she crosses to the phone . . . She picks up the phone.
(*Into phone. About to break down*): Operator . . . get me room service . . . I never got my goddamn drinks.
The lights dim and go to black.

Scene 2: *Visitor From Philadelphia*

In the same suite, mid-December morning sunlight is streaming into the living room, but the bedroom is still rather dark. A long male yawn comes from the bed, then Marvin Michaels, 42, rises wearing undershorts, T-shirt and one black sock. He is sitting on the bed vowing "Never again . . . never never never," when a female arm flops out from under the bedclothes. Startled, he investigates and finds an attractive woman lying in his bed, wearing his pajama top.

Marvin looks at the clock, sees that it is 11 a.m. and frantically but unsuccessfully tries to rouse the woman. He has forgotten to leave a call for 8 o'clock and is expecting his wife to come in on the morning plane, but he can't wake up the woman in his bed. She has drunk a whole bottle of vodka and is insensible except for an occasional groan.

Marvin throws water on her, trying desperately to arouse her, but she doesn't budge.

MARVIN: . . . All right, we're gonna get you dressed and down into a cab . . . Once you're on your feet, you'll be fine . . . I'm really sorry this happened . . . I don't remember much but it must have been a wonderful evening . . . whatever your name is . . . could you help me a little, honey? Please . . . You're not gonna help me. All right Marvin, think. Think, Marvin.
He slaps his own face to help him think.
. . . I gotta get outta here.
He picks up the phone.
Operator, get me the front desk. (*Looks at her.*) I have two wonderful children who need a father, don't do this to me. (*Into phone.*) Hello? . . . This is an *angry* Mr. Michaels in Suite 203 and 4 . . . Listen, I am very uncomfortable in my room . . . The toilet kept dripping all night. No I don't want it fixed. I want another room. I could move out immediately . . . I'm expecting my wife in from Philadelphia any minute and I *know* she's not going to be happy once she sees this room . . . *Who's* here? . . . MY WIFE???? MY-WIFE-IS-HERE??? . . . You sent my wife up without calling me? . . . How could you do such a thing? What the hell kind of a cheap hotel are you running here? . . . Can't you send someone to stop her? She's not going to like this room!!!
There is a knock on the living room door.
Oh God!!!! Oh God!!!! Oh God!!!! OH, GOD! OH, GOD . . . OH, GOD! . . . . . .
Another knock on the living room door. He crosses into living room, closing bedroom door.
(*Softly and innocently.*) Who is it?
MILLIE: It's me.
MARVIN: Millie?

MILLIE: Yes.

> *He picks up ash tray and two champagne glasses and hurls them out the patio window. He opens door.*

MARVIN: Hello sweetie.

MILLIE: Hello. What took you so long? Why didn't you pick me up at the airport?

MARVIN: Why?

MILLIE: Yes, why?

MARVIN: Why? I've been sick all night. I threw up in the other room. Don't go in there . . . . .

Anything to keep Millie out of the bedroom where the girl is still out cold. Millie of course wants to know all about his illness, entangling Marvin in a series of progressively more implausible lies. He tries to send her out for medicine, but she's too tired from her journey. He tries to persuade her to go get a cab so they can attend their nephew's bar mitzvah, but that isn't scheduled to take place for two hours yet.

Millie suddenly remembers that the airline lost her luggage, so that she has nothing to wear to the bar mitzvah — and she begins to weep. Marvin grasps at straws: they'll go out shopping for a dress, go directly to the celebration and then to San Francisco. But now all Millie wants is to go to the bathroom, and Marvin must invent all kinds of reasons to prevent this.

Millie is beginning to notice Marvin's peculiar behavior, but Marvin manages to escape to the bedroom. He locks the door behind him and, seeing that the girl is still unconscious, tries to drag her out of the bedroom door into the hall. There's someone there, though, so he has to drag the limp body back to the bed.

Millie comes over to the bedroom door and finds it locked. Marvin hurriedly hides the girl under the bed covers, throws her clothes under the bed and lets his wife in. She is on her way to the bathroom, commenting, "What took you so long? What's the matter, you got a girl in here?"

While Millie's in the bathroom Marvin thinks of putting the girl in the closet but sees that he'll never make it in time. Millie comes back and suggests that they both take a nap. Marvin stops her and gets her to sit in the armchair, where she takes off her shoes. Marvin has something to tell his wife.

MARVIN: Millie, you mean more to me than you could possibly know . . . but sometimes we transgress. Sometimes we do foolish little things that unwittingly may cause hurt and injury to the other.

MILLIE: I don't think you've ever consciously hurt me.

MARVIN: Consciously, no . . . But a careless word here, a thoughtless gesture there . . .

MILLIE: Nothing major, Marvin . . . We've had our disagreements, but nothing major.

MARVIN: I'm glad you brought that up, Millie . . . What would you consider major?

MILLIE: Major? . . . I don't know . . . I couldn't picture you doing anything "major." A couple of minors, maybe, but no major.

MARVIN: But if I did. If I were not my normal self — temporarily — if illness had caused me to act in some foolish manner, what hurt could I cause you that was major?

MILLIE: It's so hard to say . . . I guess if you were cruel to the children. I think that would be major.

MARVIN (*jumping on it*): I would put that Number One! . . . I think that would be the worst thing a man could do to his wife in a marriage . . . To be cruel to their children is unpardonable . . . *All else* could be forgiven. (*He looks at the bed.*)

MILLIE: And if I caught you with another woman. That would be major.

MARVIN: Let's not get off the children thing so fast . . . . .

Millie decides she must lie down and gets up from the chair. Marvin suggests they go into the living room and make love on the couch, or maybe on the rug. Nevertheless Millie starts in the direction of the bed, and Marvin plays his trump card, pretending to feel sick. Millie exclaims, "I'm sick, too . . . I got my period on the plane . . . The first vacation we've had together in two years and I have to get my goddamn period so don't tell me how sick you are!"

Weeping, Millie throws herself onto the bed beside the hidden body of the girl. Seeing how much this upsets Marvin, she fears she has been too irritable with him. She sits up, apologizes and invites him to lie down beside her. Marvin knows that he has lost the game and resigns himself to the worst, which immediately happens. The semi-conscious stranger in the bed pushes the covers down, revealing her presence.

MARVIN: There's something I'd like to show you, Millie . . . But I'm going to ask you to do something for me first . . . Say nothing for ten seconds . . . Whatever comes to mind, please, for the sake of both of us — say nothing for ten seconds . . . You may turn around now, Millie.
      She turns her head around to the right and sees the body in the bed.
      She looks at it, and suddenly laughs aloud.

MILLIE: . . . One . . . two . . . three . . . I'm praying, Marvin . . . I'm praying the maid came in here to clean, got dizzy from overwork and fainted in your bed . . . I pray to God the maids in this hotel wear pajamas.

MARVIN: It's not the maid, Millie.

MILLIE: Then I hope it's the doctor . . . Is this your doctor, Marvin? If it's not your doctor, then you're going to need your lawyer.

MARVIN: It's not a doctor, Millie . . . It's a woman.

MILLIE: That was my *third* guess . . . You can call American Airlines and tell them to forget my luggage. I won't be needing it. . . . Let me ask you a silly question, Marvin. Why doesn't she move?

MARVIN: I can explain that.

MILLIE: If you tell me you have been carrying on with a helpless paralytic, I won't buy it. Marvin . . . DON'T PLAY ON MY SYMPATHY!!!

MARVIN: She had six margaritas and a bottle of vodka. She won't wake up till tomorrow . . . Millie, I deny nothing.

MILLIE: Interesting, because I accuse you of EVERYTHING!! . . .

She crosses to the chair and starts to put on her shoes.

Is it a hooker, Marvin? . . . Is it someone you know or is it a hooker? If it's a hooker, I'm going to divorce you. If it's someone you know, I'm going to kill you.

Marvin admits she's probably a hooker. Millie is humiliated by the thought of having lain in the bed beside a hooker, adding to her desire for revenge. Marvin tries to save the situation and his marriage by emphasizing his guilt and confessing "I have committed adultery," but not even this pacifies irate Millie, who remarks, "Being cruel to children is number two. *This* is number one."

Millie phones for a taxi, while Marvin tries to explain that he didn't solicit the girl, she came over unbidden as a gift from his younger brother Harry who wanted to repay Marvin for a similar present Marvin gave Harry on his 15th birthday. Millie suggests they send for the official bar mitzvah photographer for a memento of their California trip.

Millie fears she will be ashamed to face Harry at the bar mitzvah (though Harry doesn't know she knows); but then she decides to brazen it out.

MILLIE: I am going to behave with more dignity than you ever dreamed of. I am going to that bar mitzvah with my head held high. I am not going to leave you, Marvin. I am not going to divorce you . . . I am going to forgive you. I am going to forget this ever happened. I am going to understand the reason *why* it happened and I will never bring it up again as long as we live . . . I am now going into Beverly Hills and spend every cent you've got.

MARVIN: Wait, Millie. Let me go with you . . . I'll get dressed, we'll go shopping, we'll go to the bar mitzvah and tonight we'll move into another hotel . . . Can we do that, Millie?

MILLIE: Yes, Marvin, I would like that . . . I would like to make a fresh start . . . I would like to try and rebuild our marriage on trust and faith . . . I don't want something like this ever to happen to us again, Marvin.

MARVIN: It won't, Millie, I promise you that.

Marvin hugs Millie and, full of contrition and gratitude, runs off to shave. The phone rings and Millie answers it — it's the children calling from home. Automatically, Millie sits on the bed while talking into the phone and then leans back. The hooker's arm flops over Millie, who is tearfully telling her children about her lost luggage as the curtain falls.

ACT II

Scene 1: Visitors From London

The same hotel suite is filled with flowers. The light of 5 p.m. in early April is pouring into the room where Sidney Nichols — *"in his early 40s and British"* — sits wearing a tuxedo, drinking a gin and tonic and reading *Daily Variety*.

Sidney's wife Diana enters fastening earrings and wearing a full-length chiffon gown. The dress is obviously very expensive but Diana is dissatisfied with a flowery bulge on her shoulder.

DIANA: It's all *bulky* on the left side. Don't you see how it bunches up?

SIDNEY: Have you taken out all the tissue paper?

DIANA: I should have worn something simple . . . My black pants suit. Why the hell didn't I wear my black pants suit?

SIDNEY: Because *I'm* wearing it . . .

DIANA: We shouldn't have come. I never know how to dress in this bloody country. It's so easy to dress in England. You just put on warm clothing . . . Why did we come, Sidney?

SIDNEY: Because it's all free, darling.

DIANA: Glenda Jackson never comes and she's nominated every goddamn year. We could have stayed in London and waited for a phone call. Michael Caine could have accepted for me. He would be bright and witty and no one would have seen my hump.

SIDNEY: Use it, sweetheart. People will pity you for your deformity and you're sure to win.

DIANA: Maybe if you put your arm on my shoulder. Keep your arm on my shoulder at all times. If I win, we'll go up together, your arm around me, and they'll think we're still mad for each other after twelve years.

SIDNEY: Oh, I thought we were. I keep forgetting.

Diana complains about the color of her hair, wonders about the amount of jewelry she's wearing. Sidney keeps trying to relieve her nervousness by making her smile and reassuring her. The phone rings, reminding them that nominees must arrive early for the benefit of the press. But before they go, Sidney makes them each a drink.

The phone rings again. This time it's Joe Levine, who is paying for everything including the dress and the flowers and is calling to wish Diana luck. Diana takes the phone and tells him, "I feel so responsible . . . I don't want to let you down tonight . . . I know how much the picture means to you and I want so much to win this for you, Joe . . . There was no picture without you . . . Well, goddamn it, it's true . . . After four studios turned it down, you deserve some special perseverance award . . . You're a chubby little man and I adore you . . . If I win tonight, darling, it's not going to be an Oscar . . . It's going to be a Joe Levine . . . You're an angel."

She hangs up, and tells Sidney that this is to be her acceptance speech — although of course she knows she doesn't stand a chance of winning. Diana has finished her drink and grabs Sidney's. He makes himself another as Diana contemplates giving up acting next year and quotes Laurence Olivier: "Acting is the finest and most noble thing you can do with your life, unless, of course, you're lucky enough to be happy."

Sidney remarks that Diana's unhappiness could be taken as a reflection upon him, but Diana assures him she didn't mean it that way.

DIANA: I envy you, Sidney. You have nothing *but* talent. You cook better than I do, you write better than I do, God knows you *dress* better than I do.

SIDNEY: Better than *I*. Do is superfluous.

DIANA: And you speak better than I do . . . Jesus, I'm glad you came. I would hate to go through this tonight alone.

SIDNEY: I don't think they allow nominees to come alone . . . They give you Burt Reynolds or someone.

DIANA: You've never liked any of this, have you? The openings, the parties, any of it.

SIDNEY: I *love* the openings. I *adore* the parties. I lead a very gay life. I mean, let's be honest, angel, how many antique dealers in London get to go to the Academy Awards?

DIANA: And I think you hate that dusty little shop. You're never there when I call. Where do you spend your afternoons, Sidney?

SIDNEY: In London? We don't have afternoons.

Sidney was once a promising actor himself and could go back to it any time, Diana assures him. As they're getting ready to leave, Sidney wishes Diana luck in his own way: "You're a gifted and remarkable woman. You've put up with me and my shenanigans for twelve harrowing years and I don't know why. But I'm grateful . . . You've had half a husband and three-quarters of a career. You deserve the full amount of everything." Diana tells him she loves him and they exit. The lights darken as day turns into night.

Scene 2: *Visitors From London (continued)*

At 3 a.m. Sidney enters, his tie askew, followed by Diana, who has had more than enough to drink and is obviously and somewhat irritably a loser. At one point, apparently, Diana threw up on the wife of a Universal V.I.P. and will probably never work there again. Diana remembers seeing Barbra Streisand in the ladies room. Later, when the Best Picture award came through, Diana was so depressed she didn't hear the announcement and wants to know who won, but Sidney won't tell her.

Diana is taking her disappointment out on Sidney, calling him names and even insisting that he has gotten them both into the wrong hotel room. Sidney is rather forbearing, without actually coddling his drunken and disappointed wife, not letting her forget that her behavior this evening was unacceptable.

DIANA: Considering that I should have won that effing award tonight, I behaved *beautifully* . . . I would like a drink, please.

SIDNEY: You *drank* everything in this state. Try Nevada.
    He crosses to the bedroom, turning out the light in the living room and on in the bedroom.

DIANA: Well, *I* had a wonderful time. (*She follows him in.*) Did you hear me? I said, *I* had a wonderful time. (*She looks at room.*) This looks just like *our* room.

SIDNEY (*sits on bed, takes off cuff links and studs*): Have you ever seen a greater assemblage of hypocrites under one roof in all your life?

DIANA: Were the hypocrites there? I missed them. Why didn't you point them out to me?

She crosses and looks into mirror.

SIDNEY: Hypocritical hypocrites . . . They all love you and fawn over you on the way in . . . And if you come out a loser, it's "too bad, darling. Give us a call when you're back in town" . . . You should have thrown up on the whole bloody lot of them.

DIANA (*looking into mirror*): Sidney?

SIDNEY: Yes?

DIANA: Was I hit by a bus? . . . I look very much as though I've been hit by a heavy, fast moving Greyhound bus . . .

SIDNEY: What really infuriated me is how quickly the winners got their cars . . . How could the winners' cars be lined up so quickly outside if they didn't know beforehand who the winners were? . . . Because it's rigged . . . We come six thousand miles for this bloody affair and they park *our* car in Vancouver.

DIANA (*still looking in mirror*): I've aged, Sidney . . . I'm getting lines in my face . . . I look like a brand new steel belted radial tire . . .

SIDNEY: That little Polish twerp who won Best Foreign Documentary got *his* car before us . . . splashed water on my trousers as he drove by . . . They must have snapped fifty photos of us going in. Coming out a little Mexican boy with a Brownie asked me where Liza Minnelli was.

Diana tries to order eggs benedict, but room service is closed for the night. Diana noticed a handsome young actor who sat next to Sidney at dinner. Sidney warns her gently to change the subject: "You're tired and smashed. Let's not get into shallow waters."

Diana also noticed that Sidney suddenly relaxed when the winner in her category was announced, and she wonders whether Sidney might have been glad she lost. Sidney doesn't want to quarrel, but Diana practically insists on it and finally annoys Sidney with her comments about the young actor.

DIANA: Adam, wasn't that his name? Adam, the first man . . . not very appropriate for you, is it? . . . He did look very Californian, I thought. Sort of a ballsy Doris Day.

SIDNEY: Oh, Christ, Diana, come off it . . . We keep up a front for everyone else, why can't we do it for ourselves?

DIANA: You mean lie to each other that we're perfectly well-mated? . . . A closet couple, is that what we are, Sidney?

SIDNEY: I have never hidden behind doors but I *am* discreet.

DIANA: Discreet? You did everything but lick his artichoke.

SIDNEY: Let's please not have a discretion contest . . . I have heard about your lunch breaks on the set . . . The only thing you don't do in your dressing room is dress . . . I'm going to take some Librium . . . If I'm not up by nine, I've overdosed.

Diana admits she couldn't do without Sidney. She is angry when she learns the young actor is coming to London next week for a film. Diana asks Sidney

"Why don't you love me?" and begs him to make love to her. Sidney is available, but far from enthusiastic. Diana declares "Jesus God, Sidney, I love you so much." She wonders why Sidney stays with her. Diana widens his circle of possibilities, Sidney tells her. He adds, "I love you more than any woman I've ever met." She must content herself with that and she does, reaching out to take Sidney's hand.

SIDNEY: You can't say we don't have fun together.
DIANA: Hell, the dinner conversations alone are worth the trouble.
    He puts his arm around her.
It's my fault for being a hopeless romantic . . . I keep believing all those movies I've made . . . And you do make love so sweetly.
SIDNEY: Would it help any if I made some empty promises?
DIANA: It never has . . . What's wrong with *me*, Sidney? We've been fighting this for years. Why haven't I ever left you for a hairier person?
SIDNEY: Because we like each other . . . And we are each a refuge for our disappointments out there.
DIANA: You *do* have a way of putting your finger right on the trouble spot . . .

Diana lies back in the bed, and Sidney turns out the light and joins her. She acknowledges the good care he takes of her.

DIANA: I love you, Sidney.
    Sidney leans over and kisses her with warmth and tenderness.
. . . Don't close your eyes, Sidney.
SIDNEY: I always close my eyes.
DIANA: Not tonight . . . Look at *me* tonight . . . Let it be *me* tonight.
    The lights dim and go to black.

Scene 3: Visitors From Chicago

Both rooms of the same suite are bright and sunny at 4 p.m. on Sunday afternoon, July 4. Mort and Beth Hollander enter in tennis clothes. Mort carrying the rackets and a can of balls, Beth with her arm around Mort's shoulder, hobbling. Beth has hurt her foot and is in pain as Mort drops the tennis equipment and lowers her into a chair. Beth wants aspirin. Mort goes to the bathroom to get it, while talking.

MORT: The thing that kills me is that they *saw* your shoe laces were untied. That's why they kept lobbing over your head.
BETH: Look at that ankle puff up. It's the size of a grapefruit. I'll have to wear your shoes on the plane tomorrow.
MORT (*in the bathroom*): And they just kept lobbing the ball over your head . . . Lob, lob, lob, the sons of bitches.
BETH: When I fell, I heard something go snap. I said to myself, "Please God, let it be my brassiere."

MORT (*comes out with water and aspirins*): That wasn't tennis out there, that was *war!* . . . They only hit it to you when the sun was in your eyes and they only hit it to me when my shorts were slipping down . . .

Beth wants a doctor. Mort looks for one in the Yellow Pages. She doesn't like the sound of any of the names, so Mort calls the desk and they promise to send one up. He also orders three buckets of ice cubes for the foot.

The phone rings. It's their tennis opponents calling to find out how Beth's ankle feels. Furiously, Mort tells them, "I want you to go to the proshop and buy two cans of Wilson yellow tennis balls, charge them to me, and shove them up your respective asses."

Mort slams the phone down in anger, although their opponents happen also to be their best friends from back home, sharing a vacation with Mort and Beth. Their friendship has been under a strain from the very first day, when the others showed up at the airport having forgotten to bring along their credit cards but bringing no less than eight pieces of luggage. Now, after three weeks of close proximity, it is past the breaking point.

There is a knock on the door. Mort opens it to Stu and Gert Franklyn, she in a white tennis dress, he in a yellow warm-up suit, carrying their tennis equipment. Gert tries to comfort Beth, reaching out to touch the sore foot.

BETH: Don't do that! I yell shit when you do that.

STU (*holds up can of balls to Mort*): Here! This is the can you told me to buy . . . You want me to take the balls out first?

Mort turns away from him in anger.

(*To Mort.*) Have you called a doctor? (*To Beth.*) Has he called a doctor?

BETH: Yes.

STU: Is he a good man?

BETH: He was listed very nicely.

GERT (*to Mort*): Shouldn't she have ice on that leg, Mort? . . . Mort? . . . Should we get some ice?

STU (*to Mort*): Gert's talking to you. What the hell's wrong with you.

MORT (*turns, hands on hips, takes a deep breath*): I'm sorry Stu . . . I'm very upset . . . Beth's foot may be broken, my temper got the best of me. I ordered some ice . . . okay?

STU: . . . I understand.

MORT: It's been a rough three weeks. After a while, you start to get on each other's nerves, you know?

STU: Sure.

MORT: I mean four people taking a vacation together can get very testy . . . You can only do it with your best friends . . . And you and Gert are our best friends . . . Christ, we don't have better friends than you . . .

Stu nods.

. . . because if we did — *I would have told you to shove a steel RACKET up your ass!*

Stu insists Beth's accident wasn't their fault, and Mort insists it was. Stu resents this, and the two quarrel in earnest, revealing the depth of their growing irritation over small matters.

Stu and Mort botch the job of carrying Beth into the bedroom because they refuse to coordinate their efforts. Gert, in the bathroom to get a wet towel to cool Beth's foot, accidentally breaks Beth's $90 bottle of perfume.

Stu and Mort struggle with Beth toward the bed. Gert appears again from the bathroom, having cut her finger on the broken glass and calling for iodine. But the men can't help her until they get Beth settled. Gert returns to the bathroom while the others maneuver Beth toward the bed. Just as they manage to lower Beth onto the bed, Gert cries out and staggers back into the room, having hit her head on the medicine cabinet. She falls to the floor, unconscious.

Mort straightens Beth out on the bed, while Stu revives Gert. Stu blames Mort for his wife's accident. Mort goes to the bathroom and brings back two wet towels, one cold compress for each wife, but not without having cut himself through his sneakers on the broken glass.

Stu and Mort manage to cooperate long enough to lift Gert onto the bed beside Beth, Mort commenting, "Jesus, it's like Guadalcanal in here." Stu is now thoroughly angry and takes out his wallet, insisting on a formal settling-up of accounts. Mort tries to calm him down.

MORT: . . . . . Take it easy. Let's not get our noses out of joint.

STU: You call this a vacation? . . . I had a better vacation when I had my hernia operation . . . I'm sick of your face . . . I'm sick of your twelve-cent cigars. After three weeks, my clothes smell like they've been in a humidor . . . I'm sick of your breakfasts . . . I'm sick of your lightly buttered rye toast and eggs over lightly every goddamned morning . . . Would it kill you to have a waffle once in a while? . . . One stinkin' little waffle for my sake?

MORT: What are you, crazy? . . . We got two invalids in bed and you're talking about waffles?

STU: We did everything *you* wanted . . . *You* made all the decisions . . . You took *all* the pictures . . . I didn't get to take *one* picture with my own camera . . . You picked all the restaurants . . . Nine Japanese restaurants in three weeks . . . I am nauseated at the sight of watching you eat tempura with your shoes off . . . I am bored following your wife into every chochkee store on the west coast looking for Mexican bracelets . . .

MORT: Hey, hey, wait a minute . . . Your wife bought too . . . What about a pair of African earrings that hang down to her navel?

STU: A year I planned for this vacation . . . You know what I got to show for it? . . . Two purple Hawaiian shirts for *my* kids that you picked out. Even *Hawaiians* wouldn't wear them . . . One entire morning wasted in Honolulu while five Chinese tailors measured you for a thirty-nine-dollar Hong Kong suit that fell apart in the box . . . I spent half an afternoon on Fisherman's Wharf watching a near-sighted eighty-four-year-old artist painting a charcoal portrait of you that looks like Charles Laughton . . . I've had enough . . . I want to go home . . . I'm a nervous wreck . . . I need a vacation.

Stu's growing anger seems to pacify Mort, who suggests they shake hands and ave a Planter's Punch. Gert leans on Beth's foot accidentally, and Mort shouts t her and calls her an idiot. Stu picks up a tennis racket and threatens to beat Mort with it unless he apologizes. Mort warns Stu that he'll defend himself, as he wives beg the husbands not to fight. Stu lunges at Mort who, much the bigger man, gets a hammerlock on his friend. The two struggling men, threatening to kill each other, stagger into the bathroom. A tremendous crash and a moan are heard. Mort comes out doubled over, having been kicked in the groin. Stu comes out holding a towel over his ballooning lip.

Mort and Stu are still threatening each other, and Mort stands up ready to continue the fight. Gert screams "Stop it!" and pulls Mort away. *"She falls back on the chair and he falls on top of her. Stu falls on the bed, right on Beth's bad leg. Beth pounds her fist on the bed. There is a long silence — a very long silence as all four lie there quietly in pain . . . Then the sobbing subsides . . . and we just hear them sigh and breathe."*

Mort is still suffering from Stu's kick. Stu is still threatening Mort unless he apologizes to Gert. Stu manages to get close enough to Mort to bite him on the calf. Mort jumps on top of Stu and holds him to the floor with his weight.

STU: Gert, hit him! . . . Get a lamp and hit him.

GERT: Don't sit on him, please . . . Get off him, you fat water tank . . . Oh, I'm sorry, Beth.

BETH: Listen, the truth is the truth.

MORT (*to Stu*): All right . . . Now nobody is leaving this room until we all make up with each other . . . We came here friends and we're leaving friends . . . Now tell me we're friends, you bastard!

> *He chokes him.*

GERT: Make up with him, Stu. It's the only chance we have.

STU: I make up . . . I surrender and make up.

MORT: Not like that. Like you mean it.

STU: I mean it . . . I can't breathe. You're cutting off my air.

BETH (*lying down flat on the bed*): I don't understand. Why is he cutting off his hair?

MORT: And tell me you had a good time on our vacation . . . *Tell me!!*

STU: I had a good time.

MORT: Especially the Japanese restaurants.

STU: Especially the goddamned Japanese restaurants. Let me up. My ribs are cracking.

MORT: . . . And you want to take another vacation with us next year.

STU: Crack my ribs!! Crush me!! I won't say that!

> *Curtain starts to fall.*

MORT, BETH and GERT: Say it!!! Say it!!! Say it!!!

> *Curtain.*

OOO
OOO
OOO
OOO THE OLDEST
OOO
OOO LIVING GRADUATE

A Play in Two Acts

BY PRESTON JONES

Cast and credits appear on page 290

PRESTON JONES was born in 1936 in Albuquerque and grew up there. H
graduated from the University of New Mexico in 1960 and two years late
joined the Dallas Theater Center as an actor (playing such roles as the Stag
Manager in Our Town, *Brutus in* Julius Caesar, *Victor in* The Price) *and direc*
*tor (*The Knack, Barefoot in the Park, *etc.). In a period of 18 months in 1973–7*
he wrote all the plays in A Texas Trilogy, *thereby adding the profession of play*
writing to his other considerable accomplishments.

All three Jones plays were first produced by and at his own group in Dallas
The first to be brought before the audience was The Last Meeting of the Knight
of the White Magnolia on Dec. 4, 1973, soon followed by Lu Ann Hampto
Laverty Oberlander *on Feb. 5, 1974. Beginning Nov. 19, 1974,* The Oldest Liv
ing Graduate *joined the other two plays in repertory under the direction of Pau*
Baker, the Dallas company's managing director. Knights *was selected by th*
American Playwrights Theater for production by its member theaters across th
country in the 1975–76 season. Kennedy Center produced the three plays i
repertory in Washington, D.C. in April, 1976, under Alan Schneider's direc
tion, and again in August prior to their opening on Broadway Sept. 21, makin
their author's New York playwriting debut and capturing two of the te
1976–77 Best Plays citations for Knights *and* Graduate.

Jones received his M.A. from Trinity University in San Antonio in 1966 and
was awarded a Rockefeller Foundation grant in playwriting in 1975. His mos
recent play, produced at Dallas Theater Center in 1976, is A Place on the Mag
dalena Flats. *He is a member of the Texas Institute of Letters, the Texas Com*

mission on the Arts and the board of governors of American Playwrights Theater. He is also an accomplished sculptor. His wife is the former Mary Sue Fridge, a member of the Dallas troupe.

Time: Summer of 1962

Place: The den of Floyd Kinkaid's ranch-style home on the outskirts of Bradleyville, Tex.

ACT I

Scene 1: A summer afternoon

SYNOPSIS: Glass doors give onto a patio upstage in the den of the Kinkaid house. The door to the living room is at right next to a huge stone fireplace. An archway at left leads to Colonel Kinkaid's bedroom. The den's furnishings include a gun rack which opens to reveal a bar, a desk with photos of the Colonel and a son in World War I and World War II uniforms, and a large sofa at center.

Colonel J. C. Kinkaid enters in a wheelchair from his bedroom, calling for his son Floyd. The Colonel is *"75, eccentric World War I vet . . . now in his dotage,"* but comfortably situated thanks to cattle, cotton and oil. The Colonel shouts for Floyd to make good his promise to take him for a drive this afternoon. Floyd's wife Maureen enters (*"42 . . . wonders why she's so goddamned bored with everything"*) to explain that Floyd has gone into town to set up a business deal with his friend Clarence Sickenger while Maureen entertains Clarence's wife Martha Ann. The Colonel doesn't think much of his son's friend Clarence. He retires to his bedroom grumbling.

Martha Ann Sickenger (27, married to 43-year-old Clarence, *"and if Clarence just happens to be one of the richest men in town, well, what the hell"*) joins Maureen in the den. The Colonel, it seems, is known to be a very difficult patient, driving away any nurse hired to take care of him. Martha Ann tells Maureen, "Clarence says the only place that can handle shell-shock business like the Colonel has is a veterans hospital." Maureen informs her that so far the family has managed to cope, with the help of ranch employees.

While the women are gossiping, the Colonel wheels himself back into the den, complaining about the fakery in TV Westerns. Introduced to Martha Ann, the Colonel wonders bluntly why a pretty girl like her married "that dumb-butted Clarence Sickenger."

On being informed that Martha Ann has two children, the Colonel complains that Floyd and Maureen have never given him a grandchild, and now it's obviously too late.

Maureen sends Martha Ann into the living room and turns to the Colonel before following her.

MAUREEN: Keep it up, Colonel, ever' time you open your mouth you're talking yourself one step closer to the old soldiers' home.
She exits.
COLONEL (*muttering*): Floyd never shoulda married that woman. Barren as a by-God thirty-year-old ewe. (*The phone rings.*) Bumble-dickin' phone! Ah'm comin'.
The Colonel wheels his chair over to the phone and picks it up.
Kinkaid here, who the hell are you? . . . Who? . . . Never heard of you . . . Hell, yes, this is the Kinkaid residence, where else would ah be?
MAUREEN (*calling from the living room*): Colonel, it's not for you. I got it out here, on the extension.
COLONEL: Damn sure is too for me. Ah answered it, didn't ah! (*Into phone.*) If you didn't want to talk to me, then why the hell did you ring up mah house! This better not be one of them-there dirty phone calls . . .
MAUREEN (*from living room*): Dammit, Colonel, hang up! The call isn't for you!
COLONEL: You mean it's for you? (*Into phone.*) You're a pretty sad-assed sex fiend, feller, if you called over here for Maureen, wasted a by-God dime . . .
MAUREEN (*appearing at the door*): Will you please get off the line! This happens to be Reverend Stone callin'. He's got a message of some kind for Floyd.
COLONEL: The hell you say. (*Into phone.*) Kinkaid here again. By God, Stone, ah'm plumb ashamed of you. What kind of a preacher makes dirty phone calls? You lose the callin' or somethin'? . . .
MAUREEN (*reaching for the phone*): Gimme that . . .
COLONEL Git away from here. (*Into phone.*) Ah seen a preacher loose the callin' over there in France. He was holy as hell till we got into the trenches. Wound up cussin' them whiz-bangs worse than any of us. Knew more cuss words than old Harry S. Truman. Never heard "Dammit to hell" said with such by-God ringin' fervor in mah life . . .
MAUREEN: Now that's jest enough!
She grabs the receiver out of his hand.
Hello . . . Hello . . . He hung up.
COLONEL: Hell, yes, he hung up. Ah let him know the truth of things.

The Colonel accuses Maureen of deliberately planning to provoke trouble with the Reverend in order to get the Colonel barred from heaven. Martha Ann comes in as the Colonel is explaining that he has already served his time in hell, in the trenches of World War I, "Over the goddamned top, over the top and the Germans all the time shootin' them damned machine guns, blappity, blappity, blap!"
Maureen calls out into the yard for Mike Tremaine to come in and take the Colonel out for a ride in the car, to distract him. Mike ("*a tall, weatherbeaten man*") wheels the Colonel out, with the Colonel directing him to drive him down to look at "mah town" by the lake.
Maureen explains to Martha Ann that there's no town there, really; it's just the old Genet farm, abandoned to the brush and jackrabbits, owned by the

Colonel, who won't let Floyd even run cattle on it. It's the Genet farm, however (Martha Ann explains to Maureen), that Floyd and Clarence are planning to develop with houses and other facilities like boat docks, calling it Mumford County Estates.

Floyd (*"a thin, nervous man"*) and Clarence (*"large and heavy-set"*) arrive and join their wives in the den, instead of in the living room which has just been expensively decorated but where nobody ever sits. Floyd fixes a round of drinks, and they all talk about barbecue pits and swimming pools. To Maureen's annoyance, Martha Ann and Clarence feel free to mention some shortcomings of the Kindaids' last Founder's Day dinner. Finally the Sickengers depart, much to Maureen's relief.

MAUREEN: . . . . . Jeezus, I've had that whiny little twang in my ear all day long.

FLOYD: Oh, hell, she never meant nuthin' by all that.

MAUREEN: The devil she didn't. Why are we such big buddies with the Sickengers nowadays? Neither one of us likes 'em very much.

FLOYD: Ah jest thought since we were goin' into this deal together that the families ought to be closer, that's all.

MAUREEN: Sure, closer to the Sickengers and further away from the Colonel. What's all this crap I hear about him givin' his Genet farm to you and Clarence?

FLOYD: Who *told* you about that?

MAUREEN: Martha Ann.

FLOYD: Big-mouthed little bitch. How the hell did she find out?

MAUREEN: Never mind about her — why didn't you tell me?

FLOYD: Because ah didn't want you talkin' to Dad before ah did.

MAUREEN: You mean you haven't even asked him yet?

FLOYD: No, ah haven't — anyway, that lake business is still in the planning stage. Ah got lots of things to do before ah get around to him.

MAUREEN: You better not let him know the Sickengers are in on it. He rates them somewhere below Herbert Hoover and the Kaiser.

FLOYD: Ah thought that spot was reserved for me.

Maureen wishes they could get away from all these Bradleyville problems. In the last two years Maureen has dragged Floyd to the Caribbean and Europe. He hated the whole thing and stayed drunk all the time. They can't go anywhere this summer, Floyd informs his wife, not because of the real estate deal, but because the Mirabeau B. Lamar Military Academy is planning to honor its oldest living graduate — Colonel Kinkaid — at a ceremony and celebration to be held here in Bradleyville. Floyd has just received a letter to this effect.

MAUREEN: . . . . . What's the big deal about a school full of little kids dressed in soldier suits coming to town?

FLOYD: The whole school isn't comin', jest the band and the honor guard. Besides that, the kids aren't important — it's the graduates and their wives.

MAUREEN: The graduates?

FLOYD: That's right. (*He looks at the letter.*) Two generals, three full colonels, one-two-three-four congressmen, six state senators, an ex-lieutenant governor and a whole raft of businessmen and such like.

MAUREEN: Interesting.

FLOYD: Damn right, it's interestin'. Hell's fire! All the people who are anybody at all go to good old M.B. Lamar. Dad graduated from there in 1905 before he went on to the A&M. As it turns out, he's the only living member of the school's first graduating class. Seems that most of his classmates were killed off in the First World War.

MAUREEN: That's kind of sad.

FLOYD: What's sad about it? This is goin' to mean a helluva lot of publicity for Bradleyville. TV and newspaper people comin' down here. The commandant told me that even the *Life* magazine people are interested.

MAUREEN: Really?

FLOYD: Damn right. There'll be people comin' here from all over the state. We're going to have a banquet, a ceremony, cocktail parties, the works. Hell's fire, it's the biggest thing to hit this town in years.

The Academy's commandant will visit Bradleyville in a couple of days to help make arrangements. Maureen starts considering: their usual caterer won't do, they'll have to hold the banquet at the country club. At some point, Floyd will put on a stag fish fry out at the lake.

Maureen is worried about how the Colonel will take it, but Floyd is sure everything will be all right when the Colonel hears there's to be a memorial service for his fallen comrades.

MAUREEN: . . . . . You know, it occurs to me that this ceremony for the Colonel is really comin' up at a good time, isn't it?

FLOYD: What do you mean?

MAUREEN: What I mean is, isn't it lucky that you were able to talk this commandant of that military academy into coming down here with all those big shots at the very time when you and Clarence are goin' into the lake-development business!

FLOYD (*raising his glass*): Damn right.

MAUREEN: Boy, you don't miss a trick, do you?

FLOYD: Ah do the best ah can.

MAUREEN: Well, I better get on over to the country club and get things started. Listen, I just remembered, Reverend Stone wouldn't have anythin' to do with the memorial service, would he?

FLOYD: I'm gonna get him to conduct it. He's spozed to call me some time today about it.

Maureen bursts into laughter.

What the hell's so funny?

Maureen continues off, laughing. Curtain.

Scene 2: An hour later

Returning from the ride, Mike Tremaine wheels the Colonel in through the patio door. Floyd and Maureen have gone off somewhere, and the Colonel urges

PATRICIA ROE, LEE RICHARDSON AND FRED GWYNNE
IN "THE OLDEST LIVING GRADUATE"

Mike to stay and talk to him. The Colonel remembers the many fishing excursions with Mike's father, now dead. The Colonel damns death: "Damn it straight to hell. Takin' things away from a feller, don't give a goddamned thing, just takes away."

Death took away the Colonel's other son Franklin (whose picture is on the desk) flying a training mission in Florida in World War II. The Colonel still has dreams that Franklin has crashed in a swamp and is calling to his father for help.

The Colonel tells Mike how it was along the big cove on the Genet farm years ago. There was a "town," or rather a settlement, of a religious sect whose members bought the land, raised a half-dozen houses and a community barn and eked out a living farming. The young folk would have dances in the barn, and the Colonel vividly remembers the two pretty Genet girls, Marie and Suzette, of French stock: "God in heaven, but Suzette was a good-lookin' girl. Kindly short, you know, with blondish hair and this little tiny waist. Ah could put both hands around it just like nuthin' at all. Ah seen lots of girls, Mike. Ah seen 'em in the Philippines, ah seen 'em in Mexico. Ah seen them madam-oselles over there to France, but none of 'em, never, any place, was as by-God good-lookin' as little Suzette Genet from right out yonder on that farm. Jesus, but ah was crazy about that girl. Betcha didn't know that, did you? Was moonin' around about her one day and fell off my horse right into a stock tank."

A severe drought forced the little community to move on, Suzette with them, and the Colonel never saw her again. The Colonel's father bought the place, razed the houses and flooded the land with the dam creating Lake Bradleyville. "But them foundations up there on that little rise, that's where ah was a young feller in love once. That's why ah don't let anybody fool with that property. Ah like to keep it for rememberin'. That's important to an old feller like me, havin' places that stay the same for rememberin' on."

Floyd comes back and dismisses Mike so that he can talk to his father. The Colonel's mind wanders all over the place. Finally Floyd pins down his attention and tells him of his plans for developing the Genet farm in partnership with Clarence Sickenger. Clarence owns a piece of adjoining property, so they can subdivide the whole north side of the lake into two-acre plots. The Colonel scoffs at Floyd: only "one of them damn Chinamen" could make a living on two acres of land. Floyd explains that the subdivision isn't for farming, it's for exclusive summer homes.

COLONEL: Summer homes?
FLOYD: That's right. Jesus, we could make a fortune.
COLONEL: You got enough money now.
FLOYD: We could dredge out the cove and put in the biggest damn marina you ever seen.
COLONEL: You cain't have the Genet farm.
FLOYD: We're goin' to call it Mumford County Estates. Nine-hole golf course, water-skiin', skeet shootin', horseback ridin', private club — the works.
COLONEL: Mumford County Estates. Who came up with that one?
FLOYD: Clarence.

COLONEL: That figures. Ah recollect as how them Sickengers is related to old Governor Mumford.

FLOYD: Ah don't know if they are or not. Now . . .

COLONEL: Why they named this county after old Governor Mumford is beyond me. Should have named it Kinkaid County.

FLOYD: Sure, Dad, now . . .

COLONEL: Ah'm proud to be from Texas, ah'm proud to be from Bradley-ville, but by God ah'm not a damn bit proud to be from Mumford County.

FLOYD: All right, all right, so it's a stupid name.

COLONEL (*chuckles*): How would you like to walk up to some feller and have to say, "Howdy, ah'm Clarence Sickenger and ah'm from Mumford County."

FLOYD: Dammit, Dad, what about the project?

COLONEL: What project?

FLOYD: The lake project.

COLONEL: Frilly, sad-assed waste of time. Ruin the land puttin' up a by-God carnival.

FLOYD: We'll have folks movin' in here from all over the country.

COLONEL: Don't graze the land, don't work the land, don't do a damned thing but throw beer bottles and little pieces of paper all over it.

FLOYD: Not if you control it. You make it exclusive and control it.

COLONEL: Best way to control crap like that is not to let it happen at all.

FLOYD: Dad, ah need that land. Clarence is goin' over to Dallas to see the architect again. Hell's fire, we wanna git started on this thing.

COLONEL: You cain't have the Genet farm.

Floyd's pleas are running up against a brick wall of obstinance, as Maureen joins them in the den. The Colonel wheels himself into his room, demanding to be left alone, declaring he wants no supper. Maureen comments on Floyd's project.

MAUREEN: Rich and exclusive. Well, there it is — the Bradleyville Country Club motto. The whole hollow useless thing all over again. A lake full of rich and exclusive, sag-bellied, loud-mouthed bores — water skis, bass boats, Chris-Crafts, everything that "rich and exclusive" can buy.

FLOYD: You're damn right they're goin' to buy — What's wrong with that? The way it is now, that damn land out there is just goin' to waste. This way the Colonel gets his ceremony, you get your picture in *Life* magazine, and old Floyd kicks off a million-dollar deal. It's a perfect plan.

MAUREEN: Perfect except for one thing.

COLONEL (*calling from offstage*): Dammit to hell, where's mah supper! You-all expect me to starve to death out here!

MAUREEN: Him.
     Curtain.

ACT II

Scene 1: Four days later

The Colonel is asleep in his wheelchair, wearing his old Army tunic. Maureen enters and wakes him up to get him ready for the imminent visit of Major Ketchum, the commandant of the Colonel's old military school. The Colonel wonders why such an exalted post should be occupied by a mere major (it was a Confederate general in his day). He is reminiscing about the post-war ill-treatment of the doughboys, when Floyd enters with Major Ketchum and one of his star pupils, Cadet Whopper Turnbull. *"The Major is a portly gentleman wearing a uniform that is closely akin to a World War II Army Air Corps officer's 'pinks' . . . . . Cadet Turnbull is a very military-looking lad of 17. His uniform is much like the Major's, only he wears large West Point-type sergeant's chevrons and shiny black riding boots."*

Cadet Turnbull salutes the Colonel smartly. Maureen exits, as the Colonel looks the cadet over.

COLONEL: How come you wearin' them boots, boy? They bringin' back the horse cavalry?

WHOPPER: No, sir, these are standard dress-uniform requirements at Mirabeau B. Lamar, sir.

KETCHUM: We feel that it gives the boys pride and military bearing.

COLONEL: Ah served in the cavalry with old Black Jack Pershing back in 1916. Betcha didn't know that, did you?

WHOPPER: Yes, sir. I've done an in-depth study of your military career, Colonel.

COLONEL: Old Black Jack. There was a general for you. Ever' inch a soldier. Ah remember once when we was chasin' that fat little greaser Pancho Villa down there in Mexico. Well, sir, ah was havin' a cup of coffee in the officers' mess. Hot as hell that day and the wind was blowin' the tent sides back and forth. Flap, flap, flap.

The Colonel is lost in his memories of the flapping tent. The others try to bring his mind back to the subject, but he's soon off on another tangent, remembering how the horses suffered in the maelstrom of 20th century warfare in France.

Ketchum reviews the details of the proposed ceremony in honor of the Colonel as the oldest living graduate of Mirabeau B. Lamar, with speeches and the band playing "Over There." The Colonel doesn't like that song, however; he'd prefer "The Old Gray Mare," the song he sang while crossing the Marne in 1918. The Colonel remembers some of the other songs of war and tries to amuse an unimpressed Whopper with variations on their lyrics.

At the ceremony, the Colonel is to be introduced, eulogized but not permitted to speak for himself (though he'd like to tell the crowd a few things about the old days in Mexico). He asks for a list of his classmates. Whopper obliges, reading the names off one by one. They are all dead and gone, of course, "Killed in action, September 12, 1918, Saint-Mihiel" or "Died April 7, 1950, in Al-

querque, New Mexico, Veterans Hospital, of lung damage caused by
ustard-gas fumes sustained in the Argonne Forest offensive, September
18." These cold facts penetrate the Colonel's emotions. Some of his class-
ates he remembers and some of them he doesn't, but he realizes that they are
as dead as the comrades left under the rows of crosses in France.

The Colonel remembers how he visited the battlefield after the war and stood
nong those crosses and wept for the young Americans who "was machine-
nned, gassed, and blowed apart, makin' the by-God world safe for Democ-
cy . . . . . whatever in the blue-balled wonder that is."

The Colonel also remembers his contempt for the souvenir-sellers exploiting
e battlefield.

COLONEL: Feller that was with me that day, American feller too, paid twenty-
ve dollars for a busted old Enfield rifle. Told me he wanted a memento of how
musta been during the fightin' there. Ah told him to stick that Enfield up his
tt sideways and march barefooted on the stickery side of the street durin' the
rmistice Day parade and that would really give him an idea of how it was.

KETCHUM: Now, now, Colonel, I don't think you're taking a very military
titude about all this.

COLONEL: Go to hell with your goddamned military attitude! You weren't
ere, dammit!

FLOYD: Dad. Please.

KETCHUM: Now, now, Colonel, we need to think about our little ceremony.

COLONEL: To hell with it! Git your ass out of here and take your by-God old-
t living graduate outfit with you. Ah don't want it, don't want no part of it.
ot worth it. Not worth a bumble-dickin', goddamned thing! It ain't no honor
be the oldest living *anything*. Oldest living *graduate*, oldest living *Indian*, old-
t living *armadillo*, oldest living *nuthin'*, 'cause that means that you're all
one! Stand around lookin' at the next-oldest livin' whippersnapper and won-
r where the hell ever'body went.

FLOYD: Now listen, Dad, you're not backin' outa this. We're havin' this cere-
ony and you're going to be there or I'll by God know the reason why!

COLONEL: The reason why? The reason why is 'cause ah flat-assed don't want
and what's more ah ain't goin' to!

Major Ketchum sees that the planned ceremony will have to be abandoned in
e face of the Colonel's flat refusal. Ketchum and Whopper depart, leaving
oyd to pick up the pieces of his collapsed publicity stunt. Bitterly, Floyd ex-
ains to his father the importance of the Academy gathering as promotion for
s lake project. The Colonel reminds Floyd that he can't have the land for his
oject, adding to Floyd's fury.

FLOYD: Quit tellin' me what ah can and can't have. Ah've looked after this
mily for seventeen years, seventeen years! Me, dammit, not you. Now, by
od, from now on, what ah say goes. The lake project, the military-school deal,
er'thing! From now on ah'm tellin' you what's by God what. *That,* Colonel,
at is an order, and *that* is a fact!

COLONEL: Mind your tongue, boy, you just mind your tongue. Franklin neve talked that way to me.

FLOYD: To hell with Franklin. I'm sick of hearin' about him. You've stuc him down my throat ever since we were boys. Your precious goddamne Franklin. You know what Franklin was, you really want to know? He was stuck-up, smart-assed twirp! My beloved big brother. My first day in hig school he sicked some of his buddies on me and they took my pants off in fror of the whole school. I was layin' there in the dirt, too goddamned ashamed t move, and he was laffin', laffin' louder than all the rest. I hated his guts and yo put him on a pedestal forty feet high . . . . .

Franklin was a football star, Floyd continues, and if he'd come home a wa hero too there would have been no life for Floyd to live. The Colonel still can get it through his head why Floyd is glad his brother is dead and wants to g against his father's wishes. Floyd exits trying to control his anger.

Maureen comes in and confides to the Colonel that she sympathizes with hin "I wouldn't wanna be the bumble-dickin' oldest livin' graduate either." Bu Maureen suggests that the Colonel might after all let Floyd have the Gene farm; it's not just a business deal, Floyd needs the project to justify his exis tence: "My God, Colonel, look at him, look at us rattlin' around in this big ol house with no purpose in life at all. The Kinkaid interests run themselve: Floyd's foremen and managers do all the work, and he just drives around an looks at things, or he sits around that damn country club and bets on ball game: He needs the deals he's gonna make to keep from goin' nuts . . . . . "

Let Floyd have the Genet land, Maureen insists, but the Colonel is now dis tracted by the thought that he doesn't want to be late for his lodge meetin; Floyd, somewhat cooled off, returns and prepares to drive his father into tow for the meeting.

> (Editor's note: This is the sequence of Bradleyville time when the events of *The Last Meeting of the Knights of the White Magnolia*, the other Best Play of Preston Jones's trilogy, take place. The next scene of *The Oldest Living Graduate* occurs during and after the lodge meeting of *Knights*, which is synopsized on the pages directly following this synopsis of *Graduate*.)

Scene 2: An hour later

Clarence and Martha Ann Sickenger have stopped by the Kinkaids' an joined Maureen in the den. Clarence is expounding on the attractions of th future Mumford County Estates. Martha Ann's admiration of her husband i one-dimensional. Maureen remains unimpressed by Clarence or his plans.

Floyd returns from driving his father to the lodge meeting and reports t Clarence that they are going to have trouble gaining the Colonel's assent to th development. But Clarence wants the land business settled.

CLARENCE: . . . . . Ah'm meetin' with some people at the bank tomorrow and ah can't go in there with a maybe.

FLOYD: What people? Dammit, Clarence, you're not tryin' to drill around me, are you?

CLARENCE: I'm not tryin' to drill around anybody! Ah'm jest tryin' to get this damn outfit on its feet, that's all.

FLOYD: Ah jest don't like the idea of you meetin' people about this deal without be bein' there.

CLARENCE: Ah didn't include you 'cause you were spozed to be makin' the arrangements about that goddamned military-school business!

MAUREEN: That's right, Floyd, you always bring the barbecue, remember?

CLARENCE (*to Floyd*): Can't you shut her up.

FLOYD: Stay outta this, Maureen.

MAUREEN: Stay out, hell! He's gonna git this deal on its feet all right, and one of them feet is going to be right on your neck!

CLARENCE: That's a damn lie. Floyd went into this deal with his eyes wide open. This whole project is split fifty-fifty and don't you forget it! Now listen, Floyd, this outfit is going to go through, but the arrangements have got to be between you and me. *You* and *me,* you understand! So just muzzle that woman you've got over there, and tell her to keep her nose outta this.

FLOYD: Now just wait a minute, Clarence. You by God watch the way you talk about Maureen!

CLARENCE: Then keep her off my back, Floyd!

Martha Ann calms the troubled waters, running on about the full-length mink coat her husband ought to buy her. Clarence returns to the point: if Floyd is still uncertain about the land, he must be backing away from their deal. Floyd denies this. Clarence reminds Floyd that he took over the managing of Kinkaid affairs from his father years ago.

CLARENCE: . . . . . 'cause your dad had some kind of spells after he came back from the war, ain't that right?

FLOYD: Yeah, that's right.

MAUREEN: What the hell you gittin' at, Clarence?

CLARENCE: Floyd doesn't need the Colonel to *give* him a damn thing. Hell, that old man's had snakes in his boots ever since the World War I. All Floyd does is go down to Judge Deckert and take that piece of property. Ain't that right, Floyd?

   Floyd doesn't answer.

Floyd?

FLOYD: Yeah, that's right.

CLARENCE: Uh-huh, and just when did you do that little old thing?

FLOYD: Last week.

MAUREEN: What!

CLARENCE: Ah figured as much. So the truth of the matter is that we got no problems at all.

Maureen is furious at Floyd for going against his father's wish to keep the Genet farm. Clarence and Martha Ann make a hurried exit to get away from the family quarrel, but not before Maureen has informed Clarence: "If bullshit was music, you'd be a by-God brass band."

Floyd tries to explain himself to Maureen.

FLOYD: I wanted Dad to give me something, just *give* me something.

MAUREEN: Seems to me that's all he's ever done.

FLOYD: No, dammit, no, he hasn't. He let me run things 'cause he didn't have no choice in it, but he's never given me anythin'. Ah wanted him to let me have the Genet farm property because he wanted me to have it, wanted to see me do somethin' with it.

MAUREEN: Floyd, he still hasn't *given* it to you. You *took* it from him.

FLOYD: Ah had to. Without that land in mah name, this deal would never have even got off the ground. Ah wanted Dad to think he'd turned it over to me. Ah wanted Clarence and the rest of them fellers to think Dad and me was in on the deal together. Ah can turn that lake property into something, Maureen. Ah know ah can. Ever'body in the whole damn state will be impressed, you'll see.

MAUREEN: Why didn't you tell the Colonel all this?

FLOYD: Ah tried to, but he went off on one of his rampages again. Somethin' about Chinamen or some damn thing. Then we got into a fight as usual and the whole blasted thing went up in smoke.

MAUREEN: But you're worse off now than you've ever been. Now you've got to tell the Colonel that whatever he does, it won't be no use. That property is gone, you've taken it.

FLOYD: Just 'cause ah've taken it don't mean it's gone. Ah mean, what the hell, ah'm not goin' to put it in my pocket and carry it off some place. Jesus, him and his damn ghost town. There never was no town out there, jest some kind of farmin' community, ah looked it up in the courthouse records. Nobody even remembers who lived out there any more. But the Colonel, the Colonel really has got a thing about it. You know, ah thought maybe there was some people buried on that land, people he knew, and he didn't want the graves disturbed. But ah looked all over and couldn't find no markers of any kind. Hell, ah don't know, maybe ah'd better git ahold of Clarence and tell him to forget the whole damn thing.

MAUREEN: No, Floyd, don't do that. You need this project, but you've got to tell your dad the truth. You're into it now and you've got to face every part of it.

FLOYD: Yeah, ah guess so. You know we could take a beatin' on this deal. The whole outfit could fall flat on its ass. We could really blow a bundle. That's a hell of a possibility.

MAUREEN (*sympathetically*): I know, Floyd, I know.

The phone rings, and Floyd answers. It's Ramsey-Eyes, the black caretaker of the hotel downtown, telling Floyd that his father has suffered a seizure of some kind at the lodge meeting.

Scene 3: Late that night

The Colonel is stretched out in the armchair, covered with a blanket, his head supported by a pillow. Maureen and Floyd are watching him as the nurse, Claudine Hampton, comes in from the Colonel's bedroom, which has been fitted out with oxygen, etc., like a hospital room.

The nurse sends Floyd and Maureen off to bed — she'll alert them if there's any change. Mike comes in, concerned about the Colonel's condition: "He oughta be in a hospital." Claudine tells him, "Don't matter where he is any more, Mike."

Their conversation rouses the Colonel, who is surprised to find himself back home — he knows something has happened to him and was dreaming about being back in the trenches facing the Germans. Claudine goes to get the others as the Colonel continues talking to Mike: he's afraid to die and become like the bodies they used to stack like cordwood in France, but he can hear "the bells of hell" ringing.

The nurse brings in Floyd and Maureen. The Colonel doesn't want anyone fussing over him and telling him not to talk about the memories flooding in: the trenches, old friends, Suzette Genet.

COLONEL: You can have that land out there, Floyd.

FLOYD: No, Dad. Please, let's never talk about that any more. That land's yours.

COLONEL: You take that land and build some houses on it. Let folks get some use out of it again. There ain't nuthin' left out there for me nowadays. The things ah seen and remember in this country is all gone now. Even the sounds of things is gone. That's right. Even the sounds of things. The creakin' noise the saddles used to make when we went to work of a mornin', men yellin', dogs barkin', horses stompin' and snortin' and fartin' around. A windmill clankin' in the night and cattle bawlin' from way off yonder some place. Ah can see my father coilin' up his rope, sittin' on that dun mare of his straight as a by-God ramrod. Ah recollect Charlie Parsons and me ridin' across that Seven Spear country on the way to the Genet place — bein' there with Suzette out by the stock tank. Listenin' to the frogs and talkin' about how things was gonna be after we got married. How good the lights looked at the ranch headquarters when you was ridin' in after dark or goin' out early of a mornin', an' hearin' the deer bump, bump through the brush. Sometimes, when we'd round up and corral some of the stock, a few deer would get mixed up with the bunch. We'd close the corral gate and them damn deer would jest jump right over the fence. Jump plumb over the fence and run off while the cattle would jest stand around lookin' dumb and stupid. Ah liked workin' on the ranch. Maybe ah should have stayed there 'stead of jumpin' the fence and runnin' off all over the damned world. The Philippines, Mexico, France — but then if ah hadn't of, ah would have never got to serve with old Black Jack. By God, that was somethin' all right. Never would have heard old Harry Truman cuss them mules there in the Herrenberg Forest. Never would have, never . . . hey, Mike, Mike.

MIKE: Yes, sir.

COLONEL: I'm the oldest livin' graduate of the Mirabeau B. Lamar Military Academy. Ain't that a helluva note. Oldest livin' graduate. Betcha didn't know that . . . did ya?

Curtain.

THE LAST MEETING
OF THE KNIGHTS
OF THE WHITE MAGNOLIA

A Play in Two Acts

BY **PRESTON JONES**

Cast and credits appear on page 290

The events of Preston Jones's The Last Meeting of the Knights of the White Magnolia *take place in the same town (Bradleyville, Tex.), with one of the same principal characters (Col. J. C. Kinkaid) and within the same time frame as the same author's* The Oldest Living Graduate, *which is synopsized in the pages immediately preceding. Both scripts opened on Broadway as part of Jones's* A Texas Trilogy, *and both were named Best Plays of 1976–77. The biographical sketch of the playwright appears at the beginning of the* Graduate *synopsis.*

Time: Summer of 1962

Place: Meeting room of the Knights of the White Magnolia on the third floor of the Cattleman's Hotel, Bradleyville, Tex.

ACT I

SYNOPSIS: Ramsey-Eyes Blankenship, *"75, black custodian of the Cattleman's Hotel,"* is humming to himself as he sweeps the stained and faded meeting room on the third floor of the ramshackle hotel. In this large room, chairs (including an old wheel chair) are scattered about, and at right is a podium on a low platform. Up left is the door into the hall and up right a windowed alcove. *"On the face of the podium is painted a rather smudged white magnolia flower. On the wall behind the podium are two flags, "The Stars and Bars" and the "Lone Star," both very old and very dirty . . . . hanging on the stage left and up-stage walls are old banners representing the sun, the moon, the west wind."* The decorations also include a cross made of light bulbs, an old trunk, a coat rack, a battered portrait of the lodge founder and dusty group photographs of large and lively lodge conventions in days gone by.

Rufe Phelps, a refinery worker, 55, dressed in khaki work clothes and a base-ball cap, and his friend Olin Potts, 56, a cotton farmer in levis and straw hat, enter bickering over their last game of horseshoes, scarcely pausing long enough to say hello to Ramsey-Eyes.

> *The door opens and Red Grover appears. Red is fat, thick-necked and cynical. He wears a rumpled blue suit with a flowered necktie. He carries a paper bag containing a bottle of cheap bourbon.*

RUFE: Hey, Red, when is a leaner a leaner?
RED: Who gives a damn!

Rufe and Olin continue their argument. Ramsey-Eyes departs and L. D. Alexander enters. He is 49, manager of the supermarket, *"big and florid; he wears a baggy J.C. Penney Western suit, scuffed black loafers with white socks, and a small white Stetson hat,"* and he greets the others: "Howdy, brothers." He notices the bottle Red has brought, calls it "Old Buzzard Puke" but allows as how Skip Hampton will want a drink of it anyway, no matter how bad it is. They plan to play a trick on Skip — hide the bottle and then when Skip arrives pretend that it was Skip's turn to bring the refreshments. They get it stashed just as Skip comes in, a young man in a greasy Texaco uniform. They prod Skip about the refreshments.

RED: You mean to say you didn't bring them?
SKIP: Me? No, ah didn't bring nuthin'.
L.D.: Well, Gawd Almighty damn!
RUFE: Now we ain't got nuthin' to drink.
SKIP: Red always brings them samples from the package store, he always does.
RED: Now, Skip. You know ah told you to pick it up for me and bring it over here for tonight's meetin'.
RUFE: Shore he did. He told you to, Skip. Didn't he, Olin?
OLIN: Shore did.
SKIP: No, you didn't, Red. Ah swear to God you never. Ah would of remembered. Hell's fire, ah'd never forgit somethin' as important as that.
L.D.: Well, looks like we just gotta do without tonight.
SKIP: No, wait. Ah'll go back and git it, Red. Ah'll just run over to your place and pick some up!

RED: Too late now. Ah done locked up the package store.

SKIP: Well, you can open it again, can't you? Give me the key, ah'll go.

RED: You? Give *you* the key to mah hard liquor. You gotta be crazy, boy, that would be like givin' old L.D. here a Charg-a-Plate to a whorehouse.

SKIP: Well, let somebody else go then. How about Rufe here?

RUFE: Why should ah go do what you was supposed to do but forgot?

He and Olin both giggle.

SKIP *(truth suddenly dawning on him)*: Whatta you guys tryin' to pull?

L.D.: Well, hell, since old Skip let us down tonight, ah guess we gotta make do with this.

He pulls out the paper bag.

RUFE: Gotcha there, Skip. We really gotcha there.

SKIP *(dully)*: Yeah, boy, that was a good one, okay.

OLIN: Rufe thought it up.

SKIP *(sarcastically)*: Damn good goin' there, Rufe.

He reaches for the paper bag.

RED *(stopping him)*: Now hold on there. All us *gentlemen* wait on refreshments till after the meetin', don't we Skip?

SKIP: Sure, sure, oh, hell, yes.

Ramsey-Eyes looks in and tells the group that Floyd Kinkaid has dropped off his father, Col. J. C. Kinkaid, to attend the meeting. Rufe and Olin go downstairs to fetch the Colonel while the others marvel at his persistence in attending his lodge meeting despite old age (he is 75), infirmity (shell shock from World War I) lameness and partial blindness.

Skip wonders why the Colonel's son Floyd has never joined their lodge. Red Grover has an answer: " 'Cause he thinks it's a bunch of bullshit, that's why. All Floyd . . . . and the rest of the rich bastards in this town wanna do is sit around the goddamned country club and play kneesies. Floyd lets the Colonel come up here to the meetings so's everyone can see how nice he is to his daddy. But you watch, the minute the Colonel kicks off, Floyd's gonna close this-here hotel before the carcass is cold . . . . You see how many payin' guests are in this-here fire trap? Probably about five. This mighta been a classy hotel way back yonder when the Colonel had it built, but that Holiday Inn out to the bypass done kicked this dump plumb outa business."

Business is pretty slow all over town, as a matter of fact, since the state highway bypassed it. Red needles his friends by suggesting that Floyd might turn this place into a "hotel for Coloreds," but they all agree he'd never do that.

Olin and Rufe carry in Colonel Kinkaid (*"dressed in gabardine Western pants, slippers and a faded, patched World War I officer's tunic"*) and set him in the old wheelchair. Ramsey-Eyes adjusts the Colonel's lap robe and then departs after making sure that the Colonel is wearing his teeth, per his son Floyd's orders.

L.D. goes to the podium and raps the meeting to order, then leads the group in their lodge oath: "Ah swear as a true Knight of the White Magnolia to preserve the merits handed to me by mah forefathers and to hold as a sacred trust the ideals of mah Southern heritage. Ah pledge mah life to the principles of White

Magnolia-ism and will obey until ah die the laws of this here so-ciety."

The formalities accomplished, Olin goes to fetch the dominoes for the usual game, but L.D. has a surprise for them all: tonight they're going to have a real lodge meeting instead of just a domino game. Someone actually wants to join the lodge, and he's coming tonight for his initiation. Recruited by Rufe, the new member-to-be is Lonnie Roy McNeil from nearby Silver City.

COLONEL: *Silver City!* Ah won't have him!

RUFE (*taken aback*): He's a real nice feller, Colonel.

COLONEL: Don't give a damn; if he's from Silver City he's no damn good!

SKIP: Well, hell, Colonel, it's not like he's from the Congo or somethin'. My God, Silver City's only three miles away.

L.D.: Ah think it's a right good idea that we branch out a little, Colonel. Ah mean, nobody from Bradleyville has joined the lodge for over five years now.

COLONEL: People from Silver City are low-down stinkin' cowards and ah flat will not have them around!

RUFE: Well, hell, ah didn't know Silver City was on our list too!

L.D.: Now, Colonel, you know we all respect your judgment in ever'thang but . . .

COLONEL: You damn well better.

L.D.: But maybe we would all understand a little better if we all knew *why* people from Silver City was no damn good.

COLONEL: Because in nineteen hundred and eighteen Staff Sergeant George Plummer from right over yonder in Silver City refused to fight, that's why! Whey-faced little coward jest stood there in the trench with his puttees floppin' around and puke all over his face, hands shakin' and spit runnin' out his mouth. Kept mumblin' over and over, "Who am ah? Who am ah?" Well, ah knew damn well who he was, he was Staff Sergeant George Plummer from over there to *Silver City.* Ah ordered that little son-of-a-bitch to climb up . . . people from Silver City are no damn good. That is an order and that is a fact.

L.D.: Well, hell, Colonel, this-here feller wantin' to join ain't no Plummer, he's a McNeil.

RUFE: That's right, Colonel, he's old Grady McNeil's boy.

COLONEL: He's from *Silver City,* ain't he?

RUFE: Well, yes, but . . .

COLONEL: Well, there you are.

L.D. pacifies the Colonel by pointing out that the new member is from *outside* Silver City, not right in the town. Olin describes the candidate's family background (Olin is the resident expert on who is who in the area), which seems to be O.K. Skip urges them all to get on with the meeting, and Red points out that Skip really means he wants to get to the refreshments.

There's a commotion outside. Ramsey-Eyes enters with Lonnie Roy McNeil in a firm grip, having mistaken him for an outsider trying to spy on the meeting. The situation is explained, and Ramsey-Eyes is sent back downstairs to keep watch.

Lonnie Roy is *"a thin, big-eyed kid in an ill-fitting suit; his hair is bowl-cut*

PATRICK HINES, HENDERSON FORSYTHE, GRAHAM BECKEL, WALTER FLANAGAN, THOMAS TONER, JOSHUA MOSTEL, FRED GWYNNE AND PAUL O'KEEFE (KNEELING) IN "THE LAST MEETING OF THE KNIGHTS OF THE WHITE MAGNOLIA"

and he wears tennis shoes." L.D. welcomes him to the meeting, reassures him that Ramsey-Eyes is not a member of the lodge and introduces him to the others. The Colonel asks Lonnie what branch of the service he was in, and Lonnie has to tell him he was turned down because of asthma and flat feet. The Colonel's comment is, "Blackball the flat-footed, asthmatic, *Silver City* son-of-a-bitch!"

L.D. assures a dismayed Lonnie that the Colonel doesn't mean anything, he's just a little crusty from time to time. Lonnie is glad to hear it, because when Rufe told him about the domino games and the lodge being for white men only, Lonnie was "sold right there on the spot."

Exasperated by the Colonel's further interruptions because they are delaying the proceedings and thus his "refreshment," Skip blurts out, "Goddammit, Colonel Kinkaid, shut up!" There is a stunned silence; but, surprisingly, the Colonel isn't angry. He's only amused as he tries to recall a time in Mexico when Black Jack Pershing gave him much the same order.

L.D. suggests that the Colonel hold the anecdote till refreshment time and proceeds to brief the new prospect on the history of the White Magnolia brotherhood. It was founded in 1902 by a splinter group of the Ku Klux Klan. The 1939 White Magnolia Convention in Tulsa boasted 2,000 delegates, but it's a long time since there has been a gathering like that. As L.D. explains to Lonnie, "People got to where they didn't want to join up any more. Can you imagine that? They didn't want to be Knights of the White Magnolia. They wanted to be Jaycees or Toast Masters or Elks or Lions or Moose, they wanted to be by-God animals, that's right, animals, but not knights. They turned around and stabbed their granddaddies square in the back. Turned up their noses on their race, started kow-towin' to all them-there mi-norities, and little by little the lodges jest sorter dried up. Nobody wanted to join. No new people."

Skip joined the lodge after serving in Korea (he tries to impress Lonnie with his wartime exploits but his storytelling too is put off until later). All other chapters of the White Magnolia have been given up — this is the last one left and these the only members — save for one Milo Crawford who is absent tonight. There are no dues, even no fee for hiring the hall, because the Colonel owns the hotel.

They make Lonnie feel important, and he *is* mighty important to them because perhaps he represents a new beginning, a new wave of interest in the Knights. Skip punctures their bubble: "We get one new member in five years, and ten minutes later we're bigger than the by-God Woodmen of the World."

Skip's sarcasm isn't appreciated by the others, the Colonel commenting "Shoot the goddamned desertin' son-of-a-bitch!" Skip clashes with Olin and then with Red, and all this hostility begins to make Lonnie Roy nervous. It occurs to him that the initiation may call for some kind of ritual physical pain. L.D. reassures Lonnie Roy that the ritual is based only on God and brotherhood.

Olin points out that they can't proceed to the initiation until after they've formally voted on the candidate.

SKIP: We didn't have no Goddamn vote when I got initiated.

RED: It's a damn good thing for you that we didn't.

SKIP: What the hell's that spozed to mean?

RED: Jest what I said, that's what.

L.D.: All right now, that's jest a by-God nuff! Ah want it quiet in here and ah mean dead quiet. (*Silence.*) That's a whole lot better. All right now, Olin, if you insist, we will . . .

COLONEL: Bumble-dick, bumble-dick, bumble-dick.

L.D. (*patiently*): Yes, Colonel, that's right. Now . . .

COLONEL: That's what old Black Jack did. Bumble-dicked all over Mexico.

Let that fat little greaser Pancho Villa make a damn fool of him. Betcha didn't know that, did you?

L.D.: No, Colonel, we didn't. Now . . .

COLONEL: Well, he did.

L.D.: Please, Colonel, we gotta get on with the vote.

COLONEL: What we votin' on?

L.D.: On Lonnie Roy, Colonel.

COLONEL: Who?

L.D.: Lonnie Roy McNeil, our new member.

COLONEL: We got a new member? Well, it's about time; who is it?

RUFE: Lonnie Roy McNeil, Colonel, Grady McNeil's boy from over there to Silver . . . from over yonder.

COLONEL: Well, ah'll be damned. You don't bumble-dick around, do you, young feller?

LONNIE: No, sir!

COLONEL: That's good. The Germans will get you if you do.

LONNIE (*with deep conviction*): Well, ah never do.

COLONEL: Come over the top and stick one of them spiky helmets right up your butt.

SKIP: Jesus H. God Almighty, that's the damndest thang ah ever heard of in my life.

COLONEL: What the hell's wrong with you?

SKIP: Them Germans ain't worn no spiky helmets in fifty years.

COLONEL: Don't mean they ain't gonna put them on again! You-all think the Kaiser's dead, don't you? Well, he ain't! Him and Crown Prince Willie is both livin' on a cattle ranch in Argentina and in secret is storin' up guns in the basements of Catholic churches all over the world.

SKIP: That ain't no Kaiser that's down there in Argentina. That there's *Hitler!* Hell, we've had a whole new world's war since the damn Kaiser was runnin' around.

Others conjecture where Hitler may be hiding. This time it's Red who pulls them back to business. Olin, a stickler for rules, insists that Lonnie leave the room during the voting. Lonnie obliges after being assured that the vote is merely a formality. Olin stands guard at the door like a sentry while the others take seats. But before they can proceed to the actual voting, a commotion is heard outside. In comes Milo Crawford, the missing member, holding fast to Lonnie Roy who has once again been mistaken for a spy. Milo is *"mild-mannered, lank, gangly and very homely. He wears a white shirt, a dark necktie and an old double-breasted brown suit."*

L.D. puts everyone straight on the situation, and Milo shakes hands with Lonnie. Milo is late because he couldn't get his pickup started. Lonnie goes outside again, and finally the lodge members proceed to their vote.

L.D.: Okay. Ever'body wantin' Lonnie Roy McNeil for a new member, put up their hand.

They all do except the Colonel.

What's wrong, Colonel, why ain't you votin'?
COLONEL: Votin? What for?
L.D.: Go over and put up the Colonel's hand, will you, Red.
RED: Shore thing.
> *He does.*
COLONEL: What's goin' on? What's goin' on?
L.D.: Nuthin', Colonel. Red's jest helpin' you to vote, that's all.
COLONEL: Oh, well, thank you, Red. Damn nice of you.
RED: Mah pleasure, Colonel.
L.D.: Fine, fine. That's real official-like. Okay, Brother Knight Potts, you can bring in Lonnie Roy now.
OLIN: Okay.
> *He opens the door.*
All right, Lonnie Roy, you-all can come in now. Lonnie Roy. Lonnie Roy? (*He steps outside.*) Well, what the hell!
L.D.: What's wrong?
OLIN (*sticking his head back into the room*): He's gone.
> *They all freeze in place as the lights fade to blackout. Curtain.*

ACT II

Seconds later, the characters unfreeze from their Act I curtain positions and set about trying to find Lonnie Roy. Ramsey-Eyes comes in to report that the candidate didn't make his escape through the lobby. He receives the Colonel's compliment "Damn good man" and returns to his post. The Colonel recalls that General Pershing once commanded "Neegrow" troops, called "Buffalo Soldiers" by the Indians.

Just as the lodge members decide to proceed to the refreshments for lack of anyone to hold a ceremony over — and Skip *"reaches frantically"* for the bottle — Lonnie Roy appears at the door. He has been in the bathroom down the hall.

Now that the new candidate is present and voted in, they seem to have mislaid the initiation book. Skip suggests they invent some new mumbo-jumbo and have done with it.

MILO: That wouldn't be right. Lonnie Roy wouldn't be a proper member.
OLIN: No, sir, somethin' like that would be agin the rules.
SKIP: What rules?
RUFE: The rules of the order of the Knights of the White Magnolia, that's what rules.
SKIP: Well, hell, there ain't no Knights of the White Magnolia but us. So what difference does it make?
L.D.: It makes plenty of difference. That rule book was writ by Maynard C. Stempco himself, way back in 1902. It's got secret valuable writin's in it.
RUFE: Damn right.
L.D.: We gotta find that book.

They try to remember what they did with the book after Milo Crawford's initiation in 1957. Skip suggests that perhaps a little drink would help them remember. Red prods him sarcastically, "Ah thought you drank to fergit." Skip insists he has plenty of Korean combat experiences to forget, but Red will have none of that: "You never was in shit! That buddy of yours that married your sister told me you guys never got closer to any front lines than fifty miles."

All at once L.D., who has been deep in thought, remembers what he did with the book after it was used last. He gave it to the Colonel.

MILO: The Colonel?
L.D.: That's right, he asked me for it and ah gave it to him.
      They all turn and look at the Colonel.
COLONEL (*after a moment, very quietly*): Ramsey-Eyes has it.
L.D.: What was that, Colonel?
COLONEL (*louder*): Ramsey-Eyes has it!
L.D.: What in the name of Christ is Ramsey-Eyes doin' with it?
COLONEL: He keeps it for me.
L.D.: Well, if that ain't the damndest thing ah ever heard of in mah life. You mean to tell me that you gave the Knights of the White Magnolia secret book to Ramsey-Eyes!
RED: Jesus Christ!
COLONEL: No, ah didn't give it to him. Ah told you-all, ah just let him keep it.
L.D.: What the hell for?
COLONEL: 'Cause ah was afraid ah would lose it. Mah memory's been givin' me some troubles lately and ah didn't want to lose it.
L.D.: But why Ramsey-Eyes? Why not one of the brothers?
COLONEL: Because for one thing he is an old and faithful employee, and for another thing ah wouldn't trust any of you bumble-dicks with the rule book if it were writ on the side of an elephant!
RED: Well, ah'll be damned.
COLONEL: Probably.
L.D. (*resigned*): Olin, would you please go down to the lobby and ask Ramsey-Eyes for the book.
OLIN: Shore thing. (*Exits.*)
LONNIE: Does this mean ah'm gonna git initiated now?
L.D.: Yes, dammit, yes! Now sit over there and shut up!
LONNIE (*sitting*): Ah never done nothing.
COLONEL: Bumble-dicks.
MILO: Gawlee, ah cain't git over it. Ramsey-Eyes with the rule book.
RUFE: You reckon he read it?
RED: Hell, no!
SKIP: How you know?
RED: 'Cause he's too damn dumb even to write his own name. Much less *read* anything.
RUFE: Well, at least we know where it is.
MILO: Yes, that's true. You know, even in the darkest moments you can always find a little good.
RUFE (*impressed*): By God, that's damn truthful, Milo.

MILO: Thank you.

RUFE: You orter write that one down some place and send it in to a magazine or somethin'.

MILO: Think so?

RUFE: Hell, yes. Whattayou think, Red?

RED: Who gives a damn!

SKIP: Why don't you write it on the shithouse wall over to Red's place?

L.D.: Shut up, Skip.

COLONEL: "Shut up, Kinkaid." That's what old Black Jack said when we was out there in Mexico. Hot as hell one day there in the officers' mess. Wind blowin' the tent sides back and forth. Flap, flap, flap . . .

Olin comes back with the book, and L.D. assigns the members to their stations for the initiation: Red beside L.D., Milo at the station of the moon, Olin at the station of the sun, Rufe by the station of the west wind. The Colonel doesn't want a role in the proceedings. He has a headache, and all he can think about is Black Jack Pershing: "Ah was havin' me a cup of coffee with the Major when old Black Jack come it. Well, sir, as luck would have it, he come in jest as I was sayin' to the Major, 'Ah don't think we're ever gonna catch that fat little greaser if we stay out here in this damn Meheeko for five hundred years . . . ' and the General he says to me he says . . . (*Voice trails off.*)."

Lonnie stands in front of Red and L.D., while Skip helps pass around cards for the ritual, together with fez-type hats with different emblems: "*A half moon, a sunburst, a cloud with streamers for the west wind, a lamp for wisdom, a series of fountain-type lines for the truth and a bolt of lightning for the wizard.*" Skip portrays Wisdom the Guide to the Mystic Mountain, Red is the Golden Fountain of Truth and L.D. is the Imperial Wizard.

Rufe will have trouble reading his West Wind role because there is a splotch on his card. L.D. informs Lonnie that he will now go on a journey guided by Wisdom "to seek the Golden Fountain of Truth that flows deep in the darkness of the Mystic Mountain." He will meet sages along the way, and to their every question his reply is to be "Stempco, Stempco, Stempco."

Skip takes Lonnie Roy over to stand before Milo.

MILO (*reading*): "Ah am the moon. By night ah cast beams down upon you, lightin' the way along your journey toward the truth."

LONNIE: Stempco, Stempco, Stempco.

L.D.: You now travel, initiate Lonnie Roy McNeil, to the blazin' realm of the sun.

Skip leads Lonnie Roy to Olin.

OLIN: "Ah am the sun. Ah bring my warmin' rays and glorious beams to warm and comfort you durin' the day as you journey toward the truth."

LONNIE: Stempco, Stempco, Stempco.

L.D.: You now travel, initiate Lonnie Roy McNeil, to the long low plains of the west wind.

Skip leads him to Rufe.

COLONEL: Flap, flap, flap . . .

RUFE (*reading with great difficulty*): "Ah am the west w . . . Ah blow my balmy bree . . . er . . . the . . . ren desert an . . . the sails of your craf . . . cross the sea of ignor . . . on your journey toward the truth." Hell, L.D., it don't make no sense readin' around this-here splotch.

L.D.: It sounded jest fine, Rufe. Anyway, we got the idea.

COLONEL: Flap, flap, flap . . .

L.D.: You now arrive, initiate Lonnie Roy McNeil, at the Mystic Mountain, wherein lies the Golden Fountain of Truth and the great white marble temple of the Imperial Wizard.

Skip brings Lonnie Roy to the podium and has him kneel down.

RED (*starting to read*): "Ah am the Golden . . ."

Just as he reads, the Colonel says the role from memory.

COLONEL: "Ah am the Golden Fountain of Truth. I welcome travelers to my magic waters. Your journey has been long and hard, but rejoice now, pilgrim, your reward is at hand."

LONNIE: Stempco, Stempco, Stempco.

L.D.: By God, Colonel, that was real fine. How was it, Red?

RED (*grinning*): Letter-perfect.

L.D.: Jesus, Colonel. You think you can remember the part of the Imperial Wizard too?

COLONEL: Shut your mouth, Lieutenant Kinkaid. You keep talkin' a lot of bull and I'll have you on the horseshit detail for the rest of the campaign.

RED: Offhand, L.D., ah'd say that wasn't it.

L.D.: Yes, well, maybe ah'd better read it. "Ah am the Imperial Wizard. You have been guided by wisdom and aided by the sun, the moon and the west wind to taste now the living waters of the Golden Fountain of Truth." Oh, hell.

RED: What's wrong?

L.D.: It says here that ah am now to give the initiate a drink of clear water from a silver cup. Ah forgot all about that.

They decide that a shot of booze will do just as well, and Lonnie takes a long swig from the bottle. Olin flips the switch to turn on the cross of light bulbs for the final bit of ritual. The bulbs are so dusty that the cross glows only dimly. Olin turns it off and Rufe proceeds to clean the apparatus while the Colonel continues wandering in memories of Black Jack Pershing, given his nickname by "smarty-assed Kay-dets there at West Point" because of his command of black troops.

With the bulbs cleaned, the cross glows like new in the otherwise darkened room. It reminds the Colonel of flares over the trenches, and of Pershing: "He told me to shut up one time. You know, he never said anythin' to me again, not one word 'cept maybe to give an order or two. Ah don't think he liked me."

L.D. proceeds to read Lonnie the final ritual, "the real meanin' of White Magnolia-ism," when suddenly the cross goes out. Rufe tries to fix it. The Colonel is afraid of the dark and suddenly reminded of the rats that infested the trenches, feeding on dead bodies and creeping close to the living in the dark. They all sit — except Lonnie, who must remain kneeling — while Rufe works on the cross.

SKIP: For Christ's sake, let's git this damn thing over with and have a drink!

RED: Why the hell don't you shut up, you goddamn little lush. You'll get a drink when ever'body else does and not until then!

SKIP: Ah'm not a lush, damn you, ah'm not! Who the hell do you think you're talkin' to anyway?

RED: Oh sure, ah plumb forgot. You're a hero, ain't you. A Korean war hero.

SKIP: Ah seen plenty of stuff over there, lot more than the Colonel ever seen; ah been in battles, big battles.

RED: Shore, shore. The battle of the Tattoo Parlor and the Beer Hall. Face it, Skip, you're nuthin' but a phony, a boozer and a phony.

SKIP: Ah'm not, damn you! ah'm not!

L.D.: All right now, all right, that's jest a goddamn nuff! This part I'm about to read is real important and ah want it quiet in here!

The cross light comes on again, this time very bright and vivid, then it goes off.

RUFE: Mah Gawd, did you see that!

COLONEL: What was that? What was that flash?

L.D.: Nuthin', Colonel, just that damn-fool cross actin' up again.

Cross sputters on and off.

COLONEL: A creepin' barrage. *Five-nines* and *seventy-sevens,* blowin' up all around us! Throwin' up bodies of Frenchmen that was killed over a year before. Old bodies and new bodies jumbled together in the air.

The cross keeps sputtering on and off, haunting the Colonel with phantoms of trench warfare, hideous memories of rotting flesh, causing Red to comment: "Don't sound too heroic when it's the real thing." The Colonel is racked by an uncontrollable recital of his Silver City comrade George Plummer's fate at the Argonne: "You was afraid and that goddamned whiz-bang hit and tore off your head, and your body jumped up and run off like it was still alive, flappin' its arms and runnin' and the boys next to me shootin' at it, shootin' at it, shootin' at it for the hell of it, shootin' and laughin' and your head rollin' around on the duckboards at the bottom of the trench like some kind of ball."

Lonnie has had more than enough of this. L.D. sends Olin off to get Ramsey-Eyes to phone the Colonel's son Floyd for help. They can't stop the Colonel, and his memories become so macabre and harrowing that even Skip is shaken. They try to bring the Colonel around with a drink of whiskey, but the old man spits it out and keeps struggling with his nightmare: "Let me go, let me go. Ah ain't crazy, damn you! It's jest them shells. Oh Jesus, they're comin', the Germans. Oh, Jesus God, ah can see their shadows up agin the wire."

Skip grabs the bottle. Red tries to take it away from him.

RED: Gimme that bottle or I'll break your goddamn neck!

SKIP (*pulling an object from his pocket and concealing it with his hand*): If you think you can git by this-here knife, you just come on ahead!

LONNIE (*jumping away*): Jesus God, he's got him a knife!

L.D.: Don't be a damn fool, Skip. Come on and give us the knife, then you can have all you want to drink.

SKIP: Ah got all ah want right now.
>*He takes a long drink.*

RED: You rotten little bastard! You stinkin' two-bit lush!

SKIP: Stay where you are, Red, or ah'll cut you! Ah ain't kiddin' now.

RUFE (*backing away*): Watch him, Red, watch him.

MILO: Maybe we'd better adjourn this-here meetin' and finish off the initiation next time.

COLONEL (*grabbing hold of Lonnie Roy, who has backed into his wheelchair*): Help me, help me. God in heaven, help me.

LONNIE (*screams and struggles to get loose*): He's got me! He's got me! Old crazy man's got me! Old crazy man's got me, help, help.
>*He tears loose from the Colonel and bolts out the door. The Colonel slumps over in his chair.*

L.D.: Stop him, Olin, don't let him get away!

OLIN: Come on, Rufe.
>*They dash out the door after Lonnie Roy.*

RED: To hell with him. Help me get the knife away from Skip.

L.D.: Come on now, Skip. Give me that knife.

SKIP (*hands L.D. a small tire gauge and grins*): What knife?

L.D.: Damn tire gauge!

RED (*advances on Skip swiftly*): You son-of-a-bitch!
>*He grabs the bottle from Skip and smashes him viciously in the stomach. Skip doubles up and falls to the floor.*

The Knights of the White Magnolia continue their downhill slide. Red throws Skip out the door so that he won't be sick in the meeting room. Milo suggests maybe they'd better adjourn the meeting, it's getting late and his mother is waiting up for him. Trying desperately to hold the crumbling meeting together, L.D. commands Milo: "Screw your mother! You're stayin' right here till Olin and Rufe get back with Lonnie Roy." Deeply shocked and affronted, Milo demands an apology. L.D. hesitates, but Red puts the lid on it: "Go to hell! . . . . Who the hell needs you. Stinkin' little mama's boy!" Milo departs, flinging back a final insult at Red: "Lard-butted booze drinker."

L.D. is sorry to see Milo go, diminishing the group, but to Red it is good riddance. Olin and Rufe return without their quarry — Lonnie Roy was running too fast for them to catch up with him.

The Colonel is now unconscious. They check his pulse to reassure themselves that he's still alive. Rufe and Olin wheel him out toward the lobby, where they'll watch over him until his son Floyd arrives to take him home.

Red now knows that there aren't likely to be any more meetings of the Knights of the White Magnolia. After the Colonel dies — and he is obviously at death's door — Floyd will surely sell this hotel and the Knights will lose their meeting place. L.D. clings to a shred of hope that the brotherhood will go on, but Red insists: "The Knights of the White Magnolia idea is gone, finished, all washed up. Did you really listen to that crap we were readin' tonight?"

L.D. insists that their ritual, the Gospel according to Maynard C. Stempco upon which this lodge was founded, continues to have meaning.

RED: Meanin'? Meanin' to who? For God's sake, take a look around you, L.D., whatta ya see? Domino players, stumble bums, mama's boys, pimple-faced kids and crazy old men.

L.D.: And you? Just where the hell do you fit in?

RED: Me? Ah don't fit in nowhere. Ah'm just a lard-butted booze drinker. Remember?

He picks up the whiskey.

So I guess that jest leaves you, L.D. The only true believer, L.D. Alexander, supermarket manager and keeper of the White Magnolias. Let me tell you somethin', brother White Knight, Imperial Wizard, you don't put down the sons-of-bitchin' freedom riders and minority bastards with all this crap any more. You got to look for the loopholes, pal. Let 'em all squawk about lunch-rooms and schools all they want. In mah place ah simply reserve the right to refuse service to anybody. You look for the loopholes, pal. Well, so long, L.D. If ah don't see you down to the bar, ah'll save a seat for you on the back of the bus.

> *He pitches the half-empty pint to L.D. and exits, leaving the door open. L.D. watches him off and glances dejectedly around; crosses to the door and closes it, then to the Stempco portrait and contemplates a moment; then he crosses to the truth banner, and after a moment rips it down and tosses it into the trunk. He takes off his hat and throws it into the trunk as well. The sound of a train passing through town makes him pause.*

Skip comes back and L.D. takes pity on him, giving him the bottle with what's left in it. Olin and Rufe re-enter and announce that Floyd Kinkaid is angry at them for letting his father get into such a frenzied state and means to close the meeting room. L.D. informs them that it doesn't matter any more. He's tired trying to hold things together; even he has had enough. L.D. tells them, "This-here lodge, this-here society, this-here brotherhood, this-here ever'thin' is now adjourned." He leaves, taking the ritual book with him.

Rufe is afraid that now that the lodge meetings are cancelled "there won't be nothin' to do." They can try the new bowling alley, Olin suggests, and they exit, bickering as usual.

> *Skip watches the exit and finishes off the rest of the bottle. He flips the bottle cap. Ramsey-Eyes enters.*

RAMSEY-EYES: Meetin' all over with, Mistah Skip?

SKIP: Yes, Ramsey-Eyes, the meetin' is all over.

RAMSEY-EYES: I'll jest straighten thangs up and lock de door.

SKIP: You jest do that little old thing, Ramsey-Eyes. (*He looks at the empty bottle.*) Christ, ah wish ah had another drink.

RAMSEY-EYES: Mistah Red Grover is over to his saloon. Ah seed him go over dere when he left the hotel here.

SKIP: Hot damn! Ah bet he'll give me a drink, sure enough, ah jest bet he will. Thanks, Ramsey-Eyes. Good night. (*Exits.*)

RAMSEY-EYES: Good night, Mistah Skip.

> *He closes the door and snaps the cross light switch a couple of times.*

When it doesn't work, he moves to the cross and raps the wall next to it with the broom handle. The cross lights up. He chuckles and moves back to the door, turning off the overhead lights. A piece of paper catches his eye. He picks it up and moves to the light of the cross to read.
"Ah am de moon. By night ah cast beams down upon you, lightin' your way along your journey toward de truth." (*He chuckles.*) "Ah am de moon." Oh, Lawdy. "Ah am de moon." (*He chuckles again.*)
The cross lights fade to blackout. Curtain.

(Editor's note: The events following Col. Kinkaid's return home with his son Floyd after the lodge meeting take place in Scene 3 of Act II of *The Oldest Living Graduate,* the other Best Play of Preston Jones's *A Texas Trilogy,* synposized in the pages directly preceding this synopsis of *Knights*)

COMEDIANS

A Play in Three Acts

BY TREVOR GRIFFITHS

Cast and credits appear on page 297

TREVOR GRIFFITHS was born in Manchester, England, in 1935. He won scholarships to a Catholic grammar school and Manchester University, where he majored in English. After two years' National Service in the infantry, he went into teaching as the head of an experimental school in Oldham, as instructor in liberal studies at Stockport Technical College and as the BBC's Further Education Officer; and into editing in a series of works issued by the Workers Northern Publishing Society.

Griffiths' first play was Wages of Thin *at the Stables Theater, Manchester, in 1969. There followed* Occupations *at the Stables in 1970 and in the experimental London season of the Royal Shakespeare Company in 1971;* Sam, Sam *at the Open Space in London in 1972 (the year Griffiths began to concentrate exclusively on writing); two short plays,* Apricots *and* Thermidor, *at the Edinburgh Festival the same year; and* The Party, *twice produced by the National Theater in 1973 (starring Laurence Olivier) and 1975.* Comedians *was first staged by the Nottingham Playhouse in February, 1975 and transferred to National Theater and West End productions. The Broadway production was its author's American theater debut, opening Nov. 28, 1976, running for 145 performances and winning a Best Play citation.*

Griffiths' work for television has included All Good Men *(also staged as a National Theater lunchtime production),* Through the Night *and a 13-part series,* Bill Brand, *about the life and career of a Labor M.P. Griffiths lives in Leeds and is married with three children.*

Time: The present

Place: A secondary school and in a workingmen's club in Manchester, England

ACT I

SYNOPSIS: A wall of windows, a blackboard, a teacher's dais and about a dozen desks are the principal features of a small classroom in an East Lancashire secondary school given over in the evenings to various adult education programs. A little old caretaker is wiping obscene graffiti from the blackboard. He takes no notice as Gethin Price enters in a wet overcoat and *"a flat Lenin-like cloth or denim hat, which he leaves on."* Price is carrying shaving materials. He sets them up and is well along with his shave when the caretaker notices him and is startled by his presence. Price has a right to be here, however — he is a member of a class that has been meeting here regularly. The caretaker guesses this must be a gents' hairdressing class, but Price will admit only "something like that."

The caretaker departs as Phil Murray (*"29, small, dapper, an insurance agent in a thick-fitting dark three-piece suit"*) enters carrying a suitcase, checking his watch, worrying about when his brother is going to show up, complaining "I've worked myself puce for tonight, I have."

George McBrain, an Ulsterman in his late 30s, *"a docker, big, beefy, wears an old parka, jeans, boots, shock of black hair, extrovert,"* makes an entrance in the classroom door, exuding confidence. Price picks up his shaving things and goes out, as Sammy Samuels — *"41, fat, Manchester Jewish, cigar, heavy finely cut black overcoat, homburg, white silk scarf"* — comes in, closely followed by Mick Connor, *"rain dripping from his donkey jacket, beneath which we glimpse hired evening dress and crumpled button-hole."*

Connor goes to the heating pipes to dry out, while McBrain pitches in to some sandwiches he's brought. Samuels notices Connor's tuxedo.

SAMUELS: Hey, that's not a bad fit. Where'd you get it, Woolworth's?
CONNOR: S'matter of fact belonged to a feller I know that passed on.
SAMUELS: Not surprised, wearing a suit like that.
CONNOR: What's wrong with the suit? It's a bit wet . . .
SAMUELS: S'hard to put your finger on . . .
McBRAIN: . . . as the actress said to the bishop . . .
    Groan.
SAMUELS (*studiously contemptuous of the interruption*): It's the sort of suit you walk into a tailor's in and ask for the cheapest suit in the shop and he says you're wearing it.
    Groan.
Don't groan, you scum, learn.

CONNOR (*studying the suit*): S'been a good suit.

SAMUELS: It was doomed the moment it left the animal. Believe me. I know about these things.

PHIL: Christ, he's doing half his bloody act.

SAMUELS: Don't worry about me, old son. Plenty more where that came from.

PHIL: That's what I'm bloody worried about . . .

McBRAIN: Right. Why should Ken Dodd worry about some obscure Manchester Jew stealing his lines? Ha!

    Samuels smiles, a little frost around the teeth, at McBrain.

SAMUELS: Why indeed. Why indeed.

CONNOR (*aware of that faint crackle*): Sure it's a detail. A detail it is.

McBRAIN (*in Waters's exact voice, assuming his manner*): Ah, but detail, friend, is all. I'd like you all to remember that now . . .

Eddie Waters is the teacher of this conglomeration of adult students, and he enters the room just as McBrain is mimicking him. Waters explains that he's a little late because he was checking to make sure there will be a piano "down at the club." He orders the others to get settled. They do so, arranging the desks in a hollow square.

Waters turns and is on his way out for a quick trip to the washroom when Price appears in the doorway, his hat off now, revealing *"an almost wholly shaven skull, the hair dense and metallic on the scalp . . . . . incomprehensible yet unmentionable."*

WATERS (*over shoulder, very dry*): Lads, lads, less noise if you would. There may be people trying to sleep in other classrooms. (*Stopping, staring at Price.*) Mr. Price. All . . . ready? All . . . ready?

PRICE: Yeah. Just about, Mr. Waters.

WATERS: Still finishing on the song . . . ?

PRICE: I'm not doing a song.

WATERS: How d'you mean? How're you gonna get off?

PRICE (*evasive, stubborn*): I've er . . . I've bin working on something else.

WATERS (*some faint concern*): Since when?

PRICE: Oh, last week. I dint like the act. I found something in the book you lent me.

WATERS: Yes, but you've not changed the basic . . . I mean a week . . .

PRICE: (*breaking deliberately into the room*): It'll be all right, Mr. Waters.

    He takes a desk. Waters watches, him, leaves.

Price takes a tiny fiddle with large bow from his bag and tunes it while McBrain mimics an MC in the area between the desks: "Ladies and gentlemen, welcome to the Factory Street Copacabana, where a feast of comedy talent on tonight's bill includes Mr. Sammy Samuels, the Golda Meier of Gagland, hot from his recent sizzling successes in the Gaza Hilton, and not forgetting, of course, the Telly Savalas of comedy, author of the highly acclaimed *The Naked Jape,* Mr. Gethin . . . . . "

McBrain breaks off. Waters comes back and takes his position at the head of the class as the others find their seats. Waters looks over his pupils, notices that Phil's brother is missing. It is by now obvious that this is a class not of gents' hairdressers or anything like it, but of aspiring comedians. Waters reminds them all that they are engaged to perform at a local workingmen's club this very evening, after which they will return here to the classroom "just to round things off and er . . . listen to the verdict," which is to be delivered by an ex-comedian, now a well-known talent agent, Bert Challenor, who is coming to see them all perform.

There is an added difficulty: in days gone by when they were both performing, the agent and Waters never liked each other's work or attitudes. Waters admits the possibility that "If I've done a good job with you lot, and he sees it, he won't like it." But when all's said and done, Waters is confident that they are all good enough now to force Challenor to approve of them despite any prejudice he may bring to the performance.

The proceedings are interrupted by the arrival of Phil Murray's brother Ged, rainsoaked but in good spirits. Ged Murray is *"pale, with bad teeth and balding. He wears a milkman's brown coat and hat. He continues, a line at a time, as he makes his way into the room, greets people with winks or smiles, finds his chair, adjusts it, sits down, apparently wholly unaware of the interruption of process he represents. A brilliant comic performance, in other words."*

Once Ged has settled down, Waters warms up his students for their coming performance by throwing them instant comic improvisations.

WATERS (*points to McBrain, immediately to his right*): Character. Stupid.

McBRAIN (*fast, in character*): Excuse me, Miss, where do I put this thing? (*Long pause.*) Oh . . .

WATERS (*to Samuels, next*): Ancient.

SAMUELS (*fast, in character*): Moses? Do I remember Moses? I was with him the day he got the tablets. The Lord said, "Anybody want any Commandments?" Moses said, "How much they going for?" The Lord said, "They're free." He said, "I'll take ten."

WATERS (*to Connor*): Silly.

CONNOR: Erm . . .

WATERS: Come on, Mick, silly.

CONNOR (*drunk Dublin*): I'd die a happy man if I could only live to see my own funeral.

Waters snorts, sustaining the speeded rhythms of the exercise.

WATERS (*to Price*): Feminine.

PRICE (*fast, perfect*): Four quid, dearie.

WATERS (*thrown a little, perhaps by the unexpected harshness*): Try another.

PRICE (*same voice*): . . . All I said was, all I *said was* . . . four quid doesn't cover sheets . . . Just take your boots off, is that a lot to ask?

WATERS (*to Ged Murray*): Aristocratic.

GED (*a strange modification, afterthought*): Could you get me some clean bread for this bacon grease, Miss . . . ?

WATERS: Nice. (*To Phil Murray.*) Absent-minded.

PHIL (*bad Robb Wilton*): I'll never forget . . .

CONNOR (*distinct whisper*): Whatsisname.

PHIL: Whasisname. Look, piss off will you, Mick . . . ?

WATERS: O.K. Coming. It's speed . . . and it's detail. It's the detail inside the speed that makes the difference.

Waters keeps throwing the improvisational ball at them, and they make comic sport with the names "Willy" and "Sammy." Then Waters gives the class a problem: "You've got a cougher in the audience . . . . . let's see how you deal with a cough." They all find ways to use the cougher for a laugh. When Price's turn comes he improvises a dirty limerick that momentarily perplexes them, particularly Waters, with the extreme vulgarity of its language and content. It seems a sort of act of hostility toward the whole exercise.

Next, Waters gives them a tongue-twister — "The traitor distrusts the truth" — which Price handles to perfection. Suddenly, discordantly, Waters changes key, first damning all Irish in a diatribe of absurd prejudicial slurs, then turning on Jews in the same offensive manner. "Gone very dark in here all of a sudden," Price remarks. Indeed, all the members of the class are disturbed and confused by Waters's abrupt outburst. It was no joke, Waters insists. The silence in the room is heavy with tension.

PRICE (*laconic, drawn out*): Lesson Three: "Stereotypes."
        *Some faint embarrassment; the sense, however obscure, of having
        let Waters down.*

SAMUELS: You were putting us on. That's a relief. I was beginning to get a bit worried.
        Some relaxation, smiles, off the hook.

WATERS (*driving home*): If I've told you once I've told you a thousand times. We work *through laughter*, not *for* it. If all you're about is getting a laugh, OK, get on with it, good luck to you, but don't waste my time. There's plenty others as'll tek your money and do the necessary. Not Eddie Waters.

McBRAIN (*conciliatory, apologetic*): So, a few crappy jokes, Mr. Waters . . .

WATERS: It's not the jokes. It's not the jokes. It's what lies behind 'em. It's the attitude. A *real comedian* — that's a daring man. He *dares* to see what his listeners shy away from, fear to express. And what he sees is a sort of truth, about people, about their situation, about what hurts or terrifies them, about what's hard, above all, about what they *want*. Any joke releases the tension. But a true joke, a comedian's joke, has to do more than release tension, it has to *liberate* the will and the desire, it has to *change the situation*. (*Pause.*) And when a joke bases itself upon a distortion — (*At Price, deliberately.*) — a "stereotype" perhaps — and gives the lie to the truth so as to win a laugh and stay in favor, we've moved away from a comic art and into the world of "entertainment" and "success." (*Pause.*) You're better than that, damn you. And even if you're not, you should bloody well want to be.

CONNOR (*trying to follow the argument*): I want to be famous. I want to be rich and famous. What's wrong with that, Mr. Waters?

WATERS: More than you want to be good?

McBRAIN: What's wrong with being all three?

WATERS: Nothing. So long as you're good *first*. Because you'll never be good later.

Price isn't satisfied with this explanation. He tries to probe deeper, asking if Waters's outburst was a reaction to the dirty limerick, and if so, why? Waters challenges Price to repeat the limerick slowly, so they can all think about it carefully. Price does so:

> "There was a young lady called Scott
> Who had a remarkable plot
> With a frightening cough
> She would jerk herself off
> By sinking her teeth in her twat."

Price tells them he made up the limerick himself on the spot, much to Ged's admiration. Waters is not amused, however. He takes Price's creation apart, writing the key words on the blackboard and examining the semantic parts so closely that the whole appears ridiculous. Finally, Waters concludes: "It's a joke that hates women and sex."

Waters goes further, probing the Freudian origins of Price's inspiration. McBrain contends that the limerick would liberate any latent fears of sex, but Waters thinks not: it "traps" a situation but does nothing to change it.

The door opens and an Asian comes in but retreats shyly when they all turn to look at him. Waters is explaining, "Comedy is medicine. Not colored sweeties to rot the teeth with," when the Asian plucks up enough courage to come back and ask for help in finding his literary appreciation course. Waters takes him out to find the Principal, and in his absence Samuels vents his anger on Price for turning these precious last-minute preparations into a philosophical dissertation. Samuels is very ambitious to do well tonight under the eye of the agent Challenor. Samuels owns a small, seedy night club where he might employ the likes of his classmates, but for himself he wants the top — the Palladium, TV.

McBrain tells a long joke about a deer-poacher and Price mimics Waters commenting on it and concluding, "It's a joke that hates *deer*." McBrain and Connor wonder how and why some sort of friction seems to have developed between the teacher Waters and his favorite pupil Price. Price feels that his individuality is being threatened. Connor sides with Waters as a brilliant artist who could, if he chose, be a popular performer instead of devoting his time and effort to teaching: "And if I get out of the building game and earn a living doing what I want to do more than anything else, always have done, I'll have him to thank and no one else. (*Deliberately.*) And that goes for everyone here, whether they know it or not." Ged immediately agrees with Connor.

GED: *We* knew next to nothing.
PHIL: Speak for yourself. I'd done clubs . . .
GED: Oh aye. Two. Ardwick and Oldham. One of 'em withheld your money. The other called a taxi to drive you off to safety.
PHIL: Like the bloody wild west, both of 'em. There was nothing wrong with *me*. My troubles started when I took you on, believe me.

GED (*quiet, toughly serious*): When are you gonna face it: you're not funny. You're a straight. You can't work on your own. (*Pause.*) But I can.
PHIL: Try it.
GED: Maybe I will.

McBrain interrupts to set the order in which they'll all perform this evening. They do so by cutting cards. Connor goes first, then Samuels, the Murrays, McBrain and finally Price. McBrain writes down the order, with asterisks for those who will need music.

Waters returns, bringing in eight teas on a tray and followed by the Asian, introduced as a Mr. Patel, who couldn't find his class and is now just tagging along. Waters instructs them all to relax, close their eyes, think about some memorable incident in their lives. Just as they're doing so, Waters commands them to open their eyes and asks Ged to tell them what he was thinking about — and make it funny. Ged was remembering when his wife went to the hospital to have their baby, the comic aspects of delay and difficulties — but then Ged's memory turns sober, even poignant, as he remembers how he feared his father's mental illness might run in the family, and how joyous he felt when his wife presented him with a baby normal in every way. Nobody understands why Ged happened to recall this particular incident on this particular occasion, and even Waters makes no attempt to analyze it.

Price was thinking about once having punched a woman music teacher who had called him a guttersnipe. He was sent to a psychiatrist who patronized him: " 'You see, Gethin, basically all any of us want is to be loved.' And I said, 'If you know so much, how come you wear a toupee?' (*Pause.*) That's when I decided I'd be a comedian."

Price twangs a string of his little violin, and Waters warns the group that whatever their mood they must not start to hate the audience or they'll wind up hating themselves. Everyone is ready, it seems, just as there is a knock on the door and the agent Bert Challenor enters. *"He's maybe five years younger than Waters, rather waxen, discreetly dressed, with a homburg and umbrella."* Challenor and Waters greet each other with friendly old-boys badinage which in spite of themselves has the suggestion of a sharp edge.

The caretaker comes in to inform Waters that the Principal will see Patel now, and Waters departs with the bewildered Asian, leaving Challenor with the class. Samuels tries to promote himself, telling the agent, "I'm *very* funny." Price asks Challenor his opinion of a comedian of the past named Frank Randle. Challenor is much less than enthusiastic. Connor asks Challenor about Waters's act, and Challenor admits, "He were brilliant . . . . . He didn't want enough."

Price persists in talking about Randle and does a monologue in imitation of him. Price gets a laugh from his classmates but fails to dazzle Challenor with his performance. Challenor gives the class some last-minute advice exactly the opposite of Waters's.

CHALLENOR (*dwells, enjoying the situation*): A couple of . . . hints. Don't try to be deep. Keep it simple. I'm not looking for philosophers, I'm looking for comics. I'm looking for someone who sees what the people want and knows how to give it them. It's the people pay the bills, remember, yours, mine . . . Mr. Waters's. We're servants, that's all. They demand, we supply. Any good comic can lead an audience by the nose. But only in the direction they're going. And that direction is, quite simply . . . escape. We're not missionaries, we're suppliers of laughter. That's what I'm here to sign up. I'd like you all to remember that. See you down there. Oh. A text for tonight. Perhaps we can't all be Bob Hope. But we can try.

> *He takes his leave. Silence . . . . . they sit looking at each other, scanning for concern or alarm.*

SAMUELS (*disgust staining his voice*): Oh, that's marvellous. That's . . . marvellous.

PHIL (*backing his chair to the floor savagely as he stands*): Jesus Christ! What the hell are we gonna do?

SAMUELS: We're gonna get the bum's rush, that's what we're gonna do.

McBRAIN: Not at all. What're you on about?

SAMUELS: Look, you heard him, Seamus . . .

McBRAIN (*thinking, already doubtful*): He had to say that. He's an old enemy of the Boss's, what else could he say?

PHIL: Sod that, what're we gonna *do?*

GED: What's that supposed to mean? We're gonna do our act.

PHIL: He'll murder us. You must be joking.

McBRAIN: That's very nearly funny.

GED (*to Phil, standing heavily*): Look, what are you talking about?

PRICE (*piercing through the din*): He means — do you not? — how can you change your act at this late stage to suit Challenor. Isn't that what you mean?

> *He takes in the whole group in the silence that follows the question. People sniff, shuffle, look at others.*

SAMUELS (*finally*): It's not such a tragedy. I can paste some'at together. Fortunately, I've managed to keep my distance . . .

CONNOR: Challenor'll get the act I came with. He don't bother me.

SAMUELS: O.K., so be the building trade's funniest shit-shoveller, then.

CONNOR (*steely, distinct*): I do not shovel shit. All right?

Phil almost panics trying to figure out what to do. He thinks maybe he and Ged should add in their "Pakistani Routine," but Ged insists they leave it out — Waters doesn't like it. Their bickering becomes so sharp that Ged warns Phil to leave off. McBrain expresses confidence in his own flexibility. Price is concentrating on his warming-up calisthenics.

> *Samuels turns to Price.*

SAMUELS: Whorrabout you then?

> *Price is doing left-leg squats on the dais. He stops carefully, swivels gracefully around.*

PRICE (*innocent*): Me?

SAMUELS: *You,* you slippy sod.

PRICE (*distinctly*): The traitor distrusts the truth. The traitor distorts the truth. The traitor destroys the truth.

SAMUELS: You're dafter than you think, you know.

PRICE (*inward*): I drive a van for British Rail all day. And if Challenor were on fire I wouldn't piss him out. Bob Hope! (*The venom muscles his throat.*)

McBrain reminds Price that he at least has already changed his act. They all gather their gear. Waters comes in with buttonhole flowers for each of them and orders them "Don't start boozing after your turn" as they troop out. Waters takes his briefcase and follows. After a beat, the caretaker comes in to inspect the empty classroom, carrying a broken chair shattered in karate class and noticing a muslin-covered package left behind by the Asian, suspicious-looking but harmless. The caretaker sniffs at it in disgust, turns out the lights and exits. *Curtain.*

ACT II

On a small stage at the workingmen's club that evening, a pianist is going through a medley of old favorites while the Concert Secretary sets himself up with his notes at a table at right. Challenor, scotch in hand, takes his place at another table, by himself.

The Concert Secretary calls for "a *brief* interval in the bingo, to listen to some new comics setting their feet on the first rung of the ladder of fame." It is more of an apology than an announcement, and it brings groans from the audience.

Waters is introduced, takes a bow and sits alone with his pint of beer at left.

SECRETARY (*checking tatty notes*): First off then, a young man from Ireland, now domiciled in Moss Side, your welcome please for . . . Mick . . . Connor.
>   *Connor appears from the wings in hired evening dress and black pumps, a white carnation and a black dickie. Pianist covers his entrance with "When Irish Eyes Are Smiling."*

CONNOR (*very Irish*): I told him not to say anythin' about me bein' Irish. I wanted to creep up on yez like. (*Own voice.*) Good evening. Sorry about the bingo.
>   *Secretary says "Sssh, sssh" out to audience.*

Wuz yez ever foreigners, any of yer? I don't mean the odd fortnight in Brighton, I mean like always? I went off looking for rooms. Your woman opens the door, a neat little thing wi' gouty eyes, I said, "Do you have any low terms for Irishmen here?" She says "Yes. Piss off." Mind you, that was before the blacks came to help us out, shoulder some of the white man's burden . . . . .

Connor's monologue proceeds to take up the practise of Catholicism, the differences between Irish and English priests and confessions, and a joke or two about birth control. Connor exits to applause, after reminding the audience of "the IRA fellow who knocks at the gates of Heaven and St. Peter says, 'Who are you?' And the fellow says, 'I'm from the IRA.' St. Peter says, 'Oh, you can't come in here,' and the IRA fellow says, 'I don't want to come in, I'm giving you all three minutes to get out!' "

Next on the bill is Samuels in a white jacket, red carnation, black bow tie, red satin handkerchief and diamond cuff links. He begins with Jewish ethnic jokes complete with accent, but they are obviously falling flat. Challenor, watching him, is stone-faced. Samuels, sweating and desperate, changes course abruptly in mid-act with "O.K., forget the Jews. Everybody else did." He tries a joke about a poacher, then switches quickly again to sexist double-entendres and begins to have better luck with his audience. He broadens his vulgarity: "I was at the bar earlier and I decided I should take a leak while it was slack . . . I'm in the bathroom and this big, black bugger rushes in, 'Aaaaah,' he says, 'Just made it!' I took a look, I said, 'There's no chance of making one in white for me, is there?' "

Samuels concludes his act with a few suggestive words to the women in the audience and exits to the tune of "When You're Smiling," taking applause and bows.

Next, it is the turn of the Murray brothers, Phil and Ged, who bill themselves as "Night and Day." A large trunk is wheeled onstage, followed by Phil dressed in a dinner jacket and carrying a small girl dummy.

Phil assumes the role of a ventriloquist trying to get his dummy, "Sophie," to sing. But strange noises of protest are coming from inside the trunk. Finally Phil opens the trunk, drops the girl dummy into it and pulls out Ged, who is dressed and made up as a life-sized dummy and mimics its floppy, loose-jointed inertia.

With considerable pulling and hauling, Phil manages to get himself seated on a stool with Ged on his knee. Ged's costume is festooned with the colors of the Manchester City football team, and soon their typical banter of ventriloquist and dummy turns to the subject of football.

GED: . . . . . My dad were a City fan. My dad said if he came home and found one of the City football team in bed with the old lady he'd brew him a cup of tea . . .
The joke dies. Ged waits for Phil to throw the next line at him.
He said if he came home and found one of the team in bed with me mother he'd brew him a cup of tea . . .
PHIL (*suddenly diverging from the act; no warning*): Look, if you're so funny, why don't you tell us all a joke?
GED (*turning his head to look at his brother and blinking a question*): What?
PHIL (*uneasy at once, but insistent*): Tell us the one about the Pakistani up on a rape charge.
GED (*half out of the act, trying to think, looking in Waters's direction, as if for help*): What you talking about?
PHIL (*faintly desperate*): Tell the joke.
Ged turns his head slowly, stares at the audience, stands, very slowly, puts his hands on his brother's shoulders, removes him from the stool, takes his place, draws his brother carefully down onto his thigh, repositions the mike.
GED (*in character*): You tell it.
PHIL (*blinks, thinks, terrified, struggling for confidence*): There's this Pakistani, see, up on a rape charge. So the coppers decide they'll have an identity parade. And they get eight or nine other Pakkies and they put this one at the

front and explain what they're doing. Then they bring in the girl and the Pakistani jumps out of the line and shouts — (*Pakistani voice.*) — she is the one, Officer. No doubt about it . . .

> *Ged and Phil stare whitely out at the audience. Neither knows where to go next. Ged gets up, repeats the procedure in reverse until he's back on Phil's knee.*

Ged and Phil try to get on with the act. Phil is now totally crushed. Ged tries another joke with little success, and then they go into their finale, a song about their brother act. Ged exits leaving Phil to carry the trunk offstage, where the loud sounds of a fight can be heard before the Secretary gets into his introduction of the next entertainer, McBrain.

McBrain comes on dressed in maroon evening jacket, horn-rimmed glasses and a frilly royal blue shirt. He was introduced as "Another Irishman . . . . . from Belfast this one," and after an opening limerick about a young lady called Tuck which deliberately chooses not to employ the obvious rhyme, he goes into a series of jokes aimed at religious and ethnic minorities, then a series of rather crude wife jokes. His frenetic performance switches back to the Irish: "Seamus, a friend of mind from Southern Ireland, he's a little thick. (*Gestures crazy in the head.*) He got a pair of water skis for Christmas. Spent the next few months looking for a sloping lake. Then he joined the IRA. Tried to blow up the Queen Elizabeth. Couldn't get his mouth around the funnel."

Quickly, McBrain switches to Western jokes and accent, then the big finish: "Well listen, I've gotta go. I'm wife-swapping tonight. I gotta fella's greyhound last week, made a change. So listen, I'll see yer, good night, God bless. (*He takes a bow, sweating, a bit concerned, not looking in Waters's direction.*)"

Following McBrain's exit, the Secretary brings on Gethin Price carrying his tiny violin and large bow. *"He wears bagging half-mast trousers, large sullen boots, a red hard wool jersey, studded and battered denim jacket, sleeves rolled to elbows, a red and white scarf folded at the neck. His face has been subtly whitened, to deaden and mask the face. He is half clown, half this year's version of bovver boy. The effect is calculatedly eerie, funny and chill."*

Price starts out with a pantomime in which, preparing to play his ridiculous violin, he notices a thin thread of gut hanging down from the bow and tries unsuccessfully to remove it by various means. Finally he burns it off, and the instrument continues to smoulder while he "plays" a number, then puts out the fire by crushing the violin underfoot.

As though the audience weren't there, Price says to himself, "I feel like smashing some cars, slashing the tires, stealing the hub caps, smashing the windows in." A spotlight comes on, lighting up his act's main prop: *"Larger than life-size dummies of a youngish man and woman: well dressed, beautiful people, a faint, unconscious arrogance in their carriage. The man wears evening dress, gloves, etc., the girl a simple, stunning white full-length dress and wrap. Her arm is looped in his. They stand, perhaps waiting for a cab to show after the theater."*

Gradually, Price notices the couple, stares at them, smiles evilly, childishly at the audience, then ambles over toward them.

Price stands by the man, measuring, then walks round to stand by the girl. We sense him being ignored. He begins to inspect the girl minutely, picks from his jacket pocket a badly rolled cigarette.

PRICE: Cigarette?

Nothing. He offers it to the man.

No? (*He withdraws the cigarette. Looking at them both again, up and down, turns, calls as though mimicking them.*) "Taxi!" (*Sharply, out front, shakes his head as it disappears. Moves 'round to the man's side again.*) Are you the interpreter then? Been to the football have we? Were you behind the goal wi' lads? Wannit? D'you see Macari with that ball? Eh? Eh? Uni-ted! Uni-ted! Great.

Silence.

P'raps I'm not here. Don't you like me? You hardly know me. Let's go and have a pint, get to know each other. Here, don't you live in Salford? I swear I've seen you at the dog track.

Deliberately, Price takes a cigarette out of the man's top pocket, lights it and blows smoke in the dummy's face. Getting no reaction, he tries again by commenting on his companion's "fair pair of knockers." Still no reaction, and Price, exasperated, tells him, "I don't know whether to smash you or what. I suppose I could just give you a clout, just to let you know I exist." He decides to "clout" them with the vulgar language of a dirty joke about a whore running naked down the street — but the elegant dummies still take no notice of him.

PRICE: . . . . . I'm *talking* to you . . . there's people'd call this *envy*, you know, it's not, it's hate. (*Now very fast.*) Are you bi-sexual or is that your sister? You'll never get a taxi here, they're all up at Piccadilly waiting for t'last train from London. Ask me how I know. I work there that's why. Don't interrupt when I'm talking, dint your mother ever tell you, it's rude?

He does a Kung Fu thrust, missing the man's head by inches.

Bruce Lee, do you like him? God, he is. You're a stuck-up bastard, aren't you? Give us a kiss then, go on, go on, Alice, give·us a kiss, I love you. Give us a kiss. (*Price halts his burble. Blinks. Pads round to stand at woman's side.*) Say something? (*In her ear.*) Listen . . . I've got a British Rail delivery van 'round the corner, ditch Alice and we'll do the town.

He notices a folded copy of the Times in the man's hand, passes behind the figures, pops his head between them.

Crosswords? (*Thinks a moment.*) Election. Nine across. Big poll in China question mark. (*Chinaman.*) E-lection.

Price looks from one to the other, laughs suddenly. He takes hold of their handles, begins to lift them up and down, to indicate their mirth.

Election! Election! Big poll in China. Laugh you buggers, laugh! (*Price laughs, throws himself around the stage, cartwheels and rolls mixed in with elaborate taichi gestures. Eventually he subsides, returns.*) Yeah. Here.

He takes a flower out of his pocket, hands it to the man.

For the lady. Allow me. I have a pin.

Pause.

No. No . . .

He pins the flower — a marigold — with the greatest delicacy between the girl's breasts, steps back to look at his work.

No need for thanks. My pleasure entirely. Believe me.

Silence. Nothing. Then a dark red stain, rapidly widening, begins to form behind the flower.

Aagh, aagh, aagh, aagh . . .

The spotlight fades slowly on the dummies, centering finally on the red stain. Price's "Aaghs" become short barks of laughter.

(*Innocence.*) I wonder what happened. I must have pierced a vein.

The light on the dummies goes altogether. We're left with Price's single, chill image.

I made him laugh, though. (*Depressed.*) Who needs them? Hunh. Who needs them? We manage. Un-*i*-ted. Un-*i*-ted. You won't keep us down, don't worry. We're coming up *there* where we can gerrat you, bastards. (*Sings.*) Lou Macari, Lou Macari . . . I shoulda smashed him. They allus mek you feel sorry for 'em, out in the open. I suppose I shoulda just kicked hum without looking at him. (*Pause. He looks after them, calling.*) National Unity? Up yours.

Pause. He picks up the tiny violin, i.e., another, switched, un-crushed, and a bow. Addresses it. Plays "The Red Flag," very simple and direct, four bars.

(*Sings, unaccompanied:*)

"The people's flag is deepest red,

It's shrouded oe'r our martyred dead." Still, I made the buggers laugh.

He walks off. The Concert Secretary is probably shocked, embarrassed, not wishing to dwell. Lights fade. Waters's face is gaunt and grey. Challenor tosses down a scotch, sheafs his notes, pockets pen.

SECRETARY: That's the lot, ladies and gentlemen. You have your bingo cards, I think. Charlie Shaw has 'em for them that hasn't, and we're starting right away, settle yourselves down now. And it's eyes down for a full card.

Lights fade gradually.

Always look after . . . Number One.

Lights fade to black. Curtain.

ACT III

It is about 9:43 the same evening, and the empty classroom slowly fills as McBrain, Samuels and Connor come in and sit, silent, drained, followed by Phil Murray. Samuels sits in his overcoat ready for getaway, and McBrain has changed back into parka and jeans. Price comes in and studies the others, noting their black mood but not sharing it, as McBrain comments: "Did you see that Challenor feller? He smiled twice all evening, and both times it was at some'at the sodding MC said."

Ged comes in bringing fish and chips for all. As he hands Price his portion, Ged remarks "Hey, that was great, Geth." But judging from the attitude of the others, Ged is the only one who appreciated Price's act.

Price tries to lighten the mood by posing as a Southern revival minister inton-
ing vulgarities. Samuels takes Price's joking personally and is quite ready to be
very angry. Price cools him off by picking up a broken chair leg left by the caretaker, taking several deep breaths and then smashing the leg into two pieces with
his forehead. Price carefully places the two pieces on Samuels's desk, saying,
"You're gonna crucify the man, do the job properly."

Samuels calls Price's performance at the club "embarrassing . . . . . putrid.
Different from bloody comedy, that's for sure."

The caretaker comes in to check on the room, points out the muslin sack left
by the Asian, then leaves as Waters enters, closely followed by Challenor. The
two men take their places briskly, Challenor at the head of the class, flicking
through his notes and saying, "I'll get cracking. Interesting evening. Lot of
promise."

Challenor takes up their performances one by one, beginning with Connor's,
which he "quite liked." He thought Connors too earnest on his too-narrow
theme of an Irishman in England, the sex jokes crude.

Challenor then turns to Samuels.

CHALLENOR: I thought you'd never get started. First thing you want to do is
ditch the first half of your act.

SAMUELS: Yeah, it's stuff I've been shedding, you know . . .

CHALLENOR: S'too Jewish. What's a Jew nowadays, eh? Who wants to know,
I mean.

SAMUELS: Yeah, I can see that.

CHALLENOR: Same mistake as the Irishman. (*Looks at notes.*) Fortunately,
you pulled out of it and got very good. It was a different act, blacks, Irish,
women, you spread it around, you can score, keep it tight they'll fall asleep on
you.
        Pause.
Liked the Women's Lib bits.
        Pause.
You need an ending, you were just sticking one after another till you'd done. No
climax. People want a climax.

SAMUELS: Yeah, I er . . . got off the rails a bit actually.

CHALLENOR: Stay on em . . . . .

About Phil and Ged Murray, Challenor states the obvious: something went
wrong with their act, and they embarrassed the audience. The brothers refuse to
explain to Challenor what happened. He pulls his pencil across their notes.

CHALLENOR: George McBrain. Cracking opening. Bang. No messing. Liked
it. Lot of sex but well handled, if you see what I mean. Near the knuckle but not
halfway up the armpit. A question of taste. Knowing when to draw back. Even
with yobboes like that lot down there.
        Pause.
Quite subtle but not too subtle . . . Yes, yes . . . Good character, I believed it,
was all of a piece. Confident, a bit aggressive, like that. Like the joke about the

thick Seamus. (*To Connor.*) See, that's what I mean, don't push your own particular prejudice, you're there on *their* terms, not your own. (*Notes again.*) Good ending. (*Nodding in Samuels's direction.*) See, it was *down*beat, but it was firm. You know, diminuendo. Well thought out . . .

> *There's a long pause now, as he stares at Price's notes. People make sweating faces on their own chances. Waters leans, half sits, against the window, staring nowhere, withdrawn, remote. Price leans almost horizontally back in his chair, staring at the ceiling. He remains like this throughout most of the following.*

(*Finally.*) Gethin Price. (*Another pause.*) Mmmmmmmmmm. Mmmmmmmmmm.

> *Looks across at Price finally, no nonsense, man to man . . . Price has buried his head in his desk. Challenor looks in Waters's direction, seeking guidance. Waters purses his lips, looks out of the window.*

Not a lot to say about your piece, Price. You have a certain talent maybe as a mime, something like that . . . What you did tonight just . . . won't do. Music hall maybe, but there *is* no music hall . . . You wanna be a comedian, you'd better start somewhere else, there's no way you'll get started with what you've got. Not viable. You've got to speak to the audience, for God's sake.

> *Pause. Studying notes.*

Personally, I found the content of your act . . . how shall I put it? . . . repulsive.

> *He stares on at his notes. Price slowly resumes an upright position in the chair.*

And aggressively unfunny. (*He looks at Price, practisedly kindly.*) If you want to get on, lad, you'd better sort a few problems out first. Get some distance, see what I mean? Don't give us your hang-ups straight. Too hot to handle.

Challenor closes his notebook and offers the group a few platitudinous pieces of advice ("You don't have to love the people, but the people *have* to love you," etc.). Finally he comes to the point: as an agent, he's interested only in McBrain and Samuels. He hands them forms to be filled out and assures them that efforts will be made to get them bookings. Then he turns to Waters.

CHALLENOR: Thanks, Eddie. Nice evening. Some good lads. Few wild notions mebbe but . . . I'm down at the Midland. How about a drink?

WATERS: Still full of shit, Bert. Fuller than a large intestine.

CHALLENOR: How's that, Eddie?

WATERS: You wouldn't know a comedian from a barrowload of crap.

CHALLENOR (*light, unruffled*): Meaning you disagree. Oh. Send in a report.

WATERS: I don't belong, remember?

CHALLENOR: What do you expect? A hundred per cent?

WATERS: They were nobbled, Bert. They're great lads.

CHALLENOR: Your opinion. Don't be ungracious . . .

WATERS: Yeah. Enjoy the Midland.

CHALLENOR (*smiling evenly*): Always do, Eddie. *Like* the best.

> *Challenor picks up his briefcase, leaves with what dignity he can*

salvage. A deep, uneasy silence.

PRICE (*without venom*): There goes nothing. A man doesn't rate Frank Randle, what does *he* know?

WATERS (*deliberately*): He knows enough, Mr. Price. He knows where the door marked In is.

PRICE: Yeah, but do you know where it leads? (*Looking at McBrain and Samuels.*) It leads to a room with a notice on the wall and the notice says "Kindly ensure that you leave this room as you found it." A shitheap.

McBrain makes a weak effort to reassure Price, who doesn't really need this kind of support. McBrain expresses his deeply-felt debt to Waters and leaves, "kiln-fired, hard inside the compromise" but refusing to have a celebratory pint with the even more compromised Samuels. Samuels takes his leave of Waters politely with "Couldn'ta done it without you" and makes a lonely exit. Phil also exits alone, after Ged, still smouldering, declines to accompany him. Connor leaves soon after, but this time it is Waters who takes the initiative of a farewell comment, telling Connor he is on the right track with his act and should stay on it.

Ged asks Waters if he can join the next class, but Waters assures him he needs no further instruction, "You need to *do* it now, Ged. You *have* it, lad." Ged has decided to work solo from now on. Tonight he deliberately threw the act off course because Phil "wanted to put something in for Challenor" and Ged wouldn't do it. Ged hands Waters a small present — a pipe — and goes out, leaving Price and Waters alone in the classroom.

Price wants to know what Waters thought of his act; Waters comments, "Terrifying." Price insists that he can't see life through Waters's eyes, he must look at it through his own. Waters protests that Price's act makes junk of love, compassion, all the sweeter side of human nature.

PRICE: You're avoiding the question, Eddie.

WATERS: What do you want me to say . . .?

PRICE: Was I good or was I crap . . .?

WATERS: You were *brilliant!*

    Pause. Price blinks. Waters glowers at the new terrain.

PRICE (*slowly*): But you . . . didn't like it. (*Waters shakes his head. Soft, slow.*) Why not?

WATERS: Look, it's late, we'll talk another time . . .

PRICE: Why not, Eddie?

WATERS: All right. It had grace, control, timing, all the things we've worked on all these weeks . . . It wasn't human. It was drowning in hate. It was ugly. People aren't dummies. I don't care what class or what race or what religion or what sex, if you make people dummies, you've stopped being interested in their reality, in their truth . . .

PRICE: Truth? What do you know about the truth, Mr. Waters? You think the truth is beautiful? You've forgotten what it's like. You knew it when you started off, Oldham Empire, People's Music Hall, Colne Hippodrome, Bolton Grand, New Brighton Palace . . . the Lancashire Lad — you knew it then all right. Nobody hit harder than Eddie Waters, that's what they used to say. Because you

were still in touch with what made you ... hunger ... diptheria, filth, un-employment, penny clubs, means tests, bed bugs, head lice ... Was all *that* truth beautiful?
> *Pause. Waters says nothing.*

Truth was a fist you hit with. Now it's like ... now it's like cowflop, a day old, hard until it's underfoot and then it's ... green, soft. Shitten.
> *Pause.*

Nothing's changed, Mr. Waters, is what I'm saying. When I stand upright — like tonight at that club — I bang my head on the ceiling. Just like you fifty years ago. We're still caged, exploited, prodded and pulled at, milked, fattened, slaughtered, cut up, fed out. We still don't belong to ourselves. Nothing's changed. You've just forgotten, that's all.

Waters has stopped laughing, Price insists, for some reason — maybe because he lost his hate somewhere in the World War II slaughterhouse. Waters warns him: "The people who run this place can handle all the hate you have and barely notice it. They were picking you off before you were born. They'll use you against yourself. It's started already."

Changing the system is what Price hopes to accomplish. *"Knowing* it is changing it," Waters declares. Price doesn't agree. He takes a book out of his bag and shows it to Waters. It's a book Waters lent him written by a clown named Grock. Price found in it the idea for tonight's act.

Grock wasn't like Chaplin, "all coy and covered in kids . . . . . he weren't even funny. He was just ... very truthful." Price remembers what Grock said about being a comedian.

PRICE (*quoting*): "A man whose life it is to turn somersaults and twist himself into knots, eat fire and ice, can't be like ordinary men ... "
WATERS (*quoting*): "He must be armor-plated as an armadillo."
PRICE: Right. It was all fire and ice out there tonight, Eddie. I loved it. I felt expressed.
> *He hands Waters the book. puts his coat on, picks up the bag.*
> *Pause. Waters stands, fastens his coat, picks up his briefcase.*

WATERS (*very quiet*): What do you do now then?
PRICE: I go back. I wait. I'm ready.
WATERS: Driving, you mean?
PRICE: Driving. It doesn't matter.
WATERS: Wait for what?
PRICE: Wait for it to happen.
WATERS (*very low*): Do you want help?
PRICE: No. I'm O.K. Watch out for me.
WATERS: How's Margaret?
PRICE (*plain*): She left. Took the kiddie. Gone to her sister's in Bolton.
WATERS (*finally*): I'm sorry.
PRICE: It's nothing. I cope.
> *Pause.*

What do you do then? Carry on with this?

WATERS: I don't know.
PRICE: You should. You do it well.

Price leaves and Waters turns to erase the blackboard. The Asian, Mr. Patel, comes into the room to get the parcel he had forgotten (it contains a chunk of beef not for himself but for a friend; the cow is sacred to Patel, who is a Hindu, though he works at the abbatoir). Patel has learned that Waters is conducting a class for comedians and offers to tell him a joke.

PATEL: (*laughing, excited*): It's very funny, it's very, very funny. A man has many children, wife, in the South. His crop fail, he have nothing, the skin shrivel on his children's ribs, his wife's milk dries. They lie outside the house starving. All round them, the sacred cows, ten, twenty, more, eating grass. One day he take sharp knife, mm? He creep up on a big white cow, just as he lift knife, the cow see him and the cow say, "Hey, aren't you knowing you not permitted to kill me?" And the man say, "What do you know, a talking horse."
    Patel laughs a lot. Waters suddenly begins to laugh too. . . . .
WATERS: What do you know, a talking horse. That's Jewish. It is. Come on, I'll give you a lift. Listen, I'm starting another class in May, why don't you join it? You might enjoy it.
    Curtain.

OTHERWISE ENGAGED

A Play in Two Acts

BY SIMON GRAY

Cast and credits appear on page 302

SIMON GRAY was born in Hayling Island, Hampshire, in 1936 and was educated at Westminster School and at universities in Canada and France before going to Cambridge, where he majored in English. His produced plays include Wise Child, *done in London in 1967 starring Alec Guinness and in New York in 1972 starring Donald Pleasence;* Dutch Uncle *(1969);* Spoiled *(1971); and* Butley *which opened in London July 14, 1971 with Alan Bates in the title role. Bates came to New York for the Broadway production opening Oct. 31, 1972, running for 155 performances and receiving a Best Play citation and a Tony nomination. Gray's second Best Play,* Otherwise Engaged, *was directed by Harold Pinter in its London premiere July 3, 1975 and again this season on Broadway, where it won the New York Drama Critics Circle Award for best play.*

Gray also adapted The Idiot *for production at the National Theater, and he is the author of three novels —* Colmain, Simple People *and* Little Portia. *His TV plays include* The Caramel Crisis, Sleeping Dog, Death of a Teddy Bear *(for which he won the British Writer's Guild Award),* Pig in a Poke *and* Man in a Sidecar. *Gray teaches English literature at the University of London's Queen Mary College. He is married, with two children.*

EDITOR'S NOTE: Simon Gray's *Otherwise Engaged* (the script of which was not available for synopsis) resembles his 1972-73 Best Play *Butley* in that it holds focus on a central character in a prolonged crisis. In the former, Butley himself comes apart under accumulating stress; in the latter, the central character — Simon Hench — keeps his cool and his elegant syntax while his relationships with other individuals — friends, family and others — fray and disintegrate. On the surface, Simon Hench shines with a high intellectual gloss. Underneath, he may be either an empty but impenetrable shell or an immoveably solid object — and a close look at the play doesn't absolutely determine which.

The setting for *Otherwise Engaged* is the book-lined living room of Simon Hench's house in London, amply furnished with such creature comforts and modest conveniences (a large hi-fi but no TV) as befit a successful publisher. Simon has brought home a new recording of *Parsifal*. In the absence of his wife Beth, Simon is looking forward to the solitary pleasure of listening to the record; but immediately there occurs the first in a continuous series of interruptions which will cause Simon to be engaged otherwise than in listening to music for the duration of the play.

The young tenant of the flat upstairs, Dave, comes in to ask Simon for a postponement of this week's rent and to borrow money for a date. Simon obliges and Dave leaves, just as Simon's brother Stephen Hench enters. Stephen is a public school teacher up for an assistant headmastership which he fears he'll lose to a rival. Simon tries to reason Stephen out of his misgivings, with little success.

The interruption continues with the arrival of a writer friend of Simon's, Jeff Golding, who stays on after Stephen leaves to confide in Simon that he's carrying on an affair with his own ex-wife under the nose of her new husband.

Jeff's regular bed-mate, Davina, also a writer, comes in to inform Jeff that his ex-wife has attempted suicide. Davina's calculated manner of reporting this disaster so exasperates Jeff that he throws the contents of his whiskey glass over her. Jeff rushes from the premises in false alarm (Davina's story of the suicide is untrue), while Davina takes off her wet shirt. Bra-less, she offers herself to Simon, trying at the same time to arouse his interest in her book. Simon declines the former honor but assures her he'll publish her book if it's good enough.

After Davina leaves, Simon switches his phone to the answering machine, only to be interrupted by still another caller. It is a former schoolmate, Wood, inquiring about his daughter who, he believes, visited Simon's office for a job interview two days before and is now missing. Wood wonders whether Simon used the opportunity of the interview to make love to her. Simon admits that he did, as the curtain falls on the first act.

The second act begins immediately following, with Wood's confession that the girl he called his "daughter" is really his beloved, the only light of his dreary life. Wood worships and scarcely dares to touch what Simon has so easily, detachedly, routinely possessed.

Simon is calm in the face of Wood's near-murderous anger. Stephen returns, his presence forcing Wood's departure. Stephen has great news: he's won the assistant headmastership after all. Simon is pleased, but not as enthusiastic as Stephen had hoped he'd be.

Stephen leaves as Dave enters on another cadging errand. This time Simon hesitates to lend Dave his special coffee-maker. The minor frustration inflames Dave into belaboring Simon with a have-not's resentful diatribe against Simon the have, after which Dave stalks out in anger.

Stephen returns to accuse his brother of despising him and the smallness of his academic ambitions. Stephen tries to unsettle Simon with insinuations about Simon's wife Beth. Simon doesn't want to listen, but Stephen insists on telling him that Beth is having an affair with another man.

Beth's entrance interrupts this confidence. Stephen leaves, and Beth perceives that Stephen has told Simon about her affair. Simon doesn't want to bring the matter out into open discussion — he is ready for tacit acceptance, for ignoring the situation in hope that it will eventually blow over. But Beth insists on communicating to him the details of her feelings as the emotionally needful wife of such an emotionally parsimonious husband. Simon's moderation and control in all things is a sign of inner decay, she believes, and calculated to drive others to frenzy. As a parting shot, Beth informs her husband that she is expecting a baby and doesn't know which man, Simon or her lover, is the father — and leaves the room.

Simon remembers that the phone rang during his session with Beth. He turns on the answering machine and hears Wood's recorded voice describing his actions in the process of committing suicide by shooting himself.

Simon switches off the recorded message just before the shot is fired and turns to face Jeff, who has come back to accuse Simon of tipping off the police that he'd been drinking, so they'd arrest Jeff for drunken driving. For Simon, this is the last straw. Indignant and out of temper at last, he throws his drink in Jeff's face.

Recovering his poise immediately, Simon offers Jeff a handkerchief to wipe his face. There is no more talk of the police. The two men are both relaxed and listening to the recording of *Parsifal* as the play ends.

This unfailingly literate and often biting satire both seduces its audience with wit and confronts it with challenge. As the play holds its focus on Simon Hench, it both reveals and conceals him. Is his balance held by some inner, untippable gyroscope of culture and self-command; or is his unflappableness merely a psychic manifestation of emotional sterility, of alienation from the rest of the human race? Is he numb as a dead nerve (Beth's judgment upon him) or quivering with cultivated, hidden sensitivities which he allows a high profile only once in the play (the drink thrown at Jeff)?

The New York Drama Critics Circle gave *Otherwise Engaged* their highest collective praise in the form of the best-play award, but as individuals they were divided on this question of Simon Hench. Those who came down on the side of self-imposed cool included Clive Barnes, who wrote of Simon in the New York *Times,* "His brilliance and his only faintly discernible snobbism are placed as barriers between himself and the world . . . . . (he) has decided it is safer, less tiring, not to join the human race . . . . . Intellectual man at bay!"

In the New York *Daily News* Douglas Watt took a similar view, calling Simon "the very model of a stoic . . . . . maddeningly reasonable." To Jack Kroll writing in *Newsweek,* Simon was "an emotional dropout . . . . . He doesn't give a damn about anybody's problems and has developed a dazzlingly comic virtuosity of sham befuddlement to fend them off."

Martin Gottfried sounded more as though he agreed with Beth when he wrote in the New York *Post,* "The play is about a man who attracts people with troubles because he is unemotional, sensible and perceptive. He is also incapable of caring about them." Edwin Wilson of the *Wall Street Journal* saw him as "a serene figure moving through life, keeping his head when all about him are losing theirs . . . . . Gradually we come to realize that for all of his charm and

TOM COURTENAY IN "OTHERWISE ENGAGED"

cleverness, Simon has no feelings, no passion. He cannot understand jealousy or anger or real love." And Richard Schickel wrote in *Time* that Simon was "testing his carefully trained incapacity for human relationships, even simple understanding . . . . . He is using words not to reveal but to conceal. He also uses them as he does his phonograph — to drown out the sounds of pain, to keep everyone at a distance from his precious, empty self."

Thus the intriguing puzzle of Simon Hench invites many solutions in Simon Gray's subtle, intelligent and distinguished *Otherwise Engaged*.

○○○ AMERICAN BUFFALO

A Play in Two Acts

BY DAVID MAMET

Cast and credits appear on page 303

DAVID MAMET was born Nov. 30, 1947 in Flossmore, Ill. and graduated from Goddard College in Vermont with a B.A. in English literature in 1969, after having observed creative theater at close quarters as a busboy at Second City in Chicago and having studied it for a year or two at a professional school in New York. From 1971 to 1973 he was artist-in-residence at Goddard. In 1974 he was a member of the Illinois Arts Council faculty and in 1975 he helped found and served as artistic director of St. Nicholas Theater Company in Chicago which first produced some of Mamet's scripts including Reunion, Squirrels, Duck Variations *and* Sexual Perversity in Chicago.

Mamet's first New York production was of Duck Variations *off off Broadway at St. Clements in May, 1975, followed by* Sexual Perversity *at the same group in September. His* American Buffalo *moved from its world premiere at the Goodman Theater Stage Two in Chicago in October to St. Clements in January, 1976, and Mamet received an Obie last year as best new playwright for these last two works.*

The off-Broadway program of Duck Variations *and* Sexual Perversity *at the Cherry Lane in June, 1976 began Mamet's career in the New York professional theater and ran for 273 performances. His* American Buffalo *was produced on Broadway Feb. 16, 1977 and was named a Best Play of its season and won the New York Drama Critics Circle Award for best American play. Mamet's long list of playwriting awards and grants includes Joseph Jefferson Awards for dis-*

tinguished Chicago shows to Sexual Perversity *in 1975 and* American Buffalo *in 1976; a New York State Council on the Arts Plays for Young Audiences grant in 1976 for* The Revenge of the Space Pandas, *or* Binky Rudich and the Two-Speed Clock; *a Rockefeller playwriting-in-residence grant in 1976, and a CBS Fellowship at Yale in 1977.*

The following synopsis of American Buffalo *was prepared by Jeff Sweet. Parentheses around lines of dialogue are the playwright's punctuation to denote the more internal expressions of the characters, the points at which they are almost talking to themselves.*

Time: The present, one Friday

Place: Don's Resale Shop, a junkshop

ACT I

SYNOPSIS: It is morning. Donny (Don) Dubrow, middle-aged owner of the store, is sitting with Bobby, the young man who is his "gofer." Bobby is apologizing for lousing up an assignment. He was supposed to wait in front of a certain building, keep his eye open for a certain guy who would be coming out. But Bobby has returned without having spotted the guy. Don tells him that when he is supposed to do a thing, he should do it and no excuses. "Action counts," he says. "Action talks and bullshit walks."

They start to clean up from a poker game held the previous night. Don tells Bobby that Fletcher, one of last night's players, is the kind of guy to be — an enterprising guy who comes through with the goods. "You take him and put him down in some strange town with just a nickel in his pocket, and by nightfall he'll have that town by the balls." Fletcher and Ruthie were the big winners of the game. One isn't born with the knack for success, Don insists, one learns: "Everything that I or Fletcher know we picked up on the street. That's all business is . . . common sense, experience, and talent." Bobby recalls that Fletcher once conned Ruthie out of a whole load of pigiron.

DON: What pigiron?
BOBBY: That he got off her that time.
DON: When was this?
BOBBY: On the back of her truck.
DON: That wasn't, I don't think, her pigiron.
BOBBY: No?
DON: That was *his* pigiron, Bob.
BOBBY: Yeah?
DON: Yeah. He bought it off her.
     Pause.
BOBBY: Well, she was real mad at him.
DON: She was.

BOBBY: Yup.

DON: She was mad at him?

BOBBY: Yeah. That he stole her pigiron.

DON: He didn't steal it, Bob.

BOBBY: No?

DON: No.

BOBBY: She was *mad* at him . . .

DON: Well, that very well may be, Bob, but the fact remains that it was *business*. That's what business *is*.

BOBBY: What.

DON: People taking *care* of themselves. Huh?

BOBBY: No.

DON: 'Cause there's business and there's friendship, Bobby . . . there are many things, and when you walk around you *hear* a lot of things, and what you got to do is keep clear who your friends are, and who treated you like what. Or else the rest is garbage, Bob, because I want to tell you something.

BOBBY: Okay.

DON: Things are not always what they seem to be.

BOBBY: I know.

> *Pause.*

DON: There's a lotsa people on this street, Bob, they want this and they want that. Do anything to get it. You don't have *friends* this life . . . You want some breakfast?

Bobby says he's not hungry. Don takes him to task for living on coffee and cigarettes, says that he should take vitamins, eat yogurt, and if he needs money for food, just to ask.

Walter Cole, called "Teach," enters in a foul mood. He's just run into Ruthie and Grace at the Riverside, a coffee shop.

TEACH: So Grace and Ruthie's having breakfast, and they're done. *Plates . . . crusts* of stuff all over . . . So we'll shoot the shit.

DON: Yeah.

TEACH: Talk about the *game* . . .

DON: . . . yeah.

TEACH: . . . *so* on. Down I sit. "Hi," "hi." I take a piece of toast off Grace's plate . . .

DON: . . . uh huh . . .

TEACH: . . . and she goes "Help yourself." Help myself. I should help myself to half a piece of toast it's four slices for a quarter. I should have a nickel every time we're over at the game, I pop for coffee . . . cigarettes . . . a *sweet roll*, never say word. "Bobby, see who wants what." Huh? A fucking *roast beef* sandwich. *(To Bobby.)* Am I right? *(To Don.)* Ahh, shit. We're sitting down, how many times do I pick up the check? But (No!) because I never go and make a big *thing* out of it — it's no big thing — and flaunt like "This one's on me" like some bust-out asshole, but I naturally assume that I'm with friends, and don't forget who's who when someone gets *behind* a half a yard or needs some help with (huh?) some fucking rent, or drops enormous piles of money at the track, or someone's *sick* or something . . .

DON (*to Bobby*): This is what I'm talking about.

TEACH: Only (and I tell you this, Don). Only, and I'm not, I don't think, casting anything on anyone: from the mouth of a Southern bulldyke asshole ingrate of a vicious nowhere cunt can this trash come. . . . . .

Don tells Teach he's sending Bobby out to the Riverside to get some breakfast. Does he want anything? Teach says no, then relents, orders crisp bacon and black coffee. He tells Bobby if he sees Ruthie not to say anything. Bobby nods, leaves.

Don and Teach talk about last night's game. Teach is still sore at Ruthie, who won, and at her partner Grace. He hints that they aren't above cheating. "We're talking about money for chrissake, huh? We're talking about cards. Friendship is friendship, and a wonderful thing, and I am all for it. I have never said different, and you know me on this point. Okay. But let's just keep it *separate* huh, let's just keep the two apart, and maybe we can deal with each other like some human beings."

Teach roams around the store, hunting for the hat he lost last night. He tells Don there's something he wants to say to Fletch and asks if Fletch will be dropping by. Don says there's no way of knowing. Teach idly picks up a souvenir from the 1933 Chicago exhibition, which cues a short discussion about the unforeseeable value of such junk. Teach comments that he would be rich today if he had kept his hands on the garbage he's thrown out over the years. The conversation deteriorates to comments on the likelihood of rain.

Bobby returns with the food and news for Teach that Ruthie isn't mad at him. Teach is initially irritated that Bobby talked to her after saying he wouldn't, but he lets the matter drop. He makes a few disparaging remarks about Don's taste for yogurt, then asks if Bobby saw Fletcher. Bobby answers no. Don notices the coffee he ordered isn't in the bag, and Bobby says he'll return to the Riv and get it.

Before leaving, Bobby tells Don that he just now spotted the man Don had wanted him to keep an eye out for. Bobby tells him that the guy came out of his building with a suitcase, got in his car and drove away. Don seems satisfied and sends Bobby off for the coffee. Teach senses that a job is in the air. He asks what Don has a line on — jewelry, maybe? After a moment's hesitation, Don tells him, "Coins." He makes a phone call.

DON (*into phone*): . . . . . Hello? This is Donny Dubrow. We were talking the other day. Lookit, sir, if I could get ahold of some of that stuff you were interested in, would you be interested in some of it?

Pause.

Those *things* . . . *Old,* yeah.

Pause.

Various pieces of various types.

Pause.

Tonight. Sometime late. Are they *what* . . . *!!??* Yes, but I don't see what kind of

a question is that (at the prices we're talking about . . .)
> *Pause.*

No, hey, no, I understand *you* . . .
> *Pause.*

Sometime late.
> *Pause.*

One hundred percent.
> *Pause.*

I feel the same. All right. Goodbye. *(Hangs up.)* Fucking asshole.

TEACH: Guys like that, I like to fuck their wives.

Under Teach's questioning, the story comes out. About a week back, a customer spotted a buffalo head nickel in Don's store, asked Don how much it was. Don had a hunch from the guy's attitude that it was valuable and haggled $90 for it. A couple of days later, the guy returned, gave Don his card and told him to give him a call if he came across another coin of interest. Don, figuring that the guy must have a valuable collection, has decided to have the coins stolen, then sell them to the man he just talked to on the phone. Bobby's report indicates that the collector has left town for a day or two, so the coast is clear to break in that night. Teach asks who he's going to send in. Don tells him Bobby.

TEACH *(pause)*: Don't send the kid in.

DON: I shouldn't send Bobby in?

TEACH: No. (Now, just wait a second.) Let's siddown on this. What are we saying here? Loyalty. *(Pause.)* You know how I am on this. This is great. This is admirable. . . . . . All I mean, a guy can be too loyal, Don. Don't be dense on this. What are we saying here? Business. . . . . . We both know what we're saying here. We both know we're talking about some job needs more than the kid's gonna skin pop go in there with a *crowbar* . . .

DON: I don't want you mentioning that.

TEACH: It slipped out.

DON: You know how I feel on that.

TEACH: Yes. And I'm sorry, Don. I admire that. All that I'm saying don't confuse business with pleasure.

DON: But I don't want that talk, only, Teach. *(Pause.)* You understand?

TEACH: I more than understand, and I apologize. *(Pause.)* I'm sorry.

DON: That's the only thing.

TEACH: All right. But I tell you. I'm glad I said it.

DON: Why?

TEACH: Cause it's best for these things to be out in the open.

DON: But I don't want it in the open.

TEACH: Which is why I apologized.

Teach continues to press his point. *He* should go in instead of Bobby. After giving 10 percent of the money to the connection who found the buyer Don just talked to, he and Don would split 45-45. If it's a big score, maybe give the kid a hundred or so. Don seems to be weakening, but he hasn't made a commitment when Bobby returns.

To underscore what he has been saying about Bobby's incompetence, Teach spends the next couple of minutes baiting the boy with questions to which Bobby can only make mumbled, confused replies. Turning from Teach, Bobby asks Don to advance him $50 on account. Teach's tactics have borne fruit. Don tells Bobby that he's decided not to go for the coins tonight.

BOBBY: You want to hold *off* on it?

DON: I was thinking that we might.

BOBBY: Oh.

DON: And, on the money, I'll give you . . . forty, you owe me twenty, and, for now, keep twenty for spotting the guy. *(Pause.)* Okay?

BOBBY: Yeah. *(Pause.)* You don't want me to do the job?

DON: That's what I *told* you. What am I telling you?

BOBBY: I'm not going to do it.

DON: Not *now.* We aren't going to do it now.

BOBBY: We'll do it later on?

DON *(shrugs)*: But I'm giving you twenty just for spotting the guy.

BOBBY: I need fifty, Donny.

DON: Well, I'm giving you forty.

BOBBY: You said you were giving me twenty.

DON: No, Bob, I did not. I said I was giving you forty, of *which* you were going to owe me twenty. *(Pause.)* And you go keep twenty . . . . .

BOBBY: . . . . . Could you let me have fifty?

DON: And you'll give me back thirty?

BOBBY: I could just give back the twenty.

DON: That's not the deal.

BOBBY: We could *make* it the deal. *(Pause.)* Donny? We could *make* it the deal. Huh?

DON: Bob, lookit. Here it is: I give you fifty, next week you pay me back twenty-five. *(Pause.)* You get to keep twenty-five, you pay me back twenty-five.

BOBBY: And what about the thing?

DON: Forget about it.

BOBBY: You tell me when you want me to do it.

DON: I don't know *that* I want you to do it. At this point. *(Pause.)* You know what I mean? *(Pause.)*

BOBBY: No.

DON: I mean, I'm *giving* you twenty-five, and I'm saying forget the thing.

BOBBY: Forget it for me.

DON: Yes.

BOBBY: Oh. *(Pause.)* Okay. Okay . . . . . I'm gonna go. *(Pause.)* I'll see you later. *(Pause, looks at Don.)*

DON: Oh.

    Reaches in pocket and hands bills to Bobby.

(To Teach:) You got two fives?

TEACH: No.

DON *(to Bobby)*: I got to give you . . . thirty, you owe me back thirty.
BOBBY: You said you were giving me fifty.
DON: I'm sorry, I'm sorry, Bob, you're absolutely right.
>   *Gives Bobby remainder of money.*

After a moment's hesitation, Bobby leaves. Teach assures Don he made the smart move. The two start talking about the job. Don begins by saying he wants the nickel he sold back. "You're going to get it back," Teach insists. "I'm going in there for his coins, what am I going to take 'em all except your nickel?" They start to wonder where the coins would be kept. Does the guy have a study? Does he have a safe or are they in a desk drawer? Of course, Teach says, he'll also have to know what he's looking for. What's valuable and what isn't. Don takes out a book listing coin prices. It's a little out of date, but it gives an indication.

TEACH: You've been looking at it?
DON: Yeah.
TEACH: You got to have a feeling for your subject.
DON: The book can give you that.
TEACH: This is what I'm *saying* to you. One thing. Makes all the difference in the world.
DON: What?
TEACH: Knowing what the fuck you're talking about. And it's so rare, Don. *So* rare. What do you think a 1929 S Lincoln head penny with the wheat on the back is worth?
>   *Don starts to speak.*
Ah! Ah! Ah! Ah! Ah! We got to know what *condition* we're talking about.
DON *(Pause)*: Okay. What condition?
TEACH: *Any* of 'em. You tell me.
DON: Well, pick one.
TEACH: Okay, I'm going to pick an easy one. Excellent condition 1929 S.
DON: It's worth . . . about thirty-six dollars.
TEACH: No.
DON: (More?)
TEACH: Well, guess.
DON: Just tell me is it more or less.
TEACH: What do you think?
DON: More.
TEACH: No.
DON: Okay, it's worth, I gotta say . . . eighteen-sixty.
TEACH: No.
DON: Then I give up.
TEACH: Twenty fucking cents.
DON: You're fulla shit.
TEACH: My mother's grave.
DON: Give me that fucking book. *(Business.)* Go beat that.
TEACH: This is what I'm saying, Don, you got to know what you're talking about.

DON: You wanna take the book?

TEACH: Naaa, *fuck* the book. What am I going to do, leaf through the book for hours on end? The important thing is to have the *idea* . . .

Don asks Teach how he figures to get into the house. Teach says he'll find a way. Don presses him for specifics. Teach says he'll know when he gets there. "You have your job, I have my job, Don," he says testily. "I am not here to smother you in theory. Think about it."

Don decides to add Fletcher to the team. Teach demands a reason. "I want some depth," Don replies. Teach doesn't like the idea. Don tries to call Fletcher but the line is busy. Teach tells Don that he's hurt that he's bringing in another guy, but Don stands firm on his decision. Teach begins to allow that Don may be right. They'll have a division of labor. "Security. Muscle. Intelligence." Don tells him to be back between ten-thirty and eleven that night. Teach nods, then asks Don, "Are you mad at me?" Don tells him no. Teach says he's off to his hotel room for a nap.

TEACH: . . . . . Anybody wants to get in touch with me, I'm over the hotel.

DON: Okay.

TEACH: I'm not the *hotel,* I stepped out for coffee, I'll be back one minute.

DON: Okay.

TEACH: And I'll see you around eleven.

DON: O'*clock.*

TEACH: *Here.*

DON: Right.

TEACH: And don't worry about anything.

DON: I won't.

TEACH: I don't want to hear you're worrying about a goddamned thing.

DON: You won't, Teach.

TEACH: You're sure you want Fletch coming with us?

DON: Yes.

TEACH: All right then so long as you're sure.

DON: I'm sure, Teach.

TEACH: Then I'm going to see you tonight.

DON: Goddam right you are.

TEACH: I am seeing you later.

DON: I know.

TEACH: Goodbye.

DON: Goodbye.

TEACH: I want to make one thing plain before I go, Don. I am not mad at you.

DON: I know.

TEACH: All right, then.

DON: You have a good nap.

TEACH: I will.

> *Teach exits.*

DON: Fuckin *business* . . .

> *Lights dim to black. Curtain.*

ACT II

That night at 11:15, Teach and Fletcher haven't shown and Don is upset. As he tries to locate them by phone, Bobby enters, telling him he's gotten hold of another buffalo head nickel and offering to sell it. Don asks if he's seen anything of Teach and Fletch. Bobby says no and brings up the subject of the nickel again, asking Don what his offer is. Don replies it's hard to make an offer without knowing things like the date and condition of the coin, but Bobby seems reluctant to show it to him. Don comes close to losing his patience, but regains his composure and asks Bobby if he needs money, and if so how much. Bobby doesn't answer. Instead he asks why Don is in the store so late. Don tells him that he and Teach and Fletch have a date to play cards.

Teach enters. He is surprised to see Bobby there and demands to know the reason for his presence. Don ignores the question and takes Teach to task for being late. Teach tells him it's because his watch broke.

DON: When did your watch break?

TEACH: The fuck do *I* know?

DON: Well, you look at it. You want to know your watch broke, all you got to do is look at it. *(Pause.)*

TEACH: I don't have it.

DON: Why not?

TEACH: I took it off when it broke. . . . . .

DON: You're going around without a watch.

TEACH: Yes. I am, Donny. What am I, you're my *keeper* all a sudden?

DON: I'm paying you to do a thing, Teach, I expect to know where you are when.

TEACH: Donny. You aren't paying me to do a thing. We are doing something together. I know we are. My watch broke, that is my concern. The *thing* is your and my concern. And the concern of Fletcher. You want to find a reason we should jump all over each other all of a sudden like we work in a *bloodbank,* fine. But it's not good business. *(Pause.)* And so who knows what time it is offhand? Jerks on the radio? The phone broad? *(Pause.)* Now I understand nerves.

DON: There's no fuckin' nerves involved in this, Teach.

TEACH: No, huh?

DON: No.

TEACH: Well, great. That's great, then. So what are we talking about? A little lateness? Some excusable fucking lateness? And a couple of guys they're understandably a bit excited? *(Pause.)*

DON: I don't like it.

TEACH: Then *don't* like it, then. Let's do this. Let's everybody get a writ. I got a case. You got a case. Bobby — I don't know what the fuck *he's* doing here . . .

Bobby explains about the nickel and hands it to Teach in a cloth. Don explains they haven't checked yet to find what it's worth. Edgy about Fletcher's lateness, Teach angrily speculates that maybe Bobby has shown up to take the missing partner's place. Teach immediately apologizes for his paranoia. Don tells Bobby to run along, but Bobby still needs money. Teach offers to buy the coin but balks at Bobby's asking price of $50. He gives back the coin and instead offers him a $5 loan. Bobby needs more. Teach gets Don to give him another ten. Heading for the door, Bobby says they'll look up the coin in the book tomorrow and, leaving, tells Teach he should talk to Ruthie "because . . . " Teach and Don are alone now.

TEACH: So where is Fletcher?
DON: Don't worry. He'll be here.
TEACH: The question is but when. Maybe his watch broke.
DON: Maybe it just did, Teach. Maybe his actual watch broke.
TEACH: And maybe mine didn't, you're saying? You wanna bet? You wanna place a little fucking wager on it? How much money you got in your pockets? I bet you all the money in your pockets against all the money in my pockets, I walk out that door right now, I come back with a broken watch.
    Pause.
DON: Calm down.
TEACH: I am calm. I'm just upset.

Teach says they should call the coin collector's house to double-check that no one is there. Don takes out the card with the phone number.

TEACH: . . . . . No look: If he *answers* . . .
DON . . . yeah?
TEACH: *Don't* arouse his fucking suspicions.
DON: All right.
TEACH: And the odds are he's not there, so when he answers just say you're calling for a wrong fucking *number,* something. Be simple. *(Pause.)* Give me the phone.
    Don hands Teach the phone.
Give me the card.
    Don hands Teach the card.
This is his number? 221-7834?
DON: Yeah.
    Teach snorts.
TEACH: All right. I dial, I'm calling for somebody named "June" and we go interchange on number. *(Pause.)* We're gonna say like, "Is this 221-7834?"
DON: . . . yeah?
TEACH: And they go, "No." (I mean "-7843." It *is* -7834.) So we go, very simply, "Is this 221-7843?" and they go "No," and right away the guy is home, we still haven't blown the shot.
DON: Okay.
    Teach picks up phone and dials.
TEACH *(into phone)*: Hi. Yeah. I'm calling . . . uh . . . is June there? *(Pause.)* Well, is this 221-7843? *(Pause.)* It is? Well, look I must of got the number wrong. I'm sorry. *(Hangs up phone.)* (This is bizarre.) Read me that number.
DON: 221-7834.

TEACH: Right. *(Dials phone. Listens.)* Nobody home. See, this is careful operation . . . check and re-check!

Teach again asks why Bobby was there. Don assures him Bobby was just trying to sell the nickel and that he knows nothing about what they're doing tonight. Don calls the Riverside, but Fletcher isn't there either.

TEACH: Cocksucker should be horsewhipped with a horsewhip.
DON: He'll show up.
TEACH: Fucking Riverside, too. (Thirty-seven cents for take-out coffee . . .)
DON: Yeah. *(Picks up phone.)*
TEACH: A lot of nerve you come in there for sixteen years. This is not free enterprise.
DON: No.
TEACH: You know what is free enterprise?
DON: No. What?
TEACH: The freedom . . .
DON: . . . yeah?
TEACH: Of the *Individual* . . .
DON . . . yeah?
TEACH: To Embark on Any Fucking Course that he sees fit.
DON: Uh huh . . .
TEACH: In order to secure his honest chance to make a profit. Am I so out of line on this?
DON: No.
TEACH: Does this make me a Commie?
DON: No.
TEACH: The country's *founded* on this, Don. You know this . . . . . Without this we're just savage shitheads in the wilderness.
DON: Yeah.
TEACH: Sitting around some vicious campfire. That's why *Ruthie* burns me up.
DON: Yeah.
TEACH: (Nowhere dyke . . .) And take those fuckers in the concentration camps. You think they went in there by *choice?*
DON: No.
TEACH: They were *dragged* in there, Don . . .
DON: . . . yeah.
TEACH: Kicking and screaming. *Gimme* that fucking phone.
       Grabs phone. Teach dials phone. Hangs up.
He's not home. I say *fuck* the cocksucker.

Teach gets more and more agitated, begins to theorize on the likelihood that Fletcher may have done the job on his own and cut them out of the action. Don insists this is impossible as Fletch doesn't have the address. Teach is all for forgetting about Fletch entirely and going on with the job right now. Don says no, that they should wait because Fletch knows how to get in. Teach waves this reason aside. It's no big trick to get in. "You break in a *window,* worse comes to worse you kick the fucking *back door* in. (What do you think this is, the Middle Ages?)" Don asks about how to handle the situation if the coins are in a safe. Teach says all you've got to do is find where the combination is written down. Don asks, what if it isn't written down? Teach goes through a convoluted and unconvincing explanation as to why it *has* to be written down some place in the room.

Don is still doubtful. Teach explodes. Doesn't Don know he can be trusted to say what is what? After all, Teach says, he isn't like Fletcher who, by the way, was cheating at cards last night. "This is nothing but poison," says Don. "I don't want to hear it." But Teach goes on to describe a particularly fishy play from the night before which he insists proves his case. Don asks why Teach didn't say anything at the time, and Teach replies he didn't want "to cause bloodshed."

DON: You couldn't say a word?

TEACH: I tell you now.

DON: He was cheating, you couldn't say anything?

TEACH: Don. Don, I see you're put out, you find out this guy is a cheat . . .

DON: According to you.

TEACH: According to me, yes. I am the person it's usually according *to* when I'm talking. Have you noticed this? And I'm not crazed about it you're coming out I would lie to you on this. *Fuck* this. On anything. Wake up, Jim. I'm not the cheat. I know you're not mad at me, who are you mad at? Who fucked you up here, Don? Who's not here? Who?

DON: . . . . . Don't fuck with me, here, Teach.

TEACH: I don't fuck with my friends, Don. I don't fuck with my business associates. I am a business man. I am here to do business, I am here to face facts. (Will you open your eyes?) The kid comes in here, he has got a certain coin, it's like the one *you* used to have. The guy you brought in doesn't show, we don't know where *he* is. *(Pause.)* Something comes down, some guy gets his house took off . . . Fletcher, he's not showing up. Let's say I don't know why, let's say *you* don't know why, but I know that we're both better off. We are better off, Don. . . . . .

Teach prepares to leave to do the job. He takes out and loads his revolver. The sight of the gun upsets Don. "We don't need a gun, Teach." "I pray that we don't," Teach replies, but he's going to take it along for security in case the collector happens to return while he's in the apartment. After all, you never know how "some crazed lunatic" will act if he "sees you as an invasion of his personal domain." They halt their argument as cops cruise by in a car. After they're gone, Teach says the cops know what's what. "Armed to the hilt. Sticks, mace, knives . . . who knows *what* the fuck they got. They have the right idea. Social customs break down, next thing *everybody's* lying in the gutter."

Another interruption — someone at the door — Bobby. They tell him to go away, but he insists it's important. Teach yanks Bobby inside and angrily demands what's so important. Bobby tells them that, according to Ruthie and

Grace, Fletch was mugged earlier this evening and had to go to the hospital with a broken jaw. Teach is skeptical of this story. Which hospital? Masonic? Bobby thinks so. Having delivered the message, he gets up to go.

TEACH: Hold on a second, Bob. I feel we should take care of you for coming here.

BOBBY: That's okay. I'll see you guys.

DON: Come here a minute, Bobby.

BOBBY: What, Donny?

DON: What's going on here?

BOBBY: Here?

DON: Yes.
        Pause.

BOBBY: Nothing.

DON: I'm saying what's happening, Bob?

BOBBY: I don't know.

DON: Where did you get that nickel from?

BOBBY: What nickel?

DON: You know what nickel, Bob, the nickel I'm talking about.

BOBBY: I got it off a guy.

DON: What guy?

BOBBY: I met downtown.

TEACH: What was he wearing?

BOBBY: Things.
        Pause.

DON: How'd you get it off him, Bob?

BOBBY: We kinda talked.
        Pause.

DON: You know what, you look funny, Bob.

BOBBY: I'm late.

DON: It's after midnight, Bob. What are you late for?

BOBBY: Nothing.

DON (*very sadly*): Jesus. Are you fucking with me here?

BOBBY: No.

DON: (Bobby.)

BOBBY: I'm not fucking with you, Donny.
        Pause.

DON: Where's Fletcher?
        Pause.

BOBBY: Masonic.

Don calls Masonic. Fletcher isn't there. Bobby says maybe it's another hospital. Teach tells Bobby he'd better come clean right now for his own "protection." What is going on? Bobby swears ignorance. *"Teach grabs a nearby object and hits Bobby viciously on the side of the head."* Bobby cries and appeals to Don, but Don tells him, "You brought it on yourself." Bobby panics. His ear is bleeding and he's scared. Teach and Don keep pressing him for the "truth."

The phone rings. Don answers with, "What? What the fuck do *you* want?" It's Ruthie with the news that Fletcher has indeed been mugged, and he and his broken jaw are in Columbus Hospital. After agreeing to go with her to visit him the next morning, Don hangs up and calls Columbus and confirms that Fletcher is a patient. He hangs up again.

Quietly, Don and Teach tell Bobby they're going to take him to the hospital to see about the ear. He's to tell the doctors that he fell downstairs. Bobby doesn't want to go. Don insists. Bobby says he wants to do the job, steal the coins. Don tells him not tonight.

BOBBY: We do it sometime else.

DON: Yeah.

TEACH: He ain't going to do no job.

DON: Shut up.

TEACH: Just say he isn't going to do no job.

DON: It's done now.

TEACH: What?

DON: I'm saying, this is over.

TEACH: No, it's not, Don. It is not. He does no job.

DON: You leave the fucking kid alone.

TEACH: You want kids, you go have them. *I'm* not your wife. This doesn't mean a thing to me. *I'm* in this. And it *isn't* over. This is for me, and this is my question:

       Pause.

Where did you get that coin?

BOBBY: What?

TEACH: Where'd you get that fucking nickel . . . . . ?

The truth comes out. Bobby bought it in a coin store for $50. "Why would you go do a thing like that?" Teach demands. Bobby replies, "For Donny."

TEACH: You people make my flesh crawl.

DON: Bob, we're going to take you out of here.

TEACH: I can not take this any more.

DON: Can you walk?

BOBBY: No.

DON: Go and get your car.

TEACH: I am not your nigger. I am not your wife.

DON: I'm through with you today.

TEACH: You are.

DON: Yes . . . . .

BOBBY: He hit me.

DON: I know, Bob.

TEACH: Yes, I hit him. For his own good. For the good of all.

DON: Get out of here.

TEACH: "Get out of here?" And now you throw me out like *trash?* I'm doing this for *you* . . . . .

DON: You get out of here.

TEACH: I am not going anywhere. I have a piece of this.

DON: You have a piece of *shit*, you fucking lame. *(Advancing on him.)* . . . . .
The stinking deals you come in here . . .

TEACH: You stay away from me . . .

DON: You stiff this one, you stiff that one . . . you come in here you stick this
poison in me . . .

     Hitting him.

. . . . . You make life of garbage.

Bobby has more to tell. He didn't really see the coin collector leave with a
suitcase that morning. He just said he did. But he didn't really. The implications of this sink in to Teach. He goes on a rampage, tearing apart the junk-
store.

TEACH: The Whole Entire World. There Is No Law. There Is No Right And
Wrong. The World Is Lies. There Is No Friendship. Every Fucking Thing. The
World. The Whole Thing. Every God Forsaken Thing. The World.

DON: Calm down, Walt.

TEACH: We all live like the cave men.

     Don, during the speech, tries to subdue Teach and finally does.

DON: Siddown.

     A pause. Teach sits still.

TEACH: I went on a limb for you.

     Pause.

You don't know what I go through. I put my dick on the chopping block.

     Pause.

I hock my fucking watch . . .

     Pause.

I go out there. I'm out there every day.

     Pause.

There is nothing out there.

     Pause.

I fuck myself.

     Pause.

DON: Are you all right?

TEACH: What?

DON: Are you all right.

TEACH: How the fuck do I know.

DON: You tire me out, Walt.

TEACH: What?

DON: I need a rest.

TEACH: This fucking day.

DON (*pause*): My shop's fucked up.

TEACH: I know.

DON: It's all fucked up.

     Pause.

You fucked my shop up.
 TEACH: Are you mad at me?
 DON: What?
 TEACH: Are you mad at me?
    Pause.
 DON: Come on.
 TEACH: Are you?
 DON: Go and get your car. Bob?
 TEACH (*pause*): Tell me are you mad at me.
 DON: No.
 TEACH: You aren't?
 DON: No.
    Pause.
 TEACH: Good.

Teach leaves to get the car, a paper hat on his head to protect him from the rain. Don rouses Bobby, who has nodded off.

 DON: Get up.
    Pause.
Bob. I'm sorry.
 BOBBY: What?
 DON: I'm sorry.
 BOBBY: I fucked up.
 DON: No. You did real good.
 BOBBY: No.
 DON: Yeah. You did real good.
    Pause.
 BOBBY: Thank you.
 DON: That's all right.
    Pause.
 BOBBY: I'm sorry, Donny.
 DON: That's all right.
    Lights dim. Curtain.

THE SHADOW BOX

A Play in Two Acts

BY MICHAEL CRISTOFER

Cast and credits appear on page 306

MICHAEL CRISTOFER was born in Trenton, N.J. Jan. 22, 1946 and grew up there and in Princeton as Michael Procaccion. He attended Catholic University in Washington, D.C. but dropped out to become an actor and playwright, taking the stage name Cristofer. His early produced plays included Plot Counter Plot *at St. Clements Space,* The Mandala *at Theater of the Living Arts Workshop in Philadelphia and* Americommedia *in a street theater production that toured during the Presidential campaign of 1972.*

The following year Cristofer began to practise both his arts at the Mark Taper Forum in Los Angeles (his first credit of record there was as an actor in a new play in October 1973; in August 1974 he was billed as Michael Ivan Cristofer in a production of Savages*). Cristofer played the leading role of Colin in the first American production of David Rudkin's British play* Ashes *at Mark Taper last season, a few months after his own play* The Shadow Box *had its first production at Mark Taper Oct. 30, 1975 under Gordon Davidson's direction. This play was subsequently produced at the Long Wharf Theater in New Haven, Conn. Jan. 21, 1976, again under Davidson's direction, then proceeding to its author's Broadway playwriting debut and winning a Best Play citation and the Pulitzer Prize. A new Cristofer play,* Ice, *was produced at the Mark Taper this season.*

Cristofer's New York debut in 1977 was a double one: while his The Shadow Box *was bowing on Broadway, he was taking his first New York bows as an ac-*

tor playing Trofimov in The Cherry Orchard *at Lincoln Center. His long list of acting credits includes other Mark Taper Forum stints, repertory credits with Arena Stage in Washington, D.C. and A Contemporary Theater in Seattle, many TV appearances and the movie* An Enemy of the People. *Cristofer lives in Los Angeles.*

Time: The present

Place: Three cottages on the grounds of a large hospital

ACT I

SYNOPSIS: The setting is a cottage secluded in the midst of trees with living room, kitchen and front porch areas which represent either a single dwelling or three different cottages inhabited by three sets of people. Downstage, away from the cottage, is a stool which marks an "Interview Area" where from time to time a voice speaks over a p.a. system to one or another of the characters.

It is morning, but only the Interview Area is lighted as Joe — *"a strong, thick-set man, a little bit clumsy with moving and talking, but full of energy"* — approaches the stool. The voice of the Interviewer addresses Joe and somewhat surprises him. The Interviewer persuades Joe to sit and reassures him that this is the routine way of keeping in touch; Joe will get used to it. Joe begins to relax and tells the Interviewer that his wife Maggie and son Steve will arrive today to join him in the cottage. The lights come up on the cottage areas, and the voices of Steve and Maggie are heard offstage now and then as the interview continues.

INTERVIEWER: Then everything is settled, right?

JOE: What? Oh, yeah. Maggie knows the whole setup. I wrote to her.

INTERVIEWER: And your son?

JOE: Steve? Yeah. I told Maggie to tell him. I figured he should know before he got here.

INTERVIEWER: Good.

JOE: It's not an easy thing.

STEVE (*offstage; overlapping*): Come on, Mom.

JOE: I guess you know that.

MAGGIE (*offstage*): Give me a chance to catch my breath.

JOE: You get used to the idea, but it's not easy.

INTERVIEWER: You seem fine.

JOE: Oh, me. Yeah, sure. But Maggie . . .

MAGGIE (*offstage; overlapping*): What number did you say it was?

INTERVIEWER (*overlapping*): What number cottage are you in?

JOE: Uh . . . one. Number one.

STEVE (*offstage; overlapping*): Number one. One, they said.

JOE: You get scared at first. Plenty. And then you get pissed off. Oh, is that all right to say?

INTERVIEWER: Yes, Joe. That's all right. It's all right for you to be angry or depressed or even happy . . . if that's how you feel. We want to hear as much as you want to tell us.

STEVE (*offstage*): Look at all these goddamn trees!

MAGGIE (*offstage*): Watch your mouth.

JOE: Yeah, cause I was. Plenty pissed off. I don't mind telling you that. In fact, I'm glad just to say it. You get tired of keeping it all inside. But it's like, nobody wants to hear about it. You know what I mean? Even the doctors . . . they shove a thermometer in your mouth and a stethoscope in their ears . . . How the hell are you supposed to say anything? But then, like I said, you get used to it . . . I guess . . .

There are a couple of other things Joe would like to discuss with the Interviewer later, but right now his wife and son are arriving. Steve, about 14, appears and runs around the cottage, checking it out enthusiastically. He sees his father and runs into his arms. The boy tries to take everything in at once but finally remembers to ask his father, very casually, how he feels. Joe tells Steve he feels fine and that they'll probably enjoy at least a couple of weeks together here at the cottage.

Steve drags his father indoors to look at his new guitar, as Maggie comes onstage carrying the luggage plus a mass of bundles and shopping bags. *"She is dressed up — high heels, bright yellow print dress — but she looks a mess. She's been walking too long, carrying too big a load."* Finally she lets everything drop and straightens up to look around. *"She walks up to the porch of the cabin and tentatively takes one step up. But the cottage seems to frighten her. She stops, looks at it and then backs away from it."*

Maggie gives a long whistle for the others, and Joe comes out. *"Surprised by Joe's sudden appearance, she doesn't move for a second. Then, very carefully, she takes a few slow steps toward him. Joe walks down to meet her. All Maggie can manage to do is reach out one hand and touch him, just to see if he's really there."*

Maggie goes back to her bundles, talking rapidly to relieve her tension. She has brought all kinds of supplies — jelly, peppers, cookies, even coffee, though Joe had assured her on the phone that the cottage was fully stocked. Maggie's first impulse is to clean the cottage, but Joe assures her it's not necessary.

Joe tries to bring Maggie inside to show her the setup, but she puts this off on one pretext or another. She shows off her new dress, complains of jet lag and then produces a huge, unneccessary ham she brought with her three thousand miles across the country. Finally Maggie lets go and weeps in Joe's arms, still clutching the ham. She's confused. Joe appears so much better than she had expected. She can only understand what she sees, and she wants to believe he's all right.

JOE: Maggie, listen . . .

MAGGIE: No. It's all right. You don't have to tell me. I can see it. You're fine. Huh? It's just I got so scared. Thinking about it. Making things up in my head. But it's all right now. I can see it's all right. I knew it would be when I got here.

JOE (*giving in*): Yes, Maggie. Everything's all right.

MAGGIE: I knew it. I knew it.

> *Our focus shifts now to the Interview Area. Brian is talking.*

BRIAN: . . . people don't want to let go. Do they?

INTERVIEWER: How do you mean, Brian?

BRIAN: They think it's a mistake, they think it's supposed to last forever. I'll never understand that. My God, it's the one thing in this world you can be sure of! No matter who you are, no matter what you do, no matter anything — sooner or later — it's going to happen. You're going to die.

> *Brian is a graceful man . . . simple, direct, straightforward . . . mind*
> *and body balanced, like an athlete.*

. . . and that's a relief — if you think about it. I should say if you think clearly about it.

INTERVIEWER: I'm not sure I follow you.

BRIAN: Well, the trouble is that most of us spend our entire lives trying to *forget* that we're going to die. And some of us even succeed. It's like pulling the cart *without* the horse. Or is that a poor analogy?

INTERVIEWER: No, Brian. I think it's fine.

Brian is keeping up his writing, he tells the Interviewer, though he seems to be losing touch with the words he's using and can only trust that they have some meaning. His former wife, bored with his continuous probing and philosophizing, wanted to stop thinking and "just dance for a few years" — he wouldn't, so she left him. He was angry and lonely at first, but then he realized, "I'd lost the energy of it, the magic of it. No wonder she left. After all, the universe isn't a, syllogism, it's a miracle. Isn't it? And if you can believe in one small part of it you can believe in all of it."

Brian's wife never returned, but now he has Mark, as the Interviewer says "a friend in the Greek sense of the word." Mark is keeping Brian company here at Brian's cottage; he is *"a young man, passionately intelligent, sexually attractive"* and he appears in the living room area as the Interviewer and Brian are talking about him. Mark throws his jacket onto a chair, sits, and makes notes as he removes a half-dozen medicine bottles from a package he has brought.

BRIAN (*checking his watch*): My watch is stopped. How long have I been babbling?

INTERVIEWER: It doesn't matter. There's no hurry.

BRIAN: Not for you, maybe. Some of us are on a tighter schedule.

INTERVIEWER: I am sorry. I didn't mean . . .

BRIAN (*laughs*): It's all right. It's all right. You mustn't take all of this too seriously. I don't . . . Our dreams are beautiful, our fate is sad. But day by day, it's generally pretty funny. We can talk again tomorrow, if you want. I don't mind. It's a bit of a shock, that's all. You always think . . . no matter what they tell you . . . you always think you have more time. And you don't. But I appreciate what you're trying to do here, and I do enjoy being a guinea pig.

INTERVIEWER: Good. Very good.

BRIAN: Tomorrow, then. If I'm still breathing. Or even if I'm not, I don't think it'll stop me from talking.
INTERVIEWER: Yes. Tomorrow.

The lights fade on the Interview Area and come up on the living room where Mark is putting the medicine in a book case with other bottles and pill boxes. Beverly comes in as though to a party. She is *"an extremely attractive woman, middle-aged, dressed curiously in what was once a very expensive, chic evening dress. But it is now soiled and torn. She also has over and around the dress about 20-odd pieces of jewelry attached wherever there is room for them. In her hand is a noisemaker that squeaks uncheerfully, and over everything a yellow slicker raincoat and rubber boots."*

Beverly is Brian's ex-wife (Brian prefers the phrase "former wife"). She had entered with noisemaker in full cry, hoping to surprise Brian, and she has certainly surprised Mark. Beverly looks around commenting, "All the comforts of home. Amazing what you can do with a coffin, if you put your mind to it." She then introduces herself, but introductions are unneccessary; she and Mark recognize each other's identity at once.

Beverly takes a swig from a half-empty bottle of whiskey from her tote bag, to the disapproval of Mark, who doesn't drink. Beverly insists on knowing about Brian's physical condition. Mark explains that Brian is officially terminal and thus removed from the hospital to this cottage. The pain is tolerable, but Brian has fainting spells: "They're harmless. Well, that's what they tell me. But it's embarrassing for him because he falls down a lot and his face gets a little purple for a minute." So far there hasn't been any problem about what others might think of this because Mark has been the only one present with Brian during this illness. He urges Beverly to be careful.

BEVERLY: About what?
MARK: That's exactly what I mean. You're ... I'm sorry, but you're very stoned, aren't you? And you're dressed in funny clothes, and you're saying a lot of funny things but I'm just not sure, frankly, what the fuck you're doing here.
BEVERLY (*flip*): Neither am I. You sure you wouldn't like a drink?
MARK: Positive. Look, please, don't you think it'd be better if you came back some other time, like tomorrow or next year or something?
BEVERLY: I'd just have to get drunk all over again.
MARK: I mean, it's sort of a delicate situation, right now. He's had a very bad time of it and any kind of, well, disturbance ...
BEVERLY: Such as me? Oh, you'll get used to it. You just have to think of me as your average tramp.
MARK: ... any disturbance might be dangerous, especially psychologically and ... shit! I sound like an idiot, the way I'm talking. But you don't seem to be understanding a goddamn word I'm saying!
BEVERLY: No. I am. I am. You know, you don't *look* like a faggot.
MARK: Oh, for Christ's sake!
BEVERLY: No, I mean it ... I mean, I didn't expect ...

MARK: Well, you'll get used to it. You just have to think of me as your average cocksucker. All right?

BEVERLY: Good. Now we're getting someplace. Are you sure you wouldn't like a drink?

MARK: No! I would not like a drink. *You* have a drink. Have two. Take off your clothes. Make yourself at home.

He grabs his jacket and heads for the door.

When you're ready to throw up, the bathroom is in there.

He exits.

The lights come up on the porch area. Steve comes out to join his mother and father, as Agnes (young middle-aged, longsuffering) wheels her mother Felicity (old, infirm, confined to her wheel chair) into sight and in the direction of the kitchen area.

Steve goes back in to get his guitar, while Joe reassures Maggie that they have plenty of time to look around and enjoy the swimming pool and other facilities. Joe wants to carry Maggie's luggage inside — exercise makes him feel good — but Maggie insists that Steve do it. While Steve's taking the things inside, Joe tries to cheer Maggie up by talking about the farm they never bought. Joe thinks he would have liked the life of a farmer, but Maggie knows that her part of it would have been all drudgery and is glad they never did it.

Joe and Steve, who has finished taking in the luggage, try to jolly Maggie into coming inside the cottage. She still resists, becoming panicky and slapping Steve when he tries to pull her by the hand. Steve, astonished, takes his guitar inside to practise.

Joe looks at Maggie, not knowing what came over her.

JOE: Maggie?

MAGGIE: I didn't tell him.

JOE: What?

MAGGIE (*still turned away from him*): I didn't tell him. Stephen. I didn't . . .

JOE: Oh. no. No, Maggie. What's the matter with you?

MAGGIE: I couldn't.

JOE: He doesn't know?

Maggie shakes her head "no."

What does he think? He thinks I'm going home with you? Maggie? Why didn't you tell him?

MAGGIE: I couldn't.

JOE: Why not?

MAGGIE: Because . . . it isn't true. It isn't true. It isn't . . .

She runs off away from the cottage. Joe is stunned. He sits down on the porch steps and puts his head in his hands.

Lights come up on the Interview Area where Felicity in her chair is singing to herself, ignoring the Interviewer's questions. Agnes leaves her there and returns to the kitchen area. The Interviewer makes no effort to force Felicity to answer.

Finally she comments, "It's a piss poor way to treat people" and proceeds to some plain speaking.

FELICITY: . . . . . You want to talk? Let's talk. "I feel fine." Is that what you want to hear? Of course it is. I feel fine, there's no pain, I'm as blind as I was yesterday, my bowels are working — and that's all I got to say about it.

INTERVIEWER: We're only trying to help.

FELICITY: Well I appreciate your concern but I don't need any more help from you. Do I?

INTERVIEWER: Well, we don't know.

FELICITY: Of course you know. I've just told you. I've just said it, haven't I?

INTERVIEWER: Yes.

FELICITY: Well, then . . . there you are. There's nothing more to say. You should learn to listen.

Felicity resents the Interviewer's smooth solicitousness. She doesn't look fine, she looks terrible, she knows, and what's more she smells. She is dying, and the Interviewer's offered help no longer seems of any use to her. Her view of the matter is, "Patient, hell! I'm the corpse. I have one lung, one plastic bag for a stomach, and two springs and a battery where my heart used to be. You cut me up and took everything that wasn't nailed down. Sons of bitches."

Felicity speaks of her absent daughter Claire who once helped her run things. Claire has been away for a long time but writes a letter nearly every day to her mother.

Finally Felicity calls for Agnes, her oldest daughter who is now accompanying her. Agnes is inside, writing. She is *a very plain looking middle-aged woman — very neat, very tense, very tired. Hair drawn back tightly. She has tried all her life to do the right thing, and the attempt has left her very confused, awkward and unsure of herself."*

When Agnes hears her mother call she folds the piece of paper into an envelope, puts it in her pocket and goes to the Interview Area, where Felicity is telling the Interviewer that her daughter Claire has twins. Felicity demands to be wheeled back to the cottage. Agnes meekly obliges.

In the living area, Brian enters and is delighted to see Beverly. She confesses that she has met Mark, probably offended him but rather likes him. Brian doesn't want to discuss his relationship with Mark, but Beverly insists that she has a right to know.

BRIAN (*singing*): "He is my sunshine, my only sunshine" . . . He's the — pardon the expression — cream in my coffee — the milk in my tea — "He will always be my necessity" . . .

BEVERLY: Ah, but is he enough?

BRIAN: More than enough.

BEVERLY: Shucks.

BRIAN (*laughs*): Sorry, but it's out of my hands. All of it. Some supreme logic has taken hold of my life. And in the absence of any refutable tomorrow, every insane thing I do today seems to make a great deal of sense.

BEVERLY: What the hell does that mean?

BRIAN: It means that there are more important things in this world.

BEVERLY: More important than what?

BRIAN: More important than worrying about who is fucking whom.

BEVERLY: You *are* happy, aren't you?

BRIAN: Ecstatic. I'm even writing again.

BEVERLY: Oh, my God. You couldn't be *that* happy!

BRIAN: Why not?

BEVERLY: Brian, you're a terrible writer, and you know it.

BRIAN: So?

BEVERLY: Outside of that wonderful book of crossword puzzles, your greatest contribution to the literary world was your retirement.

Brian has heard this from Beverly before, nevertheless he is writing voluminously: two novels, short stories, even a poem about the Firth of Forth Bridge. In addition he has taken up painting, learned to drive a car and wound up all his financial affairs including returning all his credit cards. He has decided to leave nothing undone: he has written letters to everyone telling them exactly what he thinks of them and he sleeps only three hours a day so as to experience every dawn and sunset to its fullest. He wants to use every bit of himself up before he goes, so that death will then be easy.

Brian and Beverly laugh and hold hands for a moment; then they both stop laughing.

BRIAN: It shows. Doesn't it?

BEVERLY: You're shaking.

BRIAN: I can't help it. I'm scared to death.

BEVERLY: It's a lot to deal with.

BRIAN: No. Not really. It's a little thing. I mean, all this . . . this is easy. Pain, discomfort . . . that's all part of living. And I'm just as alive now as I ever was. And I *will* be alive right up to the last moment. *That's* the hard part, that last fraction of a second — when you know that the next fraction of a second — I can't seem to fit that moment into my life . . . You're absolutely alone facing an absolute unknown and there is absolutely nothing you can do about it . . . except give in.

> *Pause.*

BEVERLY: That's how I felt the first time I lost my virginity.

BRIAN (*smiles*): How was it the second time?

BEVERLY: Much easier.

BRIAN: There. You see? The real trouble with dying is you only get to do it once.

> *Brian drifts into the thought.*

BEVERLY (*pulling him back*): I brought you some champagne.

BRIAN: I'm sorry. I must be the most tedious person alive.

BEVERLY: As a matter of fact, you are. Thank God you won't be around much longer.

BRIAN (*looking at the champagne*): I hope you don't think I'm going to pass away drunk. I intend to be cold sober.

BEVERLY: No. No. I thought we could break it on your ass and shove you off with a great bon voyage, confetti and streamers all over the grave.

BRIAN (*laughing*): Perfect. Perfect. I've missed your foolishness.

BEVERLY: You hated my foolishness.

BRIAN: I never understood it.

BEVERLY: Neither did I. But it was the only way. The only way I knew.

BRIAN: Well, all these roads, they all go to Rome, as they say.

BEVERLY: Yes. But why is it I always seem to end up in Naples?

Brian and Beverly embrace.

In the kitchen area, Agnes is singing a verse of a hymn quietly. Felicity demands instead a cheerful song like "Roll Me Over, in the Clover," and she sings the ribald verses herself as Agnes wheels her to the table and sets up a game of checkers. Finally the singing aggravates Agnes so much that she shouts at her mother to stop it, setting Felicity back into a refuge of memory, imagining she is giving Claire orders about destroying sick cattle.

Brian and Joe appear on their separate porches, as Felicity complains of pain and asks for tea with a palliative, after which she will read the latest letter from Claire.

In the other areas, Steve plays "Goodnight, Irene" on his guitar while Mark crosses to the Interview Area, telling himself he doesn't want to talk about the situation. Maggie is telling Joe about some of her father's idiosyncracies now that he is getting old. Felicity wants to know more about her daughter Claire's whereabouts.

AGNES: . . . . . They should be passing right through the center of Mexico today.

FELICITY: They're moving awfully slow, don't you think?

AGNES: Well, it's difficult for them, I imagine. Trying to get so much organized, a family, a whole family and everything else . . . You can't just drop everything and leave. Especially if you live in a foreign country, as they do.

BRIAN: I asked one of the doctors. I said, why do I shake like this? He said he didn't know . . . I said, well . . . is it a symptom or is it because of the drugs? He said, no. And I said, well, why then? I don't seem to have any control of it. I'm feeling perfectly all right and then I shake. And he said, try to think if it's ever happened before . . . that kind of thing. And I couldn't. For a long time. And then I remembered being very young . . . I was — oh — five years old. My father was taking me to Coney Island. And we got separated on the train. And I kept trying to ask for directions but I couldn't talk because I was shaking so badly. It was because I was frightened. That's . . . uh . . . That's why I shake now . . . Isn't it?

FELICITY (*in great pain*): Agnes . . . ! ! ! Agnes.

AGNES: Yes, mama, here. It's all right.

FELICITY: Agnes! Sons of bitches . . .

JOE: I get dreams now. Every night. I get dreams so big. I never used to dream. But now, every night, so big. Every person I ever knew in my life coming through my room, talking and talking and sometimes singing and dancing. Jumping all around my bed. And I get up to go with them, but I can't. The sheets are too heavy and I can't move to save my life. And they keep talking and calling my name, whispering so loud it hurts my ears . . . "Joe" and "Joe" and laughing and singing and I know every one of them and they pull at my arms and my legs and I still can't move. And I'm laughing and singing, too, inside, where you can't hear it. And it hurts so bad, but I can't feel it. And I yell back at them, every person I ever knew, and they don't hear me, either, and then the room gets brighter and brighter. So bright I can't see anything any more. Nobody. Not even me. It's all gone. All white. All gone.

FELICITY: Agnes . . . ! !

AGNES: Yes, mama.

FELICITY: When did they say they were coming?

AGNES: I don't know, mama. Soon. Soon.

FELICITY: As long as we know . . . As long as we know they're coming.

AGNES: Well, of course they're coming. You wait and see . . . One afternoon, we'll be sitting here, having tea, and that door will fly open like the gates of heaven and there they'll be . . .

> *She takes a capsule from a small bottle and adds the medication to the cup of tea.*

. . . two twin angels and our bright-eyed little girl. You wait and see, mama. You wait . . .

> *She takes the cup to Felicity and then notices that she is asleep.*

Mama? Oh, mama.

BRIAN (*going to Beverly*): Dance with me, Bev.

BEVERLY: My pleasure, sir.

MAGGIE: Joe?

JOE: We got to tell him, Maggie. We got to tell him.

AGNES: Rest, mama . . . rest . . .

MARK: It'll all be over in a minute. It just seems to take forever.

> *The lights fade out. Curtain.*

ACT II

That evening, Maggie is seated in the porch area watching the sun set. Joe, unable to persuade her to come inside yet, goes to get her a sweater.

In the living room area, Beverly is dancing by herself to record music — *"Beverly is carrying on and Brian is enjoying every minute of it. Mark is not."* Mark brings Brian a glass of milk and gives Beverly a drink. Beverly starts taking off her jewels and other adornments one by one, remembering how each was acquired.

BEVERLY (*takes off a bracelet*): This one's copper. A doctor in Colorado Springs. Said it would cure my arthritis and he'd take care of the rest. He didn't.

> *She drops the bracelet on the floor.*

BRIAN (*toasting*): Colorado Springs!

BEVERLY (*drinks*): Anyway, I didn't have arthritis. (*She points to a brooch.*) This one, God knows. A family heirloom and would I join the collection. No, thank you.

  Takes off a chain necklace with a tooth on it and swings it in a circle.

Claus. Norwegian shark tooth or something. A thousand and one positions, and each one lasted several hours. I couldn't.

  She drops it.

BRIAN: I should hope not.

BEVERLY: But I tried.

  Takes another, very similar to the previous one, but smaller.

Claus's brother. If at first you don't succeed . . . (*Points at a bracelet.*) A Russian in Paris. (*Another bracelet.*) A Frenchman in Moscow.

  Taking off an ankle bracelet.

Ah . . . a Tunisian in Newfoundland. Really. We met at an airport and made it between flights under his grass skirt.

  Drops it on the couch and then takes off two tiaras.

Two lovely ladies in Biarritz. No comment, thank you.

  Drops them on the sofa.

Oh . . . yes. The Jean Jacques collection.

  Taking off several other pieces.

Jean Jacques. Jean Jacques. Jean Jacques. Jean Jacques. Jean Jacques. You might say I took him for everything he was worth. You'd be wrong. There was a whole lot more I couldn't get my hands on. (*Toasting.*) A big one for Jean Jacques.

BRIAN (*toasting*): Jean Jacques!

BEVERLY (*a little dizzy*): I'm getting sloppy. I tried. Dear Brian, how I tried. (*To Mark.*) You're the scholar. What's the exact declension of incompatibility? I tried, they tried, we tried . . .

MARK: That's not a declension. That's a conjugation.

BEVERLY: No, it wasn't. Not once. Not a single conjugator in the bunch. Not one real dancer. Not one real jump to the music, flat out, no count, foot-stomping crazy man . . . just a lot of tired "declining" people who really didn't want to do anything but sit the next one out . . . . .

Last but not least, Beverly is wearing her favorite dress, battered and stained with experience. Mark can't resist making a hostile comment and, immediately regretting it, decides to go for a walk and leave the two alone. Beverly insists he stay because they should get to know each other. She tries again to ply him with champagne, but in opening the bottle she spills some of the wine on Mark's jacket. Beverly in her turn is immediately apologetic, but Brian intervenes, grabbing the jacket and throwing it down, telling them, "My God, it's only a jacket. Two sleeves, a collar, a piece of cloth. It was probably made by a machine in East Podunk. Why are we wasting this time?"

Brian mentions some of the important things that may be happening in the world and even the universe — such as the sun suddenly changing its course and moving out of control — in comparison to the matter of this jacket, which Brian unfeelingly hands back to a tight-lipped Mark. Brian takes Beverly in his arms, and they go into a Lindy Hop — but Brian soon falters and falls. He manages to get right back on his feet and goes to the bedroom to recover from what is obviously a symptom of his disease. Beverly follows him, while Mark turns off the music, sits, and starts drinking champagne from the bottle.

The lights center on Agnes in the Interview Area. To Agnes's surprise, the Interviewer is concerned not with the medication and care of Felicity but with Agnes's own well-being. Agnes has been having headaches but thinks perhaps they've stopped now.

Asked about her sister Claire, Agnes tells the Interviewer how close-knit her family was after her father died, working their dairy farm hard but happily. Claire and her mother were a lot alike, though they would have loud, violent quarrels which they would then reconcile lovingly: "Claire was so beautiful, and I would hide in my room. I got so frightened when they fought."

Then one day Claire left them in company with a boy. They heard nothing from her for almost a year.

AGNES: . . . . . And then one morning, finally, we received a letter from a man in Louisiana. There was an accident . . . something. And Claire was dead. They said at first they thought she was going to be all right, but she was hemorrhaging and . . . This is very hard to remember.

INTERVIEWER: But these letters from Claire.

AGNES: Yes. You see, it was after Claire died that Mama started to get sick. All of a sudden, she was "old." And she isn't, you know. But she just seemed to give up. I couldn't bring her out of it. Claire could have. But I couldn't. We lost the farm, the house, everything. One thing led to another. The letters . . . uh . . . It was after one of the last operations. Mamma came home from the hospital and she seemed very happy. She was much stronger than ever. She laughed and joked and made fun of me, just like she used to . . . and then she told me she had written a letter while she was in the hospital . . . to Claire . . . and she said she was very nice to her and she forgave her for not writing and keeping in touch and she asked her to come home to visit and to bring her children . . . Claire had been dead for a long time then. I didn't know what to do. I tried to tell her . . . I tried . . . but she wouldn't listen . . . And, of course, no letter came. No reply. And Mama asked every day for the mail. Every day I had to tell her no, there wasn't any. Every day. I kept hoping she would forget, but she didn't. And when there wasn't any letter for a long time, she started to get worse. She wouldn't talk and when she did she accused me of being jealous and hiding the letters and sometimes . . . I didn't know what to do . . . so . . .

> *Pause.*

INTERVIEWER: How long have you been writing these letters?

AGNES: Almost two years.

Felicity needs Claire's letters to keep her going, Agnes believes, and she expects Felicity will die before it becomes too obvious that Claire is never coming home. Again, Agnes is surprised that the Interviewer wants to know what sort of strain this elaborate charade may be placing on *her*. Agnes avoids an answer, instead mentioning Felicity's condition: the pain is getting worse, the medicine doesn't seem to help. The Interviewer knows this: "We hoped it wouldn't go on this long, but there's nothing we can do about it."

The Interviewer suggests that Felicity may be willing herself to stay alive, waiting for Claire. Agnes immediately grasps the implications of this and is deeply troubled. She escapes to the kitchen area, where Felicity is calling for her.

The focus shifts to the porch area, where Joe has returned with Maggie's sweater and put it around her shoulders. Maggie is still living in the past, remembering their youth in New York. She was in her school production of *The Red Mill*. Joe never touched Maggie until they were married. They used to go on motor trips after Steve was born. They could have no more children, though they both would have wanted them.

In the kitchen, Agnes looks at her sleeping mother and wonders whether she'd believe the truth if she heard it. Maggie and Joe keep talking about the little house in the country Joe built himself, while Agnes confesses (with Felicity still sleeping) that she can no longer remember the good times they all once had.

In the living area, Mark is still swigging as Beverly comes in to report that Brian is resting. Beverly starts to collect her things. Joe and Maggie remember that no sooner did they get the house built than the area suddenly was so built-up they had to put up a fence.

Mark informs Beverly that "this dying business . . . . . gets a little messy now and then," however great an effort Brian makes to keep things in order.

MARK: It's all words for Brian. And it's a little hard to keep up. One letter follows the next, one paragraph, one chapter, one book after another, close parenthesis, end of quote. Never mind what it's all about.

BEVERLY: That's not fair.

MARK: Isn't it? The way you two have been carrying on, I was beginning to think I was at a wedding. I mean, I enjoy a good joke as much as the next fellow, but dead people are pretty low on my list of funny topics.

BEVERLY: Let's not get angry, we'll spoil your metaphor.

MARK: Fuck my metaphor! It's true!
    Pause.
(*Quietly.*) My God, listen to me. You think you know something. You think you *have* something . . .
    In the porch area.

JOE: More houses, more streets.

MARK: And it all goes crazy.

JOE: So many goddamn things. Where do they go? The freezer, the washer and the dryer, a dishwasher for Christ's sake, the lawn mower, the barbecue, three bicycles, four, six lawn chairs and a chaise lounge — aluminum, last forever — the white table with the umbrella, the hammock, the bar, I put that wood paneling in the basement, we finished the attic — well, half of it, I got the insulation in — the patio, with screens . . . Jesus it was a lot to let go of.

MAGGIE: I don't want to talk about it.

JOE: Before you know it, everything you *had* is gone. Not that it was ever yours but you feel it anyway when it's gone.

MAGGIE: I'm telling you, I don't want to talk about it.

JOE (*turns from her*): All right! All right! We won't talk about it.

MAGGIE: You get tired. You get old. My hands got too big. I got too fat. I don't know how it happens, I can't remember.

In the living room, Mark is telling Beverly how he met Brian one night outside a San Francisco bar the summer after the flower-child movement: "Like everybody else, I was very hungry, very desperate . . . the whole scene. So there I was one night, like many other nights, selling it down on Market Street, I wasn't very good at it, but it was paying the rent, and Brian walks up to me . . . I didn't know him of course . . . he walks up and asks me the *time*. Right? Well, I did my little number about time for what and how much was it worth to him . . . I figured anybody who'd come on to me with an old line like that was good for a fast twenty. And all of a sudden, he starts explaining exactly what time *was* worth to him . . . Philosophy! On Market Street. And before I know it, he's into concepts of history, cyclical and lineal configurations, Hebraic and Greco-Roman attitudes, repetitive notions . . . time *warps,* even! Jesus, I thought, I've got a real freak on my hands!"

Brian was so absorbed in expressing himself and his ideas, he didn't even notice the degraded atmosphere of a bar Mark led him to. Brian bought Mark dinner and Mark lifted Brian's wallet but brought it back the next day because he was really interested in what Brian was saying and doing. Brian put a room at Mark's disposal and Mark began to take an interest in reading again, and talking, talking, probing for some kind of salvation. But in the face of death, words were not enough: "Brian looks at me and I can see it in his eyes. One stone slab smack in the face, the rug is coming out from under, the light is going *out.* You can do the pills and the syringes and the 'let's play games' with the cotton swabs and x-rays, but it's not going to change it. You can wipe up the mucous and the blood and the piss and the excrement, you can burn the sheets and boil his clothes, but it's still there. You can smell it on him. You can smell it on me. It soaks into your hands when you touch him. It gets into your blood. It's stuck inside him, filling up inside his head, inside his skin, inside his mouth . . . . . "

Mark doesn't find it easy staying here and watching Brian's death take place, cleaning up after him. But Beverly would gladly change places with him and accuses him of selfishness, going on: "Let me tell you something, as one whore to another — what you do with your ass is your business. You can drag it through every gutter from here to Morocco. You can trade it, sell it, or give it away. You can run it up a flagpole, paint it blue or cut it off if you feel like it. I don't care. I'll even show you the best way to do it. That's the kind of person I am. But Brian is different. Because Brian is stupid. Because Brian is blind. Because Brian doesn't know where you come from or who you come from or why or how or even what you are coming to. Because Brian happens to need you."

Beverly can't remember any longer exactly why she walked out on the one human being who loved and cared about her. That would be enough to keep her here now, and if it isn't enough for Mark, she declares, he should leave. But

Mark can't bring himself to go, much as he detests some of his duties — he feels an obligation to Brian. Beverly suggests that Mark is staying with Brian because of money, and Mark hits her in the face. Beverly slaps him back hard, several times, stunning him and then putting her arms around him as the truth breaks from him: "I don't want him to die. I don't . . . Please . . . "

Beverly's words of comfort are echoed in the other areas, as Maggie comforts Joe and Agnes comforts Felicity. Beverly sees that Mark has caught "a bad case of the hopes" and advises him: "Please, baby. Just one favor you owe him. Don't hurt him. Don't hurt him with your hope."

Beverly has collected all her things and has decided to leave without saying goodbye to Brian. She exits with a comment to Mark: "It's funny, he always makes the same mistake. He always cares about the wrong people."

Felicity is calling for Claire, and Agnes is wondering aloud how it all came down to this. Joe and Maggie are talking about the farm they could never afford and the little house they could. The house was important to Joe, it was something he could leave his grandchildren. His jobs meant little or nothing to him: "Twenty-four years. Two weeks a year at the beach. One week off for Christmas . . . . . Somebody walks up one day, one day, somebody walks up and tells you it's finished. And me . . . all I can say is 'what?' . . . *what's* finished? What did I have that's finished? What?"

They had their life together, Maggie remembers, and now she has nothing. She pleads: "I want you to come home. I want you to stay out four nights a week bowling, and then come home so I can yell and not talk to you, you son of a bitch. I want to fight so you'll take me to a movie and by the time I get you to take me I'm so upset I can't enjoy the picture. I want to make too much noise in the bathroom becuase you go to bed too early and I don't care if you *are* asleep because I want somebody, somebody to hug me once before I go to bed. I want to get up too early, too goddamn early, and I'll let you know about it, too, because I have to make you breakfast, because you never, never once eat it, because you make me get up too early just to keep you company and talk to you, and it's cold, and my back aches, and I got nothing to say to you and we never talk and it's six-thirty in the morning, *every* morning, even Sunday morning and it's all right . . . it's all right . . . it's all right because I *want* to be there because you need me to be there because I want *you* to be there because I want you to come home."

Joe, stricken, tries to make Maggie understand the impossibility of his coming home. He's feeling a little worse every day, and none of Maggie's promises and blandishments can change that. Joe challenges Maggie: if she wants magic, then let her make it happen. Of course she has no magic that will help.

Steve comes out and tells his father he's ready to play for him. Steve goes back into the cottage and soon a guitar solo of "Goodnight, Irene" can be heard.

JOE: I'm going inside now, Maggie. I'm going to tell him.
MAGGIE: Tell me first.
JOE: What?
MAGGIE: Tell me. Say it out loud.
JOE: I'm going to die, Maggie.

MAGGIE (*after a moment*): Why?

JOE: I don't know. I don't know. I don't know. Like everything else, I don't know. Come inside.

MAGGIE: What'll we do in there?

JOE: Try. That's all. Just try. Live with it. Look at it. Don't make me do it alone.

MAGGIE: I can't promise . . .

JOE: Don't promise. Just come inside.

> *Maggie doesn't move for a long time. Steve continues to play the guitar softly. Finally Maggie turns and walks slowly toward the cottage. Joe joins her and together they walk inside.*

In the living room area, Mark approaches the bookcase as though to get a drink of scotch, but instead he hurls the tray of medicines to the floor. The noise brings Brian in. Mark confesses that he is drunk, and Brian confesses that he's just had an accident too, wetting the bed in his sleep. He is disgusted with himself. Mark embraces Brian comfortingly and helps him into the bedroom.

In the kitchen area, Felicity asks what time it is and then wants to know if the mail has been delivered. Agnes, loathing every word of her lie, tells her mother yes, another letter from Claire. Felicity repeats "I get so lonesome for Claire" over and over until Agnes cries for her to stop. Felicity asks for tea, which Agnes supplies. Finally Agnes takes the letter she was writing earlier from her pocket and begins to read aloud to Felicity: Claire is having an adventure in Mexico and is stranded in a picturesque little mountain village.

> *Agnes watches Felicity, making up the words to the letter.*

AGNES: . . . and I can hear the wind blowing . . . outside the door, whistling and . . . and whispering . . . and when I look out the window, nothing is there . . . nothing . . . mama . . . I think . . . I think it's because I miss you . . . because it hurts not being close to you . . . and . . . and touching you . . .

> *Agnes breaks down and can't go any further.*

FELICITY: Agnes?

AGNES: Yes, mama. Yes.

FELICITY: What time is it now?

AGNES: Oh, four . . . five . . . I don't know.

FELICITY (*still holding her cup*): Could I have some tea, Agnes?

> *Agnes just looks at her.*

Could you read me the letter now?

AGNES: Mama . . .

FELICITY: Could you read me the letter now?

AGNES: Mama . . .

FELICITY: The letter from Claire?

> *Pause.*

AGNES: Yes. Yes.

As Agnes reads the letter again, Joe and Brian can be seen facing the audience and speaking as though to the Interviewer, each in his own isolation, thinking long thoughts of death — Brian: "People don't want to let go. Do they. They think it's a mistake. They think it's supposed to last forever." Joe: "You don't expect it to happen." The others appear and join in like the instruments of an orchestra playing a dead march — Mark: "You keep thinking there must be some way out of this." Beverly: "You want it to make a difference." Maggie: "You want to blame somebody." Brian: "You want to be angry." Each of the instruments has its part to play, its section of the work to inform.

MARK: Someone should have said it a long time ago.
BEVERLY: When you were young.
BRIAN: Someone should have said, this living . . .
MARK: . . . this life . . .
BEVERLY: . . . this lifetime . . .
BRIAN: It doesn't last forever.
MAGGIE: A few days, a few minutes . . . that's all.
BRIAN: It has an end.
JOE: Yes.
MARK: This face.
BEVERLY: These hands.
MARK: This word.
JOE: It doesn't last forever.
BRIAN: This air.
MARK: This light.
BRIAN: This earth.
BEVERLY: These things you love.
MAGGIE: These children.
BEVERLY: This smile.
MAGGIE: This pain.
BRIAN: It doesn't last forever.
JOE: It was never supposed to last forever.
MARK: This day.
MAGGIE: This morning.
BEVERLY: This afternoon.
MARK: This evening.
FELICITY: What time is it, Agnes?
AGNES: I don't know, mama. It's time to stop. Please, mama. It's time to stop.
BRIAN: These eyes . . .
MARK: These things you see.
MAGGIE: It's pretty.
JOE: Yes.
MARK: Yes.
BRIAN: These things you hear.
MARK: This noise.
BEVERLY: This music.
STEVE: I can play for you now. It's not good, but it's not bad either.
MAGGIE: Yes.

BEVERLY: Yes.

BRIAN: They tell you you're dying, and you say all right. But if I *am* dying . . .
I must still be alive.

FELICITY: What time is it?

MARK: These things you have.

MAGGIE: Yes.

JOE: This smell, this touch.

MARK: Yes.

BEVERLY: This taste.

BRIAN: Yes.

MAGGIE: This breath.

STEVE: Yes.

MARK: Yes.

BRIAN: Yes.

MAGGIE: Yes.

BEVERLY: Yes.

JOE: Yes.

BRIAN: This moment.

> *Long pause. Lights fade. Curtain.*

A GRAPHIC GLANCE

RALPH RICHARDSON AND JOHN GIELGUD IN "NO MAN'S LAND"

(OPPOSITE) EDWARD VILLELLA AND ELEANOR PARKER IN THE REVIVAL OF
"PAL JOEY" (MR. VILLELLA WAS REPLACED BY CHRISTOPHER CHADMAN AND
MISS PARKER BY JOAN COPELAND BEFORE THE SHOW'S OPENING)

PLAYWRIGHTS AT WORK (LOWER LEFT AND CLOCKWISE): EDWARD ALBEE,
JACK GELBER, JACK RICHARDSON, ARTHUR KOPIT

JAMES RANDOLPH, ERNESTINE JACKSON, EMETT "BABE" WALLACE, NORMA DONALDSON, ROBERT GUILLAUME, KEN PAGE AND CHRISTOPHE PIERRE IN THE REVIVAL OF "GUYS AND DOLLS"

NOMINATIONS FOR TONY AWARDS FOR 1977. PLAYS (LOWER LEFT AND CLO
"THE SHADOW BOX," DOLPH SWEET AND KENNETH MACMILLAN IN "STREAME
MUSICALS: LENNY BAKER IN "I LOVE MY WIFE," ANDREA MC ARDLE IN "ANN
"HAPPY END"

ISE): TOM COURTENAY IN "OTHERWISE ENGAGED," LAURENCE LUCKINBILL IN
RAZANA BEVERLEY IN "FOR COLORED GIRLS WHO HAVE CONSIDERED SUICIDE..."
ILLICENT MARTIN IN "SIDE BY SIDE BY SONDHEIM" AND MERYL STREEP IN

BARBARA BAXLEY IN "BEST FRIEND," CLAIRE BLOOM IN THE REVIVAL OF
"THE INNOCENTS" AND MARIA SCHELL IN "POOR MURDERER"

REX HARRISON AND ELIZABETH ASHLEY IN THE REVIVAL OF SHAW'S
"CAESAR AND CLEOPATRA"

(ABOVE) DONNIE RAY ALBERT AND CLAMMA DALE IN THE REVIVAL OF "PORGY AND BESS;" MILDRED DUNNOCK IN "DAYS IN THE TREES;" BILLY DEE WILLIAMS IN "I HAVE A DREAM;" BRAD BLAISDELL AND KIMBERLY FARR IN THE REVIVAL OF "GOING UP"

(BELOW) REPRESENTING BROADWAY: RICHARD RODGERS, LEONARD BERNSTEIN, STEPHEN SONDHEIM, TOM STOPPARD, ISAAC B. SINGER, TENNESSEE WILLIAMS. REPRESENTING OFF BROADWAY: DENNIS J. REARDON, THOMAS BABE, MICHAEL WELLER, MIGUEL PINERO, JOHN FORD NOONAN AND JOSEPH PAPP (RIGHT FRONT CENTER)

ZOE CALDWELL AND CHRISTOPHER PLUMMER IN "LOVE AND MASTER WILL"

RUTH GORDON

TRAZANA BEVERLEY, PAULA MOSS, JANET LEAGUE, AKU KADOGO, RISË COLLINS, LAURIE CARLOS AND NTOZAKE SHANGÉ IN "FOR COLORED GIRLS WHO HAVE CONSIDERED SUICIDE/WHEN THE RAINBOW IS ENUF"

(OPPOSITE) IRENE WORTH IN THE REVIVAL OF "THE CHERRY ORCHARD"

ROBERT DONLEY, LIV ULLMANN AND JOHN LITHGOW IN THE REVIVAL OF O'NEILL'S "ANNA CHRISTIE"

PAUL SORVINO AND PATTI LU PONE IN "THE BAKER'S WIFE," WHICH CLOSED
OUT OF TOWN

SYLVIA SIDNEY IN "VIEUX CARRÉ"

ROSEMARY MURPHY, ESTELLE PARSONS, AND EILEEN HECKART IN
"LADIES AT THE ALAMO"

MARY MC CARTY IN THE REVIVAL OF O'NEILL'S "ANNA CHRISTIE"

BARBARA ERWIN, ROBERT FITCH, DOROTHY LOUDON, ANDREA MC ARDLE (

ANDREA McARDLE (WITH DOG "SANDY"), REID SHELTON AND RAYMOND THORNE IN "ANNIE"

SHEPPERD STRUDWICK, NAN MARTIN, BETSY PALMER AND DAVID SELBY IN
"THE ECCENTRICITIES OF A NIGHTINGALE"

DIANE LADD IN "LU ANN HAMPTON LAVERTY OBERLANDER"

PAMELA PAYTON-WRIGHT AND PAUL RUDD IN "ROMEO AND JULIET"

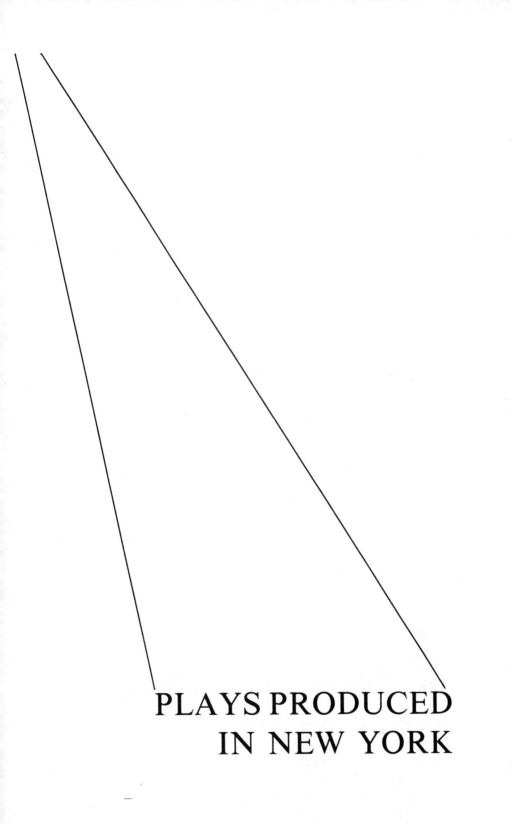

PLAYS PRODUCED
IN NEW YORK

PLAYS PRODUCED ON BROADWAY

Figures in parentheses following a play's title give number of performances. These figures are acquired directly from the production offices and do not include previews or extra non-profit performances.

Plays marked with an asterisk (*) were still running on June 1, 1977. Their number of performances is figured through May 31, 1977 (many June closings aren't marked with an asterisk and are figured for the entire run).

In a listing of a show's numbers — dances, sketches, musical scenes. etc. — the titles of songs are identified by their appearance in quotation marks (").

HOLDOVERS FROM PREVIOUS SEASONS

Plays which were running on June 1, 1976 are listed below. More detailed information about them appears in previous *Best Plays* volumes of appropriate years. Important cast changes since opening night are recorded in the "Cast Replacements" section of this volume.

*Grease (2,181). Musical with book, music and lyrics by Jim Jacobs and Warren Casey. Opened February 14, 1972.

Pippin (1,944). Musical with book by Roger O. Hirson; music and lyrics by Stephen Schwartz. Opened October 23, 1972. (Closed June 12, 1977)

*The Magic Show (1,153). Musical with book by Bob Randall; music and lyrics by Stephen Schwartz; magic by Doug Henning. Opened May 28, 1974.

*Equus (1,068). By Peter Shaffer. Opened October 24, 1974. Closed temporarily 9/11/76 after 781 performances but reopened in the same production 10/6/76 and continued.

*The Wiz (972). Musical based on L. Frank Baum's *The Wonderful Wizard of Oz;* book by William F. Brown; music and lyrics by Charlie Smalls. Opened January 5, 1975.

*Shenandoah (970). Musical based on the original screen play by James Lee Barrett; book by James Lee Barrett, Peter Udell and Philip Rose; music by Gary Geld; lyrics by Peter Udell. Opened January 7, 1975.

*Same Time, Next Year (927). By Bernard Slade. Opened March 13, 1975.

*Chicago (793). Musical based on the play by Maurine Dallas Watkins; book by Fred Ebb and Bob Fosse; music by John Kander; lyrics by Fred Ebb. Opened June 3, 1975.

*A Chorus Line (743). Musical conceived by Michael Bennett; book by James Kirkwood and Nicholas Dante; music by Marvin Hamlisch; lyrics by Edward Kleban. Opened April 15, 1975 off Broadway where it played 101 performances through July 13, 1975; transferred to Broadway July 25, 1975.

Me and Bessie (453). Musical conceived and written by Will Holt and Linda Hopkins. Opened October 22, 1975. (Closed December 5, 1976)

The Norman Conquests (228). Repertory of three plays by Alan Ayckbourn: **Table Manners** (76), **Living Together** (76) and **Round and Round the Garden** (76). Opened December 7, 1975. (Closed June 19, 1976)

Very Good Eddie (304). Revival of the musical based on a farce by Philip Bartholomae; book by Guy Bolton; revised by Guy Bolton; music by Jerome Kern; lyrics by Schuyler Greene, Elsie Janis, P. G. Wodehouse, Anne Caldwell, Frank Craven, Harry Graham, Harry B. Smith, John E. Hazzard and Herbert Reynolds. Opened December 21, 1975. (Closed September 5, 1976)

The Royal Family (232). Revival of the play by George S. Kaufman and Edna Ferber. Opened December 30, 1975. (Closed July 18, 1976)

Pacific Overtures (193). Musical with book by John Weidman; music and lyrics by Stephen Sondheim; additional material by Hugh Wheeler. Opened January 11, 1976. (Closed June 27, 1976)

Knock Knock (192). By Jules Feiffer. Opened January 18, 1976 off Broadway where it played 40 performances through February 22, 1976; transferred February 24, 1976 to Broadway where it played 152 additional performances, the final 48 in a re-staged and re-cast version. (Closed July 3, 1976)

*Bubbling Brown Sugar (524). Musical revue based on a concept by Rosetta LeNoire; book by Loften Mitchell; original music by Danny Holgate, Emme Kemp and Lillian Lopez; other music by various authors. Opened March 2, 1976.

My Fair Lady (377). Revival of the musical adapted from George Bernard Shaw's *Pygmalion;* book and lyrics by Alan Jay Lerner; music by Frederick Loewe. Opened March 25, 1976. (Closed February 20, 1977)

Who's Afraid of Virginia Woolf? (141). Revival of the play by Edward Albee. Opened April 1, 1976. (Closed August 1, 1976 matinee)

Rex (49). Musical with book by Sherman Yellen; music by Richard Rodgers; lyrics by Sheldon Harnick. Opened April 25, 1976. (Closed June 5, 1976)

The Belle of Amherst (116). One-woman performance by Julie Harris in a play by William Luce; compiled by Timothy Helgeson. Opened April 28, 1976. (Closed August 8, 1976)

Threepenny Opera (307). Revival of the musical with book and lyrics by Bertolt Brecht; music by Kurt Weill; new translation by Ralph Manheim and John Willett. Opened May 1, 1976. (Closed January 23, 1977)

The Runner Stumbles (191). By Milan Stitt. Opened May 18, 1976. (Closed October 30, 1976)

Something's Afoot (61). Musical with book, music and lyrics by James McDonald, David Vos and Robert Gerlach; additional music by Ed Linderman. Opened May 27, 1976. (Closed July 18, 1976)

PLAYS PRODUCED JUNE 1, 1976 — MAY 31, 1977

*California Suite (406). Program of four playlets by Neil Simon: *Visitor From New York, Visitor From Philadelphia, Visitors From London* and *Visitors From Chicago.*

Produced by Emanuel Azenberg and Robert Fryer at the Eugene O'Neill Theater. Opened June 10, 1976.

VISITOR FROM NEW YORK		VISITORS FROM LONDON	
Hannah Warren	Tammy Grimes	Sidney Nichols	George Grizzard
William Warren	George Grizzard	Diana Nichols	Tammy Grimes

VISITOR FROM PHILADELPHIA		VISITORS FROM CHICAGO	
Marvin Michaels	Jack Weston	Mort Hollender	Jack Weston
Bunny	Leslie Easterbrook	Beth Hollender	Barbara Barrie
Millie Michaels	Barbara Barrie	Stu Franklyn	George Grizzard
		Gert Franklyn	Tammy Grimes

Standbys: Misses Barrie, Grimes — Joan Bassie; Mr. Grizzard — John Cunningham; Miss Easterbrook — Lani Sundsten; Mr. Weston — Michael Vale.

Directed by Gene Saks; scenery, William Ritman; costumes, Jane Greenwood; lighting, Tharon Musser; production stage manager, Philip Cusack; stage manager, Lani Sundsten; press, Bill Evans.

Place: Suite 203 and 204 in the Beverly Hills Hotel. Act I, Scene 1: *Visitor From New York,* about 1 p.m. on a sunny, warm day in late fall. Scene 2: *Visitor From Philadelphia,* 11 a.m., mid-December. Act II, Scene 1: *Visitors From London* (Scene 1, about 5 p.m., early April; Scene 2, about 3 a.m.). Scene 2: *Visitors From Chicago,* 4 p.m., Sunday, July 4.

Visitor From New York: An abrasive, literate divorced couple reopen their wounds in a quarrel over their daughter. *Visitor From Philadelphia:* A prostitute is too drunk the next morning to leave the suite before the man's wife arrives. *Visitors From London:* Companionate marriage of an actress and an antique dealer stands up under the pressures of Academy Award night. *Visitors From Chicago:* Two couples are beginning to get on each other's nerves during a shared vacation. Previously produced at Center Theater Group's Ahmanson Theater in Los Angeles.

Marge Redmond replaced Barbara Barrie 1/17/77. Kenneth Haigh replaced George Grizzard 2/28/77. Rue McClanahan replaced Tammy Grimes 4/4/77. Tammy Grimes replaced Rue McClanahan 4/11/77. David McCallum replaced Kenneth Haigh 5/2/77. Joseph Leon replaced Jack Weston 5/77.

A Best Play; see page 149.

An Evening With Diana Ross (24). Musical revue with special material by Bill Goldenberg and Bill Dyer; additional material by Bruce Vilanch. Produced by Danny O'Donovan at the Palace Theater. Opened June 14, 1976. (Closed July 3, 1976)

Diana Ross	The Jones Girls:
Mimes:	Shirley
Hayward Coleman	Brenda
Don McLeod	Valorie
Stewart Fischer	

Directed by Joe Layton; lighting, John Gleason; sound consultant, Trevor Jordan; stage manager, Michael Coyle; press, Solters & Roskin, Inc., Bud Westman, Joshua Ellis.

Revue shaped around Diana Ross in musical highlights of her career including Motown, the Supremes and film and concert appearances.

ACT I: Overture, "Here I Am," "I Wouldn't Change a Thing," "The Lady Is a Tramp," "Touch Me in the Morning," "One Love in My Lifetime," "Smile," "Love Hangover," "Girls," "The Point," "Lady Sings the Blues," " 'Tain't Nobody's Bizness," "Hawaii," "Stormy Weather," "Sugar in My Bow," "My Man."

ACT II: Motown History, Supremes, "Play Me the Music," "What I Did for Love," "T & A," Theme from *Mahogany,* "Ain't No Mountain High Enough," "Reach Out and Touch."

*Godspell (392). Musical based on the Gospel according to St. Matthew; conceived by John-Michael Tebelak; music and new lyrics by Stephen Schwartz. Produced by Edgar Lansbury, Stuart Duncan, Joseph Beruh and The Shubert Organization, Inc. at the Broadhurst Theater. Opened June 22, 1976; see note.

Lamar Alford	Bobby Lee
Laurie Faso	Tom Rolfing
Lois Foraker	Don Scardino
Robin Lamont	Marley Sims
Elizabeth Lathram	Valerie Williams

Alternates: Kerin Blair, Bob Garrett, Michael Hoit, Kitty Ray (all parts in *Godspell* are interchangeable).

Band: Paul Shaffer conductor and keyboard, Mark Zeray guitar, Chris Warwin bass, Michael Redding percussion.

Directed by John-Michael Tebelak; musical director, Steve Reinhardt; costumes, Susan Tsu; lighting, Spencer Mosse; sound, Robert Minor; associate producer, Charles Haid; production supervision, Nina Faso; stage manager, Michael J. Frank; press, Gifford/Wallace, Inc., Glenna Freedman.

NOTE: This production of *Godspell* was presented off Broadway from 5/17/71 through 6/13/76 for 2,124 performances, the third longest run in off-Broadway history before being transferred to Broadway.

The list of musical numbers in *Godspell* appears on page 349 of *The Best Plays of 1970-71.*

Circle in the Square. 1975-76 schedule of programs ended with **Pal Joey** (73). Revival of the musical with book by John O'Hara; music by Richard Rodgers; lyrics by Lorenz Hart. Produced by Circle in the Square, Theodore Mann artistic director, Paul Libin managing director, at Circle in the Square Theater. Opened June 27, 1976 matinee. (Closed August 29, 1976)

Mike	Harold Gary	Vera	Joan Copeland
Joey	Christopher Chadman	Gent	David Hodo
Kid	Terri Treas	Ernest	Austin Colyer
Gladys	Janie Sell	Waldo the Waiter	Denny Martin Flinn
Gail	Gail Benedict	Victor	Michael Leeds
Murphy	Murphy Cross	Delivery Boy	Kenn Scalice
Rosamond	Rosamond Lynn	Louis	Adam Petroski
Marilu	Marilu Henner	Melba	Dixie Carter
Debbie	Deborah Geffner	Ludlow Lowell	Joe Sirola
Linda	Boni Enten	O'Brien	Ralph Farnworth

Boys and Girls: Gail Benedict, Murphy Cross, Deborah Geffner, Marilu Henner, Rosamond Lynn, Terri Treas, Denny Martin Flinn, David Hodo, Michael Leeds, Kenn Scalice.

Understudies: Messrs. Sirola, Gary — Ralph Farnworth; Miss Sell — Marilu Henner; Miss Enten — Gail Benedict; Messrs. Farnworth, Petroski — Austin Colyer; Miss Carter — Rosamond Lynn; Swing Boy — Richard Dodd; Swing Girl — Lisa Brown.

Directed by Theodore Mann; choreography, Margo Sappington; musical direction, Scott Oakley; scenery, John J. Moore; costumes, Arthur Boccia; lighting Ron Wallace; principal orchestrator, Michael Gibson; additional dance arrangements, Scott Oakley; production stage manager, Randall Brooks; stage manager, James Bernardi; press, Merle Debuskey, Susan L. Schulman.

Time: The late 1930s. Place: Chicago.

Pal Joey was first produced on Broadway 12/25/40 for 374 performances. It was revived on Broadway 10/21/41 for 104 performances, 1/3/52 for its longest run of 540 performances, 5/31/61 for 31 performances and 5/29/63 for 15 performances.

The list of scenes and musical numbers in *Pal Joey* appears on pages 302-3 of *The Best Plays of 1951-52.*

Let My People Come (108). Musical revue with music and lyrics by Earl Wilson Jr. Produced by Phil Oesterman at the Morosco Theater. Opened July 7, 1976. (Closed October 2, 1976.)

Brandy Alexander	Dianne Legro
Dwight Baxter	Allan Lozito
Lorraine Davidson	Bryan Miller
Joelle Erasme	Bryen Neves
Yvette Freeman	Don Scotti
Paul Gillespie	Dean Tait
Tulane Howard II	Lori Wagner
Bob Jockers	Charles Whiteside
Empress Kilpatrick	

Directed by Phil Oesterman; choreography, Charles Augins; musical direction and vocal arrangements, Norman Bergen; music conducted by Glen Roven; scenery and lighting, Duane F. Mazey; scenery and costumes supervised by Douglas W. Schmidt; lighting supervised by John Gleason; production stage manager, Duane F. Mazey; stage manager, Robert Walter; press, Saul Richman.

Self-described as "A sexual musical," this show began performances off Broadway 1/8/74 but never invited critics to a formal opening (though it was reviewed occasionally during the course of its run of 1,327 performances). *Let My People Come* closed off Broadway 6/13/76 and transferred to Broadway where it played 108 additional performances, again without inviting critics to a formal opening.

The list of musical numbers in *Let My People Come* appears on page 390 of *The Best Plays of 1973-74.*

Shirley MacLaine (20). Return engagement of the one-woman revue performed by Shirley MacLaine; written by Fred Ebb; additional material by Bob Wells; music composed and arranged by Cy Coleman. Produced by HMT Associates at the Palace Theater. Opened July 9, 1976. (Closed July 24, 1976).

With Shirley's Gypsies: Candy Brown, Gary Flannery, Adam Grammis, Jo Ann Lehmann, Larry Vickers. Drummer: Tom Duckworth.

Directed by Tony Charmoli; special choreography, Alan Johnson; musical direction, Donn Trenner; lighting design, Richard Winkler; lighting consultant, Graham Large; sound consultant, Steve Wooley; stage manager, Earl Hughes; press, Michael Alpert, Marilynn LeVine, Warren Knowlton.

The revue was produced on Broadway 4/19/76 for 14 performances. The list of the show's musical numbers appears on page 347 of *The Best Plays of 1975-76.*

Guys and Dolls (239). Revival of the musical based on a story and characters by Damon Runyon; book by Jo Swerling and Abe Burrows; music and lyrics by Frank Loesser. Produced by Moe Septee in association with Victor H. Potamkin at the Broadway Theater. Opened July 21, 1976. (Closed February 13, 1977)

Nicely-Nicely Johnson	Ken Page	Arvide Abernathy	Emett "Babe" Wallace
Benny Southstreet	Christophe Pierre	Agatha	Irene Datcher
Rusty Charlie	Sterling McQueen	Calvin	Alvin Davis
Sister Sarah Brown	Ernestine Jackson	Martha	Marion Moore
Harry the Horse	John Russell	Joey Biltmore; Waiter	Derrick Bell
Lt. Brannigan	Clark Morgan	Master of Ceremonies; Drunk	Andy Torres
Nathan Detroit	Robert Guillaume	Mimi	Prudence Darby
Angie the Ox	Jymie Charles	Gen. Cartwright	Edye Byrde
Miss Adelaide	Norma Donaldson	Big Jule	Walter White
Sky Masterson	James Randolph		

Guys: Derrick Bell, Toney Brealond, Jymie Charles, Alvin Davis, Nathan Jennings Jr., Mill Mackey, Sterling M^Queen, Andy Torres, Eddie Wright Jr.

Dolls: Prudence Darby, Jacquelyn DuBois, Anna Maria Fowlkes, Helen Gelzer, Julia Lema, Jacqueline Smith-Lee.

Understudies: Messrs. Guillaume, Page — Jymie Charles; Miss Jackson — Irene Datcher; Misses Donaldson, Byrde — Helen Gelzer; Mr. Randolph — Nathan Jennings Jr.; Mr. Wallace — John Russell; Mr. Pierre — Andy Torres; Mr. Russell — Bill Mackey; Mr. White — Toney Brealond; Misses Datcher, Darby — Julia Lema; Mr. Torres — Derrick Bell; Mr. McQueen — Bill Mackey, Eddie Wright Jr.; Swing Dancers — Bardell Conner, Brenda Braxton.

Musicians: Lea Richardson assistant conductor, keyboards; Herbert Lovelle percussion; Monti Ellison congas; John Cartwright bass.

Directed and choreographed by Billy Wilson; entire production under the supervision of Abe Burrows; musical direction and choral arrangements, Howard Roberts; scenery, Tom H. John; costumes, Bernard Johnson; lighting, Thomas Skelton; arrangements and orchestrations, Danny Holgate, Horace Ott; sound, Sander Hacker; associate producers, Ashton Springer, Carmen F. Zollo; presented in association with Frank Enterprises and Beresford Productions, Ltd.; production stage manager, R. Derek Swire; stage manager, Clinton Jackson; press, Max Eisen, Barbara Glenn, Judy Jacksina.

This production featured an all-black cast in the Frank Loesser musical, which was first produced on Broadway 11/54/50 for 1,200 performances and was named a Best Play of its season and won the Critics Award for best musical. It was revived by the New York City Center Light Opera Company 4/20/55 for 15 performances, 5/31/55 for 16 performances, 4/28/65 for 15 performances and 6/8/66 for 23 performances.

The list of scenes and musical numbers in *Guys and Dolls* appears on page 329 of *The Best Plays of 1950-51.*

Checking Out (16). By Allen Swift. Produced by Mathias and Myers at the Longacre Theater. Opened September 14, 1976. (Closed September 25, 1976)

Florence Grayson	Joan Copeland	Dr. Theodore Applebaum	Mason Adams
Bernard Applebaum	Hy Anzell	Dr. Sheldon Henning	Larry Bryggman
Morris Applebaum	Allen Swift	Gilbert	Tazewell Thompson
Mr. Johnson	Jonathan Moore	Schmuel Axelrod	Michael Gorrin

Standbys: Miss Copeland — Lenore Loveman; Messrs. Swift, Anzell, Adams, Gorrin — Irwin Charone; Mr. Bryggman — Kurt Garfield. Understudy: Mr. Thompson — Ron Nguvu.

Directed by Jerry Adler; scenery, David Jenkins; lighting, Ken Billington; costumes, Carol Luiken; production stage manager, Murray Gitlin; press, Susan Bloch.

Place: Morris Applebaum's apartment on West 57th Street, New York City. Act I, Scene 1: An April morning. Scene 2: 5:30 a.m. the next day. Scene 3: Four hours later. Act II: A few days later, morning.

Aging Yiddish stage actor decides to schedule and stage-manage his own death.

*For Colored Girls Who Have Considered Suicide/When the Rainbow Is Enuf (295). By Ntozake Shangé. Produced by Joseph Papp and Woodie King Jr., Bernard Gersten associate producer; a New York Shakespeare Festival production in association with the Henry Street Settlement's New Federal Theater at the Booth Theater. Opened September 15, 1976: see note.

Lady in Brown	Janet League	Lady in Purple	Risë Collins
Lady in Yellow	Aku Kadogo	Lady in Blue	Laurie Carlos
Lady in Red	Trazana Beverley	Lady in Orange	Ntozake Shangé
Lady in Green	Paula Moss		

Directed by Oz Scott; choreography, Paula Moss; scenery, Ming Cho Lee; costumes, Judy Dearing; lighting, Jennifer Tipton; music for "I Found God in Myself," Diana Wharton; production stage manager, John Beven; press, Merle Debuskey, Leo Stern.

A "choreopoem" in which a black woman explores inner space in seven facets of herself, with poetry, dance and stories.

NOTE: This work was previously produced off off Broadway at the Henry Street Settlement and then off Broadway by New York Shakespeare Festival at the Public Theater 5/17/76-8/29/76 for 120 performances, after which this production transferred to Broadway.

Seret Scott replaced Ntozake Shangé 10/16/76; Jonette O'Kelley replaced Paula Moss 2/15/77; Roxanne Reese replaced Janet League 3/8/77; Sharita Hunt replaced Seret Scott 4/5/77.

Debbie (14). Musical revue produced by Raymax Productions, Robert Fallon producer, at the Minskoff Theater. Opened September 16, 1976. (Closed September 26, 1976)

Joel Blum	Dani MiCormick
Ray Chabeau	Gene Myers
George Eiferman	Debbie Reynolds
Steven Lardas	Albert Stevenson
Bruce Lea	Penny Worth
Louis McKay	

Directed and choreographed by Ron Lewis; musical conductor, Tom Nygaard; scenery, Billy Morris; costumes, Bob Mackie; lighting, Jerry Grollnek; production stage manager, Joe Lorden; press, John Springer Associates, Louis Sica, Stephanie Buzzarté.

One-woman show built around Debbie Reynolds, with night club orientation.

ACT I: Overture — Tom Nygaard and orchestra; "Gee, But It's Great To Be Here" — Debbie Reynolds, Company; Medley of "Reach Out and Touch Somebody's Hand," "He's Got the Whole World in His Hands," "Touch a Hand," "Higher and Higher" — Reynolds, Company; Singers' Medley — Steven Lardas, Penny Worth, Dani MiCormick; Film Sequence and Medley — Reynolds; "I Ain't Down Yet" — Reynolds; Debbie's Salute to Show Business — Company. Entracte — Nygaard, Orchestra.

ACT II: *Irene* Medley of "Irene," "I'm Always Chasing Rainbows," "Alice Blue Gown," "You Made Me Love You" — Reynolds, Boys; Premier Night . . . Impressions — Reynolds; Bicentennial Salute to America — Company.

Going Up (49). Musical revival based on James Montgomery's comedy *The Aviator;* book and lyrics by Otto Harbach; music by Louis A. Hirsch. Produced by Ashton Springer, William Callahan and Stevens-Weitzenhoffer Productions in association with Stephen R. Friedman and Irwin Meyer in the Goodspeed Opera House production at the John Golden Theater. Opened September 19, 1976. (Closed October 31, 1976)

Miss Zonne	Pat Lysinger	Jules Gaillard	Michael Tartel
Alex	Calvin McRae	Hopkinson Brown	Walter Bobbie
Gus	Larry Hyman	Madeline Manners	Maureen Brennan
John Gordon	Stephen Bray	James Brooks	Noel Craig
Grace Douglas	Kimberly Farr	Robert Street	Brad Blaisdell
F. H. Douglas	Lee H. Doyle	Sam Robinson	Ronn Robinson

Dwayne ....James Bontempo		Ennis ....Teri Gill	
Faye ....Deborah Crowe		Mollie ....Barbara McKinley	
Howell .... Michael Gallagher			

Directed by Bill Gile; choreography and production numbers, Dan Siretta; musical direction and vocal arrangements, Lynn Crigler; scenery and lighting supervision, Edward Haynes; costumes, David Toser; lighting, Peter M. Ehrhardt; special consultant, Alfred Simon; musical arranger, Russell Warner; associate producer, James L. D. Roser; produced for the Goodspeed Opera House by Michael P. Price; production stage manager, Marnel Sumner; stage manager, Ron Abbott; press, Max Eisen, Irene Gandy, Barbara Glenn, Judy Jacksina.

Time: 1919. Place: Lenox, Mass.

A daring young man pretends to be a glamorous airplane pilot and takes a plane up to impress the girl he loves. Though not billed in the program as a revival, this material first appeared on Broadway 12/25/17 for 351 performances. The present production, moved forward two years to 1919 and otherwise reworked, was first produced at the Goodspeed Opera House, East Haddam, Conn. 6/22/76. The play *The Aviator* on which the musical was based was produced on Broadway 12/6/10 for 44 performances.

ACT I

Scene 1: The Gordon Inn lobby, afternoon
"Paging Mr. Street" .... Miss Zonne, Gordon, Bellboys, Ensemble
"I Want a Determined Boy" .... Madeline, Brown, Four Aviators
"If You Look in Her Eyes" ....Grace, Street, Madeline
"Going Up" ....Street, Company
Scene 2: The smoking room, later that evening
"Hello Frisco" .... Miss Zonne, Four Aviators
(From *Ziegfeld Follies of 1915;* lyrics by Gene Buck)
"Down, Up, Left, Right" .... Street, Brown, Brooks, Robinson
"Kiss Me" ....Grace, Gaillard
"The Tickle Toe" ....Grace, Ensemble

ACT II

Scene 1: The terrace, the same evening
"Brand New Hero" .... Ensemble
"I'll Think of You" ....Grace, Street
(From The Rainbow Girl; lyrics by Rennold Wolf)
"I'll Think of You" (Reprise) ....Grace, Street
Scene 2: An airfield near the Gordon Inn, 6 o'clock the next afternoon
"Do It for Me" .... Madeline, Brown
"My Sumurun Girl" ....Miss Zonne, Robinson
(From *The Whirl of Society;* lyrics by Al Jolson)
"Going Up" (Reprise) .... Company
"Down, Up, Left, Right" (Reprise) .... Company
"The Tickle Toe" (Reprise) .... Company
Finale .... Company

I Have a Dream (80). Play with music based on the words of Dr. Martin Luther King Jr.; adapted by Josh Greenfeld; conceived by Robert Greenwald. Produced by Frank Von Zerneck and Mike Wise in association with Frankie Hewitt and The Shubert Organization at the Ambassador Theater. Opened September 20, 1976. (Closed December 5, 1976 matinee)

Dr. Martin Luther King Jr. ...Billy Dee Williams	Singer/Actress .... Ramona Brooks
Woman ....Judyann Elder	Singer/Actress .... Millie Foster
Singer/Actress ....Sheila Ellis	Singer/Actor .... Clinton Derricks-Carroll
Singer/Actress ....Leata Galloway	

Directed by Robert Greenwald; scenery, Donald Harris; costumes, Terence Tam Soon; lighting, Martin Aronstein; musical direction, Fred Gripper; associate producers, Pat Lang and Theater Now, Inc.; presented by special arrangement with Mrs. Coretta King and the Martin Luther King Jr. Center for Social Change; production stage manager, David Clive; stage manager, Janyce Ann Wagner; press, Carl Samrock/Michael Alpert Public Relations, Inc., Marilynn LeVine, Warren Knowlton, Randi Cone.

Act I, Scene 1: December 1955 to December 1959. Scene 2: October 1960 to August 1963. Act II: September 1963 to April 1968.

Tribute to Martin Luther King Jr. in his own words and a dozen gospel and spiritual songs. First produced at Ford's Theater, Washington, D.C., 4/5/76.
Moses Gunn replaced Billy Dee Williams 11/30/76.

A Texas Trilogy. Repertory of three plays by Preston Jones: **Lu Ann Hampton Laverty Oberlander** (21), opened September 21, 1976; **The Last Meeting of the Knights of the White Magnolia** (22), opened September 22, 1976; and **The Oldest Living Graduate** (20), opened September 23, 1976. Produced by Robert Whitehead and Roger L. Stevens at the Broadhurst Theater. (Repertory closed October 31, 1976)

PERFORMER	"LU ANN HAMPTON LAVERTY OBERLANDER"	"KNIGHTS OF THE WHITE MAGNOLIA"	"THE OLDEST LIVING GRADUATE"
Graham Beckel	Skip Hampton	Skip Hampton	
Walter Flanagan	Rufe Phelps	Rufe Phelps	
Henderson Forsythe		L. D. Alexander	
Avril Gentles	Claudine Hampton		Clarence Sickenger
Kristin Griffith	Charmaine		Claudine Hampton
Fred Gwynne		Col. J. C. Kinkaid	Martha Ann Sickenger
Baxter Harris	Corky Oberlander		Col. J.C. Kinkaid
Patrick Hines	Red Grover	Red Grover	
Diane Ladd	Lu Ann Hampton		
William Le Massina			Maj. Leroy W. Ketchum
John Marriott		Ramsey-Eyes	
Everett McGill	Dale Laverty		
Josh Mostel	Milo Crawford	Milo Crawford	
Paul O'Keefe		Lonnie Roy McNeil	Cadet Whopper Turnbull
Lee Richardson			Floyd Kinkaid
Ralph Roberts			Mike Tremaine
Patricia Roe			Maureen Kinkaid
James Staley	Billy Bob Wortman		
Thomas Toner	Olin Potts	Olin Potts	

Standbys: Mr. Gwynne — William Le Massena; Misses Ladd, Griffith — Beverly Shatto; Messrs. Richardson, Le Massena — Donald Buka; Misses Roe, Gentles — Patricia Fay; Messrs. Hines, Flanagan, Forsythe — Joseph Warren; Mr. Beckel — Everett McGill; Mr. Marriott — Earl Sydno; Mr. Roberts — Baxter Harris; Messrs. Toner, Mostel, O'Keefe — Charles Kindl; Messrs. Staley, McGill, Harris — Stephen Nasuta.

Directed by Alan Schneider; scenery and lighting, Ben Edwards; costumes, Jane Greenwood; assistant director, Joan Thorne; production stage manager, William Dodds; stage managers, Charles Kindl, Stephen Nasuta; press, Seymour Krawitz, Patricia McLean Krawitz, Louise Ment.

LU ANN HAMPTON LAVERTY OBERLANDER — Place: Bradleyville, Texas. Act I: The Hampton House, 1953. Act II: Red Grover's bar, 1963; Act III: The Hampton home, 1973.

A West Texas small town high school queen's 20-year downhill path through two marriages and other unhappy adventures. Previously produced in repertory with the other two plays in *A Texas Trilogy* at the Dallas, Tex. Theater Center and at the John F. Kennedy Center for the Performing Arts in Washington, D.C.

THE LAST MEETING OF THE KNIGHTS OF THE WHITE MAGNOLIA — Time: 1962. Place: The meeting room of the Knights of the White Magnolia on the third floor of the Cattleman's Hotel in Bradleyville, Tex.

Members of a vanishing Ku Klux Klan-like splinter group hold their last lodge meeting.

A Best Play; see page 183.

THE OLDEST LIVING GRADUATE — Time: Summer of 1962. Place: The den of Floyd Kinkaid's ranch-style home on the outskirts of Bradleyville, Tex. Act I, Scene 1: A summer afternoon. Scene 2: An hour later. Act II, Scene 1: Four days later. Scene 2: An hour later. Scene 3: Late that night.

Family problems focusing on an old man clinging to past memories.

A Best Play; see page 168.

*Oh! Calcutta! (277). Revival of the musical devised by Kenneth Tynan; with contributions (in this version) by Jules Feiffer, Dan Greenberg, Lenore Kandel, John Lennon, Jacques Levy, Leonard Melfi, David Newman and Robert Benton, Sam Shepard, Clovis Trouille, Kenneth Tynan and Sherman Yellen; music and lyrics (in this version) by Robert Dennis, Peter Schickele and Stanley Walden; additional music by Stanley Walden and Jacques Levy. Produced by Hillard Elkins, Norman Kean and Robert S. Fishko at the Edison Theater. Opened September 24, 1976; see note.

Haru Aki	John Hammil
Jean Andalman	William Knight
Bill Bass	Cy Moore
Dorothy Chansky	Pamela Pilkenton
Cress Darwin	Peggy Jean Waller

The Band: Michael Tschudin conductor, keyboards, vocals; Dan Carter guitars, vocals; Robin Gould III drums; Jeff Gerson percussion; Harvey Swartz bass.

Understudies: Women — Peggy Jean Waller; Men — Bill Bass.

Production conceived and directed by Jacques Levy; choreography, Margo Sappington; musical direction, Stanley Walden; scenery, James Tilton; costumes, Kenneth M. Yount; lighting, Harry Silverglat; sound, Sander Hacker; assistant to the director, Nancy Tribush; projected media design, Gardner Compton; production stage manager, David Rubinstein; press, Les Schechter Associates, Herb Striesfield, Bill Miller.

This revue of erotica was first produced off Broadway 6/17/69 for 704 performances and transferred to Broadway 2/26/71 for 610 additional performances.

NOTE: This revival production of *Oh! Calcutta!* alternated performances with *Me and Bessie* at the Edison Theater until 12/7/76, when *Oh! Calcutta!* continued alone.

ACT I: "Taking off the Robe" — Company; Rock Garden: Man — William Knight, Boy — Cress Darwin; One on One — Haru Aki, Darwin; "Clarence" — Jean Andalman; Suite for Five Letters — John Hammil, Knight, Dorothy Chansky, Andalman, Pamela Pilkenton; The Paintings of Clovis Trouille; "Much Too Soon" — Darwin; Dance for George (dedicated to the memory of George Welbes) — Pilkenton; Will Answer All Sincere Replies: Sue Ellen — Chansky, Dale — Hammil, Monte — Cy Moore, Cherie — Andalman.

ACT II: Delicious Indignities: Helen — Chansky, Alfred — Moore; Spread Your Love Around — Aki, Pilkenton; "Spread Your Love Around" — Andalman; Love Lust Poem — Pilkenton, Aki; Jack and Jill — Pilkenton, Hammil; Playin' — Hammil; Was It Good for You Too?: Perlmutter — Darwin, Interviewer — Aki, Dr. Bronson — Andalman, Dr. Jaspers — Knight, Nurse — Pilkenton, Attendant — Moore, Woman — Chansky, Gypsies — Hammil, Aki; "Coming Together Going Together" — Company.

Porgy and Bess (122). Musical revival founded on the play *Porgy* by Dorothy and DuBose Heyward; libretto by DuBose Heyward; music by George Gershwin; lyrics by DuBose Heyward and Ira Gershwin. Produced by Sherwin M. Goldman and Houston Grand Opera at the Uris Theater. Opened September 25, 1976. (Closed January 9, 1977)

Jasbo Brown	Clay Fullum	(Porgy)	Donnie Ray Albert,
(Clara)	Betty Lane, Elizabeth Graham,		Abraham Lind-Oquendo, Robert Mosley
	Alma Johnson, Myra Merritt	(Crown)	George Robert Merritt,
Mingo	Bernard Thacker		John D. Anthony
(Jake)	Alexander B. Smalls, Bruce A. Hubbard	(Bess)	Clamma Dale, Esther Hinds,
Sportin' Life	Larry Marshall		Phyllis Bash
Robbins	Glover Parham	Detective	Hansford Rowe
(Serena)	Delores Ivory-Davis,	Policeman	William Gammon
	Wilma Shakesnider, Shirley Baines	Undertaker	Cornel Richie
Jim	Hartwell Mace	Annie	Shirley Baines
Peter	Mervin Wallace	Frazier	Earl Grandison
Lily	Myra Merritt	Mr. Archdale	Kenneth Barry
(Maria)	Barbara Ann Webb, Queen Yahna	(Strawberry Woman)	Phyllis Bash, Barbara Buck
Scipio	Alex Carrington	Crab Man	Steven Alex-Cole
		Coroner	John B. Ross

(Parentheses indicate roles in which the performers alternated)

Ensemble: John D. Anthony, Shirley Baines, Earl Baker, Phyllis Bash, Kenneth Bates, Barbara Buck, Steven Alex-Cole, Ella Eure, Wilhelmenia Fernandez, Elizabeth Graham, Earl Grandison, Loretta Holkmann, Bruce A. Hubbard, Alma Johnson, Christal Lockley, Roberta Long, Hartwell Mace, Patricia McDermott, Myra Merritt, Naomi Moody, Glover Parham, William Penn, Dwight Ransom, Cornel Richie, Rodrick Ross, Bernard Thacker, Mervin Wallace, Wardell Woodard, Denice Woods, Barbara L. Young.

Directed by Jack O'Brien; music director and chorus master, John DeMain; choreographer and assistant director, Mabel Robinson; scenery, Robert Randolph; costumes, Nancy Potts; lighting, Gilbert V. Hemsley Jr.; musical preparation, George Darden; conductor, Ross Reimueller; production stage manager and assistant director, Helaine Head; stage manager, Sally McCravey; press, Michael Alpert, Marilynn LeVine, Warren Knowlton.

Time: 1935. Place: Charleston, S.C. Act I, Scene 1: Catfish Row, a summer evening. Scene 2: Serena's room, the following night. Scene 3: Catfish Row, a month later. Scene 4: Kittiwah Island, late afternoon. Act II: Catfish Row, before dawn, a week later. Scene 2: Serena's room, dawn of the following day. Scene 3: Catfish Row, the next night. Scene 4: Catfish Row, the next afternoon. Scene 5: Catfish Row, a week later.

This renowned American opera-style musical about the life and times of black fisherfolk in Catfish Row, Charleston, S.C. was first produced on Broadway 10/10/35 for 124 performances. It has been revived on Broadway 1/22/42 for 286 performances; 9/13/43 for 24 performances and a return engagement 2/7/44 for 48 performances; 4/10/53 for 305 performances; 5/17/61 for 16 performances, and 5/6/64 for 15 performances. The list of musical numbers in *Porgy and Bess* appears on pages 294-5 in *The Best Plays of 1952-53*.

Andrew Smith replaced John D. Anthony 10/76; Bernard Thacker replaced Larry Marshall 12/20/76-1/3/77.

Circle in the Square. Schedule of four programs. **Days in the Trees** (62). By Marguerite Duras; translated from the French by Sonia Orwell. Opened September 26, 1976. (Closed November 21, 1976) **The Night of the Iguana** (77). Revival of the play by Tennessee Williams. Opened December 16, 1976. (Closed February 20, 1977) **Romeo and Juliet** (77). Revival of the play by William Shakespeare. Opened March 17, 1977. (Closed May 22, 1977) And *The Importance of Being Earnest,* revival of the play by Oscar Wilde, scheduled to open June 16, 1977. Produced by Circle in the Square, Theodore Mann artistic director, Paul Libin managing director, at Circle in the Square Theater.

DAYS IN THE TREES

Mother	Mildred Dunnock	Marcelle	Suzanne Lederer
Son	Joseph Maher	Dede	Ed Setrakian

Night Club Guests: Helen Harrelson, Donald Linahan, Marlena Lustik.

Standby: Miss Dunnock — Helen Harrelson; Messrs. Maher, Setrakian — Donald Linahan; Miss Lederer — Marlena Lustik.

Directed by Stephen Porter; scenery and costumes, Rouben Ter-Arutunian; lighting, Thomas Skelton; incidental music, Robert Dennis; production stage manager, James Bernardi; stage manager, Donald Linahan; press, Merle Debuskey, Susan L. Schulman, David Roggensack.

Time: The 1960s. Place: Paris. Act I: An apartment. Act II, Scene 1: The night club. Scene 2: An apartment.

An old woman losing her grip on life visits her one ne'er-do-well son — "one son in reserve for when the bad times come" — in a play which tries to explore life's hidden meanings. A foreign play first presented by the Compagnie Renaud-Barrault at the Odeon Theater in Paris 12/1/65 and in a revised version at the Théâtre d'Orsay 10/15/75 brought to Broadway 5/6/76 for a limited engagement of 11 performances in the French language as "a French contribution to the Bicentennial celebrations."

THE NIGHT OF THE IGUANA

Rev. T. Lawrence Shannon	Richard Chamberlain	Frau Fahrenkopf	Amelia Laurenson
Pedro	Gary Tacon	Hank	Matt Bennett
Maxine Faulk	Sylvia Miles	Judith Fellowes	Barbara Caruso
Pancho	William Paulson	Hannah Jelkes	Dorothy McGuire
Wolfgang	Ben Van Vacter	Charlotte Goodall	Allison Argo
Hilda	Jennifer Savidge	Nonno	William Roerick
Herr Fahrenkopf	John Rose	Jake Latta	Benjamin Stewart

Understudies: Mr. Chamberlain — John Rose; Miss McGuire — Amelia Laurenson; Miss Miles — Darlene Conley; Miss Argo — Jennifer Savidge; Messrs. Van Vecter, Paulson, Tacon — Martin Rabbett.

Directed by Joseph Hardy; scenery and lighting, H. R. Poindexter; costumes, Noel Taylor; production stage manager, Randall Brooks; stage manager, James Bernardi.

Time: The summer of 1940. Place: The Costa Verde Hotel in Puerto Barrio on the west coast of Mexico. Act I, Scene 1: Afternoon. Scene 2: Later that afternoon. Act II: That night. *The Night of the Iguana* was first produced on Broadway 12/28/61 for 316 performances and was named a Best Play of its season and won the Critics Award for Best American Play. This is its first professional New York revival.

ROMEO AND JULIET

Chorus; Musician; Guard	Jim Broaddus	Montague	Tom Klunis
Sampson; Watchman	Christopher Loomis	Lady Montague	Helen Harrelson
Gregory; Chief Watch	Dennis Lipscomb	Prince Escalus	Richard Greene
Peter	Dennis Patella	Romeo	Paul Rudd
Abram; Friar John; Watchman	Peter Van Norden	Paris	John V. Shea
Balthasar	Michael Forella	Juliet	Pamela Payton-Wright
Benvolio	Ray Wise	Nurse	Jan Miner
Tybalt	Armand Assante	Mercutio	David Rounds
Capulet	Lester Rawlins	Rosaline	Lisa Pelikan
Lady Capulet	Delphi Harrington	Cousin Capulet; Watchman	Erik Fredricksen

Friar Laurence .... Jack Gwillim	Guard .... K. C. Kelly
Apothecary .... Daniel Ben-Zali	Ladies .... Ruth Livingston, Jennifer Savidge
Paris's Page .... Mark Cohen	

Understudies: Mr. Rudd — John V. Shea; Miss Payton-Wright — Lisa Pelikan; Miss Miner — Helen Harrelson; Messrs. Rounds, Shea — Dennis Lipscomb; Messrs. Rawlins, Klunis — Daniel Ben-Zali; Misses Harrington, Harrelson — Ruth Livingston; Messrs. Greene, Van Norden — Jim Broaddus; Messrs. Loomis, Lipscomb, Patella, Forella — K. C. Kelly.

Directed by Theodore Mann; scenery, Ming Cho Lee; costumes, John Conklin; lighting, Thomas Skelton; music, Thomas Pasatieri; fights and fencing, Patrick Crean, Erik Fredricksen; production stage manager, Randall Brooks; stage manager, James Bernardi.

Place: Verona and Mantua. The play was presented in two parts.

Circle in the Square's first adventure in Shakespearean revival, in a considerably abbreviated version of the tragedy. *Romeo and Juliet* was last produced on Broadway by the Bristol Old Vic 2/21/67 for 8 performances and in Central Park by New York Shakespeare Festival 9/7/68 for 21 performances.

Siamsa (8). The National Folk Theater of Ireland. Produced by Brannigan-Eisler Performing Arts International, Inc., Robert P. Brannigan and Charles Eisler producers, at the Palace Theater. Opened September 27, 1976. (Closed October 2, 1976)

Merrymaker .... Sean O'Mahony	Shoemaker .... Sean Ahern
Gardener .... Liam Heaslip	

Solo Dancers: Patricia Hanafin, Jimmy Smith, Jerry Nolan, John McCarthy. Solo Singers: Mary Deady, Sean Ahern, Liam Heaslip, Sean O'Mahony. Folk Dancers: Philomena Daly, Susan Rohan, Catherine Hurley, Michael O'Shea, Aidan O'Carroll. Children: Mary Lyons, Marie O'Donoghue, Sandra O'Reilly, Catherine Spangler, Sean Heaslip, Oliver Hurley, John Fitzgerald.

Musicians: Pat Kennington, Gerard Buckley, Nicholas McAuliffe, Timmy O'Shea, Pierce Heaslip, Audrey O'Carroll.

Artistic director, Pat Ahern; devised and directed by Pat Ahern; choreography, Patricia Hanafin; design consultant, Lona Moran; stage manager, Jimmy McDonnell; press, Dan Langan, Langan Communications.

Act I: Samhra (Summertime). Act II, Scene 1: Cois Teallaigh (By the Fireside). Scene 2: Casadh an Sugain (The Twisting of the Rope) and Siamsa an Fomhair (A Harvest Merrymaking).

Traditional Celtic rituals, dancing and folk music presented in the context of an Irish village festival.

The Robber Bridegroom (145). Return engagement of the musical based on the novella by Eudora Welty; book and lyrics by Alfred Uhry; music by Robert Waldman. Produced by John Houseman, Margot Harley and Michael B. Kapon by arrangement with The Acting Company at the Biltmore Theater. Opened October 9, 1976. (Closed February 13, 1977)

Jamie Lockhart .... Barry Bostwick	Raven .... Carolyn McCurry
Clemment Musgrove .... Stephen Vinovich	Residents of Rodney:
Rosamund .... Rhonda Coullet	Kyle Nunnery .... George DeLoy
Salome .... Barbara Lang	Harmon Harper .... Gary Epp
Little Harp .... Lawrence John Moss	Norman Ogelsby .... B. J. Hardin
Big Harp .... Ernie Sabella	Queenie Brenner .... Mary Murray
Goat .... Trip Plymale	Rose Otto .... Melinda Tanner
Goat's Mother .... Susan Berger	Gerry G. Summers .... Dennis Warning
Airie .... Jana Schneider	K. K. Pone .... Tom Westerman

McVoutie River Volunteers: Bob Jones guitar, fiddle; Alan Kaufman fiddle, mandolin; Steve Mandell guitar, banjo; Roger Mason acoustic, electric bass; Evan Stover fiddle; Tony Trischka banjo, leader.

Understudies: Mr. Bostwick — George DeLoy; Mr. Vinovich — J. J. Hardin; Miss Coullet — Mary Murray; Miss Lang — Carolyn McCurry; Mr. Moss — Ernie Sabella; Messrs. Sabella, DeLoy, Hardin, Warning, Westerman — Gary Epp; Mr. Plymale — Tom Westerman; Misses Berger, Schneider, McCurry, Murray — Melinda Tanner.

Directed by Gerald Freedman; choreography, Donald Saddler; scenery, Douglas W. Schmidt; costumes, Jeanne Button; lighting, David F. Segal; associate producer, Porter Van Zandt; production stage manager, Mary Porter Hall; stage manager, Bethe Ward; press, The Merlin Group, Ltd., Sandra Manley.

Place: In and around Rodney, Miss. The play was performed without intermission.

This musical was originally staged off off Broadway at the Musical Theater Lab at St. Clements. It was first produced on Broadway by The Acting Company in a production similar to this one last season, 10/7/75, for 15 performances.

MUSICAL NUMBERS

"Once Upon the Natchez Trace"*	Company
"Two Heads"*	Big Harp, Little Harp
"Steal With Style"	Jamie
"Rosamund's Dream"*	Rosamund
"The Pricklepear Bloom"	Salome
"Nothin' Up"	Rosamund
"Deeper in the Woods"	Company
"Riches"	Musgrove, Jamie, Salome, Rosamund
"Love Stolen"	Jamie
"Poor Tied Up Darlin' "	Little Harp, Goat
"Goodbye Salome"	Company
"Sleepy Man"	Rosamund
"Where Oh Where"*	Jamie, Musgrove, Rosamund

*Not listed among the musical numbers of the 1975 Broadway production

Wheelbarrow Closers (8). By Louis La Russo II. Produced by Tony Conforti in association with Howard Effron and George Tunick at the Bijou Theater. Opened October 11, 1976. (Closed October 16, 1976)

Millie Grant	Norah Foster	Chet Grant	James Allan Bartz
John Mogan	Ray Serra	Chester Grant	Danny Aiello
Larry Freede	Harvey Siegel	Wilfred Dee	Tom Degidon
Beatrice Grant	Frances Helm		

Directed by Paul Sorvino; scenery, Charles Carmello Jr., supervised by Ken Billington; costumes, Jan Wallace, supervised by Carol Luiken; lighting, Leon Di Leone; associate producers, Michael Bash, Howard Wesson, Irving Warhaftig; production stage manager, Gary Stein; press, Max Eisen, Barbara Glenn, Irene Gandy, Judy Jacksina.

Time: The present. Place: The Grant household. The play was presented in two parts.

Tough sales executive comes to grips with the problem of his own retirement.

Best Friend (7). By Michael Sawyer. Produced by Marand Productions in association with Rosemary Vuocolo and Nancy Davis at the Lyceum Theater. Opened October 19, 1976. (Closed October 23, 1976)

Carolyn Parsky	Barbara Baxley	Anita Fitzgerald	Mary Doyle
Mary Tagliavini	Liz Sheridan	John McGovern	Michael M. Ryan

Understudies: Miss Baxley — Liz Sheridan; Misses Sheridan, Doyle — Ingrid Sonnischsen; Mr. Ryan — Victor Raider-Wexler.

Directed by Marty Jacobs; scenery, Andrew Greenhut; costumes, Miles White; lighting, Richard Winkler; production consultant, Doug Taylor; production stage manager, Michael Wieben; stage managers, Victor Raider-Wexler, Ingrid Sonnischsen; press, Lewis Harmon, Sol Jacobson.

Time: The present. Place: An apartment on the Upper West Side, New York City. Act I: 5:30 p.m., late August. Act II: Two hours later, the same evening.

Character study of a neurotic woman disrupting her friend's romance by falsely claiming to have a lesbian relationship with her.

Poor Murderer (87). By Pavel Kohout; based on the Leonid N. Andreyev short story *Mysl* (Thought); translated from the German version of G. and A. Baumrucker by Herbert Berghof and Laurence Luckinbill. Produced by Kermit Bloomgarden, John Bloomgarden and Ken Marsolais at the Ethel Barrymore Theater. Opened October 20, 1976. (Closed January 2, 1977 matinee)

CAST: Prof. Drzhembitsky — Larry Gates; Anton Ignatyevick Kerzhentsev, Hamlet — Laurence Luckinbill; 1st Actor, Alexey Konstantinovich Savelyov, Polonius, Hamlet II — Kevin McCarthy; 1st Actress, Tatyana Nikolayevna, Queen — Maria Schell; 2d Actor, Ignat Antonovich Kerzhentsev, Rector, Waiter, Bernardo, Others — Paul Sparer; 3d Actor, Dean, Lawyer, Maj. Count Byelitsky, Kurganov, King, Others — Ernest Graves; 4th Actor, Cashier, Newspaper Vendor, Conductor, Gypsy, Francisco, Polonius II, Others — Peter Maloney; 2d Actress, Servant Girl, Katya, Flower Vendor, Gypsy Roma, Marya Vassilyevna, Others — Julie Garfield; 3d Actress, Voluptuous Mistress, Irina Pavlovna Kurganova, Countess Byelitskaya, Others — Ruth Ford; 4th Actress, Slim Mistress, Duchess de Cliche-Turomel, Prologue, Others — Felicia Montealegre; Apprentice, Gypsy Girl — Barbara Coggin.

Four Attendants: Timothy Farmer, James Carruthers, Sean Griffin, Richard Vernon.
Musicians: Stanley Wietrzychowski, Brian Koonin, Alfonso Schipani.
Understudies: Mr. Luckinbill — Sean Griffin; Miss Schell — Felicia Montealegre; Messrs. Gates, Graves —
Harry Young; Mr. McCarthy — Ernest Graves; Mr. Sparer — James Carruthers; Misses Garfield, Coggin —
Faith Catlin; Misses Ford, Montealegre — Barbara Coggin; Mr. Maloney — Richard Vernon.
Directed by Herbert Berghof; scenery and lighting, Howard Bay; costumes, Patricia Zipprodt; musical direc-
tion, Stanley Wietrzychowski; produced in association with Don Mark Enterprises; production stage manager,
Frederick A. deWilde; stage manager, Harry Young; press, John Springer Associates, Inc., Louis Sica.
Time: 1900. Place: The great hall of the St. Elizabeth Institute for Nervous Disorders, St. Petersburg, Russia.
The play was presented in two parts.
A famous actor under treatment in a mental institution wonders: did he really kill the actor playing Polonius as
he was playing Hamlet, or was it only an illusion? A foreign play written five years ago by its Czechoslovakian
author and performed throughout Europe.

The Innocents (12). Revival of the play by William Archibald; based on *The Turn of the Screw* by Henry James. Produced by Arthur Cantor and Rose Teed at the Morosco Theater. Opened October 21, 1976. (Closed October 30, 1976)

Flora	Sara Jessica Parker	Miles	Michael MacKay
Mrs. Grose	Pauline Flanagan	Peter Quint	Dino Laudicina
Miss Bolton	Claire Bloom	Miss Jessel	Catherine Wolf

Understudies: Miss Bloom — Catherine Wolf; Mr. MacKay — Toby Parker; Miss Parker — Shelly Bruce;
Misses Flanagan, Wolf — Jane Groves; Mr. Laudicina — Paul Forste.
Directed by Harold Pinter; scenery, John Lee Beatty; costumes, Deirdre Clancy; lighting, Neil Peter Jampolis;
music, Harrison Birtwistle; costume supervisor, Mary McKinley; production manager, Mitchell Erickson; stage
manager, John Handy; press, C. George Willard, Barbara Price.
Time: The late 19th century. Place: The drawing room of an old country house in England. The play was
presented without intermission.
The Innocents was first produced on Broadway 2/1/50 for 141 performances and was named a Best Play of its
season. It was revived off Broadway in the season of 1958-59.

Don't Step on My Olive Branch (16). Musical conceived by Jonathan Karmon; book by Harvey Jacobs; music and lyrics by Ron Eliran. Produced by the Yael Company and Norman Kean at the Playhouse. Opened November 1, 1976. (Closed November 14, 1976)

Gail Benedict	Ruthi Navon
Darleen Boudreaux	Rivka Raz
Karen DiBianco	Joel Robertson
Ron Eliran	Donald Ronci
Carla Farnsworth	Lisa Gould Rubin
Riki Gal	Daniel Stewart
Hanan Goldblatt	John Windsor
David Kottke	

Directed and choreographed by Jonathan Karmon; musical direction, David Krivoshei, scenery, James Tilton;
costumes, Pierre D'Alby; lighting, William H. Bachelder; production stage manager, Daniel E. Early; stage
manager, Karen Winer; press, Max Eisen.
Israeli musical in the English language, presented without intermission in revue form with the numbers commenting on international affairs, usually satirically.

MUSICAL NUMBERS: "Moonlight," "The World's Greatest Magical Act," "I Believe," "Only Love,"
"My Land," "We Love a Conference," "Come With Me," "Tired Heroes," "Have a Little Fun," "I Hear a
Song," "I Live My Life in Color," "Young Days," "Somebody's Stepping on My Olive Branch," "It Was
Worth It," "Jerusalem."

No Man's Land (47). By Harold Pinter. Produced by Roger L. Stevens and Robert Whitehead in association with Frank Milton in the National Theater of Great Britain production at the Longacre Theater. Opened November 9, 1976. (Closed December 18, 1976)

Hirst	Ralph Richardson	Foster	Michael Kitchen
Spooner	John Gielgud	Briggs	Terence Rigby

Standbys: Messrs. Richardson, Gielgud — Ron Randell; Mr. Kitchen — Michael Miller; Mr. Rigby — Ronald Southart.

Directed by Peter Hall; designed by John Bury; stage manager, John Caulfield; press, Seymour Krawitz, Patricia McLean Krawitz.

The play was presented in two parts.

Two elderly poets, apparent strangers but possibly old friends, exchange wintry views in an enigmatic character study set in a comfortable and well-ordered but strangely hostile home environment. A foreign play previously produced at the Old Vic and National Theater and elsewhere in London.

The National Theater of Greece, Alexis Minotis director general. Repertory of two revivals in the Greek language. **Oedipus at Colonus** (3). By Sophocles; translated into modern Greek by Ioannis Gryparis. Opened November 10, 1976. **Knights** (4). By Aristophanes; translated into modern Greek by Nikos Sfyoeras. Opened November 12, 1976. Produced by Brannigan-Eisler Performing Arts International at the City Center. (Repertory closed November 14, 1976)

OEDIPUS AT COLONUS

Antigone	Olga Tournaki	Theseus	Vassilis Kanakis
Oedipus	Alexis Minotis	Creon	Ghikas Biniaris
Stranger	Grigorios Vafias	Polynices	Christos Parlas
Ismene	Maria Skountzou	Messenger	Stelios Vokovits
Chorus (see below)			

Directed by Alexis Minotis; scenery, Kl. Klonis; costumes, Dionyssis Fotopoulos; music, Theodoros Antoniou; choreography, Maria M. Horss; musical direction, Elli Nikolaidi; producers, Robert P. Brannigan, Charles Eisler; press, Langan Communications, Daniel Langan, Marshall Ballou.

Oedipus at Colonus was performed without intermission by this company whose last appearance on Broadway took place 11/24/52 for 10 performances. Its 1976 engagement is a gift from the government of Greece in celebration of the American Bicentennial. The only previous New York performance of record of *Oedipus at Colonus* was by Equity Library Theater 2/10/72.

KNIGHTS

Demosthenes	Theodoros Sarris	Paphlagon	Ghikas Biniaris
Nicias	Kostas Kokkakis	Demos	Pandelis Servos
Sausage-seller	Stelios Vokovits		

Chorus for Both Plays: Alexandros Andonopoulos, Thanos Dadinopoulos, Theodoros Dimitrief, Kostas Galanakis, Giorgos Georgiou, Kostas Kanxidis, Christophoros Kazantzidis, Kostas Kokkakis (*Oedipus* only), Giorgos Konstas, Kostas Kosmopoulos, Stephanos Kyriakidis, Christos Parlas (*Knights* only), Napoleon Roditis, Theodoros Syriotis, Dimitris Tsoutsis, Dmitris Yennimatas, Babis Yotopoulos.

Directed by Alexis Solomos; scenery and costumes, Giorgos Vakalo; music, Stavros Xarchakos; choreography, Dora Tsatsou-Symeonidi; musical direction, Ed Nikolaidi.

Knights was performed without intermission. This was the first professional New York production of record of this comedy about an ambitious and scheming servant in the household of the Athenian Demos.

The Eccentricities of a Nightingale (24). By Tennessee Williams; revised version of *Summer and Smoke*. Produced by Gloria Hope Sher in association with Neal Du Brock at the Morosco Theater. Opened November 23, 1976. (Closed December 12, 1976)

Alma Winemiller	Betsy Palmer	Roger Doremus	Peter Blaxill
Rev. Winemiller	Shepperd Strudwick	Mrs. Bassett	Jen Jones
Mrs. Winemiller	Grace Carney	Rosemary	Patricia Guinan
Mrs. Buchanan	Nan Martin	Vernon	W. P. Drémak
John Buchanan Jr.	David Selby	Traveling Salesman	Thomas Stechschulte

Directed by Edwin Sherin; scenery, William Ritman; costumes, Theoni V. Aldredge; lighting, Marc B. Weiss; original music, Charles Gross; produced in conjunction with Max W. Jacobs; production stage manager, Henry Banister; press, Seymour Krawitz, Louise Ment, Patricia McLean Krawitz.

Time: Shortly before World War I. Place: Glorious Hill, Miss. Act I (The Feeling of a Singer), Scene 1: The fountain. Scene 2: The rectory. Scene 3: The rectory. Act I (The Tenderness of a Mother), Scene 4: The Buchanan House. Scene 5: The rectory. Act II (The Tenderness of a Mother cont'd.), Scene 6: Dr. Buchanan's office. Act II (A Cavalier's Plume), Scene 7: The fountain. Scene 8: A small hotel. Epilogue: The fountain. The play was presented in two parts with the intermission between Acts I and II.

This romance of a determined young woman and a mother's boy is an extensive change of its source, *Summer and Smoke,* which was originally produced on Broadway 10/6/48 for 100 performances and rewritten for off-Broadway production in the season of 1951-52. It was previously produced under its new title at the Studio Arena Theater in Buffalo.

Comedians (145). By Trevor Griffiths. Produced by Alexander H. Cohen in association with Gabriel Katzka and Edward L. Schuman at the Music Box. Opened November 28, 1976. (Closed April 3, 1977)

Caretaker	Norman Allen	Ged Murray	John Lithgow
Gethin Price	Jonathan Pryce	Mr. Patel	Jayant Blue
Phil Murray	Jeffrey DeMunn	Bert Challenor	Rex Robbins
George McBrain	Larry Lamb	Club Secretary	Robert Gerringer
Sammy Samuels	David Margulies	Teddy	Armand Assante
Mick Connor	Jarlath Conroy	Pianist	Woody Kessler
Eddie Waters	Milo O'Shea		

Understudies: Mr. Pryce — Jeffrey DeMunn; Messrs. Margulies, Allen — John Clark; Mr. Robbins — Robert Gerringer; Messrs. Lithgow, Conroy — Jonathan Hogan; Mr. Lamb — Armand Assante; Messrs. DeMunn Gerringer — Norman Allen; Mr. Blue — Faizul Khan.

Directed by Mike Nichols; designed by John Hunter; scenery and costume supervision, James Tilton; lighting, Ron Wallace; co-producers, Hildy Parks, Roy A. Somlyo; production stage manager, Nina Seely; press, Richard Hummler, Martha Mason.

Time: The present. Place: A secondary school and in a workingmen's club in Manchester, England. The play was presented in three parts.

A class of aspiring comedians tries out before a club audience, with greatly varying degrees of success in the opinions of their teacher and of an agent come to audition them — and in their own estimation. A foreign play previously produced in London.

Jonathan Hogan replaced John Lithgow 1/24/77.

A Best Play; see page 198.

Herzl (8). By Dore Schary and Amos Elon; based on the biography by Amos Elon. Produced by Dore Schary at the Palace Theater. Opened November 30, 1976. (Closed December 5, 1976)

Theodor Herzl	Paul Hecht	Jakob Herzl	Roger DeKoven
Moritz Benedikt	Louis Zorich	Julie Herzl	Judith Light
Herman Bahr; Ibrahim	Stephan Mark Weyte	Nursemaid	Rebecca Schull
Capt. Henruach; Kaiser Wilhelm	William Kiehl	Nachum Sokolov	Ralph Byers
Heinrich Kana; Sultan	John Michalski	David Wolffsohn	Mitchell Jason
Arthur Schnitzler;		Baron De Hirsch; Pius X	Richard Seff
Russian General	Leo Bloom	Fraulein Keller	Ellen Tovatt
Rabbi Gudeman	Roy K. Stevens	Count Paul Nevlinski	Lester Rawlings
Edouard Bacher	Jack Axelrod	Menachem Issishkin	David Tress
Jeanette Herzl	Eunice Anderson	Martin Buber	Saylor Creswell

Understudies: Mr. Hecht — Robert Murch; Miss Light — Ellen Tovatt; Miss Anderson — Rebecca Schull; Messrs. Michalski, Stevens, Creswell, — Steve Karp; Misses Tovatt, Schull — Linda Selman; Mr. Byers — Stephen Mark Weyte; Messrs. Tress, Bloom — Jack Axelrod; Mr. Weyte — Saylor Creswell; Mr. Seff — Roy K. Stevens.

Directed by J Ranelli; scenery, Douglas W. Schmidt; costumes, Pearl Somner; lighting, John Gleason; production stage manager, Frank Marino; stage manager, Judith Binus; press, John Springer Associates, Inc., Louis Sica, Suzanne Salter.

Time: The years 1891 to 1897. Place: Vienna, Paris, Constantinople, Berlin, Vilna, Rome and Basel. The play was presented in two parts.

Dramatization of the life of the founder of Zionism, with characters and events based on historical fact.

*Sly Fox (194). By Larry Gelbart; based on *Volpone* by Ben Jonson. Produced by Sir Lew Grade, Martin Starger and The Shubert Organization at the Broadhurst Theater. Opened December 14, 1976.

Simon Able	Hector Elizondo	Miss Fancy	Gretchen Wyler
Foxwell J. Sly; Judge	George C. Scott	Mrs. Truckle	Trish Van Devere
Lawyer Craven	John Heffernan	Crouch's Servant	Guy King
Jethro Crouch	Jack Gilford	Capt. Crouch	John Ramsey
Abner Truckle	Bob Dishy	Chief of Police	James Gallery

1st Policeman ....Robb Webb	3d Policeman ....Joel Simon
2d Policeman; Bailiff .... Willy Switkes	Court Clerk ....Howland Chamberlin

Sly's Servants: Jeffrey Tambor, Calvin Jung, Sandra Seacat.

Understudies: Mr. Gilford — Howland Chamberlin; Mr. Scott — John Ramsey; Miss Wyler — Sandra Seacat; Messrs. Webb, Switkes, Simon, Chamberlin, Tambor, Jung — Joel Simon; Messrs. Dishy, Gallery — Willy Switkes; Messrs. Elizondo, Heffernan — Jeffrey Tambor; Mr. Ramsey — Robb Webb.

Directed by Arthur Penn; scenery and lighting, George Jenkins; costumes, Albert Wolsky; production stage manager, Henry Velez; stage manager, Steven Shaw; press, Merle Debuskey, Susan L. Schulman, Fred Hoot.

Time: One day in the late 180Cs. Place: San Francisco. Act I, Scene 1: Sly's bedroom. Scene 2: The Truckle living room. Scene 3: Crouch's office. Scene 4: Sly's bedroom. Act II, Scene 1: A jail cell. Scene 2: The courtroom. Scene 3: Sly's bedroom.

A *Volpone* updated to an American time and place as above, and rewritten in the American comic idiom, but still a farce about avarice. The last Broadway production of this story was also in an adaptation, *Foxy*, a musical version 2/16/64 for 72 performances.

Robert Preston replaced George C. Scott and Beth Austin replaced Trish Van Devere 5/10/77.

A Best Play; see page 109.

Music Is (8). Musical based on William Shakespeare's *Twelfth Night;* book by George Abbott; music by Richard Adler; lyrics by Will Holt. Produced by Richard Adler, Roger Berlind and Edward R. Downe Jr. at the St. James Theater. Opened December 20, 1976. (Closed December 26, 1976)

William Shakespeare; Feste ......Daniel Ben-Zali	Sir Toby Belch ....David Sabin
Valentine ....William McClary	Malvolio .... Christopher Hewett
Duke Orsino ....David Holliday	Olivia ....Sherry Mathis
Curio; 1st Officer ....David Brummel	Antonio .... Marc Jordan
Viola ....Catherine Cox	Sebastian ....Joel Higgins
Captain ....Paul Michael	Sir Andrew Aguecheek ....Joe Ponazecki
Maria ....Laura Waterbury	2d Officer .... Doug Carfrae

Cupids: Helena Andreyko, Ann Crowley. Court Musicians: Donald Hettinger reeds, Steve Uscher guitar. Members of the Court: Helena Andreyko, Doug Carfrae, Jim Corti, Ann Crowley, Dennis Daniels, Dawn Herbert, Dana Kyle, Wayne Mattson, Jason McAuliffe, Carolann Page, Susan Elizabeth Scott, Denny Shearer, Melanie Vaughan, Mimi B. Wallace.

Understudies: Messrs. McClary, Brummel — Doug Carfrae; Messrs. Holliday, Michael, Jordan — David Brummel; Misses Cox, Mathis — Carolann Page; Messrs. Ben-Zali, Hewett — William McClary; Mr. Ponazecki — Denny Shearer; Mr. Higgins — Jason McAuliffe; Mr. Sabin — Paul Michael; Miss Waterbury — Susan Elizabeth Scott.

Directed by George Abbott; musical numbers and dances staged by Patricia Birch; musical direction, Paul Gemignani; scenery, Eldon Elder; costumes, Lewis D. Rampino; lighting, H. R. Poindexter; orchestrations, Hershy Kay; dance and vocal arrangements, William Cox; assistant director, Judith Abbott; production stage manager, Bob D. Bernard; stage manager, Elise Warner; press, Mary Bryant, Richard Kagey.

Musical version of Shakespeare's comedy, previously produced at the Seattle Theater Center. Other recent musicals based on this play were *Love and Let Love* 1/3/68 for 14 performances and *Your Own Thing* 1/13/68 for 933 performances and a Best Play citation and Critics Prize, both shows produced off Broadway. The most recent production of the play itself was 3/2/72 at Lincoln Center for 44 performances.

ACT I

Prologue
  "Music Is" .... William Shakespeare, Company
Scene 1: Orsino's garden
  "When First I Saw My Lady's Face" ....Orsino
Scene 2: The seacoast
  "Lady's Choice" ....Viola, Captain
Scene 3: Orsino's garden
  "The Time Is Ripe for Loving" .... Company
  "Should I Speak of Loving You" ....Viola
  Dance for Six: Helena Andreyko, Ann Crowley, Mimi B. Wallace, Denny Shearer, Dennis Daniels, Jim
          Corti
Scene 4: The seacoast
  "Hate to Say Goodbye to You" ....Antonio, Sebastian
Scene 5: Olivia's garden
  "Big Bottom Betty" .... Feste

"Twenty-one Chateaux" ....Viola, Olivia, Company
"Sudden Lilac" .... Olivia
Scene 6: Olivia's orchard
"Sing Hi" ....Sir Toby, Sir Andrew, Feste, Maria
Scene 7: Orsino's palace
Dance: Blindman's Bluff" .... Viola, Orsino, Company

ACT II

Scene 1: Street with a tailor shop
"The Tennis Song" ....Orsino, Valentine, Company
Scene 2: A haystack near Olivia's house
"I Am It" ....Malvolio
Scene 3: Olivia's orchard
"No Matter Where" .... Olivia, Viola
"The Duel" .... Sir Toby, Sir Andrew, Viola, Feste
Scene 4: A room in Olivia's house
"Please Be Human" ....Olivia, Sebastian
Scene 5: Corridor — Malvolio's bedroom
Scene 6: Olivia's bedroom
Scene 7: Front of Olivia's house
"What You Will" .... Shakespeare, Company

*Your Arms Too Short to Box With God (182). Conceived from the Book of Matthew by Vinnette Carroll; music and lyrics by Alex Bradford; additional music and lyrics by Micki Grant. Produced by Frankie Hewitt and The Shubert Organization, in association with Theater Now, Inc., in the Ford's Theater production at the Lyceum Theater. Opened December 22, 1976.

Adrian Bailey	William Hardy Jr.
Salome Bey	Bobby Hill
Deborah Lynn Bridges	Edna M. Krider
Sharon Brooks	Hector Jaime Mercado
Clinton Derricks-Carroll	Mabel Robinson
Sheila Ellis	William Thomas Jr.
Thomas Jefferson Fouse Jr.	Leone Washington
Michael Gray	Derek Williams
Cardell Hall	Marilyn Winbush
Delores Hall	

Swing Dancers: Thelma Drayton, Ralph Farrington.
Musicians: Eddie Brown conductor, Denzil A. Miller Jr. keyboards, Howard L. Grate drums, Howard Hirsch percussion, Bob Fortunato horns, Van J. Gibbs guitar, Pat Perrone reeds, Thomas Michael Stevens bass.
Directed by Vinnette Carroll; choreography, Talley Beatty; scenery and costumes, William Schroder; set supervisor, Michael J. Hotopp; lighting, Gilbert V. Hemsley Jr.; orchestrations and dance music, H. B. Barnum; choral arrangements and direction, Chapman Roberts; production stage manager, Haig Shepherd; stage manager, Robert Charles; press, Henry Luhrman Associates, Anne Obert Weinberg, Terry M. Lilly.
Gospel musical developed by Miss Carroll's Urban Arts Corps for presentation at the Spoleto, Italy Festival of Two Worlds in 1975 and later produced at Ford's Theater, Washington, D.C. The play was presented without intermission.

MUSICAL NUMBERS: "Beatitudes" — Company; "We're Gonna Have a Good Time" — Clinton Derricks-Carroll, Company; "There's a Stranger in Town" — William Hardy Jr., Company; "Do You Know Jesus?/He's a Wonder" — Thomas Jefferson Fouse Jr., Company; "Just a Little Bit of Jesus Goes a Long Way" — Sheila Ellis, Company; "We Are the Priests and Elders" — Hardy, Derricks-Carroll, Bobby Hill, Michael Gray; "Something Is Wrong in Jerusalem" — Salome Bey. Mabel Robinson, Company; "It Was Alone" — Derek Williams, Fouse, Company; "I Know I Have to Leave Here" — Williams, Fouse, Company; "Be Careful Whom You Kiss" — Bey, Company; "Trial" — Company; "It's Too Late" — Company; "Judas Dance" — Hector Jaime Mercado; "Your Arms Too Short to Box With God" — Delores Hall, Cardell Hall, Company; "Give Us Barabbas" — Company; "See How They Done My Lord" — Bey, Company; "Come on Down" — Ellis, Derricks-Carroll, Gray; "Can't No Grave Hold My Body Down" — Derricks-Carroll, Williams, Company; "Beatitudes" (Reprise) — Company; "Didn't I Tell You" — Hardy, Company; "When the Power Comes" — Hardy, Company; "Everybody Has His Own Way" — Derricks-Carroll, Gray, Fouse; "I Love You So Much Jesus" — Delores Hall; "The Band" — Hardy, Delores Hall, Ellis, Company.

Fiddler on the Roof (167). Musical revival based on Sholom Aleichem's stories (by special permission of Arnold Perl); book by Joseph Stein; music by Jerry Bock; lyrics by Sheldon Harnick. Produced by The Shubert Organization, Nederlander Producing Company of America, Inc. and the John F. Kennedy Center for the Performing Arts, in association with Theater Now, Inc., at the Winter Garden. Opened December 28, 1976. (Closed May 21, 1977)

Tevye	Zero Mostel	Villagers:	
Golde	Thelma Lee	Shloime	Matthew Inge
Tzeitel	Elizabeth Hale	Yitzuk	Don Tull
Hodel	Christopher Callan	Chaim	Glen McClaskey
Chava	Nancy Tompkins	Duvidel	Wallace Munro
Shprintze	Davia Sacks	Surcha	Lynn Archer
Bielke	Tiffany Bogart	Label	Tog Richards
Yente	Ruth Jaroslow	Schmeril	David Horwitz
Motel	Irwin Pearl	Yakov	Patrick Quinn
Perchik	Jeff Keller	Hershel	Myron Curtis
Mordcha	Leon Spelman	Fredel	Hope Katcher
Lazar Wolf	Paul Lipson	Bluma	Debra Timmons
Rabbi	Charles Mayer	Mirala	Maureen Sadusk
Mendel	Paul A. Corman	Sima	Lynn Archer
Avram	Merrill Plaskow II	Rivka	Joyce Martin
Nachum	David Masters	Yussel	Duane Bodin
Grandma Tzeitel	Duane Bodin	Vladimer	Robert L. Hultman
Fruma Sarah	Joyce Martin	Sasha	Wallace Munro
Constable	Alexander Orfaly	Bascha	Shelley Wolf
Fyedka	Rick Friesen	Pinahas	Neal Thompson
Shandel	Jeanne Grant	Igor	Lorenzo Bianco
Fiddler	Sammy Bayes	Lifsha	Annette Pirrone
		Baruch	John Kirshy

Bottle Dancers: Tog Richards, Myron Curtis, Matthew Inge, Wallace Munro.

Standby: Mr. Mostel — Paul Lipson. Understudies: Miss Lee — Jeanne Grant; Mr. Pearl — Paul A. Corman; Miss Jaroslow — Lynn Archer; Misses Hale, Martin — Hope Katcher; Misses Tompkins, Sacks, Bogart — Debra Timmons; Mr. Lipson — Leon Spelman; Messrs. Mayer, Plaskow — David Masters; Messrs. Keller, Friesen — Patrick Quinn. Miss Callan — Nancy Tompkins; Mr. Corman — Matthew Inge; Mr. Orfaly — Glen McClaskey; Mr. Spelman — Merrill Plaskow II; Mr. Masters — Tog Richards; Mr. Bodin — Wallace Munro; Mr. Bayes — Neal Thompson; Swing Dancer — Vito Durante; Swing Singer — Adele Paige.

Direction and choreography, Jerome Robbins; direction reproduced by Ruth Mitchell; choreography reproduced by Tom Abbott; musical direction, Milton Rosenstock; scenery, Boris Aronson; costumes, Patricia Zipprodt; lighting, Ken Billington; orchestrations, Don Walker; vocal arrangements, Milton Greene; dance music arrangements, Betty Walberg; production stage manager, Kenneth Porter; stage managers, Tobias Mostel, Val Mayer; press, Betty Lee Hunt, Maria Cristina Pucci.

Time: 1905, on the eve of the revolutionary period. Place: Anatevka, a village in Russia. The play was presented in two parts.

Fiddler on the Roof was first produced on Broadway 9/22/64 for 3,242 performances — the all-time longest Broadway run — and was named a Best Play of its season and won the New York Drama Critics Circle Award for best musical.

The list of musical numbers in *Fiddler on the Roof* appears on page 303 of *The Best Plays of 1964-65*.

Something Old, Something New (1). By Henry Denker. Produced by Adela Holzer at the Morosco Theater. Opened and closed at the evening performance, January 1, 1977.

Cynthia Morse	Holland Taylor	Eleanor Curtis	Lois Markle
Mike Curtis	Dick Patterson	Dr. Arthur Morse	Matthew Tobin
Samuel Jonas	Hans Conried	Bruce Morse	Ahvi Spindell
Laura Curtis	Molly Picon	Angela	Cynthia Bostick

Directed by Robert H. Livingston; scenery and costumes, Lawrence King, Michael H. Yeargan; lighting, Clarke Dunham; production stage manager, Martha Knight; press, Michael Alpert Public Relations, Marilynn LeVine, Warren Knowlton, Carl Samrock, Randi Cone.

Time: The present. Place: The West Side apartment of Samuel Jonas. Act I: Thursday morning, spring. Act II: Late afternoon of the same day. Act III: The same day, immediately following.

Elderly widow and widower decide to live together out of wedlock, to the consternation of their families. Previously produced in Atlanta, Ga.

The Trip Back Down (70). By John Bishop. Produced by Philip Rose and Gloria and Louis K. Sher at the Longacre Theater. Opened January 4, 1977. (Closed March 5, 1977)

Bobby Horvath .... John Cullum	Autograph Man; Bartender;
Policeman; Dave; Mechanic;	Neighbor .... Gordon Oas-Heim
Schmidt; Man ....John Randolph Jones	JoAnn Meighan ....Jill André
Factory Worker; Richie; Man .. William Andrews	Will Horvath .... Edward Seamon
Factory Worker; Chuck .... Charles Brant	Pam ....Alexa Spencer
Frank Horvath ....Arlen Dean Snyder	Bar Girl .... Carol Chanco
Barbara Horvath .... Doris Belack	John Meeghan ....Andrew Jarkowsky
Super Joe Weller ....Anthony Call	Jan ....Blaise Bulfair
Waitress .... Gwendolyn Brown	

Party Guests: William Andrews, Gwendolyn Brown, Carol Chanco, John Randolph Jones.

Understudies: Misses André, Belack — Gwendolyn Brown; Mr. Jarkowsky — William Andrews; Misses Bulfair, Spencer — Carol Chanco; Mr. Call — John Randolph Jones; Messrs. Snyder, Seamon — Gordon Oas-Heim; Mr. Brant — Dean Vallas; General Understudy — Philip Oxnam.

Directed by Terry Schreiber; scenery, Hal Tine; costumes, Pearl Somner; lighting, Richard Nelson; production stage manager, Mortimer Halpern; stage manager, Dean Vallas; press, Merle Debuskey, Leo Stern.

Time: Spring, 1975. Place: Mansfield, Ohio. The play was presented in two parts.

Over-the-hill racing car driver comes back home to visit to renew himself.

Dirty Linen & New-Found-Land (159). By Tom Stoppard. Produced by Elliot Martin and Inter-Action Trust Ltd. at the John Golden Theater. Opened January 11, 1977. (Closed May 28, 1977)

Dirty Linen	Mrs. Ebury .... Leila Blake
Maddie ....Cecilia Hart	French .... Stephen D. Newman
McTeazle .... Francis Bethencourt	Home Secretary .... Stephen Scott
Cocklebury-Smythe .... Remak Ramsay	*New-Found-Land*
Chamberlain ....Michael Tolaydo	Arthur .... Jacob Brooke
Withenshaw .... Merwin Goldsmith	Bernard ....Humphrey Davis

Understudies: Messrs. Newman, Brooke, Tolaydo — Edmond Genest; Messrs. Scott, Goldsmith — Michael McCarty; Messrs. Ramsay, Bethencourt — Stephen Scott; Misses Hart, Blake — Lynn Welden; Mr. Davis — Daniel Keyes.

Directed by Ed Berman; original London production designed by Gabriella Falk; scenery and costume supervision, Lawrence King, Michael H. Yeargan; lighting, Martin Aronstein; production associate, Marjorie Martin; presented by arrangement with the John F. Kennedy Center for the Performing Arts; production stage manager, Wally Peterson; press, Seymour Krawitz, Patricia McLean Krawitz, Louise Ment.

Farcical treatment of a Parliamentary committee meeting to cope with sexual scandals (in *Dirty Linen*), with two other people taking over the meeting room during the committee's "lunch hour" and one of them launching into a monologue take-off of a tourist's description of a trip across America (in *New-Found-Land*). The program was presented without intermission. A foreign play previously produced in London and Washington, D.C.

Ipi-Tombi (39). A musical in South African black tribal languages conceived by Bertha Egnos; original music by Bertha Egnos; lyrics by Gail Lakier. Produced by A. Deshe (Pashanel) and Topol, by arrangement with Ray Cooney Productions, Ltd. and Academy Theater and Brooke Theater, Johannesburg, in the Bertha Egnos production at the Harkness Theater. Opened January 12, 1977. (Closed February 13, 1977)

Gideon Bendile	Count Wellington Judge
Matthew Bodibe	Andrew Kau
Busi Dlamini	Nellie Khumalo
Dorcas Faku	Jabu Mbalo
Zelda Funani	Martha Molefe
Philip Gama	Lydia Monamodi
Sam Hlatshwayo	Shadrack Moyo
Betty-Boo Hlela	David Mthethwa

Thembi Mtshali
Elliot Ngubane
Dudu Nzimande

Coreen Pike
Daniel Pule
Linda Tshabalala

Junior Tshabalala chief drummer, Ali Lerefolo drummer, Simon Nkosi drummer.

Devised by Bertha Egnos; choreography, Sheila Wartski; additional choreography, Neil McKay and members of the cast; scenery, Eliz. MacLeish; lighting, Timothy Heale, John Wain; sound, Sander Hacker; scenery supervision, Robert Mitchell; costume supervision, David Toser; lighting supervision, Jeremy Johnson; production stage manager, Patrick Horrigan; press, Max Eisen, Barbara Glenn.

South African folk dances, songs and rituals mostly of village life. A foreign play previously produced in Johannesburg, South Africa and London.

ACT I

Overture

"Ipi-Tombi" (Where Are the Girls).

Scene 1: Village of Tsomo

"Sesiyahamba" (We Are Going About Our Labors), "Hamba Bhekile" (Let the Drinks Be Served), "Uthando Luphelile" (Love Is Lost, Love Is Gone), "Madiwa-Madiwa" (Calling for Rain), "Qhobosha" (The Unfaithful One Will Die), Mokhibo (The Sotho Girls Dance), "Ntaba Zenyuka" (The Mountains Are High), "Orgy, the Temptress," "Moriva," "Shamanile," Shangaan (A Dance of Happiness).

Scene 2: The baptism (conflict between villagers and witch-doctor)

Scene 3: "Nadia" (Song of Hope)

Scene 4: E'Goli (The City of Gold)

"Emduduni" (Street Sweepers), "Oo-Le-Le," A Xhosa Proposition (a Xhosa girl converses with a man in the "click" language of the Xhosa tongue), The Refuse Collectors (Johannesburg workers doing their job at the double), "Arieni" (Let's Dance), Gum Boot Dance, "Ipi-Tombi."

ACT II

Scene 1: Sunday on the mines

"Bayakhala" (The Child, Zulu).

Scene 2: The township wedding

"Mama Tembu's Wedding," "Baby Baby," "Phata Phata" (Touch Touch), "Wishing," "Zimbaba," "Baby Baby" (Reprise).

Scene 3: Workday on the mine

"Shosholoza" (A Work Song), "Going Home."

Scene 4: The warriors (fierce dance in prelude to battle)

*Otherwise Engaged (135). By Simon Gray. Produced by James M. Nederlander, Frank Milton and Michael Codron at the Plymouth Theater. Opened February 2, 1977.

Simon	Tom Courtenay	Davina	Lynn Milgrim
Dave	John Christopher Jones	Wood	Michael Lombard
Stephen	John Horton	Beth	Carolyn Lagerfelt
Jeff	Nicolas Coster		

Understudies: Messrs. Courtenay, Lombard — Steven Sutherland; Messrs. Horton, Coster — Michael Connolly; Mr. John Christopher Jones — Jeff Rubin; Miss Lagerfelt — Catherine Wolf; Miss Milgrim — Laura Copland.

Directed by Harold Pinter; scenery, Eileen Diss; scenery supervision and lighting, Neil Peter Jampolis; costumes, Jane Greenwood; production stage manager, Ben Janney; press, Michael Alpert, Marilynn LeVine, Warren Knowlton.

Place: A house in London. The play was presented in two parts.

Poised, rather effete intellectual tries to remain aloof from a buffeting by family and friends, one after the other. A foreign play previously produced in London.

A Best Play; see page 216.

A Party With Betty Comden and Adolph Green (92). Revised version of the two-person show by and with Betty Comden and Adolph Green. Produced by Arthur Cantor and Leonard Friedman at the Morosco Theater. Opened February 10, 1977. (Closed April 30, 1977)

Piano, Paul Trueblood; Miss Comden's gowns, Donald Brooks; lighting, Andrea Wilson; production stage manager, Larry Bussard; press, C. George Willard.

Revue of numbers from the performing and writing careers of Comden & Green beginning with night clubs and continuing on Broadway and in Hollywood. A similar program under the same title was first presented by the authors off Broadway during the 1958-59 season and later on Broadway 12/23/58 for 38 performances and 4/16/59 for 44 performances.

Piaf . . . a Remembrance (21). By David Cohen; conceived by Milli Janz. Produced by Michael Ross and Eddie Vallone at the Playhouse. Opened February 14, 1977. (Closed March 5, 1977)

Theo Sarapo	Gregory Salata	Edith Piaf	Juliette Koka
Louis Leplee	Edmund Lyndeck	Loulou Barrier	Douglas Andros
Marcel Cerdan	Lou Bedford	Henri; Young Doctor	Donald Hampton

Understudies: Miss Koka — Monique Leboeuf; Messrs. Lyndeck, Andros — Owen Rachleff; Messrs. Salata, Bedford — Donald Hampton.

Directed by Lee Rachman; scenery and lighting, Ralph Alswang; costumes, Robert Troie; music arranged and conducted by John Marino; production stage manager, Robert J. Bruyr; press, David Powers, Owen Levy.

Biographical play-with-music about the life and career of Edith Piaf. The play was presented in two parts.

Prologue: "Padam." ACT I: "Bal Dans Ma Rue," "L'Étranger," "Bravo Pour le Clown," "Mon Dieu," "L'Accordioniste," "Mon Menage à Moi," "Milord." ACT II: "La Vie en Rose," "Les Trois Cloches," "Under Paris Skies," "La Goulante du Pauvre Jean," "Hymne à L'Amour," "La Foule," "Les Blouses Blanches." Epilogue: "Non, Je Ne Regrette Rien."

American Buffalo (135). By David Mamet. Produced by Edgar Lansbury and Joseph Beruh at the Ethel Barrymore Theater. Opened February 16, 1977. (Closed June 11, 1977)

Donny Dubrow	Kenneth McMillan	Walter Cole	Robert Duvall
Bobby	John Savage		

Directed by Ulu Grosbard; design, Santo Loquasto; lighting, Jules Fisher; associate producer, Nan Pearlman; production stage manager, Herb Vogler; stage manager, Joel Tropper; press, Gifford/Wallace, Inc., Glenna Freedman.

Time: One Friday. Place: Don's Resale Shop, a junkshop. Act I: Morning. Act II: 11 p.m. that night. The play was presented in two parts.

Three petty thieves plan but fail to execute the burglary of a coin collection. Previously produced in Chicago and off off Broadway at Theater at St. Clements.

A Best Play; see page 220.

New York Shakespeare Festival Lincoln Center. Schedule of two programs. **The Cherry Orchard** (62). Revival of the play by Anton Chekhov; new English version by Jean-Claude van Itallie. Opened February 17, 1977. (Closed April 10, 1977) **Agamemnon** (38). Revival of the play by Aeschylus; conceived by Andrei Serban and Elizabeth Swados using fragments of the original Greek and Edith Hamilton's translation. Opened May 18, 1977. (Closed June 19, 1977) Produced by Joseph Papp in the New York Shakespeare Festival production at the Vivian Beaumont Theater.

THE CHERRY ORCHARD

Lopakhin	Raul Julia	Charlotta	Cathryn Damon
Dunyasha	Meryl Streep	Simeonov-Pishchik	C. K. Alexander
Yepikhodov	Max Wright	Yasha	Ben Masters
Anya	Marybeth Hurt	Firs	Dwight Marfield
Ranevskaya	Irene Worth	Trofimov	Michael Cristofer
Varya	Priscilla Smith	Vagrant	Jon De Vries
Gayev	George Voskovec	Stationmaster	William Duff-Griffin

Guests, Peasants, Servants: John Ahlberg, Suzanne Collins, Jon De Vries, Christine Estabrook, C. S. Hayward, Diane Lane, Jim Siering.

Standby: Miss Worth — Jacqueline Brookes. Understudies: Messrs. Julia, Wright — Gerry Bamman; Miss Smith — Suzanne Collins; Messrs. Marfield, Voskovec — Maury Cooper; Mr. Cristofer — John De Vries; Mr. Alexander — William Duff-Griffin; Misses Hurt, Streep — Christine Estabrook; Miss Damon — Elizabeth Franz; Mr. De Vries — C. S. Hayward; Mr. Masters — Jim Siering.

Directed by Andrei Serban; scene and costumes, Santo Loquasto; lighting, Jennifer Tipton; incidental music, Elizabeth Swados; dance arrangement, Kathryn Posin; associate producer, Bernard Gersten; production manager, Andrew Mihok; press, Merle Debuskey, Faith Geer.

The Cherry Orchard was last revived in New York by the Roundabout Theater Company 4/2/76 for 56 performances and by the New York Shakespeare Festival at the Public Theater 12/7/72 for 86 performances.

AGAMEMNON

Clytemnestra; Cassandra	.........Priscilla Smith	Chorus Leader	.... George Voskovec
Agamemnon; Aegisthus	............Jamil Zakkai	Iphigenia	.... Diane Lane

Watchman and Herald: Played interchangeably by members of the chorus.

Chorus: Stuart Baker-Bergen, Patrick Ennis Burke, Suzanne Collins, Gretel Cummings, Jerry Cunliffe, Jon De Vries, Helena D. Garcia, Natalie Gray, Kathleen Harris, C.S. Hayward, Rodney Hudson, Omni Johnson, Paul Kreppel, Paula Larke, Roger Lawson, Esther Levy, Mimi Locadio, Tom Matsusaka, Valois Mickens, Joseph Neal, William Parry, Justin Rashid, Peter Schlosser, Jai Oscar St. John, Eron Tabor, John Watson, Beverly Wideman.

Musicians: Richard Centalonza woodwinds; Dan Erkkila flute; William Ruyle percussion; Andrew Schloss percussion.

Understudies: Clytemnestra — Natalie Gray; Cassandra — Valois Mickens; Chorus Leader — George Touliatos.

Directed by Andrei Serban; music, Elizabeth Swados; scenery, Douglas W. Schmidt; costumes, Santo Loquasto; lighting, Jennifer Tipton; production supervisor, Jason Steven Cohen.

The only previous Broadway production of record of *Agamemnon* was as part of the visiting Minnesota Theater Company's *The House of Atreus* 12/17/68 for 17 performances. The play was presented without intermission.

Caesar and Cleopatra (12). Revival of the play by George Bernard Shaw. Produced by Elliot Martin and Gladys Rackmil and the John F. Kennedy Center for the Performing Arts, in association with James Nederlander at the Palace Theater. Opened February 24, 1977. (Closed March 5, 1977)

Julius Caesar	.....................Rex Harrison	Lucius Septimius	................John Bergstrom
Cleopatra	.....................Elizabeth Ashley	Roman Sentinel	..................Edwin Owens
Ftatateeta	......................Novella Nelson	Apollodorus	.... Thom Christopher
Rufio	...........................Paul Hecht	Nubian Musician	.... Charles Turner
Pothinus	.... Patrick Hines	Iras	.... Fiddle Viracola
Theodotus	..................William Robertson	Charmian	.....................Linda Martin
Ptolemy	.... Roger Campo	Court Lady	.... Pawnee Sills
Achillas	.......................Mike Dantuono	Major Domo	.... Paul Rosson
Britannus	.... James Valentine		

Slaves: Cain Richards, Joseph Scalzo, Eric Booth. Priests: Cain Richards, Ian Stuart. Roman Soldiers: Phil Becker, Ken Bonafons, Gerald Graham Brown, Scott Bryce, Jim Horn, Joel Leffert, Richard Livert, Lenny Reggia, Kyle Samperton.

Understudies: Mr. Harrison — James Valentine; Miss Ashley — Linda Martin; Mr. Valentine — Ian Stuart; Misses Nelson, Viracola, Martin — Pawnee Sills; Messrs. Hines, Robertson — Paul Rosson; Messrs. Dantuono, Hecht — Edwin Owens; Mr. Campo — Christopher Weddle; Messrs. Christopher, Bergstrom — Eric Booth; Mr. Owens — Charles Turner; Mr. Turner — Cain Richards.

Directed by Ellis Rabb; scenery, Ming Cho Lee; costumes, Jane Greenwood; lighting, Thomas Skelton; movement, Al Sambogna; production stage manager, William Dodds; stage managers, Michael Schaefer, Ian Stuart; press, Betty Lee Hunt, Maria Cristina Pucci, Fred Hoot.

Time: 48 B.C. Place: Egypt. Act I, Scene 1: The Sphinx. Scene 2: The throne room. Scene 3: A council chamber in the treasury. Act II, Scene I: The lighthouse. Scene 2: Cleopatra's boudoir. Scene 3: The roof of the palace in Alexandria. Scene 4: The quay side before the palace.

Caesar and Cleopatra was first produced on Broadway 10/30/06 for 49 performances. Subsequent major revivals have taken place the season of 1913-14, 4/13/25, 12/21/49 for 149 performances and 12/13/51 for 67 performances with Laurence Olivier and Vivien Leigh in the title roles. Its most recent production was a musical version, *Her First Roman*, 10/20/68 for 17 performances. This production was previously presented at the Kennedy Center, Washington D.C.

Unexpected Guests (6). By Jordan Crittenden. Produced by Charles Grodin at the Little Theater. Opened March 2, 1977. (Closed March 6, 1977)

Vince Provenzano	.................Frank Piazza	Gordon	.........................Bill Lazarus
Harry Mullin	.....................Jerry Stiller	M. J. Nyberg	.....................Michael Vale

Mrs. Mullin ....Anne Ives	Melissa Mullin ....Zohra Lampert
Mr. Mullin .... Loney Lewis	Delivery Man ....Robert Costanzo
Susan Beckerman .... Constance Forslund	Man .... Robert Earl Jones

Understudies: Mr. Stiller — Bill Lazarus; Misses Lampert, Forslund, Ives — Sandy Gabriel; Messrs. Piazza, Vale, Lazarus, Lewis — Robert Costanzo.

Directed by Charles Grodin; scenery, Stuart Wurtzel; costumes, Joseph G. Aulisi; lighting, Cheryl Thacker; production stage manager, John Brigleb; stage manager, Ellsworth Wright; press, Michael Alpert/Marilynn LeVine, Warren Knowlton.

Time: The present, an October evening. Place: A home in Southern California. The play was presented in two parts.

Comedy about a shaky marriage.

Mark Twain Tonight! (12). Return engagement of the one-man show with Hal Holbrook; based on writings of Mark Twain. Produced by Emanuel Azenberg and Dasha Epstein at the Imperial Theater. Opened March 14, 1977. (Closed March 26, 1977)

Production supervised by Bennett Thomson; press, Bill Evans, Susan Bell, Kevin Ottem.

Hal Holbrook's characterization of Mark Twain was previously presented in an "off-Broadway" engagement at the Forty-first Street Theater in 1959 and on Broadway 3/23/66 for 71 performances.

Mr. Holbrook's 1977 program was selected from this material by Mark Twain: "Slow Train, Long Dog" and "A Moral Pauper" from *Following the Equator;* "Hunting the Water Closet," "His Grandfather's Old Ram" and "The Thin Skin" from *Mark Twain's Notebook;* "Stealing a Clerical Hat," "The Anarchist Story," "Accident Insurance," "White Suit," "Advice to Youth," "How To Be 70" and "Mary Ann" from Twain's speeches; "Virginia City," "Shovelling Sand," "A Genuine Mexican Plug" and "The Sandwich Islands" from *Roughing It;* "The Lord Will Provide," "Slavery: A Holy Thing," "Praying for Gingerbread," "Boyhood on the Farm," "My Trained Presbyterian Conscience" and "Susy's Prayer" from *Mark Twain's Autobiography;* "The German Opera" from *A Tramp Abroad;* "The Italian Guide" and "Taking Along the Window Sash" from *Innocents Abroad;* "The Supreme Art," "A Helluva Heaven," "Noah's Ark" and "The Creator's Pet" from *Letters From the Earth;* "Requesting a Hymn Book," "The Anglo-Saxon Race" and "Chief Love" from *Mark Twain in Eruption;* "The Evolution of Man," "Man, that Poor Thing" and "Halley's Comet" from biographical sources; "Huck and Jim," "Shooting of Boggs" and "Sollermun and 'Lizbeth" from *Huckleberry Finn;* "The War Prayer" from *Europe and Elsewhere;* "A Ghost Story" and "My Ancestor Satan" from the short stories; "Sunrise on the River" and "How I Stole My Name" from *Life on the Mississippi;* "The Virgin Mary" from *Ladies Home Journal.*

Also, from miscellaneous sources including sketches and essays, "Compliments Collection," "Chaucer, Sailor, Tennessee Girl," "My Cigar Habit?", "Smoke Rings," "A Cyclopedia of Sin," "San Francisco," "Crippling the Accordian," "Congress: The Grand Old Asylum," "Hunting the Cow," "My Encounter With an Interviewer," "Decay in the Art of Lying," "Taming the Bicycle," "Lynching and China," "The Christian Bible," "Is the Human Race a Joke?", "The Get Rich Quick Disease."

Lily Tomlin in "Appearing Nitely" (84). One-woman show with Lily Tomlin; written by Jane Wagner and Lily Tomlin. Produced by Ron Delsener at the Biltmore Theater. Opened March 24, 1977. (Closed June 12, 1977)

Directed by Jane Wagner and Lily Tomlin; staged by George Boyd; additional material by Cynthia Buchanan, Lorne Michaels, Patricia Resnick, Jim Rusk; music, Jerry Frankel; costume, J. Allen Highfill; lighting, Daniel Adams; sound, Jack Mann; associate producer, George Boyd; executive producer, Michael Tannen; stage manager, Brian Meister; press, The Merlin Group, Ltd.

Pot-pourri of characterizations and social comment, much of it in various veins of comedy.

*Mummenschanz (71). Program of Swiss pantomime. Produced by Arthur Shafman International, Ltd. at the Bijou Theater. Opened March 30, 1977.

Andrés Bossard	Bernie Schürch
Floriana Frassatoetto	

Production stage manager, Patrick Lecoq; production supervisor, Christopher Dunlop; press, Jeffrey Richards.

An entertainment of mime and masks, suggested by Swiss folk traditions, which has toured America annually since 1973. The program was presented in two parts.

*The Shadow Box (69). By Michael Cristofer. Produced by Lester Osterman, Ken Marsolais, Allan Francis and Leonard Soloway in the Mark Taper Forum/Long Wharf Theater production at the Morosco Theater. Opened March 31, 1977.

Interviewer	Josef Sommer	Mark	Mandy Patinkin
Cottage One:		Beverly	Patricia Elliott
Joe	Simon Oakland	Cottage Three:	
Steve	Vincent Stewart	Agnes	Rose Gregorio
Maggie	Joyce Ebert	Felicity	Geraldine Fitzgerald
Cottage Two:			
Brian	Laurence Luckinbill		

Standbys: Messrs. Oakland, Sommer — Richard Kuss; Misses Elliott, Gregorio — Pamela Lincoln; Misses Ebert, Fitzgerald — Sloane Shelton; Mr. Stewart — Dai Stockton; Mr. Patinkin — David Rasche; Mr. Luckinbill — Stephen Keep.

Directed by Gordon Davidson; scenery, Ming Cho Lee; costumes, Bill Walker; associate producers, Philip Getter, Bernard Stuchin; lighting, Ronald Wallace; production stage manager, Franklin Keysar; press, Betty Lee Hunt, Maria Cristina Pucci, Fred Hoot.

Time: The present. Place: Three cottages on the grounds of a large hospital. The play was presented in two parts.

Three terminally ill patients face death in different ways, but each more gracefully than their families. Previously produced at the Mark Taper Forum of the Center Theater Group, Gordon Davidson artistic director, in Los Angeles; and at the Long Wharf Theater, Arvin Brown artistic director, New Haven, Conn.

Mary Carver replaced Geraldine Fitzgerald 4/30/77. Clifton James replaced Simon Oakland 5/23/77.

A Best Play; see page 236.

Ladies at the Alamo (20). By Paul Zindel. Produced by Edgar Bronfman Jr. for Sagittarius Entertainment at the Martin Beck Theater. Opened April 7, 1977. (Closed April 23, 1977)

Dede Cooper	Estelle Parsons	Joanne Remington	Rosemary Murphy
Bella Gardner	Eileen Heckart	Shirley Fuller	Jan Farrand
Suits	Susan Peretz		

Understudies: Misses Parsons, Heckart — Marie Cheatham; Misses Murphy, Farrand — Jan Bowes; Miss Peretz — Maureen Sadusk.

Directed by Frank Perry; scenery, Peter Larkin; costumes, Ruth Morley; lighting, Marc B. Weiss; production stage manager, Marnel Sumner; stage manager, Maureen Sadusk; press, Michael Alpert Public Relations, Warren Knowlton.

Time: The present. Place: The Remington Room of a multi-million-dollar theater complex in Texas City, Tex. Act I: The ambush, early evening. Act II: Massacre, ten minutes later.

Women in conflict, as the rich and powerful chairman of a theater complex tries to oust the artistic director.

*Anna Christie (54). Revival of the play by Eugene O'Neill. Produced by Alexander H. Cohen, by arrangement with Gabrial Katzka and Edward L. Schuman at the Imperial Theater. Opened April 14, 1977.

Johnny-the-Priest	Richard Hamilton	Marthy Owen	Mary McCarty
Larry	Ken Harrison	Anna Christie	Liv Ullmann
Postman; Johnson	Jack Davidson	Mat Burke	John Lithgow
Chris Christopherson	Robert Donley		

Longshoremen: Edwin McDonough, Vic Polizos; Sailors: Vic Polizos, Ken Harrison.

Standby: Miss McCarty — Elsa Raven. Understudies: Messrs. Lithgow, Harrison — Edwin McDonough; Mr. Donley — Richard Hamilton; Mr. Hamilton — Jack Davidson; Messrs. Davidson, McDonough, Polizos — Alan Coleridge.

Directed by José Quintero; scenery and lighting, Ben Edwards; costumes, Jane Greenwood; coproduced by Hildy Parks and Roy A. Somlyo; production stage manager, George Martin; stage manager, Alan Coleridge; press, Richard Hummler, Martha Mason.

Time: 1912. Place: Act I: Johnny-the-Priest's saloon, near South Street, New York City, a fall afternoon. Act II: The stern of the barge "Simeon Winthrop" at anchor in the outer harbor of Provincetown, Mass., ten days later. Act III: Interior of a cabin on the "Simeon Winthrop" at dock in Boston harbor, two days later, early afternoon. Act IV: The cabin interior, two days later, 9 o'clock at night.

Anna Christie was first produced on Broadway 11/2/21 for 177 performances. Major New York revivals have occurred at the City Center 1/5/51 for 29 performances and in the musical version *New Girl in Town* 5/14/57 for 431 performances.

*I Love My Wife (51). Musical based on a play by Luis Rego; book and lyrics by Michael Stewart; music by Cy Coleman. Produced by Terry Allen Kramer and Harry Rigby, by arrangement with Joseph Kipness, at the Ethel Barrymore Theater. Opened April 17, 1977.

Cleo	Ilene Graff	Quentin	Joe Saulter
Monica	Joanna Gleason	Harvey	John Miller
Wally	James Naughton	Norman	Ken Bichel
Stanley	Michael Mark	Alvin	Lenny Baker

Understudies: Mr. Saulter — Warren Benbow; Mr. Miller — Michael Mark; Mr. Bichel — Joel Mofsenson; Mr. Mark — Michael Sergio.

Directed by Gene Saks; musical numbers staged by Onna White; musical direction, John Miller; scenery, David Mitchell; costumes, Ron Talsky; lighting, Gilbert V. Hemsley Jr.; arrangements, Cy Coleman; sound, Lou Gonzalez; associate producer, Frank Montalvo; production stage manager, Bob Vandergriff; stage manager, Tony Manzi; press, Henry Luhrman Associates, Anne Obert Weinberg, Terry M. Lilly.

Time: The present. Place: Trenton, N.J.

Comedy about two couples trying to indulge in wife-swapping and other sexual pastimes, based on a French play recently produced in Paris as *Viens Chez Moi, J'Habite Chez une Copine.*

ACT I

"We're Still Friends"	Company
"Monica"	Alvin, Monica, Four Guys
"By Threes"	Wally, Alvin, Harvey
"A Mover's Life"	Alvin, Four Guys
"Love Revolution"	Cleo
"Someone Wonderful I Missed"	Monica, Cleo
"Sexually Free"	Alvin, Cleo, Wally

ACT II

"Hey There, Good Times"	Harvey, Stanley, Quentin, Norman
"Lovers on Christmas Eve"	Monica, Wally, Norman
"Scream"	Harvey, Stanley, Quentin, Norman
"Everybody Today Is Turning On"	Alvin, Wally
"Married Couple Seeks Married Couple"	Alvin, Cleo, Wally, Monica
"I Love My Wife"	Alvin, Wally

*Side by Side by Sondheim (50). Revue with lyrics by Stephen Sondheim; music by Stephen Sondheim, Leonard Bernstein, Mary Rodgers, Richard Rodgers and Jule Styne. Produced by Harold Prince in association with Ruth Mitchell, by arrangement with The Incomes Company, Ltd., at the Music Box. Opened April 18, 1977.

David Kernan
Millicent Martin

Julie N. McKenzie
Ned Sherrin

Pianists: Daniel Troob, Albin Konopka.

Alternate: Mr. Sherrin — Fernanda Maschwitz. Standbys: Miss Martin — Carol Swarbrick; Miss McKenzie — Bonnie Schon; Mr. Kernan — Jack Blackton.

Directed by Ned Sherrin; musical direction, Ray Cook, musical staging, Bob Howe; scenery, Peter Docherty; costumes, Florence Klotz; lighting, Ken Billington; scenery supervision, Jay Moore; musical supervision, Paul Gemignani; stage manager, John Grigas; press, Mary Bryant, Bruce Cohen.

Compendium of Stephen Sondheim numbers from *A Funny Thing Happened on the Way to the Forum, Gypsy, A Little Night Music, Company, Evening Primrose, Follies, The Seven Per Cent Solution, Anyone Can Whistle, Do I Hear a Waltz? West Side Story, The Mad Show* and *Pacific overtures,* with music by Sondheim and other composers, originally produced in London by H. M. Tennent, Ltd. and Cameron MacKintosh in association with the Mermaid Theater.

PART I: "Comedy Tonight," "Love Is in the Air," "If Momma Was Married" (music by Jule Styne). "You Must Meet My Wife," "The Little Things You Do Together," "Getting Married Today," "I Remember, "Can That Boy Foxtrot," "Company," "Another Hundred People," "Barcelona," "Marry Me a Little," "I Never Do Anything Twice," "Bring on the Girls," "Ah, Paree!", "Buddy's Blues," "Broadway Baby," "You Could Drive a Person Crazy."

PART II: "Everybody Says Don't," "Anyone Can Ahistle, "Send in the Clowns," "We're Gonna Be All Right" (music by Richard Rodgers), "A Boy Like That" and "I Have a Love" (music by Leonard Bernstein),

"The Boy From . . . " (music by Mary Rodgers), "Pretty Lady," "You Gotta Have a Gimmick" (music by Jule Styne), "Losing My Mind," "Could I Leave You?", "I'm Still Here," Conversation Piece (arranged by Carl Brahms and Stuart Pedlar), "Side by Side by Side."

La Guerre de Troie N'Aura Pas Lieu (13). Revival of the play in the French language by Jean Giraudoux. Produced by Le Tréteau de Paris and Jean de Rigault with the 55th Street Dance Theater Foundation in the Le Théâtre de la Ville (Jean Mercure animateur-directeur) production at the City Center. Opened April 20, 1977. (Closed April 30, 1977)

Andromaque	Dominique Jayr	Abneos	Angelo Bardi
Cassandre	Isa Mercure	Busiris	Jean Mercure
Hector	José-Marie Flotats	Suivant; Marin	Serge Peyrat
Paris	Bernard Giraudeau	Oiax	Lionel Baylac
Demokos	Maurice Chevit	Ulysse	Jean-Pierre Aumont
Hecube	Jandeline	Gabier	Lafleur
La Paix	Djanet Lachmet	Olpides	Coussonneau
Troilus	Pascal Sellier	Garde	Georges Joannon

Servants: Virginia Duvernoy, Bernadette Lange, Hélène Zanicoli. Messengers: Michel Feder, Jean-Luc Russier.

Directed by Jean Mercure; scenery and costumes, Yannis Kokkos; incidental music, Marc Wilkinson; stage manager, Alain Tartas; press, Ted Goldsmith, Arthur Rubine.

This was the first professional New York production of the original Giraudoux play, translated by Christopher Fry as *Tiger at the Gates*, last produced by Repertory Theater of Lincoln Center 2/29/68 for 44 performances.

*Annie (46). Musical based on the Harold Gray comic strip *Little Orphan Annie;* book by Thomas Meehan; music by Charles Strouse; lyrics by Martin Charnin. Produced by Mike Nichols and Lewis Allen at the Alvin Theater. Opened April 21, 1977.

Molly	Danielle Brisebois	Lt. Ward; Morgenthau;	
Pepper	Robyn Finn	Justice Brandeis	Richard Ensslen
Duffy	Donna Graham	Harry; FDR	Raymond Thorne
July	Janine Ruane	Sophie; Cecille; Star-to-Be; Bonnie	
Tessie	Diana Barrows	Boylan; Perkins	Laurie Beechman
Kate	Shelley Bruce	Grace Farrell	Sandy Faison
Annie	Andrea McArdle	Drake	Edwin Bordo
Miss Hannigan	Dorothy Loudon	Mrs. Pugh; Connie Boylan	Edie Cowan
Bundles McCloskey; Sound Effects Man;		Annette; Ronnie Boylan	Penny Worth
Ickes	James Hosbein	Oliver Warbucks	Reid Shelton
Dog Catcher; Jimmy Johnson; Honor		Rooster Hannigan	Robert Fitch
Guard	Steven Boockvor	Lily	Barbara Erwin
Dog Catcher; Bert Healy; Kaltenborn's		Fred McCracken; Hopkins	Bob Freschi
Voice; Hull	Donald Craig	NBC Page	Mari McMinn
Sandy	Himself		

Hooverville-ites, Policemen, Warbucks's Servants, New Yorkers: Laurie Beechman, Steven Boockvor, Edwin Bordo, Edie Cowan, Donald Craig, Richard Ensslen, Barbara Erwin, Bob Freschi, James Hosbein, Mari McMinn, Penny Worth.

Standby: Miss McArdle — Kirsten Vigard. Understudies: Mr. Shelton — Raymond Thorne; Miss Loudon — Penny Worth; Miss Faison — Mari McMinn; Mr. Fitch — Steven Boockvor; Misses. Graham, Finn, Bruce, Barrows — Janine Ruane; Miss Brisebois — Shelley Bruce; Miss Ruane — Donna Graham; Mr. Thorne — Donald Craig; Miss Erwin — Edie Cowan; Messrs. Bordo, Craig — Bob Freschi; Sandy — Arf; Ensemble — Don Bonnell.

Directed by Martin Charnin; musical numbers choreographed by Peter Gennaro; musical direction and dance music arrangements, Peter Howard; scenery, David Mitchell; costumes, Theoni V. Aldredge; lighting, Judy Rasmuson; orchestrations, Philip J. Lang; producers, Irwin Meyer, Stephen R. Friedman, Alvin Nederlander Associates, Inc., Icarus Productions; associate producer, Peter Crane; production stage manager, Janet Beroza; stage manager, Jack Timmers; press, David Powers.

Time: Act I, Dec. 11-19, 1933; Act II, Dec. 21-25, 1933.

The familiar comic strip characters — Annie, Daddy Warbucks, Sandy, etc. — in a sentimental but lightly-seasoned memento of the Depression era and FDR.

A Best Play; see page 146.

ACT I

The New York Municipal Orphanage (Girls' Annex)
"Maybe" .... Annie
"It's the Hard-Knock Life" .... Annie, Orphans
"It's the Hard-Knock Life" (Reprise) .... Orphans
St. Mark's Place
"Tomorrow" .... Annie
A Hooverville Under the 59th Street Bridge
"We'd Like to Thank You" .... Hooverville-ites
The Orphanage
"Little Girls" .... Miss Hannigan
The Warbucks Mansion at Fifth Avenue and 82d Street
"I Think I'm Gonna Like It Here" ....Grace, Annie, Drake, Cecille, Annette, Mrs. Pugh, Servants
New York City
"N.Y.C." ....Warbucks, Grace, Annie, Star-to-Be, New Yorkers
The Orphanage
"Easy Street" .... Miss Hannigan, Rooster, Lily
Warbucks's Study
"You Won't Be an Orphan for
Long" .... Grace, Drake, Mrs. Pugh, Cecille, Annette, Servants, Warbucks

ACT II

The NBC Radio Studio at 30 Rockefeller Plaza and the Orphanage
"You're Never Fully Dressed
Without a Smile" .... Bert Healy, Boylan Sisters, "Hour of Smiles" Family
The Orphanage
"You're Never Fully Dressed
Without a Smile" (Reprise) .... Orphans
"Easy Street" (Reprise) .... Miss Hannigan, Rooster, Lily
Washington: The White House
"Tomorrow" (Reprise) ....Annie, FDR, Warbucks, Cabinet
The Great Hall at the Warbucks Mansion
"Something Was Missing" .... Warbucks
"I Don't Need Anything But You" .... Warbucks, Annie
The East Ballroom of the Warbucks Mansion
"Annie" .... Grace, Drake, Staff
"Maybe" (Reprise) .... Annie
"A New Deal for Christmas" ....Annie, Warbucks, Grace, FDR, Staff

*The Basic Training of Pavlo Hummel (37). Revival of the play by David Rabe. Produced by Moe Septee and Carmen F. Zollo in the Theater Company of Boston production at the Longacre Theater. Opened April 24, 1977.

Pavlo Hummel	Al Pacino	Ryan	Michael Dinelli
Yen; 2d Viet Cong	Tisa Chang	Gomez	Kevin Maung
Ardell	Gustave Johnson	Capt. Saunders; Capt. Miller;	
1st Sgt. Tower	Joe Fields	Lt. Smith	Brad Sullivan
Cpl. Jackson	Jack Kehoe	Mickey	Ron Hunter
Squad:		Sorrentino	Andrea Masters
Parker	Max Wright	Mrs. Hummel	Rebecca Darke
Kress	Larry Bryggman	Jones	Don Blakely
Pierce	Lance Henriksen	Vietnamese Boy; 1st Viet Cong	Kevin Maung
Hinkle	Paul Guilfoyle	Mamasan; Vietnamese Farmer	Anne Miyamoto
Hendrix	John Aquino	Sgt. Brisbey	Richard Lynch
Parham	Damien Leake	Sgt. Wall	Sully Boyar
Burns	Gary Bolling	Pvt. Grennel	Gary Bolling

Understudies: Messrs. Johnson, Burns — Damien Leake; Mr. Kehoe — Ron Hunter; Messrs. Leake, Guilfoyle — Kevin Maung; Miss Darke — Andrea Masters; Mr. Blakely — Gary Bolling; Mr. Bryggman — John Aquino; Mr. Henriksen — Michael Dinelli; Mr. Dinelli — Paul Guilfoyle; Miss Masters, Mr. Maung — Tisa Chang; Fields — Don Blakely; Miss Chang — Anne Miyamoto.

Directed by David Wheeler; scenery, Robert Mitchell, costumes, Domingo Rodriguez; lighting, David F. Segal; production stage manager, Patrick Horrigan; stage manager, Barbara Dilker; press, Max Eisen, Judy Jacksina, Barbara Glenn.

Time: 1965-1967. Place: The United States Army. The play was presented in two parts.

The Basic Training of Pavlo Hummel was first produced off Broadway 5/20/71 for 363 performances by New York Shakespeare Festival. This Theater Company of Boston revival production was first presented in 1972.

*The King and I (33). Revival of the musical based on the novel *Anna and the King of Siam* by Margaret Landon; book and lyrics by Oscar Hammerstein II; music by Richard Rodgers. Produced by Lee Guber and Shelly Gross at the Uris Theater. Opened May 2, 1977.

Capt. Orton .... Larry Swansen	Tuptim .... June Angela
Louis Leonowens .... Alan Amick	Lady Thiang .... Hye-Young Choi
Anna Leonowens .... Constance Towers	Prince Chulalongkorn .... Gene Profanato
Interpreter .... Jae Woo Lee	Princess Ying .... Julie Woo
Kralahome .... Michael Kermoyan	Lun Tha .... Martin Vidnovic
King .... Yul Brynner	Sir Edward Ramsay .... John Michael King

Royal Dancers and Wives: Su Applegate, Jessica Chao, Lei-Lynne Doo, Dale Harimoto, Pamela Kalt, Susan Kikuchi, Faye Fujisaki Mar, Sumiko Murashima, Libby Rhodes, Cecile Santos, Hope Sogawa, Mary Ann Teng, Patricia K. Thomas.

Princesses and Princes: Ivan Ho, Clark Huang, Annie Lam, Connie Lam, Jennifer Lam, Paul Siu, Tim Waldrip, Kevan Weber, Kym Weber, Julie Woo, Mary Woo.

Nurses and Amazons: Sydney Smith, Marianne Tatum, Patricia K. Thomas, Rebecca West.

Priests and Slaves: Kaipo Daniels, Barrett Hong, Jae Woo Lee, Ric Ornellas, Simeon Den, Chandra Tanna, Robert Vega.

Standbys: Mr. Brynner — Michael Kermoyan; Miss Towers — Margot Moser. Understudies: Mr. Kermoyan — Jae Woo Lee; Miss Choi — Sumiko Murashima; Mr. Vidnovic — Robert Vega; Miss Angela — Pamela Kalt; Mr. Profanato — Ivan Ho; Mr. Amick — Tim Waldrip; Ballet: Simon — Patricia K. Thomas; Angel — Faye Fujisaki Mar; Uncle Thomas — Hope Sogawa; Topsy — Libby Rhodes; Swing Dancers — Ching Gonzalez, Alis-Elaine Anderson.

Directed by Yuriko; original choreography, Jerome Robbins; musical supervisor, Milton Rosenstock; musical direction, John Lesko; scenery, Peter Wolf; costumes, Stanley Simmons; lighting, Thomas Skelton; sound, Richard Fitzgerald; associate producer, Fred Walker; production stage manager, Ed Preston; stage managers, Conwell Worthington, Thomas J. Rees; press, Solters & Roskin, Inc., Joshua Ellis, Milly Schoenbaum, Fred H. Nathan.

Time: The 1860s. Place: In and around the King's palace in Bangkok, Siam. The play was presented in two parts.

The King and I was first produced on Broadway 3/29/51 for 1,246 performances. Its last major New York revival was by the City Center Light Opera Company 5/23/68 for 10 performances.

The list of musical numbers in *The King and I* appears on page 360 of *The Best Plays of 1950-51*.

ACT II Ballet, "The Small House of Uncle Thomas": Narrator — June Angela; Uncle Thomas — Jessica Chao; Topsy — Lei-Lynne Doo; Little Eva — Dale Harimoto; Eliza — Susan Kikuchi; King Simon — Rebecca West; Angel — Patricia Weber; Royal Dancers — Barrett Hong, Faye Fukisaki Mar, Ric Ornellas, Libby Rhodes, Simeon Den, Cecile Santos, Sydney Smith, Hope Sogawa, Chandra Tanna, Patricia K. Thomas; Propmen — Kaipo Daniels, Jae Woo Lee, Thomas J. Rees, Robert Vega.

*Happy End (28). Musical revival based on a German play by "Dorothy Lane" (Elisabeth Hauptmann); music by Kurt Weill; lyrics by Bertolt Brecht; book and lyrics adapted by Michael Feingold; production newly conceived by Robert Kalfin. Produced by Michael Harvey and The Chelsea Theater Center, Robert Kalfin artistic director, Michael David executive director, at the Martin Beck Theater. Opened May 7, 1977 matinee; see note.

The Gang:	The Army:
Bill Cracker .... Christopher Lloyd	Lt. Lillian Holliday .... Meryl Streep
Sam Wurlizer .... Benjamin Rayson	Maj. Stone .... Liz Sheridan
"Governor" Nakamura .... Tony Azito	Capt. Hannibal Jackson .... Joe Grifasi
Jimmy Dexter .... John A. Coe	Sister Mary .... Prudence Wright Holmes
Bob Marker .... Robert Weil	Sister Jane .... Alexandra Borrie
"Baby Face" Flint .... Raymond J. Barry	Brother Ben Owens .... Christopher Cara
"The Fly" .... Grayson Hall	A Cop .... David Pursley
Miriam .... Donna Emmanuel	

The Fold: Kristin Jolliff, Frank Kopyc, Tom Mardirosian, Martha Miller, Victor Pappas.

Musicians: Dennis Anderson clarinet, tenor and bass saxophone; Mark Belair percussion; Roland Gagnon piano; Allan Jaffee guitar, banjo; Grant Keast trumpet, librarian; Billy Kerr, flute, clarinets, alto saxophone, contractor; William Rohdin trumpet; William Schimmel accordion, harmonium, associate conductor; Jonathan Taylor trombone.

Standby: Mr. Lloyd — Bob Gunton. Understudies: Miss Streep — Alexandra Borrie; Miss Borrie — Donna Emmanuel; Misses Emmanuel, Holmes — Kristin Jolliff; Mr. Grifasi — Frank Kopyc; Messrs. Barry, Pursley — Tom Mardirosian; Misses Sheridan, Hall — Martha Miller; Messrs. Azito, Weil — Victor Pappas; Messrs. Rayson, Coe — David Pursley.

Directed and staged by Robert Kalfin and Patricia Birch; musical direction, Roland Gagnon; scenery, Robert U. Taylor; costumes, Carrie F. Robbins; lighting, Jennifer Tipton; associate producer, Wilder Luke Burnap; production stage manager, Mark Wright; stage manager, Charles Kindl; press, Susan Bloch.

An unlikely twain — Salvation Army and gangsters — meet in the Chicago of the roaring 1920s. The attributed source of the book of *Happy End*, "Dorothy Lane" is fictitious; its exact source is unclear, but it may have been suggested to Brecht by his secretary, Elisabeth Hauptmann. It was first produced in Berlin in 1929 and musical excerpts have been interpolated into the New York revues *The World of Kurt Weill in Song* 6/6/63 for 245 performances and *Whores, Wars and Tin Pan Alley* 6/16/69 for 72 performances. The present adaptation was previously produced by Yale Repertory Theater, New Haven, Conn.

Note: This production was previously presented off Broadway by Chelsea Theater Center 3/8/77-4/30/77 for 56 performances, after which it transferred to Broadway.

The list of scenes and musical numbers in *Happy End* appears in its entry in the "Plays Produced off Broadway" section of this volume.

Vieux Carré (7). By Tennessee Williams. Produced by Golden Eagle Productions, Inc. and George R. Nice in association with Ruth Hercolani at the St. James Theater. Opened May 11, 1977. (Closed May 15, 1977)

Writer	Richard Alfieri	Tye	John William Reilly
Mrs. Wire	Sylvia Sidney	Photographer	Jed Cooper
Nursie	Gertrude Jeanette	1st Patrolman	Bill Perley
Jane	Diane Kagan	Judge (Voice)	Robert Colson
Painter	Tom Aldredge	Ida	Toni Darnay
Blake; 2d Patrolman	Reb Brownell	Bess	Lois Holmes
Angel	Grace Carney	Ella	Sharon Morrison
Miss Carrie	Iris Whitney	Guide	Robert Colson
Mrs. Wayne	Olive Deering		

Understudies: Misses Sidney, Deering — Toni Darnay; Mr. Alfieri — Jed Cooper; Miss Kagan — Sharon Morrison; Mr. Aldredge — William Perley; Misses Whitney, Carney — Lois Holmes; Miss Jeanette — Lil Henderson; Messrs. Perley, Colson, Brownell — William Pomeroy; Messrs. Cooper, Reilly — Reb Brownell.

Directed by Arthur Allan Seidelman; scenery and lighting, James Tilton; costumes, Jane Greenwood; incidental music, Galt MacDermot; associate producers, Milton Justice, Eleanor Fortus, May Grindrod, Christopher Rote, Myles Spector; production stage manager, Lee Murray; press, David Lipsky.

Time: In the late 1930s. Place: New Orleans, the French Quarter. Act I: January. Act II: Late April.

The acts are titled *The Angel in the Alcove* (Act I) and *I Never Get Dressed Until After Dark on Sundays* (Act II) and are complete playlets with overlapping characters (boarders in a rooming house) — the first centered on a homosexual relationship between a young writer and an elderly semi-invalid painter, the second on a stud and his sexually avid mistress.

*Toller Cranston's The Ice Show (15). Produced by Dennis Bass and Robin Cranston at the Palace Theater. Opened May 19, 1977.

Emily Benenson	Mark Hominuke
Barbara Berezowski	Candy Jones
Wendy Burge	Kath Malmberg
Jack Courtney	Gordon McKellen Jr.
Toller Cranston	Jim Millns
Don Fraser	Colleen O'Connor
Elizabeth Freeman	David Porter
Janet Hominuke	Ken Shelley

Produced and directed by Myrl A. Schreibman; executive producers, Dennis Bass, Robin Cranston; scenery, Anthony Sabatino, William H. Harris; costumes, Miles White; lighting, D. Scott Linder; sound, Jack Shirk; music supervision, Bill Courtney; skating consultant, Bill Turner; original musical, Al Kasha, Joel Hirshhorn; choreography and staging, Brian Foley; additional choreography, Ellen Burka; production stage manager, Joe Lorden; stage manager, Judith Binus; press, Seymour Krawitz, Patricia McLean Krawitz.

Ice show tailored for Canadian skating champion Toller Cranston.

ACT I: Overture and introduction (composed by Al Kasha and Joel Hirshhorn) — Company.

Trilogy: Thus Spake Zarathustra — Don Fraser, Candy Jones; Candide — Elizabeth Freeman; Somewhere — David Porter, Barbara Berezowski; Captain From Castile — Fraser, Jones, Freeman, Porter, Berezowski; Son of a Gun — Ken Shelley, Colleen O'Connor; Let's Hear It for Me — Wendy Burge; Free Again — Kath Malmberg; On the Waterfront — Emily Benenson, Jack Courtney; Nicholas and Alexandra — Toller Cranston.

Dance Medley: Rock Around the Clock — Jones, Fraser; Charleston — Courtney, Benenson; Tango — Courtney, Benenson; Nola — Jones, Fraser; Sugar Blues — Berezowski, Porter; Fascination, Varsity Drag, Dark Town Strutters Ball — Couples. My Wife the Dancer — Gordon McKellen Jr.

Russian Ode: The Young and the Restless — Jim Millns, O'Connor; Innocence — Janet and Mark Hominuke; Love Duet — Cranston, Benenson; The Warlords — McKellen, Courtney; Loneliness of War — Cranston; Vision — Porter, Berezowski; Dream of Love — Cranston, Benenson; Emptiness and Longing — Cranston.

Act II: (Toller's Ball) Le Prophète — Company; Graduation Ball I — Cranston; Corsaire I — Fraser, Jones; Graduation Ball II — Cranston; Corsaire II — Millns, O'Connor; Graduation Ball III — Cranston; Le Prophète (Reprise) — Company; Gaité Parisienne — Freeman; Raymonda — Burge; Pas de Deux — The Hominukes; Black Orpheus — Malmberg; MacArthur Park — McKellen; Tick-Tock — Fraser, Jones.

Latino: Rodrigo — Courtney, Benenson; Habanera — Millns, O'Connor; La Carioca — Porter, Berezowski; Scheherazade — Shelley; A Fifth of Beethoven — Millns, O'Connor; I Pagliacci — Cranston; Finale — Company.

*Gemini (9). By Albert Innaurato. Produced by Jerry Arrow and Jay Broad, the Circle Repertory Company (Marshall W. Mason production supervisor) and PAF Playhouse at the Little Theater. Opened May 21, 1977; see note.

Francis Geminiani	Robert Picardo	Herschel Weinberger	Jonathan Hadary
Bunny Weinberger	Jessica James	Fran Gemininiani	Danny Aiello
Randy Hastings	Reed Birney	Lucille Pompi	Anne DeSalvo
Judith Hastings	Carol Potter		

Directed by Peter Mark Schifter; scenery, Christopher Nowak; costumes, Ernest Allen Smith; lighting, Larry Crimmins; sound, Leslie E. DeWeerdt; production stage manager, Fred Reinglas; press, Rima Corben.

Place: South Philadelphia, the Geminiani-Weinberger backyard. Act I, Scene 1: June 1, 1973, early morning. Scene 2: That evening. Act II, Scene 1: June 2, 1973, morning. Scene 2: That evening.

Emotional growing pains, a brother and sister are both attracted to the same lover. Previously produced off off Broadway at Playwrights Horizons and at the PAF Playhouse, Huntingdon Sta., L.I.

NOTE: This production of *Gemini* was presented off Broadway from 3/13/77 to 5/1/77 for 63 performances before being transferred to Broadway for an additional run. See its entry in the "Plays Produced off Broadway" section of this volume.

PLAYS WHICH CLOSED PRIOR TO BROADWAY OPENING

Plays which were organized by New York producers for Broadway presentation but which closed during their tryout performances are listed below.

The Baker's Wife. Musical based on the play and film *La Femme du Boulanger* by Marcel Pagnol and Jean Giono; book by Joseph Stein; music and lyrics by Stephen Schwartz. Produced by David Merrick in pre-Broadway tryouts at the Dorothy Chandler Pavilion in Los Angeles, the Curran Theater in San Francisco, the Muni Theater in St. Louis, the Shubert Theater in Boston and the John F. Kennedy Center for the Performing Arts Opera House in Washington, D.C. Opened May 11, 1976. (Closed in Washington November 13, 1976)

Claude	Charles Rule	Antoine	Gordon Connell
Denise	Teri Ralston	Therese	Portia Nelson
Priest	David Rounds	Le Marquis	Keene Curtis
Barnaby	Pierre Epstein	Aimable	Paul Sorvino
Henriette	Darlene Conley	Genevieve	Patti LuPone
M. Robert	Timothy Jerome	Dominique	Kurt Peterson
Jean-Paul	Bill Mullikin	Raoul	Tony Schultz

Le Marquis's "Nieces": Tara Leigh, Cynthia Parva, Jean McLaughlin.

Understudies: Messrs. Sorvino, Connell, Rule — Michael Quinn; Messrs. Curtis, Rounds, Jerome, Epstein — Bill Mullikin; Misses Ralston, Nelson, Conley — Denise Lor; Miss LuPone — Teri Ralston; Messrs. Peterson, Shultz, Mullikin — Francisco Lagueruela; Nieces — Kathleen Robey.

Directed by John Berry; musical numbers staged by Robert Tucker; musical direction, Robert Billig; scenery, Jo Mielziner; costumes, Theoni V. Aldredge; lighting, Jennifer Tipton; dance music, Daniel Troob; orchestrations, Don Walker; production stage manager, Robert Borod; stage manager, Pat Trott; press, Solters & Roskin, Inc., Joshua Ellis, Milly Schoenbaum, Fred H. Nathan.

Time: The recent past. Place: A small village in Provence, France.

Musicalization of the Pagnol film *The Baker's Wife*, in which the young woman of the title runs off with a farmhand.

ACT I

Overture

"Chanson"	Denise
"Merci, Madame"	Aimable, Genevieve
"Gifts of Love"	Genevieve, Aimable
"The Baking"	Aimable, Villagers
"Bread"	Aimable, Villagers
"Not in the Market"	Dominique, Genevieve
"Serenade"	Dominique, Raoul, Aimable, Genevieve
"Meadowlark"	Genevieve
"Perfect Every Time"	Aimable
"Any Day Now Day"	Aimable, Villagers

ACT II

Entr'acte

"Chanson" (Reprise)	Denise
"Endless Delights"	Genevieve, Dominique
"The Luckiest Man in the World"	Claude, Antoine, Barnaby, Marquis, Nieces, Villagers
"What's a Man to Do?"	Aimable, Denise, Therese, Henriette
"If I Have to Live Alone"	Aimable
"Where Is the Warmth?"	Genevieve
Finale	Genevieve, Aimable

The Bed Before Yesterday. By Ben Travers. Produced by Arthur Cantor, by arrangement with H. M. Tennent, Inc., in pre-Broadway tryouts at the Playhouse in Wilmington, Del., the Locust Theater in Philadelphia, the Colonial Theater in Boston, the Morris A. Mechanic Theater in Baltimore, the Parker Theater in Ft. Lauderdale, Fla. and the Royal Poinciana Theater in Palm Beach, Fla. Opened October 22, 1976. (Closed in Palm Beach January 15, 1977)

Victor Keene	Elliott Reid	Lolly Tucker	Ludi Claire
Alma	Carol Channing	Felix	Barry Vigon
Mrs. Holly	Barbara Lester	Fred Castle	Paxton Whitehead
Aubrey	Henry Dibling	Taxi Driver	John Neville-Andrews
Ella	Caroline McWilliams		

Understudies: Miss Claire — Barbara Lester; Misses McWilliams, Lester — Lois Battle; Messrs. Vigon, Whitehead — John Neville-Andrews.

Directed by Lindsay Anderson; scenery, John Lee Beatty; costumes, Mary McKinley; lighting, Neil Peter Jampolis; associate producer, Eric Friedheim; production manager, Mitchell Erickson; stage manager, T. L. Boston; press, Solters & Roskin, Inc., Milly Schoenbaum.

Time: Spring and summer, 1930. Place: Brompton Mews, London. The play was presented in two acts and six scenes.

Comedy, a middle-aged widow's sexual emergence. A foreign play previously produced in London.

Hellzapoppin. Musical revue based on a format by Olsen and Johnson; written by Abe Burrows, Bill Heyer and Hank Beebe; music by Jule Styne and Hank Beebe; lyrics by Carolyn Leigh and Bill Heyer; additional song by Cy Coleman and Carolyn Leigh. Produced by Alexander H. Cohen, in association with Maggie and Jerome Minskoff, in pre-Broadway tryouts at the Morris A. Mechanic Theater in Baltimore, the National

Theater in Washington and the Colonial Theater in Boston. Opened November 22, 1976. (Closed in Boston January 22, 1977)

Mace Barrett	Brandon Maggart
Tom Batten	Michael Mann
Marie Berry	P. J. Mann
Terry Calloway	Dana Jo Moore
Jill Choder	Rich Pessagno
Susan Danielle	Lynn Redgrave
Herb Edelman	Rodney Reiner
Mercedes Ellington	Terry Rieser
Joey Faye	Catherine Rice
Robert Fitch	Jeff Richards
Trudie Green	Tudi Roach
Lisa Guignard	Jane Robertson
Lisa Haapaniemi	Karen St. George
Bob Harvey	Fred Siretta
Peter Heuchling	Robin Stone
Gwen Hillier	The Villams
Justine Johnston	The Volantes
Holly Jones	Bob Williams & Louie
Jerry Lewis	Melanie Winter
Leonardo	

Directed by Jerry Adler; choreography, Donald Saddler; musical conductor, John Lesko; musical supervision, Elliot Lawrence; scenery and lighting, Robert Randolph; costumes, Alvin Colt; sound, Jack Shearing; orchestrations, Ralph Burns; dance music, Gordon Lowry Harrell; co-producers, Hildy Parks, Roy A. Somlyo; production stage manager, Marnel Sumner; stage manager, Michael Turque; press, David Powers, Owen Levy; creative development, Richard Hummler.

Billed as "A Musical Circus," a new edition of the action-packed Olsen & Johnson revue concept which was produced on Broadway 9/22/38 for 404 performances.

ACT I: "Hellzapoppin" (by Jule Styne and Carolyn Leigh) — Company; The Villams; "A Husband, a Lover, a Wife" (by Hank Beebe and Bill Heyer) — Lynn Redgrave, Brandon Maggart; "Bouncing Back for More" (by Cy Coleman and Carolyn Leigh) — Jerry Lewis, Company; "Eighth Avenue" (by Jule Styne and Carolyn Leigh) — Redgrave, Ladies; Bob Williams & Louie; "Once I've Got My Cane" (by Hank Beebe and Bill Heyer) — Lewis, Ladies.

ACT II: "Hello, Mom" (by Hank Beebe and Bill Heyer) — Company; The Volantes; "Back to Him" (by Hank Beebe and Bill Heyer) — Lewis; "A Hymn to Her" (by Hank Beebe and Bill Heyer) — Redgrave, Hellzapoppin Glee Club; "A Miracle Happened" (by Hank Beebe and Bill Heyer) — Jill Choder; "Eighth Avenue" (Reprise); Leonardo; "One to a Customer" (by Jule Styne and Carolyn Leigh) — Lewis; Finale — Company.

The Dream. By Richard Lortz; from the book of Lucy Freeman. Produced by Joel W. Schenker in a pre-Broadway tryout at the Forrest Theater in Philadelphia. Opened February 7, 1977. (Closed February 12, 1977)

Dr. William Ames	Lee Richardson	James Browne	Michael Wager
Lt. Lonegan	Michael Higgins	Norma Dodd	Ann Wedgeworth
Elaine Thomas	Barbara Baxley	Jonathan Thomas	Keith Charles
Susan Michaels	Louise Sorel		

Understudies: Misses Baxley, Wedgeworth, Sorel — Lynda Myles; Messrs. Richardson, Higgins — Frank Latimore; Messrs. Wager, Charles — Wayne Carson.

Directed by Edwin Sherin; scenery, William Ritman; costumes, Theoni V. Aldredge; lighting, Marc B. Weiss; special effects, Charles Gross; production stage manager, John Actman; stage manager, Wayne Carson; press, Max Eisen, Barbara Glenn, Judy Jacksina.

Time: The present, midsummer. The play was presented in two parts.

Melodrama, a murder is solved by means of psychoanalytical techniques.

PLAYS PRODUCED
OFF BROADWAY

Some distinctions between off-Broadway and Broadway productions at one end of the scale and off-off-Broadway productions at the other were blurred in the New York theater of the 1970s. For the purposes of this *Best Plays* listing the term "off Broadway" is used to distinguish a professional from a showcase (off off Broadway) production and signifies a show which opened for general audiences in a mid-Manhattan theater seating 299 or fewer and 1) employed an Equity cast, 2) planned a regular schedule of 7 or 8 performances a week and 3) offered itself to public comment by critics at designated opening performances.

Occasional exceptions of inclusion (never of exclusion) are made to take in selected Brooklyn productions, visiting troupes, borderline cases and a few non-qualifying productions which readers might expect to find in this list because they appear under an off-Broadway heading in other major sources of record.

Figures in parentheses following a play's title give number of performances. These figures are acquired directly from the production offices and do not include previews or extra non-profit performances.

Plays marked with an asterisk (*) were still running on June 1, 1977. Their number of performances is figured from opening night through May 31, 1977 (many June closings aren't marked with an asterisk and are figured for the entire run).

In a listing of a show's numbers — dances, sketches, musical scenes, etc. — the titles of songs are identified by their appearance in quotation marks (").

Most entries of off-Broadway productions which ran fewer than 20 performances are somewhat abbreviated.

HOLDOVERS FROM PREVIOUS SEASONS

Plays which were running on June 1, 1976 are listed below. More detailed information about them appears in previous *Best Plays* volumes of appropriate years. Important cast changes since opening night are recorded in a section of this volume.

*The Fantasticks (7,115; longest continuous run of record in the American theater). Musical suggested by the play *Les Romantiques* by Edmond Rostand; book and lyrics by Tom Jones; music by Harvey Schmidt. Opened May 3, 1960.

Godspell (2,124; off Broadway's third longest run). Musical based on the Gospel according to St. Matthew; conceived by John-Michael Tebelak; music and lyrics by Stephen Schwartz. Opened May 17, 1971. (Closed June 13, 1976 and transferred to Broadway; see its entry in the "Plays Produced on Broadway" section of this volume)

Let My People Come (1,327). Musical revue with music and lyrics by Earl Wilson Jr. Opened January 8, 1974. (Closed July 5, 1976 and transferred to Broadway; see its entry in the "Plays Produced on Broadway" section of this volume)

Boy Meets Boy (463). Musical with book by Billy Solly and Donald Ward; music and lyrics by Billy Solly. Opened September 17, 1975. (Closed November 14, 1976)

Tuscaloosa's Calling Me ... But I'm Not Going (429). Musical review by Bill Heyer, Hank Beebe and Sam Dann; music by Hank Beebe; lyrics by Bill Heyer. Opened December 1, 1975. (Closed December 12, 1976)

Eden (181). By Steve Carter. Opened March 3, 1976. (Closed August 1, 1976)

*Vanities (506). By Jack Heifner. Opened March 22, 1976.

Streamers (478). By David Rabe. Opened April 21, 1976. (Closed June 5, 1977)

Women Behind Bars (311). Return engagement of the play by Tom Eyen. Opened April 25, 1976. (Closed January 26, 1977)

New York Shakespeare Festival Public Theater. So Nice, They Named It Twice (47). By Neil Harris. Opened May 5, 1976. (Closed June 13, 1976) **Rebel Women** (40). By Thomas Babe. Opened May 6, 1976. (Closed June 20, 1976). **For Colored Girls Who Have Considered Suicide/When the Rainbow is Enuf** (120). By Ntozake Shangé. Opened May 17, 1976. (Closed August 29, 1976 and transferred to Broadway; see its entry in the "Plays Produced on Broadway" section of this volume)

The Light Opera of Manhattan. The Student Prince (54). Revival of the operetta with book and lyrics by Dorothy Donnelly; music by Sigmund Romberg. Opened May 11, 1976. (Closed August 1, 1976)

PLAYS PRODUCED JUNE 1, 1976 — MAY 31, 1977

The Negro Ensemble Company. 1975-76 schedule of three programs ended with **Livin' Fat** (61). By Judi Ann Mason. Produced by The Negro Ensemble Company, Douglas Turner Ward artistic director, Robert Hooks executive director, Frederick Garrett administrative director, Gerald S. Krone director of special projects, at the St. Marks Playhouse. Opened June 1, 1976. (Closed July 18, 1976)

Big Mama	Minnie Gentry	Candy	Joyce Sylvester
Mama	Frances Foster	David Lee	Dean Irby
Daddy	Wayne Elbert	Boo	Frankie Faison

Directed by Douglas Turner Ward; scenery and costumes, Mary Mease Warren; lighting, Sandra L. Ross; production stage manager, Horacena J. Taylor; title song composed and arranged by Jothan Callins, lyrics by Douglas Turner Ward, sung by Hattie Winston; press, Howard Atlee, Clarence Allsopp, Meg Gordean.

Self-described as a "soul farce" about a poor Southern black family enjoying a morally dubious windfall of cash.

Roundabout Theater Center. 1975-76 schedule of four programs ended with **The World of Sholom Aleichem** (67). Revival of the play by Arnold Perl. Produced by the Roundabout Theater Center, Gene Feist producing director, Michael Fried executive producer, by special arrangement with Nancy Perl at the Roundabout Theater/Stage One. Opened June 11, 1976; press date July 11, 1976. (Closed August 8, 1976)

Mendel, the Book Seller .... Dick Shawn

PERFORMER	"THE FIDDLE"	"A TALE OF CHELM"	"BONTCHE SCHWEIG"	"THE HIGH SCHOOL"
Jack Aaron		Rabbi David	Bontche Schweig	Man at List; Maxl
Mark Blum	Rabbi Zorach		1st Angel	Man at Party
Ed Hall	Sholom	Stranger; Dodi	Presiding Angel	Tutor

PERFORMER	"THE FIDDLE"	"A TALE OF CHELM"	"BONTCHE SCHWEIG"	"THE HIGH SCHOOL"
Rita Karin	Raisel Klotz	Goatseller	3d Angel	Aunt Reba
Derek Meader	Pinney		4th Angel	Kholyava
Paul Regina	Belltax		5th Angel	Moishe
Dick Shawn	Father; Berodka; Colonel			Aaron Katz
Michele Shay	Bunya; Bathseba	Angel Rochele	Defending Angel	Woman at List
Suzanne Shepherd	Tante Friedl	Rifkele	2d Angel	2d Woman at List
Carol Teitel		Friend	6th Angel	Hannah
Michael Tucker		Melamed	Prosecuting Angel	Principal

Directed by Larry Arrick; scenery, Akita Yoshimura; costumes, Dianne Chapman; lighting, Cheryl Thacker; music, Robert De Cormier; musical supervision, Barbara Damashek; sculpture, Jordan Steckel; costume supervision, David Chapman; production stage manager, Douglas F. Goodman; press, David Guc.

Program of four dramatized folk tales all with a Sholom Aleichem flavor but not all his authorship, first produced off Broadway 5/1/53.

The Roundabout Theater Center also offered a workshop production of Ivan Turgenev's *A Month in the Country* in a new adaptation by David Morgan, directed by Ronald Roston, 6/9/76-6/26/76 for 12 performances.

Beware the Jubjub Bird (2). By Sandra Jennings. Produced by Pegasus III at Theater Four. Opened June 14, 1976. (Closed June 15, 1976)

Directed by Harold Guskin; scenery and lighting, Lee Goldman; music, Sandra Jennings, Richard Cameron; production stage manager, Janet Sonenberg; press, David Powers. With Jenny Sanford, Kevin Kline, Peter G. Skinner, Cheryl Scammon, Jared Sakren.

Play with five songs entangling the lives and emotions of actors with a play they are rehearsing, Chekhov's *The Seagull.*

Becoming (2). Musical by Gail Edwards and Sam Harris. Produced by Heartsong Productions in association with Drew Murphy, Dennis I. Gould associate producer, at Circle in the Square Downtown. Opened June 15, 1976. (Closed June 16, 1976)

Directed and choreographed by John Mineo; musical direction, Robert Stecko; scenery, Dan Leigh; costumes, Dee Dee Fote; production supervisor, James Zitlow; press, Max Eisen, Judy Jacksina. With Norman Meister, Anne Sward, Gail Edwards.

Musical variety show developed at University of Miami, Fla.

Sexual Perversity in Chicago and **Duck Variations** (273). Program of two one-act plays by David Mamet. Produced by Lawrence Goossen and Jeffrey Wachtel at the Cherry Lane Theater. Opened June 16, 1976. (Closed April 17, 1977)

SEXUAL PERVERSITY IN CHICAGO

Bernard Litko .... F. Murray Abraham
Deborah Soloman .... Jane Anderson
Danny Shapiro .... Peter Riegert
Joan Webber .... Gina Rogers
Time: A period of nine weeks one summer. Place: Various places around the North Side of Chicago.

DUCK VARIATIONS

George S. Aronovitz .... Michael Egan

Emil Varec .... Mike Kellin
Place: A park. The Variations: 1. "It's nice, the park is nice" 2. "The duck's life" 3. "Also they got barnyard ducks" 4. "The duck is not like us" 5. "Did you know what I was reading" 6. "What kind of a world it is" 7. "Yes, in many ways" 8. "Ahhh, I don't know" 9. "At the zoo, they got ducks" 10. "It's a crying shame" 11. "You know, I remember" 12. "Whenever I think of wild flying things" 13. "They stuff them" 14. "For centuries prior to this time."

Directed by Albert Takazauckas; music, George Quincy; scenery and costumes, Michael Massee; lighting, Gary Porto; associate producer, Jean Halbert; stage manager, William La Rosa; press, Jean Halbert.

Sexual Perversity in Chicago: Extra-marital adventures and the breakup of the marriage treated as black farce. *Duck Variations:* Two old men pass the time in conversation about the ducks flying overhead and other philosophical matters. *Sexual Perversity in Chicago* was previously produced by Chicago's Organic Theater Company and off Broadway by St. Clements in the 1975 season, when it won an Obie Award.

James Sutorius replaced F. Murray Abraham 7/76.

Actors' Alliance. Schedule of three revivals. **The Tavern** (18). By George M. Cohan. Opened June 24, 1976. (Closed July 10, 1976) **Lullaby** (13). By Don Appell. Opened July 14, 1976. (Closed July 25, 1976) **Hay Fever** (14). By Noel Coward. Opened July 30, 1976.

(Closed August 15, 1976) Produced by Actors' Alliance as a summer stock festival of comedy at the Provincetown Playhouse.

ALL PLAYS — Scenery, Vicki Paul; costumes, Peg Schierholz; lighting, Burt J. Patalano; press, William Newman.

THE TAVERN

Zach	Tom Jarus	Mrs. Lamson	Martha Miller
Sally	Robin G. Eisenman	Virginia	Sara Louise
Freeman	Robert Costanzo	Tom Allen	Terrence O'Hara
Willum	William Arrigon	Sheriff	Robert Coluntino
Vagabond	William Newman	Joshua	Peter DeLaurier
Violet	Margaret Donohue	Ezra	Martin Brandon
Lamson	Jack Poggi	Stevens	Thomas MacGreevy

Directed by Michael Posnick; stage manager, Kimberley Francis Kearsley.

The last professional New York production of *The Tavern* was by Association of Producing Artists off Broadway 3/5/64 for 12 performances.

LULLABY

Bellhop	Peter DeLaurier	Johnny	Paul Lieber
Eadie	Kathryn Arrigon	Mother	Eda Reiss Merin

Directed by William Arrigon; stage manager, Barry Kearsley.

Lullaby was first produced on Broadway 2/3/54 for 45 performances. This is its first professional New York revival.

HAY FEVER

Simon Bliss	Michael Varna	Sandy Tyrrell	Thomas MacGreevy
Sorel Bliss	Sara Louise	Myra Arundel	Isabel Grandin
Clara	Pat Maniccia	Richard Greatham	Terrence O'Hara
Judith Bliss	Nina Polan	Jackie	Margaret Donohue
David Bliss	William Newman		

Stage manager, Kimberley Francis Kearsley.

The last professional New York production of *Hay Fever* was on Broadway 11/9/70 for 24 performances.

New York Shakespeare Festival. Summer schedule of two outdoor revivals of plays by William Shakespeare. **Henry V** (28). Opened June 24, 1976; see note. (Closed July 25, 1976) **Measure for Measure** (27). Opened July 29, 1976; see note. (Closed August 29, 1976) Produced by New York Shakespeare Festival, Joseph Papp producer, at the Delacorte Theater in Central Park.

BOTH PLAYS — Associate producer, Bernard Gersten; lighting, Martin Aronstein; production supervisor, Jason Steven Cohen; press, Merle Debuskey, Bob Ullman, Bruce Cohen; produced in cooperation with the City of New York, Hon. Abraham D. Beame mayor, Hon. Martin Lang commissioner of parks and recreation, Hon. H. Claude Shostal commissioner of cultural affairs.

HENRY V

Chorus	Michael Moriarty	Scroop; Interpreter; Bates	William M. Hurt
Henry V	Paul Rudd	Grey; Salisbury; Alencon	Erik Fredricksen
Exeter	Clarence Felder	Gower	Gerry Bamman
Westmoreland	Jay O. Sanders	Fluellen	Joseph Bova
Gloucester	Gilbert Cole	Court	William Youmans
Bedford	Stephen Lang	Court's Wife	Suzanne Collins
Warwick	Jeremiah Supple	Charles VI	Jerome Dempsey
Canterbury; Harfleur Governor;		Dauphin	Lenny Baker
Erpingham	Maurice Copeland	Constable	Barton Heyman
French Ambassador; Orleans	Bruce McGill	Montjoy	Tom Klunis
Bardolph	John C. Capodice	Katharine	Meryl Streep
Nym	Ben Slack	MacMorris	Don Plumley
Pistol	Philip Bosco	Alice	Valerie French
Mistress Quickly; Isabel	Sasha von Scherler	Williams	Walter McGinn
Boy	Jaime Montilla	Le Fer	Steven Gilborn
Cambridge; Bourbon	Stephen Daley		

Ensemble: Nancy Boykin, Stephen Brennan, Joseph Carberry, Charles Clemetson, Charles Conwell, John Ferraro, F. Kenneth Freedman, Bradford Gott-lin, Gabriel Gribetz, Ron Jacobson, Dennis Krausnick, John Lordan, Christopher McHale, Robert Vincent Park, Paul John Perri, Peter Phillips, Michael Rieder, Daniel Riviera, William Sadler, Mel Shrawder, Mark Simon, Tony Simotes, Theodore Sod, Peter Van Norden, Ricardo Velez, Bernard Velinsky, Tom Villard.

Understudies: Mr. Moriarty — Tom Klunis; Mr. Rudd-Peter Phillips; Mr. Cole — William Sadler; Mr. Lang — Charles Clemetson; Mr. Felder — Jay O. Sanders; Mr. Sanders — Bradford Gott-lin; Mr. Supple — Robert Vincent Park; Messrs. Fredrickson, Daley, Hurt — John Lordan; Mr. Copeland — Stephen Daley; Mr. Bamman — Charles Conwell; Mr. Bova — Don Plumley; Mr. Plumley — Jeremiah Supple; Messrs. McGinn, Heyman — Steven Gilborn; Messrs. Youmans, Slack — Steven Brennan; Mr. Bosco — John Capodice; Mr. Capodice — Joseph Carberry; Mr. Montilla — Gilbert Cole; Misses Collins, Streep — Nancy Boykin; Miss von Scherler — Suzanne Collins; Mr. Dempsey — Maurice Copeland; Mr. Baker — F. Kenneth Freedman; Mr. McGill — Paul John Perri; Mr. Klunis — Peter Van Norden; Mr. Gilborn — Dennis Krausnick.

Directed by Joseph Papp; scenery, David Mitchell; costumes, Timothy Miller; music, William Elliott; Battle of Agincourt — choreography, Lee Breuer, combat, Erik Fredricksen; production stage manager, Louis Rackhoff; stage managers, Richard S. Viola, Robert Kellogg.

The play was presented in two parts. *Henry V* was last produced off Broadway by Royal Shakespeare Company 4/22/76 for 23 performances.

MEASURE FOR MEASURE

Vincentio	Sam Waterston	Froth	Michael Tucker
Angelo	John Cazale	Pompey	Howard E. Rollins Jr.
Escalus	Ron Randell	Abhorson	Walt Gorney
Claudio	David Haskell	Barnardine	Jay O. Sanders
Lucio	Lenny Baker	Isabella	Meryl Streep
1st Gentleman	Joseph Regalbuto	Mariana	Caroline McWilliams
2d Gentleman	Jake Dengel	Juliet	Robin Mary Paris
Provost	John Seitz	Francisca	Judith Light
Justice	Mark Simon	Mistress Overdone	Ruby Holbrook
Friar Thomas	Steven Gilborn	Servant	Harlan Schneider
Elbow	Jeffrey Tambor		

Lords, Officers, Citizens, Nuns, Monks, Attendants: Bever-leigh Banfield, Katherine Braun, Ann Bronston, Frances Hardman Conroy, Gabriel Gribetz, Cheryl Tafathale Jones, Jolly King, Michael Kolba, Christopher McHale, Marilyn McIntyre, Nathaniel Robinson, William T. Sadler, Tony Simotes.

Understudies: Mr. Waterston — Steven Gilborn; Mr. Seitz — Mark Simon; Mr. Cazale — Jeffrey Tambor; Mr. Randell — John Seitz; Mr. Haskell — Joseph Regalbuto; Messrs. Baker, Gilborn — William T. Sadler; Messrs. Regalbuto, Dengel — Michael Kolba; Mr. Tambor — Harlan Schneider; Mr. Rollins — Nathaniel Robinson; Mr. Gorney — Gabriel Gribetz; Mr. Tucker — Tony Simotes; Mr. Sanders — Christopher McHale; Miss Streep — Judith Light; Misses McWilliams, Holbrook — Ann Bronston; Miss Paris — Marilyn McIntyre; Miss Light — Bever-leigh Banfield.

Directed by John Pasquin; scenery and costumes, Santo Loquasto; Music, William Penn; production stage manager, Frank Bayer; stage manager, Joseph La Padura.

Place: Vienna. The play was presented in two parts. *Measure for Measure* was last produced off Broadway by Classic Stage Company 9/18/75 for 28 performances.

NOTE: In this volume, certain programs of off-Broadway companies like New York Shakespeare Festival in Central Park are exceptions to our rule of counting the number of performances from the date of the press coverage. When the official opening takes place late in the run of a play's public or subscription performances (after previews) we count the first performance of record, not the press date, as opening night. Press date for *Henry V* was 6/29/76, for *Measure for Measure* was 8/10/76.

Circle Repertory Company. 1975-76 schedule of six programs ended with **Mrs. Murray's Farm** (39). By Roy London. Produced by the Circle Repertory Company, Marshall W. Mason artistic director, Jerry Arrow executive director, at the Circle Theater. Opened June 30, 1976. (Closed August 1, 1976)

Barbara Warren	Nancy Snyder	Peter Roome Jr.	Michael Ayr
Willa Hooper	Sharon Madden	Lt. Dawson	Bruce Gray
Arnold Westerly Apthorpe	Burke Pearson	Mrs. Joshua Loring	Nancy Killmer
Israel James	Danton Stone	Gen. William Howe	James Perkinson
Mrs. Robert Murray	Tanya Berezin		

British Soldiers: Terence Foley, Peter Sherin.
Directed by Neil Flanagan and Marshall W. Mason; music by Michael Valenti; scenery, John Lee Beatty;

costumes, Jennifer von Mayrhauser; lighting, John P. Dodd; sound, Charles London, George Hansen; production stage manager, David Clow; press, Rima Corben.
Time: Sept. 16, 1776. Place: Murray Hill on Manhattan Island. The play was presented in two parts.
Comedy of events taking place at the time of the Battle of Manhattan. This play was followed by an afterpiece, *Wildflowers* by Richard Howard, directed by Michael Feingold, at 5 performances beginning 7/6/76.

The Light Opera of Manhattan (LOOM). Repertory of ten operetta revivals. **H.M.S. Pinafore** (46). Book and lyrics by W.S. Gilbert; music by Arthur Sullivan. Opened August 4, 1976. **The Mikado** (53). Book and lyrics by W.S. Gilbert; music by Arthur Sullivan. Opened August 11, 1976. **The Pirates of Penzance** (39). Book and lyrics by W.S. Gilbert; music by Arthur Sullivan. Opened August 18, 1976. **Ruddigore** (13). Book and lyrics by W.S. Gilbert; music by Arthur Sullivan. Opened October 6, 1976. **Princess Ida** (13). Book and lyrics by W.S. Gilbert; music by Arthur Sullivan. Opened November 3, 1976. **The Merry Widow** (40). Book by Victor Leon and Leo Stein; English lyrics by Adrian Ross; music by Franz Lehar. Opened December 8, 1976. **Naughty Marietta** (19). Book and lyrics by Rida Johnson Young; music by Victor Herbert. Opened December 29, 1976. **The Vagabond King** (13). Musical version of Justin Huntly McCarthy's *If I Were King;* book and lyrics by Brian Hooker and W. H. Post; music by Rudolf Friml. Opened January 12, 1977. **The Yeomen of the Guard** (13). Book and lyrics by W.S. Gilbert; music by Arthur Sullivan. Opened March 9, 1977. **Utopia, Limited** (32). Book and lyrics by W.S. Gilbert; music by Arthur Sullivan. Opened May 11, 1977. (Repertory closed May 29, 1977) Produced by The Light Opera of Manhattan, William Mount-Burke producer-director, at the Eastside Playhouse.

PERFORMER	"H.M.S. PINAFORE"	"THE MIKADO"	"THE PIRATES OF PENZANCE"	"RUDDI-GORE"
Raymond Allen	Porter	Ko-Ko	Stanley	Oakapple
Diane Armistead	(Buttercup)	(Katisha)	(Ruth)	
Paula Bailey	(Josephine)			Zorah
Christopher Biehn		(Pish-Tush)		
Dennis Britten	(Rackstraw)	(Nanki-Poo)		
Elizabeth Devine		(Peep-Bo)	(Kate)	Ruth
Dennis English	(Boatswain)	(Pish-Tush)		
Susan Greenleaf			Edith	
G. Michael Harvey	(Rackstraw)	(Nanki-Poo)		
Nancy Hoffman	(Josephine)	(Yum-Yum)	(Mabel)	Rose Maybud
Paul Huck	(Carpenter)			
Joan Lader	(Hebe)	Pitti-Sing	(Isabel)	Margaret
Ethel Mae Mason	(Buttercup)	(Katisha)	(Ruth)	Hannah
Georgia McEver	(Josephine)	(Yum-Yum)	(Mabel)	
Terry McNulty	(Rackstraw)	(Nanki-Poo)	(Frederic)	
Mary Moore	(Hebe)			
John Palmore			(Samuel)	
Nancy Papale	(Josephine)	(Yum-Yum)		
Kristin Paulus			(Isabel)	
Vashek Pazdera	Deadeye	Mikado	Sergeant	Sir Roderic
Steven Polcek	(Carpenter)			
Gary Ridley	(Boatswain)	(Pish-Tush)	(Frederic)	Dauntless
Julio Rosario	Corcoran	Pooh-Bah	Pirate King	Sir Despard
James Weber	(Carpenter)			Adam
Eleanor Wold	(Buttercup)	(Katisha)	(Ruth)	
Mark Wolff			(Samuel)	
Rosemarie Wright		(Peep-Bo)	(Kate)	

(Parentheses indicate role in which the performer alternated)

PERFORMER	"PRINCESS IDA"	"THE MERRY WIDOW"	"NAUGHTY MARIETTA"	"YEOMEN OF THE GUARD"
Raymond Allen	King Gama	(Popoff); (Nish)	(Slick)	Jack Point
Paula Bailey	Psyche			
Jeanne Beauvais		Sonia	Adah	Carruthers
Tom Boyd		(Popoff)		
Dennis Britten		(de Jolidon)		
Steven Brown				2d Citizen
Maureen Burns		(Natalie)		
Dennis Curran		Khadja		2d Yeoman
Elizabeth Devine	Chloe	Praskovia	Fanchon	(Kate)
Dennis English			Blake	
Susan Greenleaf	Sacharissa			
Lloyd Harris	Hildebrand	(Popoff)		
Michael Harrison		(Danilo)	Warrington	
Ed Harrison				1st Citizen
Paul Huck	Guron		Rudolfo	
Joanne Jamieson			Felice	
Joan Lader	Melissa	Olga	Lizette	Phoebe
David Mallard		(de Jolidon)		Leonard
Georgia McEver	Ida	(Natalie)	Marietta	Elsie
Terry McNulty	Hilarion			
James Nadeaux		(Nish)	(Florenze)	
Elaine Olbrycht		(Natalie)		
Kristin Paulus	Ada		Nanette	
Vashek Pazdera	Arac			Sgt. Meryll
Steven Polcek	(Scynthius)	Kovich		Cholmondeley
Gary Ridley	Cyril	de Ste. Brioche	(Slick); (Florenze)	Fairfax
Julio Rosario	Florian	(Danilo)	Etienne	Shadbolt
Kenneth Sieger		Cascada		
Richard Smithies			Grandet	
James Weber	(Schynthius)			
Eleanor Wold	Blanche			
Mark Wolff				1st Yeoman
Kathryn Zetto				(Kate)

(Parentheses indicated role in which the performer alternated)

THE VAGABOND KING

Francois Villon	Gary Ridley	Margot	Kristin Paulus
Katherine DeVaucelles	Georgia McEver	Tibaut D'Aussigny	Steven Polcek
Louis XI	Raymond Allen	Rene DeMontigny	Dennis Curran
Tabarie	Julio Rosario	Casin; Herald	Edward Hustwit
Huguette Du Hamel	Jeanne Beauvais	Johanneton	Lee Kelley
Captain	Peter Ludwig	Blanche	Joanne Jamieson
Oliver	Paul Huck	Isabeau	Mary Miller
Lady Mary	Joan Lader	Trios	Rhea Nierenstein
Tristan	Richard Smithies	Hangman	Frank Prieto
Noel	David Mallard		

UTOPIA, LIMITED

King Paramount I	Raymond Allen	Mr. Blushington	David Mallard
Scaphio	Julio Rosario	Mr. Goldbury	Gary Ridley
Phantis	Vashek Pazdera	Princess Zara	Georgia McEver
Tarara	James Nadeaux	Princess Nekaya	Rosemarie Wright
Calynx	Michael Irwin	Princess Kalyba	Joan Lader
Lord Dramaleigh	Dennis Curran	Lady Sophy	Eleanor Wold
Capt. Fitzbattleaxe	Michael Harrison	Salata	Kristin Paulus
Capt. Corcoran	Steven Polcek	Melene	Elizabeth Devine
Sir Bailey Barre	Mark Wolff	Phylla	Rhea Nierenstein

ALL PLAYS — Director and conductor, William Mount-Burke; piano, Brian Molloy; associate director, Raymond Allen; stage manager, Jerry Gotham; press, Mark J.L. Somers.

H.M.S. PINAFORE — Chorus of Sailors, Sisters, Cousins, Aunts: Elizabeth Devine, Susan Greanleaf, Barbara Gunning, Joanne Jamieson, Lisa Landis, Mary Moore, Kristin Paulus, Rosemarie Wright, Dennis Curran, Ed Harrison, Edward Hustwit, Nelson Jewell, David Margules, James Nadeaux, Mark Wolff.

The last professional production of *H.M.S. Pinafore* in New York — as well as of *The Mikado* and *The Pirates of Penzance* — was in last season's LOOM repertory.

THE MIKADO — Chorus of Schoolgirls, Nobles, Guards, Coolies: Ellen Brown, Elizabeth Devine, Constance Little, Maureem McNamara, Mary Miller, Rhea Nierenstein, Kristin Paulus, Jo Shelnutt, Eric Brothers, Ed Harrison, Rob Main, David Mallard, James Nadeaux, Steven Polcek, Kenneth Sieger, Mark Wolff, Dennis Curran.

Scenery, William Schroder; costumes, George Stinson; assistant conductor, J. Michael Bart.

For last New York production, see *H.M.S. Pinafore* above.

THE PIRATES OF PENZANCE — Chorus of Pirates, Police and Gen. Stanley's Wards: Ellen Brown, Elizabeth Devine, Joanne Jamieson, Constance Little, Maureen McNamara, Mary Miller, Rhea Nierenstein, Kristin Paulus, Jo Shelnutt, Eric Brothers, Dennis Curran, Ed Harrison, Rob Main, David Mallard, James Nadeaux, Steven Polcek.

Scenery, William Schroder; costumes, George Stinson; assistant conductor, J. Michael Bart.

For last New York production, see *H.M.S. Pinafore* above.

RUDDIGORE — Chorus: Queenie Goldman, Susan Greenleaf, Joanne Jamieson, Lisa Landis, Kristin Paulus, Vicki Piper, Rosemarie Wright, Dennis Curran, Edward Hustwit, Paul Huck, Edward Harrison, David Margules, James Nadeaux, Steven Polcek, Mark Wolff.

Scenery: William Schroder, Elinor Shanbaum; costumes, George Stinson.

The last professional New York production of *Ruddigore* was in D'Oyly Carte repertory 11/22/66 for 4 performances.

PRINCESS IDA — Chorus of Girl Graduates, Soldiers, Courtiers: Joanne Jamieson, Anne Marie Lowell, Elizabeth Spellman, Dennis Curran, Ed Harrison, Edward Hustwit, Nelson Jewell, David Margules, James Nadeaux, Mark Wolff.

Scenery, William Schroder, Elinor Shanbaum; costumes, George Stinson.

The last professional New York production of *Princess Ida* was in American Savoyards repertory 5/26/66 for 2 performances.

THE MERRY WIDOW — Chorus of Guests, Servants, Marsovian Dancers, Marsovian Troubadours: Joanne Jamieson, Lee Kelley, Connie Little, Mary Miller, Rhea Nierenstein, Kristin Paulus, Andrea Wright, Eric Brothers, Steven Brown, Jim Farnsworth, Ed Harrison, Edward Hustwit, Rob Main, David Mallard, Mark Wolff.

Scenery, Eloise Meyer; costumes, George Stinson; lighting, Peggy Clark; choreography, Jerry Gotham.

The Merry Widow was last produced by the Music Theater of Lincoln Center 8/17/64 for 40 performances. The list of musical numbers in *The Merry Widow* appears on page 298 of *The Best Plays of 1964-65*.

NAUGHTY MARIETTA — Flower Girls, Maids, Quadroon Belles, Capt. Dick's Followers: Lee Kelley, Constance Little, Mary Miller, Rhea Nierenstein, Steven Brown, Dennis Curran, Ed Harrison, Edward Hustwit, David Mallard, Steven Polcek, Frank Prieto, Mark Wolff.

Dancers: Colette Antosca, Gail August, Elizabeth Campbell, Barbara Guerard, Corrina Hall, Nyann Hurst. Choreography, Jerry Gotham; scenery, William Schroder; costumes, George Stinson.

The last professional production of *Naughty Marietta* in New York — as well as of *The Vagabond King* — was in last season's LOOM repertory.

THE VAGABOND KING — Court Ladies: Maureen Burns, Susan Greenleaf, Constance Little. Guardsmen: Mark Wolff, Steven Brown, Rob Main, Ed Harrison.

Scenery and costumes, William Schroder; choreography, Jerry Gotham; duels choreographed by Michael A. Maurice.

For last New York production, see *Naughty Marietta* above.

The list of musical numbers in *The Vagabond King* appears on page 372 of *The Best Plays of 1975-76*.

YEOMEN OF THE GUARD — Chorus of Yeomen, Gentlemen, Citizens, etc.: Eric Brothers, Steven Brown, Michael Irwin, James Nadeaux, Frank Prieto, Kenneth Sieger, Christine Batchelor, Ellen Brown, Elizabeth Devine, Joanne Jamieson, Constance Little, Maureen McNamara, Mary Miller, Kristin Paulus, Patricia Walpole, Rosemarie Wright.

Scenery, William Schroder; costumes, George Stinson.

The last professional New York production of *Yeomen of the Guard* was in City Center repertory 5/8/68 for 3 performances.

UTOPIA, LIMITED — Maidens, Guards, Citizens of Utopia: Ellen Brown, Jan Downing, Carol Felner, Joanne Jamieson, Constance Little, Mary Miller, Maureen McNamara, Jo Shelnutt, Phillip Carrubba, Ed Harrison, Edward Hustwit, Frank Prieto.

Choreography, Jerry Gotham; scenery, Eloise Meyer; costumes, George Stinson; lighting, Peggy Clark.

The only previous New York production of record of this seldom-seen Gilbert & Sullivan work was by the American Savoyards off Broadway 11/9/61.

Roundabout Theater Center. Schedule of five revivals. **The Philanderer** (50). By George Bernard Shaw. Opened September 9, 1976; see note. (Closed October 24, 1976) **The**

Rehearsal (98). By Jean Anouilh. Opened October 14, 1976; see note. (Closed January 16, 1977) **John Gabriel Borkman** (43). By Henrik Ibsen; adapted by Gene Feist. Opened December 30, 1976; see note. (Closed February 13, 1977) **Endgame** (80). By Samuel Beckett. Opened March 15, 1977; see note. (Closed May 22, 1977) **Dear Liar** (55). By Jerome Kilty. Opened April 28, 1977; see note (closed June 12, 1977) Produced by Roundabout Theater Center, Gene Feist producing director, Michael Fried executive producer at Roundabout/Stages One (*The Philanderer, John Gabriel Borkman* and *Dear Liar*) and Two (*The Rehearsal* and *Endgame*).

THE PHILANDERER

Leonard Charteris .... Donald Madden	Col. Daniel Craven .... George Ede
Grace Tranfield ....Marion Lines	Sylvia Craven ....Pamela Brook
Julia Craven .... Cara Duff-MacCormick	Dr. Percy Paramore ....Jack Bittner
Joseph Cuthbertson ....Ralph Clanton	The Page ....William Perkiss

Directed by Stephen Hollis; scenery, Eldon Elder; costumes, Christina Giannini; lighting, Dan Koetting; original score, Philip Campanella; production stage manager, Robert Neu; press, Mark Arnold.

Time: 1893. Place: London. Act I: The drawing room of a flat in the Victoria District. Act II: The library of the Ibsen Club, next day at noon. Act III: Dr. Paramore's reception room in Savile Row, the same afternoon.

Shaw's second play. Its first Broadway production took place 12/30/13 for 103 performances. Its only previous New York revival of record was off Broadway in the season of 1955-56.

THE REHEARSAL

Countess .... Elizabeth Owens	Hero ....Philip Kerr
Damiens ....Don Perkins	Villebosse .... Edward Cicciarelli
Count ....Barry Boys	Lucile ....Alexandra Isles
Hortensia .... Jean DeBaer	

Directed by Anthony Stimac; scenery, Miguel Romero; costumes, David Murin; original score, Philip Campanella; lighting, William Otterson; production stage manager, Andrew Bales.

Time: April 1952. Place: A chateau near LeMans. The play was presented in two parts.

This Anouilh play was first produced on Broadway in French under its French title *La Repetition, ou L'Amour Puni* 11/27/52 for 4 performances. It was produced on Broadway in English 9/23/63 for 110 performances.

JOHN GABRIEL BORKMAN

John Gabriel Borkman .... Robert Pastene	Fanny Wilton ....Valerie French
Gunhild Borkman ....Gale Sondergaard	Vilhelm Foldal .... Truman Gaige
Erhart Borkman ....Jeffrey David Pomerantz	Frida Foldal .... Madelon Thomas
Ella Rentheim ....Jan Farrand	Hulda ....Carolyn Sullivan

General Understudy — Carolyn Sullivan.

Directed by Gene Feist; original score, Philip Campanella; production stage manager, Robert Neu.

Time: A winter evening. Place: Rentheim Manor some distance from Christiania, the Norwegian capital. Act I: Mrs. Borkman's sitting room. Act II: John Gabrial Borkman's study. Act III: Mrs. Borkman's sitting room. Act IV, Scene 1: Outside Rentheim Manor. Scene 2: A mountain clearing overlooking the fjords. The play was presented in two parts with the intermission following Act II.

ENDGAME

Hamm ....Gordon Heath	Nagg .... Charles Randall
Clov ....Jake Dengel	Nell .... Suzanne Shepherd

Directed by Gene Feist; scenery, James Grant; costumes, Nancy L. Johnson; lighting, Frances Aronson; original score, Philip Campanella; production stage manager, Franklin Davis.

Endgame was last seen off Broadway in the Manhattan Project production 4/29/75 for 12 performances.

DEAR LIAR

Bernard Shaw ....Jerome Kilty	Mrs. Patrick Campbell ....Deann Mears

Directed by Jerome Kilty; scenery, Robin Sherman; costumes, Nancy L. Johnson; lighting, R. J. Turick; musical supervision, Philip Campanella; production stage manager, Errol Selsby.

Act I: 1899-1914. Act II: 1914-1939.

Dear Liar was first produced on Broadway 3/17/60 for 52 performances. It was revived off Broadway 3/17/62 for 40 performances.

NOTE: In this volume, certain programs of off-Broadway companies like the Roundabout Theater Center are exceptions to our rule of counting the number of performances from the date of the press coverage. When the official opening takes place late in the run of a play's public or subscription performances (after previews) we count the first performance of record, not the press date, as opening night. Press date for *The Philanderer* was 9/29/76, for *The Rehearsal* 11/4/76, for *John Gabriel Borkman* 1/19/77. For *Endgame* 3/28/77, for *Dear Liar* 5/15/77.

The American Place Theater. Schedule of six programs. **Jack Gelber's New Play: Rehearsal** (32). By Jack Gelber. Opened September 28, 1976; see note. (Closed October 4, 1976). **Comanche Cafe** and **Domino Courts** (28). Program of one-act plays by William Hauptman. Opened November 11, 1976; see note. Suspended performances 11/23/76–11/28/76. (Closed December 12, 1976) **Rodogune** (8). Revival of the play in the French language by Pierre Corneille in Le Tréteau de Paris production. Opened November 23, 1976. (Closed November 28, 1976) **Isadora Duncan Sleeps With the Russian Navy** (32). By Jeff Wanshel. Opened January 25, 1977; see note. (Closed February 20, 1977) **Jules Feiffer's Hold Me!** (100). Revue by Jules Feiffer. Opened February 14, 1977 at the Chelsea Westside Cabaret Theater; see note. (Closed May 15, 1977) **Cold Storage** (48). By Ronald Ribman. Opened March 27, 1977; see note. (Closed May 8, 1977. Produced by The American Place Theater, Wynn Handman director, Julia Miles associate director, at the American Place Theater.

JACK GELBER'S NEW PLAY: REHEARSAL

Tommy	John McCurry	Rufus	Darryl Croxton
Guard	Jack Hollander	Scott	Lane Smith
Ernst	Sam Schacht	Fat	Fred Kareman
Karl	Martin Shakar	Arlene	Grayson Hall
Danny	Robert Burgos		

Directed by Jack Gelber; scenery, Henry Millman; lighting, Edward M. Greenberg; literary advisers, Joel Schecter, Cassandra Medley; production stage manager, Errol Selsby; stage manager, Rene Mainguy; press, Jeffrey Richards Associates.

Time: The present. Act I: Five days into rehearsal. Act II: Ten days later.

Play-within-a-play, or rather, rehearsal-within-a-play, with cross-currents of effort and temperament.

COMANCHE CAFE

Ronnie	Jane Galloway	Mattie	Sasha von Scherler

DOMINO COURTS

Floyd	Guy Boyd	Roy	Conard Fowkes
Ronnie	Jane Galloway	Flo	Regina Baff

Directed by Barnet Kellman; scenery, Henry Millman; costumes, Carol Oditz; lighting, Edward M. Greenberg; production stage manager, Richard S. Viola.

Set in Oklahoma in the 1930s *Comanche Cafe* is duologue in which a woman longs to be married; then, in *Domino Courts*, she is married to a gangster. Previously produced off off Broadway.

RODOGUNE

Laonice	Jenny Alpha	Rodogune	Laure Guizerix
Timagene	Tola Koukoui	Cléopâtre	Josette Boulva
Antiochus	Gilbert Beugniot	1st Porter	Rodney Muir
Seleucus	Raphael Mattei		

Directed by Henri Ronse; scenery and costumes, Beni Montresor; produced by Le Tréteau de Paris, Jean de Rigault executive producer and founder, in association with Théâtre Oblique, with the patronage of L'Association Français d'Action Artistique of the Government of the French Republic; stage manager, Jean-Marc Colonna d'Istria.

This is the first professional New York production of record of Corneille's five-act tragedy about Cleopatra. It was performed without intermission.

ISADORA DUNCAN SLEEPS WITH THE RUSSIAN NAVY

Author	David Ackroyd	Narrator	Howard Ross
Producer	Robert Lesser	Deirdre Duncan	Daphne Youree
Isadora Duncan	Marian Seldes	Patrick Duncan	Luke Youree

Chorus: Raymond Duncan, Oscar Beregi, Paris Singer — Richard Council; Andre Beaunier, Heinrich Thode, Stanislavsky — Christopher Curry; Mother Duncan, Loie Fuller, Walt Whitman — Anita Dangler; Auguste

Rodin, Gordon Craig, Hon. Lew Shanks — Dennis Jay Higgins; Gypsy, Anna Pavlova, Angel — Annette Kurek; Alexander Gross, Sergei Essenin, Walter Rommel — Peter Lownds; Ivan Miroski, German Entrepreneur, Lenin — David Rasche.

Children, Cattleboat, Hungarians, Vienna, Sheep, Grotesque Hallucinations, Newsvendors, Daredevil Sailors of the Cruisor "Aurora" — Company.

Understudy — Tanny McDonald.

Directed by Tom Haas; costumes, Bobbi Owen; musical direction, Russell Walden; dance consultant, Linda Tarnay; assistant to the director, Joy Javits; production stage manager, Errol Selsby; stage manager, Peter Gellblum.

Free-form biography of the famous dancer (1878-1927). The play was presented without intermission.

JULES FEIFFER'S HOLD ME!

Geraldine Brooks	Dalienne Majors
Paul Dooley	Michael Tucci
Kathleen Chalfant	

Understudies: Dan Strickler, Maria Cellario.

Directed by Caymichael Patten; choreography, Dalienne Majors; scenery, Kert Lundell; costumes, Ruth Morley; lighting, Edward M. Greenberg; production stage manager, Nancy Harrington; stage manager, Rene Mainguy.

Visualization of Jules Feiffer cartoon episodes. The play was presented in two parts.

Cynthia Harris replaced Geraldine Brooks 3/22/77. Dan Strickler replaced Muchael Tucci 4/5/77.

COLD STORAGE

Freidrich Reisen	Paul Sparer	Richard Landau	Michael Lipton
Joseph Parmigian	Martin Balsam	Miss Madurga	Julie Carmen

Understudy: Messrs. Sparer, Balsam, Lipton — Sanford Morris.

Directed by Joel Zwick; scenery, Kert Lundell; costumes, Ruth Morley; lighting, Edward M. Greenberg; production stage manager, Richard S. Viola; stage manager, Jeffrey Rowland.

Time and Place: Act I, Scene 1: A police station in Portugal, 1941. Scene 2: A hospital roof garden in New York City, June 1976. Act II: The roof garden, early evening the same day.

Contemplation of the human spirit courageous and philosophical in the face of death, whether by political oppression or by cancer.

NOTE: In this volume, certain programs of off-Broadway companies like The American Place Theater are exceptions to our rule of counting the number of performances from the date of the press coverage. When the official opening takes place late in the run of a play's public or subscription performances (after previews) we count the first performance of record, not the press date, as opening night. Press date for *Jack Gelber's New Play: Rehearsal* was 10/7/76, for *Comanche Cafe* and *Domino Courts* 12/2/76, for *Isadora Duncan Sleeps With the Russian Navy* 1/30/77, for *Cold Storage* 4/6/77. *Jules Feiffer's Hold Me!* opened 1/23/77 in the American Humorists series in the Subplot Cafe and was transferred to the Chelsea Westside Cabaret Theater for a regular off-Broadway run 2/14/77.

T. Schreiber Theater. Schedule of three programs. **Does Anybody Here Do the Peabody?** (37). By Enid Rudd. Opened September 29, 1976. (Closed October 31, 1976). **All the Way Home** (37). Revival of the play by Tad Mosel. Opened December 1, 1976. (Closed January 16, 1977) **Curtains** (28). By Tom Mallin. Opened January 26, 1977. (Closed March 6, 1977). Produced by the T. Schreiber Theater, Terry Schreiber and Barbara Rosoff producers, at Wonderhorse.

DOES ANYBODY HERE DO THE PEABODY?

Polly Raisen	Betsy Von Furstenberg	Barney Steuben	Ted Forlow
Ginger Raisen	Mia Dillon	Herbert Kibble	John Aquino
Mrs. Munchen	Mary Boylan	Mr. Steinbocher	Alf Geisler
Violet Munchen	Joan Gilbert	Mrs. Steinbocher	Uta Hofmann

Directed by Terry Schreiber; scenery, costumes and lighting, Hal Tiné; choreography, Elaine Cancila; musical direction, Gregory Gilford; associate producers, David Ridings, John Bishop; production stage manager, Mark Stein; stage manager, Rita Calabro; press, Francine L. Trevens.

Time: Summer, 1938. Act I: Saturday and Sunday, late August. Act II: Sunday and two weeks later.

Nostalgic romance in the 1930s style, as a Woolworth saleswoman dreams of becoming a movie star.

ALL THE WAY HOME

Rufus Follet	Mike Brown	Jay Follet	Dan Hamilton
Boys	Brad Deutch, Lionel Chute	Mary Follet	Elizabeth Perry

Ralph Follet	Vic Polizos	Great-Great Granmaw	Jane Roberts
Sally Follet	Kathyann Peiffer	Catherine Lynch	Muriel Mason
John Henry Follet	James Sommers	Aunt Hannah Lynch	Anne Pitoniak
Jessie Follet	Eve Johnson	Joel Lynch	F. D. Herrick
Jim-Wilson	Kevin Brown	Andrew Lynch	Bob Harders
Aunt Sadie Follet	Ann Hennessey	Father Jackson	Kenny Pearl

Directed by Peter Thompson; scenery, Paul Eads; costumes, Rachel Kurland; lighting, Margaret Jennings; production stage manager, Rita Calabro; stage manager, Sari Weisman.

Time: May, 1915. Place; Knoxville, Tenn. Act I: The first day. Act II: The second day. Act III: Two days later.

Tad Mosel's dramatization of James Agee's novel *A Death in the Family* was first produced on Broadway 11/30/60 for 333 performances and won the Critics Award and Pulitzer Prize and was named a Best Play of its season. This is its first professional New York revival.

<h2 style="text-align:center">CURTAINS</h2>

Niall Scringeour	Lee Wallace	Gladys Spendlove	Eve Johnson
Mildred Wringe	Marilyn Chris		

Directed by Allen Savage; scenery and lighting, Bil Mikulewicz; costumes, Anna Hill; associate producers, David Ridings, John Bishop; production stage manager, Rita Calabro; stage manager, Sari Weisman.

Act I, Scene 1: The room one Sunday morning. Scene 2: Two o'clock in the afternoon of the same day. Act II: The same room, five days later, half past twelve in the morning.

The growing unhappiness of a couple living together is exacerbated by a third party, in black comedy fashion. A foreign play previously produced at Traverse Theater Club, Edinburgh and The Open Space in London.

Classic Stage Company. Repertory of five programs. **Heartbreak House** (23). Revival of the play by George Bernard Shaw. Opened October 1, 1976. (Closed December 19, 1976) **The Homecoming** (34). Revival of the play by Harold Pinter. Opened October 2, 1976. (Closed April 24, 1977). **Bingo** (22). By Edward Bond. Opened October 12, 1976. (Closed December 17, 1976) **Tartuffe** (19). Revival of the play by Molière; English version by Christopher Martin. Opened October 22, 1976. (Closed December 19, 1976) **The Balcony** (43). By Jean Genet; English version by Terry Hands and Barbara Wright. Opened December 4, 1976. (Closed April 10, 1977). Produced by Classic Stage Company, Christopher Martin artistic director, Leonard Edelstein managing director, at the Abbey Theater.

ALL PLAYS — Directed by Christopher Martin; scenery, Christopher Martin (*The Homecoming* with David Chapman, *The Balcony* with Harry Lines); stage manager, John Shannon (*The Balcony* with Steven Peiffer).

PERFORMER	"HEART-BREAK HOUSE"	"THE HOME-COMING"	"BINGO"	"TARTUFFE"
Sam Blackwell	Burglar	Joey	Son	Damis
Tom Donaldson	Hushabye	Teddy	Shakespeare	Cleante
Marcia Hyde	Ellie Dunn		Young Woman	Mariane
Darrie Lawrence	Nurse Guinness		Joan	Mme. Pernell
Larry Lott	Mazzini Dunn	Sam	Jerome	M. Loyal
Christopher Martin	Capt. Shotover	Max	Ben Jonson	Molière
Noble Shropshire	Utterword		Wally	Tartuffe
Karen Sunde	Hesione	Ruth	Old Woman	Dorine
Peter Van Norden			William Combe	Orgon
Ara Watson	Lady Utterword		Judith	Elmire
Wayne Wofford	Boss Mangan	Lenny	Old Man	Valère

<h2 style="text-align:center">THE BALCONY</h2>

Bishop	Peter Van Norden		(Jennifer Reed)
	(Frank Dwyer)	Torturer; Slave	Martin Treat
Penitent; Carmen	Ara Watson	General; Blood	Wayne Wofford
	(Carol Fleming)		(Harlan Schneider)
Mme. Irma	Karen Sunde	Mare	Darrie Lawrence
Judge; Tears	Noble Shropshire		(Jerri Iaia)
Thief; Chantal	Marcia Hyde	Chief of Police	Tom Donaldson

Sperm; Roger .... Sam Blackwell
                                  (Michael Kolba)
Queen's Envoy .... Christopher Martin
    Revolutionaries: Martin Treat, Noble Shropshire,

Peter Van Norden, Wayne Wofford. Photographers:
Martin Treat, Darrie Lawrence, Sam Blackwell.
(Parentheses indicate cast replacements 3/1/77)

HEARTBREAK HOUSE — Costumes, Kay Pathanky. Martin Treat replaced Larry Lott 11/76.
This Shaw play was first produced by the Theater Guild 11/10/20 and has since been revived on Broadway
4/29/38 for 48 performances and 10/18/59 for 112 performances, and off Broadway in the seasons of 1949–50
and 1955–56.
    THE HOMECOMING — Noble Shropshire replaced Larry Lott 11/76; Peter Galman replaced Wayne Wof-
ford and Kevin McClarnon replaced Sam Blackwell 4/77. This production was mounted by CSC 3/6/76 but not
introduced into repertory until this season. Its last professional New York production was off Broadway 11/6/75
for 9 performances.
    BINGO — Costumes, Evelyn Thompson. Martin Treat replaced Larry Lott 4/77. This was the New York
premiere of Bond's parable of society in a dramatic portrait of a disillusioned Shakespeare nearing the end of his
days. A foreign play previously produced in London and at the Cleveland Play house in its American premiere
10/31/75 for 22 performances.
    TARTUFFE — Costumes, Donna Meyer. Martin Treat replaced Larry Lott 4/27. This production was
mounted by CSC 1/10/76 but was not introduced into repertory until this season. Its last professional New York
production was in French 7/2/68 for 6 performances.
    THE BALCONY — The American premiere of both the complete Genet play and a new translation of it. A
previous version was produced off Broadway the season of 1959–60 for 672 performances.

Lovesong (24). Musical by Michael Valenti, based on words of James Agee, Lord Byron,
A. E. Houseman, John Lewin, Dorothy Parker, Sir Walter Raleigh, Christina Rossetti
and Richard Brinsley Sheridan; music by Michael Valenti; original idea conceived by
Henry Comor. Produced by Wayne Starr in association with Thomas Hannan and
Charles Kalan at the Top of the Village Gate. Opened October 5, 1976. (Closed October
24, 1976)

Melanie Chartoff   Ty McConnell
Sigrid Heath   Jess Richards

    Musical numbers staged by John Montgomery; musical direction, David Krane; scenery, Jack Logan; cos-
tumes, Joan Mayno; lighting, Martin Friedman; media design, Bruce Shenton; choreographic assistant, Michael
Perrier; orchestrations and vocal arrangements, Michael Valenti; production stage manager, Martin Friedman;
press, Alan Eichler.
    Revue-style musical with the numbers having the common theme of love.

Circle Repertory Company. Schedule of six programs. **The Farm** (42). By David Storey.
Opened October 10, 1976. (Closed November 11, 1976) **A Tribute to Lili Lamont** (36). By
Arthur Whitney. Opened November 28, 1976. (Closed January 2, 1977) **My Life** (36). By
Corinne Jacker. Opened January 23, 1977. (Closed February 27, 1977) **Gemini** (63). By
Albert Innaurato. Opened March 13, 1977. (Closed May 1, 1977 and transferred to
Broadway; see its entry in the "Plays Produced on Broadway" section of this volume) **Ex-
iles** (36). Revival of the play by James Joyce. Opened May 19, 1977. (Closed June 12,
1977) And *Unsung Cole,* revue with songs by Cole Porter, scheduled to open 6/23/77.
Produced by Circle Repertory Company, Marshall W. Mason executive director, Jerry
Arrow executive director at the Circle Theater.

THE FARM

Wendy .... Debra Mooney
Jennifer ....Trish Hawkins
Brenda .... Nancy Snyder
Slattery .... Jack Gwillim

Mrs. Slattery .... Ruby Holbrook
Albert .... Michael Ayr
Arthur .... Jeff Daniels

    Directed by Marshall W. Mason; scenery, John Lee Beatty; costumes, Laura Crow; lighting, Dennis Parichy;
production stage manager, Dave Clow; press, Rima Corben.
    Time: The present, November. Place: An ancient farmhouse in Northern England. Act I: Evening. Act II:
Morning. Act III, Scene 1: Evening. Scene 2: Night. Scene 3: Morning.
    To each his/her own way of life and survival in the household of a crusty Yorkshire farmer and his three attrac-
tive daughters. A foreign play previously produced in London and elsewhere.

A TRIBUTE TO LILI LAMONT

Oliver Fuller	William Hindman	Harry Shannon	Burke Pearson
Tommy Alvarez	Francis Walsh	Joe Bernstein	Jack Davidson
Bebe Bernstein	Helen Stenborg	Miss Lili Lamont	Leueen MacGrath
Pauline Johnson	Claris Erickson		

Directed by Marshall W. Mason; scenery, John Lee Beatty; costumes, Jennifer von Mayrhauser; lighting, Dennis Parichy; original music, Norman L. Berman; sound, Charles London; production stage manager, Fred Reinglas.

Time: The present. Place: A basement on a side street off Lower 4th Avenue. Act I: A rainy evening, late July. Act II: A half hour later.

Famous relic of the movies' golden age meets the members of her one remaining fan club, with some pain and disillusion on both sides. Previously produced by Players Repertory Theater, Miami, Fla.

MY LIFE

Perdita Mason	Claire Malis	Wallace Howe	Douglass Watson
Edward Howe	William Hurt	Laura Howe Winchester	Jo Henderson
Grandfather	Christopher Reeve	Young Eddie	Jeff Daniels
Father	Roger Chapman	Sally	Nancy Snyder
Mother	Tanya Berezin		

Directed by Marshall W. Mason; scenery, David Potts; costumes, Kenneth M. Yount; lighting, Dennis Parichy; original music, Norman L. Berman; sound, Charles London; stage manager, Amy Schecter.

Time: A September evening and the summers before. Place: San Francisco. The play was presented in three parts.

Young man remembers and explores his past, looking for causes and evaluating effects.

GEMINI

Francis Geminiani	Robert Picardo	Marshall Lowenstein	Jonathan Hadary
Bunny Lowenstein	Jessica James	Fran Geminiani	Danny Aiello
Randy Hastings	Reed Birney	Lucille Grande	Anne DeSalvo
Judith Hastings	Carol Potter		

Directed by Peter Mark Schifter; scenery, Christopher Nowak; costumes, Ernest Allen Smith; lighting, Larry Crimmins; production stage manager, Fred Reinglas.

Time: June, 1973. Place: The Geminiani-Lowenstein back yard in South Philadelphia. Act I, Scene 1: June 1, 1973, early morning. Scene 2: That evening. Act II, Scene 1: June 2, 1973, morning. Scene 2: That evening.

Emotional growing pains, a brother and sister are both attracted by and attractive to the same lover. Previously produced off off Broadway at Playwrights Horizons and at the PAF Playhouse, Huntingdon Sta., L.I.

EXILES

Richard Rowan	Alan Jordan	Robert Hand	Neil Flanagan
Bertha	Stephanie Gordon	Beatrice Justice	Nancy Killmer
Archie	Anthony Austin	Brigid	Eleanor Logan

Directed by Rob Thirkield; scenery, David Potts; costumes, Jennifer von Mayrhauser; lighting, Dennis Parichy; music, Norman L. Berman; sound, Charles London; production stage manager, Bob Lampel.

Joyce's only play, semi-autobiographical, was written in 1915 and first produced in New York at the Neighborhood Theater in 1925 and revived off Broadway in the seasons of 1946-47 and 1956-57.

Circle Repertory also presented special afterpieces: *The Passing of Corky Brewster,* a one-act comedy by Jerry L. Crawford, directed by Daniel Irvine, 2/8/77-2/13/77 and 3/21/77-3/27/77; *For Love or Money,* with music by Jason McAuliffe and lyrics by Jay Jeffries, directed by Susan Lehman, 3/29/77-4/10/77; and *What the Babe Said* by Martin Halpern, directed by Amy Schecter, 5/18/77-6/3/77.

Dylan Thomas Growing Up (36). Return engagement of the one-man show with and devised by Emlyn Williams; from the stories of Dylan Thomas. Produced by Chelsea Theater Center, Robert Kalfin artistic director, Michael David executive director, Burl Hash productions director, by arrangement with Arthur Cantor at Theater Four. Opened October 12, 1976. (Closed October 24, 1976) Reopened November 26, 1976. (Closed December 12, 1976)

Lighting and production supervision, Robert Crawley; assistant to Mr. Williams, Brian Stashick; press, Susan Bloch, C. George Willard, Barbara Price.

Emlyn Williams's one-man presentation of Dylan Thomas was first presented in London in 1955 and made its

American debut on Broadway as *A Boy Growing Up* 10/7/57 for 17 performances. It returned off Broadway this season, first for an engagement of 16 performances and then one of 20 beginning a national tour.

PART I — Introducing Dylan; Memories of Childhood (from *Quite Early One Morning;* Cousin Gwilym (from "The Peaches" in *Portrait of the Artist as a Young Dog*); Who Do You Wish Was With Us? and The Fight (from *Portrait of the Artist as a Young Dog*); The Hand; The Outing (from *A Prospect of the Sea*).

PART II — Reminiscence of a Schoolmaster (from "Return Journey" in *Quite Early One Morning*); Just Like Little Dogs (from *Portrait of the Artist as a Young Dog*); Self-Portrait (from "Return Journey"); Adventures in the Skin Trade; A Moment of Older Youth (from *Quite Early One Morning*).

*The Club (257). Musical by Eve Merriam. Produced by Circle in the Square (Downtown), Theodore Mann artistic director, Paul Libin managing director at Circle in the Square (Downtown). Opened October 14, 1976.

Johnny	M. Dell	Bobby	J. J. Hafner
Bertie	G. Hodes	Maestro	M. Innerarity
Algy	J. Beretta	Henry	T. White
Freddie	C. Monferdini		

Understudies: Frolic Taylor, Gerta Grunen.

Directed by Tommy Tune; musical direction and arrangements, Alexandra Ivanoff; costumes and set decor, Kate Carmel; lighting, Cheryl Thacker; stage manager, Gene Taylor; press, Merle Debuskey, David Roggensack.

Time: Circa 1905. The play was presented without intermission.

Musical spoof of attitudes and personalities in the men's clubs at the turn of the century, with all the roles male but played by women (who are billed only by last names and initials, per the cast listing above), and with all songs selected from the period 1894–1905. Previously produced by Lenox Arts Center/Music-Theater Performing Group.

Davy Jones' Locker (97). Revival of the marionette program with book by Arthur Birnkrant and Waldo Salt; music and lyrics by Mary Rodgers. And **Bil Baird's Variety.** Produced by The American Puppet Arts Council, Arthur Cantor executive producer, in the Bil Baird's Marionettes production at the Bil Baird Theater. Opened October 15, 1976. (Closed January 16, 1977)

Nick	Olga Felgemacher	First Goon	Neil Bleifeld
Billy; Miranda	Rebecca Bondor	Captain Scorn; Sea Monster	William Tost
Mr. Merriwether; Davy Jones	Peter B. Baird	Paddlefoot	Ronnie Burkett

Assorted Fishes, Ghosts, Pirates & Things: Members of the company.

Designed and produced by Bil and Susanna Baird; directed by Bill Dreyer; musical direction and arrangements, Alvy West; lighting, Peggy Clark; production stage manager, Steve Login; press, C. George Willard, Barbara Price.

DAVY JONES' LOCKER — Place: On a deserted island in the Bahamas, aboard the ship of Captain Fletcher Scorn and in Davy Jones' Locker. The play was presented in two parts.

This Baird marionette musical was last produced 12/24/72 for 79 performances.

BIL BAIRD'S VARIETY — Perennial exhibition of "puppet virtuosity embodying many styles and types."

2 by 5 (57). Musical cabaret conceived by Seth Glassman; music by John Kander; lyrics by Fred Ebb. Produced by Judy Gordon and Jack Temchin at the Village Gate Downstairs. Opened October 19, 1976. (Closed January 5, 1977)

D'Jamin Bartlett	Shirley Lemmon
Kay Cummings	Scott Stevensen
Danny Fortus	

Directed by Seth Glassman; scenery and costumes, Dan Leigh; lighting, Martin Tudor; musical direction, Joseph Clonick. Production stage manager, Mark Rubinsky; press, Jeffrey Richards.

Retrospective revue of the works of the authors of *Flora, the Red Menace, Cabaret, The Happy Time, Zorba, 70 Girls 70, Chicago,* etc.

PART I: Overture — Company; "Cabaret" — Company; "Willkommen" — Danny Fortus; "Yes" — Company; "Sing Happy" — Fortus; "Mein Herr" — Shirley Lemmon, D'Jamin Bartlett, Kay Cummings; "Seeing Things" — Scott Stevensen; "The World Goes Round" — Bartlett; "Love Song" — Fortus; "The Money Song" — Company; "Sign Here" — Cummings; "My Own Best Friend" — Lemmon; "Losers" — Fortus, Bartlett;

"Military Man" — Company; "Only Love" — Fortus; "Why Can't I Speak?" — Bartlett, Stevensen, Lemmon; "Me and My Baby" — Company; "Isn't This Better" — Cummings.
    PART II: "Home" — Company; "Maybe This Time" — Bartlett; "Ring Them Bells" — Cummings; "Mr. Cellophane" — Fortus; "Among My Yesterdays" — Stevensen; "I Don't Remember You" — Lemmon; "Class" — Lemmon, Cummings; "Broadway, My Street" — Lemmon, Cummings, Stevensen, Fortus; "New York, New York" — Bartlett; "On Stage" — Company; "Ten Percent" — Fortus; "Razzle Dazzle" — Company; "A Quiet Thing" — Stevensen; "Cabaret" (Reprise) — Company.

Chelsea Theater Center. Schedule of four programs. **The Prince of Homburg** (40). By Heinrich Von Kleist; English version by James Kirkup; adapted by Robert Kalfin. Opened in Brooklyn October 19, 1976; see note. Closed October 31, 1976 and transferred to Manhattan November 3, 1976. (Closed November 21, 1976) **Lincoln** (32). By Saul Levitt. Opened in Brooklyn November 30, 1976; see note. Closed December 12, 1976 and transferred to Manhattan December 15, 1976. (Closed December 26, 1976) **The Crazy Locomotive** (29). By Stanislaw Ignacy Witkiewicz; translated by Daniel C. Gerould and C. S. Durer. Opened in Brooklyn January 18, 1977; see note. Closed January 30, 1977 and transferred to Manhattan February 4, 1977. (Closed February 13, 1977). **Happy End** (56). Musical revival based on a German play by "Dorothy Lane" (Elisabeth Hauptmann); music by Kurt Weill; lyrics by Bertolt Brecht; book and lyrics adapted by Michael Feingold. Opened March 8, 1977; see note. (Closed April 30, 1977 and transferred to Broadway; see its entry in the "Plays Produced on Broadway" section of this volume) Produced by Chelsea Theater Center, Robert Kalfin artistic director, Michael David executive director, Burl Hash productions director, at the Academy of Music in Brooklyn and Theater Four in Manhattan.

THE PRINCE OF HOMBURG

Prince Friedrich Arthur of Homburg	Frank Langella	Baron Goltz	Peter Burnell
Count Hohenzollern	George Morfogen	Count Reuss	Frank Anderson
Friedrich Wilhelm	K. Lype O'Dell	Col. Hennings	Jon Peter Benson
His Wife	Jane Staab	Colonel Truchss	William Myers
Princess Natalia	Patricia Elliott	Field-Marshal Dorfling	Larry Swansen
		Col. Kottwitz	Roger Dekoven

Understudies: Mr. Langella — Peter Burnell; Mr. Burnell — Charles Conwell; Misses Staab, Elliott — Randy Danson; Messrs. Morfogen, Benson, Anderson, Myers — Robert Einenkel; Messrs. O'Dell, DeKoven, Swansen — William Myers.

Directed by Robert Kalfin; scenery, Christopher Thomas; costumes, Ruth Morley; lighting, Marc B. Weiss; music, Mel Marvin; special consultant, Erlo Van Waveren; period movement advisor, Cindia Huppeler; production stage manager, Sherman Warner; press, Susan Bloch, Lester Gruner.
    The play was presented in three parts.
    This was the American premiere of this foreign (German) play, written in 1811 and set in 1675, about a prince in conflict with his government after winning a great victory.

LINCOLN

Abraham Lincoln	Fritz Weaver

Directed by Carl Weber; scenery, Lawrence King; costume coordination, Carol Spier; lighting, William Mintzer; music arrangements, Mel Marvin; film consultant, Bedrich Batka; photo animation, Francis Lee; film editing, Fred von Bernewitz; sound, Edwin Pryor; production stage manager, Phillip Price.
    Multimedia study of Abraham Lincoln in visual effects, sound and actor's characterization. The play was presented in three parts.

THE CRAZY LOCOMOTIVE

Nicholas Slobok	Dwight Schultz	Mira Bean	Linda Scoullar
Julia Tomasik	Lin Shaye	Turbulence Guster	Joe Palmieri
Siegfried Tenser	Garnett Smith	Conductor	Bob DeFrank
Sophia Tenser; Jeanne Cackleson	Glenn Close	3d Thug	Lee Cotterell
1st Gendarme	John Scoullar	John Cackleson; 1st Thug	John Jellison
Valery Bean	Peter Bartlett	Dr. Riftmaker; 2d Thug	Dennis Lipscomb
Minna	Prudence Wright Holmes	2d Gendarme; Doctor's Assistant	Marc C. Peters

Understudies: Mr. Bartlett — Lee Cotterell; Messrs. Smith, Lipscomb, Palmieri, Cotterell, Scoullar —

Robert Einenkel; Misses Shaye, Close, Scoullar, Holmes — Rosalind Harris; Mr. Schultz — John Jellison; Mr. Jellison — Dennis Lipscomb; Mr. DeFrank — John Scoullar.

Directed by Des McAnuff; scenery, Douglas W. Schmidt; costumes, Carol Oditz; lighting, Burl Hash; electronic music and orchestration, Pril Smiley; production stage manager, Ginny Freedman.

Existence viewed as a train manned by lunatics, hurtling toward destruction. The play was presented in two parts. A foreign (Polish) play written between the two World Wars.

HAPPY END

The Gang:

Bill Cracker	Christopher Lloyd
Sam Wurlitzer	Benjamin Rayson
"Governor" Nakamura	Tony Azito
Jimmy Dexter	John A. Coe
Bob Marker	Robert Weil
"Baby Face" Flint	Raymond J. Barry
"The Fly"	Grayson Hall
Miriam	Donna Emmanuel

The Army:

Lt. Lillian Holiday	Shirley Knight
Maj. Stone	Liz Sheridan
Capt. Hannibal Jackson	Joe Grifasi
Sister Mary	Prudence Wright Holmes
Sister Jane	Alexandra Borrie
Brother Ben Owens	Bob Gunton
A Cop	David Pursley

The Fold: Kristin Jolliff, Frank Kopyc, Tom Mardirosian, Martha Miller, Victor Pappas.

Musicians: Mark Belair, David Gale, Allan Jaffee, Ronald A. Janelli, Grant Keast, Billy Kerr, William Schimmel, Charles Sharman III.

Understudies: Miss Borrie — Donna Emmanuel; Mr. Lloyd — Bob Gunton; Misses Emmanuel, Holmes — Kristin Jolliff; Messrs. Barry, Pursley — Tom Mardirosian; Misses Sheridan, Hall — Martha Miller; Messrs. Azito, Weil — Victor Pappas; Messrs. Rayson, Coe — David Pursley.

Produced with Michael Harvey; directed by Michael Posnick; musical numbers staged by Patricia Birch; musical direction, Roland Gagnon; scenery, Robert U. Taylor; costumes, Carrie F. Robbins; lighting, Jennifer Tipton; film, Scott Morris; production stage manager, Mark Wright; stage manager, Christopher Cara.

Time: December 1915. Place: Chicago. Act I: Bill's Beer Hall, Canal St., Dec. 22. Act III, Scene 1: The Beer Hall, Dec. 24. Scene 2: The Mission, later that night.

An unlikely twain — Salvation Army and gangsters — meet in the Chicago of the roaring 1920s. The attributed source of the book of *Happy End*, "Dorothy Lane," is fictitious; its exact source is unclear, but it may have been suggested to Brecht by his secretary, Elisabeth Hauptmann. It was first produced in Berlin in 1929, and musical excerpts have been interpolated into the New York revues *The World of Kurt Weill in Song* 6/6/63 for 245 performances and *Whores, Wars and Tin Pan Alley* 6/16/69 for 72 performances. The present adaptation was previously produced by the Yale Repertory Theater, New Haven, Conn.

ACT I

Prologue	Company
"The Bilbao Song"	Governor, Baby Face, Bill, Gang
"Lieutenants of the Lord"	Lillian, Army
"March Ahead"	Army
"The Sailors' Tango"	Lillian

ACT II

"Brother, Give Yourself a Shove"	Army, Fold
"Song of the Big Shot"	Governor
"Don't Be Afraid"	Jane, Army, Fold
"In Our Childhood's Bright Endeavor"	Hannibal
"The Liquor Dealer's Dream"	Hannibal, Governor, Jane, Army, Fold

ACT III

Scene 1:

"The Mandalay Song"	Sam, Gang
"Surabaya Johnny"	Lillian
"Song of the Big Shot" (Reprise)	Bill
"Ballad of the Lily of Hell"	Fly

Scene 2:

"The Happy End" (Finale)	Company

Chelsea Theater Center also presented Emlyn Williams as *Dylan Thomas Growing Up*, in association with Arthur Cantor, as a special addition to its season, 10/12/76 for 36 performances (see its entry elsewhere in this "Plays Produced off Broadway" section of this volume).

NOTE: In this volume, certain programs of off-Broadway companies like Chelsea Theater Center (which until this season was billed as The Chelsea Theater Center of Brooklyn) are exceptions to our rule of counting the number of performances from the date of the press coverage. When the official opening takes place late in the run of a play's public or subscription performances (after previews) we count the first performance of record, not the press date, as opening night. Press date for *The Prince of Homburg* was 10/31/76, for *Lincoln* 12/19/76, for *The Crazy Locomotive* 1/26/77, for *Happy End* 4/27/77.

The Phoenix Theater. Schedule of six programs. **Ladyhouse Blues** (12). By Kevin O'Morrison. Opened October 28, 1976; see note. (Closed November 7, 1976) **Canadian Gothic** and **American Modern** (12). Program of two one-act plays by Joanna M. Glass. Opened November 25, 1976; see note. (Closed December 5, 1976) **Marco Polo** (16). By Jonathan Levy. Opened December 26, 1976. (Closed January 2, 1977) **A Sorrow Beyond Dreams** (30). By Peter Handke; translated by Ralph Manheim; adapted by Daniel Freudenberger. Opened January 13, 1977; see note. (Closed January 23, 1977). Reopened February 8, 1977. (Closed February 20, 1977) **G. R. Point** (12). By David Berry. Opened April 7, 1977; see note. (Closed April 17, 1977). **Scribes** (12). By Barrie Keeffe. Opened May 26, 1977; see note. (Closed June 5, 1977) Produced by The Phoenix Theater, T. Edward Hambleton managing director, Marilyn S. Miller executive director, Daniel Freudenberger producing director, at the Marymount Manhattan Theater.

ALL PLAYS — Scenery, James Tilton; production stage manager, Tom Aberger; press, Gifford/Wallace, Inc., Tom Trenkle.

LADYHOUSE BLUES

Eylie	Christine Estabrook	Liz	Jo Henderson
Helen	Cara Duff-MacCormick	Terry	Gale Garnett
Dot	Mary-Joan Negro		

Directed by Tony Giordano; costumes, Fred Voelpel; lighting, James Tilton.
Time: 1919. Place: St. Louis, Mo. The play was presented in two parts.
Women waiting for their men to come home from World War I. Previously produced at Eugene O'Neill Memorial Theater Center, Waterford, Conn.

CANADIAN GOTHIC

Father	Tom Aldredge	Jean	Mary-Joan Negro
Mother	Joanna Merlin	Ben	John Kauffman

Time: The 1950s. Place: A small town on the Saskatchewan prairie.

AMERICAN MODERN

Mike	Tom Aldredge	Pat	Joanna Merlin

Time: The present. Place: A house in Oyster Bay.
Directed by Daniel Freudenberger; lighting, James Tilton; music composed and performed by Arthur Miller.
In *Canadian Gothic,* tragedy strikes the family of a dentist after his daughter has an affair with an Indian. *American Modern* pictures the madness of a suburban husband and wife. Foreign play previously produced in Canada and off off Broadway.

MARCO POLO

Harlequin	Jerry Zaks	Counselor Two	Brent Spiner
Nicolo Polo	Dick Latessa	Yellow Lama	Nicholas Hormann
Maffeo Polo	Luis Avalos	Achmed	Barry Snider
Prop Man	Joel Polis	Princess Kogatin	Christine Estabrook
Counselor One	David Berman	Kublai Khan	Bernard Frawley

Musicians: Robert Rogers, Mark Campo.
Directed by Lynne Meadow; costumes, Carrie F. Robbins; lighting, James Tilton; music, Robert Rogers; stage manager, Stephen Stewart-James.
Time: The last third of the 13th century. Place: The City of Venice, the court of Kublai Khan at Cambalu, the province of Yang Chow and everywhere in between. The play was presented without intermission.
The adventures of Marco Polo presented in a theater context designed for young audiences. Previously produced at Eugene O'Neill Memorial Theater Center, Waterford, Conn.

A SORROW BEYOND DREAMS

The Writer	Len Cariou

Directed by Daniel Freudenberger; lighting and projections, James Tilton.
Time: January, 1972. Place: Frankfurt, Germany. The play was presented without intermission.

Dramatic monologue in reflections on a mother's death by suicide. A foreign (Austrian) play previously produced in Europe.

G.R. POINT

Tito	Francisco Prado	Zan	William Russ
Deacon	Frank Adu	K.P.	Brent Jennings
Straw	Donald Warfield	Lt. Johnson	Woody Eney
Micah	John Heard	Shoulders	Joe Morton
Mama-San	Lori Tan Chinn		

Directed by Tony Giordano; costumes, Frances Ellen Rosenthal; lighting, Arden Fingerhut.

Time: April through November, 1969. Place Tay Loi, Vietnam.

Life and death in a Graves Registration outfit in the Vietnam War. Previously produced in a staged reading at Eugene O'Neill Playwrights' Conference, Waterford, Conn.

SCRIBES

Janet	Ann McDonough	Charlie	Donald Madden
Dan	Leonardo Cimino	Reg	Alan North
Roy	Jeffrey Jones	Spud	Kristoffer Tabori
Hunt	Stephen Joyce	Lorraine	Fran Brill
Arnold	Russell Horton	Dick	George Taylor
David	Don Scardino		

Directed by Keith Hack; lighting, James Tilton; costumes, Frances Ellen Rosenthal; production stage manager, Tom Aberger.

Time: A Thursday — press day — in October. Place: The newsroom of a small local weekly newspaper in a suburb of London. The play was presented in three parts.

A strike threatens an English small-town newspaper. A foreign play previously produced in England.

NOTE: In this volume, certain programs of off-Broadway companies like The Phoenix Theater are exceptions to our rule of counting the number of performances from the date of the press coverage. When the official opening takes place late in the run of a play's public or subscription performances (after previews) we count the first performance of record, not the press date, as opening night. Press date for *Ladyhouse Blues* was 11/1/76, for *Canadian Gothic* and *American Modern* 11/29/76, for *A Sorrow Beyond Dreams* 1/16/77, for *G.R. Point* 4/12/77, for *Scribes* 5/31/77.

Kraljevo (The Kermess) (2). Play in the Croatian language by Miroslav Krleza. Produced by Brannigan-Eisler Performing Arts International in association with Zagreb Concert Management in the Gavella Theater of Zagreb, Croatia, Yugoslavia production at the Brooklyn Academy of Music. Opened November 9, 1976. (Closed November 10, 1976)

Fat Citizen	Mato Ergovic	Janez	Pero Kvrgic
Master Japica	Drago Krca	Stijef	Josip Marotti
Mamica	Marija Kohn	Magician	Mladen Budiscak
Blind Man	Mirko Vojkovic	Anka	Semka Sokolovic
Madame	Nada Subotic	Hercules	Kresimir Zidaric

Others: Toll Collector — Ivo Fici; Villager — Ante Dulcic; Drunken Tanner — Zvonimir Ferencic; Tanner's Wife — Zdenka Anusic; Townsman — Bozidar Boban; Lady Citizens — Vjera Zagar-Nardelli, Helena Buljan, Ljubica Jovic; Old Turk — Djuro Utjesanovic; 1st Guest — Boris Miholjevic; 2d Guest — Ljubomir Kapor; 3d Guest — Zlatko Vitez; Peddler — Fahro Konjhodzic; Butcher — Mladen Serment; Margit — Ljiljana Gener; Stella — Zdenka Hersak; Manservant — Ivo Rogulja; Lola — Inga Apelt; Hajnal — Ljubica Mikulicic; Ruffian — Drago Mestrovic; Fortune Teller — Vesna Smiljanic; 1st Gentleman — Emil Glad; Magician's Assistant — Biserka Ipsa; Coachmen — Stevo Krnjajic, Mladen Budiscak, Slavko Brankov; Cripple — Vlatko Dulic; Peasants — Drago Mitrovic, Dusko Valentic, Mladen Budiscak; Soldier — Zorko Rajcic.

Directed by Dino Radojevic; scenery, Zlatko Bourek; costumes, Diana Bourek; language advisor, Dr. Bratoljub Klaic; stage manager, Drazen Grunwald; press, Langan Communications, Daniel Langan.

Time: The beginning of this century. Place: The annual fair, or kermess, in Zagreb.

Dead and living characters meet in this poet's version of a fair and join in the singing and folk dancing — the living finally prevailing over the dead. The Gavella Theater was founded in Zagreb in 1952 and its company toured the U.S. this season "as an expression of their wish to commemorate the Bicentennial."

The Gavella Theater also offered *The Badger in Court* by Peter Kocic, directed by Vanca Kljakovic, and *A Kajkavian Garden* compiled by M. Kuzmanovic and Z. Mesaric, directed by Z. Mesaric, in a single matinee performance at the Academy of Music 11/10/76.

The Plough and the Stars (15). Revival of the play by Sean O'Casey. Produced by Brooklyn Academy of Music in the Abbey Theater of Ireland production at the Brooklyn Academy of Music. Opened November 16, 1976. (Closed November 28, 1976)

Jack Clitheroe	Clive Geraghty
Nora Clitheroe	Sorcha Cusack
Peter Flynn	Bill Foley
Young Covey	John Kavanagh
Fluther Good	Cyril Cusack
Bessie Burgess	Siobhan McKenna
Mrs. Gogan	Angela Newman
Mollser	Bernadette Shortt
Capt. Brennan	Desmond Cave
Lt. Langon	Bryan Murray
Rosie Redmond	Maire O'Neill
Barman	Geoffrey Golden
Woman from Rathmines	Aine Ni Mhuiri
Figure	Peadar Lamb
Sgt. Tinley	Philip O'Flynn
Cpl. Stoddard	Niall O'Brien
Messenger from Arnotts	Robert Carlile

Directed by Tomas Mac Anna; scenery and costumes, Bronwen Casson; lighting, Leslie Scott; lighting supervisor, William Mintzer; sound, Nuala Golden; for The Abbey Theater, Tomas Mac Anna artistic director. Michal O hAodha chairman of directors; production manager, Brian Collins; stage manager, Tommy Woods; press, Kate MacIntyre, Kay Green.

Time: Acts I and II, November 1915; Acts III and IV, Easter Week 1916. Place: Dublin. Act I: The living room of the Clitheroes' three-room flat in a tenement house. Act II: A corner public house in the street where a meeting is being held. Act III: The outside of the Clitheroes' tenement house. Act IV: Bessie Burgess's room in the same tenement. The play was presented in two parts with the intermission following Act II.

O'Casey's comedy was last produced in New York by The Repertory Theater of Lincoln Center 1/4/73 for 44 performances.

In My Father's Time (8). One-man show devised, written and performed by Eamon Kelly. Produced by Brooklyn Academy of Music at the Brooklyn Academy of Music Lepercq Space. Opened November 30, 1976. (Closed December 5, 1976)

Directed by Michael Colgan; designed by Maebh Browne; press, Kate McIntyre, Kay Green.

Self-described as "a night of storytelling" of Irish jokes and tales, presented in two parts. A foreign play previously produced at the Abbey Theater, Dublin.

The Negro Ensemble Company. Schedule of two programs. **The Brownsville Raid** (112). By Charles Fuller. Opened December 5, 1976. (Closed February 27, 1977) **The Great Macdaddy** (56). Revival of the play by Paul Carter Harrison with music by Coleridge-Taylor Perkinson. Opened April 5, 1977; press date April 13, 1977. (Closed May 22, 1977. And *The Square Root of Soul*, one-man show conceived and acted by Adolph Caesar, scheduled to open 6/15/77. Produced by The Negro Ensemble Company, Douglas Turner Ward artistic director, Robert Hooks executive director, Frederick Garrett administrative director, Gerald S. Krone director of special projects, at the Theater de Lys.

THE BROWNSVILLE RAID

Pvt. John Holliman	Adolph Caesar	Pvt. Richard Johnson	Wayne Elbert
Pvt. James Newton	Charles Weldon	Dolly Saunders	Ethel Ayler
Sgt. Maj. Mingo		Orderly	Charles Brown
Saunders	Douglas Turner Ward	Mayor Combs	Robert Fitzsimmons
Pvt. Dorsey Willis	Reyno	Theodore Roosevelt	Owen Hughes
Cpl. Clifford Adair	Samm-Art Williams	Emmett Scott	Graham Brown
Pvt. Reuben Collins	Bill Cobbs	Maj. Blocker	William Mooney
Cpl. Boyd Conjers	Arthur French	Gen. Garlin	Frank Hamilton
Captain	Lawrence Keith	Sentry	Sam Finch

Directed by Israel Hicks; scenery, Neil Peter Jampolis; costumes, Mary Mease Warren; lighting, Sandra L.

Ross; production stage manager, Horacena J. Taylor; production assistant, Ron Lewis; press, Howard Atlee, Clarence Allsopp, Becky Flora.

Time: 1906. Place: Brownsville, Tex. Act I: Aug. 13 and 14. Act II: Several weeks later. Act III: Two weeks later.

Dramatization of an actual incident in which an entire black army regiment received a dishonorable discharge, with the collusion of everyone up to and including the President, for an incident of racial violence in which they did not take part.

Gilbert Lewis replaced Douglas Turner Ward 2/8/77.

THE GREAT MACDADDY

Charles Brown	Barbara Montgomery
Graham Brown	Reyno
Frankie R. Faison	Charles Weldon
Bill Mackey	Lynn Whitfield

Directed by Douglas Turner Ward; choreography, Dianne McIntyre; scenery, William Ritman; costumes, Mary Mease Warren; lighting, Sandra L. Ross; stage manager, Horacena J. Taylor.

The Great Macdaddy was originally produced off Broadway by The Negro Ensemble Company 2/12/74 for 72 performances. This revival was previously produced in St. Croix and St. Thomas, V.I.

A listing of the numerous scene divisions and titles appears on pages 394–5 of *The Best Plays of 1973–74*.

Joseph and the Amazing Technicolor Dreamcoat (23). Musical based on the Old Testament story; book, music and lyrics by Tim Rice and Andrew Lloyd Webber. Produced by The Brooklyn Academy of Music at the Brooklyn Academy of Music. Opened December 30, 1976. (Closed January 9, 1977)

Narrator .... Cleavon Little	Zebulum .... Craig Schaefer
Jacob .... Tony Hoty	Gad .... David Patrick Kelly
Sons of Jacob:	Benjamin ....Leonard John Crofoot
Joseph .... David-James Carroll	Judah .... Robert Rhys
Reuben .... Stuart Pankin	Potiphar .... Terry Eno
Simeon .... Adam Grammis	Mrs. Potiphar .... Virginia Martin
Levi .... Paul Kreppel	Baker ....Kurt Yahjian
Napthali .... Don Swanson	Butler .... David Patrick Kelly
Isaachar .... Ron Taylor	Pharaoh .... Jess Pearson
Asher ....William Parry	Egyptian; Ishmaelite .... Richard Seer
Dan ....Kurt Yahjian	

The Brooklyn Boys Chorus.

Ladies: Mary Jane Houdina, Marybeth Kurdock, Jill Streisant.

Musicians: Bob Mintzer flute, piccolo, clarinet; Bill Blount clarinet, bass clarinet, soprano saxophone; Danny Cahn trumpet; Sam Burtis trombone, tuba; Jim Miller guitar; Harvey Auger bass guitar; Steve Margoshes piano, harpsichord, electric organ; Allen Herman drums; Neal Boyar percussion.

Directed by Frank Dunlop; choreography, Grace Daniele; musical direction, Steve Margoshes; design, Nadine Baylis; scenery supervision, John Pitts; costumes supervision, Dona Granata; lighting, F. Mitchell Dana; sound, Abe Jacob; production stage manager, Frank Bayer; stage manager, Barbara-Mae Phillips; press, Kate MacIntyre, Kay Green.

Musicalization of the Biblical tale of Joseph's escape from slavery. Previously produced by the Young Vic in London and Playhouse in the Park, Philadelphia.

ACT I

"Jacob and Sons"; "Joseph's Coat" .... Narrator, Brothers, Choir (Boys), Jacob, Joseph
"Joseph's Dreams" .... Narrator, Joseph, Brothers
"Poor, Poor Joseph" ....Narrator, Brothers, Choir
"One More Angel in Heaven" .... Narrator, Brothers, Girl
"Potiphar" .... Choir, Narrator, Male Chorus (Adults), Mrs. Potiphar, Joseph, Potiphar
"Close Every Door" .... Joseph, Choir
"Go, Go, Go, Joseph" ....Narrator, Butler, Baker, Male Chorus, Joseph

ACT II

"Pharaoh's Story" .... Narrator, Choir
"Poor, Poor Pharaoh"; "Song of the King" ....Narrator, Lively Lad, Pharaoh, Choir, Chorus
"Pharaoh's Dreams Explained" ....Joseph, Choir, Chorus
"Stone the Crows" .... Narrator, Pharaoh, Choir, Adoring Girls, Joseph

"Those Canaan Days" .... Reuben, Brothers
"The Brothers Come to Egypt"; "Grovel, Grovel" .... Narrator, Choir, Brothers, Joseph
"Who's the Thief" ....Joseph, Choir, Brothers
"Benjamin Calypso" .... Brothers
"Joseph All the Time" ....Narrator, Joseph, Choir, Brothers
"Jacob in Egypt" .... Narrator, Choir, Chorus
"Any Dream Will Do" ....Joseph, Choir, Chorus

Nightclub Cantata (145). Revue conceived and composed by Elizabeth Swados. Produced by Charles Hollerith Jr. and Rosita Sarnoff in the Music-Theater Performing Group/Lenox Arts Center (Lyn Austin and Mary D. Silverman executive directors) production at the Top of the Gate. Opened January 9, 1977. (Closed May 15, 1977)

Karen Evans	Shelley Plimpton
Rocky Greenburg	David Schechter
Paul Kandel	Elizabeth Swados
JoAnna Peled	Mark Zagaeski

Judith Fleisher piano; William Milhizer percussion.

Directed by Elizabeth Swados; scenery, Patricia Woodbridge; costumes, Kate Carmel; lighting, Cheryl Thacker; associate producer, Martha Sturtevant; stage manager, Susan D. Greenbaum; press, Mary Bryant, Bruce Cohen, Richard Kagey.

Musical commentary on our life and times, with some literary references, previously produced off off Broadway at Westbeth and at the Lenox Arts Center in Stockbridge, Mass. The play was presented without intermission.

MUSICAL NUMBERS: "Things I Didn't Know I Loved" (words by Nazim Hikmet) — Company; "Bestiario" (words by Pablo Neruda) — Company; "Bird Chorus" — Company; "Bird Lament" — Elizabeth Swados; "Ventriloquist & Dummy" (words by Swados and Judith Fleisher) — David Schechter, Karen Evans, Mark Zagaeski, Shelley Plimpton; "The Applicant" (words by Sylvia Plath) — Evans; "To the Harbormaster" (words by Frank O'Hara) — Rocky Greenberg, Zagaeski; "Adolescents" (children's writings from *Male & Female Under 18* by Eve Merriam-Nancy Larrick) Greenberg, Evans; "Indecision" (words by Swados) — Company; "Dibarti" (words by David Avidan) — JoAnna Peled, Zagaeski; "In Dreams Begin Responsibilities" (words by Delmore Schwartz) — Company; "Are You With Me?" (words by Swados) — Plimpton; "Raga" — Schechter, Company; "Waking This Morning" (words by Muriel Rukeyser) — Plimpton, Evans, Swados, Peled; "Pastrami Brothers" — Zagaeski, Greenberg, Schechter, Paul Kandel; "The Ballad of the Sad Cafe" (words by Carson McCullers) — Peled, Evans; "Sabella" (words by Isabella Leitner) — Peled, Company; "Waiting" (words by Swados) — Greenberg, Evans, Schechter, Peled; "The Dance" (words by Swados) — Peled, Company; "On Living" (Words by Nazim Hikmet) — Company.

*New York Shakespeare Festival Public Theater. Schedule of five programs. **Marco Polo Sings a Solo** (64). By John Guare. Opened January 12, 1977; see note. (Closed March 6, 1977) ***Ashes** (145). By David Rudkin. Opened January 25, 1977; see note. **Hagar's Children** (80). By Ernest Joselovitz. Opened March 8, 1977; see note. (Closed May 15, 1977) **On the Lock-In** (62). Musical with book, music and lyrics by David Langston Smyrl; conceived by Robert Macbeth. Opened April 14, 1977; see note. (Closed June 5, 1977) **Creditors** and **The Stronger** (56). Program of revivals of one-act plays by August Strindberg; new translations by Palaemona Morner and R. Spacek. Opened April 15, 1977; see note. (Closed June 5, 1977) Produced by New York Shakespeare Festival, Joseph Papp producer, Bernard Gersten associate producer, at the Public Theater.

MARCO POLO SINGS A SOLO

Diane McBride	Madeline Kahn	Lusty McBride	Chev Rodgers
Tom Wintermouth	Chris Sarandon	Mrs. McBride	Anne Jackson
Freydis	Sigourney Weaver	Larry Rockwell	James Jansen
Stony McBride	Joel Grey	Frank Schaeffer	Larry Bryggman

Understudies: Mr. Grey — John Bottoms; Messrs. Rodgers, Bryggman — Michael Fairman; Misses Kahn, Weaver — Christine Lahti; Miss Jackson — Parker McCormick; Messrs. Sarandon, Jansen — Larry Pine.

Directed by Mel Shapiro; scenery, John Wulp; costumes, Theoni V. Aldredge; lighting, Jennifer Tipton; production supervisor, Jason Steven Cohen; production stage manager, D. W. Koehler; stage manager, Sally Campbell; press, Merle Debuskey, Bob Ullman, Richard Kornberg.

Time: 1999. Place: A garden on the island of Trollenthor, 40 miles off the coast of Norway. Act I: Early spring. Act II, Scene 1: Immediately after that. Scene 2: Three days later.

Fanciful, futuristic concept of movie making two decades from now. Previously produced by the Nantucket, Mass. Stage Company.

ASHES

Colin	Brian Murray	Man	John Tillinger
Anne	Roberta Maxwell	Woman	Penelope Allen

Understudies: Misses Maxwell, Allen — Marian Clarke; Messrs. Murray, Tillinger — Steven Gilborn.

Directed by Lynne Meadow; scenery, John Lee Beatty; costumes, Jennifer von Mayrhauser; lighting, Dennis Parichy, sound, George Hansen, Charles London; produced in association with Manhattan Theater Club; production supervisor, Jason Steven Cohen; production stage manager, Zane Weiner; stage manager, Darrell Ziegler.

Time: Now. Place: England. The play was performed without intermission.

Clinical report of a childless couple striving to have a baby, a metaphor of Northern Ireland trying to insure its heritage. A foreign play previously produced in London and at the Mark Taper Forum, Los Angeles and off off Broadway at the Manhattan Theater Club.

A Best Play; see page 131.

HAGAR'S CHILDREN

The Staff:		Sharon	Jan Dorn
Esther Roxburg	Carmen Vickers	Mervin	Tri Garraty
Oliver Davidson	Lloyd Davis Jr.	David	Thomas Simpson
The Children:		The Outsiders:	
Diana	Dorothy Hayden	Tom Hervala	Gardner Hathaway
Rob	Brian Wiese	Sheriff	Mark Simon

Guitarist: Gardner Hathaway.

Understudies: Miss Vickers — Anne Barclay; Misses Hayden, Dorn — Jacklyn Maddux; Mr. Davis — Nathaniel Robinson; Messrs. Garraty, Wiese, Simpson — Gardner Hathaway.

Directed by Robert Graham Small; music, Randy Lee Ross; scenery and lighting, Clarke Dunham; a co-production with New Playwrights Theater of Washington, Harry M. Bagdasian producing director, Paul Hildebrand Jr. artistic director; production supervisor, Jason Steven Cohen.

Time: The day and night before Christmas 1971. Place: Bridgehaven Farm.

Drama of emotionally disturbed teen-agers in an institution, written by a former staff member in such a shelter. Previously produced at The Changing Scene, Denver, and in workshop at American Conservatory Theater, San Francisco.

ON THE LOCK-IN

Houndog	David Langston Smyrl	Rock	Ezra Jack Maret
Frankie	Manuel Santiago	Guard	Leon Thomas
Mess Hall	Harold Cromer	Jazz	Alan Weeks
Home Boy	Billy Barnes	Small Times	Henry Bradley
Jerry	Henry Baker	Abdu	Don Jay
Dude	Thomas M. Brimm II		

Directed by Robert Macbeth; musical direction, George Stubbs; scenery, Karl Eigsti; costumes, Grace Williams; lighting, Victor En Yu Tan; musical arrangements, Paul Griffin; production stage manager, Toby Scott Macbeth.

Episodes of prison life. The play was presented without intermission.

MUSICAL NUMBERS

"Whatever It Happens To Be"	Company
"Dry Mouth With No Water"	Jazz, Company
"Born to Lose"	Guard, Company
"Sister Paradise"	Houndog, Company
"Peace Will Come"	Abdu, Jazz, Jerry, Rock
"Circumstances"	Dude, Company
"42d St. Blues"	Mess Hall
"Talkin' Blues"	Houndog
"Marlene"	Small Times
"Alone"	Home Boy

THE STRONGER

Mlle. Y .... Geraldine Page   Waitress .... Judith L'Heureux
Mrs. X .... Amy Wright

CREDITORS

Adolf .... John Heard   Tekla .... Geraldine Page
Gustav .... Rip Torn   Women .... Amy Wright, Judith L'Heureux

Directed by Rip Torn; scenery, John Wright Stevens; costume coordination, Carrie F. Robbins; lighting, Ian Calderon; production stage manager, James Pentecost; produced in association with the Sanctuary Theater Workshop, Inc.

Program of Strindberg one-acters previously produced off off Broadway at Hudson Guild Theater. *The Stronger* was last produced off Broadway 11/10/65 for 11 performances in tandem with Strindberg's *Miss Julie*. *Creditors* was last produced in the Roundabout's workshop program 7/4/72–7/9/72.

In addition to its regular programs, New York Shakespeare Festival Public Theater also mounted various experimental and workshop productions (including *Gogol* by Len Jenkins which suspended performances after a single preview 12/15/77). A listing appears in the "Plays Produced off off Broadway" section of this volume. The organization also provided space for a guest presentation of the Mabou Mines *The B. Beaver Animation*, text and direction by Lee Breuer.

In Joseph Papp's Public Theater there are many separate auditoriums. *Marco Polo Sings a Solo* and *Creditors* and *The Stronger* played the Estelle R. Newman Theater, *Ashes* played the Florence S. Anspacher Theater, *Hagar's Children* played Martinson Hall and *On the Lock-In* played LuEsther Hall.

NOTE: In this volume, certain programs of off-Broadway companies like New York Shakespeare Festival are exceptions to our rule of counting the number of performances from the date of the press coverage. When the official opening takes place late in the run of a play's public or subscription performances (after previews) we count the first performance of record, not the press date, as opening night. Press date for *Marco Polo Sings a Solo* was 2/5/77, for *Ashes* 2/8/77, for *Hagar's Children* 3/23/77, for *On the Lock-In* 4/27/77, for *Creditors* and *The Stronger* 5/17/77.

The Cockeyed Tiger (5). Musical by Eric Blau; musical score by Bert Kalmar and Harry Ruby; original music and lyrics by Nicholas Meyers and Eric Blau. Produced by James J. Wisner at the Astor Place Theater. Opened January 13, 1977. (Closed January 16, 1977)

Directed by Eric Blau; choreography, Gemze de Lapp, Buzz Miller; scenery and costumes, Donald Jensen; lighting, Crimmins & Smith; arrangements, Nicholas Meyers, Nicholas Archer, Jimmy Wisner; production stage manager, George Allison Elmer; press, Jeffrey Richards, Lewis Harmon. With James Nisbet Clark, Robert Matthews, Chris Campbell, Wendy Wolfe, Janet McCall, Leon Morenzie, Joseph Neal, Jack Scalici, Elly Stone.

Place: The newly refurbished facsimile of the old and celebrated Klub Kishka at Broome and Houston Streets, New York City. The play was presented in two parts.

Subtitled "The Last, Final, Farewell Peformance Tour" of a night club performer who is worried about tigers as an endangered species. Titles of original songs were "The Littleflea Hop," "Tyger, Tyger," "It's a Long, Long March to Kansas City," "We're Together," "Good Times," "You've Got To Be a Tiger, Tiger," "Daddy Oh!" and "You Were a Hell of a Crowd Tonight."

Castaways (1). Musical based on the play *She Would Be a Soldier* by Mordecai Noah; book by Anthony Stimac, Dennis Anderson and Ron Whyte; music by Don Pippin; lyrics by Steve Brown. Produced by Jeff Britton in association with Jimmy Merrill at the Promenade Theater. Opened and closed at the evening performance, February 7, 1977.

Directed by Tony Tanner; musical direction, Dorothy Opalach; scenery, Scott Johnson; costumes, Pat McGourty; lighting, Richard Winkler; press, Shirley Herz. With Gibby Brand, Stephen James, Joel Kramer, Rick Ladson, Maureen Maloney, Wayne Sherwood, June Squibb, Daniel Ziskie, Kathleen Widdoes.

Theater troupe is captured and held by Barbary Pirates, per its source, written in 1819.

Starting Here, Starting Now (120). Musical revue with music by David Shire; lyrics by Richard Maltby Jr. Produced by Steve Abrams, Mary Jo Slater and Scott Mansfield in association with Morton Schwartz at the Barbarann Theater Restaurant. Opened March 7, 1977. (Closed June 19, 1977)

Loni Ackerman   Margery Cohen
George Lee Andrews

Directed by Richard Maltby Jr.; musical direction, Robert W. Preston; choreography, Ethel Martin; costumes, Stanley Simmons; production stage manager, Joan Liepman; bassist, John Loehrke; press, Henry Luhrman Associates, Anne Obert Weinberg.

A new edition of an eclectic revue previously produced off off Broadway at Manhattan Theater Club under the title *Theater Songs by Maltby & Shire.*

ACT I: "The Word Is Love" — Company; "Starting Here, Starting Now" — Company; "A Little Bit Off" — Margery Cohen, George Lee Andrews; "I Think I May Want to Remember Today" — Loni Ackerman, Cohen; "Beautiful" — Company; "We Can Talk to Each Other" — Andrews, Cohen; "Across the River" — Company; "Crossword Puzzle" — Ackerman; "Autumn" — Cohen; "I Don't Remember Christmas" — Andrews; "I Don't Believe It" — Company; "I Hear Bells" — Andrews, Company; "I'm Going to Make You Beautiful" — Cohen; "Pleased With Myself" — Company.

ACT II: "Hey There Fans" — Andrews; "Girl of the Minute" — Company; "A Girl You Should Know" — Ackerman; "Travel" — Company; "Watching the Parade Go By" Cohen — "Flair" — Andrews; "What About Today" (lyrics by David Shire) — Ackerman; "One Step" — Company; "song of Me" — Cohen; "Today Is the First Day of the Rest of My Life" — Ackerman, Cohen; "A New Life Coming" — Company.

Monsters (61).
Program of two one-act plays: **Side Show** by William Dews and **The Transfiguration of Benno Blimpie** by Albert Innaurato. Produced by Adela Holzer at the Astor Place Theater. Opened March 10, 1977. (Closed May 1, 1977)

SIDE SHOW

Jeffrey	Richard De Fabees	Arnold	Robert Drivas

THE TRANSFIGURATION OF BENNO BLIMPIE

Benno	James Coco	Girl	K. McKenna
Old Man	Peter Carew	Father	Roger Serbagi
Mother	Rosemary De Angelis		

Standbys: Messrs. Coco, Carew — Henry Ferrentino; Messrs. De Fabees, Drivas — Steve Scott; Miss De Angelis — Marion Paone.

Directed by Robert Drivas; scenery and costumes, Rubén de Saavedra; lighting, Ian Calderon; production stage manager, Larry Forde; stage manager, Tony de Santis; press, Michael Alpert, Marilynn LeVine, Warren Knowlton, Randi Cone.

In *Side Show,* Siamese twins gloat over the murdered bodies of their parents who exploited them. In *The Transfiguration of Benno Blimpie* an unloved, misfit child fattens himself for a hideous suicide.

Movie Buff (21).
Musical with book and lyrics by Hiram Taylor; music and lyrics by John Raniello. Produced by Free Space, Ltd. at the Actors Playhouse. Opened March 14, 1977. (Closed April 3, 1977)

Spirit of the 1930s	Charlie Scatamacchia	Sally Smith	Nancy Rich
Mike Williams	Jim Richards	Tom	Mark Waldrop
Joanne Simpson	Deborah Carlson	Mildred	Marianna Doro
Velma	Nora Cole	Robert Robbins	Keith Curran

Directed by Jim Payne; musical direction and arrangements, Donald G. Jones; choreography, Jack Dyville; scenery, Jimmy Cuomo; costumes, Carol Wenz; lighting, Jo Mayer; stage manager, Jessie Frank; press, Herb Striesfield.

Time: Now. Place: New York City.

A fantasy of nostalgia for the Hollywood movies of the 1930s.

ACT I

"Silver Screen"	Spirit, Mike
"Something to Believe In"	Velma, Joanne, Sally
"Movietown, U.S.A."	Sally, Joanne, Velma, Tom
"You Are Something Very Special"	Mike, Joanne
"Where Is the Man"	Mildred
"Movie Stars"	Mike
"May I Dance With You?"	Velma, Tom, Sally
"Tell a Little Lie or Two"	Tom, Robert, Velma, Joanne

ACT II

"Song of Yesterday"	Spirit
"The Movie Cowboy"	Robert

"Reflections in a Mirror" .... Joanne
"All-Talking, All-Singing, All-Dancing" .... Joanne, Company
"Coming Attractions" .... Mike, Spirit
"Tomorrow" .... Joanne, Company
"Song of Yesterday" (Reprise) .... Spirit
"Silver Screen" (Reprise) .... Spirit, Mike

The BAM Theater Company. Schedule of two revivals. **The New York Idea** (28). By Langdon Mitchell. Opened March 18, 1977; see note. (Closed April 10, 1977). **Three Sisters** (24). By Anton Chekhov; translated by Stark Young. Opened April 26, 1977; see note. (Closed May 15, 1977) Produced by The BAM Theater Company at the Helen Owen Carey Playhouse of the Brooklyn Academy of Music.

BOTH PLAYS — Directed by Frank Dunlop; scenery, William Ritman; costumes, Nancy Potts; lighting, F. Mitchell Dana; administrative director, Berenice Weiler; production stage manager, Frank Bayer; stage manager, Barbara-Mae Phillips; press, Kate MacIntyre, Kay Green.

THE NEW YORK IDEA

Grace Phillimore	Diana Kirkwood	Rev. Matthew Phillimore	Edward Zang
Miss Heneage	Margaret Hamilton	Vida Phillimore	Rosemary Harris
Thomas	Jerome Collamore	John Karslake	Rene Auberjonois
Mrs. Phillimore	Justine Johnston	Sir Wilfred Cates-Darby	Denholm Elliott
William Sudley	Ralph Clanton	Benson	Holly Villaire
Cynthia Karslake	Blythe Danner	Brooks	Alek Primrose
Phillip Phillimore	Stephen Collins	Nogam	George David Connolly
Tim Fiddler	Leon Russom		

Understudies: Messrs. Collins, Elliott — Alek Primrose; Messrs. Zang, Auberjonois — Leon Russom; Misses Kirkwood, Harris — Holly Villaire; Messrs. Clanton, Connolly — Jerome Collamore; Misses Villaire, Danner — Diana Kirkwood.

Time: May, 1906. Place: New York. Scene 1: Living room in the house of Phillip Phillimore, 5 o'clock of an afternoon. Scene 2: Mrs. Vida Phillimore's boudoir, the next morning. Scene 3: Living room in the house of Phillip Phillimore, that evening. Scene 4: John Karslake's study and smoking room, late that evening. The play was presented in two parts with the intermission following Scene 2.

The New York Idea was first produced on Broadway 11/19/06. It was revived 9/28/15 and 3/22/33 for 3 performances.

THREE SISTERS

The Prozoroff Family:		Maid	Diana Kirkwood
Olga	Rosemary Harris	The Garrison:	
Masha	Ellen Burstyn	Lt. Col. Vershinin	Denholm Elliott
Irina	Tovah Feldshuh	Staff Capt. Solyony	Rene Auberjonois
Andrey	Stephen Collins	Lt. Baron Tusenbach	Austin Pendleton
Natalia Ivanovna	Holly Villaire	Tchebutykin	Barnard Hughes
Kulygin	Rex Robbins	2d Lt. Fedotik	Stuart Pankin
Anfisa	Margaret Hamilton	2d Lt. Roday	David Patrick Kelly
Ferapont	Ralph Clanton	Orderly	Robert Windslow

Travelling musicians: Diana Kirkwood, William Tynes, Robert Windslow.
Understudies: Misses Harris, Burstyn, Feldshuh, Villaire — Diana Kirkwood.
Place: The house of the Prozoroffs in a garrison town in provincial Russia. Act I: Spring, a living room, noon. Act II: The next February, a living room, 8:15 p.m. Act III: Several years later, an attic bedroom, just before dawn. Act IV: A few months later, autumn, the garden and the terrace, noon. The play was presented in two parts with the intermission following Act II.

The last professional New York production of *Three Sisters* was by the Acting Company on Broadway 11/4/75 for 8 performances. The music and songs in this BAM production were as chosen for the original.

NOTE: In this volume, certain programs of off-Broadway companies like The BAM Theater Company are exceptions to our rule of counting the number of performances from the date of the press coverage. When the official opening takes place late in the run of a play's public or subscription performances (after previews) we count the first performance of record, not the press date, as opening night. Press date for *The New York Idea* was 3/27/77, for *Three Sisters* 5/3/77.

Waiting for Godot (7). Revival of the play by Samuel Beckett in the German language; German translation by Elmar Tophoven. Produced by the Berlin Now Festival of Goethe

House in the Schiller Theater, Berlin production at the Lepercq Space of the Brooklyn Academy of Music. Opened March 29, 1977. (Closed April 3, 1977)

Estragon	Horst Bollmann	Pozzo	Carl Raddatz
Vladimir	Stafan Wigger	Boy	Torsten Sense
Lucky	Klaus Herm		

Directed by Samuel Beckett; scenery and costumes, Matias; lighting, Heinz Hohenwald; technical direction, Julian Herrey; press, Kate MacIntyre, Kay Green.

German-language production, directed by the author, on a visit to the U.S. from Berlin. The most recent New York professional revival of this play took place off Broadway 2/3/71 for 277 performances.

Jockeys (8). By Frank Spiering and Milton Katselas; script supervision by Michael Shurtleff. Produced by Jule Styne and Joseph Kipness, associate producers Dorothy Dicker and Charlotte Dicker, at the Promenade Theater. Opened April 11, 1977. (Closed April 17, 1977)

Directed by Milton Katselas; music, Bernardo Segall; scenery, Peter Wexler; sound, Gary Harris; martial arts choreography, Dan DiVito; choreographer and associate director, Gerald Arpino; production supervision, Fritz Holt; press, The Merlin Group, Ltd., Harriett Trachtenberg. With Chick Vennera, David Nichols, Alfred Mancini, Nicholas B. Daddario, Daniel Feraldo, John Widlock, Thaao Penghis, Simone Griffeth, Richard Forbes, Daryl Roach, Pamela Poitier, Harry Davis.

The love story of a Puerto Rican jockey and a ballerina.

The Perfect Mollusc (1). By Ben Tarver. Produced by Donald Goldman at the Players Theater. Opened and closed at the evening performance, April 20, 1977.

Directed by George Wojtasik; scenery, Richard Williams; press, Max Gendel. With Frank Anderson, Marian Clarke, Robert Lanchester, Marilyn McIntyre.

Adaptation of an English play of the early 1900s, *Dulcibella*, about a selfishly demanding woman.

***Der Ring Gott Farblonjet** (30). Musical based on the Volsung saga; book by Charles Ludlam; music by Jack McElwaine. Produced by the Ridiculous Theatrical Company, Charles Ludlam artistic director, at the Truck and Warehouse Theater. Opened April 27, 1977.

Black-Eyed Susan	Georg Osterman
John D. Brockmeyer	Lola Pashalinski
Richard Currie	Bill Vehr
Adam McAdam	

Directed by Charles Ludlam; design, Charles Ludlam; general manager, Catherine Smith; press, Alan Eichler.

Combination of various versions of the ring story (including Wagner's, Ibsen's and Nietzsche's), presented in this company's unique style.

New York City Street Show (20). Musical conceived by Peter Copani; book, music and lyrics by Peter Copani. Produced by Peter Copani and Victor Papa in The People's Performing Company production at the Actors Playhouse. Opened April 28, 1977. (Closed May 15, 1977)

Sergio	Bob Arcaro	Vernon	Hubert Kelly
Meri	Eva Charney	Xena	Deborah Malone
Jesus	Rob DeRosa	Gina	Theresa Saldana
Anita	Florie Freshman	Bob	Richard Woods

Musicians: Steven Oirich keyboard, Matthew Patuto drums, Gary Epstein bass.

Directed by Peter Copani; musical direction, Steven Oirich; scenery, Jim Chestnut; lighting, Richard Harper; stage manager, Ron Lawrence; press, Herb Striesfield.

Prologue: A community meeting. Scene 1: A community betterment center. Scene 2: One week later. Scene 3: One week later. Scene 4: Later the same day. Scene 5: Afternoon of first performance. Scene 6: The Lincoln Center Festival. Previously produced off off Broadway at Greenwich House.

MUSICAL NUMBERS

"American Dream" .... Company
(music by David McHugh)

"Who Can Say?" .... Gina, Xena
"God Is in the People" ....Sergio, Jesus, Company
"A Special Man" ....Anita
"Strawberries, Pickles and Ice Cream" .... Meri
"Hail, Hail" ....Gina, Company
"Kung Fu" .... Vernon, Bob
"One of Us" ....Xena
"When You Are Together" .... Sergio, Bob
   (music by David McHugh)
"If Jesus Walked" .... Company
"Bad But Good" .... Company
"Make Them Hate" .... Company
"Corruption" .... Gina
"Wait and See" ....Xena
   (music by Peter Copani and Ed Vogel)
"Hanging Out" .... Bob, Company
"Love Is Beautiful" .... Company

Peg o' My Heart (15). Revival of the play by J. Hartley Manners. Produced by Saul Novick, Marion Brasch and Leonard Finger in the Lion Theater Company production at Theater Four. Opened May 4, 1977. (Closed May 15, 1977)

Jarvis ....Gibson Glass	Brent ....Donovan Sylvest
Bennett .... Mary E. Baird	"Peg" ....Sofia Landon
Mrs. Chichester ....Kathleen Tremaine	Montgomery Hawkes ....Ken Costigan
Ethel ....Sandra Halperin	"Jerry" .... Allan Carlsen
Alaric .... Jim Ricketts	

Directed by Gene Nye; scenery, Miguel Romero; costumes, David James; lighting, Joseph Spencer; production stage manager, Andrea Naier; press, Shirley Herz.

Time: Early summer. Place: The living room of Regal Villa, Mrs. Chichester's House in Scarborough, England. Act I: The coming of Peg. Act II: The rebellion of Peg, one month later. Act III: Peg o' My Heart, the next morning.

This production of the 1912 comedy was previously presented off off Broadway this season. *Peg o' My Heart* was first produced on Broadway 12/20/12 for 603 performances and has since been revived 2/14/21 and 5/5/24 (in a musical version).

I Was Sitting on My Patio This Guy Appeared I Thought I Was Hallucinating (9). By Robert Wilson; music by Alan Lloyd. Produced by Richard Barr at the Cherry Lane Theater. Opened May 22, 1977. (Closed May 29, 1977)

Directed by Lucinda Childs and Robert Wilson; scenery, Robert Wilson, Christina Giannini; lighting, Beverly Emmons; film production, Greta Wing Miller; production coordinator, Robert Lo Bianco; press, The Merlin Group, Ltd., Sandra Manley. With Lucinda Childs, Robert Wilson.

Non-literal, many-sided theater effects in the unique Robert Wilson style. The play was presented in two parts.

The Sunday Promenade (14). By Lars Forssell; translated by Harry G. Carlson. Produced by Polaris Repertory Theater, Robert Horen artistic director, at the Off Center. Opened May 24, 1977. (Closed June 5, 1977)

Directed by Robert Horen; scenery, Elfie Von Kantzow; costumes and lighting, J.D. Keene; press, Max Eisen, Barbara Glenn. With Thomas Barbour, Bruce Bouchard, Suzanne Granfield, Greg Johnson, K. T. Baumann, Mary Carter.

Comedy-drama, a foreign play previously produced in Stockholm under Ingmar Bergman's direction.

PLAYS PRODUCED
OFF OFF BROADWAY

AND ADDITIONAL PRODUCTIONS

Here is a comprehensive sampling of off off Broadway and other experimental or peripheral 1976-77 productions in New York, compiled by Camille Croce. There is no definitive "off-off-Broadway" area or qualification. To try to define or regiment it would be untrue to its fluid, exploratory purpose. The listing below of about 650 programs by 78 major OOB groups and another 200-plus programs by 140 or more miscellaneous groups is as inclusive as reliable sources will allow, however, and takes in almost all Manhattan-based, new-play-producing, English-language organizations listed by the Off Off Broadway Alliance and the Theater Development Fund — plus many others.

The more active and established producing groups are identified in **bold face type,** in alphabetical order, with artistic policies and the name of the managing director(s) given whenever these are a matter of record. Examples of their 1976-77 programs — and in many cases a group's whole 1976-77 schedule — are listed with play titles in CAPITAL LETTERS. Often these are works in progress with changing scripts, casts and directors, usually without an engagement of record (but an opening or early performance date is included when available).

A large selection of other groups and shows that made appearances during the season appears under the "miscellaneous" heading at the end of this listing.

Actors' Alliance. Dedicated to bring actors and audiences together in a community of delight, understanding and humanity. William Arrigon, William Newman, Nina Polan, founding members.

> BREAK OF NOON by Paul Claudel. Directed by William Arrigon; with Nina Polan, Evan Thompson, James Higgins, William Arrigon, Michael Varna.
> UNCLE VANYA by Anton Chekhov. April 15, 1977. Directed by Bruce Jordan; with Eda Reiss Merin, William Newman, Jack Poggi, Donald Pace, Margaret Donohue, Marsha Korb.
> THE LAST WAR by David Scanlan. May 21, 1977. Directed by William Newman; with Paul Lieber, Frederick Good, Peter DeLaurier, Andrea Cullen, Nina Polan, Ceal Phelan.

The Actors Studio. Development of talent in productions of old and new works. Lee Strasberg, artistic director.

> FROM THE MEMOIRS OF PONTIUS PILATE by Eric Bentley. December 2, 1976. Directed by Ed Setrakian.
> ALFRED DIES by Israel Horovitz. January 14, 1977. (Open rehearsals supervised by Ben Levit).
> RICHARD III by William Shakespeare. May, 1977. Directed by Arthur Sherman.

Afro-American Studio. Express the black experience in terms of theater. Ernie McClintock, artistic director.

> FREEMAN by Phillip Hayes Dean. March 31, 1977. Directed by Ernie McClintock.
> TABERNACLE by Paul Carter Harrison. April 1, 1977. Directed by Ernie McClintock.
> A SON, COME HOME by Ed Bullins, directed by Glenda Dickerson; CLARA'S OLE MAN by Ed Bullins, directed by Ernie McClintock; POETRY THEATER, directed by Helmar Cooper. April 2, 1977.

A HAND IS ON THE GATE by Roscoe Lee Browne. April 3, 1977 matinee. Directed by Ernie McClintock.

EL HAJJ MALIK by N. R. Davidson. April 3, 1977. Directed by Ernie McClintock.

Amas Repertory Theater. Creative arts as a powerful instrument of peaceful change, towards healthier individuals. Rosetta LeNoire, founder and artistic director.

MIKADO AMAS (operetta) by Gilbert and Sullivan, adapted by Rosetta LeNoire. October 14, 1976. Directed by Irving Vincent.

BOJANGLES! by N. R. Mitgang. December 18, 1976. Directed by Ira Cirker; with Luther Fontaine, Billie Allen, Don Paul, James Shearwood.

COME LAUGH AND CRY WITH LANGSTON HUGHES adapted by Rosetta LeNoire and Clyde Williams from Langston Hughes's *Shakespeare in Harlem*. February 3, 1977. Directed by Bill Mason.

SAVE THE SEEDS, DARLING by Helen Powers. April, 1977. Directed by Arthur Whitelaw.

American Ensemble Company. Interested in literary value of plays; concerned with entertaining as well as stimulating thoughts of audiences. Robert Petito, artistic director.

THE HERETIC by Morris L. West. October 7, 1976.

THE HUMAN VOICE by Jean Cocteau. November 4, 1976. Directed by Robert Schwager.

THE BRICK AND THE ROSE by Lewis John Carlino. January 7, 1977. Directed by Robert Petito.

RED PEPPERS by Noel Coward. January 28, 1977. Directed by Robert Schwager.

LADIES IN RETIREMENT by Edward Percy and Reginald Denham. March 3, 1977. Directed by Barry Moss; with Jean Hafgren, Barbara Harner, Doreen Richardson, Jean Hogan.

BELL, BOOK AND CANDLE by John Van Druten. May 5, 1977. Directed by Robert Petito.

The American Place Theater Basement Space. Presents completely developed new plays (usually short) by American writers, not presented as part of the regular subscription season. Wynn Handman, director.

MANGO PLUS FAN EQUALS HAPPINESS by Steven Shea. January 5, 1977. Directed by Paul Cooper; with Amy Robinson.

American Stanislavski Theater (AST). Development of the Stanislavski technique in the American Theater. Sonia Moore, artistic director and director of all productions.

LOOK BACK IN ANGER by John Osborne. January 21, 1977.

A STREETCAR NAMED DESIRE by Tennessee Williams. March 4, 1977.

ANNIVERSARY, THE BOOR and THE MARRIAGE PROPOSAL by Anton Chekhov. April 15, 1977.

MY POOR MARAT by Aleksei Arbuzov. May 27, 1977.

American Theater Company. New works done, but accent on the American theater's heritage. Richard Kuss, artistic director.

AARON BURR by Charles Hallett. June, 1976. Directed by Ellis Santone.

MULLIGAN GUARD BALL by Edward Harrigan. January 20, 1977. Directed by Richard Kuss; with Anne Gerety, Marshall Anker, Gail Ryan, Sally Anne Tackus, Robert LeVoyd Wright.

SOLDIERS OF FREEDOM by Louis Rivers. March 4, 1977. Directed by Thurman Scott; with Hermine Bartee, O. B. Lewis, Gwendolen Hardwick, Christopher Murray, Marilyn Randall, Todd Davis.

WE AIN'T WHAT WE WAS by Isabel Monk and Gordon Gray. March, 1977. Directed by Gordon Gray.

Association of Theater Artists. Presents classical and modern plays, including new and experimental works. Roderick Nash, artistic director and director of all plays.

THE GINGERBREAD LADY by Neil Simon. November 13, 1976. With Steve Burke, Susan Kaslow, Marcia Lee Merrill, Peg Osborne, Ted Theoharous.

OLD TIMES by Harold Pinter. January 15, 1977.

A STREETCAR NAMED DESIRE by Tennessee Williams. February 19, 1977.

Circle Repertory Company Projects in Progress. Developmental program for playwrights and directors. Marshall W. Mason, artistic director, Steven Gomer, program director.

PRAGUE SPRING by Lee Kalcheim, directed by John Davis, with Pat Carey, Jordan Charney, Judy Graubart, Jim Jansen, John Jellison, Neil Flanagan; THE CONFIRMATION by Howard Ashman, directed by Stuart White, with Jean Buchalter, Alan Court, Bill Jaeger, Marion Levine, June Stein, David Swatling. June 2-6, 1976.

FOG & MISMANAGEMENT by Jeff Wanshel. June 9, 1976. Directed by Carole Rothman.
FINE PRINT by Charlie Peters. May 11, 1977. Directed by Ron Lagomarsino.
MRS. TIDINGS MASON-DIXON MEDICINE MAN by John Heuer. May 18, 1977. Directed by Susan Lehman.
CELEBRATIONS OFF RIVER STREET by James Tobin. May 25, 1977. Directed by Ann Raychel.
THE BRIXTON RECOVERY by Jack Gilhooley. May 31, 1977. Directed by Steven Gomer.
HOME FREE! by Lanford Wilson, directed by Richard Harden, with Eugenia Bostwick, David Potts; WILDFLOWERS by Richard Howard, directed by Michael Feingold; WINNERS by Brian Friel, directed by Susan Lehman, with Kate Kellery, Kevin O'Brien, James Bormann; DARK ROOM by David Epstein, directed by Bill Esper. June 16, 1976.
SUICIDE IN B FLAT by Sam Shepard. March 31, 1977. Directed by Harold DeFelice.
ALLEGRA by Allan Bates. April 14, 1977. Directed by Dick Gaffield.
TO THE LAND by Claris Nelson. April 28, 1977. Directed by Richard Mogavero.

Afterpieces
WILDFLOWERS by Richard Howard. July 6, 1976. Directed by Michael Feingold.
LISTEN, PLEASE! by Robert Abrami. July 27, 1976. Directed by Jill A. Fuchs.
DEAD SURE by Francine Stone. March 17, 1977. Directed by Carole Rothman.
THE PASSING OF CORKY BREWSTER by Jerry L. Crawford. March 22, 1977. Directed by Daniel Irvine; with Sharon Madden.
FOR LOVE OR MONEY (musical) music by Jason McAuliffe, lyrics by Jay Jeffries. March, 1977.
WHAT THE BABE SAID by Martin Halpern. May 25, 1977. Directed by Amy Schecter.

City Playworks. A company with varied ambitions and a second-year schedule of one Equity-approved showcase. Linda Brumfield, Christopher Cara, Gus Kaikkonen, Jonathan Sand, directors.

FEMALE TRANSPORT by Steve Gooch. September 8, 1976. Directed by Scott Porter.

The Classic Theater. Conceived and executed with the strictest artistic integrity and dramatic value. Maurice Edwards, artistic director.

TROPICAL MADNESS by Stanislaw Witkiewicz, translated by Daniel C. Gerould. June 24, 1976. Directed by Maurice Edwards; with Tom Bahring, Elizabeth Ballard, Woodrow Garrian, Christina Lenz, Elizabeth Reavy, Bob Whiting.
THE CONSPIRACY OF FEELINGS by Yurii Olyesha, translated by Daniel C. and Eleanor S. Gerould. January 13, 1977. Directed by Maurice Edwards; with Jerry Richkin, Ron Johnston, Linda Lodge, Albert Amateau.
SHADOW OF A GUNMAN by Sean O'Casey. February 3, 1977. Directed by Lawrence Zucker; with Linda Cook, Bettyann Leeseberg, Jack Biser, John McPeak, John Copley-Quinn, Anne-Frances Thom.
EACH IN HIS OWN WAY by Luigi Pirandello. March 11, 1977. Directed by Maurice Edwards; with Julia Curry, Thomas MacGreevy, Elaine Eldridge, Walter Wright, Donald Pace, John Archibald, Frank Askin.
AUTUMN SERENADE by Wesley St. John. April 15, 1977. With George Riddle, Gerda Shepard, Anthony Ristoff, Marilyn Rockafellow.
ROSMERSHOLM by Henrik Ibsen, translated by Rolf Fjelde. May 6, 1977. Directed by Cyril Simon; with Paul Vincent, Kathryn Harrold, Jack Axelrod, William Myers, Jeffrey Spolan, Norma Frances.

Colonnades Theater Lab. Resident repertory company with an in-training program for actors. Michael Lessac, artistic director.

WARBECK by Louis Phillips. November 17, 1976. Directed by Michael Lessac.
A FLEA IN HER EAR by Georges Feydeau. November 24, 1976. Directed by Krikor Satamian.
REFLECTIONS (musical) book by David Morgan, music and lyrics by Miriam Moses, based on Oscar Wilde's *The Birthday of the Infanta*. December 22, 1976. Directed by Michael Lessac.
SERVANT OF TWO MASTERS by Carlo Goldoni, translated and directed by Al Brooks. January 26, 1977.

Counterpoint Theater Company. Maintain high standards of excellence in the service of plays of distinction, through theatrical productions of enduring value. Howard Green, artistic director, Paulene Reynolds, managing director.

OLD TIMES by Harold Pinter. October 8, 1976. Directed by Howard Green; with Len Auclair, Jacqueline Barnett, Paulene Reynolds.
THE PLAY'S THE THING by Ferenc Molnar, adapted by P. G. Wodehouse. November 26, 1976. Directed by Howard Green; with Sam Gray, Ed Crowley, Arthur Anderson, Linda Geiser, Elek Hartman, John Seidman.

PLAYING WITH FIRE by August Strindberg and LUNCH HOUR by John Mortimer. January 28, 1977. Directed by Charles Maryan; with Alan Coates, Frencesca de Sapio, George Hall, Elizabeth Kemp, Kevin Kline, Barbara Stanton.

AWAKE AND SING by Clifford Odets. March 18, 1977. Directed by Terry Walker; with Hope Cameron, Clement Fowler, Howard Green, Elek Hartman, Michael Montel, Tanny McDonald.

HOW HE LIED TO HER HUSBAND and OVERRULED by George Bernard Shaw. May 6, 1977. Directed by Howard Green; with Fran Brill, Saylor Creswell, Tanny McDonald, John Seidman, Doug Stender.

The Courtyard Playhouse Foundation. Eclectic policy of searching for "a good play", new ones preferred but not exclusively. Houses Little People's Theater Company for quality in children's theater. Ken Eulo, artistic director.

FOOLS, FALLS & FLYING THINGS. November 18, 1976.

GREEN JULIA by Paul Ableman. February 10, 1977. Directed by Susan Schulman.

NERO by Richard Vetere. May 5, 1977. Directed by Paul Boccio.

The Cubiculo and **Cubiculo III.** Experiments in the use of theater, dance music, etc. housed in four studios and two stages. Philip Meister, artistic director.

FESTIVAL OF NEW PLAYS FROM ISRAEL HOROVITZ'S WORKSHOP: KNOW IT ALL by Daniel Lyon; MUSEUM PIECE by David Sweeney; THE SEPTEMBER MOVEMENT by David Cohen; CORNER, 28TH & BANK by Linda Segal; DECATHLON by Sean Joseph Hartley; THE REASON WE EAT (reading) by Israel Horovitz; EYES WIN by Elizabeth Wyatt. June 3-13, 1976.

FITS, SEIZURES AND SMALL COMPLAINTS (revue). June, 1976. Performed by Gelosi Company.

OTHELLO by William Shakespeare. August 4, 1976. Directed by Bill Sweeney.

A DRINK AT THE WELL (musical revue) book by Norman Matlock, music by Galt MacDermot. October, 1976. With Norman Matlock, Sheila Scott-Wilkinson.

MR. MC MANNIS, WHAT TIME IS IT? written and directed by William Schlottmann. October, 1976. With Olive Deering, Joseph Julian, Joan Kaye, Wayne Duncan.

IN THE BOOM BOOM ROOM by David Rabe. November, 1976. Directed by Peter Flood; with Mimi Bernstein, Cliff Collings, Joann Freidman, Michael Granger, Elaine LeGaro, Susan Slavin.

ONCE AND FOR ALL by Robert Gordon. November, 1976. Directed by Edward M. Cohen; with Gloria Barret, Michael Brody, Robert Haufrecht, Ron Johnston.

VAN ZANDT ELLIS AT THE PIANO. November 29, 1976.

THE AMERICAN CIRCUMFERENCE ART THEATER. December 2, 1976. Directed by David Nunemaker.

SPOON RIVER ANTHOLOGY by Edgar Lee Masters and MARK TWAIN MEDLEY. January 4, 1977. Directed by Sue Lawless.

IN BETWEEN by Albert Loftus. January 12, 1977. Directed by John Sillings; with Paul Welsh, Elaine Sulka.

PETER LOBDELL (mime). February 7, 1977.

THE RECRUITING OFFICER by George Farquhar. February 24, 1977. Directed by Philip Meister.

THE SELECTION conceived by Coda Theater Company. March, 1977. Directed by Joel Benenson; with Harvey Lieberman.

LOOK BACK IN ANGER by John Osborne. March 2, 1977. Directed by Joanna Merlin.

TWO MANY THUMBS by Robert Hivnor. April, 1977. Directed by John Olon-Scrymgeour; with Ron Carrier, Charles Lutz, Terry Markovich, Kate Weiman, Paul Andor, Renee Lippin.

NOBODY HEARD THE LIONS ROAR by Leslie Holzer. April 21, 1977. Directed by Lawrence Hoff; with Tony Kraber, Lou Quinones, Missie Zollo.

Direct Theater. A professional company of actors and other stage artists exploring new techniques. Allen R. Belknap, artistic director.

EARTH SPIRIT (musical) by Frank Wedekind, adapted and directed by Allen R. Belknap, music and lyrics by Gary Levinson. September 9, 1976. With Susan Bartels, Glynis Bell, Deborah Gordon, Christiane McKenna, Alison Mills, Petie Seals.

THIRD ANNUAL DIRECTORS' FESTIVAL. October 5-31, 1976. *Best:* HUMULUS THE GREAT by Jean Anouilh, directed by Patrick Jacobs; PHOENIX AND TURTLE by David Mowat, directed by Bruce Levitt; THE LAST ROCKETTE (musical) by Kenneth Pressman, lyrics by Jerry Murray, directed by Peter Simpson; LAURA NYRO/WOMEN OF THE CITY compiled by Roxanna Ward and Stephen Velayas, directed by Stephen Velayas.

ACTORS' FESTIVAL. November 9-28, 1976. *(Best performances, December, 1976).*

DAS LUSITANIA SONGSPIEL (Theater Songs of Bertolt Brecht). November 19, 1976. With Christopher Durang, Sigourney Weaver.

LULU (musical) book by Ross Alexander, music and lyrics by Gary Levinson, adapted and directed by Allen R. Belknap, based on Frank Wedekind's plays. January 20, 1977. With D'Jamin Bartlett, Kermit Brown, James Carruthers, Peter Jason, Charles Leader, Fred Martell.
WINTER DIRECTORS' FESTIVAL. February 8-28, 1977. *Best: The Interlude* FROM THE APPLE CART by George Bernard Shaw, directed by Charles Conwell; RATS by Israel Horovitz, directed by Gene Santarelli; PERSPECTIVE (revue) based on works by Jerry Bock and Sheldon Harnick, directed by Jim Pentecost; THE HOLY GHOSTLY by Sam Shepard, directed by Mark Harrison; AMNESIA by Bill Cook, directed by Bill Hoffman.
THE COLLECTED WORKS by David Mowat. March 21, 1977. Directed by Bruce A. Levitt; with Mathew Lewis, Bill Cwikowski, Maia Danziger, Sheila Walsh.
PHOENIX AND TURTLE by David Mowat. April 1, 1977. Directed by Bruce A. Levitt; with Henson Keys, Elinor Basescu, Kristen Lowman.
ORNAMENTS by Rodney Anderson. April 21, 1977. Directed by Charles Conwell.
THE TRAGEDY OF TALIPED DECANUS by John Barth, adapted from the novel *Giles Goat-Boy*. April 28, 1977. Directed by Ted Snowdon.

Drama Committee Repertory Theater. Performs 19th and 20th century classics of all nations and new plays. Arthur Reel, artistic director.

MAJOR BARBARA by George Bernard Shaw. June, 1976. Directed by Arthur Reel.
THE NIGHT OF THE IGUANA by Tennessee Williams. July, 1976. Directed by Laura Darius.
THE SEA GULL by Anton Chekhov. September 9, 1976. Directed by Arthur Reel; with Noreen Rauch, Joshua Rauch, Elizabeth Law, Bruce Kronenberg, Laura Darius.
THE DOCTOR'S DILEMMA by George Bernard Shaw. September 16, 1976. Directed by Arthur Kirson.
ORPHEUS DESCENDING by Tennessee Williams. October, 1976. Directed by Arthur Reel.
LEAGUE OF YOUTH by Henrik Ibsen, adapted and directed by Arthur Reel. November 28, 1976. With Michael F. Clarke, Stanley Bernstein, Paul Van Antwerp, Harris Berlinsky.
THE MAN OF DESTINY by George Bernard Shaw. December, 1976. Directed by Arthur Reel.
HOW HE LIED TO HER HUSBAND and ANNAJANSKA by George Bernard Shaw. February, 1977.
THE ANNIVERSARY by Anton Chekhov (in repertory with *How He Lied to Her Husband*). March, 1977. Directed by Arthur Reel.
HENRY IV, PART 1 by William Shakespeare. March 12, 1977. Directed by Michael Alexander.
CANDIDA by George Bernard Shaw. March 23, 1977.
HAMLET by William Shakespeare. May, 1977. Directed by Michael Alexander.

Drama Ensemble Company. Devoted to experimental plays, as outgrowths of ongoing workshops; open to new writers and directors. Peter Ehrman, artistic director.

CIRCUS written and directed by William D'Andrea. October 19, 1976.
HOME FREE and IKKE, IKKE, NYE NYE by Lanford Wilson. December 3, 1976. Directed by Robert Caprio.
FOOLS, FALLS AND FLYING THINGS. December 20, 1976.
ANIMAL FARM adapted by Nelson Bond from George Orwell's novel. February 25, 1977. Directed by Joseph Criscuoli.
SISTER'S KEEPER written and directed by Marie Scioscia. April 7, 1977.
DESPERADOES by Rebecca Ranson. May 21, 1977. Performed by Pocket Theater Co.

Dramatis Personae. Sexually oriented entertainment. Steven Baker, director.

THE NAKED ROUND by A. R. Bell. Directed by Steven Baker.
BOYS, BOYS, BOYS (revue) continued its run.

Encompass Theater. Dedicated to finding, developing and producing new playwrights and composers. Special emphasis on new and seldom performed plays and musicals by and about women. Nancy Rhodes, artistic director, Roger Cunningham, producer.

THE YELLOW WALLPAPER adapted by Gloria Albee from Charlotte Perkins Gilman works. December 2, 1976. Directed by Nancy Rhodes; with Liz Adams, Gina Barnett, Polly Brooks, Judy Hart, Martha Kearns, Martin Robinson.
THE HAPPY HAVEN by John Arden and Margaretta D'Arcy. March 31, 1977. Directed by Peter H. Clough; with Edward Conery, Steve Friedman, Dierk Toporyzek, Mary Jay, Johanna Jensen, Peter C. Johnson.
THE TENDER LAND (opera) by Aaron Copland. May 12, 1977. Directed by Nancy Rhodes, musical direction by Norman Carey; with Scott Bodie, Lisa Ann Cunningham, Nadine Olivia Earl, Jay Aubrey Jones, H. Edward Landaro, Peter J. Ludwig.

Staged Readings
PRANKS by Robert Wertheim. February 9, 1977. Directed by Nancy Rhodes.
ENDANGERED SPECIES by Elliot Caplin. February 24, 1977. Directed by Nancy Rhodes; with Kevin Conway.
WINDOW and ADORA (one-act plays) by Jean Reavey. March 3, 1977. Directed by Nancy Rhodes.
WHERE MEMORIES ARE MAGIC AND DREAMS INVENTED by Susan Nanus. March 9, 1977. Directed by Susan Einhorn.
TRUMPETS SOUNDING by Gene Ruffini. March 14, 1977. Directed by Rod Harter.
THE LIFE GAME by Bette Ziegler. March 16, 1977. Directed by Jan Crean.

Ensemble Studio Theater. Nucleus of 26 playwrights-in-residence dedicated to supporting individual theater artists and developing new works for the stage. 40-50 projects each season, initiated by E.S.T. members. Curt Dempster, artistic director, Richard Frankel, associate director.

THE CONTEST by Shirley Mezvinsky Lauro. October 21, 1976. Directed by Paul Austin; with Loren Brown, Estelle Owens, Mordecai Lawner.
GOODBYE AND KEEP COLD by John Ford Noonan. December 14, 1976. Directed by James Hammerstein.
AN EVENING WITH TWO ACTRESSES (one-woman shows) written and directed by Barbara Tarbuck. January 3, 1977. With Susan Merson, Barbara Tarbuck.
THE SOFT TOUCH by Neil Cuthbert. January 27, 1977. Directed by John Bettenbender; with Mason Adams, Jennie Ventriss, Herbert Braha, Jack Gilpin, Bill Cwikowski, Curt Dempster.
BLOOD WEDDING by Federico Garcia Lorca. May, 1977. Directed by Gary Nebiol.
WANT by A. J. Morey. May 12, 1977. Directed by William Shorr.
INNOCENT PLEASURES by Arthur Giron. May 20, 1977. Directed by Harold Stone.
New Music for Theater Series
PETER LINK AND FRIENDS — PRELUDE: A CONTEMPORARY CHORALE, and PASSAGE by Richard Peaslee. April 14, 1977.
A NIGHT IN NEW ORLEANS by Will Holt and Moogy Kingman. May 2, 1977.
AN EVENING WITH KIRK NUROCK. May 16, 1977.
JACK SOUND AND HIS DOG STAR BLOWING HIS FINAL TRUMPET ON THE DAY OF DOOM music by Steven Margoshes, lyrics by Gerome Ragni. May 23, 1977.

Equity Library Theater. Actors' Equity sponsors a series of revivals each season as showcases for the work of its actor-members and an "informal series" of original, unproduced material. George Wojtasik, managing director.

FIORELLO! (musical) book by Jerome Weidman and George Abbott, music by Jerry Bock, lyrics by Sheldon Harnick. October 14, 1976. Directed by William Koch; with Frank Kopyc, Bill Biskup, Michael McCarty, Ann Hodapp, Christopher Wynkoop, Kathryn Boule, Frank Luz, Verna Pierce, Alexandra Korey.
HEARTBREAK HOUSE by George Bernard Shaw. November 11, 1976.
THE BOYS FROM SYRACUSE (musical) book by George Abbott, music by Richard Rodgers, lyrics by Lorenz Hart, based on William Shakespeare's *A Comedy of Errors.* December 2, 1976.
TWELFTH NIGHT by William Shakespeare. January 13, 1977. Directed by Richard Mogavero; with Michael Maurice, Robert Zukerman, Dana Hart, Pam Rogers, Stan Buturla, Jared Matesky, Marie Tommon, Richard Peterson, Bill Roberts, Judy Levitt, Didi Charney, Rendee Berman, Ronald Willoughby, Michael LaGue, Jim Broaddus, Cameron Smith.
COME BACK, LITTLE SHEBA by William Inge. February 10, 1977. Directed by Ron Troutman; with Stan Lachow, Shelli Place, Joan Lowell, Edward O'Ross, Del Willard, Elaine Grollman, Allen Fitzpatrick, Stephen Stewart-James, Dave Okarski, Mark Weston, Nick Harrison.
WONDERFUL TOWN (musical) book by Joseph Fields and Jerome Chodorov (based on their play, *My Sister Eileen* and Ruth McKenney's stories), music by Leonard Bernstein, lyrics by Betty Comden and Adolph Green. March 10, 1977. Directed by Bolen High; with Cathy Brewer-Moore, Donna Liggitt Forbes.
ARSENIC AND OLD LACE by Joseph Kesselring. April 14, 1977. Directed by Susan Schulman; with William Metzo, Frances Pole, Georgia Southcotte, Chet Carlin.
SILK STOCKINGS (musical) book by George S. Kaufman, Leueen MacGrath and Abe Burrows, music and lyrics by Cole Porter. May 5, 1977. Directed by Richard Michaels; with Armin Shimerman, Neil Elliot, David St. James, Carolyn Kirsch, Carol Schweid, James Le Vaggi, Mark Zimmerman.
Informal Series
ONE-MAN SHOW with Richard Anders Ericson. September 23, 1976.
WORDS (songs) by Tony Tanner and Martin Sylvestri. October 18, 1976. Directed by Jeffrey Dunn.
PLAY ME, ZOLTAN by Lucas Myers. December 6, 1976. Directed by Charles Maggiore.
ANTIGONE (opera) by Lou Rogers. January 24, 1977. Directed by Stuart Michaels.

A TOUCH OF MARBLE by Don Potter. February 7, 1977. Directed by Jack Dyville.
SVENGALI WAS A LADY by Allen S. Huston. March 21, 1977. Directed by Sam As-Said.
MILLIONS OF MILES by Elliott Taubenslag and MOLLY BLOOM adapted by Donna Wilshire from James Joyce's work (one-act plays). April 18, 1977. Directed by Donna Wilshire.
NOT BACK WITH THE ELEPHANTS (six short pieces from *Vanity Fair* magazine, 1929-1934 by Jeffrey Kerr and Ferenc Molnar). May 16, 1977. Directed by David Pursley.

The Family. A professional theater company in its fifth year, attempting to make a tangible contribution to the Greater New York cultural community. Marvin Felix Camillo, artistic director.

FESTIVAL '77: THE BLACKS by Jean Genet and CLARA'S OLE MAN by Ed Bullins, directed by Bette Howard; LOOKING FOR TOMORROW by Ringo Reyes, STRAIGHT FROM THE GHETTO by Neil Harris and Miguel Piñero, NOAH AND THE ARK by James Weldon Johnson, THE MARRIAGE PROPOSAL by Anton Chekhov, directed by Marvin Felix Camillo. February, 1977.

4th Wall at the Provincetown Playhouse. Permanent ensemble company with an interest in developing new plays by resident playwrights. Luba Elman, Gary Palmer, executive directors.

YOU CAN'T FIGHT CITY HALL by Gary Palmer, directed by Ken Krauss; THE FALL OF THE HOUSE OF MENSCH, OR, THE YENTI by Eve Olitsky, directed by Gary Palmer; A TIME AWAY by Ken Krauss, directed by Luba Elman. December, 1976.
DON'T JUMP by Eve Olitsky, directed by Gary Palmer; ARIA DA CAPO by Edna St. Vincent Millay, directed by Luba Elman. April 15, 1977.

Gene Feist Theater Workshop. Rediscovery of neglected classics produced in an intimate showcase setting. Gene Feist, producing director, Michael Fried, executive producer.

A MONTH IN THE COUNTRY by Ivan Turgenev, adapted by David Morgan. June 16, 1976.
LOVE AND INTRIGUE by Friedrich von Schiller. August, 1976. Directed by Gavin Cameron Webb.

Gene Frankel Theater Workshop. Development of new works and revivals for the theater. Gene Frankel, artistic director, executive producer.

FEEL FREE by Nancy Henderson and Charlotte Kraft. November 4, 1976. Directed by Camille Lane.
THE MEDIUM (opera) by Gian Carlo Menotti. December 16, 1976.
NORTH ATLANTIC by Michael Colby and James Fradich. January 16, 1977. Directed by Clint Atkinson.
HALLOWEEN by Leonard Melfi and ON THE HARMFULNESS OF TOBACCO by Anton Chekhov (one-act plays). March 16, 1977. Directed by Jon Fraser; with Willi Kirkham, Robert McCullough, Robert Neilly.
KENNEDY'S CHILDREN by Robert Patrick. April 22, 1977. Directed by Lawrence Zuckerman.
FRESHWATER by Virginia Woolf. May 8, 1977. Directed by Jon Fraser.

Hudson Guild Theater. American classics interspersed with original and experimental plays. Craig Anderson, artistic director.

GARBO AND JILLIAN (magic show with music). June 12, 1976.
200 RPM (musical drama) music and lyrics by Charlotte Brody and Si Kahn. August, 1976. Directed by Chuck Portz; performed by Labor Theater (in cooperation with Hudson Guild).
THE DIARY OF ANNE FRANK by Frances Goodrich and Albert Hackett. October 13, 1976. Directed by Craig Anderson; with Susan Sharkey.
THE WOBBLIES by Stewart Bird and Peter Robilotta. November, 1976. Directed by Chuck Portz; performed by Labor Theater (in cooperation with Hudson Guild).
THE ADMIRABLE CRICHTON by James M. Barrie. December 2, 1976. Directed by Craig Anderson.
THE STRONGER, CREDITORS and MISS JULIE by August Strindberg, translated by Palaemona Morner and R. Spacek. January 12, 1977. Directed by James Kendall and Rip Torn; with Amy Wright, Geraldine Page, Judith L'Heureux, John Heard, Jeremy Peterson, Tom Hurt.
SAVAGES by Christopher Hampton. February 24, 1977. Directed by Gordon Davidson; with Joseph Mahler, Stephen Joyce, Alice Drummond, Mandy Patinkin, Leslie Barrett, Louis Beachner.
DANCE ON A COUNTRY GRAVE (musical) book, music and lyrics by Kelly Hamilton, based on Thomas Hardy's *Return of the Native*. April 21, 1977. Directed by Robert Brewer; with Sam Freed, Donna Theodore, Mike Dantuono, Fiddle Viracola, Gail Kellstrom, Kevin Kline.

Impossible Ragtime Theater (IRT). Dedicated to exploration of the director's role in all aspects of theater. Ted Story, George Ferencz, artistic directors.

PLEASE HANG UP AND DIAL AGAIN by Michael Zettler. September, 1976. Directed by Ted Story; with Stephen Moran, Celia Weston, James Otis, W. M. Hunt, Jay Devlin, Brian Hartigan.
POPULAR SUNSETS (two musicals) by Bob Jewett. September, 1976. Directed by Stephen Zuckerman.
THE DARK AT THE TOP OF THE STAIRS by William Inge. October 25, 1976. Directed by Jonathan Foster.
DYNAMO by Eugene O'Neill. October 29, 1976. Directed by George Ferencz.
LUDLOW FAIR by Lanford Wilson, directed by Jude Schanzer; THE INVESTIGATION by Rosalyn Drexler, directed by Alison Mackenzie. November, 1976.
THE MIDNIGHT RAMBLER by John Stryder. December, 1976. Directed by J. W. Roberts.
MACBETH by William Shakespeare, adapted and directed by Ted Story. January 14, 1977.
THE DYBBUK by S. Ansky. January 21, 1977. Directed by Stephen Zuckerman.
AN ARTHUR KOPIT FESTIVAL (PART ONE): THE CONQUEST OF EVEREST, directed by Penelope Hirsch; SING TO ME THROUGH OPEN WINDOWS, directed by J. W. Roberts, with Rosemary Foley, Stephen Moran; CHAMBER MUSIC, directed by Jonathan Foster; THE HERO, directed by Gideon Davis; THE QUESTIONING OF NICK, directed by Jude Schanzer; THE DAY THE WHORES CAME OUT TO PLAY TENNIS, directed by Alison Mackenzie.
CELIMARE by Labiche and Delacour, translated by Ted and Lynn Hoffman. March 18, 1977. Directed by Stephen Zuckerman.
IN THE JUNGLE OF CITIES by Bertolt Brecht, translated by Anselm Hollo. March 25, 1977. Directed by George Ferencz; with Glenn Cabrera, Margaret A. Flanagan, Jonathan Frakes, Miguel Marcott, Shelley Wyant, Michael Zuckerman.
THE REFRIGERATORS by Mario Fratti. April 22, 1977. Directed by Ted Story; with Jane Ranallo, Win Atkins, Gary McGurk.
STAGE DOOR by Edna Ferber and George S. Kaufman. April 29, 1977. Directed by Jonathan Foster.

Intar. Innovative culture center for the Hispanic American community of New York City focusing on the art of theater. Max Ferra, artistic director.

THE HOUSE OF BERNARDA ALBA by Federico Garcia Lorca. March, 1977. Directed by Max Ferra; with Caroline Thomas, Peg Osborne, Gerry Low.

Interart Theater. Showcase opportunities which provide a professional environment for women playwrights, directors, designers and performers to participate in theatrical activity. Margot Lewitin, coordinator.

CRAB QUADRILLE by Myrna Lamb. November 19, 1976. Directed by Margot Lewitin; with Joyce Aaron, Scott A. Fitzgerald, Susan Kellerman, Stan Lachow, Lily Lodge, Ilsebet Tebesli.
QUARRY (opera) conceived and directed by Meredith Monk. December 15, 1976. Performed by The House and 30 additional performers.
STILL LIFE by Susan Yankowitz and THE EXPELLED by Samuel Beckett. January 20, 1977. Directed by Rhea Gaisner; with Jenn Ben-Yacov, Philip Corner, Kathleen Gittel, Jerry Jarrett, Ellin Ruskin, Virginia Stevens.
WINE, WOMEN AND WORDS (readings). January 30, 1977. With Myrna Lamb, Vivian Gornick, Ingrid Bengis.
NEW ROOTS: AN OFF OFF BROADWAY ANTHOLOGY from the works of Kenneth Bernard, Maria Irene Fornes, Rochelle Owens, William Hoffman, Robert Patrick, Megan Terry, Sam Shepard. April 14, 1977. Directed by Margot Lewitin; with Kay Carney.
PERFORMANCE/DISCUSSION with Elizabeth Swados. April, 1977.
CROSS COUNTRY by Susan Miller. May 12, 1977. Directed by Elinor Renfield; with Bryan Gordon, Kathryn Grody, Emily Nash, Rebecca Stanley.

The Irish Rebel Theater (An Claidheamh Soluis). Dedicated to establishing an awareness among people of all ethnic backgrounds of the artistic expression of the Irish people.

A TOUCH OF THE POET by Eugene O'Neill. November, 1976. Directed by Tom Connolly.
AN EVENING OF IRISH FAIRY TALES. January 16, 1977. Directed by Virginia Glynn, Kevin MacSweeney, James Olwell; performed by the Acting Workshop.
JUNO AND THE PAYCOCK by Sean O'Casey. March, 1977. Directed by Larry Spiegel.
THE BRANDY DANCERS by Gabriel Walsh. May 5, 1977. Directed by Brian Heron.

Jean Cocteau Repertory. Located in the historic Bouwerie Lane Theater, the Jean Cocteau Repertory presents vintage and modern classics on a rotating repertory schedule. Eve Adamson, artistic director (and director of all productions).

MACBETH by William Shakespeare. September 3, 1976.

RHINOCEROS by Eugene Ionesco. September 17, 1976.
THE LESSON by Eugene Ionesco. October 1, 1976.
ANDROCLES AND THE LION by George Bernard Shaw. October 22, 1976.
THE CARETAKER by Harold Pinter. November, 1976.
THE CENCI by Percy Bysshe Shelley. January 28, 1977. With Douglas McKeown, Coral S. Potter, Chip Benjamin, Donna Rowe, Craig Smith, Olivia Virgil Harper.
SHE STOOPS TO CONQUER by Oliver Goldsmith. February, 1977.
SALOME by Oscar Wilde. April 15, 1977.
THE BRASS BUTTERFLY by William Golding. May 14, 1977.

Jones Beach Marine Theater. Each summer a musical classic is presented in this huge outdoor theater on Long Island. Guy Lombardo, producer.

SHOW BOAT (musical) book and lyrics by Oscar Hammerstein II, music by Jerome Kern, based on Edna Ferber's novel. July 1, 1976. Directed by John Fearnley; with Robert Peterson, Barbara Meister, Max Showalter, Beth Fowler, Edward Pierson, Lizbeth Prichett, Lee Roy Reams.

Joseph Jefferson Theater Company. Performs solely American plays, both revivals and new works largely drawn from their playwrights' workshop; houses Theater for Older People. Cathy Roskam, founder.

JACK FALLON FARE THEE WELL by Joseph Caldwell. June 8, 1976. Directed by Cathy Roskam; with Jevan Damadian, Jean Francis, Jan Granger, Mark Hattan, Alfred Hinckley, William Koch, Danny Landon, Barbara Mathews, Rachael Milder.
RIP VAN WINKLE (Dion Boucicault version). July 21, 1976. Directed by William Koch; with Reathel Bean, Mark Hattan, Frank Kramer, Linda Lashbrook, Paul Meacham, Suzanne Osborne, Bill Roberts, Jennifer Thompson, John Tormey.
U.S.A. by John Dos Passos and Paul Shyre. October 27, 1976. Directed by John Henry Davis; with Linda Barnhurst, Reathel Bean, Allan Carlsen, John Getz, Nita Novy, Anne C. Twomey.
THE WELL by Seymour Reiter, music by Mitsuo Kitamura. December 1, 1977. Directed by Julianne Boyd; with Richard T. Alpers, Sonya Baehr, Gary Barker, Ralph Braun, Alston Campbell, Nancy Cook, Cris Gronendaal, Martha Ihde, Leslie Middlebrook, Bill Randolph, Sheldon Silver, Bob White.
JOHNNY BELINDA by Elmer Harris. February 2, 1977. Directed by William Koch; with Reathel Bean, Jan Granger, Mark Hattan, Robert Lanchester, Frank Luz, June Stein.
SKATERS by Ted Pezzulo. April 27, 1977. Directed by Bill Herndon; with Anita Bayless, Jennifer Dawson, Roger DeKoven, Demo DiMartile, Rosemary McNamara, Richard Zavaglia.

Theater for Older People
PRIME TIME: A CELEBRATION OF AGING based on the writings of older people, adapted by Christopher Quilter and Susan Miller. November 4, 1976. Directed by John Henry Davis and Cathy Roskam; with Rae Dalven, Eleanor Cody Gould, William Da Prato.
MOTHER by Lydia Simmons. April 19, 1977. Directed by Cathy Roskam; with Judith Elder.

Staged Readings
LOVE IN A PUB by Marion Fredi Towbin, directed by Connie Abramson; FAMILY CIRCLE by Ted Pezzulo, directed by Michael Heaton; THE ROCKER by Joseph Caldwell, directed by William Koch; ROSES AREN'T FOR STRANGERS by Midge Maroni, directed by Richard Harden; AND WHAT ABOUT LOVE, PANDORA? by Marvin J. Bevans, directed by John Gillick; AH, EURYDICE by Stanley Taikeff, directed by Julianne Boyd (one-act plays). December 7, 1976.
THE SUNDAY NIGHT CREEPS by Harvey Zuckerman. February 13, 1977. Directed by Donald Warfield.
THREE EASY PIECES by Marion Fredi Towbin. February 15, 1977. Directed by Connie Abramson.
IN THE MODERN STYLE by Stanley Taikeff. March 31, 1977. Directed by Julianne Boyd.
BINGO by Harvey Zuckerman. May 26, 1977. Directed by Elaine Kanas.

The Judson Poets' Theater. The theater arm of Judson Memorial Church and its pastor, Al Carmines, who creates a series of new, unconventional musicals which are sometimes transferred to the commercial theater. Al Carmines, director.

POLITICAL THEATER SONGS by Al Carmines. July 29, 1976. Performed by Essie Borden, Lee Guilliatt, Lou Bullock, Margaret Wright.
THE BEAST: A MEDITATION ON BEAUTY (musical) by Al Carmines. November 5, 1976. Directed by Dan Wagoner; with Trisha Long, Wendell Cordtz, Gretchen Van Aken, Margaret Wright, Essie Borden, Lee Guilliatt.
CHRISTMAS RAPPINGS (annual production) by Al Carmines. December 9, 1976. Directed by Dan

Wagoner; with Theo Barnes, Martin Meredith, Alexander Galanopoulos, Christopher Banner, Trisha Long, Zoelle Montgomery.
A MANOIR (opera) by Gertrude Stein, music by Al Carmines. April 22, 1977. Directed by Lawrence Kornfeld; with Theo Barnes, James Bryan, Semina De Laurentis, Katherine Litz, David Tice, Bill Conway.
A SPRING GARLAND OF OLD SONGS (songs from the Teens, Twenties and Thirties) by David Vaughan and Al Carmines. May 15, 1977. (Seventh annual benefit).

La Mama Experimental Theater Club (ETC). A busy workshop for experimental theater of all kinds. Ellen Stewart, director.

SIGNALS conceived and directed by Michael Griggs, written by John O'Brien, music and lyrics by Ron Grant. June 14, 1976.
LORETTA STRONG written and directed by Copi. June 17, 1976.
STARSHIP TABLE written and directed by Daffi. June 24, 1976.
HEAVEN GRAND IN AMBER ORBIT by Jackie Curtis. September 23, 1976. Directed by John Vaccaro; with Playhouse of the Ridiculous.
SACRIFICE TO DAMBALLA conceived and performed by Shango-Haitian Company. October 22, 1976.
THE LITURGY conceived and directed by Cecile Guidote. October 29, 1976. Performed by Twitas Ensemble.
THE PETRO RITES conceived and performed by Shango-Haitian Company. November 5, 1976.
SUNDALO. November 12, 1976. With The Petal Ensemble.
WHO CHOOSES THE CHOICES WE CHOOSE written and directed by Nancy Gabor and Sidney Grimsley. November 12, 1976.
INOSISS adapted and directed by Hassan Wakrim. November 27, 1976.
DENSITY 1.33 by Jeff Klayman, directed by Mervyn Willis; ALMA, THE GHOST OF SPRING STREET written and directed by Ozzie Rodriguez. December 2, 1976.
ON MY CORAL ISLANDS by Somerset Maugham. December 9, 1976. Directed by George Takla.
RUN'NERS written and directed by Ivy McRay. December 22, 1976.
FRAGMENTS OF A TRILOGY: THE TROJAN WOMEN, ELECTRA and MEDEA conceived and directed by Andrei Serban, music by Elizabeth Swados. December 29, 1976.
GODSONG (musical) adapted and directed by Tad Truesdale from James Weldon Johnson's *God's Trombone*. December 30, 1976. With Marcia McBroom, Barbara Montgomery, Isaiah Smalls.
A-NON designed and directed by Joseph Dunn and Irja Koljonen. January 4, 1977.
FESTOONS & OH . . . NOTHING! by Theo Barnes, music by George Quincy. January 13, 1977. With Esteban Chalbaud, Daniel Harris, Esther Jenkins, Madeleine le Roux, Trisha Long, Bill Reynolds.
THE ARCHITECT AND THE EMPEROR OF ASSYRIA by Fernando Arrabal. January 15, 1977. Directed by Tom O'Horgan; with Nelly Vivas Company.
GOOD SEX!. January 24, 1977. With El Coyote.
THE ROMANCE AND TIMES OF MISS LAURA AND SUGAR CANE RAY by Jaime Sanchez and Mila Conway. January 31, 1977. Directed by Alba Olms.
ORGAN conceived and directed by Ken Rubenstein. February 2, 1977. With Cristobal Carambo, Ellyce Stillwater.
THE DO'S AND DON'TS OF A NATURAL THING by Billy J. Lee. March 2, 1977. Directed by Mervyn Willis.
INTERNATIONAL THEATER FESTIVAL: LA COMPETITION and SAUVAGE by Maurice Guillaud, presented by Le Centre Culturelle du Marais, March 2, 1977; THE CAUCASIAN CHALK CIRCLE by Bertolt Brecht, translated by Ralph Manheim, directed by Fritz Bennewitz, March 11, 1977; LA DOUBLE INCONSTANCE by Marivaux, March 18, 1977, directed by Jacques Rosner; HAMLET by Shakespeare and THE CYCLE by Tae Suk Oh, directed by Min Soo Ahn, presented by Korean Drama Center, March 25, 1977; HAUS VATERLAND arranged by Dieter Hildebrandt, presented by Berlin Schiller Theater, April 5, 1977; FRANZISKA by Franz Wedekind, directed by Giancarlo Nanni, presented by La Fabbrica Dell'Attore, April 6, 1977; LOCUS SOLUS conceived and directed by Meme Perlini, presented by Teatro La Maschera. April 13, 1977.
SONGS AT TWILIGHT by Maureen Howard, music by George Kent. March 8, 1977. Directed by Michael Montel; with Judith Barcroft, Richard Council, Michael Wager, Stanja Lowe.
LAMENT FOR RASTAFARI by Edgar White. March 30, 1977. Directed by Basil Wallace. With Yardbird Players.
HELLBENT FOR HEAVEN (musical) book by Jeff Tamborino, music and lyrics by John Braden. April 3, 1977. Directed by Michael Maurer.
THE SELECTION conceived by Coda Theater Company. April 21, 1977. Directed by Joel Benenson; with Harvey Lieberman.
VOX HUMANA #3: A LOVE SONG. April 21, 1977. With Cosmos.
BOO! written and directed by Sterling Harper. May, 1977.
THE FLYING DOCTOR and THE HUNGER ARTIST adapted and directed by Patrick Sciarratta from Kafka's work. May 6, 1977. Performed by Bond Street Theater Coalition.

MACBETH by William Shakespeare. May 8, 1977. Directed by Jonas Jurasas; with Barbara Montgomery, Tom Kopache.
THE LEGEND OF WU CHOW (one-act play) conceived and directed by Tisa Chang. May 19, 1977. Performed by Pan-Asian Repertory Company.

Lion Theater Company. Actors' company with an eclectic repertory. Gene Nye, producing director, Ellie Meglio, managing director.

LOVE'S LABOUR'S LOST by William Shakespeare, music by Carol Hall. July 6, 1976. Directed by Gene Nye; with Linda Carlson.
A NIGHT AT THE BLACK PIG by Charles Nolte. August 3, 1976. Directed by Larry Carpenter; with David Didawick, Wanda Bimson, Ron Van Lieu, John Arnone, Helga Kopperel, Warrington Winters.
MARATHON 33 by June Havoc. September, 1976. Directed by Garland Wright.
A BIRD IN THE HAND by Georges Feydeau, translated and adapted by Edward Stern and Ann Ward Stern. October 19, 1976. Directed by Leland Moss; with Haskell Gordon, Maria Cellario, Brian Hartigan, Laurie Heineman, Janice Fuller, David Gallagher.
VISIONS OF KEROUAC by Martin Duberman. November 26, 1976. Directed by Kenneth Frankel; with James Handy, Lane Smith, Brian Hartigan, Gregg Almquist, Tom Foley, Robert Picardo.
PEG O' MY HEART by J. Hartley Manners. January 28, 1977. Directed by Gene Nye; with Mary E. Baird, Allan Carlsen, Gibson Glass, Sofia Landon, Sandra Halperin, Jim Ricketts.
FOR THE USE OF THE HALL by Oliver Hailey (co-produced with Playwrights Horizons). April 13, 1977. Directed by Ron Van Lieu; with Evalyn Baron, Eileen Burns, David Gallagher, Sharon Laughlin, Barbara LeBrunn, Ted Tinling.

Mabou Mines. Experiment with new theater forms.

CASCANDO by Samuel Beckett. November 5, 1976. Directed by JoAnne Akalaitis.
THE B BEAVER ANIMATION text and direction by Lee Breuer, adapted by Thom Cathcart and Steve Bennyworth from Samuel Beckett's work. March 25, 1977. With Frederick Neumann, Ruth Maleczech, JoAnne Akalaitis, William Raymond, David Warrilow.
DRESSED LIKE AN EGG based on Colette's writing, designed and directed by JoAnne Akalaitis. May 6, 1977. With JoAnne Akalaitis, Ellen McElduff, Ruth Maleczech, William Raymond, David Warrilow.

Manhattan Project. A theater company in its eighth year whose experiments include Lewis Carroll and Molière as well as original writers. Andre Gregory, artistic director.

A THOUSAND NIGHTS AND A NIGHT (Richard F. Burton translation). April 19, 1977. Directed by Gerry Bamman.
Workshops included Laboratory for Theatrical Interdisciplinary Human Research, open workshops with Polish Laboratory Theater, Jerzy Grotowski.

Manhattan Theater Club. A producing organization with three stages for productions, readings, workshop activities and cabaret. Lynne Meadow, artistic director.

Downstage
CHILDREN by A. R. Gurney Jr. October 20, 1976. Directed by Melvin Bernhardt; with Holland Taylor, Dennis Howard, Nancy Marchand, Swoosie Kurtz, Gary Smith.
ASHES by David Rudkin. October 20, 1976. Directed by Lynne Meadow; with Roberta Maxwell, Brian Murray.
BOESMAN AND LENA by Athol Fugard. January 19, 1977. Directed by Thomas Bullard; with Robert Christian, Frances Foster, Paul Makgoba.
THE GATHERING by Edna O'Brian. March 2, 1977. Directed by Austin Pendleton; with Sloane Shelton, Maria Tucci, Louis Zorich.
IN THE SUMMER HOUSE by Jane Bowles. May 4, 1977. Directed by Stephen Hollis.
CLAMMA DALE IN CONCERT. May 31, 1977.

Upstage
LA VOIX HUMANE (opera) by Francis Poulenc. June 1, 1976.
CLAW by Howard Barker. November 4, 1976. Directed by Stephen Pascal.
BALLYMURPHY by Michael Neville. December 2, 1976. Directed by Ronald Roston; with Roy London, Kevin Ottem, Jay Devlin, Larry Bryggman, John C. Vennema, John Gallogly.
BILLY IRISH by Thomas Babe. January 27, 1977. Directed by Barry Marshall.
QUAIL SOUTHWEST by Larry Ketron. February 24, 1977. Directed by Andy Wolk; with Toni Kalem, Zina Jasper, Munson Hicks, Drew Snyder, Margot Stevenson, Dick Latessa.
STATUES, EXHIBITION and THE BRIDGE AT BELHARBOUR (one-act plays) by Janet Neipris. April 7, 1977. Directed by Stan Wojewodski.

THE LAST STREET PLAY by Richard Wesley. May 12, 1977. Directed by Thomas Bullard; with Roscoe Orman, Morgan Freeman, Brent Jennings, Richard E. Gant, J. Herbert Kerr, Yvette Hawkins.
Cabaret
A SALUTE TO GEORGE M. COHAN. June 2, 1976.
COMDEN AND GREEN REVUE conceived and directed by Norman L. Berman. October 27, 1976.
CRACKED TOKENS (resident improvisational group). October 29, 1976. (Late Cabaret, April 29, 1977).
SONGS OF RICHARD MALTBY AND DAVID SHIRE. November 24, 1976.
PENDLETON BROWN AND JAKE HOLMES. November 26, 1976.
BECAUSE WE'RE DECADENT (revue). January 12, 1977. Directed by Dan Goggin.
JUST ME. January 14, 1977. With Nancy Deering.
SONGS FROM "NELL" by Peter Schickele, lyrics by Diane Lampert. January 26, 1977.
NOTES: SONGS by Craig Carnelia. January 28, 1977. Directed by Bill Gile.
C. C. PRYOR AND FRIENDS. February 23, 1977.
KINKY DISCO. February 25, 1977.
DONALD SIEGAL and ROBERT JOSEPH. March 9, 1977.
MARGERY COHEN. March 11, 1977.
SONGS FROM "THE CONFIDENCE MAN" by Jim Steinman and Ray Errol Fox, based on Herman Melville's work. April 6, 1977.
SONGS by Don Scardino and Victor Garber. April 8, 1977.
FOUR YEARS AFTER THE REVOLUTION (theater songs) by Richard Peaslee, lyrics by Adrien Mitchell, Jean-Claude van Itallie, Kenneth Cavander, and others. May 4, 1977.
SALUTE TO NEW COMPOSERS. May 25, 1977. Directed by Jack Allison.

Medicine Show Theater Ensemble. Develops works that juggle incongruities of style and form, mingle wit and high physical energy. Barbara Vann, James Barbosa, directors.

OPEN REHEARSAL. November, 1976.
MISCELLANY SERIES (performances) by Margot Colbert, Robert Colbert, Ara Fitzgerald, Carol Henry, Kalvert Nelson.
MEDICINE SHOW (ensemble piece). December, 1976. Directed by Barbara Vann.
GLOWWORM (ensemble piece). February, 1977. Directed by Barbara Vann.
FROGS (collaborative creation), music by Yenoin Guibbory. May 11, 1977. Directed by James Barbosa.

National Arts Theater. To present revivals and re-adaptations of classical works. Robert Sterling, Robert Stocking, co-producers, co-artistic directors.

THE MOUSETRAP by Agatha Christie. June 5, 1976. Directed by Robert Sterling.
THE IMPORTANCE OF BEING EARNEST by Oscar Wilde. July, 1976. Directed by Robert Sterling. (Reopened January, 1977).
AN EVENING OF BRECHT: THE INFORMER, THE JEWISH WIFE and IN SEARCH OF JUSTICE by Bertolt Brecht. August 27, 1976. Directed by Bill Hux.
THE SEAGULL by Anton Chekhov. September 16, 1976. Directed by Robert Sterling; with Suzanne Toren, Mel Jurdem, Pat Kraft, Robert Marc, Jocelyne Pierrel, Martin Treat.
THE PICTURE OF DORIAN GRAY by Oscar Wilde. November, 1976. Directed by Robert Sterling.
TEN LITTLE INDIANS by Agatha Christie. March, 1977. Directed by Robert Sterling.
THIS PROPERTY IS CONDEMNED and SOMETHING UNSPOKEN by Tennessee Williams. May 20, 1977. Directed by Lucille LeClair.
National Arts on Bond
GRAND HOTEL adapted and directed by Robert Stocking, based on Vicki Baum's works. September 9, 1976.
A ONE-ACT CYCLE: QUEENS OF FRANCE by Thornton Wilder, SHOW ANGEL by Lewis John Carlino and DUST OF THE ROAD by Kenneth Sawyer Goodman (one-act plays). November, 1976. Directed by Robert Stocking.
BIRD FOOD by N. Noble Barrett, directed by Charles Pegues; AUNTS OF ANTIOCH CITY by N. Noble Barrett, directed by Cynthia Belgrave. February, 1977.
POCKET FULL OF POSIES by Sidney Morris. April, 1977. Directed by Robert Stocking.
THE MAIDS by Jean Genet. April, 1977.
HE SAID, SHE SAID (mini plays) by Anthony Cipolla, Jim Curran, Jack Henri, Steve Kalvar, Charles Pulaski, Edna Schappert. Directed by Jim Curran; performed by Actors Consort.
SUNDAY TWILIGHT MUSICALE by Charles Griffin. May, 1977.
THE BACCHAE by Euripides. May 15, 1977. Directed by Dorothy Stuart.

The New Dramatists. An organization devoted to playwrights; member writers may use the facilities for anything from private cold readings of their material to workshop stagings. Stephen Harty, administrative director, Peter Kozik, workshop coordinator.

Workshop Stagings
EVEN THE WINDOW IS GONE by Gene Radano. November 16, 1976. Directed by Shan Covey; with Shelly Batt, Laura Dowling, Mary Moon, Garnett Smith, Dorothy Wilens, Dan Ziskie.
BULL FIGHT COW by Allen Davis III. December 14, 1976. Directed by Warren Kliewer; with William Newman, Michael McCleery, Albert M. Ottenhiemer, Martha Galphin, Shirley Bodtke, Hank Smith.
THE BERSERKERS by Warren Kliewer. January 23, 1977. Directed by Cliff Goodwin; with Janine Geary, Bonnie Deroski, Paul McCrane, Barbara Tarbuck, Robert Chamberlain.
LUST by Steven Somkin. February 16, 1977. Directed by Andrew Harris; with Ronnie Harris, Ruth Baker, Richard Ehrhart, Nicholas Levitin, Ruth Gregory, Ed Crowley.
THE MUTE WHO SANG by Gene Radano. May 24, 1977. Directed by Frank Scaringi; with Anna Berger, Robert Costanzo, Paul Michael, Ralph Monaco, Phil Rubenstein, Asher Stern.

Readings
THE PROMOTION OF ARTAUD WISTAAR by Steven Somkin. September 16, 1976. Directed by Warren Kliewer; with Ruth Baker, Bill Cosgriff, Ned Farster, Lance Hewett, Terry Layman, George Salerno.
THE BESERKERS by Warren Kliewer. September 20, 1976. Directed by Cliff Goodwin; with David Aaron, Jonathan Bolt, Cathy Cieciuch, Joanne Cieciuch, Gloria Maddox.
BRIXTON RECOVERY by Jack Gilhooley. October 21, 1976. Directed by Cliff Goodwin; with Shirley Brown, Richard Stack.
THE TWO MARYS by Warren Kliewer. November 11, 1976. Directed by Cliff Goodwin; with Nancy Franklin, Bryan Hull, Peter Kozik, Michelle LaRue.
THE WAKEFIELD PLAYS (trilogy) by Israel Horovitz. December 2, 1976. Directed by John Dillon; with John Cazale, Nancy Chesney, Dominic Chianese, Joanna Miles, Michael Moriarty, Peg Murray.
LUST by Steven Somkin. January 7, 1977. Directed by Andrew Harris; with Ronnie Harris, Ruth Baker, Richard Ehrhart, George Salerno, Cyndy Aimes, Ed Crowley.
THE COUNTERPART CURE by Jeff Kindley. January 14, 1977. Directed by Bille Gile; with David Berman, Brad Blaisdell, Barbara Coggin, Georgia Creighton, Dick Pohlers, Tom O'Rourke.
THE GIRL OF THE GOLDEN WEST and THE BRIDE OF HITLER (one-act plays) by Maurice Noel. February 2, 1977. Directed by Michael Bavar; with Bonne Leu Banyard, Meredith Rile, Michael Oakes, Tony Savage, Darryl Croxton, Jane Altman.
LUNATICS AND LOVERS by Stephen Foreman. February 4, 1977. With Rusty Russ, Joe Pantaliano, Maureen Garrett, Tom Bair, Graham Beckel, Steve Ommerle.
GANDHIJI by Rose Leiman Goldemberg. February 7, 1977. Directed by Elinor Renfield; with Bob Balaban, Richard Fancy, Dana Gladstone, Katina Commings, Patricia Cray, Glenn Cabrera.
NEST OF VIPERS by Stuart Vaughan. February 10, 1977. With Paul Sparer, Gregory Abels, Kevin Kline, Sharon Laughlin, Pat Falkenhain, Tom Waites.
WHAT DO I DO ABOUT HEMINGWAY? by Enid Rudd. February 25, 1977. Directed by Barbara Rosoff; with Trip Plymale, Lin Shaye, George Riddle, Rebecca Schull, Paul Marin, Freddy Calle.
YOU ARE WHAT YOU ARE by David Trainer. February 27, 1977. Directed by Alfred Gingold; with Rich Lieberman, Susan Vare, Jack Axelrod, Katharine Manning, James Allan Bartz, Joni Fritz.
WORKING LATE by Donald Wollner. March 4, 1977. Directed by Dana Roberts; with Edmund Williams, Joan Grant, Lawrence Johnson, Anita Keal, Alfred Cherry, Carl Moebus.
MOCKING BIRD and MARY HAMILTON (one-act plays) by William Parchman. March 18, 1977. Directed by Julie Boyd; with China Chen, Anne Miyamoto, Freddy Mao, Harsh Nayyar, Harry Wong, Ernest Abuba.
LOSERS by Donald Wollner. April 1, 1977. Directed by Ellen Sandler; with David Little, Stephen Deroski, Bob Powell, Joseph Jamrog, Howard Renensland, Joan Grant.
MOTHER RYAN by Maurice Noel. April 6, 1977. Directed by Paul Schneider; with Barbara Eda-Young, Mark Metcalf, Sloane Shelton, Parker McCormick, Olympia Dukakis, John Lloyd.
ARTISTS FOR THE REVOLUTION by Eric Thompson. April 15, 1977. Directed by Thomas Gruenewald; with Peter Coffeen, David Rosenbaum, Elizabeth Franz, Edward Binns, Maurice Copeland, Nicholas Kepros.
THE TWO MARYS by Warren Kliewer. May, 1977. With Jonathan Bolt, Nancy Franklin, Michele LaRue, Peter Kozik.
A NEW WORLD! (musical) book, lyrics and direction by Marian Winters, Albert Hague. May 9, 1977.

New Federal Theater. The Henry Street Settlement's training and showcase unit for new playwrights, mostly black and Puerto Rican. Woodie King Jr., director.

THE DEFENSE by Edgar White. November 11, 1976. Directed by Dennis Scott; with Chris Campbell, Rosanna Carter, Lou Ferguson, Walter Jones, Arlene Quiyou, Lori Tan Chinn.
DIVINE COMEDY by Owen Dodson. January 14, 1977. Directed by Clinton Turner Davis; with Verona Barnes, Zaida Coles, Darryl Croxton, Jessie D. Goins, Neil Harris.
PERDIDO by Soledad. March 10, 1977. Directed by Regge Life; with Samuel L. Jackson, Patricia Mauceri-Cruz, Charles McKenna, LaTanya Richardson, Anne Saxon, R. T. Vessells.

MACBETH adapted by Orson Welles from William Shakespeare. May 12, 1977. Directed by Edmund Cambridge; with Esther Rolle, Lex Monson.

Latinos Playwrights Reading Workshop
THE LIVING ROOM by Piedro Pietri; A PAIR OF WINGS by Jaime Carrero, directed by Norberto Kerner. January, 1977.
THE JUNKIES STOLE THE CLOCK by Papoleto Melendez (reading). February 7, 1977. Directed by Marvin Camillo.

New York Shakespeare Festival Public Theater. Schedule of experimental workshop or work-in-progress productions and guest residencies, in addition to its regular productions. Joseph Papp, producer.

A MOVIE STAR HAS TO STAR IN BLACK AND WHITE by Adrienne Kennedy. November, 1976. Directed by Joseph Chaikin.
THREE SHORT PLAYS by Wallace Shawn: SUMMER EVENING, directed by Wilford Leach; YOUTH HOSTEL, directed by Leonardo Shapiro; MR. FRIVOLOUS, directed by Lee Breuer. December, 1976.
MUSEUM by Tina Howe. March, 1977. Directed by Richard Jordan.
CRACK written and directed by Crispin Larangeira. April, 1977.

New York Theater Ensemble. Organization of participating artists to encourage new theater artists and playwrights. Lucille Talayco, artistic director.

BETWEEN TIME AND TIMBUKTU by Kurt Vonnegut Jr. September, 1976. Directed by Ruth Evans.
LUDLOW FAIR, THE MADNESS OF LADY BRIGHT and THE FAMILY CONTINUES by Lanford Wilson. September 30, 1976. Directed by Pam Billig.
SHELTER ESTATES, U.S.A. written and directed by Terry Gregory. October 13, 1976.
THE FOG HORN by Ray Bradbury and MOTHERLOVE by August Strindberg. January, 1977. Directed by Ruth Evans.
THE SEAGULL by Anton Chekhov. February 9, 1977. Directed by Ann Ciccolla; performed by Renaissance Theater Company.
THE WEDDING by Stanislaw Wyspianski. February 17, 1977. Directed by Ramond Marciniak.
HOME OF THE BRAVE by Arthur Laurents. March 3, 1977. Directed by David Dreyfuss.
THE SEA by Edward Bond. March 31, 1977. Directed by John PiRoman.
ATE FROM THE APPLE (festival of one-act plays): A LIKENESS TO LIFE by Saul Zachary, WARPLAY by Howard Cruse, A DISTANCE AHEAD by Richard Garrick, GET THE ONES WITH STARS ON THE SIDE by Malik, DIMENSIONS by Ted Knite and A BAG OF MAGIC by Jim Lagona. April 28, 1977.
THE MOTION OF HISTORY written and directed by Imamu Amiri Baraka. May 27, 1977.

New York Theater Strategy. Organization of playwrights for the production of their works. Maria Irene Fornes, president.

LINES OF VISION, script by Richard Foreman, music by George Quincy, lyrics by Maria Irene Fornes. October, 1976. Directed by Lawrence Kornfeld; with Theo Barnes, John Szostek, Vicenta Aviles, John Brown, Lynn Gerb, Arlene Rothlein.
THE BONES OF BACON written and directed by David Starkweather. April 21, 1977. With Sid R. Gross, Timothy Jay O'Brien.
FEFU AND HER FRIENDS written and directed by Maria Irene Fornes. May 5, 1977. With Janet Biehl, Gwendolyn Brown, Connie Cicone, Margaret Harrington, Carolyn Hearn, Rebecca Schull.
COWGIRL ECSTASY by Michael Smith. May 26, 1977. Directed by Theo Barnes.

No Smoking Playhouse. Eclectic producing policy. Norman Thomas Marshall, artistic director.

THE NEW MAN by John von Hartz. July 19, 1976. Directed by Norman Thomas Marshall; with George Wolf Reily, Jessica Hull, Nancy Sans, Jeff Goldman, Lou Trapani, Sturgis Warner.
ASHES OF SOLDIERS by Richard Davidson. October 28, 1976. Directed by George Allison Elmer.
FORBIDDEN FRUIT by Dion Boucicault adapted by George Wolf Reily. December 7, 1976. Directed by Norman Thomas Marshall; with Jeff Marsh, Shelley Rogers, Perrin Ferris, J. R. Horne, Joan Shanagold, Nicki Kaplan.
A LITTLE WINE WITH LUNCH (revue) book and lyrics by John von Hartz, music by William Schimmel. March 16, 1977. Directed by Norman Thomas Marshall; with Ann Hodapp, Nicki Kaplan, Virginia Kruger, Tom Leo, George Wolf Reily.

Ontological-Hysteric Theater. Avant garde theater productions written, directed and designed by the group's founder, Richard Foreman.

BOOK OF SPLENDORS (PT. II) BOOK OF LEVERS: ACTION AT A DISTANCE (A CHAMBER PIECE). March 2, 1977. With Kate Manheim, Charley Bergengren, Camille Foss, Anna Jordan, Robert Schlee, Francois Thiolat.

The Open Space in Soho. Focus in presenting new plays and developing new playwrights. Lynn Michaels, Harry Baum, directors.

FANTASIES AT THE FRICK by Leonard Melfi. November 9, 1976. Directed by Lynn Michaels; with Justin Deas, Jody Catlin, William Russ, Ilene Kristen.
WOMEN PLAYWRIGHTS' FESTIVAL (staged readings): THE RIGHT KIND OF people by Carol Manago; WOMAN WITH A GUN by Florence Hunt; DIALOGUE BETWEEN DIDEY WARBUCKS AND MAMA VASELINE by Ilsa Gilbert; SOUL OF A STRIPPER by Ilsa Gilbert; CLANCY by Ronnie Paris; NEW WORLD MONKEY by France Burke; THE TORTOISE AND THE YARROW by Julien Berk; WHEN BANANAS GROW IN THE CHERRY TREE by Melba Thomas; THE MARRIAGE MUSEUM by Elyse Nass. December, 1976.
SOLITAIRE and THE VACUUM CLEANER (one-act plays) by Julien Berk; THE ELIZABETH STUART COMPANY PRESENTS by Jean Nichtern; DIALOGUES OF THE SHADOW WOMEN by Denise Bell; AN ACT OF LOVE by Pamela Lengyel; IN SICKNESS AND IN WEALTH by Anita Hart and Ruth King. February, 1977.
PLAYWRIGHTS GROUP FESTIVAL 3 schedule included THE BRAIN by Helen Duberstein, directed by Jerry Heymann, March 3, 1977; SLIGHT by Richard Foreman, interpreted by Stuart Sherman; STUART SHERMAN'S EIGHTH SPECTACLE; WITNESSES by Arthur Sainer; THE IGNORANCE OF QUEEN VICTORIA'S HABITS by Victor Lipton, directed by Geraldine Court, March 5, 1977; THE SHAGGY DOG ANIMATION, PART I by Mabou Mines, March 8, 1977.
BENNY LEONARD AND THE BROOKLYN BRIDGE by Paul Leaven, music by William Finn. March 30, 1977. Directed by Edward M. Cohen.
SHAYNA by Mordecai Siegal. May 10, 1977. Directed by Richard Karp; with Bernard Anello, Sharon Heffler, Keith Kermzian, Jean Sage, Dan Tyra, Pegge Winslow.

The People's Performing Company. New, socially significant musicals. Peter Copani, Vince Gugleotti, Denise Bonenfant, directors.

NEW YORK CITY STREET SHOW written and directed by Peter Copani. January, 1977.

The Performance Group. Experiments with new, collaborative and non-verbal creative techniques. Richard Schechner, director.

RUMSTICK ROAD composed and directed by Spalding Gray and Elizabeth LeCompte. March, 1977. With Spalding Gray, Libby Howes, Bruce Porter, Ron Vawter.
MOTHER COURAGE AND HER CHILDREN by Bertolt Brecht, translated by Ralph Manheim. April, 1977. Directed by Richard Schechner; with Joan MacIntosh, Elizabeth LeCompte, Spalding Gray, James Clayburgh, Leeny Sack, Bruce Porter.

Perry Street Theater. Dual emphasis placed on producing scripts by new playwrights and on experimentation with other contemporary and classical scripts. Vasek Simek, producer and artistic director, Susan Gregg, managing director.

THE DUMBWAITER by Harold Pinter. June, 1976. Directed by Susan Gregg; with Vasek Simek, Cole Stevens.
HOME BOY by Ed Bullins. September 23, 1976. Directed by Patricia Golden; with Thommi Blackwell, Rodney Hudson, Dana Manno, Pamela Poitier.
DEATH AND DEVIL by Frank Wedekind, directed by Vasek Simek and THE EXCEPTION AND THE RULE by Bertolt Brecht, translated by Eric Bentley, directed by Louis Rackoff. October 21, 1976.
RITA HOLLY by Abraham Tetenbaum. November 18, 1976. Directed by Alan Fox.
THE WINTER GARDEN THEATER PROUDLY PRESENTS A SPECIAL PERFORMANCE OF "JULIUS CAESAR" BY THE BROTHERS BOOTH by Erik Brogger. December 16, 1976. Directed by Louis Rackoff; with Stephen Daley, Pedro Silva, Stanley Flood, Juergen Kuehn, Tom McLaughlin, Pamela C. Lewis.
BOZ! by John M. Benders. December 21, 1976. Directed by Dick Gaffield.
HE WHO GETS SLAPPED by Leonid Andreyev. January 13, 1977. Directed by Vasek Simek; with Maurice Blanc, Owen Rachleff, Juergen Kuehn.
THE PURIFICATION by Tennessee Williams, directed by Susan Gregg; with Marilyn Dossey, Jacqueline

Jacobus, Linda Kane, Martin Marinaro, Robert Nersesian, Wyman Kane and DUTCHMAN by Leroi Jones, directed by Anita Khanzadian. February 10, 1977.

THE UNDERPANTS by Carl Sternheim, translated by Eric Bentley. March 10, 1977. Directed by Dick Brukenfeld; with Peter Brouwer, Faith Catlin, Sylvia Gassell, Pat McNamara, Dan Szelag, Donald Warfield.

COWBOYS #2 and THE UNSEEN HAND (one-act plays) by Sam Shepard. March 31, 1977. Directed by Jim O'Connor; with John Archie, Paul Craggs, Sam Freed, Bill Kornovsky, Dana Mills, David Wohl.

SIX CHARACTERS IN SEARCH OF AN AUTHOR by Luigi Pirandello. April 28, 1977. Directed by Larry Speigel.

DANTON'S DEATH by Georg Buechner. May 26, 1977. Directed by Louis Rackoff.

Playwrights Horizons. Give playwrights the opportunity to see their work produced by professionals in an atmosphere devoid of commercial pressure. Robert Moss, executive director.

Manhattan Full Productions (asterisk indicates also performed at Queens Theater in the Park)

PARADISE by Steven Shea. June 3, 1976. Directed by Paul Cooper; with Jillian Lindig, John Guerrasio, Ron Johnston, Kathleen Chalfant, Greg Johnson, Elliot Burtoff.

BOO HOO by Philip Magdalany. September 29, 1976. Directed by Michael Flanagan; with Patricia O'Connell, Ann Shaler, Elaine Kerr.*

RIO GRANDE by Martin Sherman. November 11, 1976. Directed by Leland Moss; with Irene Dailey.*

GEMINI by Albert Innaurato. December 8, 1976. Directed by Peter Mark Schifter; with Jon Polito, Jessica James, Reed Birney, Sigourney Weaver, Jonathan Hadary, Tom Mardirosian, Anne DeSalvo.

REBECCAH by Karen Malpede. December 9, 1976. Directed by Tina Shepard.*

STOP THE PARADE by Marsha Sheiness. February 3, 1977. Directed by Harold Scott; with Robert Sevra, Joseph Mays, Jayne Haynes, Steve Simpson, Dallas Greer, Ernest Lehrer.*

FAIR WEATHER FRIENDS by Philip Magdalany and Kenneth Pressman. March 10, 1977. Directed by Richard Place.*

FOR THE USE OF THE HALL by Oliver Hailey (co-produced with Lion Theater Company). April 13, 1977. Directed by Ron Van Lieu; with Evalyn Baron, Eileen Burns, David Gallagher, Sharon Laughlin, Barbara LeBrunn, Ted Tinling.

S.W.A.K. (SEALED WITH A KISS) by Sally Ordway. April 28, 1977. Directed by Geraldine Court.

EARTHWORMS by Albert Innaurato. May 17, 1977. Directed by David Schweizer; with Richard Hayes, David Keith, Jeffrey Knox, Michael Egan, Cara Duff-MacCormick, Jonathan Frakes.

Manhattan Workshops

WORKSHOP FESTIVAL *(new plays):* THE INVESTIGATION OF JT by Richard Ploetz, directed by Lew Pshena; REUNION by Dennis Andersen; STORMBOUND by Larry Ketron, directed by Jessica Levy; OCTOBER WEDDING by Dorothy Louise, directed by William Shorr; MONTPELIER PIZAZZ by Wendy Wasserstein, directed by Donald Warfield. June 15, 1976 (festival opening).

MAD DOGS by George Shea. October 13, 1976. Directed by Stuart Ross; with Nick LaPadula.

JUST LIKE THE NIGHT by David Rimmer. January 19, 1977. Directed by Barry Keating.

RAMBLINGS by Gus Kaikkonen. February 10, 1977. Directed by Michael Montel.

Staged Readings

TRANSATLANTIC BRIDGE by Ann Commire. November, 1976. Directed by Anna Smith.

MADEMOISELLE COLOMBE (musical) book and directed by Albert Harris, music by Michael Valenti, lyrics by Edwin Dulchin, based on Jean Anouilh's play. February 7, 1977.

TRADE-OFFS by Lonnie Carter. February 8, 1977. Directed by Richard Vos.

THE WHITE PIANO conceived and directed by Christopher Adler. March 4, 1977.

UNCOMMON WOMEN by Wendy Wasserstein. March 19, 1977. Directed by Christopher Cox.

INNOCENT THOUGHTS AND HARMLESS INTENTIONS by John Heuer. March 26, 1977. Directed by James Nicola.

A TALE FOR CHRISTMAS EVE by Susan Jack. May 12, 1977. Directed by Alfred Gingold.

Queens Theater in the Park

DEAR RUTH by Norman Krasna. June 2, 1976. Directed by Robert Moss.

THE TAVERN by George M. Cohan. June 24, 1976. Directed by Ron Miller.

BORN YESTERDAY by Garson Kanin. July 15, 1976. Directed by Caymichael Patten; with Harry Goz, Lynne Lipton, Richmond Hoxie, Stan Edelman, Kathleen Chalfant.

THE DYBBUK by S. Ansky. October 30, 1976. Directed by Philip Himberg.

THE RIVALS by Richard Brinsley Sheridan. December 4, 1976. Directed by Robert Moss.

HAY FEVER by Noel Coward. January 22, 1977. Directed by Marshall Oglesby.

THE MOUSETRAP by Agatha Christie. February 26, 1977. Directed by Larry Carpenter.

JACQUES BREL IS ALIVE AND WELL AND LIVING IN PARIS (musical) by Eric Blau and Mort

Shuman, based on Jacques Brel's lyrics and commentary, music by Jacques Brel. April 8, 1977. Directed by Stuart Ross.
STAGE DOOR by Edna Ferber and George S. Kaufman. May 7, 1977. Directed by Robert Moss.

Puerto Rican Traveling Theater. A professional company presenting bilingual productions of Puerto Rican and Hispanic playwrights, emphasizing subjects of relevance today. Miriam Colon, founder and producer.

EVERYTHING NOT COMPULSORY IS STRICTLY FORBIDDEN by Jorge Diaz and THE DINNER GUEST by Manuel Martinez Mediero. July 7, 1976. Directed by Alba Olms.
THE OXCART by Rene Marques, translated by Charles Pilditch. April 30, 1977. Directed by Miriam Colon.
I TOOK PANAMA by Luis A. Garcia and El Teatro Popular de Bogota, translated by Tony Diaz, music by Galt MacDermot. May, 1977. Directed by Alba Olms; with Juan M. Aguero, Eduouard DeSoto, Norberto Kerner, Teresa Yenque, Carlos Carrasco, Luis Avalos.

Quaigh Theater. Primarily a playwrights' theater, devoted to the new playwright, the established contemporary playwright and the modern (post-1920) playwright. William H. Lieberson, artistic director.

THE LAST RESORT by Marvin Pletzke. January, 1977. Directed by Sherwood Arthur; with Louise Larabee, Russell Horton, Annette Hunt, Bob Levine.
THE LIFE AND TIMES OF SHOLOM ALEICHEM by Felix Leon. February, 1977. Directed by Tony DeVito.
INDEPENDENCE DAY by Richard Mansfield. March 16, 1977. Directed by Thom Molyneaux; with James Nesbit Clark, James Galvin, John Leighton, Larry Rosler, Jim Stubbs, H. Richard Young.
NIGHT FEVER by Sebastian W. Stuart (workshop). March 18, 1977. Directed by Ted Mornel.
HEAT by William Hauptman. April 11, 1977. Directed by Sharon Barr.
I AM A CAMERA by John Van Druten. May 11, 1977. Directed by Dorothy Stuart.
THE BLOOD KNOT by Athol Fugard. May 25, 1977. Directed by J. C. Ross.

Lunchtime Theater
HOLDING ACTION by Mark Zalk. June 2, 1976. Directed by Doug Popper.
A PERFECT ANALYSIS GIVEN BY A PARROT by Tennessee Williams. June 7, 1976.
AUGUSTUS by Jean Anouilh and AVENUE OF DREAM by Elyse Nass. October, 1976. Directed by Doug Popper.
THE TATAMI by David Shapiro. December 29, 1976. Directed by Ted Mornel.
THE TEASERS written and directed by Hiram Taylor. January 12, 1977.
PLAYING WITH FIRE by August Strindberg. January 24, 1977. Directed by Peter del Valle; with Dale Corman, Dale Copps, Mary Feeney, John Ingle, Diane Tarleton, Marcia Wood.
THREE ACTORS AND THEIR DRAMA by Michel de Ghelderode. February 7, 1977. Directed by Dale Copps.
THE GRAVE ROBBER by William Kushner. March 7, 1977. Directed by Ted Mornel.
TAPESTRY by Alexis de Veaux. March, 1977. Directed by Kimako Baraka.
UNTIL FURTHER NOTICE, TOMORROW IS CANCELLED by Elyse Nass and Jim Struthers. April, 1977. Directed by Jim Struthers.
THE DODO BIRD by Emanuel Fried. April 4, 1977. Directed by Dale Copps; with J. P. Clark, Alfred Cherry, Paul Merrill, Frank Robinson.
SWIMMING IN THE SAND BOX by Jim Justice. May 4, 1977. Directed by Bruce Payton.
THE EASY ASSIMILATION OF FREDI DUNDEE. May, 1977. Directed by Rhoda Roberts.
THE RETURN by Mario Fratti. May 16, 1977. Directed by Doug Popper.
THE TOP LOADING LOVER (one-act opera) by Raymond Allen and Glenn Allen Smith. May 31, 1977. Directed by Ted Mornel.

Richard Morse Mime Theater. To create a home for a permanent mime repertory theater in America. Richard Morse, artistic director.

GIFTS. December 22, 1976.
DUET and VOYAGES. February 18, 1977. (re-opened).

Shirtsleeve Theater. Full productions of new works. John A. Vaccaro, James J. Wisner, artistic directors.

SCRAMBLED FEET (musical revue) by John Driver and Jeffrey Haddow. December, 1976. Directed by John Driver.

CHILDREN OF ADAM (songs) by Stan Satlin, conceived and directed by John Driver. March, 1977. With Ralph Bruneau, Kate Draper, Elizabeth Lathram, Robert Polenz, Carole Schweid, James Seymour.
ALIVE AND KICKING (one-woman show). May 11, 1977. With Eliza Ward.

Soho Rep. Classics, old and new, freshly staged in an airy loft arena space. Marlene Swartz, Jerry Engelbach, artistic directors.

PRIVATE LIVES by Noel Coward. June 5, 1976. Directed by Jack Cunningham.
THE BIRTHDAY PARTY by Harold Pinter. August 6, 1976. Directed by Marlene Swartz.
JULY 2 and THANKSGIVING by Stan Kaplan. August 21, 1976. Directed by Jerry Engelbach.
GHOSTS by Henrik Ibsen, adapted and directed by Marlene Swartz. September 18, 1976.
UNDER MILK WOOD by Dylan Thomas. September 25, 1976. Directed by Harrison Ewing.
DRACULA adapted and directed by Jerry Engelbach from Bram Stoker's novel. November 5, 1976.
BLACK COMEDY by Peter Shaffer. November 12, 1976. Directed by Frank Cento.
THE MERCHANT OF VENICE by William Shakespeare. December 11, 1976. Directed by Marlene Swartz; with Mary Eileen O'Donnell, Judy Jurgaitis, Bernard Mantell, John Snyder, Peter Manzione, Daniel Snow.
YOU THE JURY: THE DOCK BRIEF by John Mortimer, directed by Steven Burch; THE PUBLIC EYE by Peter Shaffer, directed by Stephen R. Lieb. January 8, 1977.
WHAT THE BUTLER SAW by Joe Orton. February 18, 1977. Directed by Marlene Swartz.
FAUSTUS X 7 adapted by Jerry Engelbach and Carol Corwen from Christopher Marlowe's *Doctor Faustus*. February, 1977. Directed by Jerry Engelbach and Carol Corwen.
BACK TO METHUSELAH by George Bernard Shaw, interludes by Donald Rifkin. March 19, 1977. Directed by Stephen R. Lieb.
SPRING'S AWAKENING by Frank Wedekind, translated by Mary Eileen O'Donnell, adapted and directed by Carol Corwen. April 16, 1977.
UNCLE VANYA by Anton Chekhov, adapted and directed by Marlene Swartz. April 30, 1977.
RAIN by Somerset Maugham, adapted by John Colton and Clemence Randolph. May 21, 1977. Directed by Jack R. Cunningham.

South Street Theater. Developing an outdoor environmental theater on Pier 17 at the South Street Seaport Museum. Michael Fischetti, artistic director, Jean Sullivan, executive director.

A TIDE OF VOICES by Suzanne Granfield. June 24, 1976. Directed by Michael Fischetti; with Jean Sullivan, Peter Jensen, Robert Foresta, Michael Fischetti.

Stage Company. Endeavors to produce new plays as well as classics and to provide an opportunity for Queens residents to enjoy legitimate theater in their own community. Robert D. Simmons, artistic director.

TWELFTH NIGHT by William Shakespeare. November, 1976. Directed by Robert D. Simmons.
CHILD'S PLAY by Robert Marasco. December, 1976. Directed by Lucia Victor.
WHAT THE BUTLER SAW by Joe Orton. March, 1977. Directed by Lucia Victor.
EYE FOR AN I by Lucia Victor. March 30, 1977.
I DO! I DO! (musical) book and lyrics by Tom Jones, music by Harvey Schmidt, based on *The Fourposter* by Jan de Hartog. May 19, 1977. Directed by Joseph D. Rodgers.

Stage Directors and Choreographers Workshop Foundation. Experimental showcase. Madolin Cervantes, director.

NOBODY, MY MOTHER, OR WHO WAS THAT ON THE TELEPHONE? by Gerald Kean. September 20, 1976. Directed by Madolin Cervantes.
THE FARTHEST STAR by Madolin Cervantes. October 18, 1976. Directed by John Sillings.
DEATH IN THE COUNTRY and THE DROWNING by Elaine Dundy. November 1, 1976. Directed by Robert Haddad.
THE TROGLODYTIC SERENDIPITERS by John P. Dunn. November 15, 1976. Directed by Madolin Cervantes.
WITNESS by Florence Stevenson. November 13, 1976. Directed by Frank Wayne.
WINNERS by Brian Friel. December 13, 1976. Directed by Frank Scaringi.
BACKWARDS by Elyse Nass. December 18, 1976. Directed by Kimako Baraka.
PENNINGTON'S PRIDE by Milli Janz. January 8, 1977. Directed by Madolin Cervantes.
SCENES OF LOVE AND LUST (from Shakespeare).January 8, 1977. Directed by Joan White.
PENSION PLAN by Verna Woskoff. January 22, 1977. Directed by Madolin Cervantes.
A MEANINGFUL RELATIONSHIP by Don Flynn. February 26, 1977. Directed by S. C. Hastie.

SWEET ANNA MELLISSA AND THE GETTYSBURG ADDRESS by Lewis Colick. March 12, 1977. Directed by William E. Hunt.
CHARLES II, OR THE MERRY MONARCH by John Howard Payne. March 26, 1977. Directed by Warren Kliewer.
JUST KEEP LISTENING by John Kendrick. April 4, 1977. Directed by Clifford Ammon.
BOARDWALK WITH TWO HOUSES by Mark Eisman. April 9, 1977. Directed by Dan Duckworth.
A MATTER OF CHOICE by Susan Cain. April 23, 1977. Directed by Madolin Cervantes.
COME, LIBERTY by Beth Turner. May 21, 1977. Directed by Charles Turner.

T. Schreiber Studio. Establishing a close bond with the audience with all productions, with the widest range possible. Original scripts and plays deserving a second chance produced. Terry Schreiber, artistic director.

ALL RUNNERS, COME by James Childs. June 16, 1976. Directed by Dick Gaffield; with Frank A. Ammirati, K. T. Baumann, Mary Carter.

Theater at St. Clements. Concerned with the development of new plays in workshop, experimental and showcase situations. Steve Roylance, Michael Hadge, producers.

TESTIMONIES by James Edward Shannon. June, 1976. Performed by Black Experience Company.
THE EMERGENCE GROUP/HEALING THEATER — THE 50 DAYS: A PENTECOSTAL PILGRIMAGE. June 6, 1976.
ECHOES OF SPOON RIVER adapted and directed by Valerie Bettis, based on Edgar Lee Masters's poems. June 17, 1976.
THE SPICE OF LIFE (musical revue) by Bill Cunningham. June 24, 1976. Directed by James Wigfall.
VIRILITY by Ed Setrakian (workshop). June, 1976. Directed by Kevin O'Connor.
3 WARNER AND SARAH PETERSON PLAYS by Kenneth L. Shan. July 8, 1976. Directed by Jay S. Hoffman.
THE DANCE OF MATA HARI by Bart Midwood. August, 1976. Directed by Robin Hirsch; with Elaine Sulka, David Naughton.
HAMLET and AS YOU LIKE IT by William Shakespeare. September, 1976. Directed by Margrit Roma; performed by New Shakespeare Company of San Francisco.
THE MAN WITH A FLOWER IN HIS MOUTH and DEATH AS A LIFE FORCE by Luigi Pirandello. October, 1976.
THE BALLYGOMBEEN BEQUEST by John Arden and Margaretta D'Arcy. November 11, 1976. Directed by Omar Shapli.
1950 by Steve Friedman. November 24, 1976. Directed by Denny Partridge; with Jack J. Caputo, David Dean, Kathryn Grody, Lyle Kessler, Emily Nash, Andrea Snow.
MEMPHIS IS GONE by Richard Hobson. January 27, 1977. Directed by Robert Allan Ackerman; with Kevin O'Connor, John Kellogg, William Snikowski, Jean DeBaer.
MACBETH by William Shakespeare. March 2, 1977. Directed by Barbara Forst.
THE CURSE OF DEATH! by Jeffrey M. Jones, music by Ken Guilmartin. April, 1977. Directed by Matthew Elkan.
THE CRUCIBLE by Arthur Miller. May 4, 1977. Directed by Allan Winthrop.
THE BOOK OF LAMBERT by Leslie Lee. May 26, 1977. Directed by Dick Gaffield.

Theater for the New City. Specializing in serious, dramatic musical form. George Bartenieff, Crystal Field, artistic directors.

BERCHTESGADEN by Jacques Levy. June, 1976. Directed by Barbara Loden; with Joanne Dorian, Lane Smith.
THE COLONIZATION OF AMERICA (PRODUCED BY THE LONDON COMPANY UNDER THE DIRECTION OF JAMES I) by Joan Durant. June 10, 1976. Directed by Bob Pesola.
BRAVO, ISABEL by Ga-Ga LeGault. July 15, 1976. Directed by Richard Busch.
MAMA LIBERTY'S BICENTENNIAL PARTY (musical street theater) by Crystal Field, George Bartenieff and TFNC Company, music by David Tice. August, 1976.
THE RICH MAN, POOR MAN PLAY (street theater) by Arthur Sainer, music by David Tice and Paul Dver. August 9, 1976.
HERZL (one-man show) by Harold Herbstman. September 9, 1976.
SEED FROM THE EAST by Geraldine Lust. September 11, 1976. Directed by Martin Oltarsh; with Molly Adams, Chev Rodgers, David Tabor, Carole Leverett.
NEW YORK FLESH AND FANTASY (musical) by Lee Kissman, music by Steve Cohen. September 23, 1976. Directed by David McKenna; with Paul Cohen, Daniel Herris, Katherine Cordes, Alvin McCall, Yole Sommer, Peter Yoshita.
A UNIQUE & AMAZING 2 WEEKS FESTIVAL VILLAGE WRITERS ON THE VILLAGE scheduled

included A PASSAGE THRU BOHEMIA by Sally Ordway, directed by Crystal Field; THE INTERNATIONAL STUD by Harvey Fierstein, directed by Harvey Tavel; THE LIFE & TIMES OF . . . by Joan Durant; PLAYBIRTH by Ronald Tavel, directed by Harvey Tavel; THE LEGEND OF SHERIDAN SQUARE written and directed by H. M. Koutoukas; SIMPLIFIED SITE ENGINEERING by Chryse Maile, directed by Donald L. Brooks; POEMS OF KENNETH PATCHEN, with James Leon; BELLA'S LAMENT by Dolores Walker and Andrew Piatrowski, directed by Richard Foreman; . . . a poem by Joel Oppenheimer; PAPER DOLL by Helen Duberstein; GREENWICH VILLAGE SONG by Paul Dver; AMERICAN HAMBURGER, directed by Robert Dahdah; BREAKING OPEN (poems) by Muriel Rukeyser; NEW POEMS by Robert Nichols; A SHORT STORY by Grace Paley; STREETS (song) by John Herbert McDowell; THE FUTURE OF CONGLOMERATES by Sybil Claiborne; POEMS by Hart Crane; WASHINGTON'S SQUARE by Hugh Seidman; GET LOST (A BICENTENNIAL DIRECTION) by Victor Lipton, directed by Bob Pasola; KHADDISH by Allen Ginsberg; A READING FROM KEROUAC by George Bartenieff; LOVE SONGS TO N.Y.C. composed and performed by Al Carmines; WASHING by Maria Irene Fornes; SIDEWALKS by Amlin Gray. November 11, 1976.
STUART SHERMAN'S EIGHTH SPECTACLE. November 18, 1976. With Richard Foreman, Kate Manheim, Charles Ludlam, Stuart Sherman.
BEAUTY KILLS, OR, THE BIL BIKE STORY (musical) by Emilio Cubeiro, music and lyrics by Marie D'Antoni December, 1976.
STRAIGHT FROM THE GHETTO by Neil Harris and Miguel Piñero. January 10, 1977. Directed by Marvin Felix Camillo.
WAITING FOR THE MOON, MELANCHOLY BABY and PEARLS by Arthur Williams, music by David Tice. January 19, 1977. Directed by Robert Dahdah.
A TRIPLE BILL by Arthur Williams. January 20, 1977. Directed by Robert Dahdah; with Mary Boylan, Jerry Jaffe, Bill Daniels.
CLARA'S OLE MAN by Ed Bullins. January 22, 1977.
TWENTY YEARS AFTER THE MAN IN THE IRON MASK by Leo Rutman. February 17, 1977. Directed by Scott Redman; with George Bamford, Armand Dahan, Michael Fischetti, Mary Mitchell, Frederick Ponzlov, Christopher Schario.
WOMEN IN VIOLENCE and THE LYSISTRATA NUMBAH! (work-in-progress) by Spider Woman Theater Workshop. February 24, 1977. With Lisa Maya, Gloria Mojica, Muriel Miguel, Brandy Penn, Pam Verge, Lois Weaver.
HIGH INFIDELITY by John Dooley. February 28, 1977. Directed by Martin Oltarsh; with Jack Betts, Alice Evans, John McComb, Patricia Mertens, Chev Rodgers.
THE SEVEN DAYS OF SHIVA by Sidney S. Antebi. March 17, 1977. Directed by Ronald Roston; with Leonard Di Sesa, Nancy Franklin, Richard Glover, Vivian Kaye, Valerie Ososky, Shemo Sassoon.
CAROL IN WINTER SUNLIGHT by Arthur Sainer, music by George Prideaux. April 28, 1977. Directed by Crystal Field; with Kristin Steen, George Bartenieff, Shelley Desai, Rachael Milder, Sandra Dudley, Jake Maille.
RED FOX SECOND HANGIN' (multi-media ensemble piece) conceived and performed by Roadside Theater. May 12, 1977.
CLAY CAMPBELL'S TRIP WITH THE ELEPHANT GODDESS, POPEYE, ELEANOR ROOSEVELT, AND OTHERS by Tom LeBar, music by Stewart Powell. May 26, 1977. Directed by John Herbert McDowell and Jacquelyn Colten.

Theater Genesis. Writers' theater; production of new American plays. Walter Hadler, artistic director.

AUTO-DESTRUCT by Jeff Wanshel. November 26, 1976. Directed by Scott Redman; with John Bottoms, Tony Diaz, Arthur Erickson, Pinocchio Madrid, Michael Moran, Stuart Sherman.
THE KALEVALA (based on Finnish epic), music by Elizabeth Swados and The Talking Band. January 27, 1977. With Sybille Hayn, Ellen Maddow, Tina Shepard, Margo Lee Sherman, Charles Stanley, Arthur Strimling.
SILVER BEE by Walter Hadler. February 10, 1977. Directed by Raymond Barry. Performed by Quena Company.
BLUE HEAVEN (writings) by R. D. Laing, Miguel Algarin, Barry Stevens and Quena Company; A STRANGE BEAST by Phil James and Quena Company. February 11, 1977. Directed by Raymond Barry; performed by Quena Company.
JO ANN IN THE WHITE HOUSE (stage reading) by Irving Stettner. March 30, 1977.
ATTACK OF THE ANDROGYNES and THE HONKY TONK PIANO IN THE ALL NIGHT CAFÉ by Stephen Policoff. May 12, 1977. Directed by Ron Nash.
METAPHYSICAL VAUDEVILLE (five one-act plays) written and directed by Rob Cassatt. May 19, 1977.
CELL BLOCK 162 by Stuart Silver. May 26, 1977. Directed by Scott Redman; with Richard Dubin, Bruce Kornbluth, Robert Lesser, Joseph Davison, Sam Affoumado.

Theater of the Open Eye. Total theater involving actors, dancers, musicians and designers working together, each bringing their own talents into a single project. Jean Erdman, artistic director.

GAUGIN IN TAHITI (collaborative piece) by Jean Erdman and John Fitzgibbon. December 2, 1976. With Kevin O'Connor.
OP ODYSSEY II (mixed-media performance) poems by Diane Wakoski, music by Robert Mahaffay. March 9, 1977. With Gloria Tropp, Valerie Hammer, Jonathan Hollander, Nancy Cohen.
RAVEN'S DANCE (music, dance, puppetry) music by Robert Mahaffay, Didi Charney, Anne Sheedy, choreography by Ari Darom, Nancy Cohen. April, 1977. Directed by Eric Bass.

Theater of the Riverside Church. Maintains high professional standards. Anita Thomas, artistic director.

THE GARDEN written and directed by Al Asermely. June 10, 1976.
JO ANNE! by Ed Bullins. October 7, 1977. Directed by Carl Weber; with Robbie McCauley, I. M. Hobson, Thomas Carson, David Connell, Frankie Faison, Richard E. Gant.
BREAD AND ROSES by Marissa Gioffre. December 2, 1976. Directed by Tom Ellun.
THE DOUBLE INCONSTANCY by Marivaux, translated and directed by Al Asermely. February 3, 1977.
TUSCARORA by Joe Waddington, directed by Michael Holmes; CURTAIN adapted by Roy Finamore from Jean Cocteau's *Opium — Diary of a Cure,* directed by Rosemary Foley (one-act plays). May 5, 1977.

Theater Off Park. Theater for the community, attempting to reach as wide an audience as possible through as wide a variety of productions as possible. James Howe, Martin deMaat, executive directors.

SIX CHARACTERS IN SEARCH OF A PLOT (improvisational revue). August 5, 1976. Directed by Martin deMaat.
THE LOVER by Harold Pinter. August 18, 1976. Directed by Lynn Thomson.
KRAPP'S LAST TAPE and COME AND GO by Samuel Beckett; NIGHT by Harold Pinter. November, 1976. Directed by James Howe.
THE SNAFU REVUE written and performed by the Nasty, Short & British Players. November 7, 1976.
THE LAST DAYS OF THE WICHITA KID! by Carla Joseph Conway. December, 1976. Directed by Donald Warfield.
JOURNEY by Ronn Tombaugh. February, 1977. Directed by Lester Malizia.
EMIGRES by Slawomir Mrozek. April, 1977. Directed by Tim Curnen; with Marcus Smythe, Kelly Monaghan.

Thirteenth Street Repertory Company. A musical company focusing on new work; also children's programs. Edith O'Hara, artistic director.

TWO IN REVUE by Steve Clements and RATS by Israel Horovitz. June, 1976. Directed by Jim Payne.
BIRTHDAY by Gio Marsico. July, 1976. Directed by Armand Fillian.
MIND BENDING written and directed by Richard Townsend. August, 1976. With Lynn Powell, Pat Edwards, Elinor Jones.
CLOUD NINE by Nancy Heikin. October, 1976.
COMEDY TONIGHT, IMAGE AND LIKENESS and MISSES (one-act plays) by John Raniello. November, 1976.
THE MADNESS OF LADY BRIGHT and LUDLOW FAIR (one-act plays) by Lanford Wilson. November, 1976. Directed by Pamela Caren Billig.
LOVE AND THE WINNER by Tom Milliot. February, 1977.
POOR LOST LAMBS (revue) by Jeff Lantos. March, 1977. Directed by Mordecai Newman.
CHEERS by Richard Castagna. March, 1977. Directed by Pamela Caren Billig.

Time and Space, Ltd. Express theater in terms of form and process — focusing much of the current work on the novel — to express the word and the idea as a priority via the actor. Linda Mussman, artistic director (and director of all productions).

CREDITORS by August Strindberg, adapted by Linda Mussman. February 16, 1977.
THE WAVES (CHAPTER 1) adapted by Linda Mussman from Virginia Woolf's work. May 11, 1977. With Graham Bellin, Bilo Bryant, Cheryl Kilgren, Betty LaRoe, John Mintun, Ron Mutz.

TRG Repertory Company. Theater revival group, presenting original and professional revivals of rarely seen plays. Marvin Kahan, artistic director.

THE REAL INSPECTOR HOUND by Tom Stoppard. June 4, 1976. Directed by John Fournier.
SAVED by Edward Bond. October 1, 1976. Directed by Marvin Kahan.
STALAG 17 by Edmund Trzcinski and Donald Bevan. April, 1977. Directed by Marvin Kahan.

Urban Arts Corps. Dedicated to the development of theater arts and craft skills in the black community. Vinnette Carroll, artistic director.

THE UPS AND DOWNS OF THEOPHILUS MAITLAND adapted and directed by Vinnette Carroll from a West Indian folk tale, music and lyrics by Micki Grant. October, 1976. With Jeffrey Anderson-Gunter, Neville Richen.
I'M LAUGHIN' BUT I AIN'T TICKLED conceived and directed by Vinnette Carroll, music by Micki Grant. December, 1976.
THE LAST STREET PLAY by Richard Wesley. February, 1977.
ALICE written and directed by Vinnette Carroll, music by Micki Grant. May, 1977.

West Park Theater. Cooperative, accessible laboratory theater founded in 1975. Clark Kee, artistic director.

A SPY FOR THE BRITISH by William Dunlap, based on Maj. André. June 23, 1976. Directed by Clark Kee; with James Feldman, Rachel Hockett, Celia Lee, Mark C. Peters, Catherine Schreiber, Joel Wald.
ARMS AND THE MAN by George Bernard Shaw. October 27, 1976. Directed by Rachel Hockett; with Cindy Ames, Stefan Hartman, Celia Lee, Nancy Mette, George Salerno, Andre Schefman.
THE LOWER DEPTHS by Maxim Gorky. December 1, 1976. Directed by Michael Maines.
NIGHT MAIL AND OTHER SKETCHES by Ted Tally. January 5, 1977. Directed by Gary Pearle; with Maeve Kinkead, Ralph Martin, Paul McCarren.
OLMSTED! written and directed by Clark Kee. February 9, 1977. With John Briggs, Barry Burns, Steve Liebman, Marilyn Redfield, Judith Townsend.
THE GREAT NEBULA IN ORION by Lanford Wilson. February 22, 1977. Directed by Kim Rosen.
THE PUZZLE OF THE OLD PURDY PLACE by Ted Tally. March 26, 1977. Directed by Peter Glazer; with Cayce Blanchard, F. Kenneth Freedman, Nancy Mette, Stanley Schwartz, Alan Wasserman.
WAYS OF LOVING adapted by Drew Denbaum from Brendan Gill's short stories. May 4, 1977. Directed by Victor Bucnick.

West Side Community Repertory Theater. Contemporary approaches to classical plays. Andres Castro, director (and director of all productions).

THE CHERRY ORCHARD by Anton Chekhov. June 25, 1976.
A DOLL'S HOUSE by Henrik Ibsen. September 24, 1976.
MAN AND SUPERMAN by George Bernard Shaw. February 18, 1977.

The Wooden O. Repertory selected and staged so as recapture the atmosphere of New York playgoing in the 1700s. Clif Dowell, director, and director of productions.

THE CONTRAST by Royall Tyler. March 8, 1977. With Messrs. Roller, Ewert, Dowell, Misses Schembri, Brookner, Rittenhouse.
THE FAIR PENITENT by Nicholas Rowe. March 12, 1977. With Messrs. Wampler, Pinella, Roller, Dowell, Ewert, Miss Schembri.

The York Players. Each season, three or four productions of classics are mounted with professional casts; concerned with bringing classics to neighborhood residents. Janet Hayes Walker, artistic director.

WHAT DID YOU SAY "WHAT" FOR? by J. P. Dey; THE CLUB BEDROOM by Louis Auchincloss; THE LOVE COURSE by A. R. Gurney Jr. June 18, 1976. Directed by James Morgan; with Wayne Flower, Dan Jesse, Edith Larkin, Mary Lou Mahiman, Janice Sizemore, Edward White.
SHE LOVES ME (musical) book by Joe Masteroff, based on Miklos Laszlo's play *Parfumerie*, music by Jerry Bock, lyrics by Sheldon Harnick. November 19, 1976. Directed by Janet Hayes Walker.
MURDER IN THE CATHEDRAL by T. S. Eliot. January 14, 1977. Directed by Janet Hayes Walker.
LANDSCAPE and SILENCE by Harold Pinter. March 4, 1977. Directed by Stuart Howard; with Bella Jarrett, John Newton, Susan Sharkey, David Snell.
TWELFTH NIGHT by William Shakespeare. May 13, 1977. Directed by Janet Hayes Walker; with Daniel Blessing, George Crowley, Gregory Keenan, Merle Louise, Peter Saputo, Don Whisted.

Miscellaneous

In the additional listing of 1976-77 off-off-Broadway productions below, the names of the producing groups or theaters appear in CAPITAL LETTERS and the titles of the works in *italics*. This list consists largely of new or reconstituted works and excludes most revivals, especially of classics.

ABSOLUTE REALITY MIME THEATER. November, 1976.

ACADEMY ARTS THEATER COMPANY. *How Do You Spell Watergait?* by James Darrah. January 5, 1977. *An Evening of Fun and Games* (one-act plays): *The Perfect Game* and *Fly, Crow, Fly* by Anthony Cipolla; *Roger Ashley Here* by John Hart; *Teasing* by Emshalom Mamom Smith. March 25, 1977. Directed by Gary K. Sales. *Lady Macbeth in the Park* by Susan Slade. May 18, 1977. Directed by William J. West. *Borders* by David Ives. May, 1977. Directed by Truman Kelly.

ACTOR'S ANNEX. *The Glass Banana House East* (revue) by Mark Egan and Mark Solomon. June, 1976. Directed by Ted Weiant.

ACTORS FOR ACTORS. *Snow Angel* (one-act play) by Lewis John Carlino. September, 1976. Directed by Alaire Mitchell.

ACTORS REPERTORY THEATER. *Cacciatore* (three one-act plays) by Joseph Pintauro. May, 1977. Directed by Warren Robertson, Barnet Kellman, Peter Flood; with Kenneth Olin, Jay Thomas, Elaine Grollman, Hy Anzell, Frank A. Ammirati.

ADAM CLAYTON POWELL II REPERTORY. *Shoeshine Parlor* by James Lee. July, 1976.

AIRLINE THEATER WING. *Scenario of Death* by Richard Eckert. April 12, 1977. Directed by Ron Nash. *Dancing with Strangers* by Edward Six and Thomas Darien. April 22, 1977. Directed by Thomas Darien.

AMDT. *Variety Show* by Hogan Levermann. May 25, 1977.

AMERICAN JEWISH CONGRESS. *Reflections of a China Doll* (one-woman show) by and with Susan Merson. May 16, 1977.

AMERICAN MIME THEATER. *Hurleyburley* and *Six*. January 28, 1977.

AMERICAN WRITERS THEATER FOUNDATION. *An Awfully Big Adventure* by Thomas Fontana, music by Mark Hardwick. March 29, 1977. Directed by Tom Mardirosian.

BIJOU THEATER *The Left-Hand Mirror* by William McQueen. February 15, 1977. Directed by Jeffrey Buchman.

BILLIE HOLIDAY THEATER. *The Last Chord* written and directed by Charles Gordone. August, 1976. *Winti Train* by Lennox Brown. March 12, 1977. Directed by Glenda Dickerson.

BILLYMUNK THEATER. *The Long and the Short and the Tall* by Willis Hall. July 21, 1976. Directed by Jack Corliss; with James Handy, Pat Callaghan, William Cohen, Thomas Ikeda, Tom Ryan, Anthony Watts. *Other People's Tables: Breakfast, Lunch and Dinner, Chinese Restaurant Syndrome* and *Among Friends* (one-act plays) by Corinne Jacker. October 20, 1976. Directed by Bob Mandel; with Carol Nadell, Christina Pickles, Richard K. Weber, William Wise. *The Days of the Turbins* by Mikhail Bulgakov. January 13, 1977. With Roy Barry, David Kimball, Mark Cohen, Mark Jacobson. *A Couple of Blaguards.* March, 1977. With Malachy McCourt, Frank McCourt.

BLACK THEATER ALLIANCE 5TH ANNUAL FESTIVAL OF THEATER. July 14-25, 1976. Included *Movin' On Up,* presented by Voices, Inc.; *One-Woman Show* with Lynn Bell, presented by New Heritage Repertory Theater.

BLACK THEATER AT COLUMBIA UNIVERSITY. *Wine in the Wilderness* by Alice Childress, directed by Clifton Smith; *A Warning: A Theme for Linda,* directed by Jeanette McDaniel. November 5, 1976.

BOND STREET THEATER COALITION. *Charlie McDeath* by Lars Forssell and *The Hunger Artist* adapted by Patrick Sciarratta from Kafka's work. March 31, 1977.

BREAD AND PUPPET THEATER. *White Horse Butcher* and other pieces from the 5th Annual Domestic Resurrection Circus. August 20, 1976.

BRIEFCASE THEATER COMPANY. *We the People.* February 22, 1977. *The Impotent Guru* and *Dealer's Choice* by Joseph MacLaren. May 4, 1977. Directed by George Petalis.

THE BROOK. *10-Minute Platform* (six works-in-progress). June 23, 1976. *Saratoga* by Thomas Caulfield Goltz, music by Stephen Sturk. September, 1976. *Hunter Green* by Ed Kelleher. November 11, 1976. Directed by

Richard Ryder. *Boxcar* by Ted Knipe. February, 1977. Directed by Gary Cox. *The Maker of Dreams* by Oliphant Down. December 28, 1976. Directed by Victoria Berdy; with Charles McKenna, Hugo Napier, Lillian Silverstone.

BROOKLYN MUSEUM THEATER IN THE BACK. *The Great American Sucker Family* (musical) by Peter Copani. August 1, 1976. Directed by Frank Carucci.

BYRD HOFFMAN STUDIO. *Dialogues with a Single Performer* (three solo theater-dance pieces) by Tannis Hugill. March, 1977. *Ostal* by Cfr. Theater Lab. May, 1977. Directed by Aldo Rostagno.

CATHEDRAL OF ST. JOHN THE DIVINE. *The Devil Catcher* by Ed Bullins. October 17, 1976. Directed by Robert Macbeth.

CENTRAL SYNAGOGUE. *The Rise of David Levinsky* adapted and directed by Isaiah Sheffer from Abraham Cahan's novel. November, 1976.

CITHAERON. *A Handful of Watercress* adapted from a John Arden trilogy. September, 1976. Directed by Steven Brant.

COLLATION CENTER. *The Secret of Rented Island* adapted by Jack Smith from Henrik Ibsen's *Ghosts*. October 31, 1976.

COMBINATION CABARET. *On the Lock-In* by David Langston Smyrl. October, 1976. Directed by Robert Macbeth.

COMMON GROUND. *Round Dance* by Norman Taffel. June 4, 1976.

CONSTRUCTION COMPANY STUDIO. *Hamlet Kathakali* and *Shunkan in Exile* by Fred Curchack. May 13, 1977.

CORNER LOFT THEATER. *Coming to Terms* by Michael Shurtleff. January 14, 1977. Directed by Gail Kellstrom.

DESTINY PLAYERS. *The Realities of the Business* by Richard Monaco. March 30, 1977.

DRAMATIC WORKSHOP. *The Actor at Work* (one-act plays in repertory). July 9, 1976. *A Company of Wayward Saints* by Geo Herman. November, 1976. Directed by Maria Mollinedo.

DOUBLE IMAGE THEATER. *Life in Excellence* by Anthony Calandra. March 23, 1977. Directed by Helen Warren.Mayer. *Annual Metropolitan Short Play Festival.* May 10-15, 1977.

DRAMATIKA MAGAZINE (Sponsor). *Never Give a Lady a Restive Horse* by Robert Kangas; *Double Vision* by Dennis Moritz and Audrey Bookspan; *A Vocabulary for Carl Fernbach-Flarshein* by Jackson MacLow; *Newspapers* by William Burrison; *He/She Pizza Pie* by Lanie Robertson. February 4, 1977.

EDEN'S EXPRESSWAY. *Dreams of Survival* (theater-dance play) by Micki Goodman. September 9, 1976. *In Side Out Side In* by Irene O'Brien. September 17, 1976.

18TH STREET PLAYHOUSE. *Wine Untouched.* June 2, 1976. With JoAnne Belanger, Erle Bjornstad, Susan Kellerman, Elizabeth Sturges, Conchata Ferrell. *Treadmill* written and directed by Robert Rolf Randall. February 10, 1977.

ETC THEATER. *Precious Stones: Delicious Leek and Her Sister Helpless* and *Marijuana and Other Precious Stones* by Michael Shaffer. June 15, 1976. Directed by Ron Abbott; with Kathryn Grody, Carol Potter, Barbara eda-Young, Tony Paulazzo.

ETI (Ente Teatrale Italiano). New Theater Festival April 14-May 1, 1977. Schedule included *Three Monkeys in a Glass* by Mario Moretti, directed by Rina Elisha.

FEDERAL HALL NATIONAL MEMORIAL. *It Happened Here — The Case and Trial of John Peter Zenger.* July, 1976.

FOUR SEAS PLAYERS. *Water Margin* adapted from a 16th century Chinese novel. July 4, 1976.

FRANK SILVERA WORKSHOP. *Dialogues of the Shadow Women* by Denise Bell. January 27, 1977. Directed by David Shephard.

FRANKLIN THOMAS LITTLE THEATER. *Brace Yourself.* July, 1976. Directed by Franklin Thomas. *Community Kitchen* by Alex Foster. October 15, 1976. Directed by Franklin Thomas. *An Evening of Three One-Acts.* March 25, 1977. Directed by Gwendolyn Ketchen, Kenneth Freeman.

FREDERICK DOUGLASS CREATIVE ARTS CENTER. *Emily T* by Daniel Owens and *Transcendental Blues* by Aishah Rahman. July 29, 1976. Directed by Kimako Baraka; with Nadyne C. Spratt, Elizabeth Van Dyke.

GAP THEATER COMPANY. *Night Over the Tiber* by Richard Vetere. August 18, 1976. Directed by Tony

Napoli; with Steven Edwards, Myra Quigley, Russ Banham, Natalia Chuma, Sal Allocco, Hubert Kelly. *The Second Shepherd's Play* (musical) music and lyrics by Steve Kitsakos. December 15, 1976. Directed by Tony Napoli; with Greg Cesario, Doug Holsclaw, Joel Stevens, Myra Quigley, Richard Woods, Karen Haas. *The Affair* by Jeff Rubin and Ron Naar; *Are We in Love* by Anthony Cipolla, directed by Gary Sales; *Jack & Jill* by Richard Vetere, directed by Anthony Cipolla. January 19, 1977.

GARDEN VARIETY MIME THEATER. March 18, 1977.

GARRIS THEATER. *M'Liss* (musical) based on Bret Harte's work. July 1, 1976. Directed by Robert Dahdah.

GATE THEATER. *Mayfly* by Merrick Bursuk, music by Edrian Winters. June, 1976. Directed by Lawrence Harbison; with Stephen Geiger, Janice Kay Young. *Ubu/Jarry* by Michael Chipiga. September 22, 1976. Directed by Gary Trout; with Andy Wood, Maurice Blanc, Owen Rachleff. *On Again-Off Again* (musical) book by Duane Bondy, music and lyrics by Renee Bondy, based on William Wycherley's *The Country Wife*. October 16, 1976. Directed by David Berman. *Strange Cargo* by Ed Kelleher, directed by William Shorr; *Listen to the Duchess* by Bruce Feld, directed by Michael Diamond. March 30, 1977. With Mary Carter, Robert O'Herron, Alfred Cherry, Toby Tompkins. *Yangtze Gunboats* (revue). April, 1977. Performed by Swamp Fox.

THE GLINES. *Fascination* (musical) book by Michael Bottari, music and lyrics by Quitman Fludd III and Michael Green. June 3, 1976. Directed by Quitman Fludd III. *Swap* by Richard Lortz, *Special Gifts* by Robin Jones and *Trevor* by John Bowen (one-act plays). July 8, 1977. Directed by David Logan Morrow. *Something Hopeful* (revue) conceived by Loretta Lotman, written by Mark Bentley, Regina Kahney, James Saslow, Loretta Lotman, Jimmy Zepp, directed by Jimmy Zepp; *Women on Mars;* August 12, 1976. *All American Movin' Muscle* (revue). October 7, 1976. Directed by Seamus Murphy. *Marriage A La Mode* (one-act play) by Graham Jackson. October 28, 1976. Directed by Roy De Nunzio. *Queer Things* by Ed Kuczewski. November 4, 1976. *Once Below a Lighthouse* by Ramon Delgado. February 2, 1977. Directed by Howard Lipson. *The Love Match* by Richard Hall. February 2, 1977. Directed by Peter Dowling. *Last Chance at the Brass Ring* by Sidney Morris. March 3, 1977. Directed by Peter Dowling. *Unnatural Acts* (revue) by May 21 Gay Action Coalition. April, 1977. *Gulp!* (musical) book by J. B. Hamilton and Stephen Greco, music by Scott Kingman, lyrics by J. B. Hamilton and Robin Jones. April 28, 1977. Directed by John Glines; with Ben Cassara, Bill Errigo, Rip Grier, Lawrence Lane, John Michel, Sal Piro.

GOLDEN LION PUB. *It's What Makes the World Go Round* by Don Weiss. July 21, 1976. Directed by Sally Gavin.

GOLDEN THEATER. *The Exstasy of St. Zero* written and directed by Matthew Causey. April, 1977.

GREENWICH MEWS THEATER. *An Evening of Mime and Dramas.* October 12, 1976. Directed by Gabriel Oshen; with New York Mime and Drama Company. *Riding with the Devil* by Joseph Renard. November 11, 1976. Directed by Alan A. Gabor; with Kathleen Tremaine, Ronald Ballard, Ivett Ashley, Vivian Schindler Gabor, Barbara Landegger.

GROMMET ART THEATER. *Regardless of Circumstances* by Elaine Hernett. April 28, 1977. *Stroking Lullabye* by Wendy Greenberg. April 29, 1977.

GUGGENHEIM MUSEUM. *Explosion of Loneliness* (evening of music, songs and poetry) by Sandra Hochman, music by Galt MacDermot. May 24, 1977. With Rita Gam, Phyllis Newman, Florence Kennedy.

GUILD LITTLE THEATER. *My Brother, Cain* written and directed by Nomi Rubel. March 26, 1977.

HARLEM PERFORMANCE CENTER. *Deep Heat* by Sharon Stockard Martin. October 10, 1976. Directed by Candy Mabry.

HARTLEY HOUSE. *That's a Heavy Crown, Mr. Jones* (musical revue) by Phyllis Lynd. June, 1976. Directed by Robert Dahdah; with Memrie Innerarity, Lee Torchia, Bev Johnson, Penny Dennis, Phyllis Lynd, Alan Sorenson. *Psychiatric Service* by Joyce Carol Oates. September 30, 1976. Directed by Jane Hoffman. *Soho Promenade* (musical) book by Jerry Heymann, Joseph Gerena and Howard Harris. February 9, 1977. Directed by Jerry Heymann; with Jane Blackstone, Arthur Erickson, Sue Katz, Faith Minton, Jane Ranallo, Christine Vadnais.

HENRY STREET SETTLEMENT HOUSE. *Don't Cry, Child, Your Father's in America* by Herb Schapiro, adapted from Isaac Metzker's *A Bintel Brief: 60 Years of Letters to the Jewish Daily Forward.* January, 1977. Directed by C. R. Portz. *The In Crowd* (musical) by J. E. Franklin and Julius P. Williams. February, 1977. Directed by Lynn Rogoff. *A Husband for May* (musical) written and directed by Karl Friedman, music by Barry Alan Heimowitz. March, 1977. *J. B. Weaver's One-Ring Circus* (musical) by Robert Reiser. April, 1977. Directed by Jeff Schecter. *The Jewish Woman* (one-woman show). April, 1977. With Martha Schlamme.

HUNTER PLAYWRIGHTS. *High Wire* by Bill Cook. November 13, 1976. Directed by Ira Zuckerman. *Dirty Gerty* by Eileen Smith (staged reading). February 11, 1977. Directed by Kathleen Claypool. *Crossed Wires* by Frank Simon (straged reading). February 18, 1977. Directed by Robert Haddad. *Becoming Eve* by Rae Edelson. April 26, 1977. Directed by Thom Molyneaux.

INNER TRANSIT THEATER COMPANY. *This Is Your Scribble, John Q. Public* by John Bakos. July, 1976. Directed by Barbara Press.

JEWISH REPERTORY THEATER. *Jonah* by Guenter Rutenborn, music by Jeremy Storch. October 21, 1976. Directed by Chuck Selber.

KAVOOKJIAN AUDITORIUM. *The Armenian Question* written and directed by Anna Antaramian and William Rolleri. April, 1977.

KUKU RYKU THEATER LAB. *Babbling* (work-in-progress). January, 1977. *The Wise Woman and/or Babbling and Its Treatment.* April, 1977.

LAMBS CLUB. *The Chance of a Lifetime* (musical) book and lyrics by D. G. Welch, music by B. E. Cowley. June, 1976. Directed by Dennis McDonald.

LEE STRASBERG THEATER INSTITUTE. *Mrs. Minter* by Donald Kvares. April, 1977.

LITTLE BROADWAY THEATER. *The Mystery and Inner Life of Emily Dickinson.* July, 1976.

LITTLE CHURCH AROUND THE CORNER. *Haunting at Dow'do Landing* written and directed by Larry O'Connel. April 28, 1977.

LITTLE FLAGS THEATER COLLECTIVE. *Fanshen* by David Hare, based on a documentary by William Hinton. February 5, 1977.

THE LOFT. *T*ts D*amond* by Mark Bramble, music by Lee Pockriss, lyrics by Steve Brown. January, 1977. Directed by Anthony Stimac.

MALACHY COMPANY. *The Paschal Mystery.* April, 1977. *Women in Love* (cabaret). May, 1977.

MAX'S KANSAS CITY. *Time Takes a Cigaret* by David Street. February, 1977.

M. ELSON GALLERY. *In Memory of Long John Silver.* March, 1977.

MANHATTAN LAMBDA PRODUCTIONS. *Ramshackle Inn* by George Batson. June, 1976. *Lily, the Felon's Daughter* by Tom Taggart. October 1, 1976. *Not Just Another Love* by Robert Rolf Randall. November, 1976. *Seven Fabulous Nights* by Arthur Thomas. April, 1977. *Murder, My Sweet Matilda* by Janet Green. May, 1977. All productions directed by Edmund W. Trust.

MEAT AND POTATOES COMPANY. *Rendezvous* and *Lunch* (one-act plays) by Benjamin Bradford. October 7, 1976. Directed by Neal Weaver.

MIDNIGHT EPICUREAN PRODUCTIONS. *The Circus Play* by Roberto Monticello. November 19, 1976. Directed by Erle Bjornstad.

NAGRIN STUDIO THEATER. *Humboldt's Current* by Ping Chong and Fiji Company. April 21, 1977.

NAMELESS THEATER. *Traps* (two plays) by Donald Kvares. June 9, 1976. Directed by Larry Locke. *Your Place or Mine?* by Sam McClanahan. September 9, 1976. *God Isn't Home Tonight* by Irving Gold. October 7, 1976. Directed by Lester Goldman. *Screwing Out From Under* by Michael Bergmann and M. Francis Sivy; *Every Wise Man's Son Doth Know* by Michael Bergmann, from Shakespeare's plays. November 4, 1976. *We Ain't What We Was* (one-man show) by Isy Monk and Gordon Gray. March, 1977. With Isy Monk. *A Better Place* by Robert Hogan. May 5, 1977. Directed by Thomas Connolly.

NAT HORNE THEATER. *Tatiana Golikova Is Real* by Kay Kynlon. June, 1976. Directed by Steve Elmore; with Donald Madden, Frank Bongiorno, John Copeland, Paul J. Darby, Regina David, Sharon Laughlin. *The Late Late Show* (musical revue). July, 1976. Directed by Nat Horne. *Homeseekers* (musical) by Allen Deitch. July 23, 1976. Directed by Jeri Kaplan. *I Murdered My Finch One Day Last Spring* by Jerome Walman. August 19, 1976. Performed by Nettle Creek Players. *Ham* (musical) by Nikki Stern and John Faro PiRoman. October 7, 1976. Directed by Albert Reyes. *Onica Mitchell Is in Double Jeopardy: She's Black and Female* by Aarion Brown. January 28, 1977.

NECESSARY LUXURY COMPANY. *In Praise of the Common Woman.* January 15, 1977. Directed by Dolores Brandon; with Jennifer Dunning, Marcia Rappaport, Eniko Runde, Laury Tatz, Roberta Pikzer.

NEW CONSERVATORY THEATER. *The New Farce of the Meatloaf and the Pie* and *The Play of Anti-Christ.* January 17, 1977. Directed by Joan Langue.

NEW HERITAGE REPERTORY. *The Long Black Block* written and directed by Roger Furman.

NEW MEDIA STUDIO. *Sophie* written and directed by Miranda McDermott. June 3, 1976. *Dreams* (mixed-media play). December, 1976.

NEW WORLD THEATER. *Pieces.* July 16, 1976.

N.Y. FEMINIST THEATER TROUPE. *In Transit* by Lucy Winer. June 4, 1976. Directed by Eileen Mitchell.

NEW YORK PUBLIC LIBRARY PROGRAMS. *Byron* (one-man show) with Richard Williams. September 20, 1976. *Despite the Odds* (one-woman show) by Maureen Hurley.

NEW YORK STAGE WORKS. *Pecos Bill Meets the Trickster* and *Slingsong* (one-act plays) by Jim Magnuson. March 12, 1977. Directed by Randi Klein; with Mark Hoyt. *Auto-Destruct* by Jeff Wanshel. April, 1977. Directed by Craig LaPlount. *The Wolves and the Lambs* written and directed by Frieda Lipp. May, 1977.

NEW YORK STREET THEATER CARAVAN. *Sacco and Vanzetti* written and directed by Marketta Kimbrell and the Company. September, 1976. *Bitter Harvest.* February 10, 1977.

THE NIGHTHOUSE. *Her Hair Down Singing* by Paul J. Stevens. August 26, 1976. *Happy Birthday at Throgg's Point* written and directed by Paul J. Stevens. October 14, 1976. *A Very Stylish Affair* by Paul J. Stevens. December, 1976.

NIGHTINGALE PRODUCTIONS. *Don't Trust Life* by Ken Friedman. May, 1977. Directed by Joanne Bongiovanni.

NOHO. *Meet Lucy Stone* (one-woman show) with Edna Toney. June 24, 1976.

NUYORICAN POETS' CAFE, *The Murder of Pito* written and directed by Miguel Algarin. July, 1976. *The Guntower* (one-act play) by Miguel Piñero. August 26, 1976.

OFF-CENTER THEATER. *Hope for Life.* July 5, 1976. *Connections* by Irene Tractenberg (reading). January 24, 1977. *Heaven & Earth* by Gerlind Reinshagen. March, 1977. Directed by Carl Weber.

OOB BAND COMPANY. *She Lays Eggs for Gentlemen* by Bonnie Snow. May 4, 1977.

THE OPEN EYE. *Play Me, Zoltan* by Lucas Myers. January, 1977. Directed by Charles Maggiore. *Natures* (two verse-dialogues) developed from Richard Howard's *Two Part Invention.* May 31, 1977. Directed by Michael Feingold; with Kathryn Walker, Kevin O'Connor.

OKC THEATER COMPANY. *200 Years of American Poetry and Song.* October 21, 1976. Directed by Donald Keyes.

ORPHANS OF THE STORM. *The Radio Show* (revue) written, directed and performed by Orphans of the Storm. December, 1976.

PAD COMPANY. *Open House* (etudes based on improvisational material). April, 1977.

PENTHOUSE THEATER. *Herzl* (one-man show) with Harold Herbstman. November 12, 1976. Directed by Sylvia Mann.

THE PERFORMING GARAGE. *Of a Silence in the Sun* written and directed by Mark J. Dunau. June, 1976. Performed by Flying Dust Company. *Female Transport* by Steve Gooch. September 8, 1976. Directed by Scott Porter. *Working: Daily Life Rhythms* conceived and performed by Chris Torch. January, 1977. *You're Gonna Be Alright, Jamie Boy* by David Freeman. May, 1977. Directed by Paul Schneider.

PLAYERS WORKSHOP. *Young Marrieds at Play* by Jerome Kass and *On a Cambodian Highway* by Brent Filson. September 24, 1976. Directed by Clay Stevenson. *Summer Ghost* by Claude Frendricks. October, 1976.

POLARIS REPERTORY COMPANY. *The Sunday Promenade* by Lars Forssell, translated by Harry G. Carlson. April 4, 1977. Directed by Bob Horen; with Mary Carter, K. T. Baumann. *Wine Untouched* by Bjorg Vik. April 25, 1977. Directed by Erle Bjornstad.

POTATO PLAYERS. Season of one-act Plays: *Pecos Bill Meets the Trickster* by Jim Magnuson, directed by Randi Klein; *The Locked Room/Night Shift* by George Naylor, directed by Sharon Carnicke; *A Merry Death* by Nikolai Evreinov, translated by Christopher Collins, directed by Sharon Carnicke. July 12-28, 1976.

POVERTY PRODUCTIONS. *Kripples* by Max Welles. January 27, 1977. Directed by Lawrence Bandini.

PRETENDERS THEATER. *Tuxedos for Rent* (musical revue). Directed by J. D. Sheehan. *Directors' Festival.* September, 1976. *Confetti and Carnivore.* October, 1976. Directed by Gene Santarelli.

PRIMAL THEATER WORKSHOP. *Theater Within* (improvisation). November, 1976. Directed by Alex Rubin.

PROPOSITION THEATER. *Taxi Sales* (musical satire). July, 1976.

PROVINCETOWN PLAYHOUSE. *Pavilion* by Marshall Yaeger. June 9, 1976. Directed by Eve Brandstein. *Stone Soup* adapted by Ronnie Berman.

PUBLIC PLAYERS. *Bohemian Summer* adapted by Charles McDonough from Henri Murger. June 2, 1976. Directed by J. Perry McDonald. *Mr. Dorain, Sir; or Prof. Chen-Tung's Magic Lantern Horror Show.* February 17, 1977. Directed by J. Perry McDonald.

QUENA COMPANY. *A Strange Beast, Silver Bee* and *Blue Heaven.* June, 1976. Directed by Raymond Barry.

QUOG MUSIC THEATER. *Civilization and Its Discontents* (opera) written, composed and directed by Eric Salzman and Michael Sahl; *An Old-Fashioned Girl* (dance drama) based on Theodore Dreiser's *Sister Carrie*, music by Michael Sahl, choreographed by Anne Sahl. May 19, 1977.

RAFT THEATER. *Silent Murders and Musical Chairs* (collaborative work). September, 1976. Directed by Anna Antaramian.

ROYAL PLAYHOUSE. *Gaslight Recitations* (one-woman show) with Monona Rossol. February, 1977.

ST. JOHN STREET THEATER. *Drum Beat* by Barbara Monicure. August 25, 1976.

ST. PETER'S CHURCH. *Emmanuel* (musical) by Dorothy Davidson Hausske. May 21, 1977.

SHARED FORMS THEATER. *The Illustrated Journal* based on writings of G. I. Gurdjieff, Maurice Nicoll and Frederick Chopin. May 27, 1977.

SHELTER WEST. *The Totem Pole* by Paul Smith. June, 1976. Directed by Dan Mason. *Compulsion* by Meyer Levin. March 11, 1977. Directed by Dan Mason; with Joel Freedman, Peter Reznikoff. *Stoop & London Loo* by Stephen Holt. April 14, 1977. Directed by Joseph Siracuse; with Helen Hanft. *Landslide at North Station* by Ugo Betti. May, 1977. Directed by Dan Mason.

SOLARON PRODUCTIONS. *Mandragola* (musical) translated by J. R. Hale, music by Pat Cook, lyrics by Joe Cook, adapted and directed from Machiavelli's play by Dan Held. December 3, 1976.

SHOWPLACE. *Lovesong* (revue), music by Michael Valenti. July 8, 1976. Directed by Albert Harris.

SOBOSSEK'S. *Bicentennial Suicide* by Bob Holman and Bob Rosenthal. July, 1976.

SOHO ARTISTS THEATER. *Brothers* by Eric Krebs. January 12, 1977. Directed by Dino Narizzano; with Mark Blum, John Corey, Aleen Malcolm, Robert McIlwaine, Bronwyn Rucker. *Heavenz* by Pat Kaufman. May 4, 1977. Directed by Dino Narizzano.

SPEAK-EASY CABARET THEATER. *Speak Easy: A Legend of the Life of Frank Costello*. October, 1976.

SPECTRUM THEATER. *A Hit on Wall Street* by Denise Collette Bishop. October, 1976. Directed by Benno Haehnel; with Jacqueline Bertrand, Rebecca Darke, Suzanne Gilbert, George Hall, Ralph Redpath, Liz Thackston.

SPIDER WOMAN WORKSHOP. *Women in Violence*. October 14, 1976. (Reopened February 24, 1977).

STAGE 73. *The Really Portable Hamlet Company*. June 10, 1976.

STRUCTURALIST WORKSHOP. *Noh Structure* by Mickey Levy; *Transportation: #10* by Kay Davy; *Li Po* by Wu Bon-Tien; *Operating Angle* by Robb Crease. July 21, 1976. *Photoanalysis* by Michael Kirby. November, 1976. *Revolutionary Dance* by Michael Kirby. January 14, 1977.

STUART SHERMAN: *Sixth Spectacle*. June 7, 1976.

THEATER 9. *The Book*. November 12, 1976.

TOSOS. *Handmade Guns* by Martin Calabrese. May, 1977. Directed by David Logan-Morrow.

20TH STREET THEATER. *The Snob* by Carl Sternheim. September 8, 1976.

THEATER 126. *Yankee Daddy* by Evelyn Clark. October, 1976. Directed by Voight Kempson.

THEATER IN CHELSEA. *Infinity* written and directed by Donald L. Brooks. July 8, 1976.

THEATER LABORATOIRE VICINAL (of Belgium). *I* by Frederic Baal. February 4, 1977. With Anne West.

THEATER OF CHAOS. *Blood, Fire and Bone* (Antonin Artaud program). May 25, 1977.

THEATER OF UNIVERSAL IMAGES. *Sam Carter Belongs Here* by Wade Hudson. July 29, 1976. Directed by Clarence C. Lilley.

TITLE THEATER. *Exits* by Daniel Gabriel. July, 1976. Directed by Shelly Desai; with Stanley Sayer, Michael Dattore, Shelly Desai, Carolyn Geer, Carol Ann Kessler. *Where the Onus Falls* by Stephen Holt. September 16, 1976. Directed by Pat LaVelle. *The One-Way Omnibus* by David Haviland. October 21, 1976. Directed by Robert Crompton. *Cold Winds from Canada* and *Out There* by Tardu. October, 1976. *Night Shift* by William Rolleri, Martin Zurla and Anna Antaramian. November, 1976. Directed by Anna Antaramian. *Wall, Prize, Redemption: A Trilogy* by Vincent Viaggio. February 24, 1977. Directed by Peter Rothman. *Don't Trust Life* by Ken Friedman. May, 1977. Directed by Joanne Bongiovanni.

U.N. CHURCH CENTER. *Allegories* by Mel Yosso. November 4, 1976. Directed by Ron Troutman.

UNIVERSALIST CHURCH. *On Toby Time* (musical) book and lyrics by Harley Hackett, musical by Herschel Dwellingham. January, 1977. Directed by Robert M. Cooper.

VANDAM THEATER. *Seven Scandalous Theater Pieces by Mark Twain,* music by Jack Easton. November, 1976.

VENTURE THEATER. *Desmond and Sim* (one-woman show) with Mary Bozeman. April 9, 1977.

WALDEN THEATER. *With the Girls Be Handy* (musical). June 17, 1976. *Fedora's Navel* and *The Gilded Fig* by Walter Wilson. September 30, 1976. Directed by Chris Kane. *Incident in New York* by Bernard Myers. February 24, 1977. *Day One* (musical) by Robert W. Preston. April 14, 1977. Directed by Robert N. Nigro.

WARD NASSE GALLERY. *Harry and Larry* by Richard Taylor, directed by Thom Mitchell; *Settings* written and directed by Wayne Mahler. June 24, 1976. *Incidental Music* written and directed by Wayne Mahler; *Waiting Room* (musical) by Richard Taylor, directed by Craig Barisch. January 21, 1977. *Hit Tunes From Flop Shows.* February 3, 1977. Directed by Vincent Napoli; with Atlantic Players. *All in Ones* (one-act plays): *Sorry Tongue* and *Poet* by Richard Taylor, directed by Hank Flacks; *Summer's Room* written and directed by Wayne Mahler. May 19, 1977.

WASHINGTON SQUARE METHODIST CHURCH. *S-1* written and directed by Imamu Amiri Baraka. July, 1976. *Shakespeare/After Words* conceived and directed by Robert Smith. April, 1977

WEST GLADE OPEN AIR POETS FORUM. *The Other Emily* and *Slax* written and directed by Larry O'Connel. July, 1976.

WHITE MASK THEATER. *Performance and Poetry* by Daniela Gioseffi and Matthew Paris. October 10, 1976. *Fish Joy* by Doloris Holmes. May 7, 1977. Directed by Donald Kvares; with James Howley, Barbara Vaccaro, Deborah Beck, Robert Scott.

WONDERHORSE THEATER. *Shelter Estates, U.S.A.* written and directed by Terry Gregory. July 2, 1976.

WORKING THEATER. *Richard Plantagenet* (based on Shakespeare). December 3, 1976. *Coo-Me-Doo, or, They're Only Made of Clay* by Kristin Linklater and Caroline Du Crocq. May, 1977. Directed by Leo Shapiro.

WORKSHOP OF THE PLAYERS ART (WPA). *Lotsa Ladies* with Irene Dailey, Beverly Shimmin. June 2, 1976. Directed by Jamie Brown. *Fifth Annual New Plays Festival* schedule included *Faith Healer* by Brian Friel; *Life Guard* by Louis Phillips; *The Silent Catastrophe* by Cliff Harville; *The Mom and Pop Store* by Robert Lerner; *Ice* by Lane Batman; *You've Changed* by Robert Somerfeld; *A Sneaky Bit to Raise the Blind* by John Ford Noonan; *Mime Piece* by Gabriel Oshen; *Office Temp* by Joseph Renard; *The Mind of Mary Dugan* by Stephen Holt; *Pickers* by Richard Taylor. June 9, 1976.

CAST REPLACEMENTS AND TOURING COMPANIES

Compiled by Stanley Green

The following is a list of the more important cast replacements in productions which opened in previous years, but were still playing in New York during a substantial part of the 1976–77 season; or were still on a first-class tour in 1976–77; or opened in New York in 1976–77 and went on tour during the season (casts of first-c/ass touring companies of previous seasons which were no longer playing in 1976-77 appear in previous *Best Plays* volumes of appropriate sears).

The name of each major role is listed in *italics* beneath the title of the play in the first column. In the second column directly opposite appears the name of the actor who created the role in the original New York production (whose opening date appears in *italics* at the top of the column). Indented immediately beneath the original actor's name are the names of subsequent New York replacements, together with the date of replacement when available.

The third column gives information about first-class touring companies, including London companies (produced under the auspices of their original Broadway managements). When there is more than one roadshow company, #1, #2, etc., appear before the name of the performer who created the role in each company (and the city and date of each company's first performance appears in *italics* at the top of the column). Their subsequent replacements are also listed beneath their names, with dates when available.

A note on split-week touring companies appears at the end of this section.

THE BELLE OF AMHERST

	New York 4/28/76	*Washington 9/13/76*
Emily Dickinson	Julie Harris	Julie Harris

BUBBLING BROWN SUGAR

	New York 3/2/76	*Chicago 6/22/76*
John Sage; Rusty	Avon Long	Vernon Washington
Irene Paige	Josephine Premice	Mable Lee
Checkers; Dusty	Joseph Attles	John Flash Riley
Marsha; Young Irene	Vivian Reed	Ursuline Kairson
	Ursuline Kairson 2/15/77	Vivian Reed 2/15/77
Bill; Time Man; Bumpy; Emcee	Vernon Washington	Charles "Honi" Coles
	David Bryant 6/22/76	

CALIFORNIA SUITE

	New York 6/10/76	*Palm Beach, Fla. 3/7/77*
Hannah; Diana; Gert	Tammy Grimes	Penny Fuller
	Rue McClanahan 4/4/77	
	Tammy Grimes 4/11/77	

William; Sidney; Stu	George Grizzard Kenneth Haigh 2/28/77 David McCallum 5/2/77	David McCallum Kenneth Haigh 5/7/77
Marvin; Mort	Jack Weston Joseph Leon 5/77	Vincent Gardenia
Millie; Beth	Barbara Barrie Marge Redmond 1/7/77	Rosemary Prinz

CHICAGO

New York 6/3/75

Roxie Hart	Gwen Verdon Lenora Nemetz 7/30/75 Liza Minnelli 8/8/75 Gwen Verdon 9/15/75 Ann Reinking 2/7/77
Velma Kelly	Chita Rivera Lenora Nemetz 7/28/76
Billy Flynn	Jerry Orbach
Matron	Mary McCarty Alaina Reed 1/10/77
Amos Hart	Barney Martin Rex Everhart 2/20/76 Barney Martin 3/1/76 Rex Everhart 9/76
Annie	Michon Peacock Joan Bell 5/10/76
Go-to-Hell Kitty	Charlene Ryan Fern Fitzgerald 3/76
Mona	Pamela Sousa Debra Lyman 12/76

A CHORUS LINE

		#1 Toronto 5/3/76 *London 7/22/76* *#2 San Francisco 5/11/76* *#3 Baltimore 2/9/77*
	N.Y. Off-Bway 4/15/75 *N.Y. Bway 7/25/75*	
Roy	Scott Allen Danny Ruvolo 8/76 Scott Allen 1/77 Danny Ruvolo 2/77	#1 Donn Simione Gerry Davis 2/77 #2 Tim Cassidy Timothy Smith 12/76 #3 Donn Simione
Kristine	Renee Baughman Cookie Vazquez 4/26/76 Deborah Geffner 10/76	#1 Christine Barker Vicki Spencer 2/77 #2 Renee Baughman Cookie Vazquez 10/76 #3 Christine Barker
Sheila	Carole Bishop (name changed to Kelley Bishop 3/76) Kathrynann Wright 8/76	#1 Jane Summerhays Geraldine Gardner 2/77 #2 Charlene Ryan #3 Jane Summerhays
Val	Pamela Blair Barbara Monte-Britton 4/26/76 Karen Jablons 10/76 Mitzi Hamilton 3/1/77	#1 Mitzi Hamilton Linda Williams 2/77 #2 Pamela Blair #3 Mitzi Hamilton Karen Jablons 3/1/77

Mike	Wayne Cilento	#1 Don Correia
		    Jeff Hyslop 7/10/76
		    Michael Howe 2/77
		#2 Don Correia
		#3 Jeff Hyslop

Butch	Chuck Cissel
	    Edward Love 10/76
		#1 Ken Rogers
		    Richard Lloyd-King 2/77
		#2 Sam Tampoya
		#3 Ken Rogers

Larry	Clive Clerk
	    Jeff Weinberg 10/76
	    Clive Clerk 1/77
	    Adam Grammis 2/77
		#1 T. Michael Reed
		    Jack Gunn 2/77
		#2 Roy Smith
		#3 T. Michael Reed

Maggie	Kay Cole
	    Lauree Berger 4/26/76
	    Donna Drake 2/77
		#1 Jean Fraser
		    Veronica Page 2/77
		#2 Kay Cole
		    Donna Drake 10/76
		    Lisa Donaldson 2/77
		#3 Betty Lynd

Richie	Ronald Dennis
	    Winston DeWitt Hemsley 4/26/76
		#1 A. William Perkins
		    Roy Gayle 2/77
		#2 Ronald Dennis
		# A. William Perkins

Tricia	Donna Drake
	    Jo Speros 10/76
	    Cynthia Carrillo Onrubia 4/77
		# Nancy Wood
		    Nicky Croydon 2/77
		#2 Rebecca York
		    Linda Dangcil 10/76
		#3 Nancy Wood

Tom	Brandt Edwards
	    Timothy Smith 10/76
	    Tim Cassidy 12/76
	    Rene Clement 2/77
		#1 Mark Dovey
		    Ronald Stafford 7/10/76
		    Kenn Oldfield 2/77
		#2 Danny Taylor
		#3 Ronald Stafford

Judy	Patricia Garland
	    Sandahl Bergman 4/26/76
		#1 Yvette Mathews
		    Judy Gridley 2/77
		#2 Patricia Garland
		#3 Murphy Cross

Lois	Carolyn Kirsch
	    Vicki Frederick 4/26/76
	    Pamela Sousa 12/76
	    Cheryl Clark 1/77
	    Patti D'Beck 4/77
		#1 Wendy Mansfield
		    Jo-Ann Robinson 2/77
		#2 Carolyn Kirsch
		    Lee Wilson 5/76
		#3 Wendy Mansfield

Don	Ron Kuhlman
	    David Thomé 4/26/76
		#1 Ronald Young
		    Lance Aston 2/77
		#2 Ron Kuhlman
		    Dennis Edenfield 10/76
		#3 Brandt Edwards

Bebe	Nancy Lane
	    Gillian Scalici 4/26/76
		#1 Miriam Welch
		    Susan Claire 2/77
		#2 Nancy Lane
		#3 Miriam Welch

Connie	Baayork Lee
	    Lauren Kayahara 4/26/76
	    Janet Wong 2/77
		#1 Jennifer Ann Lee
		    Cherry Gillespie 2/77
		#2 Baayork Lee
		    Lauren Kayahara 2/77
		#3 Jennifer Ann Lee

Diana	Priscilla Lopez
	    Barbara Luna 4/26/76
		#1 Loida Iglesias
		    Diane Langton 2/77

	Carole Schweid 5/7/76 Rebecca York 8/76 Loida Iglesias 12/76	#2 Priscilla Lopez Chris Bocchino 10/76 #3 Gina Paglia

Zach	Robert LuPone
	  Joe Bennett 4/26/76
	  Eivind Harum 10/76
	  Robert LuPone 1/31/77
	  Kurt Johnson 5/77
		#1 Eivind Harum
		  Jean-Pierre Cassel 10/76
		#2 Robert LuPone
		  Joe Bennett 10/76
		#3 Eivind Harum

Mark	Cameron Mason
	  Paul Charles 10/76
		#1 Timothy Scott
		  Peter Barry 2/77
		#2 Paul Charles
		  Jimmy Roddy 10/76
		#3 Timothy Scott

Cassie	Donna McKechnie
	  Ann Reinking 4/26/76
	  Donna McKechnie 9/27/76
	  Ann Reinking 11/29/76
	  Pamela Sousa 1/77
	  Vicki Frederick 2/9/77
		#1 Sandy Roveta
		  Petra Siniawski 2/77
		#2 Donna McKechnie
		  Ann Reinking 9/27/76
		  Vicki Frederick 11/29/76
		  Pamela Peadon 2/9/77
		#3 Pamela Sousa

Al	Don Percassi
	  Bill Nabel 4/26/76
	  John Mineo 2/77
	  Ben Lokey 4/77
		#1 Steve Baumann
		  Jeffrey Shankley 2/77
		#2 Don Percassi
		#3 Steve Baumann

Frank	Michael Serrecchia
	  Tim Cassidy 2/77
		#1 Troy Garza
		  John Chester 2/77
		#2 Claude R. Tessier
		  Jim Wolfe 4/77
		#3 Troy Garza

Greg	Michel Stuart
	  Justin Ross 4/26/76
		#1 Andy Keyser
		  Mark Dovey 7/10/76
		  Stephen Tate 2/77
		#2 Michel Stuart
		  Andy Keyser 10/76
		#3 Mark Dovey

Bobby	Thomas J. Walsh	#1 Ron Kurowski
		  Leslie Meadows 2/77
		#2 Scott Pearson
		  Michael Austin 4/77
		#3 Ron Kurowski

Paul	Sammy Williams
	  George Pesaturo 4/26/76
		#1 Tommy Aguilar
		  Michael Staniforth 2/77
		#2 Sammy Williams
		#3 Tommy Aguilar

Vicki	Crissy Wilzak	#1 Nancy Dafgek
		  Olivia Breeze 2/77
		#2 Mary Ann O'Reilly
		  Deborah Henry 1/77
		# Nancy Dafgek

EQUUS

	New York 10/24/74	*#1 Boston 11/18/75* *#2 Washington 9/14/76*

Dr. Martin Dysart	Anthony Hopkins
	  Anthony Perkins 6/30/75
	  Richard Burton 2/16/76
	  Anthony Perkins 5/11/76
	  Douglas Campbell 8/6/76
		#1 Brian Bedford
		#2 Douglas Campbell

	Anthony Perkins 10/5/76	
	Alec McCowen 2/15/77	
	Anthony Perkins 3/15/77	
Alan Strang	Peter Firth	#1 Dai Bradley
	Thomas Hulce 6/30/75	Michael Snyder
	Jacob Milligan 1/6/76	Ralph Seymour 2/15/77
	Keith McDermott 2/16/76	Michael Snyder 3/15/77
	Ralph Seymour 10/5/76	#2 Keith McDermott
	Michael Snyder 2/15/77	
	Ralph Seymour 3/15/77	
Dora Strang	Frances Sternhagen	#1 Delphi Lawrence
	Marian Seldes 6/15/76	#2 Catherine Byers
	Frances Sternhagen 10/5/76	
	Beverly May 1/77	
Frank Strang	Michael Higgins	#1 Humbert Allen Astredo
	Page Johnson 10/5/76	#2 Dalton Dearborn
Hester Salomon	Marian Seldes	#1 Sheila Smith
	Louise Troy 6/15/76	#2 Jillian Lindig
	Lorinda Barrett 10/5/76	
Jill Mason	Roberta Maxwell	#1 Penelope Willis
	Jeanne Ruskin	#2 Roxanne Hart
	Betsy Beard 10/5/76	
	Nancy Frangione 2/77	
	Ellen Parker 4/4/77	

THE FANTASTICKS

New York 5/3/60

El Gallo   Jerry Orbach
Gene Rupert
Bert Convy
John Cunningham
Don Stewart 1/63
David Cryer
Keith Charles 10/63
John Boni 1/13/65
Jack Metter 9/14/65
George Ogee
Keith Charles
Tom Urich 8/30/66
John Boni 10/5/66
Jack Crowder 6/13/67
Nils Hedrick 9/19/67
Keith Charles 10/9/67
Robert Goss 11/7/67
Joe Bellomo 3/11/68
Michael Tartel 7/8/69
Donald Billett 6/70
Joe Bellomo 2/15/72
David Rexroad 6/73
David Snell 12/73
Hal Robinson 4/2/74
Chapman Roberts 7/30/74
David Brummel 2/18/75
David Rexroad 8/31/75
Roger Brown 9/30/75
David Rexroad 9/1/76
Joseph Galiano 10/14/76
Keith Charles 3/22/77
Joseph Galiano 4/5/77

Luisa   Rita Gardner
Carla Huston
Liza Stuart 12/61
Eileen Fulton
Alice Cannon 9/62
Royce Lenelle
B. J. Ward 12/1/64
Leta Anderson 7/13/65
Carole Demas 11/22/66
Leta Anderson 8/7/67
Carole Demas 9/4/67
Anne Kaye 5/28/68
Carolyn Magnini 7/29/69
Virginia Gregory 7/27/70
Leta Anderson
Marty Morris 3/7/72
Sharon Werner 8/1/72
Leilani Johnson 7/73
Sharon Werner 12/73
Sarah Rice 6/24/74
Cheryl Horne 7/1/75
Sarah Rice 7/29/75
Betsy Joslyn 3/23/76

Matt   Kenneth Nelson
Gino Conforti
Jack Blackton 10/63
Paul Giovanni
Ty McConnell
Richard Rothbard
Gary Krawford
Bob Spencer 9/5/64
Erik Howell 6/28/66
Gary Krawford 12/12/67
Steve Skiles 2/6/68
Craig Carnelia 1/69
Erik Howell 7/18/69
Samuel D. Ratcliffe 8/5/69
Michael Glenn-Smith 5/26/70
Jimmy Dodge 9/20/70
Geoffrey Taylor 8/31/71
Erik Howell 3/14/72
Michael Glenn-Smith 6/13/72
Phil Killian 7/4/72
Richard Lincoln 9/72
Bruce Cryer 7/24/73
Phil Killian 9/11/73
Michael Glenn-Smith 6/17/74
Ralph Bruneau 10/29/74
Bruce Cryer 9/30/75

Note: As of May, 1977, 25 actors had played the role of El Gallo, 18 actresses had played Luisa, and 19 actors had played Matt.

GODSPELL

N.Y. Off-Bway 5/17/71
N.Y. B'way 6/23/76

Jesus   Stephen Nathan
Andy Rohrer 6/6/72
Don Hamilton
Ryan Hilliard
Don Scardino 1/73
Jeremy Sage 2/74

	Don Scardino
	Tom Rolfing 8/74
	Don Scardino 6/23/76
	Jeremy Sage
Judas	David Haskell
	Bart Braverman 5/72
	Lloyd Bremseth
	Don Scardino
	Michael Hoit 4/75
	Tom Rolfing 6/23/76
	Michael Hoit

GREASE

	New York 2/14/72	*Millburn, N.J. 9/1/76*
Danny Zuko	Barry Bostwick	Adrian Zmed
	Jeff Conaway 6/73	
	John Lansing 11/74	
	Treat Williams 12/75	
	Lloyd Alann 6/14/76	
	Treat Williams	
Sandy Dumbrowski	Carole Demas	Andrea Walters
	Ilene Graff 3/73	
	Candice Earley 6/17/75	
	Robin Lamont	
Betty Rizzo	Adrienne Barbeau	Loralle Brina
	Elaine Petrikoff 3/73	
	Randee Heller 5/74	
	Karren Dille 12/1/75	
	Livia Genise	
	Judy Kaye 5/10/77	
Kenicke	Timothy Meyers	Paul Regina Jr.
	John Fennessy	
	Jerry Zaks	
	Timothy Meyers	
	Danny Jacobson	
	Michael Tucci	
	Matt Landers	
	Danny Jacobson	
Vince Fontaine	Don Billett	Douglas Barden
	Gardner Hayes	
	Jim Weston	
	John Holly	
	Walter Charles	
	Jim Weston 1/76	
Marty	Katie Hanley	Char Fontane
	Meg Bennett	
	Denise Nettleton	
	Marilu Henner	
	Char Fontane	
	Diane Stilwell 8/76	

JULES FEIFFER'S HOLD ME!

	New York 1/23/77	*#1 San Francisco 4/6/77* *#2 Los Angeles 4/18/77*
	Geraldine Brooks	#1 Rose Arrick
	Cynthia Harris 3/22/77	Elaine Heilveil
	Kathleen Chalfant	Maria Cellario
	Paul Dooley	Anna Levine

Dalienne Majors
Michael Tucci

William Snikowski
Ray Stewart
#2 Julie Kavner
Nan Martin
Leland Palmer
Richard Schaal
Ray Stewart
Michael Tucci

THE MAGIC SHOW

New York 5/28/74

Doug*	Doug Henning
	Joe Abaldo 3/30/76
	Doug Henning 7/21/76
	Joe Abaldo 11/3/76
Cal	Dale Soules
	Dara Norman 10/29/75
	Dale Soules
Charmin	Anita Morris
	Loni Ackerman 8/75
	Louisa Flaningam 3/76
Feldman	David Ogden Stiers
	Kenneth Kimmins 12/29/74
	Timothy Jerome 7/25/75
	Stephen Vinovich 4/14/76
	Rex Robbins 5/23/76
	Kenneth Kimmins 10/27/76

*Name of character changed to Joe when Mr. Abaldo played role.

A MATTER OF GRAVITY

	New York 2/3/76	*Denver 9/29/76*
Mrs. Basil	Katharine Hepburn	Katharine Hepburn
Dubois	Charlotte Jones	Charlotte Jones
Nicky	Christopher Reeve	Richard Kelton
Herbert	Paul Harding	Paul Harding
Elizabeth	Wanda Bimson	Wanda Bimson
Shatov	Elizabeth Lawrence	Peggy Croft

ME AND BESSIE

	New York 10/22/75	*Los Angeles 3/7/77*
Bessie Smith	Linda Hopkins	Linda Hopkins

PACIFIC OVERTURES

	New York 1/11/76	*Los Angeles 8/31/76*
Reciter; Shogun; Jonathan Goble	Mako	Mako
Tamate; Samurai; Storyteller; Swordsman	Soon-Teck Oh	Soon-Teck Oh

PIPPIN

	New York 10/23/72
Pippin	John Rubinstein
	Michael Rupert 11/74
	Dean Pitchford 12/1/75
	Michael Rupert 12/8/75
Charles	Eric Berry
Catherine	Jill Clayburgh
	Betty Buckley 6/11/73
	Joy Franz 2/10/76
Fastrada	Leland Palmer
	Priscilla Lopez 1/6/74
	Patti Karr 8/5/74
	Antonia Ellis 1/5/76
Berthe	Irene Ryan
	Lucie Lancaster 4/73
	Dorothy Stickney 6/11/73
	Lucie Lancaster 7/74
	Fay Sappington 8/18/75
	Lucie Lancaster 9/1/75
	Fay Sappington 12/75
Leading Player	Ben Vereen
	Northern J. Calloway 2/18/74
	Ben Vereen 5/7/74
	Samuel E. Wright 12/74
	Irving Lee 6/75
	Ben Harney 1/12/76
	Northern J. Calloway 5/24/76

PORGY AND BESS

	New York 9/25/76	Boston 3/15/77
Porgy	Donnie Ray Albert	Donnie Ray Albert
	Abraham Lind-Oquendo	Robert Mosley
	Robert Mosley	Bruce A. Hubbard
Bess	Clamma Dale	Clamma Dale
	Esther Hinds	Wilhelmenia Fernandez
	Irene Oliver	Gail Nelson
		Naomi Moody
Sportin' Life	Larry Marshall	Larry Marshall
Crown	Andrew Smith	Andrew Smith
	George Robert Merritt	George Robert Merritt

Note: Multiple names of actors following name of character indicate role was alternated.

RAISIN

	New York 10/18/73	Wilmington 12/9/75
Lena Younger	Virginia Capers	Virginia Capers
		Sandra Phillips 3/30/77

THE ROYAL FAMILY

	Brooklyn 12/17/75 New York 12/30/75	Boston 10/12/76
Fanny Cavendish	Eva Le Gallienne	Eva Le Gallienne

Julie Cavendish	Rosemary Harris	Carole Shelley
Tony Cavendish	George Grizzard Ellis Rabb 1/12/76 Richard Council 5/76	Leonard Frey
Oscar Wolfe	Sam Levene	Sam Levene
Herbert Dean	Joseph Maher	Richard Woods
Kitty Dean	Mary Louise Wilson Peg Murray 6/76	Laura Stuart

SAME TIME, NEXT YEAR

New York 3/13/75

#1 Toronto 12/1/75
#2 San Francisco 6/26/76
#3 Los Angeles 4/19/77

| *Doris* | Ellen Burstyn
Joyce Van Patten 10/20/75
Loretta Swit 12/1/75
Sandy Dennis 6/21/76
Hope Lange 5/30/77 | #1 Joyce Van Patten
Barbara Rush 8/3/76
#2 Gail Strickland
#3 Carol Burnett
Diahann Carroll 5/18/77 |
| *George* | Charles Grodin
Conrad Janis 10/20/75
Ted Bessell 12/1/75
Don Murray 3/8/77 | #1 Conrad Janis
Tom Troupe 8/3/76
#2 John Lithgow
#3 Dick Van Dyke
Cleavon Little 5/18/77 |

SHENANDOAH

New York 1/7/75

Charlie Anderson	John Cullum William Chapman 11/2/76
Jenny	Penelope Milford Maureen Silliman 9/8/75 Emily Bindiger 5/31/77
Anne	Donna Theodore Leslie Denniston 10/12/76
James	Joel Higgins Wayne Hudgins 2/17/76 Paul Myrvold 2/4/77
Jacob	Ted Agress Roger Berdahl 7/29/76
Sam	Gordon Halliday
Gabriel	Chip Ford Brent Carter 10/20/75 David Vann 3/29/76 Donny Cooper 6/29/76 Tony Holmes 10/5/76
Robert	Joseph Shapiro Mark Perman 4/26/76 Steve Grober 8/16/76
Henry	Robert Rosen
John	David Russell
Nathan	Jordan Suffin Craig Lucas 9/26/76 Kevin Wilson 5/31/77

STREAMERS

	New York 4/21/76
Billy	Paul Rudd Mark Metcalf 6/14/76 Peter Weller 9/76
Carlyle	Dorian Harewood Kene Holliday
Richie	Peter Evans Thomas A. Stewart 4/77
Sgt. Cokes	Dolph Sweet Philip Bosco 2/15/77

THREEPENNY OPERA

	New York 5/1/76
Mack the Knife	Raul Julia Philip Bosco
Polly Peacham	Caroline Kava Blair Brown
Lucy Brown	Blair Brown Penelope Bodry
Tiger Brown	David Sabin Jerome Dempsey
Jenny Towler	Ellen Greene

TRAVESTIES

	New York 10/30/75	Washington 1/10/77
Henry Carr	John Wood	John Wood

VANITIES

	New York 3/22/76	Washington 10/21/76
Joanne	Kathy Bates Sally Sockwell 12/76	Lucie Arnaz Priscilla Lopez 1/4/77
Kathy	Jane Galloway	Stockard Channing Valorie Armstrong 1/4/77
Mary	Susan Merson	Sandy Duncan Kathy Bates 1/4/77

VERY GOOD EDDIE

	New York 12/21/75	Cleveland 10/4/76
Elsie Darling	Virginia Seidel	Virginia Seidel
Eddie Kettle	Charles Repole	J. J. Jepson
Georgina Kettle	Spring Fairbank	Spring Fairbank
Percy Darling	Nicholas Wyman	John Sloman
Mme. Matroppo	Travis Hudson	Travis Hudson
Dick Rivers	David Christmas	Russ Beasley
Elsie Lilly	Cynthia Wells	Sharon Werner
Al Cleveland	James Harder	Benny Baker
De Rougemont	Joel Craig	Ed Dixon

THE WIZ

	New York 1/5/75	*Los Angeles 6/15/76*
Tinman	Tiger Haynes	Ben Harney
Lion	Ted Ross James Wigfall 5/11/76	Ted Ross
Scarecrow	Hinton Battle Gregg Burge 12/76	Valentino
Dorothy	Stephanie Mills	Ren Woods Renée Harris 10/76
Glinda	Dee Dee Bridgewater Deborah Burrell 4/12/76	Dee Dee Bridgewater Roz Clark 10/76
Evillene	Mabel King Irene Reid Theresa Merritt 4/12/76 Ruth Brisbane 9/76	Ella Mitchell
The Wiz	Andre De Shields Alan Weeks 5/4/76 Andre De Shields 1/25/77	Andre De Shields Kenneth Scott 1/25/77
Addaperle	Clarice Taylor	Vivian Bonnell
Aunt Em	Tasha Thomas Esther Marrow	Dee Dee Bridgewater Roz Clark 10/76

WOMEN BEHIND BARS

	New York 4/25/76
Matron	Divine
Guadalupe	Vira Colorado Fanne Foxe 11/76

SPLIT-WEEK

These are touring productions designed for maximum mobility and ease of handling in one-night and split-week stands (with occasional engagements of a week or more). The one-man show is an attraction, because it is not required to give eight performances weekly (per Equity rules) and thus can be played for only one or two stands per week. The number of large-scale bus-truck tours has tended to diminish in recent seasons because 1) there have been fewer Broadway hits available and 2) the obligatory stars have been slow to commit themselves the necessary many months in advance for college and commercial bookings.

Among shows on tour in the season of 1976-77 were the following, listed in alphabetical order of titles:

Absurd Person Singular, 12/5/76-5/15/77.
The Belle of Amherst with Julie Harris, 1/10/77-5/28/77.
Don't Bother Me, I Can't Cope, 9/16/76-12/2/76.
Equus with David Leary, Bill Barrett, 9/16/76-12/6/76.
A Little Night Music with Julie Wilson, 9/18/76-12/11/76.
Plaza Suite, 9/76-5/29/77 (intermittent bookings).
Shenandoah with John Raitt, 10/1/76-3/20/77.
Sherlock Holmes with Kurt Kasznar, John Michalski, 12/31/76-5/3/77.
The Young Vic Company, 9/16/76-12/12/76.

FACTS AND
FIGURES

LONG RUNS ON BROADWAY

The following shows have run 500 or more continuous performances in a single production, usually the first, not including previews or extra non-profit performances, allowing for vacation layoffs and special one-booking engagements, but not including return engagements after a show has gone on tour. Where there are title similarities, the production is identified as follows: (p) straight play version, (m) musical version, (r) revival.

THROUGH MAY 31, 1977

(PLAYS MARKED WITH ASTERISK WERE STILL PLAYING JUNE 1, 1977)

Plays	Number Performances	Plays	Number Performances
Fiddler on the Roof	3,242	Cabaret	1,165
Life With Father	3,224	Mister Roberts	1,157
Tobacco Road	3,182	*The Magic Show	1,153
Hello, Dolly!	2,844	Annie Get Your Gun	1,147
My Fair Lady	2,717	The Seven Year Itch	1,141
Man of La Mancha	2,328	Butterflies Are Free	1,128
Abie's Irish Rose	2,327	Pins and Needles	1,108
Oklahoma!	2,212	Plaza Suite	1,097
*Grease	2,181	Kiss Me, Kate	1,070
Pippin	1,944	*Equus	1,068
South Pacific	1,925	Don't Bother Me, I Can't Cope	1,065
Harvey	1,775	The Pajama Game	1,063
Hair	1,750	The Teahouse of the August	
Born Yesterday	1,642	Moon	1,027
Mary, Mary	1,572	Damn Yankees	1,019
The Voice of the Turtle	1,557	Never Too Late	1,007
Barefoot in the Park	1,530	Any Wednesday	982
Mame (m)	1,508	*The Wiz	972
Arsenic and Old Lace	1,444	*Shenandoah	970
The Sound of Music	1,443	A Funny Thing Happened on	
How To Succeed in Business		the Way to the Forum	964
Without Really Trying	1,417	The Odd Couple	964
Hellzapoppin	1,404	Anna Lucasta	957
The Music Man	1,375	Kiss and Tell	956
Funny Girl	1,348	*Same Time, Next Year	927
Oh! Calcutta!	1,314	Bells Are Ringing	924
Angel Street	1,295	The Moon Is Blue	924
Lightnin'	1,291	Luv	901
Promises, Promises	1,281	Applause	896
The King and I	1,246	Can-Can	892
Cactus Flower	1,234	Carousel	890
Sleuth	1,222	Hats Off to Ice	889
1776	1,217	Fanny	888
Guys and Dolls	1,200	Follow the Girls	882

Plays	Number Performances	Plays	Number Performances
Camelot	873	Gypsy (m)	702
The Bat	867	The Miracle Worker	700
My Sister Eileen	864	Cat on a Hot Tin Roof	694
No, No, Nanette (r)	861	Li'l Abner	693
Song of Norway	860	Peg o' My Heart	692
A Streetcar Named Desire	855	The Children's Hour	691
Comedy in Music	849	Purlie	688
Raisin	847	Dead End	687
That Championship Season	844	The Lion and the Mouse	686
You Can't Take It With You	837	White Cargo	686
La Plume de Ma Tante	835	Dear Ruth	683
Three Men on a Horse	835	East Is West	680
The Subject Was Roses	832	Come Blow Your Horn	677
Inherit the Wind	806	The Most Happy Fella	676
No Time for Sergeants	796	The Doughgirls	671
Fiorello!	795	The Impossible Years	670
*Chicago	793	Irene	670
Where's Charley?	792	Boy Meets Girl	669
The Ladder	789	Beyond the Fringe	667
Forty Carats	780	Who's Afraid of Virginia	
The Prisoner of Second Avenue	780	Woolf?	664
Oliver	774	Blithe Spirit	657
State of the Union	765	A Trip to Chinatown	657
The First Year	760	The Women	657
You Know I Can't Hear You		Bloomer Girl	654
When the Water's Running	755	The Fifth Season	654
Two for the Seesaw	750	Rain	648
*A Chorus Line	743	Witness for the Prosecution	645
Death of a Salesman	742	Call Me Madam	644
Sons o' Fun	742	Janie	642
Candide (mr)	740	The Green Pastures	640
Gentlemen Prefer Blondes	740	Auntie Mame (p)	639
The Man Who Came to Dinner	739	A Man for All Seasons	637
Call Me Mister	734	The Fourposter	632
West Side Story	732	Two Gentlemen of	
High Button Shoes	727	Verona (m)	627
Finian's Rainbow	725	The Tenth Man	623
Claudia	722	Is Zat So?	618
The Gold Diggers	720	Anniversary Waltz	615
Jesus Christ Superstar	720	The Happy Time (p)	614
Carnival	719	Separate Rooms	613
The Diary of Anne Frank	717	Affairs of State	610
I Remember Mama	714	Star and Garter	609
Tea and Sympathy	712	The Student Prince	608
Junior Miss	710	Sweet Charity	608
Last of the Red Hot Lovers	706	Bye Bye Birdie	607
Company	705	Irene (r)	604
Seventh Heaven	704	Broadway	603

Plays	Number Performances	Plays	Number Performances
Adonis	603	Good News	551
Street Scene (p)	601	Let's Face It	547
Kiki	600	Milk and Honey	543
Flower Drum Song	600	Within the Law	541
A Little Night Music	600	The Music Master	540
Don't Drink the Water	598	Pal Joey (r)	540
Wish You Were Here	598	What Makes Sammy Run?	540
A Society Circus	596	The Sunshine Boys	538
Absurd Person Singular	592	What a Life	538
Blossom Time	592	The Unsinkable Molly Brown	532
The Me Nobody Knows	586	The Red Mill (r)	531
The Two Mrs. Carrolls	585	A Raisin in the Sun	530
Kismet	583	The Solid Gold Cadillac	526
Detective Story	581	*Bubbling Brown Sugar	524
Brigadoon	581	Irma La Douce	524
No Strings	580	The Boomerang	522
Brother Rat	577	Follies	521
Show Boat	572	Rosalinda	521
The Show-Off	571	The Best Man	520
Sally	570	Chauve-Souris	520
Golden Boy (m)	568	Blackbirds of 1928	518
One Touch of Venus	567	Sunny	517
Happy Birthday	564	Victoria Regina	517
Look Homeward, Angel	564	Half a Sixpence	511
The Glass Menagerie	561	The Vagabond King	511
I Do! I Do!	560	The New Moon	509
Wonderful Town	559	The World of Suzie Wong	508
Rose Marie	557	The Rothschilds	507
Strictly Dishonorable	557	Sugar	505
A Majority of One	556	Shuffle Along	504
The Great White Hope	556	Up in Central Park	504
Toys in the Attic	556	Carmen Jones	503
Sunrise at Campobello	556	The Member of the Wedding	501
Jamaica	555	Panama Hattie	501
Stop the World — I Want to		Personal Appearance	501
Get Off	555	Bird in Hand	500
Florodora	553	Room Service	500
Ziegfeld Follies (1943)	553	Sailor, Beware!	500
Dial "M" for Murder	552	Tomorrow the World	500

LONG RUNS OFF BROADWAY

Plays	Number Performances	Plays	Number Performances
*The Fantasticks	7,115	Godspell	2,124
The Threepenny Opera	2,611	Jacques Brel	1,847

Plays	Number Performances	Plays	Number Performances
You're a Good Man Charlie Brown	1,547	Scuba Duba	692
The Blacks	1,408	The Knack	685
Let My People Come	1,327	The Balcony	672
The Hot l Baltimore	1,166	America Hurrah	634
Little Mary Sunshine	1,143	Hogan's Goat	607
El Grande de Coca-Cola	1,114	The Trojan Women (r)	600
One Flew Over the Cuckoo's Nest (r)	1,025	Krapp's Last Tape & The Zoo Story	582
The Boys in the Band	1,000	The Dumbwaiter & The Collection	578
Your Own Thing	933	Dames at Sea	575
Curley McDimple	931	The Crucible (r)	571
Leave It to Jane (r)	928	The Iceman Cometh (r)	565
The Mad Show	871	The Hostage (r)	545
The Effect of Gamma Rays on Man-in-the-Moon Marigolds	819	Six Characters in Search of an Author (r)	529
A View From the Bridge (r)	780	The Dirtiest Show in Town	509
The Boy Friend (r)	763	*Vanities	506
The Pocket Watch	725	Happy Ending & Day of Absence	504
The Connection	722	The Boys From Syracuse (r)	500
Adaptation & Next	707		
Oh! Calcutta!	704		

DRAMA CRITICS CIRCLE VOTING, 1976-77

The New York Drama Critics Circle voted the British play *Otherwise Engaged* by Simon Gray the best play of the season on the fourth ballot (weighted to produce a consensus by points with 3 points given to a critic's first choice, 2 for second and 1 for third) with 22 points in a close contest with *American Buffalo* (21), *No Man's Land* (21) and *Ashes* (20). *Otherwise Engaged* also received a small plurality of 5 first choices from John Beaufort, Glenne Currie, William Glover, Allan Wallach and Edwin Wilson on the first ballot, on which by the Critics' rules a play could win outright with a majority of first choices. Other first-choice votes on this ballot were widely distributed, as follows: *American Buffalo* 3 (Howard Kissel, Julius Novick, Alan Rich), *Ashes* 3 (Harold Clurman, Jack Kroll, Emory Lewis), *Comedians* 3 (Ted Kalem, William Raidy, Marilyn Stasio), *The Shadow Box* 3 (Walter Kerr, Norman Nadel, George Oppenheimer), *No Man's Land* 2 (Clive Barnes, Edith Oliver), *The Trip Back Down* 1 (Douglas Watt) and *The Transfiguration of Benno Blimpie* 1 (Martin Gottfried).

After the first ballot, a new point-scoring rule adopted by the Critics last fall required a winning play to receive not merely a plurality of points as in the past, but a point total equal to the number of voting members (in this case 21 including proxies) multiplied by three, divided by two, plus one, making this year's plurality minimum 31 points. *Otherwise Engaged* received only 23 points on the second ballot, but instead of declaring an impasse and no award under the new rule, the majority of those present voted to restrict third and fourth ballot candidates to plays that had already received ten points on the previous ballot. This eliminated 6 proxy voters and brought the winning point total down to the 22 points finally eked out by *Otherwise Engaged,* to 21 for *American Buffalo* and *No Man's Land* and 20 for *Ashes* (see the record of the balloting below).

Having named a foreign play best of bests, the Critics then voted *American Buffalo* by David Mamet the best American Play of the year, by the same rules as above. First-choice distribution on the first ballot was as follows: *American Buffalo* 6 (Currie, Kissel, Novick, Oliver, Raidy, Rich), *The Shadow Box* 6 (Glover, Kerr, Nadel, Oppenheimer, Wallach, Wilson), *A Texas Trilogy* considered as a single play 6 (Beaufort, Clurman, Kroll, Lewis, Stasio, Watt), *Cold Storage* 1 (Barnes), *Gemini* 1 (Kalem) and *The Transfiguration of Benno Blimpie* 1 (Gottfried). *American Buffalo* received a winning plurality of 32 points on the second ballot, against 26 for *A Texas Trilogy,* 23 for *The Shadow Box* and scattered points for other candidates.

In the best-musical category, *Annie* by Thomas Meehan, Charles Strouse and Martin Charnin won on the first ballot with a majority of 10 first choices (after an abstainer, Julius Novick, and a *The Club* voter, Marilyn Stasio, agreed to become non-voters in order to reduce the number of voters to 19 and thus avoid the ordeal of a second, point ballot). The actual first ballot for best musical went as follows: *Annie* 10 (Beaufort, Clurman, Glover, Gottfried, Kissel, Lewis, Nadel, Oppenheimer, Rich, Wallach), *I Love My Wife* 7 (Barnes, Currie, Kalem, Kerr, Oliver, Raidy, Watt), *The Club* 1 (Stasio) and abstain 3 (Kroll, Novick, Wilson).

Three other members of the Circle — Brendan Gill of the *New Yorker,* Hobe Morrison of *Variety* and John Simon of *New Leader* — were absent and not voting. Here's the way the votes were distributed on the point ballots:

SECOND BALLOT FOR BEST PLAY

Critic	1st Choice (3 pts.)	2d Choice (2 pts.)	3d Choice (1 pt.)
Clive Barnes *Times*	No Man's Land	Ashes	Otherwise Engaged
John Beaufort *Monitor*	Otherwise Engaged	No Man's Land	A Texas Trilogy
Harold Clurman *The Nation*	Ashes	Comedians	For Colored Girls
Glenne Currie *UPI*	Otherwise Engaged	American Buffalo	For Colored Girls
William Glover *AP*	Otherwise Engaged	A Texas Trilogy	A Sorrow Beyond Dreams
Martin Gottfried *Post*	The Transfiguration of Benno Blimpie	American Buffalo	No Man's Land
Ted Kalem *Time*	Comedians	Ashes	Otherwise Engaged
Howard Kissel *Women's Wear*	American Buffalo	The Shadow Box	The Trip Back Down
Jack Kroll *Newsweek*	Ashes	Otherwise Engaged	A Texas Trilogy
Emory Lewis *Bergen Record*	Ashes	No Man's Land	For Colored Girls
Norman Nadel *Scripps-Howard*	The Shadow Box	American Buffalo	For Colored Girls

Critic			
Julius Novick *Village Voice*	American Buffalo	Otherwise Engaged	Comedians
Edith Oliver *New Yorker*	No Man's Land	Ashes	A Texas Trilogy
George Oppenheimer *Newsday*	The Shadow Box	Savages	Ashes
William Raidy Newhouse	Comedians	Otherwise Engaged	American Buffalo
Alan Rich *New York*	American Buffalo	The Shadow Box	Ashes
Marilyn Stasio *Cue*	Comedians	Ashes	A Texas Trilogy
Allan Wallach *Newsday*	Otherwise Engaged	No Man's Land	The Shadow Box
Douglas Watt *Daily News*	The Trip Back Down	No Man's Land	For Colored Girls
Edwin Wilson *Wall St. Journal*	Otherwise Engaged	The Shadow Box	American Buffalo

THIRD BALLOT FOR BEST PLAY

Critic	1st Choice (3 pts.)	2d Choice (2 pts.)	3d Choice (1 pt.)
Barnes	No Man's Land	Ashes	Otherwise Engaged
Beaufort	Otherwise Engaged	No Man's Land	Comedians
Clurman	Ashes	Comedians	American Buffalo
Currie	Otherwise Engaged	American Buffalo	Ashes
Gottfried	American Buffalo	No Man's Land	Otherwise Engaged
Kissel	American Buffalo	The Shadow Box	Comedians
Lewis	Ashes	No Man's Land	Comedians
Novick	American Buffalo	Otherwise Engaged	Comedians
Oliver	Ashes	No Man's Land	American Buffalo
Oppenheimer	The Shadow Box	Otherwise Engaged	Ashes
Rich	American Buffalo	The Shadow Box	Ashes
Stasio	Ashes	Comedians	American Buffalo
Wallach	Otherwise Engaged	No Man's Land	The Shadow Box
Watt	Otherwise Engaged	No Man's Land	Comedians

FOURTH BALLOT FOR BEST PLAY

Critic	1st Choice (3 pts.)	2d Choice (2 pts.)	3d Choice (1 pt.)
Barnes	No Man's Land	Ashes	Otherwise Engaged
Beaufort	Otherwise Engaged	No Man's Land	Ashes
Clurman	Ashes	American Buffalo	No Man's Land
Currie	Otherwise Engaged	American Buffalo	Ashes
Gottfried	American Buffalo	No Man's Land	Otherwise Engaged
Kissel	American Buffalo	No Man's Land	Otherwise Engaged
Lewis	Ashes	No Man's Land	American Buffalo
Novick	American Buffalo	Otherwise Engaged	Ashes
Oliver	No Man's Land	Ashes	Otherwise Engaged
Oppenheimer	Ashes	Otherwise Engaged	No Man's Land
Rich	American Buffalo	Otherwise Engaged	Ashes
Stasio	Ashes	American Buffalo	No Man's Land
Wallach	Otherwise Engaged	No Man's Land	American Buffalo
Watt	Otherwise Engaged	No Man's Land	American Buffalo

SECOND BALLOT FOR BEST AMERICAN PLAY

Critic	1st Choice (3 pts.)	2d Choice (2 pts.)	3d Choice (1 pt.)
Barnes	Cold Storage	Benno Blimpie	For Colored Girls
Beaufort	For Colored Girls	A Texas Trilogy	The Shadow Box
Clurman	A Texas Trilogy	For Colored Girls	American Buffalo
Currie	American Buffalo	For Colored Girls	Cold Storage
Glover	For Colored Girls	A Texas Trilogy	The Shadow Box
Gottfried	American Buffalo	Benno Blimpie	The Shadow Box
Kalem	Gemini	American Buffalo	The Shadow Box

Kissel	American Buffalo	The Shadow Box	Cold Storage
Kroll	A Texas Trilogy	For Colored Girls	Cold Storage
Lewis	A Texas Trilogy	American Buffalo	For Colored Girls
Nadel	The Shadow Box	American Buffalo	For Colored Girls
Novick	American Buffalo	For Colored Girls	The Shadow Box
Oliver	American Buffalo	A Texas Trilogy	Cold Storage
Oppenheimer	The Shadow Box	A Texas Trilogy	Ashes
Raidy	American Buffalo	The Shadow Box	Benno Blimpie
Rich	American Buffalo	The Shadow Box	Gemini
Stasio	A Texas Trilogy	American Buffalo	Sly Fox
Wallach	The Shadow Box	A Texas Trilogy	Cold Storage
Watt	A Texas Trilogy	For Colored Girls	The Trip Back Down
Wilson	The Shadow Box	American Buffalo	A Texas Trilogy

CHOICES OF SOME OTHER CRITICS

Critic	Best Play	Best Musical
Judith Crist	Otherwise Engaged	Side by Side by Sondheim
Brendan Gill *The New Yorker*	No Man's Land	Abstain
Hobe Morrison *Variety*	A Texas Trilogy	Annie
Stewart Klein WNEW-TV	Sly Fox	I Love My Wife
Bob Lape WABC-TV	Gemini	Annie
Pia Lindstrom WNBC-TV	The Shadow Box	Annie
Jeffrey Lyons WPIX-TV	The Shadow Box	Annie
Leonard Probst WNBC	Otherwise Engaged	Abstain

NEW YORK DRAMA CRITICS CIRCLE AWARDS

Listed below are the New York Drama Critics Circle Awards from 1935–36 through 1976–77 classified as follows: (1) Best American Play, (2) Best Foreign Play, (3) Best Musical, (4) Best, regardless of category (this category was established by new voting rules in 1962–63 and did not exist prior to that year).

1935–36—(1) Winterset
1936–37—(1) High Tor
1937–38—(1) Of Mice and Men, (2) Shadow and Substance
1938–39—(1) No award, (2) The White Steed
1939–40—(1) The Time of Your Life
1940–41—(1) Watch on the Rhine, (2) The Corn Is Green
1941–42—(1) No award, (2) Blithe Spirit
1942–43—(1) The Patriots
1943–44—(2) Jacobowsky and the Colonel
1944–45—(1) The Glass Menagerie
1945–46—(3) Carousel
1946–47—(1) All My Sons, (2) No Exit, (3) Brigadoon
1947–48—(1) A Streetcar Named Desire, (2) The Winslow Boy

1948–49—(1) Death of a Salesman, (2) The Madwoman of Chaillot, (3) South Pacific
1949–50—(1) The Member of the Wedding (2) The Cocktail Party, (3) The Consul
1950–51—(1) Darkness at Noon, (2) The Lady's Not for Burning, (3) Guys and Dolls
1951–52—(1) I Am a Camera, (2) Venus Observed, (3) Pal Joey (Special citation to Don Juan in Hell)
1952–53—(1) Picnic, (2) The Love of Four Colonels, (3) Wonderful Town
1953–54—(1) Teahouse of the August Moon, (2) Ondine, (3) The Golden Apple
1954–55—(1) Cat on a Hot Tin Roof, (2) Witness for the Prosecution, (3) The Saint of Bleecker Street

1955-56—(1) The Diary of Ann Frank, (2) Tiger at the Gates, (3) My Fair Lady
1956-57—(1) Long Day's Journey Into Night, (2) The Waltz of the Toreadors, (3) The Most Happy Fella
1957-58—(1) Look Homeward, Angel, (2) Look Back in Anger, (3) The Music Man
1958-59—(1) A Raisin in the Sun, (2) The Visit, (3) La Plume de Ma Tante
1959-60—(1) Toys in the Attic, (2) Five Finger Exercise, (3) Fiorello!
1960-61—(1) All the Way Home, (2) A Taste of Honey, (3) Carnival
1961-62—(1) The Night of the Iguana, (2) A Man for All Seasons, (3) How to Succeed in Business Without Really Trying
1962-63—(4) Who's Afraid of Virginia Woolf? (Special citation to Beyond the Fringe)
1963-64—(4) Luther, (3) Hello, Dolly! (Special citation to The Trojan Women)
1964-65—(4) The Subject Was Roses, (3) Fiddler on the Roof
1965-66—(4) The Persecution and Assassination of Marat as Performed by the Inmates of the Asylum of Charenton Under the Direction of the Marquis de Sade, (3) Man of La Mancha
1966-67—(4) The Homecoming, (3) Cabaret
1967-68—(4) Rosencrantz and Guildenstern Are Dead, (3) Your Own Thing
1968-69—(4) The Great White Hope, (3) 1776
1969-70—(4) Borstal Boy, (1) The Effect of Gamma Rays on Man-in-the-Moon Marigolds, (3) Company
1970-71—(4) Home, (1) The House of Blue Leaves, (3) Follies
1971-72—(4) That Championship Season, (2) The Screens, (3) Two Gentlemen of Verona (Special citations to Sticks and Bones and Old Times)
1972-73—(4) The Changing Room, (1) The Hot l Baltimore, (3) A Little Night Music
1973-74—(4) The Contractor, (1) Short Eyes, (3) Candide
1974-75—(4) Equus, (1) The Taking of Miss Janie, (3) A Chorus Line
1975-76—(4) Travesties, (1) Streamers, (3) Pacific Overtures
1976-77—(4) Otherwise Engaged, (1) American Buffalo, (3) Annie

PULITZER PRIZE WINNERS, 1916-17 to 1976-77

1916-17—No award
1917-18—Why Marry?, by Jesse Lynch Williams
1918-19—No award
1919-20—Beyond the Horizon, by Eugene O'Neill
1920-21—Miss Lulu Bett, by Zona Gale
1921-22—Anna Christie, by Eugene O'Neill
1922-23—Icebound, by Owen Davis
1923-24—Hell-Bent fer Heaven, by Hatcher Hughes
1924-25—They Knew What They Wanted, by Sidney Howard
1925-26—Craig's Wife, by George Kelly
1926-27—In Abraham's Bosom, by Paul Green
1927-28—Strange Interlude, by Eugene O'Neill
1928-29—Street Scene, by Elmer Rice
1929-30—The Green Pastures, by Marc Connelly
1930-31—Alison's House, by Susan Glaspell
1931-32—Of Thee I Sing, by George S. Kaufman, Morrie Ryskind, Ira and George Gershwin
1932-33—Both Your Houses, by Maxwell Anderson
1933-34—Men in White, by Sidney Kingsley
1934-35—The Old Maid, by Zoë Akins
1935-36—Idiot's Delight, by Robert E. Sherwood
1936-37—You Can't Take It With You, by Moss Hart and George S. Kaufman
1937-38—Our Town, by Thornton Wilder
1938-39—Abe Lincoln in Illinois, by Robert E. Sherwood
1939-40—The Time of Your Life, by William Saroyan
1940-41—There Shall Be No Night, by Robert E. Sherwood
1941-42—No award
1942-43—The Skin of Our Teeth, by Thornton Wilder
1943-44—No award
1944-45—Harvey, by Mary Chase
1945-46—State of the Union, by Howard Lindsay and Russel Crouse
1946-47—No award
1947-48—A Streetcar Named Desire, by Tennessee Williams
1948-49—Death of a Salesman, by Arthur Miller
1949-50—South Pacific, by Richard Rodgers, Oscar Hammerstein II and Joshua Logan
1950-51—No award
1951-52—The Shrike, by Joseph Kramm
1952-53—Picnic, by William Inge
1953-54—The Teahouse of the August Moon, by John Patrick
1954-55—Cat on a Hot Tin Roof, by Tennessee Williams
1955-56—The Diary of Anne Frank, by Frances Goodrich and Albert Hackett
1956-57—Long Day's Journey Into Night, by Eugene O'Neill
1957-58—Look Homeward, Angel, by Ketti Frings
1958-59—J. B., by Archibald MacLeish
1959-60—Fiorello!, by Jerome Weidman, George Abbott, Sheldon Harnick and Jerry Bock
1960-61—All the Way Home, by Tad Mosel
1961-62—How to Succeed in Business Without Really Trying, by Abe Burrows, Willie Gilbert, Jack Weinstock and Frank Loesser
1962-63—No award
1963-64—No award
1964-65—The Subject Was Roses, by Frank D. Gilroy
1965-66—No award

1966–67—A Delicate Balance, by Edward Albee
1967–68—No award
1968–69—The Great White Hope, by Howard Sackler
1969–70—No Place to Be Somebody, by Charles Gordone
1970–71—The Effect of Gamma Rays on Man-in-the-Moon Marigolds, by Paul Zindel
1971–72—No award

1972–73—That Championship Season, by Jason Miller
1973–74—No award
1974–75—Seascape, by Edward Albee
1975–76—A Chorus Line, by Michael Bennett, James Kirkwood, Nicholas Dante, Marvin Hamlisch and Edward Kleban
1976–77—The Shadow Box, by Michael Cristofer

THE TONY AWARDS

The Antoinette Perry (Tony) Awards are voted by members of the League of New York Theaters and Producers, the governing bodies of the Dramatists Guild, Actors' Equity, the American Theater Wing, the Society of Stage Directors and Choreographers, the United Scenic Artists Union and members of the first-night and second-night press, from a list of four nominations in each category.

These nominations are made annually by a committee whose personnel changes annually at the invitation of the abovementioned League, which sponsors the Tony Awards under an agreement with the American Theater Wing. The 1976-77 nominating committee was composed of John Beaufort of the *Christian Science Monitor*, Harold Clurman of *The Nation*, Martin Gottfried of the New York *Post*, Claude Lewis of the Philadelphia *Bulletin*, Paul Myers, curator of the New York Public Library Theater Collection, Seymour Peck of the New York *Times*, Joan Rubin of *Playbill*, Marilyn Stasio of *Cue*, Alan Wallach of *Newsday*, Douglas Watt of the New York *Daily News* and Edwin Wilson of the *Wall Street Journal*.

These nominations are made from a list of those eligible in each category, provided by the Tony administration's Eligibility Committee consisting of Jesse Gross, executive director of the American Theater Society, Susan Harley, executive secretary of the League, and Stuart Little, a free-lance critic and editor.

The list of 1976-77 nominees follows, with winners in each category listed in **bold face type:**

BEST PLAY. *For Colored Girls Who Have Considered Suicide/When the Rainbow Is Enuf* by Ntozake Shangé, produced by Joseph Papp; *Otherwise Engaged* by Simon Gray, produced by Michael Codron, Frank Milton and James M. Nederlander; **The Shadow Box** by **Michael Cristofer,** produced by **Allan Francis, Ken Marsolais, Lester Osterman** and **Leonard Soloway;** *Streamers* by David Rabe, produced by Joseph Papp.

BEST MUSICAL. **Annie** produced by **Mike Nichols** and **Lewis Allen;** *Happy End* produced by Michael Harvey and Chelsea Theater Center; *I Love My Wife* produced by Terry Allen Kramer and Harry Rigby.

BEST BOOK OF A MUSICAL. *Annie* by **Thomas Meehan;** *Happy End* by Elisabeth Hauptmann; *I Love My Wife* by Michael Stewart; *Your Arms Too Short to Box With God* by Vinnette Carroll.

BEST MUSICAL SCORE. *Annie*, music by **Charles Strouse,** lyrics by **Martin Charnin;** *Happy End*, music by Kurt Weill, lyrics by Bertolt Brecht; *Godspell*, music and lyrics by Stephen Schwartz; *I Love My Wife*, music by Cy Coleman, lyrics by Michael Stewart.

BEST ACTOR — PLAY. Tom Courtenay in *Otherwise Engaged;* Ben Gazzara in *Who's Afraid of Virginia Woolf?;* **Al Pacino** in *The Basic Training of Pavlo Hummel;* Ralph Richardson in *No Man's Land.*

BEST ACTRESS — PLAY. Colleen Dewhurst in *Who's Afraid of Virginia Woolf?;* **Julie Harris** in *The Belle of Amherst;* Liv Ullmann in *Anna Christie;* Irene Worth in *The Cherry Orchard.*

BEST ACTOR — MUSICAL. **Barry Bostwick** in

The Robber Bridegroom; Robert Guillaume in Guys and Dolls; Raul Julia in Threepenny Opera; Reid Shelton in Annie.

BEST ACTRESS — MUSICAL. Clamma Dale in Porgy and Bess; Ernestine Jackson in Guys and Dolls; Dorothy Loudon and Andrea McArdle in Annie.

BEST FEATURED ACTOR — PLAY. Bob Dishy in Sly Fox; Joe Fields in The Basic Training of Pavlo Hummel; Laurence Luckinbill in The Shadow Box; Jonathan Pryce in Comedians.

BEST FEATURED ACTRESS — PLAY. Trazana Beverley in For Colored Girls, etc.; Patricia Elliott and Rose Gregorio in The Shadow Box; Mary McCarty in Anna Christie.

BEST FEATURED ACTOR — MUSICAL. Lenny Baker in I Love My Wife; David Kernan and Ned Sherrin in Side by Side by Sondheim; Larry Marshall in Porgy and Bess.

BEST FEATURED ACTRESS — MUSICAL. Ellen Greene in Threepenny Opera; Delores Hall in Your Arms Too Short, etc.; Millicent Martin and Julie N. McKenzie in Side by Side by Sondheim.

BEST DIRECTOR — PLAY. Gordon Davidson for The Shadow Box; Ulu Grosbard for American Buffalo; Mike Nichols for Comedians and Streamers.

BEST DIRECTOR — MUSICAL. Vinnette Carroll for Your Arms Too Short, etc.; Martin Charnin for Annie; Jack O'Brien for Porgy and Bess; Gene Saks for I Love My Wife.

BEST CHOREOGRAPHER. Talley Beatty for Your Arms Too Short, etc.; Patricia Birch for Music Is; Peter Gennaro for Annie; Onna White for I Love My Wife.

BEST SCENIC DESIGNER. Santo Loquasto for American Buffalo and The Cherry Orchard; David Mitchell for Annie; Robert Randolph for Porgy and Bess.

BEST COSTUME DESIGNER. Theoni V. Aldredge (tie) for Annie and Threepenny Opera; Santo Loquasto (tie) for The Cherry Orchard; Nancy Potts for Porgy and Bess.

BEST LIGHTING DESIGNER. John Bury for No Man's Land; Pat Collins for Threepenny Opera; Neil Peter Jampolis for The Innocents; Jennifer Tipton for The Cherry Orchard.

MOST INNOVATIVE PRODUCTION OF A REVIVAL. The Cherry Orchard produced by Joseph Papp; Guys and Dolls produced by Moe Septee; Porgy and Bess produced by Sherwin M. Goldman and Houston Grand Opera; Threepenny Opera produced by Joseph Papp.

SPECIAL AWARDS (voted by the Tony Administration Committee): Second annual Lawrence Langner Award for lifetime achievement in the theater to Cheryl Crawford. Special Tony Awards to the Mark Taper Forum, Los Angeles (designated by the American Theater Critics Association) as an outstanding regional theater; Barry Manilow; Diana Ross; Lily Tomlin; Equity Library Theater and National Theater of the Deaf.

THE OBIE AWARDS

The Village Voice Off-Broadway (Obie) Awards are given each year for excellence in various categories of off-Broadway shows — and frequently off-off-Broadway shows, as close distinctions between these two areas are ignored in Obie Award-giving. The Obies are voted by a committee of Village Voice critics and others, whose 1976-77 members were Michael Feingold, Dan Isaac, Erika Munk, Julius Novick, Arthur Sainer, Marilyn Stasio and Ross Wetzsteon. 1976-77 Obie Awards were as follows:

LIFETIME ACHIEVEMENT. Joseph Chaikin.

BEST NEW AMERICAN PLAY. Curse of the Starving Class by Sam Shepard.

DISTINGUISHED PLAYWRITING. David Berry for G. R. Point; Maria Irene Fornes for Fefu and Her Friends; William Hauptman for Domino Courts; Albert Innaurato for Gemini and The Transfiguration of Benno Blimpie; David Rudkin for Ashes.

DISTINGUISHED PRODUCTIONS. Eve Merriam (playwright), Tommy Tune (director) Kate Carmel (costume designer), entire cast of The Club; Ntozake

Shangé (author), Oz Scott (director), entire cast of For Colored Girls Who Have Considered Suicide/When the Rainbow is Enuf; Mabou Mines for Dressed Like an Egg.

MISCELLANEOUS. Barbara Garson for The Dinosaur Door; Manhattan Theater Club, New York Street Theater Caravan and Theater for the New City for sustained excellence; Philip Glass for the music for Einstein on the Beach; Ping Chong for Humboldt's Current; creators of Nightclub Cantata; Charles Ludlam for the design of Der Ring Gott Farblonjet; Carol Oditz (costumes), Douglas W. Schmidt (scenery), **Burl Hass** (lighting) for *The Crazy Locomotive;* **Henry Millman** (scenery), **Edward M. Greenberg** (lighting) for *Domino Courts.*

DISTINGUISHED DIRECTION. **Melvin Bernhardt** for *Children;* **Gordon Davidson** for *Savages.*

DISTINGUISHED PERFORMANCES. **Danny Aiello** and **Anne DeSalvo** for *Gemini;* **Martin Balsam** for *Cold Storage;* **Lucinda Childs** for *Einstein on the Beach;* **James Coco** for *The Transfiguration of Benno Blimpie;* **John Heard** for *G. R. Point;* **Jo Henderson** for *Ladyhouse Blues;* **William Hurt** for *My Life;* **Joseph Maher** for *Savages;* **Roberta Maxwell** and **Brian Murray** for *Ashes;* **Lola Pashalinski** for *Der Ring Gott Farblonjet;* **Marian Seldes** for *Isadora Duncan Sleeps With the Russian Navy;* **Margaret Wright** for *A Manoir.*

ADDITIONAL PRIZES AND AWARDS, 1976-77

The following is a list of major prizes and awards for achievement in the theater. In all cases the names of winners — persons, productions, contributions or organizations — appear in **bold face type.**

1976 MARGO JONES AWARD for the professional producer and theater deemed to have made the most significant contribution to the American theater. **Gordon Davidson** and the Center Theater Group's **Mark Taper Forum.**

1977 JOSEPH MAHARAM FOUNDATION AWARDS for distinguished New York theatrical design by American designers. Scenery design — **Douglas W. Schmidt** for *Agamemnon;* **Santo Loquasto** for *American Buffalo.* Costume design — **Santo Loquasto** for *Agamemnon.*

CLARENCE DERWENT AWARDS for the most promising female and male actors on the metropolitan scene. **Rose Gregorio** in *The Shadow Box.* **Barry Preston** in *Bubbling Brown Sugar.*

ELIZABETH HULL-KATE WARRINER AWARD to the playwright whose work produced within the 1975-76 season dealt with controversial subjects involving the fields of political, religious or social mores of the time, selected by the Dramatists Guild Council. **David Rabe** for *Streamers.*

OUTER CRITICS' CIRCLE AWARDS for distinctive achievement in the New York theater, voted by critics of out-of-town and foreign periodicals. **Liv Ullmann** for *Anna Christie.* **Ntozake Shangé** for *For Colored Girls,* etc. **Annie** as "most refreshing musical." **Dorothy Loudon** and **Andrea McArdle** in *Annie.* **David Mitchell** for the *Annie* scene design. **John Gielgud** and **Ralph Richardson** in *No Man's Land.* **Andre Serban** for "virtuoso direction" and **Santo Loquasto** for scene design of *The Cherry Orchard.* **Elizabeth Swados** for musical contribution to *The Cherry Orchard, Nightclub Cantata* and *Agamemnon.* **Gordon Davidson** for direction of *The Shadow Box* and *Savages.* **Brooklyn Academy of Music Theater Company** for *Three Sisters* and *The New York Idea.* John Gassner Prize for new playwrights to **Preston Jones** for *A Texas Trilogy.*

33d ANNUAL THEATER WORLD AWARDS for the outstanding new performers in Broadway and off-Broadway productions during the 1976-77 season.

Trazana Beverley in *For Colored Girls,* etc. **Michael Cristofer** in *The Cherry Orchard.* **Joe Fields** in *The Basic Training of Pavlo Hummel.* **Joanna Gleason** in *I Love My Wife.* **Cecilia Hart** in *Dirty Linen.* **John Heard** in *G. R. Point.* **Gloria Hodes** in *The Club.* **Juliette Koka** in *Piaf . . . a Remembrance.* **Andrea McArdle** in *Annie.* **Ken Page** in *Guys and Dolls.* **Jonathan Pryce** in *Comedians.* **Chick Vennera** in *Jockeys.*

ACTORS FUND MEDAL to **Joseph Papp** "in recognition of his outstanding achievements in the American theater and his exceptional cooperation with the Fund."

LOS ANGELES DRAMA CRITICS CIRCLE 1976 DISTINGUISHED ACHIEVEMENT AWARDS. Production — *A Chorus Line, Equus.* Performance in a major role — **Brian Bedford** in *Equus,* **Mary Jo Catlett** in *Come Back, Little Sheba,* **Carole Shelley** in *The Royal Family.* Performance in a supporting role — **Barbara Lang** in *The Robber Bridegroom,* **Tamara Long** in *The Great American Backstage Musical.* Direction — **John Allison** for *Medea,* **Michael Bennett** for *A Chorus Line,* **William Devane** for *The Changing Room,* **John Dexter** for *Equus,* **Danny Goldman** and **Julia Steiny** for *Skyjack '76: Entebbe.* Playwriting — **Peter Shaffer** for *Equus.* Book for a musical — **James Kirkwood** and **Nicholas Dante** for *A Chorus Line.* Music and lyrics — **Stephen Sondheim** for *Pacific Overtures.* Choreography — **Michael Bennett** and **Bob Avian** for *A Chorus Line.* Lighting design — **Tharon Musser** for *A Chorus Line* and *Pacific Overtures.* Set design — **Boris Aronson** for *Pacific Overtures,* **David Lukas** and **James Riddle** for *Come Back, Little Sheba.* Costume design — **Geoffrey Holder** for *The Wiz,* **Florence Klotz** for *Pacific Overtures.* Margaret Harford Award "for continuing distinguished achievement in the Los Angeles theater" — **The Los Angeles Actors Theater.** Special awards "for continuing excellence in theatrical production" — **Company of Angels** and **Colony Productions** at the Studio Theater Playhouse.

DRAMA DESK AWARDS for outstanding achievement. Director of a play — **Mike Nichols** for

Comedians, Alan Schneider for *A Texas Trilogy.* Director of a musical — Martin Charnin for *Annie,* Gene Saks for *I Love My Wife.* Book of a musical — Thomas Meehan for *Annie.* Lyrics — Martin Charnin for *Annie.* Musical score — Cy Coleman for *I Love My Wife.* American play — *A Texas Trilogy* by Preston Jones. Foreign play — *Otherwise Engaged* by Simon Gray. Musical — *Annie.* Choreography — Peter Gennaro for *Annie.* Actor in a musical — Lenny Baker in *I Love My Wife.* Actress in a musical — Clamma Dale in *Porgy and Bess.* Featured actress in a musical — Dorothy Loudon in *Annie.* Featured actor in a musical — The Band (John Miller, Michael Mark, Joseph Saulter, Ken Bichel) in *I Love My Wife.* Actor in a play — Al Pacino in *The Basic Training of Pavlo Hummel.* Actress in a play — Irene Worth in *The Cherry Orchard.* Featured actor in a play — Bob Dishy in *Sly Fox.* Featured actress in a play — Rosemary De Angelis in *The Transfiguration of Benno Blimpie.* Costumes — Theoni V. Aldredge for *Annie.* Scenery — Santo Loquasto for *American Buffalo* and *The Cherry Orchard.* Lighting — Jennifer Tipton for *For Colored Girls,* etc. and *The Cherry Orchard.* Outstanding theatrical experience of the season award — Ralph Richardson and John Gielgud in *No Man's Land.*

1976-1977 PUBLICATION OF RECENTLY-PRODUCED PLAYS

A-A-America! and *Stone.* Edward Bond. Methuen (paperback).
Angel City, Curse of the Starving Class and Other Plays. Sam Shepard. Urizen (also paperback).
Belle of Amherst, The. William Luce. Houghton, Mifflin.
California Suite. Neil Simon. Random House.
Candide. Leonard Bernstein, Richard Wilbur, Stephen Sondheim, John Latouche, Hugh Wheeler. Schirmer (also paperback).
Contemporary Chicano Theater. Roberto J. Garza, editor. University of Notre Dame (paperback).
Cyrano de Bergerac. Christopher Fry's translation of Edmond Rostand. Oxford.
Dirty Linen and *New-Found-Land.* Tom Stoppard. Grove Press (also paperback).
Female Transport. Steve Gooch. Pluto Press (paperback).
Fool, The/We Come to the River. Edward Bond. Methuen. (paperback).
For Colored Girls Who Have Considered Suicide/When the Rainbow Is Enuf. Ntozake Shangé. Macmillan.
Forever Yours Marie-Lou. Michel Tremblay. Talon (paperback).
Gorf. Michael McClure. New Directions (also paperback).
Guthrie New Theater (Volume One). Eugene Lion and David Ball, editors. Grove Press (paperback).
Hitting Town/City Sugar. Stephen Poliakoff. Methuen (paperback).
Hosanna. Michel Tremblay. Talon. (paperback).
I Am a Woman. Viveca Lindfors and Paul Austin. Natalie Slohm (paperback).
India Song. Marguerite Duras. Grove Press (paperback).
Knock Knock. Jules Feiffer. Hill & Wang (also paperback).
Magnificence. Howard Brenton. Eyre Methuen (paperback).
Marcus Brutus/Silver Queen Saloon. Paul Foster. John Calder.
Mound Builders, The. Lanford Wilson. Hill & Wang (also paperback).
Old Flames. E.A. Whitehead. Faber & Faber (paperback).
Otherwise Engaged and Other Plays. Simon Gray. Viking (also Penguin Paperback).
Pacific Overtures. John Weidman and Stephen Sondheim. Dodd, Mead.
Painters, The. Heinrich Henkel. Davis-Poynter (paperback).
Phaedra Britannica. Tony Harrison. Rex Collings (paperback).
Plays of Copi (Volume One). Copi. John Calder (paperback).
The Pleasure Principle: The Politics of Love, the Capital of Emotion. Snoo Wilson. Methuen (paperback).
Ritz, The and Other Plays. Terrence McNally. Dodd, Mead.
Runner Stumbles, The. Milan Stitt. James T. White (also paperback).
Sizwe Banzi Is Dead/The Island. Athol Fugard with John Kani and Winston Ntshona. Viking.
Streamers. David Rabe. Knopf.
Suzanna Andler/La Musica/Tamante Anglaise. Marguerite Duras. John Calder (also paperback).
Sylvia Plath: A Dramatic Portrait. Barry Kyle. Harper & Row (paperback).
Tales from the Vienna Woods. Christopher Hampton's translation of Odon von Horvath. Faber & Faber (paperback).
Teeth 'n' Smiles. David Hare. Faber & Faber (paperback).
Texas Trilogy, A. Preston Jones. Hill & Wang (also paperback).
Thunder: A Play of the Brontës. Richard Crane. Heinemann (paperback).
Three Plays. Alan Ayckbourn. Chatto & Windus.
Three Plays. Peter Shaffer. Penguin (paperback).
Treats. Christopher Hampton. Faber & Faber (paperback).

A SELECTED LIST OF OTHER PLAYS PUBLISHED IN 1976-77

Andromache and Other Plays. John Cairmcross' translation of Jean Racine. Penguin (paperback).
Best Short Plays of 1976, The. Stanley Richards, editor. Chilton.
Collected Plays of Euripides. Gilbert Murray's translation of Euripides. Allen & Unwin (paperback).
Complete Plays of Aeschylus, Gilbert Murray's translation of Aeschylus. Allen & Unwin.
Country Gentleman, The: A "Lost" Play and Its Background. Robert Howard and George Villiers. University of
    Pennsylvania.
Crucible, The. Arthur Miller. Penguin (paperback).
Ends and Odds. Samuel Beckett. Grove Press (also paperback).
Freshwater. Virginia Woolf. Harcourt Brace Jovanovich.
Great Musicals of the American Theater: Volume Two. Stanley Richards, editor. Chilton.
Maxim Gorky Plays. Margaret Wellin, Bernard Isaacs and Robert Daglish translation of Maxim Gorky.
    Imported Publications.
Plays of Arnold Wesker (Volumes One and Two). Arnold Wesker. Harper & Row.
Plays of Ionesco (Volume Ten). Eugene Ionesco. John Calder.
Plays of Strindberg (Volumes One and Two). August Strindberg. Vintage (paperback).
Revenger's Tragedy, The. Cyril Tourneur, edited by R. A. Fookes. Barnes & Noble (paperback).
Sea Gull, The. Anton Chekhov. Harper & Row (paperback).
1776: A Musical Play. Peter Stone and Sherman Edwards. Penguin (paperback).
The Theater of Tennessee Williams (Volume Five). Tennessee Williams. New Directions.
Tony Winners, The. Stanley Richards, editor. Doubleday.
Vegetable, The. F. Scott Fitzgerald. Scribners (also paperback).

MUSICAL AND DRAMATIC RECORDINGS OF NEW YORK SHOWS

Title and publishing company are listed below. Each record is an original cast album unless otherwise indicated. An asterisk (*) indicates recording is also available on cassettes. Two asterisks (**) indicate it is available on eight-track cartrïdges.

Annie. Columbia. (*) (**).
Ballad of Baby Doe, The (reissue of original New York City Opera production). Deutsche Grammophon.
Belle of Amherst, The. Credo.
Boy Meets Boy. JO.
Cole (original London cast). RCA.
Cowardly Custard (original London cast). RCA.
For Colored Girls Who Have Considered Suicide/When the Rainbow is Enuf. Buddah.
Goodtime Charley. RCA.
Guys and Dolls (1976 original cast). Motown.
Gypsy (original London cast). RCA.
I Am a Woman (Viveca Lindfors). Natalie Slohm Associates.
Ipi-Tombi. Ashtree.
Jesus Christ Superstar (original London cast). MCA.
Leave Him to Heaven (original London cast). Chrysalis.
Let My People Come. Libra.
Little Night Music, A (original London cast). RCA.
Mardi Gras (original London cast). EMI (Capitol).
Murder in the Cathedral (Royal Shakespeare Company). Argo.
My Fair Lady (original Spanish cast). (*) (**). Columbia Special Products.
My Fair Lady (1976 original cast). Columbia. (*) (**).
Oh, Captain. Columbia Special Products.
Rex. RCA. (*) (**).
Rocky Horror Show, The. Ode.
Shenandoah. RCA.
Side by Side by Sondheim (original London cast). RCA.

Shirley MacLaine Show, The. Columbia.
Threepenny Opera (1976 original cast). Columbia.
Tuscaloosa's Calling Me . . . But I'm Not Going. Vanguard.
Turnabout. Pelican.
Your Arms Too Short to Box With God. ABC. (*) (**).

THE BEST PLAYS, 1894-1976

Listed in alphabetical order below are all those works selected as Best Plays in previous volumes in the *Best Plays* series. Opposite each title is given the volume in which the play appears, its opening date and its total number of performances. Those plays marked with an asterisk (*) were still playing on June 1, 1977 and their number of performances was figured through May 31, 1977. Adaptors and translators are indicated by (ad) and (tr), the symbols (b), (m) and (l) stand for the author of the book, music and lyrics in the cast of musicals and (c) signifies the credit for the show's conception.

NOTE: A season-by-season listing, rather than an alphabetical one, of the 500 Best Plays in the first 50 volumes, starting with the yearbook for the season of 1919-1920, appears in *The Best Plays of 1968-69.*

PLAY	VOLUME	OPENED	PERFS.
ABE LINCOLN IN ILLINOIS—Robert E. Sherwood	38-39.	.Oct. 15, 1938. .	472
ABRAHAM LINCOLN—John Drinkwater	19-20.	.Dec. 15, 1919. .	193
ACCENT ON YOUTH—Samson Raphaelson	34-35.	.Dec. 25, 1934. .	229
ADAM AND EVA—Guy Bolton, George Middleton	19-20.	.Sept. 13, 1919. .	312
ADAPTATION—Elaine May; and NEXT—Terrence McNally	68-69.	.Feb. 10, 1969. .	707
AFFAIRS OF STATE—Louis Verneuil	50-51.	.Sept. 25, 1950. .	610
AFTER THE FALL—Arthur Miller	63-64.	.Jan. 23, 1964. .	208
AFTER THE RAIN—John Bowen	67-68.	.Oct. 9, 1967. .	64
AH, WILDERNESS!—Eugene O'Neill	33-34.	.Oct. 2, 1933. .	289
AIN'T SUPPOSED TO DIE A NATURAL DEATH—(b,m,l) Melvin Van Peebles	71-72.	.Oct. 7, 1971. .	325
ALIEN CORN—Sidney Howard	32-33.	.Feb. 20, 1933. .	98
ALISON'S HOUSE—Susan Glaspell	30-31.	.Dec. 1, 1930. .	41
ALL MY SONS—Arthur Miller	46-47.	.Jan. 29, 1947. .	328
ALL OVER TOWN—Murray Schisgal	74-75.	.Dec. 12, 1974. .	233
ALL THE WAY HOME—Tad Mosel, based on James Agee's novel *A Death in the Family*	60-61.	.Nov. 30, 1960. .	333
ALLEGRO—(b,l) Oscar Hammerstein II, (m) Richard Rodgers	47-48.	.Oct. 10, 1947. .	315
AMBUSH—Arthur Richman	21-22.	.Oct. 10, 1921. .	98
AMERICA HURRAH—Jean-Claude van Itallie	66-67.	.Nov. 6, 1966. .	634
AMERICAN WAY, THE—George S. Kaufman, Moss Hart	38-39.	.Jan. 21, 1939. .	164
AMPHITRYON 38—Jean Giraudoux, (ad) S. N. Behrman	37-38.	.Nov. 1, 1937. .	153
ANDERSONVILLE TRIAL, THE—Saul Levitt	59-60.	.Dec. 29, 1959. .	179
ANDORRA—Max Frisch, (ad) George Tabori	62-63.	.Feb. 9, 1963. .	9
ANGEL STREET—Patrick Hamilton	41-42.	.Dec. 5, 1941. .	1,295
ANIMAL KINGDOM, THE—Philip Barry	31-32.	.Jan. 12, 1932. .	183
ANNA CHRISTIE—Eugene O'Neill	21-22.	.Nov. 2, 1921. .	177
ANNA LUCASTA—Philip Yordan	44-45.	.Aug. 30, 1944. .	957
ANNE OF THE THOUSAND DAYS—Maxwell Anderson	48-49.	.Dec. 8, 1948. .	286
ANOTHER LANGUAGE—Rose Franken	31-32.	.Apr. 25, 1932. .	344
ANOTHER PART OF THE FOREST—Lillian Hellman	46-47.	.Nov. 20, 1946. .	182
ANTIGONE—Jean Anouilh, (ad) Lewis Galantière	45-46.	.Feb. 18, 1946. .	64
APPLAUSE—(b) Betty Comden and Adolph Green, (m) Charles Strouse, (l) Lee Adams, based on the film *All About Eve* and the original story by Mary Orr	.69-70.	.Mar. 30, 1970. .	896
APPLE TREE, THE—(b, l) Sheldon Harnick, (b, m) Jerry Bock, add'l (b) Jerome Coopersmith, based on stories by Mark Twain, Frank R. Stockton and Jules Feiffer	66-67.	.Oct. 18, 1966. .	463
ARSENIC AND OLD LACE—Joseph Kesselring	40-41.	.Jan. 10, 1941. .	1,444
AS HUSBANDS GO—Rachel Crothers	30-31.	.Mar. 5, 1931. .	148

NECROLOGY

MAY 1976-MAY 1977

PERFORMERS

Adams, Stanley (62) — April 27, 1977
Adamsons, Arnold (69) — September 13, 1976
Alexander, Alex (66) — April 24, 1977
Allison, Ted (57) — April 12, 1977
Anderson, Eddie "Rochester" (71) — February 28, 1977
Anderson, Warner (65) — August 26, 1976
Armengod, Ramon (68) — October 31, 1976
Atkinson, Rosalind (76) — Winter 1977
Avenell, William (66) — October 11, 1976
Ayres, Queenie (74) — October 8, 1976
Badia, Leopold (74) — July 2, 1976
Baker, Stanley (49) — June 28, 1976
Balin, Betty (61) — November 18, 1976
Balshofer, Cecil (Cecil Weston) (86) — August 7, 1976
Bannerman, Margaret (83) — June 14, 1976
Barrett, Edith (64) — February 22, 1977
Barry, Merna (51) — October 31, 1976
Baum, Harry (77) — November 29, 1976
Baxter, George David (72) — September 10, 1976
Becker, Harry (57) — June 25, 1976
Ben, David (82) — August 28, 1976
Bennett, Dorothy C. (86) — Winter 1977
Benton, Steve (79) — August 4, 1976
Berger, Andre (63) — February 6, 1977
Berle, Rosalind (64) — May 14, 1977
Bermudez, Alfonso Aragon — June 22, 1976
Bettis, Frank (35) — January 5, 1977
Betts, Fred (63) — March 16, 1977
Bleiberg, Bernard (55) — April 11, 1977
Bloom, Lloyd G. (60) — August 11, 1976
Bohn, Marty (76) — November 12, 1976
Boles, Jim (63) — May 26, 1977
Bonehill, Selina (97) — September 27, 1976
Bonn, Issy (74) — April 21, 1977
Boswell, Connee (68) — October 10, 1976
Bowlus, Joan (86) — July 2, 1976
Bracken, Denis (45) — March 27, 1977
Bradbury, Saxe (33) — November 13, 1976
Brent, Romney (74) — September 24, 1976
Broderick, Johnny (83) — April 14, 1977
Brogan, Harry (72) — May 20, 1977
Buckridge, Kenneth W. (61) — August 17, 1976
Bull, Aurora Stewart (80) — July 6, 1976
Burstein, Celia (77) — December 20, 1976
Burton, Martin (71) — August 4, 1976
Callahan, Lillian Hill (78) — June 29, 1976
Cambridge, Godfrey (43) — November 29, 1976
Cassidy, Jack (49) — December 12, 1976
Clark, Bobby (53) — July 10, 1976
Clarke, Paul (28) — September 12, 1976
Clooney, Betty (45) — August 5, 1976
Coleridge, Ethel (93) — August 15, 1976
Colt, Ethel Barrymore (65) — May 22, 1977
Cooper, Lillian Kemble (85) — May 4, 1977
Corrigan, Ray (73) — August 10, 1976

Cortez, Ricardo (77) — April 28, 1977
Cotton, Larry (65) — January 12, 1977
Crawford, Joan (69) — May 10, 1977
Crews, C.S. (95) — February 16, 1977
Cutting, Brenda (42) — September 9, 1976
Dana, Dick (75) — July 10, 1976
Daniels, John E. (78) — April 1, 1977
Darro, Frankie (59) — December 25, 1976
Dashington, Alvera (75) — March 22, 1977
Davies, Rupert (59) — November 22, 1976
Davis, Spencer — September 13, 1976
De Camp, Gayle S. — December 30, 1976
Dega, Igor — July 5, 1976
Dermo, Pierre (65) — June 15, 1976
Devine, Andy (70) — February 18, 1977
Devore, Dorothy (77) — September 10, 1976
DeWitt, Alan (52) — June 2, 1976
Dexter, Bert (77) — February 17, 1977
Dix, Geraldine J. — Summer 1976
Doherty, Marie (83) — March 22, 1977
Doran, Carrie A. (92) — May 3, 1977
Dow, Al Kerner (86) — March 15, 1977
Drubin, Charles (82) — September 23, 1976
Drum, James (58) — November 28, 1976
Dunlap, Florence (94) — May 3, 1977
Dunlop, Billy (68) — September 28, 1976
Dupray, Gaston (91) — December 12, 1976
Dutt, Surya Kumar (103) — April 23, 1977
Dwyer, Donald Lynn (48) — September 3, 1976
Eason, Myles (61) — January 8, 1977
Egan, Carolyn Porter — October 11, 1976
Eggleston, David (26) — September 7, 1976
Eubanks, Gene (81) — July 10, 1976
Evans, Edith (88) — October 14, 1976
Farren, Mary (69) — May 9, 1977
Fay, Robert M. (74) — August 28, 1976
Ferguson, Helen (76) — March 14, 1977
Field, Frances Fox (64) — January 3, 1977
Field, Walter (101) — June 5, 1976
Finch, Peter (60) — January 14, 1977
Fisher, Alex — June 9, 1976
Fisher, Irene (89) — June 18, 1976
Fitzgerald, Walter (80) — December 20, 1976
Flavin, Lucile Browne (69) — May 10, 1976
Fletcher, Vida (72) — April 26, 1977
Flynn, Bernadine (73) — March 10, 1977
Foster, Norman (72) — July 7, 1976
French, Hugh (66) — November 2, 1976
Gabin, Jean (72) — November 15, 1976
Garasa, Angel (71) — August 27, 1976
Gardner, Jack (77) — February 13, 1977
Garrett, Fredda (82) — October 14, 1976
Gateson, Marjorie (86) — April 17, 1977
Gibbons, Robert — February 21, 1977
Gibson, Norman (26) — September 29, 1976
Gordon, Patti (Milbanks) (50s) — January 17, 1977
Graham, David Scottie (58) — July 15, 1976

Grannis, Anita Louise — July 20, 1976
Graves, Kathryn (78) — February 26, 1977
Graves, Ralph (75) — February 18, 1977
Gray, Joan Barton (52) — May 1977
Greene, Al (70) — January 19, 1977
Greene, Madeline (55) — May 30, 1976
Gresham, Edith F. (79) — December 31, 1976
Guild, Bill (80) — October 25, 1976
Hadley, Alvan Cordell (81) — August 4, 1976
Hafez, Abdel (46) — March 30, 1977
Halop, Billy (56) — November 9, 1976
Hanna, Betty (73) — October 25, 1976
Hardey, Bill (82) — September 5, 1976
Harris, Arlene (77) — June 12, 1976
Hawley, William E. (66) — August 22, 1976
Hayes, Allison — February 27, 1977
Hayes, Margaret (61) — January 26, 1977
Holly, Mary (89) — May 17, 1976
Hotaling, Frank (77) — April 13, 1977
Howard, Jules (76) — June 16, 1976
Hull, Henry (86) — March 8, 1977
Hunt, Edward E. (54) — May 17, 1977
Hurt, Mary (87) — October 6, 1976
Hyland, Diana (41) — March 27, 1977
Idzikowski, Stanislas (82) — February 12, 1977
Imhoff, Marcelle (88) — January 15, 1977
Johnston, Mac (71) — March 22, 1977
Jones, Freda M. (79) — October 24, 1976
Jones, Isabel Rose (72) — December 26, 1976
Jones, Mary Anissa (18) — August 28, 1976
Josen, Margaret (88) — August 24, 1976
Joyce, Jolly (75) — October 7, 1976
Kamen, Milt (55) — February 24, 1977
Kauffman, Frank (92) — March 27, 1976
Kean, Harold — Summer 1976
Kelly, John Gerard (73) — May 19, 1977
King, Carlton (William Davison) (81) — May 21, 1977
Knight, Charlotte (83) — May 16, 1977
Koellen, Helmut (27) — May 5, 1977
Konstam, Phyllis (69) — August 20, 1976
Kurstin, Frances (Raeburn) — December 26, 1976
Laing, Alfred B. (86) — August 3, 1976
Landers, Muriel R. (55) — February 19, 1977
Landon, Avice (65) — Summer 1976
Langley, Ethyl Sloat (86) — April 28, 1977
Lastfogel, Frances (Arms) (83) — September 1, 1976
Latimer, Sally (66) — Winter 1977
Latinovits, Zoltan (44) — June 1976
Laws, Jerry (64) — September 7, 1976
Leaf, Maury (79) — June 6, 1976
Leeds, Augusta Glose (99) — September 24, 1976
Lehmann, Lotte (88) — August 26, 1976
Lenihan, Liam — December 5, 1976
Lenz, Theodore J. (62) — December 26, 1976
Leoning, John (50) — March 23, 1977
Lewis, Fran (68) — October 13, 1976
Lewman, Hiram W. (72) — August 27, 1976
Lifton, Lillian S. (80) — August 8, 1976
Lindsay, Pat (43) — June 9, 1976
Lobit, Elva Stephens — May 13, 1977
Lowry, Judith (86) — November 29, 1976
Lucker, Leo (84) — February 1, 1977
Lumet, Julia (68) — October 15, 1976
Mack, Jennie (100) — April 18, 1977

MacNanamy, Sue (84) — June 10, 1976
Magallanes, Nicholas (54) — May 2, 1977
Maguire, Francis (64) — August 21, 1976
Mairena (Jose Garcia Perez) (43) — September 7, 1976
Mannheim, Lucie (77) — July 28, 1976
Manning, Frenchy (76) — September 4, 1976
Mark, Julia (49) — Spring 1977
Marks, Rita (68) — November 11, 1976
Marr, Raymond A. (79) — February 23, 1977
Marriott, John (83) — April 5, 1977
Martini, Nino (72) — December 10, 1976
Marx, Gummo (84) — April 21, 1977
Mason, Charles (53) — December 8, 1976
Matthews, Dorothy (65) — May 18, 1977
Matthews, Edward (69) — September 25, 1976
Maynard, Harry (78) — July 23, 1976
Maypole, Roy (62) — July 4, 1976
McCoy, George B. (72) — December 22, 1976
McDevitt, Ruth (80) — May 27, 1976
McGinn, Walter (40) — March 31, 1977
McGowan, Jack (81) — May 28, 1977
Merli, Francesco (90) — December 11, 1976
Mervyn, William (64) — August 6, 1976
Meyer, Eve Turner (44) — March 27, 1977
Milan, Frank (71) — April 8, 1977
Mills, James E. (73) — October 18, 1976
Monclova, Felix (42) — April 15, 1977
Monkman, Phyllis (84) — December 2, 1976
Montgomery, Marian (80) — February 7, 1977
Moore, Clarence J. (63) — November 16, 1976
Morelli, Michael (66) — August 14, 1976
Morelli, Rina (67) — July 17, 1976
Mossman, Earl P. (82) — September 25, 1976
Mourning, Sidney Abbett (62) — September 12, 1976
Moussouris, Costas (73) — December 7, 1976
Muller, Richard (48) — December 11, 1976
Mustin, Burt (92) — January 28, 1977
Nash, Mary (92) — December 3, 1976
Nelson, Lou (60) — May 15, 1977
Newton, Ralph (76) — March 14, 1977
Nichols, Anthony (69) — Winter 1977
Nichols, Barbara (47) — October 5, 1976
Nock, Charles A. (55) — June 1, 1976
North, Mary (79) — September 9, 1976
North, Robert (92) — August 13, 1976
O'Halloran, Michael (66) — July 2, 1976
Olman, Peggy Parker (78) — June 18, 1976
Owens, Tex (54) — May 23, 1976
Paget, Peter (92) — November 8, 1976
Panzera, Charles (80) — June 6, 1976
Parker, Warren — July 31, 1976
Parkison, Charles A. Jr. (31) — November 23, 1976
Parsons, Morris (69) — September 12, 1976
Payant, Lee (52) — December 14, 1976
Payne, Virginia (66) — February 10, 1977
Peregrina, Eddie (31) — May 9, 1977
Perryman, Lloyd (60) — May 31, 1977
Pisu, Mario (66) — Summer 1976
Plunkett, Charles E. (91) — April 28, 1977
Polanski, Goury (83) — October 17, 1976
Powers, Florence C. (90) — June 24, 1976
Printemps, Yvonne (82) — January 18, 1977
Prinze, Freddie (22) — January 29, 1977
Prowse, Peter (52) — Winter 1976

Pryor, Maureen — May 5, 1977
Rasp, Fritz (85) — November 30, 1976
Redfield, William (49) — August 17, 1976
Redondo, Marcos (82) — July 18, 1976
Reed, Jimmy (50) — August 29, 1976
Reid, Ed (47) — March 6, 1977
Remson, Deborah (45) — April 7, 1977
Rethberg, Elisabeth (81) — June 6, 1976
Reynolds, Floy-Margaret (64) — July 4, 1976
Rich, Robert (89) — October 9, 1976
Richard, Florence (79) — November 22, 1976
Richmond, Ruth (75) — February 26, 1977
Roman, Dick (39) — October 19, 1976
Roman, Gene — February 11, 1977
Ronan, Robert A. (41) — April 6, 1977
Roosevelt, Emily Hubbard (82) — September 14, 1976
Rothlein, Arlene (37) — November 20, 1976
Roy, Mike (63) — June 26, 1976
Russell, Rosalind (64) — November 28, 1976
Russo, Norma Tina (74) — February 15, 1977
St. Clair, James Walter (80) — May 27, 1976
Salvaneschi, Mario (65) — April 26, 1977
Sauberlich, Lu (64) — Fall 1976
Sawyer, Hal (62) — January 9, 1977
Schilling, Margaret — July 1976
Schmidt, Wolf (64) — January 17, 1977
Scordino, Teresa M. (74) — September 30, 1976
Scott, Mabel Julienne (83) — October 1, 1976
Sewall, Lucile (88) — December 15, 1976
Shaw, Buddy (70) — August 29, 1976
Sidney, Jack Sr. (88) — May 15, 1977
Silva, David (60) — September 21, 1976
Sim, Alastair (75) — August 19, 1976
Simba, Janco (30) — February 10, 1977
Smith, Ruby (73) — March 24, 1977
Sobrido, Eva (26) — August 2, 1976
Soler, Julian (72) — May 5, 1977
Soloviev, Uri (36) — January 16, 1977
Spivey, Victoria (68) — October 3, 1976
Stanitsyn, Viktor (79) — Winter 1977
Starke, Pauline (76) — February 3, 1977
Stevens, Onslow (70) — January 5, 1977
Stone, Betty (63) — April 30, 1977
Stoneman, Hatti Frost (75) — July 22, 1976
Stuart, Gene (47) — August 14, 1976
Stuewe, Hans (75) — Spring 1976
Tannen, William (65) — December 2, 1976
Teyte, Maggie (88) — May 27, 1976
Thomas, Blanche (54) — April 21, 1977
Thommen, Edward (59) — February 1, 1977
Thorndike, Sybil (93) — June 9, 1976
Tilden, Freda A. (Ann Sterling) — June 23, 1976
Tinelli, Alberte (54) — November 30, 1976
Tubb, Carrie (100) — September 20, 1976
Van Sickel, Dale (69) — January 25, 1977
Vanderveer, Ellinor (89) — May 27, 1976
Varconi, Victor (80) — June 16, 1976
Vegeres, Joe (82) — March 31, 1977
Vernon, Jimmy (72) — September 19, 1976
Vestry, Art (36) — November 7, 1976
von Hoyer, Natalie (68) — March 8, 1977
Vye, Murvyn Wesley Jr. (62) — August 17, 1976
Watkins, Linda — October 31, 1976
Welch, Niles (88) — November 21, 1976

White, Alice Brewer (77) — August 9, 1976
Williams, Roy (69) — November 7, 1976
Wise, Vic (76) — Fall 1976
Woreman, Vivian (Crawley) (65) — February 23, 1977
Worsley, Julia Taylor (98) — December 4, 1976
Wynant, Patrecia (37) — March 31, 1977
Zavadsky, Yuri (82) — Spring 1977

PLAYWRIGHTS

Andrews, Robert Hardy (73) — November 11, 1976
Bellah, James Warner (77) — September 22, 1976
Bernstein, Elliot (41) — May 22, 1977
Bissell, Richard (63) — May 4, 1977
Bronson, William (49) — July 13, 1976
Coit, Dorothy (87) — October 20, 1976
de Roly, Rene (59) — Summer 1976
Dehn, Paul (63) — September 30, 1976
Donavan, Hobart (71) — December 3, 1976
DuBois, Shirley Graham (69) — March 27, 1977
Duffy, Albert J. (73) — September 15, 1976
Freeman, Lea David (89) — August 22, 1976
Garland, Charles Talbot (66) — September 11, 1976
Garment, Grace R. (49) — December 3, 1976
Gilbert, Edwin (69) — August 24, 1976
Greene, Paul (70) — January 1, 1977
Hale, Lionel (67) — May 15, 1977
Hussein, Rashed (40) — February 1, 1977
Hyland, Dick Irving (70) — September 5, 1976
Johnson, Nunnally (79) — March 25, 1977
Kahn, Kermit (82) — December 20, 1976
Khandekar, V. S. (79) — Fall 1976
Locke, Charles (81) — May 1, 1977
MacDougall, Hugo (74) — May 15, 1976
Mahoney, Wilkie (78) — July 30, 1976
Mainwaring, Daniel (74) — January 31, 1977
March, Joseph (78) — February 14, 1977
McGinn, Matt (48) — Winter 1977
Merrick, Laurence (50's) — January 26, 1977
Miller, Abner A. (75) — September 16, 1976
Moore, Carroll B. (63) — February 5, 1977
Pipe, Archie (70) — December 4, 1976
Prevert, Jacques (77) — April 11, 1977
Rodgers, Robert (52) — October 10, 1976
Rogers, Lela (86) — May 25, 1977
Savage, George M. (72) — January 24, 1977
Segal, Fred (51) — May 28, 1976
Sherman, Charles (77) — December 25, 1976
Skinner, Jane (54) — September 16, 1976
Smith, Fred (88) — August 14, 1976
Smith, Robert Paul (61) — January 30, 1977
Tanner, Edward E. (Patrick Dennis) (55) — November 6, 1°
Thompson, Jim (70) — April 7, 1977
Totheroh, Dan (82) — December 3, 1976
Trumbo, Dalton (79) — September 10, 1976
Tzavellas, George (60) — October 19, 1976
Wilmot, Seamus (75) — January 21, 1977
Zuckmayer, Carl (80) — January 18, 1977

COMPOSERS, LYRICISTS

Baer, Abel (83) — October 5, 1976
Battle, Edgar (69) — February 6, 1977

Britten, Benjamin (63) — December 4, 1976
Burwell, Cliff (78) — October 10, 1976
Cheiffetz, Hyman (74) — January 6, 1977
Dark, Harold (88) — November 28, 1976
De Los Rios, Waldo (43) — March 29, 1977
De Vocht, Louis (90) — March 27, 1977
Durlet, Emmanuel (83) — Winter 1977
Edmonds, Dixie Lee (52) — February 25, 1977
Frank, Ruth Kantz — March 6, 1977
Gray, Jerry (61) — August 10, 1976
Hagen, John M. (85) — February 12, 1977
Hanighen, Bernie (68) — October 19, 1976
Hanson, Raymond (63) — December 5, 1976
Holzer, Lou (63) — April 6, 1977
Howard, Tash (36) — April 15, 1977
Hug, Armand (66) — March 19, 1977
Jerome, M.K. (83) — January 8, 1977
Johnson, Woodrow Wilson (62) — February 9, 1977
Kenessey, Jeno (71) — Summer 1976
LaMure, Pierre — December 28, 1976
Lockyer, Malcolm (52) — June 28, 1976
Lopatnikoff, Nikolai (73) — October 7, 1976
Lubin, Ernest (60) — March 15, 1977
Mann, Michael (57) — January 1, 1977
McDiarmid, Don Sr. (78) — February 27, 1977
Mercer, Johnny (66) — June 25, 1976
Miller, Eddie (67) — April 10, 1977
Myers, Richard (75) — March 12, 1977
Newman, Herbert (51) — June 21, 1976
Nordoff, Paul (67) — January 18, 1977
Pedtke, Daniel H. (70) — December 10, 1976
Piston, Walter (82) — November 12, 1976
Ramirez, Rafael Jr. (63) — May 21, 1976
Revutsky, Lev N. (87) — March 30, 1977
Romero, Federico (89) — June 30, 1976
Sanjuan, Pedro (89) — October 18, 1976
Semmler, Alexander (76) — April 24, 1977
Shuken, Leo (69) — July 24, 1976
Todaro, Tony (61) — July 28, 1976
Twardy, Werner (50) — January 16, 1977
Vincent, John N. (74) — January 21, 1977
Washington, Ned (75) — December 20, 1976
Zador, Eugene (82) — April 3, 1977

PRODUCERS, DIRECTORS
CHOREOGRAPHERS

Alessandro, Victor (61) — November 27, 1976
Alexander, Brooks (59) — July 27, 1976
Asmus, Harry C. (57) — March 24, 1977
Aufricht, Jack W. (51) — Winter 1976
Baar, Tim (64) — March 9, 1977
Bailey, G. Rex (75) — February 4, 1977
Ballin, Robert Walden (73) — March 21, 1977
Barber, Clarence H. (57) — January 3, 1977
Barna, Yon (49) — November 28, 1976
Bates, John (68) — February 3, 1977
Bennett, Cyril (48) — November 7, 1976
Birkmayer, Richard L. (43) — December 9, 1976
Bloomgarden, Kermit (73) — September 20, 1976
Boyce, George (77) — February 4, 1977
Buzby, J. Howard (82) — Summer 1976
Cannon, Thomas (66) — January 21, 1977

Castle, William (63) — May 31, 1977
Chandler, Gloria (78) — August 16, 1976
Clouzot, Henri-Georges (69) — January 12, 1977
Coburn, Anthony (49) — April 27, 1977
Dallamano, Massimo (59) — Fall 1976
Del Ruth, Richard (54) — December 24, 1976
Digangi, C.J. (65) — August 26, 1976
Doughty, Charles L. (48) — April 4, 1977
Edgar, George P. (53) — August 16, 1976
Esser, Wright (69) — August 12, 1976
Feldman, Milton (65) — October 8, 1976
Finos, Philopoemen (69) — January 26, 1977
Fogle, George L. (76) — September 29, 1976
Foy, Bryan (82) — April 20, 1977
Frend, Charles (67) — January 8, 1977
Friedkin, David (64) — October 15, 1976
Fromkess, Leon (69) — March 11, 1977
Gagliardo, Ezio (57) — Summer 1976
Garcia, Joel (36) — May 30, 1977
Gardiner, James W. (57) — November 6, 1976
Gering, Marion (73) — April 19, 1977
Gries, Tom (53) — January 3, 1977
Hall, Howard (55) — December 7, 1976
Hamlisch, Max (69) — February 13, 1977
Hanson, Herdis P. (79) — April 1, 1977
Heidt, Charles P. (82) — January 24, 1977
Henderson, Claire (51) — August 17, 1976
Herren, Eric Albert Richard (59) — August 30, 1976
Hibler, Winston (65) — August 8, 1976
Hornblow, Arthur Jr. (83) — July 17, 1976
Horwitz, Howie (58) — June 25, 1976
Hyman, Joseph M. (80) — February 25, 1977
Inkpen, Ron (42) — February 18, 1977
Kerz, Leo (64) — November 4, 1976
Kellogg, Ray (70) — July 5, 1976
Knaster, Ira H. — August 26, 1976
Kopalin, Ilya P. (76) — Summer 1976
Lang, Fritz (85) — August 2, 1976
Langlois, Henri (62) — January 12, 1977
Lerner, Irving (67) — December 25, 1976
Levitan, Paul (60) — October 1, 1976
Lippert, Robert L. (67) — November 16, 1976
Lisemore, Martin (36) — February 3, 1977
Lloyd, Ted (61) — February 6, 1977
Luby, Roy (71) — August 19, 1976
Machiz, Herbert (57) — August 27, 1976
Macian, Francisco (47) — October 23, 1976
Mayo, Waldo (75) — July 8, 1976
McEveety, Joseph L. (50) — October 15, 1976
McNaught, Herbert (61) — November 28, 1976
Murphy, L. John (82) — July 26, 1976
Nelson, John (61) — November 3, 1976
Nunes, Abraham R. (70) — February 27, 1977
Peter, Will (69) — Fall 1976
Poppe, Harry H. Sr. (86) — August 25, 1976
Poss, Stanley (56) — January 11, 1977
Radok, Alfred (62) — Spring 1976
Richards, Tan (50) — March 21, 1977
Room, Abram M. (82) — Summer 1976
Rosen, Kenneth M. (47) — July 2, 1976
Rust, Gordon A. (69) — May 23, 1977
Salvia, Rafael J. (61) — June 21, 1976
Samish, Adrian (66) — October 14, 1976
Schaumer, Adolph (72) — April 6, 1977

Schreiber, Taft B. (68) — June 14, 1976
Seghers, E. Boyd Jr. (54) — June 6, 1976
Seltzer, Frank N. (77) — April 7, 1977
Serratore, Boris (57) — July 9, 1976
Shaw, Frank X. (59) — March 15, 1977
Sieber, Rudolph (77) — June 24, 1976
Small, Edward (85) — January 25, 1977
Solow, Victor D. (59) — November 14, 1976
Starkie, Walter (82) — November 2, 1976
Strode, Hudson (83) — September 22, 1976
Underwood, Cecil (76) — September 27, 1976
Valde, Pierre (69) — February 26, 1977
Vesota, Bruno (54) — September 24, 1976
Vorkapich, Slavko (84) — October 20, 1976
Weiss, Noel R. (44) — June 13, 1976
Wilcox, Herbert (85) — May 15, 1977
Wolf, Jay (47) — June 11, 1976
Woolner, Bernard (66) — February 21, 1977
Worth, Claude (74) — November 23, 1976

DESIGNERS

Boyle, Edward G. — February 17, 1977
Fegte, Ernst (76) — December 15, 1976
King, Muriel (76) — March 21, 1977
Patterson, Russell (82) — March 17, 1977
Roper, Robert St. John (64) — April 29, 1977
Roup, Helen Scovil (62) — August 16, 1976
Schulze-Mittendorf, Walter (83) — August 20, 1976
Soloviov, Nikolai (66) — July 12, 1976
Timmins, Gertrude Gass — June 27, 1976
Wenger, John (89) — August 24, 1976
Woodall, Mark B. (29) — July 1, 1976

CRITICS

Beaumont, Cyril (86) — May 24, 1976
Berg, Louis (77) — April 8, 1977
Bianchi, Pietro (67) — Fall 1976
Cooper, Jack (72) — June 9, 1976
Dahlberg, Edward (76) — February 27, 1977
Daugherty, George (68) — June 14, 1976
Doyle, Peggy (75) — March 22, 1977
Frankel, Ruth Leipziger (81) — February 4, 1977
Galantière, Lewis (81) — February 20, 1977
Ihering, Herbert (88) — January 15, 1977
Leonard, William (64) — January 6, 1977
Lyons, Leonard (70) — October 7, 1976
Savio, Francesco (50) — October 27, 1976
Sayre, Syd (64) — January 31, 1977
Shain, Sam (75) — July 17, 1976
Stern, Harold S. (53) — May 25, 1976
Thomas, Freddie — Spring 1977
Wasserman, Jack (50) — April 7, 1977
Worsley, T. C. (69) — February 23, 1977

CONDUCTORS

Bigelow, Jack (83) — February 3, 1977
Brall, John A. (88) — November 6, 1976
DeAngelis, Harry (67) — March 7, 1977

Dixon, Dean (61) — November 3, 1976
Evans, Paul W. (69) — January 10, 1977
Garnett, Joseph (77) — January 2, 1977
Geiger-Torel, Herman (69) — October 6, 1976
Gordon, Gray (72) — July 23, 1976
Hall, John Nelson (77) — February 21, 1977
Horton, Wayne L. (82) — September 30, 1976
Hudgens, Ray (66) — March 21, 1977
Hunt, Brad (Norman J. Auth) (58) — February 15, 1977
Jacoby, Elliott (75) — March 28, 1977
Juneau, Thomas (61) — November 24, 1976
Karp, Richard (74) — February 2, 1977
Kerr, Charles E. (86) — October 7, 1976
Lanin, Samuel (85) — May 5, 1977
Moro, Domenico (91) — December 22, 1976
Paquette, Arthur H. (74) — April 26, 1976
Raymond, Lee (43) — November 11, 1976
Rothschild, Leonard J. (63) — April 26, 1977
Sanford, Charles (71) — April 22, 1977
Somohano, Arturo (66) — March 23, 1977
Tarrasch, William (75) — May 30, 1976
Ternent, Billy (77) — March 25, 1977
Welborn, Adam Clark (73) — April 18, 1977

MUSICIANS

Acksworth, Harry F. (77) — December 3, 1976
Ald-Williams, Ron (28) — July 25, 1976
Anda, Geza (55) — June 13, 1976
Aronin, Bertha (64) — Winter 1976
Ashlock, Jesse (61) — August 9, 1976
Avellone, Charles J. (75) — August 29, 1976
Bachauer, Gina (63) — August 22, 1976
Baron, Hyman (73) — Winter 1977
Bennett, John III (60) — October 3, 1976
Bernstein, Joseph (62) — November 3, 1976
Biggs, E. Power (70) — March 1, 1977
Bolin, Tommy (25) — December 4, 1976
Bonnie, Joe (70) — October 8, 1976
Braun, Edith Evans (89) — November 7, 1976
Brennand, Charles (47) — July 29, 1976
Burbank, Albert (74) — August 15, 1976
Burke, Walter V. (63) — January 9, 1977
Byrd, Dessa (79) — May 19, 1977
Candoli, Joe (75) — February 15, 1977
Chandler, Lori (27) — Summer 1976
Chotzinoff, Pauline (73) — August 3, 1976
Cochran, Wallace Daniel (55) — December 28, 1976
Cooper, Stoney (58) — March 22, 1977
De Angelis, Joseph (72) — November 2, 1976
Deeley, Jason Gregory (27) — January 25, 1977
Desmond, Paul (52) — May 30, 1977
Downs, Leo (75) — June 19, 1976
Dushkin, Samuel (82) — June 24, 1976
Dvonch, Frederick (64) — November 18, 1976
Elisha, Dorothy Kestner (60) — March 22, 1977
Erle, Broadus, (59) — April 6, 1977
Espen, Anthony S. (62) — November 12, 1976
Evans, Gene (54) — October 18, 1976
Featherstonhaugh, Rupert E.L. (67) — July 12, 1976
Fitzwater, Delmar J. (68) — November 30, 1976
Fleming, Herb (75) — October 2, 1976

Foster, Sidney (59) — February 7, 1977
Freundlich, Irwin (66) — March 13, 1977
Fuchsova, Liza (63) — February 27, 1977
Furmansky, Harold (70) — January 25, 1977
Garner, Erroll (53) — January 2, 1977
Giampietro, Horace S. (88) — April 16, 1977
Graffman, Vladimir (85) — December 22, 1976
Guerra, Michael (88) — August 6, 1976
Hackett, Bobby (61) — June 7, 1976
Hawes, Hampton (48) — May 22, 1977
Hayes, Roland (89) — December 31, 1976
Henriques, Sara Schwatlo (72) — Winter 1977
Hittler, Louis — February 7, 1977
Hulihan, Olive Kline (89) — July 29, 1976
Hungerford, Bruce (54) — January 26, 1977
Jackson, Quentin (67) — October 2, 1976
Johnstone, G.W. (76) — February 5, 1977
Jones, Brian W. (21) — July 27, 1976
Jones, H. Truett (70) — May 11, 1977
Jones, Mendel (73) — January 30, 1977
Joyce, Giorgio (70) — June 12, 1976
Kaopuiki, James (54) — July 30, 1976
King, Freddie (42) — December 28, 1976
Kirkpatrick, Jess (78) — August 9, 1976
Knox, Emile (74) — August 20, 1976
Kullberg, Richard (65) — March 11, 1977
Kurta, George A. (61) — May 26, 1976
Lane, Lewis (73) — January 24, 1977
Lanzarone, Gloria W. (35) — June 21, 1976
Leibert, Richard (73) — October 22, 1976
Lhevinne, Rosina (96) — November 9, 1976
Loder, James P. (76) — May 15, 1977
Martin, Hugh Edwards (47) — December 23, 1976
McDermott, Edward M. (81) — January 1, 1977
Megerlin, Frances W. (90) — December 8, 1976
Miller, Bettye (49) — February 28, 1977
Moore, Harold C. (73) — December 19, 1976
Munz, Mieczslaw (75) — August 25, 1976
Peiffer, Bernard P. (53) — September 7, 1976
Pellettieri, Vito (87) — April 14, 1977
Peterson, Charles (76) — August 4, 1976
Phillips, Leon M. (61) — January 10, 1977
Piatigorsky, Gregor (73) — August 6, 1976
Politis, James (56) — December 2, 1976
Ponti, Leo (75) — August 9, 1976
Powell, Everard Stephen (69) — October 30, 1976
Pryor, George H. (65) — June 6, 1976
Reher, Kurt (63) — July 7, 1976
Rehm, Matthew M. Sr. (71) — July 17, 1976
Robertson, Arthur Glenn (78) — Winter 1977
Rosner, Ady (67) — August 8, 1976
Rudolph, Walter J. (86) — January 5, 1977
Schertzer, Hymie (67) — March 22, 1977
Schlamm, Murray (67) — December 5, 1976
Schmit, Lucien S. (78) — July 20, 1976
Schnabel, Ethel C. (69) — June 21, 1976
Scott, Dorothy P. — September 16, 1976
Shertzer, Herman (67) — March 22, 1977
Shiroff, Hubert D. (66) — May 26, 1976
Smith, Jeanette P. — August 1, 1976
Stango, John Victor (72) — February 26, 1977
Stepney, Charles (45) — May 17, 1976
Stevens, Teddy (66) — March 31, 1977
Strassner, Isidor (80) — June 13, 1976

Szanto, Jani (89) — March 24, 1977
Taylor, Helen — August 14, 1976
Teller, Jacob J. (68) — September 12, 1976
Wallace, Lucille (79) — March 21, 1977
Watkins, Julius (55) — April 4, 1977
Weis, Lawrence B. (66) — August 1, 1976
Whallon, Jean B. (51) — February 4, 1977
Willi, Arthur F. (81) — March 31, 1977
Wolf, Leo (71) — March 2, 1977
Yak, Yakov (62) — June 28, 1976

OTHERS

Abrams, Benjamin (83) — September 22, 1976
  Manager, Meyer Davis orchestras
Allen, Lorraine (50) — September 3, 1976
  Wife of Marty Allen
Anderson, Harvey J. (75) — May 1977
  Press agent
Ansell, Jack (40) — September 20, 1976
  Special Projects director, ABC-TV
Applebaum, Sada Rothman (72) — August 18, 1976
  Music writer, teacher
Ayling, Keith (77) — August 9, 1976
  Author, journalist
Baker, Mary (67) — July 29, 1976
  Hollywood agent
Bambridge Elsie Kipling (80) — May 23, 1976
  Daughter of Rudyard Kipling
Barker, Shirley R. (45) — September 25, 1976
  Talent co-ordinator, "Tonight"
Beadle, Sir Gerald C. (77) — November 6, 1976
  BBC television
Bell, Robert (82) — May 11, 1977
  Teacher, American Academy
Bercovici, Rion (73) — August 6, 1976
  Newspaperman
Bevacqua, Phyllis D. (58) — April 27, 1977
  Press agent
Bodrero, Geraldine — September 10, 1976
  Founder, San Francisco Ballet Guild
Bohn, Joyce Illig (36) — August 22, 1976
  Reporter
Brandt, Mary (92) — February 17, 1977
  Widow of Joseph Brandt
Bronstein, Leo (72) — June 1, 1976
  Fine arts author
Brown, Milton (61) — July 23, 1976
  NBC news information services
Brownstone, Laura T. (78) — August 19, 1976
  Mother of Alexander H. Cohen
Burke, Thomas F. Jr. (33) — October 4, 1976
  Talent agent
Bush, Bill — February 28, 1977
  Columnist
Calamari, Rose (76) — April 15, 1977
  Wardrobe mistress
Carlton, Sam — July 7, 1976
  Associate of George Jessel
Carmer, Carl (83) — September 11, 1976
  President, Authors Guild
Carney, Phil — December 18, 1976
  Brother of Art Carney

Carr, John Dickson (70) — February 27, 1977
  Mystery writer
Carter, Edgar (71) — May 22, 1977
  Aide to Ira Gershwin
Civit, Jose Maria (42) — February 2, 1977
  Spanish impresario
Clark, Anthony (52) — November 22, 1976
  Minneapolis Institute of Arts
Cohen, Sid (77) — April 12, 1977
  Road manager
Cohn, Gala Jane (52) — September 2, 1976
  Woodstock Playhouse
Connor, Frank H. (74) — April 1, 1977
  President, Carl Fischer Inc.
Cowan, Louis G. (67) — November 18, 1976
  Creator, radio, tv programs
Devlin, (Msgr.) John J. (79) — April 6, 1977
  Roman Catholic Legion of Decency
Draper, John W. (83) — November 30, 1976
  Shakespeare expert
Dresser, Davis (Brett Halliday) (72) — Feb. 4, 1977
  Mystery writer
Dunn, Nat (75) — March 31, 1977
  Personal manager
Federico, Giuseppe (75) — July 29, 1976
  Owner, Capri Restaurant
Foote, William J. (71) — September 6, 1976
  Editor, The Hartford *Courant*
Fowler, George, (55) — August 18, 1976
  Vice president, Hurok Concerts
Frank, Fredric M. — May 9, 1977
  Founding member, Screen Writers Guild
Friedlander, Emil (88) — September 27, 1976
  President, Dazian's Inc.
Friedman, Edgar H. (89) — February 9, 1977
  Brother of Ted Lewis
Furlong, Thomas (71) — March 10, 1977
  Executive editor, Chicago *Tribune*
Gallico, Paul (78) — July 16, 1976
  Author
Geoly, Andrew (69) — April 20, 1977
  President, Eaves Costume Co.
Gingrich, Arnold (72) — July 9, 1976
  Founder, *Esquire* magazine
Giovannini, Sandro (62) — April 26, 1977
  Italian musical comedy impresario
Goldwyn, Frances Howard (73) — June 2, 1976
  Widow of Samuel Goldwyn
Grauer, Ben (68) — May 31, 1977
  Announcer, newsman, commentator
Greben, Harry (77) — January 17, 1977
  Talent agent
Greer, William Sr. (70) — August 20, 1976
  Publisher, *Fortune, Life*
Guido, Domingo (84) — January 24, 1977
  Arranger
Head, Francis — July 4, 1976
  London literary agent
Hill, John W. (86) — March 17, 1977
  Founder, Hill & Knowlton
Hinman, Charlton J.K. (66) — March 16, 1977
  Expert on Shakespeare first editions
Hoffenberg, Jack (70) — March 23, 1977
  Novelist

Holden, Theodore L. — September 5, 1976
  Editor, The Hartford *Times*
Holt, Emily Schultze (80) — August 24, 1976
  Counsel, Actors' Equity
Houston, Clyde (51) — May 1, 1977
  Company manager
Howe, James Wong (76) — July 12, 1976
  Cinematographer
Howe, Quincy (76) — February 17, 1977
  News commentator, radio and television
Hull, Mrs. Lytle (83) — December 11, 1976
  Music patron
Jackson, Phyllis (69) — March 20, 1977
  Literary agent
Joseph, Nannine (87) — July 9, 1976
  Literary agent
Judd, George E. (90) — May 2, 1977
  Manager, Boston Symphony
Kantor, Bernard R. (53) — November 21, 1976
  Dean, USC School of Performing Arts
Keller, (Father) James (76) — February 7, 1977
  Founder, The Christophers
King, Floyd (87) — August 24, 1976
  Circus owner
Kitcat, Cecil — December 30, 1976
  Teacher, movement for the stage
Lawrence, Bert (73) — December 30, 1976
  Gag writer
Lee, George W. (83) — August 1, 1976
  "Sage of Beale Street"
Lewis, Merlin C. (73) — January 17, 1977
  Theater Equipment Supply Association
Lieberson, Goddard — May 29, 1977
  President, Columbia Records
Lowenfels, Walter (79) — July 7, 1976
  Editor, *Worker*
Mack, Ted (72) — July 12, 1976
  "Amateur Hour" emcee-host
Magnus, Finn Haakon (70) — August 29, 1976
  President, Magnus Organ Corp.
Malraux, Andre (75) — November 23, 1976
  Art historian, writer
Manuel, Alvin G. (68) — October 12, 1976
  Literary Agent
Maren, Tommy (71) — November 12, 1976
  Owner, Dinty Moore's
Meiklejohn, Jean (85) — July 2, 1976
  Vaudeville booker
Merrill, Scott (24) — February 23, 1977
  Writer
Meynert, Monika (38) — May 14, 1976
  Music journalist
Nixon, Billy (79) — November 9, 1976
  Boston theater treasurer
O'Brien, Edward (58) — August 10, 1976
  Public relations executive
Oddie, Frank (67) — Fall 1976
  Blackpool theater manager
Odlum, Floyd B. (84) — June 17, 1976
  Financier
Pell, Howland H. Jr. (79) — November 23, 1976
  Active in Connecticut theater
Popplewell, Eric (77) — October 8, 1976
  Vaudeville, revue impresario

Proctor, Jack (78) — August 1, 1976
Publicist
Pulaski, Lillion (95) — January 21, 1977
Widow, Jack Pulaski
Queneau, Raymond (73) — October 25, 1976
French novelist
Ramsaur, Edmund A. (51) — December 18, 1976
President, Multimedia Inc.
Ritz, Charles (84) — July 11, 1976
Director, Ritz Hotel, Paris
Robertson, Johnnie (48) — October 15, 1976
Manager, Royal Lyceum Theater, Edinburgh
Roslavleva, Natalia (69) — January 3, 1977
Soviet dance historian
Rudnick, Louis (84) — March 6, 1977
Founder, Williamstown summer theater
Saldutti, Vincent J. (82) — June 20, 1976
Head tailor, Western Costume Co.
Sandburg, Lillian (93) — February 18, 1977
Widow of Carl Sandburg
Sasser, James W. (51) — January 14, 1977
Public relations executive
Schenck, Janet (93) — October 12, 1976
Founder, Manhattan School of Music
Shapiro, Meyer H. (76) — May 27, 1977
Public relations
Shor, Bernard "Toots" (73) — January 23, 1977
Restaurateur
Shribman, Charles (84) — December 27, 1976
Manager, big bands
Sicari, Joseph L. (59) — May 31, 1977
Public relations
Sidelle, Ira (52) — May 24, 1976
Road manager for Frank Sinatra
Sinatra, Natalie (82) — January 6, 1977
Mother of Frank Sinatra
Smith, C. Duryea III (73) — May 5, 1977
Chairman, Alfred drama department

Smokey the Bear (26) — November 9, 1976
Internationally known symbol of fire prevention
Starr, Milton (80) — June 5, 1976
President, Theater Owners Booking Assn.
Strelsin, Alfred A. (78) — August 25, 1976
Supporter New York Shakespeare Festival
Sylvanus, Al (59) — February 28, 1977
Executive secretary, ANTA-West
Taylor, Donald (59) — August 17, 1976
Chief of news, *Voice of America*
Temple, Gertrude A. (84) — January 3, 1977
Mother of Shirley Temple
Thody, Henry (59) — March 7, 1977
British show business reporter
Tierney, James (65) — August 5, 1976
Stagehand
Tobin, Phil (75) — December 8, 1976
"Father of Nevada gambling"
Tonkins, Irvin (65) — August 1, 1976
President, Campus Concerts Ltd.
Van Remoortel, Edouard (51) — May 26, 1977
Director, St. Louis Orchestra
Vaugnan, Bill (61) — February 26, 1977
E 'or, Kansas City *Star*
Welch, Constance (77) — June 20, 1976
Drama Professor, Yale University
Wenzel, Robert G. (59) — May 19, 1976
Theater columnist
Williams, Annie L. (80's) — May 17, 1977
Authors' agent
Williams, Leroy B. — Spring 1977
Club Harlem, Atlantic City
Yeager, Charles U. (75) — January 25, 1977
Promoter, Depression-era Bank Nights
Zeckendorf, William (71) — September 30, 1976
Broadway backer
Zukor, Adolph (103) — June 10, 1976
Paramount executive

INDEX

Play titles appear in **bold face**. *Bold face italic* page numbers refer to those pages where complete cast and credit listings for New York productions may be found.

421